GIOVANNI RUCELLAI ED IL SUO ZIBALDONE

II

A FLORENTINE PATRICIAN AND HIS PALACE

STUDIES OF THE WARBURG INSTITUTE

EDITED BY J. B. TRAPP

VOL. 24, II

Anon. (? Giacomo Coppi), Imaginary Portrait of Giovanni Rucellai. Florence, Rucellai Palace.

GIOVANNI RUCELLAI ED IL SUO ZIBALDONE

II

A FLORENTINE PATRICIAN AND HIS PALACE

STUDIES BY

F. W. KENT, ALESSANDRO PEROSA,
BRENDA PREYER, PIERO SANPAOLESI &
ROBERTO SALVINI

WITH AN INTRODUCTION BY NICOLAI RUBINSTEIN

LONDON
THE WARBURG INSTITUTE
UNIVERSITY OF LONDON
1981

CONTENTS

FOREWORD

Twenty years have passed since the publication by the Warburg Institute in 1960 of Alessandro Perosa's edition of *pagine scelte* from the *Zibaldone* of Giovanni Rucellai. Though this lapse of time has brought certain changes in content and in emphasis in the companion volume of studies then promised, the centre of interest remains Giovanni himself and the palace which embodied the aspirations of this Florentine patrician.

The companion volume was originally intended to comprise three studies. Alessandro Perosa, of the University of Florence, was to deal with Giovanni's life and historical position; Roberto Salvini, also of the University of Florence, with the then newly discovered frescoes in the *altana* of the Rucellai Palace; and Rudolf Wittkower was to make a new assessment of Giovanni's building activities. In the interval, a new generation of scholars has made available much new material, which we have been fortunate in being able to use in the volume as it is now published. Professor Perosa's account of Giovanni's intellectual milieu is supplemented by F. W. Kent, of Monash University, with a characterization of the interior and exterior forces which combined to form a Florentine patron of the arts. Professor Salvini contributes his study of the *altana* frescoes. The death of Rudolf Wittkower having deprived us of the account which he was uniquely qualified to write of Rucellai as builder and as patron of Leon Battista Alberti, we have been fortunate to secure, besides the collaboration of Dr. Kent, the assistance of Brenda Preyer, of the University of Texas at Austin, and of the late Piero Sanpaolesi, of the University of Florence. Professor Sanpaolesi has provided a chapter on the architecture of the Rucellai Palace, as well as the measured drawings of its façade made under his supervision by the Istituto di Restauro dei Monumenti[1]. The close co-operation between Dr. Preyer and Dr. Kent, in particular, has been as important to our undertaking as it has in itself been a model of scholarly collaboration. These two authors, working constantly together, have freely exchanged findings and documents, so that each has contributed substantially to the other's chapter. Occasional differences of opinion—notably concerning the role of Alberti in the building of Giovanni Rucellai's palace—and a small degree of overlap between contributors have been allowed to remain, without, it is hoped, impairment of the whole.

To the five who have combined to make this assessment of Giovanni Rucellai both as an individual and in his social context as head of a family, patron and builder, the Warburg Institute is under the greatest of obligations, not least because they have enabled the Institute to fulfil its undertaking to Count Bernardo Rucellai. To Count Rucellai's own sympathetic interest, and above all to his patience, the Institute is also much indebted. It is a great satisfaction that Professor Perosa's edition of the *Zibaldone* is now complemented by a group of studies which will place Count Rucellai's remarkable ancestor even more firmly in his deserved place in the history of his native city during the fifteenth century.

Much credit for this volume is due to its *soprintendente*, Nicolai Rubinstein, who not only gave the project fresh life but has watched over it from first to last. Two other 'Florentines' are also to be gratefully remembered: Felix Gilbert, who originally suggested that Giovanni Rucellai was worth

---

[1] It is sad to have to record that Professor Sanpaolesi died in March 1980, while this volume was in the final stages of preparation for the press.

intensive study; and the late Gertrud Bing, whose enthusiasm ensured that the suggestion was followed up and whose mediation secured Count Rucellai's blessing.

Particular help is acknowledged at the beginning of each contribution. The Warburg Institute owes thanks, for indispensable and much appreciated aid of various kinds, to many others, chief among them Francis Ames-Lewis, Michael Baxandall, Howard Burns, Caroline Elam, Isabelle Hyman and Margot Wittkower.

This book is published with the aid of a contribution from the Erasmus Prize Fund of the Warburg Institute.

J. B. Trapp

LIST OF ILLUSTRATIONS

The frontispiece and Plates 40–48, 49a, 51, 53, 54a, 55–60, 61a and 62–64 are reproduced by kind permission of Count Bernardo Rucellai. Grateful acknowledgement of leave to reproduce objects in their charge is also made to the Musée des Beaux-Arts, Dijon; the Soprintendenza alle Gallerie, Florence; and the Trustees of the National Gallery, London. All photographs for Plates 16–18, 21, 22, 23a and b, 24, 26, 28 and 29 were taken by Dr. Brenda Preyer and for Plates 36, 37a and 38 by Professor Piero Sanpaolesi. Photographs for Plates 5–11, taken by Artini, were kindly supplied by the Kunsthistorisches Institut, Florence.

LIST OF ABBREVIATIONS

All manuscript references are to collections in the Florentine State Archives, unless otherwise indicated. Dates are shown in modern style, unless qualified by *s.f.*

ARCHIVES AND LIBRARIES

AR	Archivio Rucellai
ASF	Archivio di Stato, Florence
AS Ferr.	Archivio di Stato, Ferrara
BL	British Library
BN	Bibliothèque Nationale
BNC	Biblioteca Nazionale Centrale, Florence
Cat.	Catasto
Conv. Sopp.	Conventi Soppressi (ASF)
CS	Carte Strozziane (ASF)
Laurenziana	Biblioteca Medicea Laurenziana
MAP	Archivio Mediceo avanti il Principato (ASF)
NA	Notarile Antecosimiano (ASF)
Pupilli	Pupilli avanti il Principato (ASF)
Vaticana	Biblioteca Apostolica Vaticana

BOOKS AND JOURNALS

AB	*Art Bulletin.*
ASI	*Archivio Storico Italiano.*
Biagi, *Men and Manners*	G. Biagi, *Men and Manners of Old Florence,* London, 1909.
BM	*Burlington Magazine.*
Boll. Arte	*Bollettino d'Arte.*
Brucker, *Civic World*	Gene A. Brucker, *The Civic World of Early Renaissance Florence,* Princeton, 1977.
DBI	*Dizionario Biografico degli Italiani.*
Dezzi Bardeschi, "Complesso monumentale"	M. Dezzi Bardeschi, "Il complesso monumentale di S. Pancrazio a Firenze ed il suo restauro (nuovi documenti)", *Quaderni dell'Istituto di storia dell'architettura,* ser. XIII, 73–8 (1966), pp. 1–66.
Dezzi Bardeschi, *Facciata*	*id., La Facciata di Santa Maria Novella a Firenze* (Collana di rilievi architettonici a cura dell'Istituto di Restauro dei Monumenti dell' Università di Firenze), Pisa, 1970.
Goldthwaite, *Private Wealth*	Richard A. Goldthwaite, *Private Wealth in Renaissance Florence: A Study of Four Families,* Princeton, 1968.
GSLI	*Giornale Storico della Letteratura Italiana.*
GW	*Gesamtkatalog der Wiegendrucke.*
H	L. Hain, *Repertorium bibliographicum* (and Supplements).
IMU	*Italia Medioevale e Umanistica.*
JSAH	*Journal of the Society of Architectural Historians.*
JWCI	*Journal of the Warburg and Courtauld Institutes.*
Kent, "Due Lettere"	F. W. Kent, "Due lettere inedite di Giovanni di Bernardo Rucellai", *GSLI,* CXLIX (1972), pp. 565–9.

Kent, *Household and Lineage*	*id.*, *Household and Lineage in Renaissance Florence: The Family Life of the Capponi, Ginori and Rucellai*, Princeton, 1977.
Kent, "Letters"	*id.*, "The Letters genuine and spurious of Giovanni Rucellai", *JWCI*, XXXVII (1974), pp. 342–9.
Kent, "Loggia"	*id.*, "The Rucellai Family and its Loggia", *JWCI*, XXXV (1972), pp. 397–401.
Kent, " 'Più superba' "	*id.*, " 'Più superba de quella de Lorenzo': Courtly and Family Interest in the Building of Filippo Strozzi's Palace", *Renaissance Quarterly*, XXX (1977), pp. 311–23.
Kent, "Poggio a Caiano"	*id.*, "Lorenzo de' Medici's Acquisition of Poggio a Caiano in 1474 and an early Reference to his architectural Expertise", *JWCI*, XLII (1979), pp. 250–7.
D. V. Kent, *Rise of the Medici*	Dale V. Kent, *The Rise of the Medici: Faction in Florence, 1426–1434*, Oxford, 1978.
Mancini, *Alberti*	G. Mancini, *Vita di Leon Battista Alberti*, 2nd ed., Florence, 1911.
Marcotti, *Mercante fiorentino*	G. Marcotti, *Un mercante fiorentino e la sua famiglia nel secolo XV*, Florence, 1881.
MARS	*Mediaeval and Renaissance Studies.*
Martines, *Social World*	Lauro A. Martines, *The Social World of the Florentine Humanists, 1390–1460*, Princeton, 1963.
MKHIF	*Mitteilungen des Kunsthistorischen Institutes in Florenz.*
Molho, *Florentine Public Finances*	Anthony Molho, *Florentine public Finances in the early Renaissance, 1400–33*, Cambridge, Mass., 1971.
Orlandi, *Necrologio*	S. Orlandi, O.P., "*Necrologio*" *di Santa Maria Novella*, Florence, 1955.
Passerini, *Rucellai*	L. Passerini, *Genealogia e storia della famiglia Rucellai*, Florence, 1861.
Perosa	*Giovanni Rucellai ed il suo Zibaldone. Part I: 'Il Zibaldone Quaresimale'. Pagine scelte*, a cura di A. Perosa, London, 1960.
	Migne, *Patrologiae . . . cursus completus*
PG	*Series graeca*
PL	*Series latina.*
Preyer, *Giovanni Rucellai*	Brenda Preyer, *Giovanni Rucellai and the Rucellai Palace*, unpub. thesis presented to the Department of Fine Arts, Harvard University, 1976.
Rochon, *Jeunesse*	André Rochon, *La Jeunesse de Laurent de Médicis, 1449–78*, Paris, 1963.
de Roover, *Rise and Decline*	Raymond de Roover, *The Rise and Decline of the Medici Bank, 1397–1494*. 2nd ed., Cambridge, Mass., 1963.
RR.II.SS.	L.A. Muratori, *Rerum italicarum scriptores,* 1723–1751; n. ed. 1900–
Rubinstein, *Government*	Nicolai Rubinstein, *The Government of Florence under the Medici, 1434–94* (Oxford-Warburg Studies), Oxford, 1966.
Zibaldone	MS. *Zibaldone Quaresimale di Giovanni Rucellai* in possession of Count Bernardo Rucellai.

NICOLAI RUBINSTEIN

INTRODUCTION

INTRODUCTION

Giovanni Rucellai's contribution to the adornment of his native city has been evident for five centuries. On the façade he gave to the church of Santa Maria Novella an inscription prominently records his patronage, and his palace on Via della Vigna Nuova, together with the Rucellai Loggia near by, less explicitly but equally eloquently proclaim him a wealthy citizen and a patron of architecture. Yet he is not so much as mentioned in Jacob Burckhardt's *Civilization of the Renaissance in Italy*, and even a hundred years ago he was almost unknown to historians of Florence.

The picture that emerged in 1881 from the first publication of extracts from Rucellai's *Zibaldone Quaresimale* was that of a great Florentine merchant of the Quattrocento, who was also interesting for his connexion with the Medici. This connexion, it was subsequently believed, he had emphasized by placing the Medici emblem of a diamond ring on the façade of his palace. On the façade of Santa Maria Novella and the Rucellai Loggia, as well as in the courtyard of the palace, his personal *impresa* of a wind-filled sail is also several times displayed. Aby Warburg was the first, in 1907, to interpret this device in the light of Marsilio Ficino's reply to Giovanni's question about the nature of Fortune and the remedies against her power. For Warburg, the merchant's request was an expression of a deep concern with the problems of fortune and prudence, necessity and freedom of action, and of an ability to 'reconcile his belief in the power of the pagan goddess with his traditional devotion'[1].

Warburg gave Giovanni Rucellai a lasting place in the history of Renaissance culture. For the economic historian, on the other hand, the 'überseeische Kaufmann'—a figure which must have been familiar enough to the native of Hamburg—could also be representative of early capitalism[2]. It was not until the edition, in 1960, by Alessandro Perosa of a large part of the *Zibaldone* that it became clear how fitting Giovanni Rucellai's personal device was in reflecting not only his preoccupation with the moral problems posed by the concept of Fortune, but the vicissitudes of his mercantile enterprises.

The edition of the *Zibaldone*, judiciously balanced in its selection, provided a much fuller picture of Rucellai's life and ideas than had hitherto been obtainable, as well as new evidence of the public and private attitudes of a Florentine patrician of the Quattrocento. We have moved away from Warburg's emphasis on Giovanni Rucellai's preoccupation with Fortuna; and we are no longer solely interested in him as a patron of the arts. The publication of the *Zibaldone* coincided with a growing interest, represented by a number of historical studies, in the structure of the Florentine upper class and its place in Florentine politics during the fifteenth century. Gene Brucker, consequently, could even see Rucellai as 'a spokesman for the Florentine patriciate of the mid-Quattrocento'[3]. This class no longer had the political power it had possessed before the Medici régime was established, but it remained its principal social ingredient. The varied fortunes of Giovanni Rucellai's public life bear out the problems Florentine *ottimati* had to face under the Medici, and in their turn help us to unravel the complex network of public and private relationships which enabled the Medici to

---

[1] A. Warburg, "Francesco Sassetti's letztwillige Verfügung", in *Gesammelte Schriften,* ed. G. Bing, Leipzig, 1932, I, pp. 146–50 = *La Rinascita del paganesimo antico,* Florence, 1960, pp. 232–8; I quote E. H. Gombrich, *Aby Warburg. An Intellectual Biography,* London, 1970, p. 173.

[2] W. Sombart, *Der Bourgeois. Zur Geistesgeschichte des modernen Wirtschaftsmenschen,* Munich, 1913, pp. 282–3.

[3] *Renaissance Florence,* New York, 1969, pp. 125–7.

found and consolidate their ascendancy. Deprived of eligibility for government office in 1455, he recovered it by special dispensation two years after his son Bernardo's engagement to Lorenzo de' Medici's sister Nannina. In September 1466 his election to the Balìa which ended a brief period of republican reaction launched him late in life on a political career which was crowned, a year before his death, by his election to the powerful council of Seventy.

Another field of study in which Giovanni's *Zibaldone* has achieved fresh significance is that of the family and its place in Renaissance society. The vast amount of documentary material available for these studies in Florence, above all in the *catasti*, offers opportunities unequalled anywhere in late medieval Italy and Europe. The work of Philip Jones, Richard Goldthwaite, F. W. Kent, Dale Kent, David Herlihy and Christiane Klapisch has thrown a flood of light on a subject which not so long ago was almost exclusively the business of genealogists. A major question which has emerged in the course of these explorations relates to the role, in Florentine society during the fifteenth century, of the 'extended family'. Was it, following a pattern which can be observed elsewhere in Europe, being gradually displaced by the smaller domestic group of the 'nuclear family', usually consisting only of the parents and their children? In contrast to Professor Goldthwaite, Dr. F. W. Kent has argued that the wider family group of the *casa* or *consorteria* survived as an important social unit after the end of the fourteenth century, and in his *Household and Lineage in Renaissance Florence* has drawn on the rich, and mostly unpublished, material on the Rucellai family in the *Zibaldone*, compiled by Giovanni and his descendants[1]. The study he has contributed to this volume explores the role of family and lineage in Giovanni Rucellai's life within the wider context of his place in the city: it shows the patrician as private and public citizen.

Much the same regard for the 'famiglia de' Rucellai' as in the *Zibaldone* is revealed by Giovanni Rucellai's building projects, in particular his palace and its Loggia. In his last will he stipulated that the ownership of the palace must never leave the *consorteria* of the Rucellai; the Loggia was designed for the communal use of the whole family, not only for the private use of his household; and following an ancient Florentine tradition, he transformed part of the Via della Vigna into a Rucellai enclave. At the same time, he showed great pride in his personal role as a benefactor of his family, and pointed out that while in general spending money well had brought him greater honour than acquiring it, this was especially true of his buildings, first among them his palace, and of his additions to the two Rucellai churches, the façade of S. Maria Novella and his chapel in S. Pancrazio[2]. More than any other form of art patronage, such building activities could combine the sense of personal status and social ambition with loyalty to the family and its heritage. They could also be seen as a service to the city.

Florence, wrote Matteo Palmieri a few years before Cosimo de' Medici began the construction of his palace, is enriched by the 'bellezza de' privati abituri', the 'beauty of private dwellings'[3]. The following decades were marked by a veritable boom in palace building, due partly to the example set by Cosimo, partly to the exemptions granted by the new taxation system introduced in 1427 and to the lightening of the tax burden following on the peace of 1454 which concluded a period of thirty years of intermittent wars. One after another of the great Florentine families would rebuild and extend their houses, or build new and more splendid ones. Luca Pitti, and later Filippo Strozzi, were certainly not alone in bringing competition and rivalry to an enterprise in which art patronage was closely tied up with social prestige and political status. Like Cosimo de' Medici,

---

[1] Kent, *Household and Lineage,* esp. pp. 274–8.
[2] Perosa, p. 118.   [3] *Della vita civile,* ed. F. Battaglia, Bologna, 1944, p. 164.

Giovanni Rucellai saw his palace as only one part, although probably the most important and demanding, of his architectural patronage; unlike Luca Pitti and other great citizens, he did not attempt to imitate Cosimo's palace, but created a unique building whose style was in keeping with his admiration of that 'risucitatore delle muraglie antiche alla romanescha', Brunelleschi[1]. He would no doubt have agreed with Leon Battista Alberti's statement that 'we build sumptuously in order to demonstrate our greatness to posterity', but also in order 'to do honour to our fatherland and to our family'[2]. In fifteenth-century Florence, a palace could serve as a physical testimony to the individual patron's wealth and power as well as a symbol of his family's place in the city. Three of the studies contained in this volume reflect this close relationship between a patrician citizen and his palace.

Giovanni Rucellai's admiration for classical antiquity and his pride in its revival in early Quattrocento Florence, borne out by his *Zibaldone* as well as by the façade of his palace, raise the question of his attitude to contemporary humanism. This is a question which is fully discussed in Professor Perosa's study in this volume of the *Zibaldone* as a document of Giovanni's cultural formation. Unable to read Greek and probably even Latin, he draws widely on classical sources to provide moral teachings, and he turns to leading representatives of humanist learning for the solution of the philosophical problem which troubled him most of all, that of the power of Fortuna. Other sections of the *Zibaldone* have more in common with the popular culture of Trecento and early Quattrocento Florence than with the new classicism. Giovanni's interest in the history of his city, shown by the insertion in the *Zibaldone* of large extracts from Domenico Buoninsegni's historical compilation, as well as by his personal memoirs, is quite untouched by the humanist historiography of Bruni and Poggio. In relying, for his moral advice to his sons, on the abridged version of the third book of Alberti's *Della Famiglia*, which was ascribed to Angelo Pandolfini, he was seeking guidance from a fellow patrician rather than from a humanist representing the philosophy of classical antiquity. Yet in his ideal picture of a citizen, that of Palla Strozzi, he singles out as particularly noteworthy Palla's knowledge of Greek and Latin. In his own way he tried to live up to the humanist belief in the reconciliation between the *vita activa* and the *vita contemplativa*, although during much of his adult life the former meant for him, rather than participation in the government of Florence, the activities of a great merchant-banker.

How far was Giovanni Rucellai 'typical' of his social group, the patriciate, or, for that matter, of Florentine Quattrocento culture? A shrewd businessman, he believed that spending one's wealth was more satisfactory and honourable than acquiring it; belonging to a class which was accustomed, and considered itself entitled, to ruling Florence, he was excluded from government under Cosimo until, after the engagement of his eldest son to one of Piero's daughters, he was admitted to the inner circle of the Medici regime. As an innovating patron of the arts, he built a palace which, while serving as a model for Pius II's palace at Pienza, found, like his Loggia, no imitator in Florence. In the *Zibaldone*, though he praised Florentine painters and architects, he did not so much as mention the name of the architect of his palace, nor, for that matter, that of the painter of the frescoes in its *altana*. It may be argued that these contrasting aspects of his life and thought were characteristic of the Florentine patriciate of the mid-Quattrocento. Rather than regard him as a typical representative of that class, we may see him as exemplifying its richly diverse contribution to the civilization of Renaissance Florence.

---

[1] Perosa, p. 61.
[2] *De re aedificatoria*, ed. G. Orlandi and P. Portoghesi, Milan, 1966, II, p. 783: 'uti aiebat Tuchidides, magna struimus, ut posteris magni fuisse videamur . . . patriae familiaeque condecorandae non minus quam lautitiae gratia nostra ornamus'.

F. W. KENT

THE MAKING OF A RENAISSANCE PATRON OF THE ARTS

THE MAKING OF A RENAISSANCE PATRON OF THE ARTS

I. INTRODUCTION

Giovanni Rucellai's mixed and unsteady reputation both with his contemporaries and with later historians mirrors his enigmatic career. He is known today to anybody interested in the Italian Renaissance—if not as a 'typical' figure, a rich patron of the arts who wrote a charming common-place book, then at least as Palla Strozzi's son-in-law and Bernardo Rucellai's father—yet there is something elusive about him in the Quattrocento sources. He is rarely mentioned in the chronicles and great letter collections of the period. Not even Alessandra Strozzi, who lived near Rucellai in town and country and shared a common acquaintance, refers to him more than casually, save for one incident in which his role was ambiguous[1]. Giovanni's absence from the political scene for a quarter of a century helps to explain contemporaries' neglect, but his far from anonymous building pro-gramme attracted little comment by comparison with Cosimo de' Medici's[2]. Vasari gave his palace to a Rucellai other than Giovanni[3], who has himself inconvenienced generations of art historians by his own silence as to his architect's identity. A number of Rucellai's closest relations and friends were praised by Vespasiano da Bisticci, but Giovanni himself went unnoticed.

We do not even know what he looked like. A man so self-absorbed, with such artistic connections, must surely have commissioned a portrait bust—as did his acquaintance Giovanni Chellini[4]—or have had his likeness smuggled into a painting. There remain to us, however, only a suggestion that he or his son Bernardo may be lurking somewhere in Cosimo Rosselli's *Adoration of the Magi*[5], and a sixteenth-century portrait, not even—so far as one can tell—taken from a death mask (Frontispiece). The portrait turns this vigorous banker (who once repeated the Albertian dictum that man is not

I am grateful to Brenda Preyer, Diane Zervas, Heather Gregory and Nicolai Rubinstein for reading and commenting upon these chapters in typescript; more generally I should like to thank Count Bernardo Rucellai, and Professors Rubinstein and Alessandro Perosa, for the support they have given me and the entire project. I have received financial help from the History Department at Monash University and from the Australian Research Grants Committee, whose grant enabled me to enjoy the benefits of Gino Corti's archival expertise. As on other occasions Dr. Corti has been more than generous with his time and knowledge. A period of leave, during which I was a fellow of the Harvard University Center for Italian Renaissance Studies in Florence, alone made it possible to complete the manuscript which Signora Fiorella Gioffredi Superbi quickly and efficiently typed for me. I owe less specific but important debts to Gene Brucker, who some years ago encouraged me to pursue further my interest in Giovanni Rucellai, and to my final honours "special subject" classes at Monash University between 1973–77 with whom I talked over—indeed formulated—many of the arguments that follow. It has been a pleasure to collaborate with Dr. Brenda Preyer, with whom I have constantly exchanged information. Dr. Preyer's contribution to this volume, and the thesis on which it is based, add much to our knowledge of Giovanni's life and have provided me with a number of my points. Dale Kent shared her knowledge of the field, read and typed successive drafts, and even came to accept Rucellai's unexpectedly long stay in *casa nostra*. I believe it will be obvious how much my portrait of Giovanni Rucellai draws on her past, and our present, research.

[1] Alessandra Macinghi degli Strozzi, *Lettere di una gentildonna fiorentina del secolo XV ai figliuoli esuli*, ed. C. Guasti, Florence, 1877, pp. 37, 386 (but cf. p. 70 below). For some other contemporary references in the Strozzi papers and elsewhere, see below, p. 77, n. 4, and CS, III, 131, f. 101ʳ (24 February 1463).

[2] For contemporary references, see below, pp. 84–85. Cf. K. W. Forster, "The Palazzo Rucellai and Questions of Typology in the Development of Renaissance Buildings", *AB*, LVIII (1976), pp. 109–13.

[3] See p. 43, n. 4 below.

[4] Rucellai borrowed silver plate from Chellini for the marriage of a daughter to Bernardo Manetti in 1452: see R. W. Light-bown, "Giovanni Chellini, Donatello, and Antonio Rossellino", *BM*, CIV (1962), p. 103.

[5] R. Hatfield, *Botticelli's Uffizi Adoration*, Princeton, 1976, pp. 73, n. 20, 92, n. 83, 98, n. 108.

born 'per vivere dormendo, ma per vivere facendo')[1] into an immobile patriarch, dignified and bearded, surrounded by his commissions and holding a book with the portentous title *Delle Antichità*[2].

Giovanni has left from his own pen a capital source for his life and character, the *Zibaldone Quaresimale* begun in 1457, but it is still in some respects a reticent book which raises as many questions as it generously resolves. Explicit about what Giovanni was eating on 17 July 1458 (prematurely ripe *fichi albi*)[3], it neglects to tell us how precisely the dramatic betrothal of Bernardo di Giovanni to Cosimo de' Medici's grand-daughter in 1461 was engineered; frank about its author's great admiration for Palla Strozzi, it is in effect silent on the very existence of precise and elaborate bonds between the two long after the older man's exile from Florence in late 1434. Uniquely revealing of a patron's attitudes and background, it yields very little practical information about his patronage. Moreover the *Zibaldone*, by presenting its author's achievements, considered opinions and paternal advice in carefully selected phases of his later life, tends to underplay and even to eliminate—whether by design or not one cannot say—the struggles and tensions of a long and difficult career.

There are no account-books, no collection of private papers, with which to compare and supplement the intriguing information in the *Zibaldone*. The archive of the Rucellai family contains some useful clues, but the mass of Giovanni's papers—the correspondence and registers he sometimes mentions, and much else no doubt—have gone beyond recall[4]. As early after his death as 1495 his archive was in disarray, perhaps because his sons Pandolfo and Bernardo, so unlike each other in almost every other respect, had in common, at least, a cavalier approach to their affairs. Paolo di Pandolfo was unable to find a certain *libro rosso*, he reported to his father on 26 September, 'chè ò rivolto tutta la chasa'; when a month later the book was found, with the help of friends, among sacks of letters 'sopra l'armario grande', Paolo commented that 'è suto uno miracolo'[5]. There appear to have been further gaps in the archive a century or so later; one could almost sympathize with the gifted forger of documents concerning Giovanni Rucellai, at work in the archive in the late seventeenth or early eighteenth century, had he not further muddied the waters[6]. It is certainly explicable that he gave some of his expert attention to producing letters supposedly written by his hero, for Giovanni's twenty odd genuine surviving letters are as reticent in their way as the *Zibaldone* itself, though they complement it. Of Giovanni's ruling passions only his acquisitive drive emerges clearly from the letters, which are impersonal, business-like and even bland (there is

---

[1] Perosa, p. 43.

[2] Published as 'derivazione da Giorgio Vasari' in *Mostra dei Tesori segreti delle case fiorentine*, Florence, 1960, pp. 25–26, and tav. 39. Older writers have accepted the portrait as a genuine likeness: Marcotti, *Mercante fiorentino*, pp. 40–41; Biagi, *Men and Manners*, p. 129. See also now Perosa, below, p. 99, n. 1.

[3] *Zibaldone*, f. 66ᵛ.

[4] Some were presumably still there in 1574, when Giovanni di Pandolfo di Paolo Rucellai noted in his *ricordanze*, without further detail, that he had made an inventory 'di tutte le mia scritture, lettere di diversi et libri antichi et moderni di conti et altro dove sono . . .' (Acquisti e Doni, 315, f. 43ᵛ). For a description of the modern archive, see S. Camerani, "Notizie degli archivi toscani", *ASI*, CXIV (1956), p. 430. I thank Renzo Ristori for the information that the Rucellai papers which were held by the Goggi family and then by John Temple Leader in the mid-nineteenth century all found their way back to their original owners, the *Zibaldone Quaresimale* by purchase in London in 1923, and the rest by gift. Apparently only the commonplace book went to England with Temple Leader's heir; I am grateful to the present Lord Westbury for confirming that his family possesses no Rucellai papers from this inheritance.

[5] Spedale di S. Matteo, 30, ff. 357ʳ⁻ᵛ, 361ʳ. Two years earlier, some Strozzi papers in the archive could not be found (see CS, III, 139, f. 21ʳ⁻ᵛ, and for the circumstances p. 92, n. 4 below).

[6] On this man, whom Brenda Preyer calls 'the Archivist', see her interesting remarks, below, p. 163, n. 3 and Kent, "Letters", pp. 342–9.

only one touch of irony)[1]. Reading them in isolation, one would not dream that their author was a major patron of the arts[2].

Perhaps because of this inaccessibility, which is however not always recognized by historians understandably and properly grateful for the *Zibaldone*, Giovanni Rucellai has received a mixed and often a bad press since the publication of Giovanni Marcotti's *Un mercante fiorentino e la sua famiglia nel secolo XV* in 1881. Even though he has been admired as 'le type du marchand éclairé de la Renaissance'[3], a 'rich and liberal bourgeois'[4], there has been little agreement about what constituted Rucellai's typicality. For Werner Sombart Alberti and Rucellai were quintessential middle-class merchants whose writings heralded the triumph of bourgeois individualism and capitalist values over older aristocratic mores and ideals[5]. Recently, in a sensitive sketch of Giovanni, an American historian has found in the *Zibaldone* statements which 'define and justify an aristocratic mode of life; they reflect a milieu of leisure and enjoyment, and also of withdrawal and disengagement from affairs'[6]. Rucellai's public spiritedness has not gone unpraised, but Girolamo Mancini, in his life of Alberti, went out of his way violently to attack the banker for his political opportunism. In particular, he censures Rucellai's ingratitude to Palla Strozzi whom, by Mancini's account, he deserted after 1434 to court favour with the Medici[7]. This 'change of party', according to Luigi Passerini, the family's genealogist, 'non forma il più bell'elogio della sua fermezza d'animo e della sincerità del suo amore di patria'[8].

It was Passerini, in 1861, who first formulated the view of Rucellai's role in fifteenth-century Florence which, though strongly challenged from time to time, has become more coherent, explicit and popular with the years. In Passerini's opinion, the support given by Rucellai and other aristocrats to the Medici and their preference for private over public interests, helped 'to enchain Florence' and to initiate the decline of their own class[9]. Even a more sympathetic writer saw Giovanni as a symbol—to be compared unfavourably with a simple *popolano* such as Ser Lapo Mazzei—of the Quattrocento's loss of innocence[10]. In 1906 an Englishman, Wood Brown, joined this adverse judgement on Giovanni's political conduct to a denunciation of the misuse by the individualist and selfish Medici and their followers of their patronage of the arts; it was a sign of social and cultural decline when, as the popular guild regime gave way to a more autocratic rule, 'the Arts swallowed up the Arti'[11]. Arnold Hauser's more refined version of this account pictured Giovanni as 'perhaps

---

[1] Of Betto Rustichi, with whom he was in litigation, Rucellai wrote to Lorenzo de' Medici on 15 October 1468 that 'quando mi dava una schusa e quando un'altra, e che al presente gli dava noia la vendemmia, e anchor dava schusa alla madre che non lo chonsentiva etc. Dipoi è achaduto che tre dì fa egli à fatto citare noi alla chorte dell'arciveschovado . . . E a questo non gli dà noia la vendemia . . .' (MAP, XXI, 109).

[2] Kent, "Letters", pp. 342–9. To the letters described on p. 342, n. 2, one must add several more, discovered by Brenda Preyer and by me, cited below.

[3] Rochon, *Jeunesse*, p. 90. See too Biagi, *Men and Manners*, p. 125, and most recently M. Bucci, *Palazzi di Firenze: Quartiere di S. Maria Novella*, Florence, 1973, p. 93.

[4] E. Londi, *Leon Battista Alberti architetto*, Florence, 1906, p. 49.

[5] *The Quintessence of Capitalism*, London, 1915, pp. 103 ff. Cf. A. von Martin, *Sociology of the Renaissance*, London, 1944, pp. 29–30.

[6] G. A. Brucker, *Renaissance Florence*, New York, 1969, p. 126.

[7] *Vita di Leon Battista Alberti*, 2nd edn., 1911, reprint Rome, 1967, pp. 419 ff.

[8] L. Passerini, *Genealogia e storia della famiglia Rucellai*, Florence, 1861, p. 118.

[9] *Ibid.*

[10] A. d'Ancona, "Due antichi Fiorentini: Ser Jacopo Mazzei e Bernardo Rucellai", *Varietà storiche e letterarie*, seconda serie, Milan, 1885, pp. 189–222. Marcotti, *Mercante fiorentino*, portrays Giovanni as the quintessential 'uomo di transizione' (p. 10) overcome by political forces beyond his control (pp. 18–19).

[11] *The Builders of Florence*, London, 1906, p. 229. See in general pp. 203 ff.

the best representative of the new type of secularly-minded patron', whose generosity was inspired more by private and personal concerns than by family pride, 'much more keenly occupied with their palaces than with their family chapels'. Rucellai, Hauser goes on, 'comes from a patrician family which had made its money in the wool industry and he belongs to the generation devoted to the enjoyment of life which begins to withdraw from business during the regime of Lorenzo de' Medici'[1]. Giovanni's 'second generation' mentality, his pursuit of the aristocratic life in which spending is more important than earning, has also been held to be explained by economic rather than political causes; he was, according to R. S. Lopez and Yves Renouard, a worried Renaissance businessman whose patronage of the arts was an investment in culture, a response to economic depression[2].

Several of these strands have been pulled together, and the weaker ones rejected, in Gene Brucker's very interesting characterization of Rucellai as 'a spokesman for the Florentine patriciate of the mid-Quattrocento' whose 'credentials are impeccable'. Carefully noting the 'thicket of conventional attitudes and viewpoints' in the *Zibaldone,* Brucker emphasizes 'the novel elements in this value system'. Giovanni is a-political and opposed to his sons' engaging in trade. He is above all complacent, an emergent aristocrat who defends liberality and the *vita signorile*. 'There is little trace in this diary of the drives and impulses to action, involvement, and acquisition which marked the careers (and the memoirs) of Florentine patricians in the fourteenth and early fifteenth centuries'[3]. As Lauro Martines put it, though not speaking of Rucellai himself, 'the courtier had made his appearance in Florence'[4]. Beside (if not synonymous with) him, Giovanni emerges as a chief actor in a drama in which the Medici, abetted by a contracting and ultimately enfeebled oligarchy, became virtual rulers of Florence. One version of this scenario—that of Martines who here follows Eugenio Garin—also implies the explanation of certain major changes in the intellectual history of the later fifteenth century when there occurred, it has been brilliantly argued, a flight from reality to metaphysics, from civic humanism to Neoplatonism[5]. Rucellai, not a humanist, has been given a minor role in this last act, dominated by the 'complaisant' Neoplatonist Marsilio Ficino, busily administering his 'Platonic poison' to the 'merchant tyranny' of which the banker was a member[6].

Even if Rucellai's clearly controversial personality and career did not arouse our curiosity, his prominence in these influential explanations of the connections between Renaissance society and the arts would invite a brief biography with which to test, and perhaps to refine them. We have been reminded that, because it is difficult to define 'the links between economics, politics, literature and the arts' without resorting to rhetoric, it may be time to touch earth again by looking hard at

---

[1] *The Social History of Art*: *Renaissance, Mannerism, Baroque,* London, 1962 edn., ii, p. 34.

[2] There is no reference to Rucellai in R. S. Lopez's "Hard Times and Investment in Culture", in *The Renaissance. A Symposium* (*February* 8–10, 1952), Metropolitan Museum of Art, New York, 1953. In Lopez's *The Three Ages of the Italian Renaissance,* Charlottesville, 1970, however, Giovanni is used as an example of a man 'losing money for many years' for whom 'art had become a good investment, if only as the credit card of the élite' (p. 14). See too Y. Renouard, "L'Essor et le déclin de la banque des Médicis", *Annales E.S.C.,* XX (1965), pp. 166–7.

[3] *Renaissance Florence,* pp. 125–6. See too Brucker's review of Perosa in *Speculum,* XXXVI (1961), pp. 346–8.

[4] *The Social World of the Florentine Humanists, 1390–1460,* Princeton, 1963, p. 294.

[5] *Ibid.,* pp. 263 ff., where reference is made to Garin's work on this theme.

[6] E. Wind, "Platonic Tyranny and the Renaissance Fortuna: On Ficino's Reading of Laws IV, 709A–712A", in *De artibus opuscula XL: Essays in Honor of Erwin Panofsky,* ed. M. Meiss, New York, 1961, i, pp. 491–6. I am grateful to Jaynie Anderson for sending me the revised version which will appear in the collection of Wind's essays she is editing.

individuals and their activities[1]. Wallace Ferguson, concerned to account for the vitality of Renaissance culture in a period of economic stagnation, has also urged a return to biographical studies of businessmen and their expectations and attitudes—a particularly happy suggestion when one remembers Giovanni Rucellai's optimism about Florence's economy, even amidst the crises of the late 1420s and the failures of the 1460s[2]. That this approach can yield results which are at once convincingly precise and interestingly broad Richard Goldthwaite has shown in a recent monograph on Filippo Strozzi and his palace[3].

Despite the limitations and ambiguity of the evidence, there is still much to be said about Giovanni Rucellai. His letters, if unexciting, provide much information for the years 1437–1480. The extensive unpublished parts of the *Zibaldone* give a fuller sense of Giovanni's activities and vicissitudes than the printed selections can convey. The resources of the Florentine State Archives have not yet been systematically exploited to throw light on Rucellai, as Brenda Preyer has been the first to show[4]. Apart from the information in the more accessible taxation and *tratte* records, there is precious if scattered material in the notarial protocols, the Strozzi papers and elsewhere, especially in the archive of the convent of San Pancrazio, already used by Marco Dezzi Bardeschi[5]. Outside Florence, in Ferrara and Padua, one can find vital clues concerning Rucellai's ties, important for an understanding of his life and patronage, with his exiled Strozzi relations.

From all these sources Giovanni emerges, as Aby Warburg realized in 1907[6], a more complex, indeed a more consistent, even a more admirable, character than has often been implied. He reveals himself as a man so obsessed with building that, having in his own words done nothing for fifty years but earn and spend[7], he chose to pour his earnings into architectural patronage. In the *Zibaldone* he quotes the aphorism 'Due cose principali sono quelle che gl'uomini fanno in questo mondo: La prima lo'ngienerare: La seconda l'edifichare'[8], and it is hardly an exaggeration to say that an account of his life must also be largely an exploration of the origins and workings of this second passion which, unlike most of his Florentine contemporaries, he lived long enough and was shrewd enough to gratify before his death.

---

[1] E. H. Gombrich, "Renaissance and Golden Age", in *Norm and Form*, London, 1966, p. 29 (here quoting and commenting upon a point made by D. Cantimori). R. Fubini saw in Perosa's edition of the *Zibaldone* an opportunity to re-examine 'una tipologia ormai trita' (*GSLI*, CXXXVII [1960], p. 466).

[2] "Recent Trends in the economic Historiography of the Renaissance", *Studies in the Renaissance*, VII (1960), pp. 7–26. For Rucellai's attitudes, see Perosa, pp. 61–62, 117–20, and G. Ponte, "Etica ed economia nel Terzo Libro 'Della Famiglia' di Leon Battista Alberti", *Renaissance Studies in Honor of Hans Baron*, ed. A. Molho and J. A. Tedeschi, De Kalb, Illinois, 1971, pp. 299–300, n. 47.

[3] "The Building of the Strozzi Palace: The Construction Industry in Renaissance Florence", *Studies in Medieval and Renaissance History*, X (1973), pp. 97–104.

[4] Preyer, *Giovanni Rucellai*, *passim*.

[5] Dezzi Bardeschi, "Complesso monumentale", pp. 1–66. Inevitably, many notarial records concerning Giovanni's life, scattered as they are throughout the numerous uncatalogued protocols for the Quattrocento, will have escaped my attention.

[6] "Francesco Sassettis letztwillige Verfügung", in *Gesammelte Schriften*, Leipzig, 1932, I, pp. 145 ff. = *La Rinascita del paganesimo antico*, Florence, 1966, pp. 231 ff. Cf. Perosa, below, pp. 134 ff.

[7] Perosa, p. 121.

[8] *Zibaldone*, f. 83ᵛ. I now find the passage also in Giannozzo Salviati's *Zibaldone*, begun in 1484: 'Due sono le principali chose che fanno gli uomini in questo mondo, cioè la prima si è lo'ngienerare, la sechonda si è lo edifichare. Ma debbesi edifichare per neciesità non per volontà' (BNC, II, IX, 42, f. 12ʳ). Cf. p. 52, n. 6 below for Giovanni's version of this last sentence.

II. EARLY LIFE, 1403–33

The facts of Giovanni's early life, sparse and not always easily interpreted, are abundant enough to suggest that his paradoxical character—vigorously self-assertive, but reliant upon the support provided by others—was formed in an atmosphere of uncertainty and disruption. His twenty-five-year-old father Paolo di Messer Paolo died in 1406, when Giovanni was only three, leaving a young widow, Caterina (née Pandolfini), who already had borne 'quattro figluoli maschi in termine di 40 mesi, che ongni 10 mesi ne faceva uno. . .'[1]. This 'notable mother', who lived to be over eighty, was a very determined young woman. To ensure that her infant family was not 'abandoned'—the children lacked the close Rucellai relations (grandfather, uncles or first cousins) who normally might have protected their interests—Caterina 'fè gran risistentia di non rimaritarsi contro al volere de' fratelli e della madre'[2]. Seventy years afterwards Giovanni describes his debt to her in a passage which is emotionally revealing to an unusual degree:

> e monna Chaterina nostra madre rimase vedova d'età d'anni 19, e per non ci abandonare non volle rimaritarsi e puossi dire che nnoi non chonoscessimo Paghola nostro padre, perchè nel tenpo che morì Govanni aveva 3 anni, Filippo 2 anni, Donato uno anno (Pagholo era in chorpo e naque poi dopo la morte di nostro padre), e però monna Chaterina ci fu madre e ppadre, di che gli siamo ubrighati più che a madre di preghare Idio per lei[3].

The very fact that Caterina had to withstand pressure from her Pandolfini brothers suggests what other evidence confirms, that for some years the fatherless family moved within the domestic orbit of this small but wealthy and distinguished lineage from the quarter of San Giovanni. The precise details of where and with whom the young Rucellai lived are not clear. In the second decade of the century, they cannot have stayed in their ancestral house, in the Via della Vigna Nuova in the parish of San Pancrazio where almost all of their many Rucellai kinsmen were settled, because at that time this house and their country villa were both rented out. Perhaps the brothers had left their own house almost at once, in later 1406 when most of their furniture was ordered to be sold by the authority of the Ufficiali dei Pupilli, the magistracy in charge of the estate[4]. If so, they probably lived with or near their Pandolfini relatives, two of whom were compensated for the wards' living expenses during this time. One such reference of 1408 suggests that the two eldest boys, Giovanni

---

[1] *Zibaldone*, f. 223ʳ.

[2] Perosa, p. 118; see also p. 177, n. 9. On the customary role of *proximi consorti*, see Kent, *Household and Lineage*, Part I.

[3] *Zibaldone*, f. 223ʳ. After her death in 1471, Rucellai was anxious to have the details of 'uno lascio che monna Chaterina mia madre fecie alla chiesa di Sancto Branchazio d'uno champo di terra e d'uno pezzo di vigna', so that he would know 'quello ch'e' monaci sono obrighato di fare ciaschun anno per rimedio dell'anima di detta monna Chaterina'. This passage occurs in an undated note to Salvestro, brother of the notary Ser Antonio Salamone, requesting 'che tu sia operatore di fare ciercare nelle imbreviature di Ser Antonio . . . dal 1460 al 1470'. The note is autograph and is bound in at f. 76ʳ of NA S 20 (Ser Antonio Salamone, 1462–70). The year of the bequest was probably 1457 (see p. 60, n. 1 below).

[4] The villa at Quaracchi was leased by 'Benedicto Comi [Federighi]', a neighbour in San Pancrazio, from July 1406: Pupilli, 17, f. lvʳ. There appears to be no reference to the renting of the Florentine house in these official records (see *ibid.*, f. lviʳ, however, for the sale of its effects); in November 1414 it was rented to Cambio di Tano Petrucci, according to his *ricordanze* (CS, II, 10, f. 29ᵛ), which correctly describes its position as 'alato' the house of Piero di Giovanni Rucellai and brothers.

and Filippo, may have then lived apart from the younger ones[1]; they were again united by 1418 when they all rented a house, where we do not know, from the Guild of Notaries[2].

Pandolfini support and influence endured far beyond the boys' childhood. When Giovanni fled the plague in 1424, it was to Agnolo Pandolfini's villa at Ponte a Signa; this same uncle represented him at his betrothal ceremony in 1428[3]. (These would be suggestive details indeed were it likely that Agnolo wrote the well-known vulgarization, first used by Giovanni in 1457, of the third book of Alberti's *Della Famiglia*!)[4]. One of the executors of Giovanni's first will of 1437 was his cousin Giannozzo Pandolfini[5]. Another cousin, Carlo d'Agnolo, was the 'amicus communis et amicabilis compositor' appointed by the four brothers in February 1442 to preside over the dissolution of the joint household which his kin and he had earlier helped to keep together; as Messer Carlo, he was also to be prominent at Bernardo's wedding over twenty years later[6]. Giovanni Rucellai unmistakably acknowledged his domestic debt to, and affection for, the Pandolfini when he named his first son not Paolo, after his own father, but Pandolfo which had never been a Rucellai Christian name. One source of his knowledge about the fourteenth-century history of his own lineage was 'mona Dora, donna che fu di Filippo Pandolfini, mia avola'[7]; Caterina's Pandolfini mother and brothers had certainly accepted graciously their early defeat at her capable hands, and her sons had good reason to remember these maternal relations gratefully.

Despite Pandolfini support *in loco parentis*, however, and despite Caterina's successful effort to be 'more than a mother', the position of Giovanni and his brothers was vulnerable and unsettling, as his early interest in Rucellai traditions suggests. If it is usually unsatisfactory to be left fatherless when very young, it could be positively dangerous in fifteenth-century Florence, where unscrupulous guardians and kinsmen were, according to Giovanni Morelli[8], very much to be feared. There were other disadvantages, less material but crucial. The father–son relationship was an idealized one in that patrilineal society, and a fatherless Florentine boy had no solid ground from which to begin his ascent, no paternal mirror in which to observe himself, no direct and tangible link to connect him with the important world of his male ancestors[9]. The *Zibaldone* provides good evidence that Giovanni Rucellai, whose own father had also been a young ward, missed this paternal example and guidance. 'Diciesi', he wrote, 'che il maggiore amore che ssia è quello del padre verso il figliuolo' and went on to give examples and to draw up a timetable for the development of an ideal father-son relationship[10]. In an age of high and sudden mortality, Giovanni, always very conscious of

---

[1] Pupilli, 18, f. 134ᵛ: Giovanni di Filippo di Ser Giovanni [Pandolfini] was paid 30 florins 'pro alimentis datis Iohanni et Filippo'. A notarial act of 8 December 1407 had given this Giovanni authority in his sister's affairs; it was drawn up, possibly significantly, 'in populo Sancti Proculi', the Pandolfini parish (NA, C 187 [Ser Tommaso Carondini, 1406–8], f. 96ʳ). The Pandolfini tax report of 1427 throws no retrospective light on this question: Cat., 56, ff. 106ʳ–109ʳ.

[2] Pupilli, 27, f. 88ᵛ. In early 1416 Agnolo di Filippo di Ser Giovanni [Pandolfini] was compensated 'pro alimentis per eum datis domine . . . [sic] uxori olim dicti Pauli et filiis suis . . .' (*ibid.*, 24, f. 188ᵛ).

[3] *Zibaldone*, f. 26ʳ; NA, C 189 (Ser Tommaso Carondini, 1428–31), f. 14ʳ.

[4] F. C. Pellegrini, "Agnolo Pandolfini e il 'Governo della Famiglia' ", *GSLI*, VIII (1886), pp. 1–52; Judith Ravenscroft, *A Fifteenth-Century Guide to Household Management: The 'Trattato del Governo della Famiglia' ascribed to Agnolo Pandolfini*, unpublished M. Phil. thesis, University of London, 1972, pp. 85 ff. I am grateful to Miss Ravenscroft for permission to read her thesis. On Agnolo Pandolfini and Giovanni's use of the vulgarization, see now Perosa, below, pp. 111 ff.

[5] NA, C 190 (Ser Tommaso Carondini, 1435–38), f. 123ᵛ.

[6] *Ibid.*, B 1994 (Ser Matteo Boccianti, 1441–42), f. 84ʳ; Perosa, pp. 28, 53.

[7] Pub. by Marcotti, *Mercante fiorentino*, p. 58. The Pandolfini arms appear in the *altana* frescoes; see R. Salvini, below p. 247.

[8] Cited by C. Klapisch, " 'Parenti, amici e vicini': il territorio urbano d'una famiglia mercantile nel XV secolo", *Quaderni storici*, XXXIII (1976), p. 973, n. 1.

[9] Kent, *Household and Lineage*, Part I.

[10] Quoted *ibid.*, p. 56, n. 130; see too pp. 55–60.

the plague's depredations[1], was determined that his own sons should not be left as isolated and uninformed as he had been; in part we owe the *Zibaldone*, begun during an outbreak of plague in the year after his elder son married, to this passionate desire to 'dare notitia et amaestramento a Pandolfo et a Bernardo miei figliuoli di più chose, ch'io credo abbia a essere loro utile'[2]. They at least should not experience Donato Acciaiuoli's feelings, which his friend and kinsman Giovanni would have known and shared, for the father he had never known: 'I could not draw on the experience of his life . . .', Donato wrote to Rucellai's cousin Pandolfo Pandolfini, 'nor did I know any happiness thanks to him, nor did I receive any aid in my career, nor inspiration to lead a virtuous life'[3].

Giovanni may also have felt isolated from, and ignorant about, his other Rucellai ancestors and kinsmen. Certainly he began the *Zibaldone* by carefully introducing his sons to the history of their lineage and its achievements, and he provided a genealogy of some hundred *consorti*, living and dead. This information, perhaps not so early or easily acquired by one who had no close Rucellai kin and had spent at least some of his first years outside the circle of more distant cousins, Giovanni discovered later in discussion with 'più antichi huomini di casa nostra' and with others, and by some elementary documentary research[4]. It is possible that the young brothers had experienced a certain indifference from some of their kinsmen—this might help to explain the central role of the Pandolfini and Giovanni's own anxious and rather competitive commitment to the Rucellai—but even so they had remained in touch with their closest paternal cousins. Paolo Rucellai, and his two first cousins Iacopo di Messer Giovanni di Bingeri and Cardinale di Piero di Bingeri, had formally received Caterina's dowry in January 1402[5]; all these descendants of Bingeri owned some urban property in common until the middle of the century[6]. Earlier, Iacopo had been Paolo's guardian, in which capacity he was involved with the administration of the boys' paternal estate in December 1408[7], and it was his own nephews, Piero di Giovanni and brothers, who rented out the wards' house for them in November 1414, into friendly hands so far as one can tell[8]. The marriage in 1442 of Iacopantonio di Bingeri, from this Rucellai line, to one of Giovanni's Pandolfini cousins may reflect an earlier shared interest in the affairs of Paolo's young sons[9].

Such contacts would have served to remind the brothers as they grew older that it was among their paternal kinsmen that they were most likely to find a sense of public, and even private, identity. Despite any indifference there may have been, they returned to live in their ancestral *gonfalone* of Lion Rosso, perhaps as early as 1421, certainly by 1427 at the latest[10]. Their mother sanctioned this step towards reintegration into the Rucellai *consorteria* by moving with them, and was to continue for the rest of her long life to be part of that local Rucellai world. One suspects that, like another

---

[1] *Zibaldone*, ff. 25ᵛ–26ʳ, 81ʳ; Perosa, pp. 44 ff., 147–8. See too below, p. 66.

[2] Perosa, p. 2.

[3] Quoted by E. Garin, "Donato Acciaiuoli", *Portraits from the Quattrocento*, New York, 1963, p. 103, n. 7.

[4] Quoted in Kent, *Household and Lineage*, p. 278, n. 197. In general see Marcotti, *Mercante fiorentino*, pp. 53 ff. (on pp. 58–9 there is a quotation 'a verbo a verbo' from 'uno libro de' frati di Santa Maria Novella in carta pecorina'), and *Zibaldone*, ff. 1ʳ–2ᵛ. Giovanni noted of a collateral ancestor, Messer Guglielmo, that 'ancora dura la fama sua nel reame di Napoli' (Marcotti, *Mercante fiorentino*, p. 57), information he probably had from his brother Paolo, long established there (see below, p. 36).

[5] The reference is in a document of December 1407 in NA, C 187 (Ser Tommaso Carondini, 1406–08), f. 96ᵛ.

[6] Pupilli, 17, f.liiiʳ; Cat., 42, f. 453ᵛ; 43, f. 867ʳ; 707, f. 124ᵛ.

[7] Pupilli, 19, f. 1ʳ–ᵛ; Conv. Sopp., 88, 62, f. 27ʳ.

[8] CS, II, 10, f. 29ᵛ. Cambio Petrucci's *ricordanze* has a number of references to Paolo di Vanni Rucellai and other Rucellai friends and neighbours.

[9] *Zibaldone*, f. 223ᵛ; Passerini, *Rucellai*, tav. xi.

[10] Petrucci leased the brothers' house for a further three years in November 1420 (CS, II, 10, f. 58ᵛ; cf. ff. 29ᵛ, 40ʳ, 49ᵛ), but in fact took another one year later (ff. 70ᵛ, 71ᵛ). Their tax report of 1427 shows the four firmly established there (Cat., 43, f. 867ʳ).

redoubtable widow, her neighbour Alessandra Strozzi, Caterina actively fostered that sense of the patrilineage and its importance to which her dead husband would have subscribed[1]. The district of the Red Lion comprised an area of irregular shape centred on the churches of San Pancrazio and San Paolino. Confined to the north and south by Via della Scala and Borgo Ognissanti, it stretched in the west from Via Santa Caterina eastwards as far as Via de' Vecchietti. There lived in this *gonfalone* in 1427 some 535 households or about 2,200 people[2], a small community quite dominated by the Strozzi and Rucellai families. In the scrutiny held in 1433 to determine eligibility for Florence's chief magistracies, the two families won twenty-three and twenty-two majorities respectively, far more than their nearest patrician rivals, the smaller Federighi, Minerbetti, Berardi and Temperanni[3]. Several of the greatest Strozzi lived there; to a district meeting held on 4 July 1428 came Lorenzo, son of Florence's richest man Messer Palla, and his kinsman Matteo di Simone, also a prominent member of the ruling group[4]. The twenty-three households of Rucellai, some of them prosperous wool merchants and bankers and generous patrons of the local church of San Pancrazio, lived *en masse* in the section of the *gonfalone* where the house of Giovanni and his brothers stood. Here, in the year the boys' father had died, two of their kinsmen had assaulted some humbler neighbours and when they made peace did so 'pro se ipsis et eorum fratribus et consortibus'[5]. Relations between neighbours were not always so strained. In the *gonfalone* of his own lineage a young aristocrat could usually hope to find support in the first stage of the electoral process by which office was attained, favourable discrimination for those taxes still administered by representatives of the districts and, less tangible but just as encouraging, a sense of belonging[6].

After their move to Lion Rosso, acceptance of the brothers into the wider Rucellai community came quickly. Though quite young, Giovanni was among the five Rucellai tutors for his children named by Cardinale di Piero, a family elder and his first cousin once removed, in his will of August 1428[7]. A year later the young men lent 525 florins to more distant cousins, whose house they occupied as compensation. The tax records mention other financial transactions, including a sizable one with Paolo di Cardinale[8]. Filippo, the second brother, was an official of Lion Rosso for part of 1428[9], about which time the four began to enjoy the wider benefits of local political support. Giovanni's success in a minor scrutiny in 1427 gave him several administrative offices from 1429 onwards; the three elder brothers attained majorities in the 1433 scrutiny to the *Tre Maggiori*[10].

On 6 June 1428, in the church of Santa Trinita, Giovanni was betrothed to Iacopa, one of Messer Palla Strozzi's daughters, and this splendid match must have contributed to his increasingly secure place in the local community. Iacopa's dowry of 1,200 florins, received upon the marriage in 1431,

---

[1] I owe this point about Alessandra to Heather Gregory's unpublished honours thesis (Monash University). For a rather different account of 'feminine influences' on fatherless boys, see D. Herlihy, "Mapping Households in medieval Italy", *Catholic Historical Review*, LVIII (1972), p. 18. On Caterina, see Kent, *Household and Lineage*, pp. 24, 181.

[2] I am grateful to Marian Murphy for these details from her unpublished master's thesis (La Trobe University, 1978).

[3] D. V. Kent, "The Florentine *Reggimento* in the Fifteenth Century", *Renaissance Quarterly*, XXVIII (1975), p. 636; cf. Kent, *Household and Lineage*, p. 180.

[4] NA, A 798 (Ser Antonio di Luca Franceschi, 1428–31), f. 13ʳ⁻ᵛ.

[5] *Ibid.*, C 187 (Ser Tommaso Carondini, 1406–08), f. 44ʳ⁻ᵛ. On the Rucellai position in Lion Rosso, see Kent, *Household and Lineage, passim*.

[6] On this theme see D. V. Kent, *Rise of the Medici*; Kent, *Household and Lineage*, chaps. 4–5; G. A. Brucker, *Civic World*, pp. 15, 21–30, 311.

[7] NA, C 189 (Ser Tommaso Carondini, 1428–31), f. 33ᵛ.

[8] Cat., 405, ff. 63ʳ, 65ᵛ; 460, ff. 495ᵛ–96ʳ.

[9] NA, A 798 (Ser Antonio di Luca Franceschi, 1428–31), f. 13ʳ.

[10] Tratte, 80, ff. 49ʳ, 70ᵛ, 176ʳ, 341ʳ: Donato too was an office-holder in 1432 (f. 214ʳ); Manoscritti, 555, unfoliated.

would also have been welcomed by a man making his own way[1]. It was a happy binding together of the Pandolfini and Rucellai strands in Giovanni's upbringing: Messer Palla was 'a friend and kinsman' of Agnolo Pandolfini[2], and the Rucellai had intermarried, and were to intermarry, more with their Strozzi neighbours, with whom they had many other ties, than with any other Florentine house. Early in the fourteenth century Dino Compagni had already described the Strozzi and Rucellai (with the Acciaiuoli and Altoviti, also connections of Giovanni's, from the quarter of Santa Maria Novella) as allies[3]. More personally, Rucellai was now related to a man he was always deeply to admire, one who in 1428 was not only 'il più potente et maggiore cittadino della terra nostra et il più richo' but, according to Lionardo Bruni, the 'più felice huomo, non tanto della nostra città, ma quanto mai avessi il mondo, però ch'egli à tutte a sette le parti della felicità. . . '[4]. There may have been more affection in this desirable match than was usual. Our authority for this is not an often quoted and probably apocryphal account of the betrothal but an extract from a slightly earlier version of the *Zibaldone,* where in 1456 Giovanni wrote that all of Palla's children 'parevano angnoli di Paradiso'[5]. If he later appreciated his 'degnissima donna' in rather conventional and self-centred terms 'per essere molto amorevole della persona mia e di buono ghoverno per la chasa e per la famigla', Giovanni was also to write of her death, more feelingly than most Florentine husbands, that 'riputai mi fusse la maggior perdita che mai abbi avuto o potessi avere'[6].

According to Giovanni, Palla's children married so well 'perchè stava a lui il chiedere'[7]. Strozzi presumably singled out the young Rucellai not only because he was, like his other sons-in-law, 'di degnissima istirpe, e de' primi della città e ricchi'[8], but for the exceptional energy and business acumen which he had already displayed. However, the frequently repeated story that Giovanni began in business with Palla is not strictly true[9], though his early activities and the Strozzi's were entwined. It was as the twenty-year-old associate of Pierozzo della Luna, whose family had close Strozzi ties by marriage and friendship, that Giovanni makes his first modest appearance as a man of affairs in the books of Lorenzo di Palla in 1423[10], the year in which he matriculated as a member of the Bankers' Guild[11]. Even after 1428, though the older man increasingly relied on Giovanni's help, particularly perhaps in their *gonfalone,* there appear to have been no formal business ties between

---

[1] For the betrothal, see NA, C 189 (Ser Tommaso Carondini, 1428–31), f. 14ʳ. Still in her father's household in 1430 (Cat., 405, f. 152ʳ), Iacopa apparently married Giovanni in mid-1431, according to a document copied by Passerini (BNC, Collezione Genealogica Passerini, 226 [35], unfoliated). Messer Palla was buying jewellery for his daughter in April 1431 (CS, IV, 345, f. 57ʳ).

[2] Vespasiano da Bisticci, *Vite di uomini illustri del secolo XV*, ed. P. d'Ancona and E. Aeschlimann, Milan, 1951, p. 468. Agnolo had married Giovanna di Francesco Strozzi in 1393: Alessandra Strozzi, *Lettere*, p. 84; cf. p. 81.

[3] *La Cronica di Dino Compagni,* ed. I. Del Lungo, Città di Castello, 1916, p. 142.

[4] Perosa, p. 63; see too p. 61.

[5] CS, III, 79, f. 58. On this 1456 book, see Kent, "Letters", p. 343. Marcotti, *Mercante fiorentino,* p. 11, publishes the romantic version of the much repeated engagement story, which derives from the anonymous late sixteenth-century continuation of the *Zibaldone* (see *Zibaldone,* f. 296ʳ⁻ᵛ, and Kent, "Letters", p. 346).

[6] Perosa, p. 119.

[7] CS, III, 79, f. 58 (see n. 5 above).

[8] Vespasiano, *Vite, ed. cit.,* p. 389.

[9] See, e. g., Marcotti, *Mercante fiorentino,* p. 11; Mancini, *Alberti,* pp. 418–19.

[10] CS, III, 289, f. 58: 'Pierozo dela Luna e chonpagnia deono dare a dì XIIIᵒ di giugno [1423], fiorini mile d'oro porto Giovanni di Pagholo . . .'. There is a reference to Donato di Paolo in another Strozzi account book for 1426 which suggests that he too worked for della Luna (*ibid.,* 287, f. cxxiiᵛ). On the Strozzi connections of a number of the della Luna, see Martines, *Social World,* p. 342; Alessandra Strozzi, *Lettere,* pp. 57, 64, 69, 77, 102, 112, 156, 296, 382, 458; A. Della Torre, *Storia dell' Accademia Platonica di Firenze,* Florence, 1902, pp. 293 ff. However, Giovanni did not include the della Luna in his *parentado* (*Zibaldone,* ff. 223ʳ–24ᵛ).

[11] Arte del Cambio, 12, f. lxxxxiᵛ.

Palla and his neighbour and son-in-law. There, as early as 1422, Strozzi had felt discriminated against by the taxes demanded of a massive fortune soon to be drastically diminished[1].

The beginnings of Giovanni Rucellai's business career are obscure, but they predate his first formal partnership 'cum Pierozo Francisci della Luna et aliis' in 1423[2]; he started, he much later recalled, 'da raghazzo, cioè da picholo fancullo', with the 'poche sustanze che mi furno lasciate. . .'. His patrimony was not, however, so insubstantial as it appeared from the distorting perspective of his later 'bella richezza'[3]. His father Paolo had paid the respectable tax of twelve florins in 1403 and three years later had left, besides expensive personal effects, a well furnished town house of average size, some urban property undivided with his Rucellai kinsmen, a villa and estate, several other farms and almost 2,000 florins invested in the communal debt (*Monte*). There is no evidence that Paolo's Pandolfini and Rucellai kinsmen, and the three or four *attori* mentioned in the early sources[4], despoiled this patrimony, which was essentially intact at the time of the first *catasto* in 1427, the shares having earned considerable interest[5]. Later Giovanni was to quote, probably from his own satisfactory experience, the maxim that landed assets were most useful 'a' popilli et altri cittadini, che non sono usitati nè sanno trafficare il denaio'[6].

While still very young Giovanni somehow acquired this financial expertise—between 1413 and 1423, a flourishing time for the Florentine economy. He tells us that there were then no fewer than seventy-two bankers operating in the Mercato Nuovo[7]. With his and his brothers' patrimony (and perhaps with 400 florins he had borrowed from his faithful mother), he was already in 1423 a partner in the fourth largest bank of the city[8]. His banking association with the able Pierozzo della Luna, not much older than himself, continued until at least 1434 and included general trading 'in perpignani, e in seta e in altre chose'[9]. By the late 1420s, Giovanni was beginning to dissociate his own investment from the joint patrimony. The brothers did not fall out, however, nor did they finally

---

[1] See Palla's letter of 1422 cited in D. V. Kent, *Rise of the Medici*, p. 62. On 22 September 1432, and again on 11 May 1433, Giovanni and Lorenzo di Palla were made Strozzi's *procuratores* (NA, C 190 [Ser Tommaso Carondini, 1432–34], ff. 20ʳ, 58ᵛ). The first reference in tax reports to financial dealings with these Strozzi is in Rucellai's for 1433 (Cat., 460, f. 496ᵛ; cf. Palla's *portata*, *ibid.*, 461, f. 450ᵛ), and there are others mentioned in Palla's accounts for 1430–33 (CS, IV, 345, ff. 99ᵛ, 106ʳ). A. Molho, *Florentine Public Finances*, pp. 157 ff., analyses Strozzi's financial position in this decade.

[2] NA, B 1994 (Ser Matteo Boccianti, 1441–42), f. 84ᵛ.

[3] Perosa, pp. 117, 120.

[4] These were administrators of the estate appointed by the Ufficiali dei Pupilli. From 1406 to 1417 Niccolò di Marco Spinellini had the position which after his death went successively, until 1422, to Nofri di Giovanni da Castiglione and Francesco di Ser Tommaso: there are references to these men in Pupilli, 17–31, *passim*, and CS, II, 10, ff. 40ʳ, 49ᵛ, 58ᵛ, 64ʳ, 71ᵛ. In 1427, the Rucellai brothers did claim, however, that they were still owed money by two of these men or their heirs (Cat., 43, f. 869ᵛ).

[5] Pupilli, 17, ff. 1ʳ–lviiʳ, has an inventory of Paolo's possessions on his death in July 1406; Martines, *Social World*, p. 360, gives his assessment three years earlier. For details of their *Monte* credits and for the estate in 1427, when Giovanni and his brothers had the fifteenth richest household in their *gonfalone* (information from Murphy, p. 17, n. 2 above), see Cat., 43, ff. 867ʳ–70ᵛ. For some examples of the *attori* buying land and investing money for their charges, see Carte Gondi, Pergamene, 32 (17 December 1410): Pupilli, 18, f. 134ʳ; 24, f. 188ᵛ; 26, f. 116ʳ; though most of the administrators' time was spent disbursing money for the wards' living expenses, the rentals from the villa, town house and other urban property, and the returns from their lands must have gone a long way towards keeping them. No important property was alienated in this period.

[6] Perosa, pp. 8, 140, n. 55; cf. C. Grayson's review in *Italian Studies*, XVI (1961), p. 113, n. 1.

[7] Perosa, pp. 46, 62. But see Brucker's qualifications in *Civic World*, pp. 396 ff.

[8] On the bank's size, see Preyer, *Giovanni Rucellai*, pp. 3, 235–6, n. 6, and, for the debt to Caterina, Cat., 43, f. 869ᵛ (cf. *ibid.*, 405, f. 66ʳ, for one still larger in 1430). She also mentioned the 400 florins in 1427 when it was already an old debt: 'e' quali gli prestai più tenpo fa' (*ibid.*, 42, f. 455ʳ).

[9] *Ibid.*, 43, f. 870ʳ. According to his father's 1427 return, Pierozzo, then aged 31, was also in partnership with one Oddo del Buono; Pierozzo 'à ritrarre dal bancho . . . fiorini mille dugiento dieci . . .' (*ibid.*, 46, f. 509ʳ; cf. Oddo's 1433 report in *ibid.*, 454, f. 412ᵛ). Giovanni's returns for 1430 and 1433 have a number of references to Pierozzo (*ibid.*, 405, f. 65ʳ–ᵛ; 460, ff. 496ʳ–ᵛ, 497ʳ). The last reference to their partnership I have found occurs on 31 July 1434 (Capitani di Parte Guelfa, numeri rossi, 67, f. 85ᵛ). On Pierozzo, see Molho, *Florentine Public Finances*, pp. 168, n. 31, 181, 184, 220.

divide their estate until 1442[1]. Fraternal cooperation continued in two trading and manufacturing ventures of which we hear between 1427 and 1433, the most important with Simone di Giovanni Altoviti, their young first cousin through the Pandolfini connection, with whose company in 1433 in 'panni e drapi e altra merchatantia trafichano per lo paese di Napoli e altrove. . .'[2]. Giovanni was extremely busy in this early period; he had time to sell grain in Pisa on behalf of his cousin's firm, and to enter into partnership in a company in Venice (where much of his money was later to be made) with one of the foremost businessmen of the day, Galeazzo Borromeo[3]. He was assiduously using all the social ties at his disposal—his relationship with the Strozzi, his Pandolfini connections, and, in the case of the Borromeo, his neighbours[4].

These business successes after 1423 were the more remarkable for the difficult conditions in which they were achieved. Many companies failed in 1425 and the commune, almost continuously at war and with a soaring national debt, imposed high and constant taxes[5]. Giovanni knew these problems at first hand, because his father-in-law's difficulties were extreme: between 1423 and 1433 Palla paid 160,000 florins 'di gravezze ordinarie, per cagione di guerre', according to Rucellai, who attributed Strozzi's collapse to this and to his political misfortunes[6]. Palla's situation, Florence's external problems, and the growing partisan conflict within the city must have disturbed Rucellai but, at the time of his marriage in 1431, he was probably more contented privately than ever before.

---

[1] Giovanni must early have realized how far his abilities and reputation outstripped his brothers'. Alive and dead, Donato was to be known as 'fratello di Giovanni'. Alessandra Strozzi, *Lettere*, p. 37: in the San Pancrazio *ricordo* concerning his funeral, he is 'Donato fratello di Giovanni Rucellai nostro popolano': Conv. Sopp., 88, 23, f. 46ʳ. The document of division, dated 14 February 1442, and Giovanni's first will of 20 September 1437 provide the business details: NA, B 1994 (Ser Matteo Boccianti, 1441–42), ff. 84ʳ–92ᵛ; *ibid.*, C 190 (Ser Tommaso Carondini, 1435–38), f. 123ʳ. Cf. Preyer, *Giovanni Rucellai*, pp. 3, 236, nn. 7–8. Paolo died at Naples in 1458 in financial confusion (see below, p. 36. n. 3); Giovanni was still in touch with him (see Paolo's letters in Perosa, pp. 57–60), and indeed made out his youngest brother's last *catasto* report (Cat., 816, f. 1044ʳ). Donato was in business with his more talented brother in the 1450s (see p. 33 below). Despite the division Filippo lived with Giovanni still in 1442 (Cat., 620, parte ii, ff. 574ʳ–ᵛ, 579ʳ), no doubt because, according to Palla Strozzi's will, at this time 'come è d'usanza, egli [Giovanni] era in alcuna differentia con Filippo suo fratello', and believed 'poterlo accordare avendo da dargli casa et habitatione'. Without Palla's knowing it, and much to his later annoyance, Rucellai bought one of his father-in-law's houses from Strozzi's wife, defending himself with the excuse that his strong desire was 'per uscire di contesa col fratello' (AS Ferr., Archivio Bentivoglio, lib. 6, 34, ff. 43–44). In 1446 Filippo lived in Bologna 'su l'abergho per non potere istare nela patria mia per le gravezze'; he had neither house 'nè maserizia nè posessioni nè danari di monte' (Cat., 372, f. 910ʳ). In the next decade he was again at home, with a house and family, and rather better off (*ibid.*, 707, f. 296ʳ–ᵛ; 816, ff. 497ʳ–98ʳ).

[2] *Ibid.*, 454, f. 248ᵛ (report of Giovanni di Simone Altoviti, with whom Simone, aged 33, still lived). Altoviti wrote that his son traded 'a chomune chon Giovanni di Pagholo Rucellai overo chon Pagholo suo fratello. . .'. It is indeed hard to separate the brothers' activities in this company, in which Giovanni was certainly involved: half of the profit of 400 florins went to 'Giovanni di Pagholo Rucellai e fratelli' (f. 253ᵛ), with which compare his own note (*ibid.*, 460, f. 495ᵛ). Filippo Rucellai was active in a wool *bottega* with Oddo del Buono (one of his brother Giovanni's banking partners), as references in the fraternal returns show (*ibid.*, 43, f. 869ᵛ; 405, f. 65ʳ–ᵛ). Later, Giovanni also had a partnership with his cousin Ruberto di Giovanni Altoviti which was finished by 1446 (*ibid.*, 672, f. 570ᵛ). The mothers of Giovanni and these Altoviti were Pandolfini sisters (*Zibaldone*, f. 223ᵛ).

[3] Cat., 454, f. 252ʳ. The partnership with Borromeo, referred to in the document of division, would have been made between 1427 and 1436, the year of Galeazzo's death: F. Edler de Roover, "Galeazzo Borromeo", *DBI*, XIII (1971), pp. 48–49; NA, B 1994 (Ser Matteo Boccianti, 1441–42), f. 85ʳ. Giovanni does not refer to it in his tax reports, but in 1433 he mentions land bought from Galeazzo and a debt to him (Cat., 460, ff. 494ʳ, 496ᵛ) which Borromeo also noted (*ibid.*, 500, f. 257ᵛ; cf. f. 216ʳ). Rucellai was one of Galeazzo's executors (Preyer, *Giovanni Rucellai*, p. 237, n. 25). On Borromeo, see F. Edler de Roover, above, and T. Zerbi, *Le origini della partita doppia*, Milan, 1952, pp. 31 ff.

[4] Galeazzo submitted his tax reports from the district of Vaio, in the quarter of San Giovanni, but a large Borromeo household filed its *portata* from Lion Rosso and some of its members lived in the Via Vigna Nuova (Cat., 43, ff. 803ʳ–24ʳ). Rucellai much later tried to further the career of Giovanni Borromeo, a monk of San Pancrazio (see below, p. 83).

[5] Molho, *Florentine Public Finances*, pp. 6 ff., and *passim*; U. Procacci, "Sulla cronologia delle opere di Masaccio e di Masolino tra il 1425 e il 1428", *Rivista d'arte*, XXVIII (1953), pp. 3–55. For Florence in this period, see now Brucker's indispensable *Civic World*, chaps. VII–VIII.

[6] Perosa, p. 63.

If the desire to assert himself, to find a powerful ally and to become part of his ancestral community, had been the central drives of his unsettled youth, his position in that year was an enviable resolution of these early needs. The Chancellor of Florence himself, 'quello famoso poeta messere Lionardo d'Arezzo', had been kind enough to congratulate personally this coming young man on his fine match with the daughter of Palla Strozzi[1] whom, a later notarial act stated, Giovanni and his son Pandolfo 'semper in patrem habuerunt et in summa reverencia'[2].

---

[1] *Ibid.*

[2] AS Ferr., Archivio Bentivoglio, lib. 6, 10, unfoliated. For this act see below, p. 49, p. 4.

III. 'TEMPO D'AVERSITÀ', 1434–61

When Palla Strozzi was exiled from Florence to Padua on 9 November 1434[1] any sense of serenity his Rucellai son-in-law had achieved disappeared with him down the road to Ferrara. Giovanni's account in the *Zibaldone* is impersonal enough, though he mentions Palla first among the *principali* exiled on account of 'ghare et divisioni cittadinesche'[2] and would have agreed with Vespasiano da Bisticci that the Strozzi were hostages of fortune. It is perhaps to this period that we can trace the origins of Giovanni's intense curiosity about the workings of that Fortuna which so buffeted Palla and himself[3], for his connection with the Strozzi—and with other men distrusted by the Medicean regime, such as his cousin Stoldo Frescobaldi and partner Pierozzo della Luna—was directly responsible for his 'tempo d'aversità' when he was 'non acetto ma sospetto allo stato anni 27, cioè dal 1434 al 1461'[4]. This much later description of his public and political position in the city was not exaggerated. For a quarter of a century Rucellai held no executive office and was largely unsuccessful in scrutinies for Florence's three chief offices. A few administrative and fiscal posts came his way but they were not, with one important exception, politically sensitive[5].

This was prolonged discrimination against a man whose relatives also included influential Mediceans—almost all his Rucellai kinsmen, his uncle Agnolo Pandolfini and his cousins' branch of the Altoviti[6]—and who apparently had not been personally active in the partisan struggles of 1433–34, though he was a member of the Otto from June 1434[7]. The explanation must be sought not only in the fact of Giovanni's ties with Palla Strozzi, but in his determined and enduring cultivation of them long after 1434. Far from 'ungratefully' deserting his father-in-law because 'spinto da calcolo

---

[1] For details see Otto di Guardia e Balìa, 224, ff. 46ᵛ–48ʳ.

[2] Perosa, pp. 49, 63.

[3] Vespasiano's life of Alessandra, Palla's daughter-in-law, several times makes this point (*Vite, ed. cit.*, pp. 549 ff.). His account of Palla ends with the moral that 'non si fidino troppo della prosperità della fortuna' (*ibid.*, p. 403). The Strozzi shared this view of their own misfortune; on 21 June 1450 Lorenzo di Palla told Michele di Felice Brancacci that his new son had been given the family name Carlo: 'A Dio piaccia somigli di bontà, virtù e gratia per chi 'gli à nome, ma abbi miglior fortuna' (Acquisti e Doni, 140, inserto 8 [3]). For Rucellai's concern with Fortuna, see Perosa, pp. 103–16, and below, pp. 37, n. 70; 85ff.; 94.

[4] Perosa, p. 122. Frescobaldi, long to be Giovanni's banking partner (see below, p. 33), was forbidden to hold office for ten years in November, 1434; earlier in that year, the anti-Medicean regime had made him, from a magnate family, a *popolano* (D. V. Kent, *Rise of the Medici*, p. 296, n. 31). Pierozzo and Giovanni della Luna were still regarded in 1458 as belonging to the anti-Medicean group of 1433 (Rubinstein, *Government*, p. 103, n. 6). The family had ten majorities in the scrutiny to the *Tre Maggiori* of 1433, and none in the Medicean period (D. V. Kent, "Florentine *Reggimento*", *Renaissance Quarterly*, XXVIII (1975), p. 637). In a statute of 1355, there was a prohibition against business partners, or factors from their company, being Priors at the same time (see D. Marzi, *La Cancelleria della Repubblica Fiorentina*, Rocca S. Casciano, 1910, p. 566), a *divieto* identical in intention to that against paternal kinsmen who would, it was assumed, have shared interests to pursue.

[5] See below, pp. 28–31. For his offices, see Tratte, 80, ff. 25ʳ, 339ʳ, 447ʳ, 466ʳ, 472ʳ; 115, letter J; and Preyer, *Giovanni Rucellai*, pp. 5, 236, n. 13; cf. also Perosa, below, p. 132.

[6] For the Rucellai, see Kent, *Household and Lineage*, esp. chap. 4. Pandolfini's pro-Medicean position, despite Vespasiano, is described in Pellegrini, "Agnolo Pandolfini", pp. 1–52. There were Altoviti among Cosimo's enemies (see D. V. Kent, *Rise of the Medici*, p. 355), but the sons of Giovanni Altoviti enjoyed high office after 1434 (L. Passerini, *Genealogia e storia della famiglia Altoviti*, Florence, 1871, pp. 103, 117–18).

[7] Tratte, 80, f. 14ʳ; he was also one of the coopted members of the anti-Medicean Balìa of late 1433: Giovanni Cavalcanti, *Istorie fiorentine*, ed. G. di Pino, Milan, 1944, p. 274 (as 'Giovanni de messer Paolo Rucellai'; cf. Francesco Giovanni's *priorista* for that year in BNC, Fondo Magliabechiano, XXV, 379). In her work for her study of the *Rise of the Medici*, D. V. Kent found no evidence of his being a committed partisan, despite the often repeated claim that he was 'one of the most violent of the party which exiled Cosimo . . .' (L. Scott, *The Orti Oricellari*, Florence, 1893, p. 6).

o da bassezza d'animo' as Mancini maintained[1], Rucellai at once publicly identified himself with the administration of the exile's Florentine affairs. Nine days after the ban against Palla he was appointed, with his brother-in-law Lorenzo, Strozzi's *procuratore*, in which capacity he was to act many times again[2]. The major responsibility at this early stage was Lorenzo's. As his father later acknowledged, he experienced a perilous time, having to burn a master account-book on one occasion, presumably to avoid investigation by communal magistracies avid for Palla's property[3]. Giovanni was increasingly to take over Lorenzo's unenviable position, and with it many of Palla's papers during the next two decades, after Lorenzo's own exile from Florence on 19 December 1438[4]. Furthermore, in the early 1440s, with Cosimo de' Medici's increasingly confident ascendancy in Florence, there came more and extended confinements for the regime's enemies, including Palla Strozzi, who had apparently expected to be recalled[5]. Already an old man, Strozzi was never likely again to hold office in, or even to return to, the city. Indeed, Palla needed further help, and from the son-in-law who not so long before had anticipated looking to him for support, if his affairs at home were not utterly to collapse from neglect and malicious attack[6]. This Giovanni gave with an increasing commitment which, despite the financial benefits he was to receive, made his position in the city vulnerable, though not untenable.

His ever growing intimacy with the Strozzi he so admired was a compensation. It was easy for

---

[1] *Alberti*, pp. 419, 421. Until recently Palla's biographers have had no inkling of Rucellai's key role in his life (see, e.g., A. Fabronio, *Pallantis Stroctii vita*, Parma, 1802). Now L. W. Belle, *A Renaissance Patrician: Palla di Nofri Strozzi, 1372–1462*, unpublished Ph.D. dissertation (University of Rochester, 1972), pp. 60, 317, 319, alludes to it. I saw Dr. Belle's dissertation only after completing this contribution.

[2] Diplomatico, Strozzi Uguccione, 18 November 1434; see below, pp. 24, 46 ff. On 13 May 1437 the *gabella* on a forced sale of some of Palla's property was paid by Giovanni's bank (NA, C 190 [Ser Tommaso Carondini, 1436], f. 15ᵛ). In 1440 Giovanni stood surety in a sale of dowry property belonging to one of Palla's daughters (Archivio di Stato, Padua, Istr. di Giovanni Pinto, lib. 21, f. 278).

[3] In his will of 24 August 1447 Palla wrote that: 'dopo e' mie confini ... decto Lorenzo rimase a Firenze e stettevi alcuni anni e fece tutte le faccende di là e di possessioni e d'altro. Et molte cose gli convenne fare di che mal potrebbe render ragione spetialmente essendosi aceso certo libro o quaderno dove aveva scritto tutto'. AS Ferr., Archivio Bentivoglio, lib. 4, 2, f. 18: Lorenzo 'à portato di grandi et gravi pericoli, come è manifesto', his father added (f. 19). The will of 1462 makes a similar point: *ibid.*, lib. 6, 34, ff. 15–16. Dated June 1462, the will must be earlier, Palla having died on 8 May 1462.

[4] Otto di Guardia e Balìa, 224, f. 73ᵛ. On Palla's books, see CS, III, 139, f. 18ʳ (letter of Bardo di Lorenzo Strozzi, Palla's grandson, to Michele Strozzi, 22 July 1493: 'sechondo che già intesi Govanni Rucellai ave[va] molte sue scritture quando Messer Palla fu chonfinato e anche n'ave[va] l'abate di San Branchazio ... I libri di Messer Palla del bancho gli ave[va] certo Govanni Rucellai che chosì n'ò questa mattina trovato richordo...'). Early in the next century Lorenzo Strozzi consulted a diplomatic diary of Messer Palla's still in Rucellai hands: (*Vite di alcuni della famiglia Strozzi descritte da Lorenzo Strozzi* [Nozze Strozzi-Corsini], ed. P. Stromboli, Florence, 1890, p. 36). In Palla's 1447 will Rucellai, who also had control of certain of Marietta Strozzi's money, was one of five executors; he and Strozzi's wife had especial authority 'del comperar le possessioni' (AS Ferr., Archivio Bentivoglio, lib. 4, 2, ff. 8, 30).

[5] Lorenzo Strozzi, *Vite di alcuni della famiglia Strozzi*, ed. cit., p. 50; no date is given, however, and Strozzi may refer to 1454 (see p. 61, n. 1 below). On the proscriptions, see Rubinstein, *Government*, pp. 109–10. It is possible that Strozzi, and then Giovanni, suffered from the fact that a 'sworn conspiracy' of citizens had been formed in 1444 in Messer Palla's chapel in Santa Trinita (*The 'Trattato Politico-Morale' of Giovanni Cavalcanti*, ed. M. T. Grendler, Geneva, 1973, p. 196). Rucellai does not, however, mention this particular incident (Perosa, p. 51).

[6] The 1447 will refers to Palla's few assets 'per rispecto delle impositioni factemi e graveze fuor d'ogni dovere e dello exilio e rilegatione factami...' (AS Ferr., Archivio Bentivoglio, lib. 4, 2, f. 7). The final testament adds that these taxes were imposed 'sol per vedere l'ultima mia disfaction...' (*ibid.*, lib. 6, 34, f. 10). While it is clear that much of Palla's property went to sympathetic hands (see pp. 26, 46–49 below), some did not. The villa at Petraia, for example, was sold to one 'Brunetto beccaio', whereupon Lorenzo 'andò a Firenze e per la via de' consigli et uficiali delle leggi gliel trasse di mano' (*ibid.*, lib. 4, 2, f. 17). This is one of several incidents which show that not all communal authorities were unsympathetic to Palla's case; cf. Preyer, *Giovanni Rucellai*, pp. 9–10. Certainly Lorenzo Strozzi and Rucellai were often permitted to be *procuratori* at these forced sales, which must have protected Palla's interests to some extent; see, e.g., Capitani di Parte Guelfa, numeri rossi, 70, ff. 5ʳ, 9ᵛ; 73, ff. 9ᵛ, 13ᵛ, 14ʳ. However, Palla disapproved of one such sale, made to Giovanni himself by Strozzi's wife, and of another made by Rucellai to Giovanni Minerbetti (AS Ferr., lib. 6, 34, ff. 43–45, 52).

Giovanni, often in Venice and Lombardy on business, to see Palla in Padua. One such meeting, apparently in the mid-1440s, is described in detail in Palla's last will, and the two corresponded in the next decade[1]. With Giovanfrancesco di Palla, his brother-in-law, Giovanni had a Venetian firm from the mid-1440s to 1464[2]; one of his two companions on his Jubilee visit to Rome in early 1450, after which he fled the plague to the Strozzi estate at Petraia, was his old ally Lorenzo, whose widow he represented many times in the 'fifties[3]. The first and last letters Giovanni Rucellai has left us are addressed respectively to Pazzino Strozzi, a cousin of Messer Palla, and to one of the knight's grandsons[4]. When in 1476 he wrote down his large *parentado*, the Strozzi were basic to it—even his mother-in-law had been born a Strozzi and so Iacopa 'ssi tira drieto gran parentado'[5].

So major a commitment to the Strozzi kept Rucellai in touch with other men distrusted by the regime. One of Messer Palla's favourite notaries, Ser Tommaso Carondini from their district of Lion Rosso, is said to have been confined outside Florence 'per sospetto' in 1438, the year after he had drawn up Giovanni's will[6]. The Brancacci, exiled in 1434, were still friends of the Rucellai in the very early 1450s, at which time Giovanni was personally arranging the marriage, and assuring the dowry, of Felice Brancacci's daughter[7]; Felice was Palla's son-in-law and the bridegroom, Francesco Caccini, was to be exiled in 1458[8]. Connected to this politically tainted Strozzi-Brancacci group was Felice's step-son Donato Acciaiuoli, a man devoted to his maternal grandfather Palla; like his older friend and cousin Giovanni Rucellai, Donato was allowed to remain in Florence, but

---

[1] *Ibid.*, ff. 43–45: 'E vegnendo Giovanni decto da Venegia qua a Padova a vicitarmi innanzi l'andata sua a Firenze dove andava, et essendo in casa nella camera appresso alla sala allato alla mia camera la Marietta [his wife] e Giovanni e io . . .' (*ibid.*). This meeting must have taken place between early 1442 (Giovanni's division with his brothers of that date is mentioned, in the past tense, as part of the conversation) and 1447, the year of Marietta's death. A private document between the two men of 1445 implies that Giovanni, then in Venice, personally handed over some cash to Palla 'più dì fa' (Archivio di Stato, Padua, Istr. di Giacomo Polenton, lib. 1, f. 166 [kindly sent me on film by Dr. Rita Collavo Buggio]). A seventeenth-century copy of entries from a book of *ricordanze* of Giovanni, dated 1456 (CS, III, 79, f. 57; see p. 18, n. 5 above) yields a number of references to Palla, including: 'Chopia di una lettera mi scrisse Messer Palla degli Strozzi da Padova per mia chiarezza di sua faccende fatte per lui, la qual lettera è nel mazzo di febbraio 1452. . .'; '. . . e ancora del mese di gennaio 1452 [Palla] mi scrisse una lettera ch'egl'era ben contento di più cose fatte per lui di commissione di Giovanfrancesco suo figlo. . .'; 'Et questo dì 20 di novembre 1456 ebbi un'altra lettera dal detto Messer Palla. . .'. A number of notarial acts concerning the two men's relationship between 1434 and Palla's death are summarized in G. Fiocco, "La casa di Palla Strozzi", *Atti della Accademia Nazionale dei Lincei, Memorie*, s. VIII, V (1954), pp. 379 ff. CS, III, 116, f. 22r, is a late document of May 1460 giving Rucellai authority in Palla's affairs.

[2] See below, p. 35.

[3] Perosa, pp. 67, 160, n. 14. There are a number of references to Giovanni's acting as Alessandra's *procuratore* (see, to give only one example, NA, G 616 [Ser Simone Grazzini, 1460–62], f. 53r, 20 August 1460). Palla's 1462 will reveals Rucellai's central role in preserving the widow's financial position (AS Ferr., Archivio Bentivoglio, lib. 6, 34, *passim*).

[4] CS, III, 120, f. 330r–v (23 June 1437); *ibid.*, 139, f. 24r, which is a 'Chopia d'una lettera di Govanni detto de dì 12 d'[a]ghosto 1480' in Bardo Strozzi's hand, addressed to Messer Lorenzo, the copyist's brother. See below, p. 93.

[5] *Zibaldone*, f. 224r.

[6] According to one *priorista*: BNC, Fondo Magliabechiano, XXV, 379, unfoliated. I could find no reference to Carondini in Otto di Guardia e Balìa, 224.

[7] See Giovanni's letter to Lorenzo di Palla Strozzi, in Gubbio, in Acquisti e Doni, 140, inserto 8 (2): '. . . Solo questa per avisarti chome abiamo fatt[o] concrusione [sic] del parentado dela Ginevra di Filicie con Francesco Chaccini, che a dD[i]o piaccia sia in buon [sic] punto e di consolazione di ciaschuna delle parti. Siamo stati parecchi dì su una diferanza ch' egl'à voluto essere cierto d'avere fiorini mille contanti, e non n'à voluto avere a ffare chol Monte. . .'. Rucellai offered to guarantee the money should the commune fail to do so, explaining that 'ò preso questa gravezza perchè la chosa non resti indrieto, del quale rischo fo pocho conto perchè le dote si rendono molto bene al presente'. The letter bears the date 27 April, but the year is missing; it belongs to 1450, judging by the bridegroom's note of 9 May 1450 (*ibid.*, [1]). On 7 June 1455 Giovanni wrote familiarly to Michele Brancacci concerning a sum owed Rucellai by 'L'amicho tuo da Todi' (*ibid.*, [3]). Heather Gregory has kindly drawn my attention to MS. 4009 in Biblioteca Riccardiana, Florence, an unfoliated collection of letters illustrating the close ties between Michele Brancacci, Giovanfrancesco Strozzi and Francesco Caccini at this time; Giovanni Rucellai is several times mentioned (see, e.g. below, pp. 29, n. 6; 36, n. 2.) See now the invaluable Brancacci biographical information in A. Molho, "The Brancacci Chapel: Studies in its Iconography and History", *JWCI*, XL (1977), pp. 50–98.

[8] Otto di Guardia e Balìa, 224, ff. 84v, 85r.

was also long out of office on account of his presumed guilt by association[1]. It is arguable that Rucellai's early support of the Strozzi in the 'thirties, when Cosimo de' Medici's position in Florence was novel and unsecured, sprang from a belief that the exiles' eclipse was only temporary. Even if this were so, however, his later developed relationships with them and their friends not only absolve him from the charge of inconstancy but make more interesting and subtle the story of his experiences in, and feelings about, Medicean Florence. For during his long period of adversity Rucellai not only managed to stay in Florence (a feat in itself) but was able to help his Strozzi relations and to make himself one of the very richest merchants in the city. These achievements argue a flexible strategy—much later he said that he had had 'to navigate very precisely and without error'[2]—carried out with courage and style. It was also supported by a number of friends in an atmosphere which was not always or totally hostile to his virtuoso efforts.

Giovanni's local base in Lion Rosso was to prove a sanctuary in a largely suspicious world. Among his strongly pro-Medicean Rucellai kinsmen the position he had sought to establish earlier was still a secure one, which survived his poor view of the business abilities of most of his young cousins[3]. Several prominent Rucellai took a hand in a matter requiring arbitration between Giovanni and his brothers and a distant branch of the lineage in the mid-thirties (not apparently or at least permanently acrimonious, as the two lines were later very intimate)[4]. These elders were assisted by two of Rucellai's closest business associates (Pierozzo della Luna and Giovanni's first cousin Simone Altoviti)[5]. Simone's brother Ruberto, and Giannozzo Pandolfini, cousin to both Giovanni and these Altoviti, were among the executors (who also included the arch-Medicean Piero di Cardinale Rucellai and Giovanni's three brothers) of the young banker's first will made in 1437[6]. The large Rucellai *consorteria* proclaimed its sense of corporate well-being in the next decade, when it commissioned a pulpit (Pl. 1) for the principal church of the family's quarter, Santa Maria Novella. Giovanni did not take a leading part, according to the extant documents, but since he would have been much in Venice at this time there is no reason to exclude him from the number of 'the family and men of the house of Rucellai' for whom the commission was made[7]. He was to show concern in 1445 for the lineage's rights of patronage over the chapel of St. Catherine the Martyr in Santa Maria Novella, and in the same decade joined his many kinsmen and neighbours in the campaign to rebuild their parish church of San Pancrazio[8].

The corporate life of the *gonfalone* as a whole increasingly claimed Giovanni's attention. It was a mark of local respect that he and Andrea Minerbetti were asked to arbitrate between several members of the Berardi family in 1440[9]. On 11 June of the same year Rucellai joined others of his

---

[1] Garin, "Donato Acciaiuoli", pp. 57, 103, and *passim*; A. Della Torre, *Storia dell'Accademia Platonica*, pp. 322–6; Perosa, pp. 91–102. Donato wrote to Giovanni in August 1464 that 'sempre per le vostre virtù et per molte chagioni' he had felt for him 'affectione et reverentia chome a singulare padre' (*ibid.*, p. 91), and the friar Giovanni da Viterbo called Donato 'vostro familiare' in a letter to Rucellai (p. 135). Giovanni's paternal grandmother was one of these Acciaiuoli (*Zibaldone*, f. 223v).

[2] Perosa, p. 122.

[3] *Ibid.*, p. 5; see also Kent, *Household and Lineage*, pp. 67–68.

[4] *Ibid.*, pp. 181, 243, 269; Cat., 672, ff. 413v, 535r.

[5] There are several such agreements for 1435–37 between the two groups, none of which mentions the subject of the dispute (NA, C 190 [Ser Tommaso Carondini, 1432–34], f. 136v; *ibid.*, [1435–38], ff. 84r, 121v).

[6] *Ibid.*, f. 123v. Donato di Paolo was one of several Rucellai witnesses to the will of Paolo di Vanni, then the family's greatest man, in November 1435 (*ibid.*, ff. 28v–29r).

[7] Quoted in Kent, *Household and Lineage*, p. 283; in general, see G. Poggi, "Andrea di Lazzaro Cavalcante e il pulpito di S. Maria Novella", *Miscellanea d'arte*, III (1905), pp. 77–85.

[8] Kent, *Household and Lineage*, p. 257; Dezzi Bardeschi, "Complesso monumentale", *passim*.

[9] NA, N 127 (Ser Niccolò di Francesco di Niccolò, 1444–48), unnumbered folio after f. 269r. The Minerbetti and Berardi were both Lion Rosso families.

neighbours at a formal meeting of the district, held as was customary in San Pancrazio, and was made one of several syndics responsible for discharging the *gonfalone*'s collective business[1]. This was largely financial; since some taxes were still assessed within each of the sixteen Florentine districts, the affairs of defaulters from those levies also came into local hands. Giovanni's concern with the fiscal policies of his district was not only inspired by his personal needs but by the difficulties experienced by Palla Strozzi, who was among Lion Rosso's most notable tax delinquents.

As early as July–August 1438 Giovanni was acting as a financial intermediary between his father-in-law and his *gonfalone*[2]; by the 1440s—the details are obscure—he had worked out a scheme with Benedetto Toschi, the Vallombrosan abbot of San Pancrazio, by which Palla's financial interests were to be protected whenever possible. Several of the documents concerning this collaboration are registered in Giovanni Rucellai's hand[3], and he was present at the crucial district meeting on 1 April 1444, with the Gonfalonier of Company Albizzo d'Ugolino Rucellai in the chair, at which Benedetto was made permanent procurator of Lion Rosso's affairs. This was the essential enabling act for his and Giovanni's project[4]. The two men had perhaps first co-operated over Giovanni's obligations, under his grandfather's will, to the main chapel of the Vallombrosan church, and were to continue to do so, not only in Messer Palla's name. It was a long and mutually advantageous local alliance between two men who, apparently alike in several respects, may also have enjoyed a close personal friendship. Benedetto Toschi deserves to be better known than he is, for his careful account books and his artistic patronage. His *ricordi* show him to have been a vigorous man-of-affairs, an engagingly sensible monastic administrator: his (presumed) donor-portrait by Neri di Bicci reveals few signs of an intense spiritual life but several admirable worldly qualities of the sort which would have much recommended themselves to his parishioner Giovanni Rucellai[5].

---

[1] *Ibid.*, A 799 (Ser Antonio di Luca Franceschi, 1438–40), f. 128[r–v]. A much fuller account of these and other activities by the *gonfalone* of Lion Rosso will soon be available in a study D. V. Kent and I have written. On the continuing strength of neighbourhood ties in the Renaissance, see J. Heers, *Le Clan familial au moyen age*, Paris, 1974, and D. O. Hughes, "Kinsmen and Neighbours in Medieval Genoa", *The Medieval City*, ed. H. A. Miskimin, D. Herlihy and A. L. Udovitch, New Haven, 1977, pp. 95–111.

[2] CS, III, 116, f. 60[r]. The notary to Lion Rosso's *sindachi* noted in this declaration that they had sold the harvest from Palla's Empoli lands to a miller, who then paid Rucellai's bank, which was in turn responsible for discharging Strozzi's tax debt for a *novena* to the Camera delle Prestanze. This document is one of an important series on Strozzi's relations with the *gonfalone*, on which see below, pp. 46 ff.

[3] In general see below, pp. 46 ff. *Ibid.*, at f. 48[r], there is a document in this series described in Giovanni's autograph (f. 48[v]) as 'Chose apartenenti a San Branchazio pel ghonfalone'; cf. f. 45[v] for a summary description by Rucellai of another, not in his hand, concerning the 'Incorporazione di possessioni di Messer Palla per l'abate'. Two undated (probably draft) pleas to the *Monte* officials by Benedetto give a vivid impression of the close collaboration between the abbot and banker. At f. 58[r] Toschi's arguments to retain certain goods which had belonged to Marietta, Palla's wife, are bolstered by a memorandum, in Giovanni's own hand, beginning 'Ancora si può aleghare . . .', and we find this last point incorporated verbatim in another version at f. 36[r]. Rucellai still could not leave the matter alone, adding in autograph the shrewd argument: 'Priegovi abiate riguardo a questo ricorso perochè la detta madonna Marietta à altro debito chol chomune e quello che si giudichasse di questo si giudicherebbe del'altro e sareste chagione di gran danno di San Bra[n]chazio. Piaciavi avendo dubbio alchuno mandiate per me'. Giovanni's hand also appears in the related, and occasionally identical, series of documents in San Pancrazio's archive: Conv. Sopp., 88, 53, ff. 35[v], 36[r].

[4] *Ibid.*, f. 38[r]. Albizzo Rucellai's chairmanship presumably did not hinder proceedings. He was apparently something of a fixer, for during that same tenure of office he prevailed against Francesco Giovanni in a lawsuit, 'unjustly' according to the latter, who explained Albizzo's success by his holding office and by the fact that he had no less than '3 parenti stretti' (two cousins and a man 'nato per madre de' Rucellai') among the five officials responsible for the case (CS, II, 16, f. 28[r], an interesting story I owe to Barbara Wilson). In 1458 Giovanni Rucellai noted financial dealings with Albizzo (Cat., 816, f. 686[v]; 817, f. 653[v]), who witnessed a notarial act in the palace in early 1462 (NA, B 1184, [Ser Girolamo Beltramini, 1457–78], inserto 6 [35]).

[5] Toschi is however prominent in Dezzi Bardeschi's "Complesso monumentale", *passim*. There are also references to his activities as a patron in M. Haines, "Documenti intorno al Reliquiario per San Pancrazio di Antonio del Pollaiuolo e Piero Sali", *Scritti di storia dell'arte in onore di Ugo Procacci*, ed. M. G. Ciardi Dupré dal Poggetto and P. dal Poggetto, Milan, 1977, i, pp. 264–9;

Giovanni's network of local friendships enabled him to protect himself, as well as his father-in-law, from his economic environment. Any businessman's fortune was hard to preserve in the volatile and unpredictable circumstances of late medieval Italian trade. 'Nella nostra città di Firenze', Rucellai told his sons in 1457, 'si conservano et mantengono le richezze non con pichola dificultà ma con grandissima'[1]. Giovanni had begun his mature career in trying times, and remained keenly aware of 'danni di falliti'. He had taken a considerable loss in May 1451 when 'e' Viniziani acchonmiatorono di Vinegia e' nostri merchatanti . . .'[2]. The consistently high taxation demanded by the commune's 'almost continuous' wars was, according to Giovanni, the major cause of economic disruption. Since by 1473 he estimated that he had paid taxes amounting to 60,000 florins[3], it was understandable that his longing for peace (he was anyway not a bellicose man) was as palpable as his happiness in the 'fifties and afterwards when Florence finally achieved it. 'La pace è sopra tutte le richeze e grandeze del mondo', goes one of his maxims[4].

In addition to the occupational hazards of a merchant, Giovanni had to contend with his own precarious position in Florence: Palla Strozzi had suffered punitive taxation at the hands of his and Giovanni's enemies, and Palla's son-in-law was naturally conscious of the 'nimicitie et discordie, contese et offese' around him, the economic threat posed by anyone who 'con superbia o alterigia si volesse soprastare. . .'. He was still too highly taxed in May 1453, according to Giovanfrancesco Strozzi, who was hoping 'pure Giovanni avesse maggiore sgravo, e troppo alto resta, e non so come si possa reggiere'[5]. In 1458 he was again treated unsympathetically (and perhaps vindictively) by the *catasto* officials[6]. It is not at all clear how much or how often the Medici regime overtaxed its enemies (the charge is traditional). Nevertheless, the situation of a rich man 'sospetto allo stato' was at best unsafe and harrowing, as Lorenzo de' Medici himself was to concede when he wrote that he accepted leadership of the regime in 1469 'solo per conservazione degli amici e sostanze nostre, perchè a Firenze si può mal vivere senza lo stato. . .'[7].

Giovanni found some relief from a burdensome and potentially discriminatory tax system in Lion Rosso. He disliked the *catasto*, introduced in 1427, because 'offendeva più le richeze grandi che lle mezane o lle picchole'. The *catasto* officials had neither 'albitrio nè discrezione', he claimed with some exaggeration, when assessments were made openly ('a lume') from written reports submitted to them by the citizens. Better, because easier to control with the help and connivance of friends and

---

M. Levi d'Ancona, *Miniatura e miniatori a Firenze dal XIV al XVI secolo*, Florence, 1962, pp. 61, 266–7; Neri di Bicci, *Le Ricordanze (10 marzo 1453–24 aprile 1475)*, ed. B. Santi, Pisa, 1976, pp. 22–23, 26-27, 58-59. It seems likely that Neri di Bicci's 'Santo Giovanni Ghualberto chon dieci tra Santi e beati de[l] loro ordine e da pie' uno abate ginochioni', commissioned 'dall'abate Benedetto' for San Pancrazio in 1455 and now in Santa Trinita (*ibid.*, pp. 26–27), portrays Toschi as the kneeling abbot. See below, p. 42, for Rucellai's preoccupation with the main chapel of San Pancrazio. There is little direct evidence of the two men's having a personal friendship. However, Giovanni's brother Filippo did Toschi a service in early 1451 (Conv. Sopp., 88, 23, f. 104ʳ), and the abbot gave young geese for Pandolfo's wedding several years later (BNC, II, IV, 374, f. 131).

[1] Perosa, p. 9; cf. p. 8.

[2] *Ibid.*, pp. 6, 53; Kent, "Letters", pp. 347–8.

[3] Perosa, pp. 9, 121.

[4] *Zibaldone*, f. 37ʳ; see too, on the theme of peace, ff. 29ʳ, 34ʳ, 36ᵛ, and Perosa, pp. 118, 122. The cost of war appalled him (*Zibaldone*, ff. 61ʳ, 95ᵛ).

[5] Perosa, p. 9, has the first quotation. The second is from a letter to Francesco Caccini of 5 May 1453 in Riccardiana 4009, unfoliated. Strozzi continued: 'Iddio provegha al bisognio suo, perchè son cierto non s'è restato far nulla per suo utile e bene'. On 28 April Strozzi had been pleased to hear of Giovanni's *sgravo* but thought it insufficient.

[6] See below, p. 57.

[7] Pub. in W. Roscoe, *The Life of Lorenzo de' Medici, called the Magnificent*, 2nd ed., London, 1796, i, App. I, p. li. Even so, Giovanni reported in 1458 that for the *cinquina* he was taxed 18 florins 'ridotto per grazia de' Signori e Chollegi per le xxviii fave' (Cat., 816, f. 60ʳ).

relatives, were those assessments—and there were a number of them after 1434 when the *catasto* was replaced by the older system—made 'al buio per oppenione' by officials who allocated individual assessments within each *gonfalone*. Those responsible for giving tax relief (*sgravatori*) usually came from the local community[1], and in 1457 Giovanni described the advantages he derived from this system in a passage which perhaps more than most reveals his activities and his preoccupations during this trying period:

> Non ci ò trovato migliore rimedio a difendersi quanto a guardarsi da non avere nimici, perchè nuoce più uno nimico che non giovano quattro amici; appresso, d'essere in gratia et in benivolentia de' consorti et de' parenti et de' vicini et del resto degl'uomini del tuo gonfalone, de' quali io m'ò molto da lodare, perchè sempre ne li sgravi che si sono fatti per 'l gonfalone m'ànno servito et aiutato et avuto conpassione di me[2].

Some of these local 'buoni amici e buoni parenti' had indeed helped Giovanni 'to keep his head above water' by lowering his assessment for a *decina*[3]. A number of the influential Mediceans among them, who had also at least acquiesced in the indirect protection extended to the exiled Messer Palla by his *gonfalone*, also 'compassionately' supported his son-in-law's attempts to achieve eligibility for office. Rucellai was nominated there in a scrutiny for the internal offices as early as 1439, and again for the external posts in 1454; perhaps his neighbours also put his name forward for several scrutinies to the three chief magistracies, though there is definite evidence of only one such nomination[4]. On that occasion, Giovanni was successful later in the electoral process, but not for long; on 21 June 1455 his name ticket was taken out of the bags, with some others, by the *Accoppiatori* for 'frankly political' reasons, 'admodum quod utile futurum pro rei publice florentine quiete ac pace'[5]. Clearly he still did not enjoy the confidence of those members of the regime outside the circle of his *consorti*, *parenti* and *vicini*. These facts suggest the complexity and ambiguity of political allegiance in Quattrocento Florence, where local traditional bonds and affections could cut across other loyalties to party or even to the commune, and help to explain why the politically suspect Giovanni Rucellai's affairs could prosper in a district most of whose men were firm adherents of the Medici.

Outside his *gonfalone*, however, Giovanni did not always have to face a regime of which all members were equally or consistently hostile. Nicolai Rubinstein has reminded us that the *stato* was not synonymous with Cosimo de' Medici, who 'may have derived as much influence from his ability to bridge differences among the *uomini principali* as from any effective leadership of them'[6], and seems

---

[1] Perosa, pp. 9, 46–47. The 'Libro di Ricordi' of Matteo Palmieri records the imposition of a number of these taxes, and the names of the officials concerned with them and the *sgravi* (Acquisti e Doni, 7, *passim*). For the taxation system at this time, and the suspension of the *catasto* after 1434, see now D. Herlihy and C. Klapisch-Zuber, *Les Toscans et leurs familles*, Paris, 1978, chap. 1.

[2] Perosa, p. 9.

[3] *Ibid.* In his 1451 tax return, Rucellai reports that 'Avevo di decina fiorini 20s.16d.11 a oro, poi fui sgravato fiorini 2s.2d.3 a oro . . .' (Cat., 707, f. 402r). This decision would have been a local one; in general see Palmieri's *ricordi* (Acquisti e Doni, 7, and f. 44v), where the reference may be to this particular *sgravo* that 'si facesse per 5 per gonfalone chome s'usa'.

[4] Tratte, 80, supplies the information that for two offices he held Giovanni's nomination had come 'ex [14]39' (ff. 25r, 339r), as confirmed in *ibid.*, 49, ff. 41r–52v, a scrutiny-list for the offices of 1445 in which he was apparently rejected. See BNC, II, IV, 346, ff. 115r, 116r, for his and Pandolfo's 1454 success. Giovanni's removal from the electoral bags in 1455 (see next note) means of course that he had been nominated for, and then successful in, a scrutiny to the *Tre Maggiori*, perhaps in 1453, when he appears ambiguously in a scrutiny list (Tratte, 1151, ff. 414r–17r). Among the protocols of Ser Baldovino Baldovini, a notary who lived in Lion Rosso and did much of its official business, there is what appears to be a partial draft of a list of nominations from the *gonfalone* for a scrutiny, and Rucellai's name heads the 'Non veduti'; it may belong to late November 1448, the date of a document very near to it: NA, B 384 (Ser Baldovino Baldovini, 1446–49), ff. 220r–v, 224r. For the electoral role of the *gonfalone*, see Kent, *Household and Lineage*, pp. 171 ff.

[5] Quoted by Rubinstein, *Government*, p. 45.

[6] *Ibid.*, p. 133.

to have given Rucellai tentative encouragement in his efforts 'd'uno nimicho farselo amicho', as he put it in 1457[1]. One should not perhaps make too much of Cosimo's deciding the dowry when Giovanni's eldest daughter was betrothed to Domenico di Giovanni Bartoli, apparently warmly Medicean, in May 1445[2]. There is, however, evidence, both firmer and more suggestive, of an entente when three years later Piero di Cosimo was godfather to Bernardo. This intriguing story, often told by older writers but recently ignored, is now confirmed unimpeachably. Bernardo and his bride Nannina de' Medici had to obtain a papal dispensation to marry on account of the consanguinity created by Piero de' Medici's role as godfather in 1448[3]. (This technicality may solve a problem that has concerned art historians: Giovanni's use of a Medicean heraldic device—if such it was—well before the 1461 betrothal)[4]. The two families also had commercial ties at this time and Giovanni trusted Pigello Portinari, the Medici manager in Milan[5]. Hardly surprisingly, the beginnings of political and social acceptance, of 'buona volontà', came early in the next decade, when Giovanni was one of '3 agiunti ali uficiali del monte' and was successful, with Pandolfo, in scrutinies[6]. Pandolfo, the elder son, was betrothed to Buonaccorso di Luca Pitti's daughter in 1453—a significant alliance with a Medicean family whose leader, Luca, Giovanni pointedly praised as 'grandissimo cittadino . . . e di grande seghuito e fra l'altre chose era il più chaldo e più amorevole uomo che si trovasse per li parenti e amici suoi'[7]. Probably the increasing divisions within the regime explain why, despite such endorsement, Rucellai's public advancement stopped in 1455. Perhaps, indeed, there was resentment at the tentative gestures Cosimo had made towards this friend of the Strozzi, for in 1465, admittedly in a tenser atmosphere, the Medici faced opposition from their own allies in winning preferment for Giovanni, by then almost a relation[8]. Rucellai's great admiration for Cosimo in 1457, the nadir of his own political fortunes, suggests that his real enemies in the regime were others, though he presumably believed that the man who 'disponeva del governo della

---

[1] Perosa, p. 9.

[2] NA, I, 95 (Ser Iacopo di Ser Stefano, 1445–49), unfoliated, 4 May 1445. There were a number of families named Bartoli, but the Giovanni di Domenico Bartoli who became Gonfalonier of Justice in July–August 1447 was probably Domenico's father, or a close relation: G. Cambi, *Istorie*, in *Delizie degli eruditi toscani*, XX, ed. Fr. Ildefonso di San Luigi, Florence, 1785, p. 258. This man was very close to Cosimo: Rubinstein, *Government*, p. 134.

[3] NA, B 397 (Ser Baldovino Baldovini, 1465–8), ff. 27r–28r, 31 March 1466. I am grateful to Alison Brown for the reference to this archiepiscopal ratification of the papal dispensation of December 1463. One finds this story, without a source and with Cosimo named as the godfather, in L. Passerini, *Curiosità storico-artistiche fiorentine*, Florence, 1866, p. 8, and in his *Rucellai*, p. 122, whence (presumably) it was repeated by Scott, *Orti Oricellari*, p. 6, and Wood Brown, *Builders of Florence*, p. 226.

[4] Preyer, pp. 198 ff. below, is sceptical about the necessity of a connection between the use by the Medici and Giovanni of the device of a ring with three feathers. My suggestion supports her conclusions about the palace's dates, which have been doubted on this emblematic evidence alone.

[5] R. de Roover, *Rise and Decline*, pp. 90–91, 129; Cat., 817, 220r. Giovanfrancesco Strozzi and Giovanni sent a letter from Ferrara to Portinari in Milan on 7 February 1454 giving him 'plenissima libertà' in deciding a dispute between them and Antonio Moroni and brothers, and recognizing 'la vostra virtù e bontà': MAP, CXXXVIII, 304. Pigello again fulfilled this role in 1457: Pergamena Medicea, 31 August 1457. For a later example, see too MAP CXXXVII, 142, Rucellai to Lorenzo de' Medici, 27 April 1465, where Lorenzo is asked to be 'operatore in quello modo che parrà a Pigiello di farmi rischuotere cierti danari. . .'.

[6] For the scrutiny information, see above, p. 28, n. 4. On 12 February 1453 (possibly 1452 if the writer was not using Florentine style) Giovanfrancesco Strozzi wrote to Francesco Caccini from Ferrara that: 'Gran piaciere arei auto che Giovanni avesse ottenuto di essere de' 3 agiunti ali uficiali del monte. Bastali per ora aver visto la buona volontà e altra volta aver l'effeto . . .'. Strozzi was probably sceptical about the regime's motives, for he asked Caccini to inform him 'a che fine si fanno questi 3 aroti e s'egli ànno a prestar danari e se ànno l'aministrazione del ghoverno del monte come li altri uficiali' (Riccardiana 4009).

[7] *Zibaldone*, f. 5v. The wedding was on 30 May 1456 (BNC, II, IV, 374, f. 131). Another 'Medicean' marriage was made in 1455, when Giovanni's daughter Margherita became the wife of Iacopo di Francesco Venturi (Passerini, *Rucellai*, tav. xvi; Rubinstein, *Government*, p. 134; and G. Carocci, *La famiglia Venturi di Firenze*, Florence, 1915, pp. 33–4).

[8] *Ibid.*, p. 165, n. 6. There is also the possibility that the criticisms Giovanni expressed in the *Zibaldone* of the pro-Sforza foreign policy of the *principali cipttadini* were somehow known to them (Perosa, pp. 52–53).

ciptttà come se propio ne fussi stato singniore' was somehow implicated in recent discrimination against him. Even so for him Cosimo was, with Messer Palla, one of Florence's few really notable men, for his wealth, his following and his power[1].

Such suggestions that the Medici were less suspicious of, if not more warmly disposed towards, Rucellai than some of their allies may have made his earlier situation not so much tolerable as tenable. He had in fact quite early provided an earnest of his devotion to Florence that must have allayed or even cancelled fears about the practical implications of his other main allegiance, to the Strozzi. Giovanni's bad relations with some men of the regime did not diminish—indeed they may even have intensified—his devotion to the welfare of Florence and its community. The attack on the city in 1439–40 by the Milanese, and some Florentine rebels led by Rinaldo degli Albizzi, confirmed him in a patriotic commitment which had been nurtured earlier in the century during a period of similar crisis. Brought up among several notable 'civic humanists', Rucellai at least subscribed to what has been called their propagandist view of early fifteenth-century Florentine history, even reporting that in 1402 'era oppenione che la libertà nostra fusse a gravissimo pericolo'[2]. Despite his close connections with a number of the exiles of 1434, Giovanni deeply disapproved of this assault by the more recalcitrant of them upon the city he regarded as the most beautiful in the world, and rejoiced in its failure at the battle of Anghiari in May 1440 where, with God's grace, 'lla vettoria fu grandissima'[3]. In the next month he would have given material help, for he was made one of the Ufficiali del Banco, a magistracy whose members were themselves expected to lend large sums to the commune at a time when 'il danaio per la difesa si facieva con grandissima difichultà'[4]. Rucellai was three times more an Ufficiale del Banco in that decade[5], which suggests not only that he was known to have considerable resources but also that he had a reputation for patriotism without serious partisan stain, at least at a time of emergency. He himself later claimed, in a draft passage of his second will, that:

> decto testatore tucto il tempo della vita sua quanto à potuto s'è ingegniato favorire l'onore et dignità del comune di Firenze e della sua libertà, no[n] mancando cura ad alcuno pericolo nè a spesa quando fu di bisognio[6].

This passage probably reflects the influence on Giovanni of the high-minded political tradition of two of his mentors, the friends Palla Strozzi and Agnolo Pandolfini, who found themselves in opposing camps in the intricate events of 1433–34 but were not, and despite their different fates did not apparently become, men of a fundamentally partisan cast of mind. Like them Giovanni believed above all in public service for the city's welfare, and he may have shared their reputation (with Vespasiano da Bisticci at least) for a certain patriotic disinterestedness. This was not undeserved if one takes into account his activities in the 'forties: the Florentine ambassadors to the king of

---

[1] *Ibid.*, p. 61. However, Filippo di Paolo, when a Guelf Party Captain, was in the Balìa of 1458 (Rubinstein, *Government*, p. 282). The marriage of Giovanni's daughter Marietta to Girolamo di Luca degli Albizzi in July 1459 (Passerini, *Rucellai*, tav. xvi) was also a new step in the Medicean direction, Luca having long been Cosimo's ally despite his brother Rinaldo's position (D. V. Kent, *Rise of the Medici*, pp. 59, 197).

[2] Perosa, p. 44, and for his admiration of Bruni, pp. 48, 54–55, 61, 63.

[3] *Ibid.*, pp. 49–50. Rucellai was writing in 1457, but there is no reason to doubt that the passage faithfully reflects his attitude seventeen years before.

[4] *Ibid.*, p. 50. See Tratte, 80, f. 447ʳ. On this magistracy, see Molho, *Florentine Public Finances*, pp. 166 ff.; D. V. Kent, *Rise of the Medici*, pp. 284 ff.

[5] Preyer, *Giovanni Rucellai*, p. 236, n. 13.

[6] NA, L 130 (Ser Lionardo da Colle, 1441–95), busta 121 of 'Testamenti mancanti di principio e fine'. See, however, p. 29, n. 6 above.

Naples, one of whom was admittedly his cousin Giannozzo Pandolfini, did not hesitate to ask Rucellai to deliver a letter to the Signoria in March 1450[1]. It is arguable that Giovanni was not profoundly curious about, or overwhelmingly eager to participate in, day-to-day domestic politics, a commoner attitude among his countrymen than some recent writers—more political animals than even the Florentines themselves—have suggested. One should not overstate the point. Giovanni of course saw the desirability of being acceptable to the regime—and happily took high office in the 1460s—but he may not have experienced the intense sense of deprivation after 1434 that a Cosimo de' Medici, a Neri di Gino Capponi or an Agnolo Acciaiuoli would have suffered in similar circumstances. When in 1457 he came to present his own version of the pseudo-Pandolfini's views of political and civic life, Giovanni was neither as garbled nor as pessimistic as his source. He believed that virtuous men could and should be found in public life—for his sons he drew up a (very conventional) list of 'certi utili amaestramenti a uno cittadino che attendi al governo della republica'[2]— but made it clear that practical politics, even when conducted by good and patriotic men, exasperated him. 'Perchè uno solo non può provedere', he wrote in a passage not taken from his authority, 'e molti non s'acordano a farlo, però vi conforto . . . a lasciare lo stato a chi piace'[3]. This view cannot perhaps be wholly attributed to his own harsh experience, which would however have confirmed any a-political tendencies he may have had as a very young man. None of his letters, even those to the Medici after 1461, gives much impression of a man deeply interested in or expert at the time-absorbing minutiae of Florentine communal politics (they almost all seek help for himself and relatives), and his account of his participation in the activities of the *Accoppiatori* in 1471 has been described as 'naive'[4]. It is not perhaps wholly inexplicable that his indubitable enemies in the regime still tolerated Giovanni Rucellai, a patriot whose principal energies after 1434 were manifestly devoted to making money from his growing business concerns.

It was politic of this a-political man to do so, but he was perhaps already committed to this course. A near-professional politician in Renaissance Florence, even if he were rich in his own right, normally had the financial support of one or more close paternal relations who devoted themselves to the family's welfare. Giovanni Rucellai, who had only an average patrimony, conspicuously lacked this backing. Without a father or paternal uncles, he could not even rely on his brothers, men

---

[1] See Vespasiano's lives of Palla and Agnolo, *Vite, ed. cit.*, pp. 387 ff., 458 ff., and Pellegrini's "Agnolo Pandolfini", pp. 1–52. Later, Donato Acciaiuoli would probably have reinforced Palla's influence on Giovanni (see Garin, "Donato Acciaiuoli", p. 57). For Strozzi's role in 1433–34, see D. V. Kent, *Rise of the Medici*, pp. 204–5, 333–4, 343. I am grateful to Heather Gregory for allowing me to read her paper on the *Vite* of Palla by Vespasiano and Lorenzo Strozzi, and for her suggestion that he could hardly have been quite the paragon they portrayed. I owe the reference to the diplomatic letter to Anthony Molho (Signoria, Dieci di Balìa, Otto di Pratica, Legazioni e Commissarie, Missive e responsive, 18, f. 4ʳ). The letter, written in Perugia, was admittedly not top secret.

[2] *Zibaldone*, f. 34ʳ. Some samples: 'A signore somma reverenza s'abbia; a compagni humile e piacevole conversatione; a tutti si facci piacere di benificio, ma prima agli amici e parenti'; 'Ogni cosa di grande importanza si facci con consiglio de' cittadini'.

[3] Perosa, p. 42, and in general pp. 39–43. I am indebted to Judith Ravenscroft's thesis (cited on p. 15, n. 4 above) for the point that Rucellai's section on politics 'is a series of analytical and refreshingly brief essays which gain considerably over their model in lucidity and attack' (p. 77). Grayson has argued, against those who have judged Rucellai's political behaviour harshly, that he was 'primarily a man of business and of the family . . . and not of politics' (review of Perosa, *Italian Studies*, XVI (1961), p. 112). F. Edler de Roover has said of Andrea Banchi, the rich *setaiuolo*, that he 'was not a political man . . .' ("Andrea Banchi, Florentine Silk Manufacturer and Merchant in the Fifteenth Century", *Studies in Medieval and Renaissance History*, iii, ed. W. M. Bowsky, Lincoln, Nebraska, 1966, p. 280).

[4] Preyer, *Giovanni Rucellai*, p. 6; see below, pp. 69–70.

considerably less talented than he, who were indeed to be increasingly his responsibility[1]. When in mid-1437 Rucellai assured Messer Pazzino Strozzi in Rome that in the urgent letter he was asking him to forward to Gaeta there was nothing 'se non di chose merchantili'[2], he used a phrase that might stand as his credo both before and after 1434. Certainly for a decade or so after that date he gave himself up almost ostentatiously to 'chose merchantili', often outside Florence. A plague in 1437–38 sent him to Genoa 'in exercitio mercantile' while his family stayed in Pisa[3]. The contract of a Venetian company he and several others formed in January 1442 stated that Giovanni was to stay in Venice and to devote himself to it 'night and day'. Neither of the two principals was able 'aciettare niuno uficio nella città di Firenze o nel suo territoro se ggià non fussino tratti a uficio che non si potesse rifiutare'—which was not to make a virtue of necessity since Giovanni had by then been successful in a minor scrutiny[4].

A 'solicitous and diligent' merchant banker, Rucellai regarded his proud *mestiero* as almost a vocation: he and his *compagni* in Venice prayed God to concede them 'ventura e buon ghuadangno chon salvamento dell'anima e del chorppo'[5]. Giovanni was as ready to derive his surname from the wool dye orchil (*oricello*), which his ancestors had brought to Italy, as to assert in the manner of the times the chivalrous, indeed northern European, origins of his family's founder[6]. 'Trading is what has made our city great and honoured', one of Rucellai's contemporaries wrote[7]; and Pandolfo Rucellai, who as a Dominican friar came to have serious theological scruples about many banking procedures, was still his father's son when he said that without trading 'l'humana specie non potrìa vivere'[8]. Giovanni, delighted to possess those essential qualities of the medieval merchant, 'good faith' and a 'good name', was quick to pursue some defaulting Milanese debtors 'e' quali sono ricchi e possono paghare', and to puzzle over the behaviour of another who 'è huomo da bene e di buona fama'[9]. The *Zibaldone* is full of advice—ranging from the banal traditional 'scripta leggibile di buono inchiostro' to material as useful to the historian as to his sons—on how to become the good, efficient and honourable merchant he himself was[10]. The commonplace book leaves the impression of a man unable to repress, even had he wanted to, the mercantile instincts of his family and class. In the chronicle of his own times, which also suggests that his one strong political interest was the

---

[1] On this theme, see D. V. Kent, "Florentine *Reggimento*", p. 600. For references to Giovanni's brothers and nephews, see above, pp. 16–20, and below, pp. 33, 35, 76–77. Giovanni several times makes the point, from the pseudo-Pandolfini, that it is foolish to neglect private for public concerns: Perosa, p. 41; *Zibaldone*, f. 21ʳ: 'Per le facciende publiche del comune conforto a non lasciare le private perochè a chi mancherà in casa meno troverà fuori di casa. . .'.

[2] CS, III, 120, f. 330ʳ (27 June 1437): the context was a political prohibition against letters sent to the area. Rucellai twice says the matter 'm'importa assai', as in two similar letters (*ibid.*, f. 343ʳ [13 July]; f. 351ʳ [23 July]).

[3] *Zibaldone*, f. 26ʳ.

[4] MAP, LXXXIX, 289, f. 304 bisᵛ. Dated 21 November, the contract gives 1 January 1442 as the company's starting day.

[5] *Ibid.*, f. 304ʳ; Perosa, p. 120.

[6] Pub. in Marcotti, *Mercante fiorentino*, pp. 53–54. The forms "Oricellai", or "Ricellai", were used even in the vernacular in the Trecento (*La cronica domestica di Messer Donato Velluti*, ed. I. Del Lungo and G. Volpi, Florence, 1914, pp. 39, 294).

[7] Niccolao degli Albizzi, in a letter of 27 November 1414, printed in *Commissioni di Rinaldo degli Albizzi*, ed. C. Guasti, Florence, 1873, i, p. 281.

[8] Pub. in R. de Roover, "Il Trattato di Fra Santi Rucellai sul cambio, il monte comune e il monte delle doti", *ASI*, CXI (1953), p. 26. See now an improved edition by E. Fumagalli, "I Trattati di Fra Santi Rucellai", *Aevum*, LI (1977), pp. 289–332. Santi Rucellai concluded of banking that 'ciascheduno che può vivere senza fare tale exercitio, che lo facci perch'è a me assai sospecto per molte ragioni et cagioni . . .' (de Roover, p. 34).

[9] The two quotations from letters are respectively in MAP, XVII, 343 (7 November 1462), and Acquisti e Doni, 140, inserto 8 (3) (7 June 1455). For Rucellai's 'gran credito' and 'buona fede', see Perosa, pp. 117, 120, and his sons' affirmation in *Zibaldone*, f. 66ʳ. The 1441 contract (MAP, LXXXIX, 289) insists on the firm's making 'senpre liciti e honesti chontratti', and sets aside two Venetian gold ducats each year 'per l'amore di Dio' (f. 304ʳ).

[10] *Zibaldone*, f. 96ʳ; Perosa, pp. 3–19.

economic implications of foreign policy[1], Giovanni cannot resist ending his account of the Jubilee of 1450 with an anecdote of the sort he relished—the story of a Polish pilgrim 'alto braccia 4, che si disse era discieso di gighanti'—and the information that other northerners had left 'grandissimo tesoro di danari contanti . . . per modo che tutte le zecche d'Italia batterono in quello anno grandissimo numero d'oro'[2].

The details are obscure, but it was by his single-minded efforts in the late 1430s and in the 'forties that Rucellai made his fortune. Moderately well-off in 1427, he was very rich by 1451 and the third wealthiest man in Florence (after Cosimo de' Medici and the manager of the Medici bank) only seven years later, when the total taxable value of his 'trafichi e merchatante e conti' was estimated at no less a sum than 8,500 florins[3]. Without account-books and other business records one can give only an impressionistic (and almost certainly imprecise if not misleading) analysis of Giovanni Rucellai's economic activities in this, his hey-day. However the attempt must be made for a man who throughout his life-time was always identified, in formal documents, as 'Florentine merchant and banker' or 'Florentine citizen and merchant'[4]. In the characteristic Florentine way Rucellai combined banking and mercantile activities to produce his high profits; he gave the fullest summary of his past interests 'nel mestiero della merchatantia e del chanbio' in 1473:

> . . . e ne' miei dì ò fatte più chonpagnie in Firenze di bancho chon variati chonpangni e avuto chonpangnie e tenuto chase fuori di Firenze in più luoghi, cioè in Vinega, in Genova, in Napoli e in Pisa, e ssono intervenuto per chonpangno in Firenze in sette botteghe d'arte di lana in variati tenpi e chon variati chonpangni'[5].

The first reference to Giovanni as a banker in his own right occurs in 1437[6] and thereafter he was established in the Mercato Nuovo, where for some twenty years from about 1445 onwards his maternal first cousin once-removed, Stoldo di Lionardo Frescobaldi (a Pandolfini connection) was his principal partner[7]. In the 1440s and early 1450s Giovanni's brother Donato was another associate, as was Pandolfo in the next decade[8]. Even if he later felt he had contradicted his own advice to employ paternal kinsmen as factors, Giovanni's major associates throughout his life were

---

[1] See, e.g., *ibid.*, pp. 52–53, It is, however, an exaggeration to say, with R. Klein, that Rucellai had 'une seule idée politique personnelle, très simple', namely 'le pacifisme motivé par des raisons d'économie': review of Perosa in *Bibliothèque d'Humanisme et Renaissance*, XXIII (1961), p. 178.

[2] Perosa, p. 52. See too pp. 45, 46, 47.

[3] Cat., 817, f. 212ʳ; he was taxed 102 florins (f. 74ʳ). His 1451 assessment had been 94 florins (*ibid.*, 707, f. 403ᵛ), that of 1430 only twenty (*ibid.*, 405, f. 66ᵛ). For the comparative figures, see de Roover, *Rise and Decline*, p. 31.

[4] For example, see Consigli della Repubblica, Emancipazioni, 7 (1456–63), f. 45ᵛ; NA, C 190 (Ser Tommaso Carondini, 1435–38), f. 122ʳ. Rucellai begins the *Zibaldone* by describing himself as 'mercatante et cittadino fiorentino' (Perosa, p. 2); in a formal letter by the Signoria to the Duke of Milan (15 June 1461), he is called 'nostro egregio mercatante e citadino': Signori—Carteggio, Missive, Registri, 43, f. 141ᵛ. I owe this reference to Gino Corti.

[5] Perosa, pp. 120–21.

[6] NA, C 190 (Ser Tommaso Carondini, 1436), f. 15ᵛ (13 May 1437): a certain payment had been made 'per banchum Iohannis Pauli domini Pauli de Oricellariis et sotiorum. . .'.

[7] A notarial act of 1445, drawn up in Giovanni's bank in the Mercato Nuovo, was witnessed by Stoldo, the first reference I have found to his connection with the bank (Diplomatico, Strozzi Uguccione, 7 March 1444). Both cousins declare their partnership in their tax reports of 1451 (Cat., 689, f. 250ᵛ; 707, f. 402ʳ). Arte del Cambio, 15, f. 2ʳ, lists one of their companies as beginning in April 1460. I thank John Najemy for the information that there appear to be no Quattrocento partnership records in the Bankers' Guild archive before 1460. Giovanni's mother and Stoldo's grandmother were Pandolfini sisters (*Zibaldone*, f. 223ᵛ). Later in the partnership, Rucellai drew two-thirds of the profit, Stoldo the rest (Cat., 919, f. 377ᵛ).

[8] See his tax report for 1451: *ibid.*, 707, f. 290ʳ. In early 1456 Donato appealed to the Bankers' Guild about a certain 'deferenzia' he had with the other partners (Archivio Frescobaldi, 56, unfoliated. I thank Marchese Dino Frescobaldi for permission to consult his private archive). See too Cat., 816, f. 136ʳ; 817, f. 62ᵛ. A notarial document of June 1462 was drawn up 'in the bank of the undermentioned Giovanni Rucellai and his son Pandolfo' (NA, B 1184 [Ser Girolamo Beltramini, 1457–78], inserto 7 [6]).

usually in some sense *parenti* (the pseudo-Pandolfini had once said that factors could come 'della casa vostra et di vostro parentado') on whom he could rely to protect his interests[1]. Scattered references, and a list of debtors and creditors in his *catasto* report of 1458, suggest that Rucellai's clients, for sums large and small, were not only Florentines but men and companies from elsewhere in Italy (especially Milan) and even beyond[2]. The firm's operations were various. Giovanni was, for example, the banker for the convent of San Pancrazio during building operations there, and for other transactions[3]: Bernardo Rossellino deposited money with Rucellai's bank, another man used its services to pay his rent[4].

In 1457 Giovanni suggested his sons look more kindly upon a banker 'chi sta sul denaio corrente che di chi mette in mercatantia il suo et l'altrui, perchè il cambio comunemente è di minore pericolo, et sempre state sospesi et sospettosi in credere a chi è molto pigliatore'[5], but it is unlikely that he followed his own cautious advice to concentrate upon exchange operations and short-term loans. In another respect he appears to have taken large risks as a speculator in *Monte* shares, whose value fluctuated dramatically during the period, as Giovanni himself noted in the *Zibaldone*. In 1423 shares in the communal debt were worth 61% of their face value, but only 10% in 1452–53, according to this banker who six years later had a sizable proportion of his wealth tied up in them[6]. Despite his non-Florentine contacts, and the exchange activities of at least one of his Venetian companies[7], Giovanni's bank apparently had no branches outside the city. In one of the most vivid passages of the *Zibaldone* he emerges as a man snugly settled 'in mercato', constantly and cannily quizzing merchants, factors, and agents about their own and others' activities, reliant for foreign news upon the young men just arrived home 'chi da Vinegia, chi da Roma, chi da Ginevra, chi da Bruggia'. It was Giovanni's technique to congratulate them upon their safe return, then, drawing them aside, to question them closely. He was obviously very good at it, for his bank was to become one of the largest in Florence[8].

In 1451 part of the bank's funds went to provide the capital for a wool firm, founded in partnership with two other men to take advantage of better trading conditions anticipated 'in su le buone

---

[1] Perosa, p. 4; see above, p. 25.

[2] Cat., 817, ff. 213ʳ–220ᵛ. These accounts are not identified (ff. 208ʳ–211ᵛ belong to the Venetian firm of Giovanni and Giovanfrancesco Strozzi), but f. 220ᵛ has a reference to Stoldo Frescobaldi and Donato Rucellai which makes it certain they are the bank's. Giovanni is called 'nostro magiore' at f. 218ʳ.

[3] See Conv. Sopp., 88, 23, f. 98ʳ, and *passim*, for a number of references in the abbot's account book for 1446–64; for one example, see f. 114ᵛ: 'A dì 27 di novembre [1451] fece Don Matheo nostro una poliza a bancho di Giovanni Rucellai che pagassi a Bandecho nostro maestro di murare lire quaranta, i qua' danari achattiamo da decto Giovanni per la muraglia nostra. . .'. See too Dezzi Bardeschi, "Complesso monumentale", pp. 13, 15, 16, 19, 42. For other examples of Giovanni's financial role at San Pancrazio, building aside, see Conv. Sopp., 88, 23, ff. 71ᵛ, 149ᵛ; *ibid.*, 41, ff. 1ᵛ, 2ʳ, 10ʳ, 22ᵛ, 25ʳ, 33ᵛ; 57, f. 7ʳ; NA, M 569 (Ser Piero Migliorelli, 1454–58), ff. 17ᵛ–18ʳ. Conv. Sopp., 88, 24, f. 64ʳ, shows him dealing with another Vallombrosan community in 1452.

[4] For the reference to Rossellino, see F. Hartt, G. Corti, and C. Kennedy, *The Chapel of the Cardinal of Portugal, 1434–1459*, Philadelphia, 1964, p. 182. The other is from Guido Baldovinetti's *ricordi* in Acquisti e Doni, 190 (3), f. 15ʳ. I have found numerous other isolated references to banking transactions of Giovanni's.

[5] Perosa, p. 6.

[6] *Zibaldone*, f. 81ʳ; cf. Perosa, pp. 46, 62. In 1458 the *Monte* shares in Rucellai's control (they were in a number of names) had a face value of over 40,000 florins and were worth, according to the annotations of the *catasto* officials, some 8,250 florins; his total assets amounted to 21,464 florins before, and 19,406 after, deductions (Cat., 816, ff. 60ʳ–63ᵛ). Cosimo de' Medici's bank had shares with a nominal value of 105,950 florins in 1460 (de Roover, *Rise and Decline*, p. 236). There is a reference to Giovanni's selling *Monte* shares in early 1436 in Francesco Giovanni's *ricordi* (CS, II, 16, f. 12ᵛ). On the market in this stock, see de Roover, *Rise and Decline*, p. 22; Molho, *Florentine Public Finances*, pp. 157 ff.

[7] See p. 35 below.

[8] Perosa, p. 6. Mancini, *Alberti*, p. 419, says that Rucellai also had banks in Pisa and Rome; Passerini, *Rucellai*, p. 119, adds (also without giving evidence) Lyons and Constantinople. Other members of the Rucellai family certainly had companies in at least some of these places.

novelle della pacie'[1]. We have only bare details about several other of the 'seven wool shops' in which Giovanni had a share, but it is unlikely that they brought him in more than a steady income[2]. Profits were very much higher in silk manufacture, on the other hand, and there is intriguing evidence of his being interested in it. Indeed, Rucellai provides figures for Florence's total output of silk in 1459–60 which are apparently unique and may conceivably be accurate. Several of his firms traded in silk, and he owned extensive mulberry groves in 1474[3].

Banking aside, much of Giovanni's profit may have come not from Florence but from the Venetian interests he had had since his partnership with Borromeo. The company to devote itself to 'merchatantia e traffichare de' chanbi e fare arte di seta e chosì altre chose che ssi credesse che fusse utile e bene' founded in late 1441 with three partners had the large capital (suggestive of higher expectations) of 12,000 gold florins, half of it subscribed by Giovanni himself[4]. This company was replaced by one with his brother-in-law Giovanfrancesco di Palla, who became Giovanni's formal partner in Venice and Ferrara in 1445–46. The two worked together, later with the help of a Rucellai cousin Filippo d'Amerigo, until about 1462[5]. From what one can gather these Venetian companies traded in skins, leather and slaves, and presumably in anything else, particularly textiles, which could be turned to profit[6]. The close Strozzi connections with Ferrara, where a number of them lived in exile, were exploited by the two brothers-in-law who, in a letter of 10 September 1446 written by Lionello d'Este, were with 'soi compagni e compagnia per ogni e singule robbe' granted a safe-conduct throughout his principality. According to the Marquis Giovanni had been a faithful servant of his house[7]. Several passages of the *Zibaldone* reveal that Rucellai knew Venice well and believed indeed that 'è meglio posta ciptà per fare merchatantia che alcuna altra ciptà del mondo'. This was not so much because it was a great port, Giovanni continued, but because it was an unrivalled clearing house for goods to be sent, cheaply and easily, to populous Lombardy and to a

---

[1] Giovanni reported in August 1451: 'E del detto nostro chorpo ne mettemo cierta parte in una bottegha d'arte di lana che facciamo in Sa[n] Martino insieme chon Brancha di Ghostantino da Perugia e chon Antonio Giuntini . . .' (Cat., 707, f. 404ʳ). It was Antonio who said that his shop 'è stata serrata più d'anni cinque e non se ne trattò nulla e in su le buone novelle della pacie m'achonpangniai con Brancha . . . e Giovanni Ruciellai . . .' (*ibid.*, 705, f. 663ᵛ); the reference must be to the peace with Naples (Perosa, p. 51). In the *tassa* of that year, this company paid 36 gold florins, Rucellai contributing 20 and Branca the rest (A. Molho, "The Florentine 'Tassa dei Traffichi' of 1451", *Studies in the Renaissance*, XVII [1970], p. 103).

[2] See the comments of R. de Roover, "Labour Conditions in Florence around 1400: Theory, Policy and Reality", *Florentine Studies*, ed. N. Rubinstein, London, 1968, pp. 298–99; Brucker, *Renaissance Florence*, pp. 68 ff.

[3] Published below by Perosa, p. 128, n. 7. Judith Brown kindly points out that, while the figures for looms cannot be right if those for production are accurate, the total output is not an impossible one. Certainly Giovanni, who had ties with a number of the city's leading silk merchants, could well have been generally familiar with the subject. He was, for example, Andrea Banchi's banker according to F. Edler de Roover, "Andrea Banchi, Florentine Silk Manufacturer and Merchant", pp. 239–40. See too below, p. 82.

[4] MAP, LXXXIX, 289, 2 November 1441, f. 304ʳ. A passage on this folio ('si debbi seghuire e fare nel modo che s'è fatto per l'adietro') implies an earlier company. The partners were Giannozzo di Bernardo Manetti (whose son was to marry Giovanni's daughter in 1452), Mariotto Banchi and Giovanni di Francesco della Luna, the brother of Rucellai's first partner Pierozzo della Luna. Banchi reported in 1458 that this partnership had lasted 'insino l'anno 1445' (Cat., 785, f. 98ᵛ).

[5] For the 1446 reference, see below n. 7. A note in Francesco Giovanni's diary implies an association between Strozzi and Rucellai by October 1445 (CS, II, 16 bis, f. 4ʳ). For Filippo d'Amerigo, see de Roover, *Rise and Decline*, p. 129; Kent, *Household and Lineage*, pp. 67–68, n. 21; below, pp. 76, 78, 80, n. 8. In 1451 Rucellai reported 'una chonpagnia a Vinegia, insieme chon altri . . .' (Cat., 707, f. 402ʳ).

[6] For slaves, see CS, II, 16 bis, f. 4ʳ. In general, see Perosa, p. 53.

[7] The letter is quoted in full below by Preyer, p. 199, n. 6. For the one example I know of Giovanni's service to the Estensi —by implication an important subject given Alberti's close ties with Lionello in the 1440s (cf. below, p. 44)—see *ibid.* There is evidence of the Ferrarese activities of the two brothers-in-law in Cat., 817, ff. 208ʳ ff.; see too MAP, CXXXVIII, 304, letter of February 1454 signed 'Giovanni Ruciellai e Giovanfrancesco Strozzi di V[enezi]a in Ferrara', and Pergamena Medicea, 31 August 1457. For the Strozzi in Ferrara, see Kent, " 'Più superba' ", pp. 311–23.

Germany eager for textiles and other merchandise. Perhaps Giovanni himself traded with Germany, as he certainly did in Lombardy. Of Venice he believed—the sentence deserves a wider audience— 'che quando fusse disfatta, o per guerre o per altro, fino a' fondamenti, che sarebbe nicistà di nuovo riedificharla'[1].

This analysis of Venice's advantages suggests that Giovanni was not deeply committed to maritime trade. Only one reference connects him with the Levantine traffic, and his interest in the Florentine galley fleet appears to have been patriotic as much as commercial[2]. To be sure we know nothing of his Genoese activities, and little of his affairs in Pisa and Naples. There is, however, scattered evidence of a long association with his youngest brother, Paolo, who lived in Naples, where Rucellai sent textiles, perhaps for the local market[3]. There need be no specifically maritime allusion in Giovanni's choice of the sail of fortune as a personal emblem; it served quite as well to refer, among other possible associations, to the 'buona fortuna' God had conceded him in his highly competent mercantile activities in various parts of the Italian peninsula[4].

The sense of achievement in his business successes Rucellai was later to express, the pleasure he had found in acquisition[5], presumably were with him earlier but they would have been no more than a powerful consolation in a long period of unrelenting effort and strain. Even these riches could only be safeguarded 'non con pichola dificultà ma con grandissima,' and there was as well the struggle to help the Strozzi while not too much alienating a regime which in 1455 was to repulse his

---

[1] *Zibaldone*, f. 84r–v; see Perosa, below, p. 125, n. 5. Cf. f. 47v for a reference to an unusual Easter Mass Giovanni had seen in a Venetian church. On the same folio he mentions religious practices at Cologne, without making it clear if he had been there; his enthusiasm about Germany's 'grandissimo consumare di spazierie e cotoni e altre merchatantie' (f. 84r) in itself cannot be taken as evidence of his having German interests.

[2] According to Benedetto Dei, one 'Gilio Ganberegli' represented Giovanni in Turkey in 1470. Several others, including Lorenzo Rucellai, were there 'for the Rucellai' (Bayerische Staatsbibliothek, Munich, "Memorie storiche", cod. ital. 160, ff. 141r–v, 144v). Giovanni is, however, nowhere mentioned in Dei's letters concerning the area (P. Orvieto, "Un esperto orientalista del '400: Benedetto Dei", *Rinascimento*, s. 2, IX [1969], pp. 207–75). It is suggestive that, on hearing 'della perdita di Chonstantinopoli', Rucellai's partner Giovanfrancesco Strozzi hurriedly told his informant, Francesco Caccini, that '. . . scrivo a Giovanni apieno . . .' (Riccardiana 4009, 2 July 1453, unfoliated). On the question of the maritime trade, see Preyer, *Giovanni Rucellai*, pp. 6–7, and Kent, "Letters", pp. 346–47, to which add the minor reference in Cat., 817, f. 209r. A late, chance find in the notarial archives suggests that a long search there might produce new evidence of Rucellai's substantial participation in international maritime trade. Late in 1461, he gave very wide powers to a Pisan agent in a dispute with a Genoese galley master over unspecified 'mercantias et res mobiles' which the captain was carrying for Giovanni (NA, B 1184 [Ser Girolamo Beltramini, 1457–78], inserto 6 [22]).

[3] The brothers' tax report of 1430 suggests that Paolo was already operating from Naples (Cat., 367, f. 599r), as he certainly was in 1433 (see p. 20, n. 2, above); cf. NA, C 190 (Ser Tommaso Carondini, 1435–38), f. 84r, for his absence from Florence in the 1430s. There is a reference to two Neapolitan companies formed by Paolo in the division of 1442 (*ibid.*, B 1994 [Ser Matteo Boccianti, 1441–42], f. 85r). His tax return of 1458 reveals him still established there ('abito familiarmente a Napoli dove ò fatto e fo traficho di taglo . . .' [Cat., 816, f. 1044r]), but almost destitute, as indeed he had been in 1451, when he wrote: 'Fo traficho a Napoli e non n'ò conpangnia. O a ddare e avere da più persone ma più a ddare, perchè le ghurre [sic] tra il nostro chomune e il re di 'Raona m'ànno fatto gran danno per medo ch'io resto chon più debito che mobile' (*ibid.*, 707, f. 407r). Several letters from Lorenzo di Messer Palla Strozzi to Filippo Strozzi, from mid-1450 to early 1451, mention Paolo's difficulties but with compassion, out of consideration for his brother-in-law perhaps. On 30 August 1450 Lorenzo mentioned ten florins Paolo owed him and asked Filippo to tell him 'in che termini si truova i fatti sua e se credi con dolceza e sollecitudine gli ritragha . . .' (CS, III, 131, f. 53r; cf. ff. 56r, 61r, 64r). Giovanni's 1458 accounts have references to dealings with Paolo—e.g. 'Panni e drapi a Napoli in mano di Paolo Rucellai' (Cat., 817, f. 208r; cf. ff. 209r, 218v, 219r–v)—and to a Rucellai company there (ff. 215v, 218v), but there was perhaps no formal connection between Giovanni's flourishing, and Paolo's confused, Neapolitan affairs (see p. 35, n. 1 above). The entry at f. 214r for a debit account of 2,342 florins for 'Unna mandata di più robba a Napoli' presumably referred to a transaction in which Paolo was not concerned. Giovanni's Venetian firm, with Giovanfrancesco Strozzi, also dealt with Filippo Strozzi's Neapolitan company (NA, B 1184 [Ser Girolamo Beltramini, 1457–78], inserto 7 [8], 13 July 1462).

[4] Perosa, pp. 117, 120; see below, p. 86. Mancini, *Alberti*, pp. 422–23, thought the sail alluded to Giovanni's maritime commerce.

[5] Perosa, pp. 117–121.

tentative overtures to a modest reconciliation. The 'Zibaldone vetus' of 1457, identified in Alessandro Perosa's edition[1], preserves the atmosphere of tension, threats and unresolved conflicts through which its author had lived and was still living, despite his seeing more clearly by that date how to order his life and the world around him. Giovanni had obviously been working out his attitude to the attractions and snares of public life, and to the virtues and the vices of the statuali who took part in it[2]. He had in fact decided by 1457 what to do with his hard-won wealth, but even then he marshalled the opposing texts he had been reading, on the pros and cons of conspicuous liberality and conservative financial management, without really disclosing what the dramatic outcome of his mental struggle had been[3]. Above all there was Rucellai's unsophisticated collection of learned and poetic opinions on how, and to what extent, a man might resist 'a' casi della fortuna', a consuming interest which reflected his own past efforts to understand, and to grapple with, an unpredictable existence full of unpalatable decisions. While agreeing with the majority of his authorities that fortune existed only in name and 'il buono ghoverno e il senno e la prudenza giova molto a ogni caso averso', he did not conceal from his sons that these prized qualities were acquired only with difficulty and long experience (an important concept for Giovanni)[4], that for survival careful calculation and deliberation were necessary at every step:

> vi do questo per consiglio e per ricordo, che tutti e' partiti che avete a pigliare nella vita vostra, così de' mezzani come delle cose grandi d'inportanza, voi dobiate molto bene et sottilmente esaminagli et pensarvi et per diritto et pe' rovescio, e di ciò avere consiglio da chi stimate ve lo sappi dare buono et che sia persona v'abbi amore e affection; e se così farete et governerete, rade volte v'arete a dolere della fortuna[5].

There is an autobiographical flavour in this passage, all the more precious since the Zibaldone is more reticent about Giovanni's personal experiences and feelings than its wealth of information might seem to promise. This makes more plausible the suggestion in other evidence that some of his own difficulties had concerned not just his public but his frustrating personal position in his 'time of adversity'. By the mid 1440s, when the renewed exile of Strozzi made Rucellai's increasing commitment to them and to Florence even harder to reconcile, it was becoming clearer that he faced a prolonged period of public indifference if not hostility, despite the support of his relations and friends and one or two gestures of goodwill from the Medici. He was now in his forties, fully mature by the standards of his day (one could be Gonfalonier of Justice at this age) and possessed, by his own account[6], of excellent health and exceptional vigour. Above all Giovanni Rucellai had a rich sense of his own powers, and a longing somehow to express them and to have them acknowledged by others, which in his present predicament seemed likely to be frustrated. As he made more money he seems to have enjoyed acquiring it less; he was literally wondering what to do with his increasing

---

[1] Perosa, pp. xii–xiii.

[2] Ibid., pp. 39–43; see too pp. 30–31 above.

[3] Ibid., pp. 10–13; at p. 12 he comes near to doing so, however. But see too his 'nota di più auctori che ànno detto dello spendere moderatamente e del servire gli amici e parenti' (Zibaldone, f. 20ᵛ), and at f. 22ᵛ the 'nota di detti di più autori che ànno scripto dello spendere con largeza e del servir gli amici con grande liberalità forse più che non richiede la ragione'. There are still further passages at ff. 37ᵛ–38ʳ.

[4] Ibid., f. 24ʳ: 'Uno nostro cittadino, savissimo huomo, disse che voleva così tosto sapere quello che sapeva come gli dimostravano le pratiche e le sperienze che come gli dimostrasse la scienza ... E però volgarmente si dice "la lunga sperientia fa scientia e arte"'.

[5] Perosa, p. 103. While staying in San Gimignano in 1457, Rucellai had consulted a local scholar on the subject of Fortuna (pp. 112–14, 175–76, n. 40).

[6] Ibid., pp. 117, 120.

wealth in this period, when he perhaps stayed at home more than ever before[1]. He was also a patriot without public place or recognition, one suspected by many influential citizens: this social isolation was perhaps particularly hard to bear for a man who had once felt (if not been) something of an outsider to his own kin, and had early manifested a need to insert himself into the community and to find a powerful ally there. Giovanni had, he wrote thankfully in 1457, the 'gratia et . . . benivolentia' of his Lion Rosso neighbours, a key phrase in his emotional vocabulary which, in different versions, he used more than once[2]. In a passage he added almost wistfully to one of the pseudo-Pandolfini's more violently pessimistic accounts of 'la vita civile' he told his sons:

> Non dico che non mi piaccia che voi siate nelle borse e onorati come gli altri cittadini, se non fusse per altro che per mostrare non essere a sospetto al reggimento, ma essere accetti e in gratia de' cittadini[3].

If political action and a public career had ever seemed a means of much needed self-expression for Giovanni Rucellai, by 1457 he was left with only one political ambition: to hold office as a sign of the public approval he so desired. He was no doubt then more pessimistic about his specifically political prospects than he had been earlier, but this need to be honoured and accepted by the wider Florentine community was an old and deep one springing from the earlier vicissitudes of his life. He mentioned this, perhaps his major ambition, yet again in the psychologically interesting passage which described his good standing with the 'consorti et . . . parenti et . . . vicini' of his district, and went on to offer his sons precise counsel on how to broaden that local base 'per essere in gratia et benivolentia de' cittadini et de' parenti et degli amici':

> vi conforto, figliuoli miei, essere buoni, giusti et honesti, darvi alle virtù e alle buone opere, imparare, intendere, farvi amare e farvi tali d'essere amati et onorati: niuna cosa è tanto in gratia quanto le cose virtuose, grate et degne. Et così facciendo, non dubito punto, prima colla gratia di Dio et poi colla vostra buona fama et col vostro buono nome che aquisterete, non vi difendiate da chi cercasse o operasse farvi male[4].

Though it occurs in a passage concerned with the art of economic self-defence, this advice implies a broader programme of personal and public rehabilitation than any mercantile activity, however honest, zealous and patriotic, could realize. When Giovanni wrote it he had recently perfected his plans for the magnificent building campaign, for himself and his city, which he had decided was the best way for a man in his position to become loved and honoured and secure. We cannot be far wrong, however, in placing the first conception of this programme in the middle and late 1440s[5], when it came as a happy and creative response to the sense of crisis and frustration Giovanni Rucellai was then experiencing, perhaps more intensely than at any other time. His earliest project

---

[1] See above, pp. 31 ff. Giovanfrancesco Strozzi, and later Filippo d'Amerigo Rucellai, presumably attended to Venetian affairs Giovanni had earlier handled personally.

[2] Perosa, p. 9. Cf. the aphorism 'Alla giustitia si dia favore e i vicini in benivolenza s'abbino' (*Zibaldone*, f. 34r).

[3] Perosa, p. 39.

[4] *Ibid.*, p. 9. Among mankind's greatest pleasures, he noted on f. 34r of the *Zibaldone*: 'Ancora disse ch'essere in gratia degl'uomini del mondo e massimamente di quegli della sua patria era grandissima dolceza e piacere'. See too p. 29, n. 6 above for Giovanfrancesco Strozzi's comment that Giovanni's appointment to public office was a sign of 'buona volontà'. Interestingly, Carlo Marsuppini was using the word *benivolenza* in a sense cognate to Rucellai's, as Salvatore Camporeale makes clear in a note which he generously allows me to quote here: 'Il termine *benivolentia* sembra esser parola-chiave nella scrittura cancelleresca fiorentina di Carlo Marsuppini negli anni '40/'50 del sec. XV. Particolarmente nelle transazioni diplomatiche, la parola si carica via via di senso politico e civile: indica "rapporto multilaterale di alleanza e collaborazione tra le diverse città-stato, ai fini di un equilibrio politico da instaurarsi *in tucta Italia*". Cf. Signori Missive 1ª Cancelleria, Reg. 36, ff. 90v–91r, 104r; Signori Missive Legazioni e Commissarie, Reg. 11, ff. 41v–43r, 54v–55r'.

[5] See chap. IV below.

was the palace, begun about 1450, and he was no doubt excited to discover, probably some years later, that what he had hoped for at that time had been in fact achieved by another palace-builder, the Roman Gnaeus Octavius who, according to Cicero, had gained 'honore grandissimo . . . per la edificazione d'uno bellissimo palazzo' which 'fu chagione di farli aquistare nel populo grandissima benivolenzia e grazia'[1].

[1] *Zibaldone*, f. 63ᵛ; see also below, pp. 54–55.

IV. THE GENESIS OF THE BUILDING PROGRAMME

I

During the first phase of work on his palace Giovanni Rucellai's building plans became more ambitious. Certainly by 1448 he wanted to found a chapel of the Holy Sepulchre, either in San Pancrazio or Santa Maria Novella. Probably the beginnings of his activities at the villa and garden of Quaracchi also belong to this fertile period[1]. What Marco Dezzi Bardeschi has called Rucellai's 'ambizioso, unitario programma edilizio'[2] was not fully developed in the 1440s—the hesitation concerning the site of the chapel is suggestive—but he had settled upon and organized a coherent campaign by about 1457 at the latest. The subtly façaded palace was to be set off by a family 'piaza e logia chomune', and his tomb and its chapel was to be given to San Pancrazio, which stood just behind this small complex. Moving beyond his parochial world, Giovanni was planning a marble façade for Santa Maria Novella (Pl. 33), a focus of his family's patronage but also the major church of his quarter and one of the most celebrated Dominican centres in Christendom[3]. This was not the first ambitious building programme devised by a private citizen in Florence—before Cosimo de' Medici's there had been, for example, Nicola Acciaiuoli's in the 1350s, and his explicit, almost 'Renaissance' justification[4]—but it was one of the earliest and most interesting Quattrocento projects. It is exceptional for its rational conception, with the pleasingly finished ensemble in the parish of San Pancrazio at its centre, and for the spirit of magnificent (even joyous) liberality, nicely calculated to satisfy private passions and public needs, in which it was undertaken and successfully completed at 'grandissime spese'.

Contemporary justifications of private building on this scale, disapproved of by earlier and some Quattrocento theorists, were borrowed above all from Cicero. Giovanni, fascinated by the period when 'e' Romani signioreggiorono il mondo'[5], had a taste for buildings which were self-consciously

---

[1] I am assuming that Giovanni more or less simultaneously turned his attention to rural and to urban domestic building. Quaracchi was certainly substantially finished by 1464 (Perosa, pp. 20–23, 118), earlier than any other of his undertakings save parts of the palace itself; it is even possible that 1456 may be a significant year in its history, when 'fessi le nozze [of Pandolfo] a Quaracchi' (BNC, II, IV, 374, f. 131). I have found very little about this villa. Some building went on there (Perosa, p. 118), and it may have been more substantial than improvements to the apparently rather modest villa whose contents were inventoried in Pupilli, 17, ff. liiii ff., in 1406. Giovanni himself called Quaracchi a 'buona e bella chasa' (Perosa, p. 20), and the late sixteenth-century continuator of the *Zibaldone* described it as 'un palagio grande' (*Zibaldone*, f. 247ʳ); it was 'un bellissimo loco et apto ad essere ogni cosa', a friend of the family had written in 1520: pub. by G. Mazzoni, *Le opere di Giovanni Rucellai*, Bologna, 1877, p. xvi.

[2] "Complesso monumentale", p. 17.

[3] See below, pp. 62–65.

[4] See Nicola's letters in G. Gaye, *Carteggio inedito d'artisti dei secoli XIV, XV, XVI*, Florence, 1839, reprint edn. 1968, i, pp. 57 ff. In 1356 he wrote that 'imperò che tutte altre sustantie che iddio me ave concedute, rimaneranno ali posteri, e non so a cui; solo lo dicto munisterio [Certosa] con tutti li suoi adornamenti sarà mio in ogni tempo, e farà plu essere verzicante e duratoro lo mio nome in cotesta cittate, e se lanima è immortale . . . la mia anima di ciò sarà letificante . . .' (p. 61). 'Tutte le mie consolationi si riposano alo nostro santo munisterio . . .', he said later, 'e per certo se io avessi denari, io lo farei lo plu notabile loco a tutta ytalia' (p. 64). A letter by Rinaldo degli Albizzi of 9 June 1426 shows the success of Nicola's plans; Acciaiuoli was so famous 'in superlativo grado, *et in memoriam longinquam*, . . . pe' lasci pii magnifici e discreti, *et inter alia*, della fabrica di Certosa . . . . (*Commissioni*, II, p. 595). Rucellai was very proud that he was closely connected with these Acciaiuoli (see Perosa, p. 145, n. 1, and *Zibaldone*, f. 223ʳ⁻ᵛ), but he does not refer to the 'gran sinischalcho's' building activities.

[5] Perosa, p. 55. See *Zibaldone*, f. 25ᵛ, for the phrase 'nel tenpo ch'e'Romani dominavono il mondo'. In general see A. D. Fraser Jenkins, "Cosimo de' Medici's Patronage of Architecture and the Theory of Magnificence", *JWCI*, XXXIII (1970), pp. 162–70; J. Onians, "Alberti and Φιλαρετη: A Study in their Sources", *JWCI*, XXXIV (1971), pp. 96–114.

all'antica. One thinks in particular of the Rucellai palace, with its 'facciata dinanzi composta di pietre lavorate, e tutta fatta al modo antico', which Filarete cited explicitly as an example of building which followed 'la pratica e maniera antica' favoured by Brunelleschi, 'famoso e degnissimo architetto e sottilissimo imitatore di Dedalo, il quale risuscitò nella città nostra di Firenze questo modo antico dello edificare'[1]. This was praise which must have delighted a patron who also regarded Brunelleschi as the most brilliant architect of the generation which had transformed the city 'con bellissimi addornamenti di conci alla romanesca, cioè al modo facievano gli antichi romani'. In one of the earliest contemporary eulogies of Brunelleschi, by whom 'lle muraglie antiche alla romanescha furono ritrovate', Giovanni called him:

> maestro d'architettura e di scoltura, perfetto gieometrico, di grande ingiengnio naturale e fantasia nelle dette arti quanto niuno altro che fusse mai dal tenpo de' Romani in qua, risucitatore delle muraglie antiche alla romanescha[2].

Presumably Rucellai would have wanted to employ Brunelleschi had the architect lived longer. The model for the Rucellai pulpit was made by Brunelleschi, and Piero di Cardinale, Giovanni's cousin, was on the committee of the Wool Guild given the task of honourably burying the architect.[3] Brunelleschi being dead, Giovanni chose Alberti, for his commitment to the same classicizing tradition. Nor were Rucellai's interests confined to building. He was fully aware that his was a period of unusual artistic innovation and intellectual distinction, in which flourished learned classical scholars whom he believed to have 'rivochato a lucie [l']anticha leggiadria dello stile perduto e spento', and artists who had gone beyond even Giotto and Cimabue[4]. He may have set out to 'collect' these new masters in a spirit unusually appreciative for the period. Notably, his list of the paintings and sculpture 'di mano de' migliori maestri che siano stati da buono tenpo in qua' which he had 'in chasa nostra' in 1471 is precisely that, for despite the typically eclectic taste it displays, it ignores several minor painters who had worked for Giovanni[5]. One of the distinctive features of Giovanni Rucellai's patronage was that so often he expressly chose the best and (what he took to be) the most classical, whether he sought this admired past in Apollonio di Giovanni's *cassone* paintings—which introduced many of his contemporaries to classical themes in late Gothic disguise—or in the novel

---

[1] See passage quoted below by Preyer, Doc. XVI; and cf. Salvini, below, pp. 248–50.

[2] Perosa, pp. 55, 60, 61; cf. E. Luporini, *Brunelleschi: forma e ragione*, Milan, 1964, p. 205, n. 46.

[3] S. Orlandi, *S. Antonino. Studi bibliografici*, Florence, 1960, II, p. 185. In 1443, Brunelleschi received one gold florin for the model; the pulpit was executed by his adopted son Andrea Cavalcante, whose influence on part of the sculptural work in the Rucellai palace *cortile* has been discerned (Preyer, below, p. 165). For Piero Rucellai, see C. Guasti, *La cupola di Santa Maria del Fiore*, Florence, 1857, reprint edn., 1974, p. 56. For two differing accounts of Alberti's attitude to Brunelleschi, see now C. Grayson, "Leon Battista Alberti, Architect", *Architectural Design*, XLIX (1979), pp. 7–17 (especially pp. 8–9), and H. Burns, "A Drawing by L. B. Alberti", *ibid.*, pp. 45–56 (especially pp. 47–48).

[4] Perosa, pp. 60–61. When in Rome in 1450, Giovanni twice noted works by Giotto (pp. 68, 69). See Perosa's assessment that Rucellai 'ha colto ... con gran lucidità, l'importanza del grande momento storico-culturale in cui era vissuto e viveva' (below, p. 128).

[5] *Ibid.*, pp. 23–24. The painters not mentioned are Apollonio di Giovanni and Marco del Buono, who worked in the palace in 1452 and made *cassoni* for Giovanni's daughters' marriages (see E. Callmann, *Apollonio di Giovanni*, Oxford, 1974, pp. 35, 76–81; cf. Preyer, below, pp. 165–6); Neri di Bicci (*ibid.*, p. 165, 166, n. 1), whose father's *compagno* Stefano d'Antonio may also have been employed by the Rucellai (see my "Art Historical Gleanings from the Florentine Archives", *Australian Journal of Art History*, ii, 1980); and the fresco master now identified by Professor Salvini as Giovanni di Francesco (below, p. 249). Among others, R. and M. Wittkower have suggested that Rucellai was proud of 'the artists who served him and [had] an interest in their individuality; ... a man who seemed less concerned with assembling anonymous decorations for his palace, than in collecting works by famous masters' (*Born under Saturn*, New York, 1969 edn., p. 32; cf. F. Haskell in *Encyclopedia of World Art*, London, 1966, xi, col. 120).

Roman lettering, favoured by Alberti, that distinguishes Giovanni's tomb and the façade of Santa Maria Novella[1].

Until the 1440s Rucellai's activities as a patron had been modestly and decently traditional both in conception and scale. An early reference to his paying fifty florins to 'più persone', including a 'dipintore' and 'maestri di murare' among other tradesmen, almost certainly suggests no more than that he was making house repairs or additions[2]. The first will of 1437 reveals little trace of a great patron in the making. Giovanni left the interest from one thousand florins in *Monte* shares (not a large sum) to the main chapel of San Pancrazio because his grandfather's bequest to it was not yet fully honoured, despite an earlier deduction from the brothers' patrimony. This was anyway in one respect a family project to which other Rucellai had contributed[3]. The young banker apparently did not covet a special sepulchre or chapel; his desire to be buried 'in the tomb of his ancestors' was as traditional as those charitable bequests he made to poor girls and prisoners 'in onorem Dei'[4]. These frugal and pious provisions conformed to his family's pattern. Like most of their peers, the Rucellai had done no more in the fourteenth century than build and decorate tombs and chapels in their local churches and a hospital and oratory near their rural home. When early in the next century they employed painters, it was as skilled artisans. One of Giovanni's distant Rucellai cousins dealt with Giovanni dal Ponte in the 1420s[5]; and his own father, who had the usual taste for decorative furniture, commissioned a picture from one 'Luca, painter', to whom he was still in debt at the time he died. Even if this had been a painting to excite an exceptional interest in Giovanni, it was sold in 1407 when the paternal home was broken up[6].

There might seem to be a hint of conversion in Giovanni's apparently rather rapid transition from an interest in pious charity to a preoccupation with self-absorbed liberality. It is understandable that Leon Battista Alberti has in this been given the role of missionary, a piece of casting which not only suits the traditional though not undisputed attribution to Alberti of some or all of Rucellai's buildings but accords with the rather modest reading of his patron's intellectual grasp implied by several historians. Unfortunately, there is still no evidence directly linking the two men in the 1440s, which is indubitably the key decade for an understanding of the genesis of Giovanni's programme. The recent suggestion that they met at the Council of Florence between 1439 and 1443, when Alberti was there as a papal abbreviator, is based upon the false testimony of a document, in fact of

---

[1] E. Callmann, *Apollonio di Giovanni*, pp. 23–24, and chap. 4; see too the preceding note. G. Mardersteig, "Leon Battista Alberti e la rinascita del carattere lapidario romano nel Quattrocento", *IMU*, II (1959), pp. 285–307.

[2] Cat., 462, f. 518ᵛ (1433): 'Abiano a dare a più persone, cioè lengniaiuolo, lastraiuolo, fornaciaio, maestri di murare, al dipintore, al fabro e per lengniame cho[m]perato per tutto fiorini 50'. Perhaps some alterations were necessary after the brothers had rented a house beside their own, which 'era pichola chasa' (*ibid.*, 405, f. 63ʳ), in 1429.

[3] Later, of course, when Toschi restored this chapel 'faccendovi la finestra del vetro chon aiuto e favore' of Giovanni Rucellai, the abbot conceded him the right to put 'l'arme sua in detta finestra sotto quella di San Pancrazio, e fugli chonceduto l'arme sculta sopra la finestra' (Conv. Sopp., 88, 68, f. 91ᵛ). See too Kent, *Household and Lineage*, p. 267. Details of the 1408 deduction are in Conv. Sopp., 88, 62, f. 27ʳ. Parishioners other than the Rucellai had also contributed to this chapel (Dezzi Bardeschi, "Complesso monumentale", p. 8). Giovanni's will is in NA, C 190 (Ser Tommaso Carondini, 1435–38), f. 124ʳ.

[4] *Ibid.*

[5] H. P. Horne, "Appendice di documenti su Giovanni dal Ponte", *Rivista d'arte*, IV (1906), pp. 171, 177.

[6] Upon Paolo's death we find that his estate owed 'Luce pictori, pro pictura facta in camera dicti Pauli libras . . .[sic] parvorum' (Pupilli, 17, f. lviʳ). 'In camera maiori Pauli' there was indeed 'una tabula nr̄e dn̄e', later sold with a painting from another room (*ibid.*, ff. liʳ, liiiʳ, lviᵛ). This man could be one of several minor Lucas active at this time (Thieme-Becker, *Künstler-Lexikon*, Leipzig, 1929, XXIII, pp. 426–27). For Rucellai patronage in the Trecento, see Kent, *Household and Lineage*, pp. 235, 261–2, 267–70, 280. In 1457 Giovanni did note, however, that one of his fourteenth-century ancestors 'murò Charcheregli dilà dal Ponte a Grieve, che in quel tempo fu riputato la più degna et la più magnifica fortezza del contado nostro' (*Zibaldone*, f. 5ʳ). This, perhaps a public commission, still survives; see the Touring Club Italiano's guide, *Firenze e dintorni*, Milan, 1964, 5th edn., p. 457.

1448, which seemed to show that Giovanni had devised the project for a Holy Sepulchre chapel as early as 1440; he may have done so at this time of increased contact between East and West (and with or without Alberti's inspiration) but there is no warrant for our saying that he did[1]. The same is true of another scrap of evidence which provides a new and more precise context in which Alberti and Giovanni might have met. According to Santa Maria Novella's chronicler Borghigiani, the papal abbreviators, who customarily gathered in the Rucellai chapel in the church, voted a *limosina* to repair its roof in 1440, the year as it happens that the convent's treasurer was Fra Andrea Rucellai, a man interested in patronage of the arts and almost certainly a close associate of his distant kinsman Giovanni[2]. Even much later the documentable bonds between Alberti and Rucellai are similarly indirect or what one can only call contextual—that in 1466 Bernardo Rucellai was on intimate terms with Francesco d'Altobianco Alberti, the friend and benefactor of his famous kinsman; that Alberti guided Bernardo round Rome in 1471[3]. Clues which come even later—for example Palla di Bernardo's ownership of a self-portrait by Alberti in the sixteenth century—are very likely attempts (there were certainly others) to give authority to the oral tradition linking Alberti to the Rucellai which Vasari first put on paper[4]. There are many Albertian echoes in the *Zibaldone*, but the only obvious literary borrowing, Giovanni's use of the pseudo-Pandolfini's *rifacimento* of the

---

[1] For this document and suggestion, see Dezzi Bardeschi, *Facciata;* and the same author's "Sole in Leone: Leon Battista Alberti: astrologia, cosmologia e tradizione ermetica nella facciata di Santa Maria Novella", *Psicon*, I (1974), pp. 33 ff. It has been accepted by F. Borsi, *Leon Battista Alberti*, Milan, 1975, p. 61. Brenda Preyer first pointed out to me the dating problem; cf. my *Household and Lineage*, p. 101, n. 168. See too below, pp. 57 ff. If C. Seymour is right in connecting the Rucellai's pulpit project in Santa Maria Novella with the papal stay there during the Council (*Sculpture in Italy, 1400–1500*, Harmondsworth, 1966, p. 119), this is evidence of a family ferment which may indeed have touched Giovanni.

[2] This information was published by Orlandi, *Necrologio*, II, p. 577. Under 1440 we find: 'Limosina dei Scrittori del Papa che adunavano nella Cappella di S. Caterina V. e M. [i.e. the Rucellai chapel] per riparare i tetti della Cappella'. However, since the patronage of the Rucellai was apparently still in dispute (see below, p. 58), the point is not a strong one. Furthermore, Rucellai was probably much in Venice at this time (see pp. 32 ff. above). For Fra Andrea, see *ibid.*, p. 576, and below, p. 64. On Alberti's movements at this time, see C. Grayson's article in *DBI*, Rome, 1960, i, pp. 702 ff. I am grateful to Professor Grayson for his opinion that Alberti was very likely present at such a meeting, though he knows of no other relevant evidence.

[3] See Borsi, *Alberti*, p. 364, for the 1471 visit. On 13 March 1466 Bernardo Rucellai informed Lorenzo de' Medici that 'abbiamo ordinato una gita piacevole domenicha che si va al Paradiso; andremo a desinare con Bernardo Manetti . . . e fo conto ci daremo buon tempo fra luogo di Francesco d'Altobiancho [Alberti, owner of the villa and garden at Paradiso] e quivi, chè sai quella sua mogle fa buona festa . . .' (MAP, XXIII, 19; cf. CXXXVIII, 134, two days later). Francesco Alberti, as patron of an oratory near this estate, made Leon Battista its rector in October 1468: see A. Parronchi, "Otto piccoli documenti per la biografia dell' Alberti", *Rinascimento*, s. 2, XII (1972), pp. 233–34. For the cousins' friendship, see too R. N. Watkins, *The Family in Renaissance Florence*, Columbia, South Carolina, 1969, pp. 5–6, 19, 151–4. Francesco Alberti's 1458 *catasto* throws no light on his relations with the Rucellai and Leon Battista (Cat., 804, ff. 267r–78r).

[4] Referring to the façade of Santa Maria Novella, Vasari says that Giovanni 'ne parlò con Leon Batista suo amicissimo'; however, he wrote that Cosimo Rucellai commissioned the palace and Loggia from Alberti, who also did the Holy Sepulchre chapel for 'i medesimi Rucellai' (*Le opere di Giorgio Vasari*, ed. G. Milanesi, Florence, 1906, reprint edn. 1973, II, pp. 541, 543). It is also Vasari who informs us that Giovanni's grandson Palla owned a 'self portrait [of Alberti], done with the aid of a mirror, and a panel with large figures in chiaroscuro' (ed. and trans. in C. Grayson's edition of Alberti's *On Painting and On Sculpture*, London, 1972, p. 144). It is tempting to believe that Alberti himself gave the self-portrait to Rucellai for, according to the 'anonymous' life now thought to be autobiographical, Alberti had done such a self-portrait so that 'he should be more readily known to visitors who had not met him' (quoted in *ibid.*, p. 143), a motive which Rucellai, the proud palace owner, could well have shared. There seems, however, no reason to identify the Rucellai portrait with the one Alberti mentions (*ibid.*, p. 153: I am again grateful to Professor Grayson for his cautionary advice on this question). Further, it seems inconceivable that Rucellai would have neglected to mention in his list of 1471 (Perosa, pp. 23–24) graphic works by one so celebrated as Alberti, even if they were comparatively amateurish. Presumably the portrait came into Rucellai hands later; Palla, and probably his father Bernardo, appear to have been collectors, since the younger man also owned a lost Masaccio, according to Vasari (Berti, *Masaccio*, pp. 19, 97, 166), to which Giovanni had made no reference. For the palace collection in 1548, unfortunately not specifically described, see Preyer, below, pp. 171–4. See too, Kent, "Letters", pp. 342–9, on the question of Rucellai and Alberti.

third book of *Della Famiglia*, is second-hand and, as Cecil Grayson has pointed out, notably unacknowledged[1].

These silences are disconcerting and have not been satisfactorily explained. Rucellai makes them more intriguing by his failure to mention Alberti while so praising Brunelleschi (as well as painters and sculptors who, by comparison with architects, did not generally enjoy great esteem). A frustrated longing for documentary confirmation of the two men's collaboration does not, however, constitute grounds for rejecting the stylistic attributions to Alberti, especially the latest discriminating one by Dr. Preyer, of at least some of Rucellai's buildings[2]. The two men had the opportunity to meet in the 'forties—a time of ferment for them both when Alberti was working out his architectural ideas [3]—as much perhaps (if this is not to multiply hypothetical contexts beyond necessity) through the Estensi connection[4] as at the Council of Florence. This said, the absence of all evidence other than the buildings themselves makes it impossible to be at all precise about the timing and extent of Alberti's contribution to Rucellai's education as a patron.

There are other grounds for rejecting the 'conversion' theory. Unless Giovanni met and was deeply influenced by Alberti much earlier than has ever been suspected (in the early 'thirties), one should probably envisage the humanist's contribution as one among several whose confluence in the 1440s refined, shaped and perhaps activated a taste for painting, classicizing architecture and grand patronage to which the young banker was first exposed from the late 1420s onwards. For Rucellai grew up in a circle passionately interested in the arts, especially the new century's experiments, and eager and able to spend on them. Most of the personal links are firm if the intellectual and artistic ones are not. They encourage us to think that it was in the company of Palla Strozzi and other relatives, several of them major patrons, that Giovanni first saw 'modern' painting and architecture, and heard discussed—he was perhaps, being no Latinist, more impressed than genuinely enlightened—the new humanistic assessment of classical themes and their relevance. As Richard Krautheimer has suggested, Messer Palla was an important bridge between the humanistic and artistic circles who were both sharply interested in the antique in the very early Quattrocento. As such, Strozzi was one of three citizen *operai* chosen in November 1403 to treat with Ghiberti concerning the north door of the Baptistery[5]. Himself a patron of the sacristy and chapel with a tomb for his father in Santa Trinita, he may have used Ghiberti in this ambitious project[6], which has recently been said to

---

[1] In his review of Perosa, *Italian Studies*, XVI (1961), p. 114. In general see J. Ravenscroft, "The Third Book of Alberti's *Della Famiglia* and its two *rifacimenti*", *ibid.*, XXIX (1974), pp. 45–53. Perosa does not believe that Rucellai knew Alberti's work (below, pp. 111 ff).

[2] Preyer, below, pp. 184 ff.

[3] C. Grayson, "The Composition of Leon Battista Alberti's *'Decem libri de re aedificatoria'*", *Münchner Jahrbuch der bildenden Kunst*, XI (1960), pp. 152–61.

[4] See *ibid.*, pp. 153, 155–6, for Alberti's ties with Lionello d'Este, for whom the *Ten Books on Architecture* were probably intended; Rucellai was praised by Lionello in a letter of 1446 (see p. 35, n. 7 above). This lead would be well worth following up in the archives of Ferrara and Modena. I am struck, for example, by Lionello's use of the device of the sail of fortune in 1444 (Preyer, below, p. 201), and Giovanni's later passion for putting it on his buildings.

[5] *Lorenzo Ghiberti*, Princeton, 1956, i, pp. 105 ff., 279, 299; ii, 368–9; see too H. W. Janson, *The Sculpture of Donatello*, Princeton, 1963, 2nd edn., p. 59, for Palla's playing a similar role in 1421. A. Della Torre, *Storia dell' Accademia Platonica*, pp. 286 ff., describes the intellectual circle around the Strozzi.

[6] According to U. Middeldorf, "Additions to Lorenzo Ghiberti's Work", *BM*, CXIII (1971), pp. 75–76. See now R. Jones, "Documenti e precisazioni per Lorenzo Ghiberti, Palla Strozzi e la Sagrestia di Santa Trinita", in the proceedings of the *convegno*, *Lorenzo Ghiberti nel suo Tempo*, held at Florence in October 1978, Florence, 1980, pp. 507–21. For further material on Ghiberti as Palla Strozzi's artistic adviser, see J. Russell Sale, "Palla Strozzi and Lorenzo Ghiberti: New Documents", *MKHIF*, XXII (1978), pp. 355–8.

reflect 'the avant-garde tastes of its designer and patron'[1]. When in 1422 Palla employed Gentile da Fabriano to paint the gorgeous *Adoration of the Magi*, he had chosen 'the greatest modern painter' in Italy at precisely the time when Masaccio was dramatically to alter the meaning of that phrase[2]. Even so, it was through his father-in-law that Giovanni was exposed to both the old and the new currents in contemporary painting. In 1431 Felice Brancacci, Masaccio's principal Florentine patron, also became Strozzi's son-in-law. How close a relationship existed between Rucellai and the Brancacci then we do not know, but they were certainly intimate twenty years later[3]. One should perhaps add that Giovanni brought to this distinguished company that down-to-earth mercantile training which, Michael Baxandall has suggested, unconsciously prepared contemporaries to look for certain qualities in pictures. His shrewd guess that 'Giovanni Rucellai was good at the Rule of Three' is charmingly confirmed by the banker's repetition in the *Zibaldone* of a common riddle—about the testamentary difficulties of a widow and her unborn twins—which demonstrated the workings of a mathematical rule that may have made patrons very aware of geometric proportion in paintings. As a man much concerned with trading, Rucellai was probably one of Baxandall's expert 'barrel gaugers' as well[4].

Messer Palla provided one of the several channels through which Giovanni may have received both a personal knowledge of Brunelleschi and a passionate concern for building. Even if the architect's work at the villa of Petraia was done before Strozzi acquired it in 1422, Rucellai knew well this estate on which Palla lavished attention[5]. His father-in-law's devotion to his villa at Tresiano which 'da' fondamenti fu edificato dagli nostri antichi e padri' and had been 'grande e bella e magnifica', suggests an attitude to monumental building which Giovanni would have understood instantly if indeed he did not imbibe it from that very source. In 1462 Strozzi insisted that the villa be kept 'nella casa nostra e ne' nostri discendenti per memoria di chi lo edificò e fu principio . . .', a sentence which might come from Rucellai's own will made three years later[6]. Giovanni's partnerships with Pierozzo and Giovanni della Luna, not least because they were Strozzi connections, may also have opened a path to Brunelleschi, for Rucellai would have known, if he was not a friend of, the brothers' kinsman Francesco. The expertise of Francesco della Luna as a builder and disciple of Brunelleschi has been inflated, but he was many times an *operaio* for the Spedale degli Innocenti and may reasonably be

---

[1] D. D. Davisson, "The Iconology of the S. Trinita Sacristy, 1418–1435: A Study of the private and public Functions of religious Art in the Early Quattrocento", *AB*, LVII (1975), p. 318. On Palla's patronage, see too G. Poggi, *La cappella e la tomba di Onofrio Strozzi nella chiesa di Santa Trinita (1419–23)*, Florence, 1903.

[2] Berti, *Masaccio*, pp. 58–61. On Palla's possible patronage of Fra Angelico, see S. Orlandi, *Beato Angelico*, Florence, 1964, pp. 45 ff.

[3] See p. 24 above. On Felice, see C. Carnesecchi, "Messer Felice Brancacci", *Miscellanea d'arte*, i (1903), pp. 190–2, and Berti, *Masaccio*, pp. 22–23, 62, 101–2. For a new, very cautious and well documented assessment of Felice's precise role, see now Molho, "The Brancacci Chapel", pp. 50–98. See postscript, p. 95 below.

[4] *Painting and Experience in Fifteenth-Century Italy*, Oxford, 1972, p. 109; pp. 86 ff.; *Zibaldone*, f. 80ᵛ.

[5] 'Dicesi che avendosi a murare la Petraia, Filippo da chi era quella posessione ne fu richiesto di consiglio, e che fece quella torre che v'è, con suo parere . . . la quale muraglia non si seguitò poi per mutamenti di fortuna': Antonio Manetti, *Vita di Filippo Brunelleschi preceduta da La Novella del Grasso*, eds. D. de Robertis and G. Tanturli, Milan, 1976, p. 54. The editors very sensibly point out that the last passage could be a reference to Palla Strozzi's exile (p. 54, n. 6), though in context the passage appears to refer to juvenile work which Brunelleschi could hardly have done after 1422; according to Lorenzo Strozzi, who was often very well informed about Palla (see pp. 46–7, n. 7 below), Petraia was 'da lui edificata' (*Vite di alcuni della famiglia Strozzi*, ed. cit., p. 50). One of Palla's account books (CS, IV, 345) has a number of references to painters employed at Petraia (e.g. f. 106ʳ), some of them published in Orlandi, *Beato Angelico*, pp. 181–82; see also p. 48 below, and now Sale, "Palla Strozzi and Lorenzo Ghiberti" (pp. 355–8 above). The villa was imposingly described in 1463 as 'Unam tenutam, palatium sive fortilitium, cum turri et domo pro domino' (NA, C 407 [Ser Pierozzo Cerbini, 1456–65], f. 341ʳ).

[6] AS Ferr., Archivio Bentivoglio, lib. 6, 34, f. 51; cf. below, pp. 53–4. Palla's Paduan *palazzo* was apparently a modest one (Fiocco, "La casa di Palla Strozzi", pp. 361–82).

called 'a leading silk merchant with architectural interests'[1]. Stoldo Frescobaldi was yet another patrician with architectural concerns about whose relationship with Giovanni we can be quite certain. The two were on the closest terms in the 1440s and presumably much earlier since they were first cousins through the Pandolfini and each was 'sospetto allo stato'. In the late 1420s and 1430s Stoldo, 'uno atto uomo e valente ed amorevole della chiesa per più interessi'[2], was one of the most energetic entrepreneurs of the Brunelleschian rebuilding of Santo Spirito, advancing his own money to begin a project in which he took the closest interest for the rest of his life[3]. Stoldo's cousin certainly knew about, and may have profoundly admired, this generous example and this decided expression of taste. By the time the two were banking partners in the Mercato Nuovo in the 'forties their conversation, stimulated perhaps by the proximity of Brunelleschi's palace for the Guelf Party (where indeed Francesco della Luna had made one of the two architectural mistakes which have put him into the literature!)[4], would not only have been about their flourishing business[5].

Rucellai's background had already disposed him towards a sharper and more informed interest in building and magnificent liberality than one might have supposed from reading his 1437 will when, in the 1440s, his developing relationship with Messer Palla provided him with the means—and it may be the encouragement—to undertake large scale ecclesiastical patronage. This came at a time when his attention was already directed towards the campaign at San Pancrazio and his family's donation of the pulpit to Santa Maria Novella. During this decade and the next Giovanni acquired at modest cost more and more Strozzi property ('ex variis titulis, rationibus et causis' as a much later document conveniently summarized an immensely complex process)[6], almost always with Palla's consent and usually on the understanding that on request it should revert to the Strozzi at the same prices. By 1462 Palla could write that most of his remaining estates 'si può dire quasi tutte ritrovarsi nelle mani di Giovanni. . .'[7]. These sales kept Palla's lands in sympathetic hands while

---

[1] H. Saalman's comment in his edition of Manetti's *The Life of Brunelleschi*, Philadelphia, 1970, p. 142, n. 117. However, see C. Gilbert's shrewd marshalling of the evidence to show that Francesco 'has been subjected to a transformation from rich merchant to minor builder that cannot be called one of our successes' ("The earliest Guide to Florentine Architecture, 1423", *MKHIF*, XVI [1969], p. 37, n. 12). Manetti does not refer to della Luna by name (see *Vita di Filippo Brunelleschi, ed. cit.*, pp. 100, n. 6, 105). To Vasari he was Brunelleschi's 'amicissimo' (*Opere, ed. cit.*, ii, p. 366). His role as a leading *operaio* is not, however, in doubt; see now E. Battisti, *Filippo Brunelleschi*, Milan, 1976, pp. 335, 338, 345, 346, 347, 366, and for the cupola of the Duomo, Guasti, *Cupola*, pp. 76–77.

[2] Manetti, *Vita di Filippo Brunelleschi, ed. cit.*, pp. 121–2.

[3] *Ibid.*, p. 122; cf. Vasari, *Opere, ed. cit.*, ii, p. 381. See Luporini, *Brunelleschi*, pp. 147–8, 149, 155, 230–1. On 19 January 1434 Stoldo and another man were appointed 'ambos in concordia operaios et pro operariis et constructores ed edificatores opere ecclesie capitali et conventus Sancti Spiritus predicti cum plenissima balia auctoritate et potere . . .' (p. 230). For his later activities as a chapel patron there, see M. Bori, "L' 'Annunziazione' di Piero del Donzello . . .", *Rivista d'arte*, III (1906), pp. 121–3. Rucellai's relations with Frescobaldi are described above, p. 33, and below, p. 80. Stoldo had also been a ward, his father having died about the time Giovanni's had: Cat., 18, ff. 1431r–4r.

[4] Manetti, *Vita di Filippo Brunelleschi, ed. cit.*, pp. 104–5. On the palace, see Battisti, *Filippo Brunelleschi*, pp. 69 ff. In 1469 Giovanni rented his banking premises from the Guelf Party (below, p. 80).

[5] In fact, as I have only lately discovered, business and patronage were combined. From a list of 1482, compiled from the records of the *opera* of Santo Spirito, it is clear that, for some twenty years after 1445, Rucellai's bank made payments there on behalf of the Frescobaldi chapel builders. This information, on a loose folio among papers written and collected by another Stoldo Frescobaldi in the early sixteenth century, is in the Archivio Frescobaldi, 48.

[6] Diplomatico, Strozzi Uguccione, 5 April 1475. This document summarises the properties thus acquired, for which see p. 47, n. 1 below.

[7] AS Ferr., Archivio Bentivoglio, lib. 6, 34, f. 49. He went on: 'con conditione di poterle col tempo riavere, pagandogli e' suo danari pagati da llui in diversi tempi, come per gli pacti e convegne facte con esso e come per le scritte tra lui e noi si contiene'. I have found one such private pact, made in Giovanni's hand in 1445, concerning a Pisan house and a farm at Santa Maria a Nuovoli which Rucellai bought for 300 florins on the condition that Palla could repurchase it any time after 25 March 1451

absolving him from paying the taxes that were destroying him, and in return for this favour, Strozzi allowed Giovanni to use the income 'piis operibus' which meant, or came to mean, ecclesiastical building.

It is not certain when the two men made this ingenious (and I think extremely unusual) arrangement, nor who took the initiative. The first explicit description of it occurs only in 1471, which allows the possibility that the scheme developed after Giovanni acquired the lands and their revenues. However there is good reason to date the understanding to the early and mid-1440s—even perhaps to 1438, the year in which the first property later to be included in the scheme was exchanged[1]—when the principle of using ex-Strozzi lands for ecclesiastical patronage was born, Giovanni Rucellai and Benedetto Toschi acting as midwives. In 1442, according to an unconfirmed reference in his tax report, Giovanni had committed half of two properties bought 'come beni furono di Messer Palla Strozzi' from the *Monte* officials 'per fornire la chapella magiore [of San Pancrazio] per tenpo d'anni cinque salvo 'l vero'[2]. Two years later, at a meeting of the men of the district in December 1444, Toschi, as administrator of Lion Rosso's affairs, devoted local tax defaulters' money, which must certainly have included some of Messer Palla's, to providing a handsome choir in San Pancrazio 'pro salute animarum hominum et personarum' of the *gonfalone*[3]. Friendly intervention by the abbot on Palla's behalf is quite explicit in an agreement of 23 February

(Archivio di Stato, Padua, Istr. di Giacomo Polenton, lib. i, f. 166). This document makes it clear that tax avoidance was one of Palla's aims: 'et durante questo tempo d'anni sei, decto Messer Palla non habia a soportare su decte possessione niuna graveza di comune, ma tuto debia andare sopra decto Giovanni' (from a copy, made in May 1458, in AS Ferr., Archivio Bentivoglio, lib. 5, 32). The prices are described as 'modest' in the 1471 documents mentioned on p. 77 n. 5, below, and there is good reason to believe, comparing purchase prices with taxable value, that Giovanni received a number of bargains. Benedetto Toschi was often associated with Rucellai in these schemes (for details, see below, pp. 48–9), and it was to friends of Palla's such as these that Lorenzo Strozzi later alluded when he compared bad citizens who 'sotto nome di pubblica gravezza le comperassero' [Palla's properties] with 'alcuni più costumati' who 'li comperorno con licenzia del prefato Messer Palla, e con condizione di restituirgliene ogni volta che riavessero i loro denari: atto veramente degno di commendazione. . .': *Vite di alcuni della famiglia Strozzi*, ed. cit, p. 50. It is striking that many of Palla's alienated properties mentioned in the documents I have seen went to persons or their kinsmen also mentioned in Giovanni's *parentado* of 1476 (*Zibaldone*, ff. 223r–24v). For just one prime example, there is the acquisition by Iacopo di Iacopo Venturi of the villa at Poggio a Caiano, eventually sold to Rucellai in 1469. The Venturi were Mediceans (see above, p. 29, n. 7) but this Iacopo was married to Palla Strozzi's grand-daughter (*Zibaldone*, f. 224v); in 1455, Giovanni's own daughter Margherita wed Iacopo di Francesco Venturi. See my "Lorenzo de' Medici's Acquisition of Poggio a Caiano in 1474, and an Early Reference to his architectural Expertise", *JWCI*, XLII (1979), pp. 250–7.

[1] According to the *compositio* between Giovanni and Bardo and Messer Lorenzo Strozzi of 4 August 1471 (AS Ferr., Notarile Antico, Giacomo Vincenzi, matricola 177, pacco 16/5, unfoliated), this was the Pisan house bought in fact by Giovanni 'sub alio nomine' in November for 200 florins from another Strozzi, though Palla in truth owned it; however, the private pact between the two men (described in the preceding note) implies that if the house, and the farm, were already in Rucellai's hands, he did not pay for them until 1444/45. Yet the house first appears in Giovanni's tax return in 1442 (Cat., 620, parte ii, f. 574v). I am not sure how to explain this and a number of other aspects of the dealings between Palla and Giovanni. The other sales were: (i) a farm at Santa Maria a Nuovoli again bought from a Strozzi other than Palla by Iacopa, Giovanni's wife, in February 1444; (ii) ex-Strozzi properties bought from Ruberto Altoviti (see p. 49, n. 2 below), including part of the Poggio a Caiano estate, a farm and ruined villa at Tresiano, near Carmignano, and two *botteghe* in Florence in November 1448; (iii) an inn and houses at Poggio, promised by Altoviti in 1448 and then sold not by him but by Messer Lionardo Salutati to Giovanni in November 1453 (1452 according to the document in Dezzi Bardeschi, *Facciata*, p. 21); (iv) ex-Strozzi land at San Giorgio a Castelnuovo, near Poggio, sold by the abbot of San Pancrazio as procurator of Lion Rosso, to a nominee of Rucellai's (who then consigned it to yet another party to pay for the Santa Maria Novella façade) in March 1461. Giovanni had further ex-Palla property—see, e.g., Cat., 919, ff. 376r–80v—though whether tied by such agreements I have not discovered. For a very useful brief discussion of this whole matter, see Preyer, *Giovanni Rucellai*, pp. 9–10.

[2] Cat., 620, parte ii, f. 574r–v. A notarial reference, without date, is given ('Ser Nicholò di Francesco'), but I can find it neither in the protocols of Ser Niccolò di Francesco di Niccolò da Carmignano nor of Ser Niccolò di Francesco Galeotti. So far as I can see there is no reference to the matter in the San Pancrazio papers.

[3] Diplomatico, San Pancrazio di Firenze, 21 December 1444. Though Giovanni Rucellai was not present, three of his kinsmen were, one of them as 'pennonerius' of the *gonfalone*. The choir, which was to bear the arms and insignia of the *gonfalone*, is now at Vallombrosa.

1447, described by Giovanni Rucellai in his own hand as 'scripta di certi patti cum Messer Palla'. In this Strozzi wiped away his debt to the *gonfalone* by ceding to Benedetto certain rights over part of his estate and income, thereby in fact preserving control of his town house and certain estates and acquiring a vigorous estate administrator and debt collector into the bargain[1]. Two thousand florins in interest from shares consigned by Messer Palla went by means of Giovanni's bank 'per murare il chiostro di detta chiesa' in early 1451, as painless an extraction of his money as Palla, who was devoted to the Vallombrosans of nearby Santa Trinita, could have hoped for[2]. Strozzi might reasonably have expected to enjoy more directly—but in the event did not—Benedetto's activities at the villa of Petraia, which the abbot carefully protected for him. There too, in March 1448, Toschi employed the artist Giovanni di Guccio 'per dipignere sei fighure di Messer San Pancratio nostro al luogo della Petraia di Messer Palla, perchè ricade a nnoi per la morte di madonna Marietta [Strozzi's wife] per la donagione ci fece il gonfalone nostro. . .'[3].

These were perhaps tentative steps towards the formulation of a policy—fully worked out by Giovanni and Messer Palla (no doubt with advice from Toschi) by 1448—which combined some protection of Strozzi's interests, and the promotion of his son-in-law's, with plans for patronage that would directly answer the younger man's needs and, presumably, give the older some vicarious consolation and pleasure. In that year and again in 1452 Rucellai acquired parts of the estate at

---

[1] Conv. Sopp., 88, 53, ff. 36ʳ–37ʳ. Lion Rosso had actually paid certain of Messer Palla's 'graveze residiate', whereupon Strozzi put into Toschi's hands, as the district's legal representative: (i) his house and the shop below 'acciochè altro uficio di comune o altri per debiti di Messer Palla non possa andarvi'; Palla could nominate who was to live in the house, rent-free, and retained possession of it, the abbot receiving the rent of the shop; (ii) certain income from Strozzi land in Toschi's hands should go to Alessandra, his daughter-in-law. There were other clauses which in effect made Toschi an administrator of parts of Palla's estate, even giving him the right to pursue Strozzi's own debtors. The Strozzi copy of this agreement is in CS, III, 116, ff. 42ʳ–43ʳ.

[2] According to the 1447 agreement (preceding note), Toschi could request Strozzi 'a potere permutare ogni danaio di monte scripto in detto Messer Palla', to collect his interest from such investments and in particular 'permutare ongni quantità di paghe sostenute . . . solamente quelle del 1419 al 1423 che sono circha fiorini tremila o più oltre'; such moneys, and those from any Strozzi estates in the abbot's hands, were to be his. It was explicitly some of this income, namely 'fiorini dumila cinquantanove di paghe sostenute dal 1419 al 1423 alle 143 migliaia i qua' danari n'era creditore Messer Palla', that Giovanni and San Pancrazio used for the cloister (Conv. Sopp., 88, 53, f. 41ʳ), cf. Dezzi Bardeschi, "Complesso monumentale", pp. 12, 42, n. 68. The 750 florins Giovanni paid Toschi in March 1461 for some of Palla's former property at Poggio a Caiano, the abbot had converted 'in ornamentis abbatie Sancti Pancrati . . .' (Diplomatico, Strozzi Uguccione, 14 March 1461; and see p. 49, n. 4 below).

[3] Conv. Sopp., 88, 23, f. 78ʳ. Petraia presumably came into Toschi's hands as a result of the 1447 pact. At f. 81ʳ we find him making further payments on behalf of the estate and enjoying its fruits (ff. 83ʳ, 122ᵛ–23ᵛ and *passim*). In November 1456 it was rented to Alessandra, Palla's daughter-in-law; half of the rent went to Rucellai 'riicievente per detto Messer Benedetto', the rest to Felice Brancacci's daughter 'per nome di Messer Palla'; see CS, III, 116, f. 41ʳ (in Rucellai's hand). Toschi, on behalf of Lion Rosso, then sold Petraia, very cheaply it would seem, to Alessandra, whom Giovanni represented, on 10 June 1458 (NA, A 313m [inserto 1, by Ser Giovanni Allegri], ff. 65ʳ–69ᵛ). Again (see preceding note), Toschi had to use the proceeds for the building of San Pancrazio. Just before his death, Palla mentioned 'una pratica si tiene con Messer Benedecto Abate di San Brancatio di Firenze per mezo di Giovanni Rucellai decto ch'egli e'l convento de' monaci di decto luogo comperino con certe conditioni e tempo l'abituro della Petraia e poderi . . .' (AS Ferr., Archivio Bentivoglio, lib. 6, 34, ff. 48–49). In 1463, after Strozzi's death, the villa was sold by Alessandra to Agnolo di Nerone di Nigi Dietisalvi (CS, III, 116, fol. 55ʳ; and NA, C 407 [Ser Pierozzo Cerbini, 1456–65], ff. 340ʳ–43ᵛ, 347ʳ); the farms had been sold in 1460, through Rucellai 'come prochuratore di Monna Alessandra donna fu di Lorenzo di Messer Palla di Nofri Strozzi', to Bernardo Rinieri (Conv. Sopp., 95, 212, f. clviiʳ). Here see too F. Chiostri, *La Petraja: villa e giardino. 700 anni di storia*, Florence, 1973, pp. 13–14.

A later document both gives another example of these subtle machinations and makes the protagonists' motives quite clear. In 1485 Pandolfo Rucellai acknowledged possession of some woods in the Pistoian *contado* which San Pancrazio had acquired 'più tenpo fa (overo aquistò Giovanni di Pagholo Rucellai i[n] nostro nome) . . . e' quali boschi si sono senpre tenuti per detto Giovanni Rucellai e sui figliuoli perchè chosì ne fu d'achordo choll'abate e monaci a quello tenpo . . . perchè detti beni erono suti di Messer Palla di Nofri degli Strozi, e detto Giovanni Rucelai sapeva e intendeva de' deti sua beni q[u]elli erono suti posseduti chontro a ragione nelle mani di molti cittadini, de' quali pe' tenpi passati per mezo di detto Giovanni Rucelai se ne ritrattò per buona soma . . .' (Conv. Sopp., 88, 65, f. 25ᵛ). Giovanni noted these lands in 1469, held of the abbot 'per danari avevo avere da llui' (Cat., 919, f. 378ʳ). For other references, see p. 79, n. 4 below, and the study by D. V. and F. W. Kent referred to on p. 26, n. 1 above.

Poggio a Caiano, all of which had belonged to Messer Palla in 1427, and put them in the hands of the Bankers' Guild with the condition that the revenues should be used for the building of the Holy Sepulchre chapel. The published documents[1] concerning this transaction do not reveal what Palla's will of 1462 makes explicit, that Giovanni bought this and other important ex-Strozzi property from his cousin Ruberto di Giovanni Altoviti in 1448 in order to regain control for his wife's family, who had almost certainly sold it to Altoviti on favourable terms in the mistaken belief that as a relative of both parties he would be sympathetic to their concerns[2]. One of the notarial acts which later listed these and similar protective purchases by Giovanni confirms that 'omnia predicta in veritate processerunt de voluntate dicti domini Palle'. The same document dispels any suspicion that Giovanni had not consulted his father-in-law about how the revenues from the estate at Poggio and other properties were to be used, one condition having been that: 'licet pro magna parte eorum fructus deserviant piis operibus ut fuit de voluntate dicti domini Palle et etiam dicti Iohannis quando fuerunt dicta bona ut supra transalata [sic]'[3].

In the event the Poggio revenues did not contribute to the building of the Holy Sepulchre chapel (perhaps the income from other 'tied' properties was put to this use). They went towards paying for the façade of Santa Maria Novella, for which project there is direct evidence of Palla's approval. By an extraordinarily complex process, two other parcels of land from the large *possessione* at Poggio were acquired by Giovanni in 1460–61, and their fruits devoted to the façade. Since Giovanni had used dummy buyers, the Strozzi notarial act of 1471 was at some pains to insist that he was the real purchaser and that the income 'debebat deservire et volebat dictus Ioannes quod deservirent edificationi et structioni et seu structioni marmoree faciei anterioris ecclesie sancte Marie Novelle de Florentia'. Moreover, 'erat de consensu dicti domini Palle' that the confraternity of St. Peter the Martyr, attached to the church, could use the lands for that purpose[4].

---

[1] Dezzi Bardeschi, *Facciata*, p. 21, has published the documents, the first of which should be dated 1448 (see above, p. 43, n. 1); see too Perosa, p. 25. Cat., 76, f. 185ᵛ, lists Strozzi's Poggio a Caiano estate in the first *catasto*.

[2] AS Ferr., Archivio Bentivoglio, lib. 6, 34, ff. 17–18: '. . . Ruberto Altoviti si trovava nelle mani più mie possessioni e ancor, di ragion di Lorenzo mio figliuolo, si trovava nelle suo mani fiorini settemila cinquecento, cioè 7500, di monte commune colle paghe d'alcun tempo, quegli ch'io gli aveva assegnati per la dota [of Alessandra, Lorenzo's wife; cf. f. 10], e non volendo lui ristituire e' detti beni (allegando che alle graveze di commune gli avevan facto gran danno), et eran per fare dopo molte pratiche per mezo d'esso Giovanni Rucellai si rimase d'accordo con lui in questo modo, cioè: che a me et a Lorenzo egli desse la possession del Poggio a Chaiano con gli alberghi e case, e la possession di Tresiano e le due botheghe nella Via Larga de' Legnaiuoli, e fu finito per me e per Lorenzo come constretti per non poter fare altro, delle quali possessioni e botheghe io fece vendita a Giovanni di Pagolo di Messer Pagolo Rucellai per pregio di fiorini mille correnti di Firenze, con questa conditione, che che [sic] passato certo tempo fossono in mia libertà di ricomperarle per fiorini mille correnti di Firenze come appare scripta fra noi che una n'è appresso di me e l'altra appresso di decto Giovanni'. In an earlier account of the deal at f. 17, Strozzi wrote: 'E fecesi decto accordo per trarre di mano di Ruberto di Giovanni decto decte possessioni nelle cui mani erano, e per dare commodità a Lorenzo decto ch'egli potesse vivere colla sua donna e figliuolo. . .', which may further have disposed Strozzi to trust him; notably he was also a connection of Palla himself, his wife Lionarda Soderini being one of Strozzi's granddaughters: *Zibaldone*, f. 224ᵛ.

[3] AS Ferr., Notarile Antico, Giacomo Vincenzi, matricola 177, pacco 16/5, 4 August 1471, unfoliated. Elsewhere the point is repeated that the fruits of such property 'deputabantur per dictum Ioannem in effectu ad opera pia et ornamenta ecclesiarum'. Rucellai's 1480 tax report refers to his financial arrangements concerning the façade of Santa Maria Novella 'e altri legati a[d] pias chausa[s]' (Cat., 1011, f. 343ᵛ).

[4] See the Ferrarese document referred to in the preceding note. These complex transactions are contained in the following notarial acts and other documents: NA, C 407 (Ser Pierozzo Cerbini, 1456–65), unfoliated, 20 April 1461; AS Ferr., Archivio Bentivoglio, lib. 6, 10, undated and unfoliated; Conv. Sopp., 102, 308, f. 95ᵛ; 309, f. 33ʳ; NA, G 616 (Ser Simone Grazzini, 1458–59), ff. 261ʳ–63ʳ, 265ʳ, 3 January 1460; *ibid.*, B 391 (Ser Baldovino Baldovini, 1460–61), f. 39ʳ⁻ᵛ; Diplomatico, Strozzi Uguccione, 14 March 1461. The two parcels were bought from Alessandra Strozzi and Benedetto Toschi (as procurator of Lion Rosso) by Marco di Bartolo, who was Giovanni's trusted manservant (see below, p. 73). Palla again kept the right of repurchase for himself and heirs.

This new information does not permit more than speculation on how loud a voice Messer Palla's indirect vested interests, let alone his seniority, his experience as a patron, and his infinitely wider intellectual range, gave him in the creation and working out of parts of Giovanni's programme. His constant background presence, and what we know of the two men's relationship are, however, suggestive of a considerable if indefinable influence. Such an influence is all the more plausible because, despite Giovanni's obvious fascination with buildings of all sorts in the *Zibaldone*, and his 'modern' tastes, there appears to be no evidence of his having, or being considered to have, that practical and theoretical architectural expertise which a number of his aristocratic contemporaries possessed. According to published sources he was, unlike a number of his kinsmen and friends, not an *operaio* on a major public building project (political discrimination might conceivably explain this fact)[1]. Nor is there reason to believe that he was himself a designer of buildings, as Cosimo and Lorenzo de' Medici may have been, or even a gifted amateur like his own son Bernardo[2]. Giovanni's silence as to his architect's identity presumably reflects not his own authorship but his acceptance of one contemporary's belief that the patron was the 'father' of the project and the architect the 'mother'[3]. Only one (admittedly intriguing) piece of evidence could possibly be taken to imply that Rucellai's creative or directive role was decisive. In a notarial document of 20 April 1461 the Santa Maria Novella façade is described as having been begun 'per dictum Iohannem de Oricellariis et construendam designandam et ordinandam per dictum Iohannem eo modo et forma et prout dicto Ioanni videbitur et placebit, seu per Pandolfum eiusdem Iohannis filium[4].' It is true that all these verbs, according to Pevsner, can 'allude to architectural designing and planning and not to purely clerical work', but Pevsner's reading in this instance is not confirmed by anything else we know[5]. Rather, since Giovanni apparently kept the funds both for the Holy Sepulchre chapel and the façade in his own hands, the passage probably refers to the close administrative interest in their projects maintained by him and by certain other patrons[6]. If there has sometimes seemed a gap between the

---

[1] Preyer, *Giovanni Rucellai*, p. 158. For Piero di Cardinale and Paolo di Vanni Rucellai as *operai*, see respectively Krautheimer, *Ghiberti*, ii, pp. 387–8, and above, p. 41; Guasti, *Cupola*, pp. 13, 39. Three mid-Trecento *operai* of the Duomo had been Rucellai (M. Trachtenberg, *The Campanile of Florence Cathedral: "Giotto's Tower"*, New York, 1971, pp. 184 [Cennes Nardi], 189 [Lapo di Vanni], 195).

[2] See for Bernardo and for some of the literature on this point, my "Poggio a Caiano".

[3] Filarete, quoted in Kent, " 'Più superba' ", p. 322; see pp. 311–23 for this theme and for references to some of the relevant literature. There have been a number of explanations of Giovanni's silence. Marcotti, e.g., in *Mercante fiorentino*, pp. 43–44, suggests modesty, which seems unlikely, and E. G. Holt that 'he may have disliked him [Alberti], or he may have assumed everyone knew of his connection with the palace': *A documentary History of Art*, New York, 1957 edn., i, p. 248, n. 8.

[4] NA, C 407 (Ser Pierozzo Cerbini, 1456–65), unfoliated. Interestingly, Pandolfo Rucellai was later given a certain administrative-cum-artistic discretion concerning a chapel, in the will of his brother-in-law, Domenico Bartoli (*ibid.*, B 398 [Ser Baldovino Baldovini, 1468–72], f. 67r–v).

[5] "Terms of architectural Planning in the Middle Ages", *JWCI*, IV–V (1941–2), p. 236; see in general pp. 232–37.

[6] See below, p. 58; cf. R. A. Goldthwaite, "Building of the Strozzi Palace", pp. 114 ff.; and, for another type of patron, R. A. Goldthwaite and W. R. Rearick, "Michelozzo and the Ospedale di San Paolo in Florence", *MKHIF*, XXI, 1977, pp. 267 ff. Rucellai's first agreement of 1448 with the Bankers' Guild stated that the fruits of Poggio a Caiano, and the property itself if sold, 'si debbino diporre in su uno bancho come parrà al decto Giovanni Rucellai', though the money could only be used for the agreed purpose: Arte del Cambio, 105, f. 16v, and not in the version published by Dezzi Bardeschi, *Facciata*, p. 21. Even in 1479, when the situation had rather changed, the Rucellai seem to have controlled the actual cash 'in su uno bancho' (*ibid.*, p. 22). The terms of an agreement with the Company of St. Peter the Martyr on 15 May 1461 are more explicit. The tenant who held the income-producing land, bought by Giovanni and put in the Company's name, 'debbe rispondere per nome della conpagnia a Giovanni di Pagolo Rucellai per invertirgli [sic] nella muraglia de' marmi della faccia della nostra chiesa, perchè siamo rimasti [d'accordo] co[n] llui tenga conto della rendita et della spesa': Conv. Sopp., 102, 308, f. 95v; cf. document of 20 April 1461 in NA, C 407 (Ser Pierozzo Cerbini, 1456–65). It is true, however, that in 1471 Giovanni gave to the consuls of the Bankers' Guild powers over the façade, in the event of his death, which implied their making decisions at once administrative and aesthetic; whether the façade should be said to be finished 'debbi stare alla dischrezione de' chonsoli . . . e quando della facciata predetta si restassi a ffare alchuna chosa, che detti chonsoli abbino a vedere e possino farla fornire . . .' (Perosa, p. 26).

character of Giovanni Rucellai, who was not an educated man, and the sophistication of the buildings he commissioned, it may be that the figure of Messer Palla fills it. He and Alberti were perhaps
the mediators in some sense that only future research, into both Rucellai's ecclesiastical buildings
and Messer Palla's life and ideas, can hope to define. It is even conceivable that Palla was exercising
patronage by proxy, but to suggest this is almost certainly to simplify and to distort beyond
recognition a relationship of a much more subtle kind.

Moreover, the size of the gap can easily be exaggerated. For whatever reasons, the Rucellai who
went to Rome for the Jubilee between 10 February and 8 March 1450 was already a man deeply
interested in building, as much a serious architectural tourist 'cerchando et veggiendo tutte quelle
muraglie antiche et cose degne di Roma' as a pilgrim seeking the remission of his sins[1]. He did not
'discover' the 'world of the arts' there as has been suggested, but may have sharpened and increased
his knowledge of it[2]. His account, significantly described in the contemporary index of the *Zibaldone*
as 'della bellezza e antichaglia di Roma'[3], both reflects and foreshadows his personal concerns as an
architectural patron. Not, seemingly, of real importance to specialists in Roman topography, it
certainly reveals still more about Giovanni than that he had 'a lay interest in the antique'[4]. He
described not only ancient but more recent palatial buildings: the pope's 'bellissima habitatione', the
commission of a French cardinal 'murata alla moderna, bella et gentile casa'. Tombs of all sorts,
including Martin V's, caught his eye, which was sharpened perhaps by his preoccupation with his
own chapel and sepulchre. A church built by 'uno privato cittadino' was no doubt an encouraging
precedent: one would like to know what passed through his mind as he noted that the church whose
size he compared explicitly with Santa Maria Novella's had a very fine 'musaico . . . nella facciata di
fuori. . .'[5].

If Giovanni's reactions at least imply some of his future activities one can say little more about the
precise impact upon him of his Roman journey, and recent speculation on the subject is at best
inconclusive. The visit might have left him with a firmer and more articulate desire to elaborate a whole
programme if Nicholas V's building campaign had indeed been begun, but the suggestion that Giovanni's own account is evidence of its actual inception is rather unconvincing[6]. Curiously, however,
Giovanni had several likely sources of information, in 1450 or afterwards, on papal plans. The best
account of these was written by the pope's secretary, the Florentine Giannozzo di Bernardo Manetti,
who had been Rucellai's business partner between 1442–45 and whose son was to marry his
daughter in 1452[7]. Giovanni may also have been acquainted with Nicholas himself, who as

---

[1] Perosa, p. 68.

[2] A. Chastel, *Art et humanisme à Florence au temps de Laurent le Magnifique*, Paris, 1961, p. 32. Benedetto Toschi also made the
pilgrimage between 24 November and 13 December 1450 (Conv. Sopp., 88, 23, ff. 103r, 104r), and his reactions may have been
important to his Rucellai colleague.

[3] Perosa, p. xx.

[4] R. Weiss, *The Renaissance Discovery of Classical Antiquity*, Oxford, 1969, p. 60; but cf. pp. 73–75, where the point is notably
softened. See too R. Valentini and G. Zucchetti, *Codice Topografico della Città di Roma*, Rome, 1953, iv, pp. 399–419, who call
Rucellai's account an 'arida enumerazione' (p. 401). Cf. Perosa, below, pp. 126–27.

[5] Perosa, pp. 67 ff.

[6] C. W. Westfall, *In This Most Perfect Paradise: Alberti, Nicholas V, and the Invention of conscious urban Planning in Rome, 1447–55*,
University Park and London, 1974, pp. 174–9.

[7] *Ibid.*, chap. 3. See above, pp. 9, n. 4; 35, n. 4; 43, n. 3 for Manetti and the Rucellai. Giannozzo was also an admired associate
of Giovanni's friend Donato Acciaiuoli (Garin, "Donato Acciaiuoli", pp. 58 ff.); and in August 1448 on his way home from
Venice, where he had been on an embassy, Manetti had gone to Padua, receiving after dinner a visit from Messer Palla Strozzi
(see p. 278 of the diary of Manetti's chancellor, Griso di Giovanni, published by N. Lerz in *ASI*, CXVII [1959]).

Tommaso Parentucelli had once briefly been tutor to Palla Strozzi's children[1]. By 1455—if one accepts the stylistic attribution of the Rucellai façade—he also knew Alberti who is usually associated with the papal projects[2]. Like some minor character in a novel by Evelyn Waugh, Alberti here makes yet another of his mysterious half-appearances, for there may be reason to suppose that he was in some sense Giovanni's guide to Rome in 1450, through his brief description of the city if not personally[3]. The Jubilee visit, which certainly comes between the inception and the mature working out of Giovanni's own programme, may prove to have been quite central to the precise consolidation of Giovanni's plans. Until further information is forthcoming, however, it is more properly regarded as evidence of his already intense and wide interest in matters architectural in 1450, and as only one among several contributions to his continuing education as a patron.

Events outside his own life served further to encourage Giovanni to turn to major building in the 1440s and 1450s. By then the building boom about which Richard Goldthwaite has written so stimulatingly was well (if not always uninterruptedly) under way, first in the public sphere and increasingly, after Cosimo de' Medici's palace was begun in 1445, in the private[4]. At the same time there came from Cosimo's circle an apologia for his activities which others could find, among other places, in the pages of Alberti and in Matteo Palmieri's *Della vita civile*[5]. Rucellai's struggle with the traditional texts that counselled moderate spending, especially on building which could become, according to the pseudo-Bernardine letter he transcribed, a ruinous obsession, was probably resolved in favour of virtuous liberality in this decade[6]. In 1457 he quoted Seneca as saying that 'il giovane debba attendere a guadagnare e aquistare, e il vechio debbe godere usando quello ch'egli à aquistato nella giovaneza'[7], a personally appropriate dictum which was also recommended by contemporary circumstances. Nicolai Rubinstein has recently pointed out that the introduction of the *catasto*, which exempted the tax payer's personal dwellings, made domestic building more attractive than ever before because the rich could escape some of the special burden the new system imposed upon them[8]. And one may add that one of the more practical motives which had inspired the traditional fourteenth-century strictures on conspicuous display, including fine buildings, had been the desire

[1] Vespasiano da Bisticci, *Vite, ed. cit.*, p. 390, who adds that the tutor remained so grateful to Messer Palla that when his son Carlo went to Rome 'lo fece suo cubiculario segreto'.

[2] Westfall, *This Most Perfect Paradise*, "Epilogue"; cf. T. Magnusson, *Studies in Roman Quattrocento Architecture*, Stockholm, 1958, pp. 88–9, 97.

[3] Borsi, *Alberti*, pp. 33–34; Westfall, *This Most Perfect Paradise*, p. 175.

[4] "The Florentine Palace as domestic Architecture", *American Historical Review*, LXXVII (1972), pp. 977–1012; I. Hyman, "Notes and Speculations on S. Lorenzo, Palazzo Medici, and an urban Project by Brunelleschi", *JSAH*, XXXIV (1975), pp. 98–120; N. Rubinstein, "Palazzi pubblici e palazzi privati al tempo del Brunelleschi: problemi di storia politica e sociale", in *Atti del Convegno internazionale di studi Brunelleschiani* [Florence, 1977] = *Filippo Brunelleschi. La sua opera e il suo tempo*, Florence, 1980, I, pp. 27–36.

[5] Fraser Jenkins, "Cosimo de' Medici's Patronage of Architecture", pp. 162–70. Rucellai actually reproduced parts of Palmieri's work (Perosa, pp. 13–15) though not on this theme. Possibly Giovanni's careful distinction between his 'public and private' buildings in his petition of August 1474 (see below, p. 83) reflects the usage of contemporary writers such as these.

[6] See above, pp. 37–38. *Zibaldone*, f. 93ᵛ: 'Se tu vuoi edificare casa, fa che la necessità t'induca e non la volontà [etc]' (Rucellai ascribes this very popular text to Donato Acciaiuoli: Perosa, pp. 173–4). Elsewhere, immediately after the splendid dictum that building is one of life's two 'cose principali' Giovanni wrote: 'Ma San Bernardo dicie che si debbe hedifichare più per neciessità che per volontà, perchè hedifichando la volontà non mancha ma crescie' (*Zibaldone*, f. 83ᵛ); cf. Preyer, below, p. 184. St. Bernard, a Rucellai patron saint, presumably had considerable influence with Giovanni. For an edition of this passage from the "Lettera a Raimondo", see *Prosatori minori del Trecento*, I, *Scrittori di religione*, ed. G. De Luca, Milan and Naples, 1954, p. 822.

[7] *Zibaldone*, f. 25ʳ.

[8] Forthcoming article. Certainly at the end of the century Domenico Cecchi suggested that there should be passed 'una leggie che chiunche vuole murare possa e che in su tali muramenti non vi si possa mai porre su alchuna gravezza' (U. Mazzone, "*El buon governo*": *un progetto di riforma generale nella Firenze savonaroliana*, Florence, 1978, p. 191).

not to seem too rich at a time when most taxes were assessed by one's watchful and often envious neighbours, a fear which would have faded though not disappeared after 1427[1]. These are economic reasons (which would have appealed to the over-taxed Rucellai) for the Quattrocento boom, but neither for him nor many others did it become an investment in culture by cautious businessmen, nor a withdrawal from trade which reflects their development of a rentier mentality. Giovanni Rucellai at least conceived, began and pursued his programme while at the very height of his economic powers, and for motives which included but also transcended economic considerations. These cannot fully explain his or others' major building projects, more reckless undertakings—witness the number of uncompleted plans and bankruptcies—than we sometimes allow. Like many of his contemporaries, Giovanni more often advocated the 'via di mezzo'[2] than he followed it; he genuinely prized prudence and calculation[3], but in a number of respects he was as calculatedly daring as he was prudently careful. This was not least the case in his building programme which was a well organized and finely calculated attempt to realize an audacious dream.

II

Rucellai devoted the 1450s to working out more precisely this building campaign, already several decades in the making. A full discussion of his activities in that decade—his choice of individual projects and his decisions about what priority to give them—demands a close study of each building by an architectural historian who has looked for and found unpublished documents. What follows can be only a preliminary sketch, largely from a biographer's point of view, of the chronological development of his ideas and of the various personal and public aspirations which they expressed[4]. Thanks to Brenda Preyer, we at least know the complicated building history of Giovanni's first project, and with her help can infer what a significant place the palace, well under way by the 'fifties if not finished until the next decade, had in Rucellai's life.

Giovanni's second will of 13 December 1465, which gives much more space to the *palazzo* than to any other subject, confirms the impression that the project had been designed to answer several of the banker's emotional needs in the 1440s, above all his desire to assert and affirm his own importance during his lifetime and beyond. The newly completed palace, which 'totam edificari fecit et a fundamentis ferme erexit propriis sumptibus', was never to leave his paternal lineage by any means whatsoever (a theme repeated with many legal variations) as much for his own as for his wider family's sake. Giovanni reasoned that Rucellai ownership *ad infinitum* would ensure him a kind of immortality. It was most desirable that his direct descendants keep his house 'per immensum et longissimum tempus' so that 'ipsius testatoris memoriam conservetur', but he believed that the palace, even in the hands of his collateral kinsmen, would ensure the perpetuation of his memory. When the commune of Florence inherited the palace on the extinction of the Rucellai clan the

---

[1] For examples of this watchful attitude to neighbours and others, see G. Corti, "Consigli sulla mercatura di un anonimo trecentista", *ASI*, CX (1952), pp. 114–9; pseudo-Bernardine "Lettera a Raimondo", in *Prosatori minori del Trecento, ed. cit.*, pp. 819–24; Herlihy and Klapisch-Zuber, *Les Toscans*, pp. 26–7.

[2] *Zibaldone*, f. 96[r]; on f. 95[v] he admitted that 'Dificilissimo è a tenere in tutte le chose il modo overo il mezo'.

[3] *Ibid.*, ff. 38[v]–39[r]. Of Michelangelo Tanagli, whom he recommended to Piero de' Medici on 15 February 1464, Rucellai wrote 'e benchè lui sia giovane, chome forse sapete egli è di buona prudenzia . . .' (MAP, XVII, 360).

[4] Rucellai's programme has been summarized many times before, more recently by Dezzi Bardeschi, "Complesso monumentale", espec. pp. 17 ff.; by Borsi, *Alberti*, chap. 4 and—most convincingly—by Preyer, *Giovanni Rucellai*, chap. 1, and *passim*.

property, again to be inalienable, could never be inhabited by anyone of Florentine birth[1]. This clause reflects the contemporary belief that family houses were in a sense sacred[2], an idea which for Giovanni had an even more specific meaning—the association of his palace with another Florentine might obliterate his 'memory'. In several drafts of those parts of the will which concerned the palace, Rucellai was undecided about its ultimate heir. In one version he nominated the Duke of Milan. Always, however, his concern was, as he wrote when proposing to bequeath it to Santa Maria del Fiore, 'per conservare la memoria del detto testatore'[3], 'eternally' as one clause of the final will explicitly stated.

These passages provide a neat gloss on the nature of Rucellai's 'Renaissance individualism'; his egotism, the preservation of his memory, were as important motives for his palace-building as they were to be half a century later for Filippo Strozzi, a rich man similarly without public recognition[4]. Theirs was, however, a sense of self which, expressing itself in a wider family context, was to be transmitted and preserved by association with a long line of paternal kinsmen, the 'ancestors, and . . . the living and . . . those who by grace are to come' as one contempory defined a lineage[5]. Giovanni's palace was in several respects a Rucellai house, even before it was complemented by the clan loggia opposite. On its façade appear strikingly the arms of his *consorteria*, as well as devices more personal to the patron. He would have been pleased, judging by his will, that in a later sixteenth-century diary the palace, today still lived in and cherished by his direct descendants, was described as '[la] casa detta "de' Rucellai" '[6]. This 'large and agreeable edifice', which stands on the site of several older houses of the lineage including Giovanni's own more modest seven- or eight-roomed, two-storied ancestral home[7], both provided handsomely for his growing family—one should not ignore the domestic motive for major palace building—and gave it a conspicuously secure place amidst his kinsmen, whose many households clustered around this ancestral area.

In this Rucellai enclave, through which ran a major street, the Via della Vigna Nuova, Giovanni's palace was at once a private family house and a public building. According to Alberti, the liberal and virtuous patron brought honour not only to himself but to his family, to his descendants and to the city[8], a constellation which Rucellai clearly had in mind when he dictated the elaborate terms of his will. His civic intention was not merely or exclusively to assure his own commemoration but more immediately, in Dr. Preyer's words, to 'call attention to himself'[9] by building a superb palace which, Filarete thought, showed ancient Roman architecture reborn. When about 1464 Giovanni quoted the example of the Roman citizen who had been honoured for his 'bellissimo palazzo', he emended his source, Cicero's *De officiis*, in two telling ways. That Gnaeus Octavius had been the first

---

[1] NA, L 130 (Ser Lionardo da Colle, 1441–95), no. 31, unfoliated. His sons summarized Giovanni's intentions in a brief passage, which does not enough emphasize their father's 'memory', pub. by Marcotti, *Mercante fiorentino*, pp. 69–71. According to G. Richa, *Notizie istoriche delle chiese fiorentine*, Florence, 1760; reprint edn. 1972, iii, p. 315, Giovanni made a 1470 will with the notary Ser Niccolò di Piero Bernardi; however, I can find no such document in Ser Niccolò's protocols (NA, B 1445, B 1446), and notably Pandolfo Rucellai later made reference only to the 1465 testament: Decima Repubblicana, 22, f. 195r.

[2] Kent, *Household and Lineage*, pp. 75–77, 142–44.

[3] NA, L 130 (Ser Lionardo da Colle, 1441–95), busta 121, unfoliated.

[4] Goldthwaite, "Building of the Strozzi Palace", pp. 97 ff.; Kent " 'Più superba' ", pp. 311–23.

[5] Quoted in Kent, *Household and Lineage*, p. 252. On 'individualism' see pp. 288 ff.

[6] Acquisti e Doni, 315, ff. 44v–45r.

[7] This phrase is from an important notarial document of 1458, quoted by Preyer, below p. 214: on the old house, see *ibid.*, p. 157.

[8] See Fraser Jenkins, "Cosimo de' Medici's Patronage of Architecture", p. 167: cf. Matteo Palmieri, *Della vita civile*, ed. F. Battaglia, Bologna, 1944, pp. 123, 154, 164.

[9] Preyer, *Giovanni Rucellai*, p. 153.

of his family to become consul 'per chagione della edificazione' Giovanni's version allowed. He played down, as Dr. Preyer has observed[1], Cicero's reference to the Roman as an upstart, which was inappropriate to the Rucellai, a lineage of decent antiquity. Giovanni was more interested, for good personal reasons, in Cicero's general point that building could be a means to 'acquistare nel populo grandissima benivolenza e grazia'. He conveniently ignored his author's related warning— as Palmieri had not when he used part of the same passage—that a man should only enhance his reputation by building a fine palace, not seek to have the 'fine seat bring honour to its master'. This story probably only came to Giovanni's attention after the palace was almost finished[2]. His careful handling of it reflects, however, his awareness that when he began his own house one of his motives had been to make so convincing and pleasing a public point about his personal worth, taste and distinction as to transform his uncertain position in Cosimo's Florence, and by means which Cicero, and after him Palmieri, regarded as indecorous.

How far, and in what sense, Giovanni's undoubted desire for increased public recognition was also a bid for political office (or at least acceptance) is very difficult to decide. The political significance contemporaries gave to the new wave of palace-building still eludes us. Dr. Preyer is surely right in stressing that there was a direct relationship between Giovanni's palace and Cosimo de' Medici's, begun just before by a man whose buildings, Rucellai was to write, 'basterebbono a uno re di chorona'[3]. Stylistically the Rucellai palace is 'paying homage' to the Medici, she has further argued, as part of a move towards Cosimo in the late 1440s in a medium he would understand[4]. The suggestion receives support from precisely contemporary evidence of a personal entente between the two families[5]. It is possible, however, that any approach Giovanni Rucellai made to the Medici and to the *stato* they led was also tinged by competitiveness, by a subtle mixture of flattery and challenge to which any Florentine party leader would have been sensitively accustomed. Palace building had always been competitive, since the days of the crazily ascending magnate towers (about which Giovanni knew)[6], or the Black-White Guelf struggle of the early fourteenth century. Then, a vital ingredient of communal factionalism was the pretensions of the newer Cerchi family, who broke the not inexhaustible patience of their Donati neighbours by buying a palace from the even more aristocratic Counts Guidi, whereupon, seeing 'i Cerchi salire in altezza, avendo murato e

---

[1] *Ibid.*, pp. 156–57.

[2] *Zibaldone*, f. 63ᵛ. The passage reads in full: 'Tulio nel primo chiamato *De offitiis* dice lui avere inteso essere stato honore grandissimo a Gneo Ottavio cittadino romano per la edificazione d'uno bellissimo palazzo edificato a Roma nel Monte Palatino. E avendo detto Tulio a scrivere al figliuolo, ch'era in istudio atene per inanimarlo alle virtudi con esempli de' magnanimi e virtuosissimi huomini, gli si dice chosì, cioè: Noi avemo inteso essere stato a honore grandissimo a Gneo Ottavio ciptadino romano, il quale fu facto consolo di Roma il primo che fossi mai della famiglia sua per chagione della edificazione d'uno bellissimo palazzo facto per lui nel Monte Palatino, lo quale palazzo era pieno di riputazione e di degnità per avere in sè buono ordine e chosa misurata, e intesa che fu chagione di farli aquistare nel populo grandissima benivolenza e grazia'. The entry comes not long after the *ricordo* of 1464 (ff. 61ᵛ–62ᵛ) and the account of Quaracchi (ff. 62ᵛ–63ᵛ), which makes it even more likely that Rucellai had his own new palace in mind: for evidence that he may have known the passage in 1457, see p. 84, n. 6 below. Cf. Cicero, *De officiis*, ed. W. Miller, London and New York, 1913, pp. 140–3. Palmieri's *Della vita civile* mentions only that 'non il signore per la casa, ma la casa pel signore si vuole e debbe onorare' (*ed. cit.*, p. 164). On the *De officiis* as a basic source of Alberti's *Ten Books*, see Onians, "Alberti", pp. 96 ff. See also, Preyer, below, p. 203.

[3] Perosa, p. 157, n. 34. Rucellai naturally associated regal power with building, as when he noted that 'llo imperadore Carlo-magno di Francia' when in Italy 'fece edificare molte citte et castella. Et ancora molti luoghi di religione' (*Zibaldone*, f. 47ʳ). The clearing of the site for the Medici palace was under way in March 1445. See D. V. and F. W. Kent, "Two Comments of March 1445 on the Medici Palace", *BM*, CXXI (1979), pp. 795–6.

[4] Preyer, below, p. 202 and her *Giovanni Rucellai*, p. 154.

[5] See above, pp. 28–30.

[6] *Zibaldone*, f. 99ʳ, a passage which perhaps significantly also makes the point that 'le torri alte' were 'le torri de' privati ciptadini che erano per la città'.

cresciuto il palazzo, e tenendo gran vita. . .', the proud Donati were shamed, with disastrous results for the city[1].

Cosimo showed more finesse, but the same political instinct, when he came to build, and contemporaries such as Donato Acciaiuoli, Benedetto Dei and Giovanni Rucellai himself recognised the contribution of his programme to his public position, as indeed did Lorenzo de' Medici[2]. The subject has not been comprehensively studied, but it is possible that future work will show that Cosimo's notable activities as a patron were in part a response to the achievements, in the first part of the Quattrocento, of men who were to become his political rivals—Niccolò da Uzzano, the arch anti-Medicean, whose palace was a prototype of Renaissance development[3], one of the Barbadori[4], Palla Strozzi, Felice Brancacci and others. Further research may also confirm the impression that after 1434 some aristocratic builders, including such Medicean *amici* (notably to become enemies in the 1460s) as Luca Pitti and Dietisalvi Neroni, responded to Cosimo's example as much out of a desire to keep up with him, to counter his unspoken claims to pre-eminence, as to flatter him in the way patrons from newer client families may very well have done[5]. To regard Cosimo as exercising what Caroline Elam, speaking of his grandson Lorenzo, has happily called 'meta-patronage'[6], as being in Niccolò Tignosi's phrase 'quasi gubernator omnium', including other citizens' buildings, may be to put too much faith in humanist eulogies[7] which over-estimated Cosimo's influence over the touchy and watchful patricians, jealous of their own and their ancestors' status, who made up the regime. Considerable as Cosimo's informal authority was, a very long and increasingly firm Medicean ascendancy was neither predictable—nor to many 'Mediceans' desirable—in the 'forties, 'fifties and 'sixties[8], when the palace boom, a complex process to be sure, was probably in part an oligarchic jockeying for position in a race which if started was not yet won.

If this was indeed the atmosphere in which Giovanni began one of the very first Renaissance palaces, his initiative was both more daring, and less easily interpretable, than one might have supposed. Probably the Rucellai palace was nicely calculated to say enough, but not too much, to the Florentine community at large. One recalls Rab Hatfield's description of Cosimo's palace, all

---

[1] Dino Compagni, *Cronica, ed. cit.*, p. 55.

[2] Lorenzo thought the 663,755 florins spent by his family on building, charity and taxes 'essere gran lume allo Stato nostro e pajommi ben collocati e ne sono molto ben contento'; in W. Roscoe, *Life of Lorenzo de' Medici*, 2nd ed., London, 1796, I, App. I, p. li. See too Dei's comments, ed. G. degli Azzi, "Un frammento inedito della cronaca di Benedetto Dei", *ASI*, CX (1952), pp. 104–5, and Acciaiuoli's, cited by Garin in "Donato Acciaiuoli", pp. 107–108, n. 33. On this aspect of Medici patronage, see E. H. Gombrich, "The early Medici as Patrons of Art: A Survey of primary Sources", *Italian Renaissance Studies*, ed. E. F. Jacob, London, 1960, pp. 279–311; Fraser Jenkins, "Cosimo de' Medici's Patronage of Architecture", pp. 162–70; R. Hatfield, "Some unknown Descriptions of the Medici Palace in 1459", *AB*, LII (1970), pp. 237–49; I. Hyman, "Notes and Speculations", pp. 105 ff.

[3] N. Rubinstein, "Palazzi pubblici e palazzi privati al tempo del Brunelleschi: problemi di storia politica e sociale", *Filippo Brunelleschi. La sua opera e il suo tempo*, Florence, 1980, I, pp. 27–36.

[4] Manetti's *Vita di Filippo Brunelleschi, ed. cit.*, pp. 102–3, refers to his designing 'la casa de' Barbadori' and the Santa Felicita chapel usually identified with the Barbadori chapel; see the editors' careful note at pp. 103–4, n. 2, and Battisti, *Filippo Brunelleschi*, pp. 98–101, pp. 357–8. Several of the Barbadori were leading anti-Mediceans (D. V. Kent, *Rise of the Medici*, p. 355). Davisson has suggested that Strozzi's sacristy chapel at Santa Trinita might have been a model for Cosimo at San Lorenzo ("Iconology of the Santa Trinita Sacristy", p. 323).

[5] As is well known, Machiavelli later described Pitti's palace and villa of Rusciano as 'tutti superbi e regj": *Istorie fiorentine*, in *Opere complete*, ed. E. Oliva, Milan, 1850, i, p. 189.

[6] In an unpublished lecture on "Lorenzo de' Medici's architectural patronage" given at the Courtauld Institute in February 1976. See now her article "Lorenzo de' Medici and the Florentine Building Boom", *Art History*, I, 1978, pp. 43–66.

[7] Cited by Alison M. Brown, "The Humanist Portrait of Cosimo de' Medici, Pater Patriae", *JWCI*, XXIV (1961), p. 197, n. 56; the whole article (pp. 186–221) is fundamental to this theme. On Tignosi, who certainly knew Florence well, see A. Della Torre, *Storia dell' Accademia Platonica*, pp. 495–500.

[8] Rubinstein, *Government*, pp. 88 ff.

'dignified restraint' externally, and within ornately fit for princes[1]. With its expensive and classicizing façade, the Rucellai palace exalted the patron and enriched the city. Unrusticated and unforbidding, modest in size by comparison with most other *palazzi*, it gave notice to the regime, without really threatening it by a show of *superbia*, that Rucellai was a good citizen, a man to take account of and to be 'acceto'. Contemporaries read buildings in this way—witness the Ferrarese comment in 1489 that Filippo Strozzi's palace 'sarà più superba de quella de Lorenzo [de' Medici]'. It may thus not be too far-fetched to suggest that Rucellai, apparently not so alienated from the Medici as from certain of their lieutenants, intended that his palace should at once mildly challenge and 'pay homage' to Cosimo while perhaps making a sterner point to the other leading *ottimati* who denied him the community's 'grace and benevolence'[2].

If so, growing tensions within the regime made this an unfortunate strategy, for whatever the Medici's own attitude to him and his palace it is striking that Giovanni's specifically political fortunes were never lower than at the time when the first five bays of the façade were conspicuously finished[3]. A little later, in 1458, his building programme—it may even have been the palace itself—was not notably encouraged by the *catasto* officials, who taxed him for the Poggio a Caiano estate held in the name of the Bankers' Guild because, in Lorenzo de' Medici's presumably informed later account, though 'la charta dicieva nell'Arte del Chanbio per l'ubrigho della faccia di Santa Maria Novella . . . gl'uff[icial]i, intendendo che lla richolta andava a cchasa sua, agiunseno alla scritta di Giovanni dette posessioni per fiorini i^mc. . .'[4]. The charge is clear in outline if obscure in detail. Before the façade was begun in or after 1458 Giovanni, while claiming tax exemption, had diverted the fruits of the estate to his own use, either generally if 'cchasa sua' means 'his household' or should read 'cassa [coffers]', or more specifically, as one is quite justified in interpreting the phrase, to help pay for the palace. Giovanni said that he had been wronged but, since he controlled the income, the breach was technically possible[5]. Even so, one imagines that in political circumstances other than his the matter might well have been overlooked, if not by the guild, which was to remain jealous of its rights, at least by the tax officials.

Giovanni's concern in the late 1440s with this-worldly things, his palace and his 'memory', was matched by an interest in his chapel and hopes of resurrection in the after-life. The first reference, of 1448, is to his desire to build 'una cappella con uno sipolcro simile a quello di geRusalem del

---

[1] "Some unknown Descriptions", p. 240. Alessandra Strozzi, with her usual irony, in a sense reversed this formula *avant la lettre* when she wrote of the della Luna, whose affairs were thought to be in disorder, 'E' murano una bella casa, a vedere di fuori; drento non so' (*Lettere*, p. 458, 17 August 1465).

[2] When quoting this (" 'Più superba' ", p. 315), I assumed that it was a reference to the Medici palace. A comment in a letter of 18 September 1490 that the villa at Poggio was being built so quickly that 'la vorrà vedere p[r]esto e p[r]ima ch[e] non farà lo Strozo' suggests the intriguing possibility that the Ferrarese letter-writer rather had Poggio in mind. The above passage is published by P. Foster, *A Study of Lorenzo de' Medici's Villa at Poggio a Caiano*, New York, 1978, vol. i, p. 111. Mancini, *Alberti*, pp. 424–5, comments that the palace's 'relatively modest' character reflects Giovanni's timorous desire not to offend the Medici. It might be appropriate to ask here why Rucellai did not employ Michelozzo if he so wanted to flatter them; or did he rather wish to make some sort of independent statement by avoiding what Saalman has colourfully called Michelozzo's ' "every man a Medici" style'?: "Tommaso Spinelli, Michelozzo, Manetti and Rossellino", *JSAH*, XXV (1966), p. 158.

[3] Between 1455–58, according to Preyer, below, pp. 179–84, 202; and *passim*. See above, pp. 28–30, 38.

[4] The passage is from the section of Lorenzo's tax report of 1480 (Cat., 1016, parte ii, f. 467^r) which mentions his recent purchase of Poggio a Caiano.

[5] In 1469 Rucellai noted: 'Nel chatasto del 1457 mi fu acchatastato una possessione posta al Poggio a Chaiano chon abrigho [i.e. albergho] e chasette, le quali non erano in me e fumi fatto torto. Dovene notizia perchè non vi venisse fatto il simile, perchè le dette chose sono nell'Arte del Chanbio chome a ttenpo e luogho si mosterrà'. There is a clerk's mutilated annotation, apparently referring by way of confirmation to the 1448 document (*ibid.*, 919, f. 379^r). Indeed, in a special addition to the calculations, Giovanni had been taxed florins 5-4-6 extra in 1458 (*ibid.*, 817, ff. 62^v, 74^r). For his financial control, see above, p. 50.

nostro Signore . . .', either 'nella chiesa di Sancta Maria Novella o di Sancto Branchatio . . . dove più gli aglerà. . .'. Further land to pay for the project was put aside in the name of the Bankers' Guild four years later, but when the chapel had not been begun in early 1456 the guild consuls ruled that they themselves would make a start within five years if Giovanni had not, though he would still be able to choose the site[1]. The chapel was presumably begun in San Pancrazio in or soon after 1458, when the decision to give a façade to Santa Maria Novella, using the incomes previously allocated to the earlier project, was approved by the guild and by Giovanni. The monastery's excellent books have no accounts concerning the construction, which was certainly under way in 1464–65 and probably substantially finished two years later[2]. Dezzi Bardeschi has plausibly suggested that Giovanni kept his own financial records of the project[3]. The banker would have paid for it from money strictly his own or perhaps, since this was a pious work which Palla had already approved, with income from ex-Strozzi lands other than Poggio a Caiano.

One can only speculate as to why Giovanni was so long undecided about the site. It is possible that Messer Palla's wishes had somehow to be taken into account or, alternatively, if Lorenzo de' Medici's story was correct, that Rucellai deliberately procrastinated in order to use the income for his palace, perhaps without his father-in-law's knowledge because this was hardly what Strozzi had in mind. Where in Santa Maria Novella Giovanni might have planned a chapel is another mystery which the present writer is not competent to solve. The possibility is, however, that if Rucellai was not hoping to make a new chapel or to assume another family's patronage rights, he may have intended to convert the lineage's chapel of Saint Catherine to his purposes (Pl. 2). This suggestion would help to explain the delay and the ultimate decision in favour of San Pancrazio, since Rucellai rights over the Trecento chapel were in dispute until 1464, according to a Dominican chronicler. As early as 1445 Giovanni himself had modernized the archaic family arms there in an attempt to scotch false rumours 'che la no[n] si murassi per noi'[4], and in the same period he had cultivated the small line of his distant kinsmen whose members had a special interest in the chapel's patronage[5]. With time and the guild consuls pressing in the mid-1450s, and changes at San Pancrazio perhaps creating the possibility of building a new chapel, these specific difficulties at Santa Maria Novella and the approval of the scheme for its façade (a handsome compensation if such it was!), may together have persuaded Giovanni to turn away from the Dominicans to his neighbourhood church, especially since at this time his activities in that district had become more ambitious with the Loggia project. It may however be incorrect to assume that San Pancrazio was always Giovanni's second choice. If he had early decided to furnish the Santa Maria Novella façade but was waiting to be given the rights of patronage, he may have intended the chapel for his parish church while leaving himself the option of giving it to the larger one if his more ambitious plans there misfired.

This and related questions would be easier to resolve if one knew why the banker wanted to make 'uno sipolcro simile a quello di geRusalem del nostro Signore'—apparently a common

---

[1] The relevant documents are published, from Arte del Cambio, 104, by Dezzi Bardeschi, *Facciata*, p. 21. My transcriptions are from Arte del Cambio, 105, ff. 16ᵛ–18ᵛ, the text of which differs in important respects (see above, pp. 43, n. 1; 50, n. 6 and below, p. 63).

[2] Perosa, p. 118 (1464). In his will of the next year, Giovanni elected to be buried in San Pancrazio 'in cappella quam ibidem fecit edificari, que nondum est finita . . .' (NA, L 130 [Ser Lionardo da Colle, 1441-95], no. 31). The sepulchre bears the date 1467. For the possibility that the decision in favour of San Pancrazio was made by mid-1457, see p. 60, n. 1 below.

[3] "Complesso monumentale", p. 16. Dezzi Bardeschi has discussed the whole project in some detail at pp. 19–25. See now Borsi, *Alberti*, pp. 105 ff.

[4] Quoted in Kent, *Household and Lineage*, p. 268: in general see pp. 267 ff.

[5] *Ibid.*, pp. 181, 243, 268–70, and above, p. 25, nn. 4, 5.

medieval concern but not so popular in the fifteenth century, save in Germany and England[1]. Here Rucellai's biographer can only offer clues for the art historian to follow, particularly as to Giovanni's knowledge about, as distinct from his attraction to, the Holy Sepulchre theme before 1448. There were several plausible sources for this knowledge. His banking partner Stoldo Frescobaldi, whose kinsman had been to Jerusalem and had left an account of the holy places, including the Sepulchre itself, was one[2]. Personal contacts during the Council of Florence which made it 'possible for anybody who was interested to find out for himself what the Holy Sepulchre was like' were another[3]. A third was Germans, or merchants operating in Germany, whom Rucellai would have met in Venice, so convenient a gateway to and from the north as he himself wrote[4], and for ideas as much as for merchandise. However his information came to him—it now appears unlikely that he sent a special expedition to the Holy Land to take 'il giusto disegno e misure del Santo Sepolcro'[5]—the theme may have had a family meaning, as it certainly had a personal, for Rucellai. Twice in the *Zibaldone* Giovanni emphasized that the Rucellai had once been called the 'de' Tempiali' after their founder Messer Ferro, supposedly a 'cavaliere dell'ordine de' Militi Templari'[6]. His Holy Sepulchre chapel may refer to this tradition, for the Templars were defenders of pilgrims and the holy places. Giovanni may even have thought that there was a closer connection between the forms of the knights' prolific architecture and that of the Holy Sepulchre than appears usually to have been the case[7]. A reference to this family tradition would have been appropriate in the clan chapel in Santa Maria Novella. The fourteenth-century founder, Cenni di Nardo Rucellai, had left a special offering to be distributed to the friars on Good Friday, as Giovanni noted in the *Zibaldone*[8]. When

---

[1] For its medieval popularity and significance, see R. Krautheimer, "An Introduction to an 'Iconography of Medieval Architecture' ", *JWCI*, V (1942), pp. 1–20. See too N. C. Brooks, "The Sepulchre of Christ in Art and Liturgy", *University of Illinois Studies in Language and Literature*, VII (1921), pp. 1–110, who also emphasizes fifteenth-century English interest in the Holy Sepulchre. I am grateful to Andrew Morrogh for helpful suggestions, particularly about German preoccupation with the theme.

[2] Lionardo Frescobaldi's pages on the subject do not, however, give a detailed description of the Sepulchre (Lionardo Frescobaldi and S. Sigoli, *Viaggi in Terrasanta*, ed. C. Angelini, Florence, 1944, pp. 139–43). See too above, p. 46.

[3] S. Lang, "The Programme of the SS. Annunziata in Florence", *JWCI*, XVII (1954), p. 293 and, in general, pp. 288–300. Rucellai was certainly interested in the Council as early as June 1437, when he reported to Pazzino Strozzi: 'Quelli di Vingnone vorrebbono il concilio: ànno fatto ducati 40 mila per mandare pe' Greci, e ànno in ordine 4 ghalee e armava[n]lle per mandare per loro in Ghostantin[opoli] e avevano eletti 4 anbasciadori per montare su dette ghalee, cioè 4 veschovi. Qui si delibe[ra] in ogni modo mandare 2 ghalee per le dette genti con provedimento di fiorini 50 mila se voran[no]' (CS, III, 120, f. 330r). See too his remarks on the Council itself (Perosa, p. 48). Cosimo de' Medici's building activities at Jerusalem, when told by 'frati di Gerusalem' that 'il luogo dove venne il sanctissimo Spirito era rovinato e sarebbe bene a rifarlo' (Vespasiano da Bisticci, *Vite*, ed. cit., p. 412), may also have aroused Giovanni's interest.

[4] See above, pp. 35–36. Borsi, *Alberti*, pp. 35, 109, mentions two possible Roman models for Rucellai's project, a suggestion I am not competent to comment on.

[5] Kent, "Letters", p. 348, and pp. 342–9. This was a common medieval claim (Krautheimer, "Introduction to an 'Iconography of Medieval Architecture' ", pp. 4–12).

[6] See the rather damaged *nota* appended to f. 1r (Rucellai's account of his ancestors) of the *Zibaldone*, and reproduced as Tav. 2 by Perosa. Among Rucellai's informants was 'Federigo Comi huomo che passa settanta anni', conceivably one of the Federighi, his San Pancrazio neighbours, some of whom were called 'di Como': see p. 14, n. 4 above. Later, when again speaking of Messer Ferro, Rucellai added in his own hand to the scribe's notes: 'fu de' kavalieri del Tenpio' (f. 3v); cf. Marcotti, *Mercante fiorentino*, pp. 53–54, 117–18). I have come across no basis for Rucellai's claim, which may, however, reflect an old Rucellai tradition. St. Bernard encouraged the Templars (see K. J. Conant, *Carolingian and Romanesque Architecture, 800–1200*, Harmondsworth, 1974 edn., p. 333) and he was a Rucellai patron saint; the lineage's *spedale* at Osmannoro, 'St. Bernard's hospital of the Rucellai', may well have served pilgrims (Kent, *Household and Lineage*, pp. 235, 243, 255, 267). It is clear from a letter by Nannina Rucellai of 1474 that pilgrims received a warm welcome at Quaracchi; she recommended to her mother 'uno de' nostri peregrini da Quaracchi' who, though treated 'come amico', needed still more help 'che possi seguire il suo viaggio . . .'; pub. by D. De Robertis, "Supplementi all'epistolario del Pulci", *GSLI*, CXXXIV (1957), p. 568.

[7] E. Lambert, "L'Architecture des Templiers", *Bulletin monumental*, CII (1954), pp. 7–60, 129–60. I owe this reference to Andrew Morrogh. See too Conant, *Carolingian and Romanesque Architecture*, pp. 334–41.

[8] Published in Marcotti, *Mercante fiorentino*, p. 59.

the Holy Sepulchre chapel was given to San Pancrazio, the marble tomb bore the Rucellai arms as well as Giovanni's insignia, and older funeral slabs of the lineage were carefully incorporated into its floor (Pl. 3).

Even so, for Giovanni the Holy Sepulchre was probably much more 'a symbol of promised salvation' for himself and his beloved mother, whose soul was also to be prayed for there[1], than 'a memento of a venerable site'[2]. His was apparently a particularly pressing need to be pardoned sins the precise nature of which he never disclosed. On his visit to Rome in early 1450—where there was to be found, he wrote, 'una remissione prenaria di tutti e' tuoi peccati'—Rucellai explicitly noted, among his several references to Jerusalem and holy objects brought back from there, 'una gentile cappelletta, adornata di marmi, porfido et musaico' where 'dicesi v'è il medesimo perdono che il sepolcro di Gerusalem'[3]. Pope Paul II later granted to the San Pancrazio chapel, built with such 'ssinghulare devozione', a bull which released the faithful from 'sette anni e altrettante quarantane delle iniunte penitenze' if every year they visited it on Good Friday and Holy Sunday[4]. In 1481, when his death must have seemed long overdue, Giovanni himself went to a special mass, conceded him by the abbot, said every Friday in this chapel where he had provided that there should be 'due lampane che abbino a stare accese dì e notte nel sepolchro di Santo Branchazio'[5]. One hopes that Giovanni, by associating himself however discreetly with Christ's resurrection, felt reassured about his own. It may be that his qualms on the issue were well known. Luigi Pulci, a friend of the younger Rucellai and a guest at Quaracchi, mischievously chose the pious Pandolfo as the recipient of his lines, 'per ridere', against Ficino's doctrine of the immortality of the soul; Giovanni Rucellai's had been a pointless though beautiful exercise if: 'noi ce n'andremo, Pandolfo, in valle buia/senza sentir più cantar alleluia'[6].

Rucellai announced major decisions in the years 1456–58: first the Loggia project, then the scheme for Santa Maria Novella's façade with the attendant allocation of the chapel to San Pancrazio. According to a Dominican tradition, his way had become clear at Santa Maria Novella in 1457, the year of the decision against the Baldesi family's claim to patronage rights over the façade. While it seems likely that he had harboured explicit plans for some time—his having to wait to overcome this obstacle would help to explain his apparent indecision about the Holy Sepulchre chapel[7]—it is

---

[1] Perosa, p. 26. This *ricordo* refers to Caterina's having helped to endow the chapel; perhaps her donation to San Pancrazio, on 13 August 1457, of some land 'pro amore Dei et pro remedio anime sue' constituted this endowment, in which case August 1457 may be close to the date of Rucellai's allocation of the Holy Sepulchre chapel to that church (NA, S 16 [Ser Antonio Salamone, 1434–57], f. 273r–v).

[2] Krautheimer, "Introduction to an 'Iconography of Medieval Architecture' ", p. 17. The sepulchre bears the inscription YHESVM QVERITIS NAZARENVM CRVCIFIXVM. SVRREXIT NON EST HIC. ECCE LOCVS VBI POSVERVNT EVM (Richa, *Notizie istoriche delle chiese fiorentine*, iii, p. 314). Giovanni noted in the *Zibaldone* that in a Venetian church 'ò veduto il sabato sancto tra le ventitre et ventiquattro hore dirvi la messa pasquale solempne proprio come la mattina della pasqua . . .', a practice also current in Siena and after 1458 'nella chiesa de' Servi' in Florence (*Zibaldone*, f. 47v).

[3] Perosa, pp. 67, 68, 70, 71, 73.

[4] *Ibid.*, pp. 24–25. Cf. Borsi, *Alberti*, pp. 61–62.

[5] Perosa, p. 26, and below, p. 94.

[6] Published by S. S. Nigro, *Pulci e la cultura medicea*, Bari, 1972, p. 66. The sonnet apparently dates from the mid-1470s (pp. 64–65). There seems no reason to doubt the tradition that it was addressed to Giovanni's son (see, e.g., E. O. Lebano, "Luigi Pulci and late fifteenth-century Humanism in Florence", *Renaissance Quarterly*, XVII [1974], p. 493), for Pulci knew the Rucellai well (see below, p. 81).

[7] Orlandi, *Necrologio*, ii, p. 262. Giovanni Baldesi's reference to the dispute in his tax report of early 1458 implies that it had gone on some time. Explaining why he and his brothers lived, in effect, rent free in a house belonging to the Company of St. Peter the Martyr, Baldesi wrote, interestingly but imprecisely: 'Naghue tra noi e detti fratti una diferenza della porte e marmi di Santa Maria Novella, della quale porta i detti frati levorono l'arme nostra stata g[i]à è molto tempo, e doppo più e ghuistioni fue rimesa in Giovanni di Francesco della Luna, el qualle per chonpesazione lodò che lla pigione di detta chasa per xv anni i detti

also true that in these seminal years, which also saw the *Zibaldone* begun, past ideas and enthusiasms crystallized in response to a series of personal and external circumstances that are not now fully recoverable. Since some or perhaps all of these decisions hung upon each other, their sequence will defy precise analysis until more specific evidence comes to light. Again, for instance, Palla Strozzi's shadow lies across these events. In early 1454, when his term of exile was again renewed, it became clear as never before to his shocked relations that the old man was not to see Florence again[1]. The realization might have encouraged him and Giovanni to use the income of the ex-Strozzi lands on the façade, a more ambitious and less personal ecclesiastical project than the chapel.

Amidst these conjectures only one thing appears certain. Giovanni's building plans came to maturity, and were acted upon, precisely at the time he was as rich and as vigorous as he would ever be, and as isolated from public and political recognition. It was no coincidence that the project to build a family Loggia belongs to such a period. Giovanni may have taken the initiative, for he says that his second cousin once-removed Ugolino di Francesco Rucellai donated the site in April 1456 'per mio conforto e d'altri di casa nostra'[2]. He certainly paid for it, as the notarial act had anticipated. Brenda Preyer has shown that building was delayed until 1463 so that the patron could take advantage of a bigger site which would better set off the palace[3], an intention perhaps grasped by Giovanni's one Rucellai critic who, believing himself unjustly deprived of his share of a house knocked down on the Loggia site, said that he would be 'chontento se della sua chasa avenisse il simile'[4]. Even if Giovanni had early seen the aesthetic advantages to himself, there is no reason to doubt the sincerity of his parallel commitment to a scheme also undertaken 'per honore della nostra famiglia' (he would have seen little conflict of interest) and with the active co-operation of many of his kinsmen. All but one willingly gave up their share of Ugolino's home, the destruction of which made possible the larger site[5]. Giovanni received the shop 'per tutta la famiglia de' Rucellai' and, as Ugolino's act of donation stated, the Loggia, to be used 'pro omnibus eorum letitiis et tristitiis et honoribus quibuscumque . . .', must be named 'la loggia de' Rucellaj'[6]. If in 1469 a clerk of the tax officials called it, in a marginal note, 'la loggia di Giovanni di Pagholo Rucellai', it appears as 'lodiam de Oricellariis' in a notarial document of 1492[7], and bears both the Rucellai arms and Giovanni's devices.

It is not impossible that the decision to build a Loggia was in some sense arrived at after family discussions. Though Alberti and Palmieri praised the civic usefulness of 'porticoes', few family loggias were built in the Quattrocento. The Rucellai decision to create a clan meeting-place of a

fratti non dovesino avere, ma che a noi restassi per murare una chapella o altra chosa piatosa chome a noi paressi . . .' (Cat., 818, f. 22ᵛ. I owe the reference to Brenda Preyer). Rucellai's involvement in these *ghuistioni* is implied by the appointment of Giovanni della Luna as arbiter in the dispute (see above, pp. 19; 22; 25; 35, n. 4; 45–46, and below, pp. 72; 83, n. 4).

[1] I am grateful to Heather Gregory for the reference to this matter in Giovanfrancesco Strozzi's letter to Francesco Caccini dated 21 March 1453 (Riccardiana, 4009, unfoliated). I have assumed that Strozzi, though writing from Ferrara, used Florentine style and that the year was 1454. On 18 October 1453 Giovanfrancesco had written in distress about the possibility that his branch's period of exile would be renewed. Cf. Rubinstein, *Government*, pp. 109–10; Fiocco, "La casa di Palla Strozzi", p. 381.

[2] Perosa, p. 20.

[3] Preyer, below, pp. 205–06. See now her "The Rucellai Loggia", *MKHIF*, XXI (1977), pp. 183–98.

[4] Published by Kent, "Loggia", p. 399. Another Rucellai, Giovanni d'Antonio, may also have disapproved of his more powerful cousin's activities; see Preyer, below, pp. 183–84.

[5] Kent, "Loggia", pp. 397–401; Perosa, p. 20.

[6] The quotations are respectively from *ibid.*; and Kent, "Loggia", p. 397.

[7] Cat., 919, f. 121ᵛ, and cf. the scribal note in *ibid.*, 816, f. 895ʳ, where Ugolino's old house is said in 1469 to be 'a chonto di Giovani Rucellai che ne fè la logia'. The 1492 reference is in NA, F 237 (Ser Antonio Ferrini, 1470–99), Busta 1492–5, f. 50ʳ.

sort so popular in the preceding century may have been influenced by the dynastic if not architectural predilections of the site's donor, Ugolino, who was eighty years old in 1456[1]. In the event,
Giovanni managed to please himself and almost all his kinsmen with whom, despite his other
difficulties at this time, he continued to share satisfyingly cordial relations. Indeed, as the Loggia
project itself suggests, there was the consolation of having become one of the family's leaders. In
1460 when Piero di Cardinale, in the name 'omnium suorum consortium et agnatorum de domo et
familia de Rucellariis', saw to the appointment of a new rector to the family's rural *spedale*, which
also required considerable repairs, Giovanni, who was otherwise interested in this clan property,
was his lieutenant[2]. By about 1466 the 'piaza e logia chomune' was finished, one of the first
Florentine Renaissance piazzas associated directly with a private palace[3], which it enhanced while
providing tangible evidence of Giovanni's solidarity with, and benevolence towards, the kinsmen
and neighbours who had treated him so compassionately.

When on 19 April 1458 the Bankers' Guild gave Giovanni permission to use the income from
Poggio 'nello ornamento della porta et faccia della chiesa di Sancta Maria Novella'[4], he had
decisively committed himself to a project which was, unlike his others, unambiguously public. In
retrospect at least, Rucellai gives the impression of having carefully worked out from himself and
his family to wider civic concerns, from his parish to his quarter and to the city at large. It was by
any standards a major undertaking, the successful completion of which would (and indeed did)
bring its patron's name literally before an international audience. During the fifteenth century
several crowned heads, Italian statesmen and popes stayed at Santa Maria Novella, including Pius II
who in late April or early May 1459 must have become personally and admiringly acquainted with
Giovanni's palace and other projects, just as he formally received Rucellai's colleague Benedetto
Toschi[5]. Church façades proved troublesome for Florentine patrons in the Quattrocento. Castello
Quaratesi is supposed earlier to have offered a huge sum to furnish Santa Croce's, but to have been
refused because he wanted vaingloriously to place his arms there[6]; the Medici themselves were
later apparently so embarrassed by San Lorenzo's stark façade that in an early sixteenth-century
miniature it is shown as completed[7]. Giovanni's coup was considerable, for he not only finished
Santa Maria Novella's façade but impressed upon it the family arms and his own devices. Even more
strikingly his name and the date 1470, in fine Roman letters which according to Giovanni Marder-

[1] Kent, "Loggia", p. 398; *id.*, *Household and Lineage*, pp. 242, 278, 286; Preyer, *Giovanni Rucellai*, p. 223.

[2] NA, B 385 (Ser Baldovino Baldovini, 1450–9), ff. 327r–328r; Kent, *Household and Lineage*, pp. 234–6, 243, has references to the
hospital.

[3] Quoted in Kent, "Loggia", p. 399; see also Preyer, *Giovanni Rucellai*, p. 227; below, pp. 205–06, who is cautious about the
extent to which the piazza was Giovanni's creation. On piazzas in general, see the unpublished paper by C. Elam, "The Piazza
Strozzi: Two Drawings by Baccio d'Agnolo for a private Renaissance Piazza" (I thank Miss Elam for permission to refer to it); and
Hyman, "Notes and Speculations", pp. 105 ff. Dr. Preyer believes the Loggia was built between 1463 and 1466 (above, p. 61, n. 3).

[4] Arte del Cambio, 105, f. 17v; cf. Dezzi Bardeschi, *Facciata*, p. 21, which gives 18 April. His is the most recent account of the
whole project; see too his "Sole in Leone", pp. 33–67.

[5] Haines, "Documenti intorno al Reliquiario per San Pancrazio", pp. 264, 266, 267, mentions this interesting fact, which makes
contact between Rucellai and Pius even more likely. I am assuming here that Preyer, *Giovanni Rucellai*, pp. 121 ff., is correct in
regarding Pius' palace at Pienza as having been inspired by Rucellai's, and not vice versa as has again been very recently argued:
C. R. Mack, "The Rucellai Palace: Some new Proposals", *AB*, LVI (1974), pp. 517–29. On Santa Maria Novella's outstanding
position, see Borsi, *Alberti*, p. 61. Rucellai's public initiative is all the more striking if M. Weinberg is right in suggesting a direct
link between Arnolfo di Cambio's design for the façade of Florence's cathedral and Alberti's scheme at Santa Maria Novella
("The first Façade of the Cathedral of Florence", *JWCI*, IV–V [1941–42], p. 79).

[6] F. Moisè, *Santa Croce di Firenze: illustrazione storico-artistica*, Florence, 1845, pp. 90–91, 492. On contemporary opposition to
placing arms in and on churches, see Brucker, *Civic World*, pp. 7–8.

[7] C. H. Krinsky, "A View of the Palazzo Medici and the Church of San Lorenzo", *JSAH*, XXVIII (1969), pp. 133–5.

steig have lost a good deal of their clarity over the centuries, still dominate the building, as boldly as Sigismondo Malatesta's inscription on San Francesco at Rimini[1]. When in 1469 the bishop of Cortona told Giovanni that Santa Maria Novella was the most beautiful Dominican church in Christendom, and Santa Croce the finest Franciscan 'ecietto la facciata dinanzi', he was paying a gracefully oblique compliment to the patron[2].

Such display was only possible after Giovanni's alliance with the Medici. He was able to begin the project at all because the old Rucellai ties to the major church of their quarter gave his initiative an acceptable traditional context, and because personal bonds with several influential Dominicans helped him to implement it at a time when he was still *sospetto*. According to the convent's chronicler Borghigiani, the friars themselves asked for Rome's intercession in the patronage dispute with the Baldesi[3] and, a guild document informs us, it was 'di consenso dello Arcivescovo di firenze', the Dominican Antoninus Pierozzi, that the Bankers' Guild and Giovanni arranged the financing of the façade in April 1458. A second, in other respects more reliable, version of this document reads: 'di consiglo' which, if it is not a fifteenth-century copyist's misreading, gives the saintly archbishop an even more decisive and intriguing role in the affair[4]. St. Antoninus may have had a keen understanding of modern painting, and experience as a patron at San Marco, but he rated the architect and his works much lower. He disliked 'spacious palaces and excessive buildings' because they were displeasing to God, and condemned the invasion of ecclesiastical patronage by laymen with their heraldic paraphernalia[5]. He must, however, have somehow been able to reconcile these well-known views with Giovanni's proposals. Very likely the banker concealed his desire—if indeed he had formulated it—so firmly to stamp his identity upon the façade. A close reading of the documents confirms, however, that from the beginning it was arguable if not understood that he could 'porre l'arme' there[6]. The archbishop may have felt justified in favouring a pious work, unostentatiously described in the guild document and, it could be said, intended not so much for his own order *per se* as for one of its great public churches[7]. Perhaps, however, Antoninus' position

---

[1] "Leon Battista Alberti e la rinascita del carattere lapidario romano", pp. 294–5.

[2] Perosa, p. 65. For the bishop's interest in building, see the letters of early 1471 published by Gaye, *Carteggio*, i, pp. 226–7, 232; and G. Mirri, *I vescovi di Cortona dalla istituzione della diocesi (1325–1971)*, Cortona, 1972, p. 117 (Fra Mariano Salvini). According to Moisè, *Santa Croce*, p. 91, there was a strong renewed interest in the 1470s in providing a façade for the Franciscan church—a response, one might think, to Rucellai's successful initiative. Brenda Preyer has kindly brought to my attention the relevant law of 28 September 1476 (Provvisioni, Registri, 167, ff. 146ᵛ–148ʳ), which begins: 'si conosce manifestamente per experienta che uno de' più begli templi di questa città si è la chiesa di Santa Croce et solo v'è uno mancamento, il quale quando fusse riparato si potrebbe dire et sarebbe uno de' più begli templi d'Italia, e questa si è la faccia . . .' (f. 147ʳ). The initiative came from the friars of Santa Croce themselves. See now the interesting suggestion by Goldthwaite and Rearick, *op. cit.*, p. 50, n. 6 above, concerning the 'confrontation of façades [at San Paolo and Santa Maria Novella] between the rival orders of friars' (p. 226) from the 1450s onwards.

[3] Orlandi, *Necrologio*, II, p. 262. The friars' active role is also implied by Giovanni Baldesi's account (p. 60, n. 7 above).

[4] Dezzi Bardeschi, transcribing from Arte del Cambio, 104, correctly gives 'di consenso dello Arcivescovo di firenze et di volontà et consenso di decto Giovanni Rucellai' (*Facciata*, p. 21); Arte del Cambio, 105, f. 17ᵛ (on which see above, p. 58, n. 1), reads: 'di consiglo di messer l'archiveschovo di Firenze e di volontà e consentimento del dito [sic] Giovanni Ruciellai'. According to Borghigiani, cited by Orlandi, *Necrologio*, ii, p. 262, the original dispute with the Baldesi 'andò a banco all'Arcivescovado' before the friars had recourse to Rome.

[5] The quotation from Antoninus is in G. G. Coulton, *Art and the Reformation*, Oxford, 1928, p. 335; see in general, pp. 83–4, 334–5, 463. See too C. Gilbert, "The Archbishop on the Painters of Florence, 1450", *AB*, XLI (1959), pp. 75–87.

[6] The 19 April 1458 document giving Rucellai permission to use Poggio a Caiano's income for the façade and not the Holy Sepulchre chapel, adds 'stando ferme l'altre condizione tute che in dette chompere e chommessione si contenghono' (Arte del Cambio, 105, f. 17ᵛ), one of which (23 March 1456) was that Giovanni or his heirs could 'porre l'arme di decto Giovanni Rucellai' in the chapel (*ibid.*). See p. 42, n. 3 above for Giovanni's placing of his arms in the main chapel of San Pancrazio.

[7] The 1458 act speaks only of 'ornamento' (*ibid.*), while documents of three years later concerning further financing of the project are quite explicit about a 'parietem et primam faciem marmoream' (NA, C 407 [Ser Pierozzo Cerbini, 1456–65], unfoliated,

on these questions requires further analysis. He was also one of the four arbiters who on 30 December 1448—in a ruling against the Minerbetti family which explicitly used aesthetic criteria and in a sense condoned aristocratic competitiveness—awarded the Rucellai rights of patronage over the column in Santa Maria Novella to which their pulpit, with its prominently displayed coat-of-arms of the *consorteria*, was to be attached[1]. The saint also knew Giovanni Rucellai personally, and may have been persuaded of his genuine piety. The two, with some other notable citizens, had ridden out together in August 1456 to examine the damage caused by a fierce storm which had fallen on the upper Valdarno. Giovanni's own account of the event characteristically omits the Archbishop's name[2]. Another link between them would have been Antoninus's secretary and loving hagiographer, the notary Ser Baldovino Baldovini, who worked a great deal for Giovanni, his banker and neighbour in Lion Rosso[3].

Within the convent itself Giovanni almost certainly had, as Father Orlandi has suggested, the backing and advice of his very distant cousin from a collateral branch, Fra Andrea Rucellai, the last of his line, whose death Giovanni noted in the *Zibaldone*[4]. Fra Andrea was committed to his family's affairs within the church and, apart from being a minor patron in his own right, was long one of its highly competent financial officials. 'Multa bona fecit fieri a civibus ecclesia sua prochuratione', the convent's necrology said of this Rucellai friar, who had been a *gubernator* of the Company of St. Peter the Martyr, the lay confraternity which was in early 1461 to assume an important role in Giovanni's financing of the façade campaign[5]. At that point another distinguished friar, Stefano Benincasa, several times prior, took a hand. This successful confessor to a number of Florentine noblemen and women[6], and one of the four captains of the company who ratified the banker's donation[7], appears to have had a personal relationship with Giovanni, who left 'amore Dei . . . unam vestem ad usum et dorsum ipsius magistri Stefani condecentem' in his will of 1465[8].

---

20 April 1461) and '[la] muraglia de' marmi della faccia della nostra chiesa' (Conv. Sopp., 102, 308, f. 95ᵛ). Salvatore Camporeale of Santa Maria Novella kindly discussed this matter with me.

[1] See the terms of the judgement, published by Orlandi, *S. Antonino*, ii, pp. 308–10, and Kent, *Household and Lineage*, p. 282. The Rucellai arms were placed there with the approval of the arbiters, two of whom, Martino dello Scarfa and Domenico Petrucci, were neighbours of the Rucellai and Minerbetti. See the comments of W. Braunfels on the friars' receptivity to secular patronage (*Monasteries of Western Europe: The Architecture of the Orders*, London, 1972, pp. 137 ff.). Sir Nikolaus Pevsner has suggested that it may have been the medieval Dominicans of Florence who diffused the word 'architect', in its original dignified meaning, 'among the scholars and the humanists from whom the initiators of the Italian Renaissance then took it over '("The Term 'Architect' in the Middle Ages", *Speculum*, XVII [1942], pp. 560–1).

[2] Perosa, pp. 78–82; he says simply 'montai a cavallo in compagnia di Bartolomeo Ridolfi et altri' (p. 79). Antoninus' presence was noted by a chronicler cited by Orlandi, *S. Antonino*, ii, pp. 227, n. 23, 304. St. Antoninus was close to the Medici (see A. d'Addario in *DBI*, Rome, 1961, III, pp. 524–28), despite his public protest in July 1458 against Medicean attempts to control the Council of the People by having open voting there (*ibid.*, and Rubinstein, *Government*, p. 98); his approval of the Rucellai scheme might also reflect Medicean influence on Giovanni's behalf. Both the Rucellai and the Medici were powerful in the counsels of the Bankers' Guild, according to *partiti* surviving from 1462–76 (Arte del Cambio, 19, largely unfoliated).

[3] See Rucellai's undated autograph note to Ser Baldovino, loose and unfoliated among his protocols for 1463–65 (NA, B 396, at f. 92ᵛ in 1974), which begins 'Kᵐᵒ amico', asks him for 'una fede d'una chiarigione che feron e' sindachi del ghonfalone de' Lio[n] Rosso', and ends abruptly: 'Anchora vi ricordo il chanciellare la ragone vostra quando prima potete'. Baldovino and his father lived in Lion Rosso in 1442 (Cat., 620, parte i, f. 363ʳ), and the notary was later much employed on the district's business. For Baldovini's relationship with the saint, see R. Morçay, *Saint Antonin, 1389–1459*, Tours-Paris, 1914.

[4] *Necrologio*, ii, p. 261; Kent, *Household and Lineage*, p. 275.

[5] For this information, see *ibid.*, pp. 268, 270, 282, 283; Orlandi, *Necrologio*, i, p. 168; ii, pp. 168, 173, 191, 230, 255–63.

[6] On Benincasa, see *ibid.*, i, pp. 193–4; ii, pp. 320–4.

[7] Conv. Sopp., 102, 308, f. 95ᵛ. See above, p. 50, n. 6.

[8] NA, L 130 (Ser Lionardo da Colle, 1441–95), no. 31. There is a gap after the reference to 'magistro Stefano', but since he is then called 'fratri predicatori, sacre theologie magistro', my identification seems certain.

Benincasa was a doctor of theology. Should art historians wish to look for the influence on Giovanni's project of a theological expert, Fra Stefano is as likely as not to be their man.

With his building plans essentially complete by 1458, Giovanni wasted as little time as possible over the next few years in implementing them. The façade was under way by 20 April 1461 at the latest[1]. Rucellai's major interest had now become and was to remain his *muraglie*, into which he had put his hopes of personal commemoration and public rehabilitation and recognition. (If Giovanni in part had begun to build to catch the eye of the Medici, a decade later the means had in a sense become the end, not the least of a Medici match's attractions being the protection it gave his mature activities as a patron). His commonplace book, begun at this time during his enforced leisure at San Gimignano, reflects this sense of commitment, this awareness of having begun to order his ideas and his world. But the '*Zibaldone* vetus' was still very much an interim report—which says very little even indirectly about his buildings and plans—on his hopes for the future. Giovanni did not yet know that he would live to enjoy, or be enabled by changed circumstances to delight in, his achievements as a builder[2]. In 1457 his central mood is one of stoic pride at having survived so well in an often hostile environment. As if not to tempt providence, he allowed himself only the modest hope that were his sons to follow his advice and practice in the matter of winning friends and public approval, they would be able to defend themselves 'da chi cercasse o operasse farvi male. . .'[3].

---

[1] NA, C 407 (Ser Pierozzo Cerbini, 1456–65), unfoliated, 20 April 1461, describes the façade as 'iam inceptam construi', and Dezzi Bardeschi is probably right in assuming, in the light of the documents he discovered, that the project was begun in 1458 (*Facciata*, pp. 18, 21). See Hatfield, *Botticelli's Uffizi Adoration*, p. 24, n. 55, for further evidence of a pre-1462 start.

[2] Perosa, p. 121.

[3] *Ibid.*, p. 9.

V. 'ONORATO, STIMATO E RIGHUARDATO', 1461–73

In November 1461 Bernardo, Rucellai's younger son, was betrothed to Cosimo de' Medici's granddaughter Nannina and Giovanni's time of adversity was over. One would dearly like more information on how the marriage came about. A letter from Cosimo to his nephew Pierfrancesco di Lorenzo implies, as one would expect, that the Medici took the initiative, but beforehand there would have been the usual approaches and bargaining conducted by friends and relatives, perhaps by the Pandolfini or the Pitti[1]. Even more than most contemporary matches, it was a *mariage de convenance* between two very young people and not as it turned out a happy one, for Bernardo's arbitrary behaviour later forced from Nannina one of the few surviving self-conscious statements by a fifteenth-century woman about her position: 'o pure non si vole nascere femina chi vuole fare a suo modo,' she wrote to her mother on 12 July 1479[2]. The alliance was presumably acceptable to both men and to the Medicean *stato* because by 1461 the figure of Palla Strozzi no longer stood between Giovanni and Florence. In 1460 Messer Palla had become a Paduan citizen, his renunciation of the city that had rejected him made even more pointed in the last will he drew up just before his death at the great age of ninety in May 1462. He was not to be buried in his father's chapel in Santa Trinita, as his testament of 1447 had required, but in Padua. A nostalgia for ancestral ways shows itself in Strozzi's request that his corpse be dressed in a Vallombrosan habit[3]. Palla had never rebelled against his homeland, as his son Giovanfrancesco was to do in 1467, and as late as 1458 had repudiated force as a means of regaining his place in Florence[4].

Giovanni welcomed the betrothal for reasons that were personal as well as public. Judging by his attention to the welfare of his own and Cosimo's family during an outbreak of plague in mid-1464[5], he dreaded that the alliance would still elude him. Bernardo and Nannina married only in June 1466. Now he was able to concentrate on his new *parente* Cosimo the surpassing admiration—almost hero-worship—he had always had for his father-in-law Palla. He had no need to feel disloyal, for Strozzi in effect signalled his acceptance of Giovanni's action by making him the chief executor of his last will[6]. The praise the *Zibaldone* had given Cosimo in 1457 acquired by 1464 a new fervour comparable with the passages on Messer Palla. Among the 'many and infinite graces' God

---

[1] Letter quoted by Dr. Preyer, below, p. 215. I can find no answer from Pierfrancesco. According to the papal document of dispensation, the marriage had been arranged by 'common friends' (NA, B 397 [Ser Baldovino Baldovini, 1465–68], f. 27ᵛ).

[2] Pub. by G. Pieraccini, *La stirpe de' Medici di Cafaggiolo*, Florence, 1924, i, p. 147 (translated in Y. Maguire, *The Women of the Medici*, London, 1927, pp. 115–16). Nannina states explicitly that Bernardo does not care for her.

[3] AS Ferr., Archivio Bentivoglio, lib. 4, 2, ff. 5–6; lib. 6, 34, ff. 5–6. See Fiocco, "La casa di Palla Strozzi", p. 365, for his becoming a Paduan citizen.

[4] Rubinstein, *Government*, p. 136. Otto di Guardia e Balìa, 224, f. 146ᵛ, declares Giovanfrancesco a 'rubello del comune'.

[5] On 27 June Giovanni wrote to Piero de' Medici with the news that 'la Caterina donna di Pandolfo è in termine della sua malatia d'avere pocha speranza o non punto della salute sua. Il male suo gli cominciò a dì 18 che siamo oggi nel 9 dì, e con tutto ch'e' medici dicano non essere male pistilenziale (chè ci sono stati 6 medici), a me ne resta pure nel'animo qualche sospezione, masimamente per avere fatto senpre l'orina molta torbida e di mala condizione, e per questa chagone vi conforto che maestro Mariotto [the Medici doctor] non vi pratichi in chasa per parechi dì perchè lui gl'è stato più a boccha che gli altri. Sono tanti quelli che gli sono stati a boccha in questa sua malatia, e di dì e di notte, che non potrà essere sendo stato male pistilenziale che non se ne vegha qualche segno; che Dio per sua grazia conservi gl'altri' (MAP, XVI, 157). Bernardo had indeed already been sent to Volterra, where he informed Piero on 21 April 'a Giovanni mio è paruto che io sia venuto qui per parecchi giorni, tanto che si vegha quello che questa morìa abbi a ffare' (*ibid.*, XVII, 405).

[6] See below, p. 78.

had granted him, Giovanni wrote, was to have been alive at 'la più gioconda età' for Florence, especially:

> per essere stato al tempo del magnifico ciptadino Cosimo di Giovanni de' Medici, el quale è stato ed è di tanta richeza e di tanta virtù e di tanta grazia e riputazione e seguito, chosì fuori della ciptà come dentro, che mmai nel Cristianesimo non fu simile ciptadino nè di tante buone parti e chondizioni quanto sono state e sono in lui. E in fra l'altre grazie che Iddio m'à conceduto è stato che m'à facto parente del detto Cosimo[1].

About the public advantages of the marriage Rucellai was quite explicit, in words which recall his now happily banished sense of social isolation during the preceding decades, in the *ricordo* of 1473:

> ppoi ch'io fui parente di Piero di Chosimo de' Medici e di Lorenzo e Guliano, suoi figluoli, sono stato onorato, stimato e righuardato, e lla loro felicità e prosperità me l'ò ghoduta e ghodo insieme cho. lloro, di che ò preso grandissimo chontentamento[2].

In 1457 Giovanni had been right to see political advancement as evidence of being 'accetti e in gratia de' cittadini'[3], for the Medici brought their new relative in from the cold with a speed and efficiency which shows how delicately the machinery of government could respond to their touch. Specially added to the bags for the *Tre Maggiori* on 19 April 1463[4], Giovanni became a Prior at the age of sixty just a fortnight later. Rather naively he revealed his pleasure at being for the first time in this 'degnissimo magistrato' by grandly giving himself four, rather than the usual two or three, patronymics in the *priorista* of his family which he kept year by year in the *Zibaldone*[5]. In the same year he was a *Monte* official, and held this sensitive and powerful financial office again in 1467[6]. A Medici *parente* required even greater political distinctions than these. At Piero's express wish, and not without opposition, Giovanni was made *veduto* Gonfalonier of Justice in June 1465. A year later, and again in 1472, his and others' names were specially put in the bags for this, the commune's supreme office, by the *Accoppiatori*. Before he died he was to become Gonfalonier (in 1475) and five years later a member of the Council of Seventy, the cornerstone of Lorenzo's political system[7]. Other political responsibilities came his and his sons' way: Pandolfo was Prior in 1469[8] and in a letter written on 29 March 1466 Bernardo, still very young, gives the impression that he had been preoccupied with the current scrutiny[9].

Giovanni's well known and detailed description of the wedding-feast (what one would give for similar precision about just one of his buildings!) shows how determined an effort he made proudly

---

[1] Perosa, p. 118.

[2] *Ibid.*, p. 121.

[3] *Ibid.*, p. 39.

[4] Rubinstein, *Government*, p. 124, n. 2. On 1 September 1462 he had been made Consul of the Bankers' Guild (Arte del Cambio, 19, f. 10v). The volume shows Giovanni and Pandolfo active in guild affairs between 1462 and 1476.

[5] *Zibaldone*, f. 6v; Perosa, p. 91.

[6] Tratte, 81, ff. 65r–v.

[7] See Rubinstein, *Government*, pp. 139, n. 1, 317; *Zibaldone*, f. 6v; CS, III, 3, ff. 59r ff.; MAP, LXXXVI, ff. 324v–25v. Heather Gregory kindly refers me to a letter by Filippo Strozzi of 26–27 June 1475, which, interestingly enough, shows foreknowledge of Rucellai's triumph: 'Domattina si tragheno e' nostri priori e areno Gonfaloniere Govanni Ruciellai, e forse Niccolò Ghuaschoni de' priori' (CS, III, 247, f. 19v).

[8] *Zibaldone*, f. 6v. For Pandolfo's career, see R. Ristori, "Un mercante savonaroliano: Pandolfo Rucellai", in *Magia, Astrologia e religione nel Rinascimento: Convegno polacco-italiano*, Florence, 1972, pp. 30–47; and E. Fumagalli, "I Trattati di Fra Santi Rucellai", *Aevum*, LI (1977), pp. 289–332.

[9] MAP, CXXXVII, 243: 'e chome ti dissi ora che lo squittino non ci dà brigha nè noia, spero andremo [to Quaracchi]'. Other offices held by Giovanni and Pandolfo are in Tratte, 81, ff. 56r–v, 68v, 100v, 151r.

to advertise his recent acceptance by the Medici. The festivities, dancing and dining, were held on a great platform 'che teneva tucta la piazzuola' between the palace and the *loggia*, shade from the summer sun being provided by a *cielo* decorated with, among other things, the Rucellai and Medici arms. The whole display, which was considered as it was meant to be 'il più bello e 'l più gientile parato che si sia mai facto a ffesta di nozze . . .', and the scale on which the many guests were entertained, must have contravened the sumptuary laws at almost every point. The food and drink alone—the biggest bills were for poultry and wine—cost the huge sum of 6,638 lire, well over three times the annual income, some years later, of the entire rich estate of Poggio a Caiano[1]. This was a private celebration which became in effect a public ceremony. Not only the Via Vigna Nuova would have been inaccessible to through traffic but also the street 'dirieto alla chasa nostra, faccendo chiuderla con assi', where in an open-air kitchen fifty cooks and their assistants laboured away. On one day a number of aristocratic youths playfully skirmished their way with the new bride down the Via della Vigna Nuova, past the homes of her mother's Tornabuoni and Tornaquinci relations to the Medici palace in Via Larga[2]. No ceremony, no route, could better have demonstrated the newly cordial relations between the owners of the two finest Renaissance palaces in Florence.

Cosimo's motives for seeking the marriage are far obscurer than Giovanni's. His letter of November asking for Pierfrancesco de' Medici's opinion is almost studiously laconic. Commenting on the 'scharsi partiti' there were, he made it plain that to choose 'a son of Giovanni Rucellai' was only 'fare il meglio che ssi può'[3]. However, with Strozzi in effect removed, and given Rucellai's record of prudent navigation and public-spiritedness, Bernardo was not an illogical choice. As Machiavelli later noted, Cosimo always carefully married into prominent *popolani* families in order not to offend public opinion[4], and by the late 'fifties there were few citizens as eligible as Giovanni, the third wealthiest man in the city and from a lineage comparable in antiquity to the Medici. Without an explicit statement from one of the Medici there is no way of assessing what contribution Giovanni's building activities and plans may have made to Cosimo's decision. If the palace indeed conveyed a subtle message, Cosimo would have been the first to take the point. The new project for the façade of Santa Maria Novella perhaps prepared the way by making Giovanni a civic benefactor whom any of his detractors would have to regard as acceptable.

It is possible that Cosimo himself was not (perhaps had never been) as lukewarm to Giovanni's aspirations as even the letter to his kinsman implies. The acquisition of a rich new ally perhaps seemed a particularly attractive prospect at that time, when so astute a politician as Cosimo may have had some inkling of the problems his successor would soon have with some of the family's increasingly restive traditional *amici,* including the Pierfrancesco de' Medici branch itself. As it happened, the Medici found in Giovanni a conveniently unambitious and inexperienced elder statesman and in Bernardo an extremely able and energetic partisan, a major figure in the *stato* who worked very closely with his brother-in-law for two decades before mutual disenchantment set in towards the

---

[1] For Poggio's income, see the figures in Spedale di San Matteo, 30, f. 299ᵛ. P. F. Watson has noted Rucellai's infringement of the sumptuary laws in his very useful Appendix II, part B ("A Concordance of Sumptuary Laws 1356–1415") of his *Virtù and Voluptas in Cassone Painting*, unpublished Ph.D. dissertation (Yale University, 1970), p. 361; and see pp. 322 ff. I thank Dr. Watson for permission to cite his thesis. Cf. J. Heers, *Le Clan familial au moyen âge*, Paris, 1974, p. 243.

[2] Perosa, pp. 28 ff.; cf. C. Molinari, *Spettacoli fiorentini del Quattrocento*, Venice, 1961, pp. 19–20.

[3] See p. 66, n. 1, above. It seems quite possible that Cosimo was being less than frank with Pierfrancesco; see below, p. 69, n. 2; and now Alison M. Brown, "Pierfrancesco de' Medici, 1430–76: A radical Alternative to elder Medicean Supremacy?", *JWCI*, XLII, 1979, pp. 81–103.

[4] *Istorie fiorentine*, ed. P. Carli, Florence, 1927, ii, p. 124.

end of Lorenzo's life[1]. Even if the Medici were genuinely only moderately enthusiastic about the Rucellai match the wedding ceremony itself, in June 1466, could not have been better timed for their political purposes, coming as it did between the anti-Medicean May declaration—signed by a number of Mediceans, including several prominent Rucellai and Pierfrancesco de' Medici himself—and the open conflicts within the regime of July and August[2]. Certainly Piero and Lorenzo de' Medici did not lose the propagandist opportunity provided by Giovanni's magnificent display, at once a timely compliment to them and a proud statement about his own worth as an ally. The young Lorenzo wore a cloak, described by Pigello Portinari as 'tanto bella quanto veruna che n'habbi may vista', given him by the Duke of Milan whose own 'divisa . . . del cane' it bore by express permission of Sforza himself. Pigello made sure that the cloak reached Florence in time for the Rucellai wedding, as Lorenzo was able to tell the Duke and his wife on the 9 June in a letter thanking them for their 'tanto excellente et magnifico dono' and swearing that not so much on his shoulders 'ma in nel mezo del cuore le vostre insengne et divise ci staranno sculte et infisse'[3]. Those dissident *ottimati* at the wedding who, amidst the festivities, did not take the point must have remembered it two months later when the threatened intervention of Milanese troops played an essential part in the preservation of the Medici regime[4].

Despite the political advantages the Medici may have derived from the marriage and the high offices he subsequently held, Giovanni himself gave little time to politics, and exercised no real authority, after 1461. One or two references suggest a new social prominence—according to Benedetto Dei he was at a joust in 1470, dreaming perhaps of his own triumph fifty years before[5]— but such an informed contemporary as Dei does not mention Rucellai among the leaders of the regime, and his contributions to the *Consulte e Pratiche*, the forum for its discussions, were negligible[6]. Giovanni's surviving letters to the Medici are not those of a man privy to the secrets of the regime. It is true that he described his term as *Accoppiatore* with some gusto, and knew that in 1471 this magistracy enjoyed special authority, but his account is an almost innocent one—without backward-looking irony he mentions the officials' powers 'di potere trarre delle borse e' sospetti e

---

[1] On Bernardo's career, and his relations with Lorenzo, see F. Gilbert, "Bernardo Rucellai and the Orti Oricellari", *JWCI*, XII (1949), pp. 101–31.

[2] For these events, see Rubinstein, *Government*, pp. 154 ff. The *sottoscrizione* with its signatories is published by G. Pampaloni, "Il giuramento pubblico in Palazzo Vecchio a Firenze e un patto giurato degli antimedicei (Maggio, 1466)", *Bullettino senese di storia patria*, LXXI, s. 3, XXIII (1964), pp. 213–38.

[3] The exchange of letters is pub. by R. Magnani, *Relazioni private tra la Corte Sforzesca di Milano e Casa Medici 1450–1500*, Milan, 1910, pp. xxxv–vii; cf. now Lorenzo de' Medici, *Lettere*, i, ed. R. Fubini, Florence, 1977, p. 24. On p. xxxvi of Magnani the phrase 'mandate la nomina a marito' must read 'la Nanina'. The Medici may have been partly responsible for the timing of the wedding; Piero de' Medici had written to Lorenzo on 4 May 1465 that 'intorno alle nozze sua [Nannina's] ragionanmo alla tornata tua da Napoli': pub. by A. Fabroni, *Laurentii Medicis Magnifici vita*, Pisa, 1784, ii, p. 52. The *cassone* for the wedding may survive at Paris (see Preyer, *Giovanni Rucellai*, p. 254, n. 13), though Ellen Callmann has kindly told me that she is not certain of this identification.

[4] Rubinstein, *Government*, pp. 155, 161–62, 164.

[5] Benedetto Dei, "Memorie storiche", in Bayerische Staatsbibliothek, Munich, cod. ital. 160, f. 116; Rucellai, then 67, was presumably not a participant (cf. f. 138). On 26 February 1421, at a joust-cum-ball in the Mercato Nuovo, 'l'onore diedono alla figliuola di Salvestro Orlandi, e l'altro al figliuolo di Pagolo di messer Pauolo [sic] Rucellai', who would most probably have been Giovanni, the eldest of the four brothers: G. O. Corazzini, "Diario fiorentino di Bartolommeo di Michele del Corazza, anni 1405–1438", *ASI*, ser. 5, XIV (1894), p. 277.

[6] I can find no political references to Rucellai in the Munich manuscript cited in the preceding note, nor in Dei's "Cronica" (Manoscritti, 119), nor in his "Memorie curiosissime" (BNC, II, II, 333), unless one "Ser [?] Zanni Ruciellai" is to be identified with Giovanni (f. 18r). Consulte e Pratiche, 60 (1467–80), yields several contributions by a Giovanni Rucellai (ff. 1v, 3r, 9r, 63v, 95v, 96r, 163v), some of which may even belong to his kinsman Giovanni di Cardinale, who also spoke (see ff. 47v, 49v). Contributions to the *consulte* were, however, in general much thinner in this period than earlier.

niminici e nimici [sic] dello stato quel numero che a nnoi pareva e chi a nnoi piaceva'—which reveals his delight in simply holding high position as much as in exercising power[1]. When he was Prior in 1463 his political style was certainly relaxed, unless Donato Acciaiuoli's description is all literary artifice: the two friends, until recently both suspect, talked much 'di chose morali' during their joint tenure, the younger man learning much from Giovanni's 'prudence and counsel' and taking 'grande iocondità . . . della vostra iocondissima conversatione'[2]. Committed to his Medici relations he was, but there is little reason to believe with Edgar Wind that at about this time Giovanni, who was not a learned man, knowingly accepted the full Platonic implications of Marsilio Ficino's pro-Medicean account of the role in human affairs of Fortuna, and thereby approved of rule by an absolute if benevolent prince[3]. This is to make Rucellai at once more politically alert and sophisticated, and more subservient to his Medici *parenti*, than he was.

Giovanni's intense personal admiration for Cosimo he had confined to the private pages of the *Zibaldone*, save for his naming Bernardo's first child, born in 1468, 'Chosimo, per memoria di Chosimo di Govanni de' Medici, suo bisavolo' rather than Paolo or Giovanni, his own line's Christian names[4]. He kept (or was kept) a certain distance from the Medici, to whom his letters are almost stilted until the time of Lorenzo, his 'karissimo parente', when social relations were perhaps paradoxically eased by a marked difference in age and experience which made older awkwardnesses and tensions seem increasingly irrelevant[5]. Nor did Giovanni hesitate to confront his newest with his oldest allegiances. If Nannina's first son was named Cosimo and her third Piero, the second boy was called Palla (hardly a reference to the *palle*, or balls, in the Medici arms) and the fourth Giovanni; Rucellai's request in March 1465 to have the exiled Niccolò Ardinghelli granted special permission to visit Florence may have indirectly helped along Lorenzo de' Medici's love affair with Ardinghelli's wife but was probably inspired by the banker's desire to please an intimate connection of the Strozzi[6]. When Lorenzo visited Quaracchi in autumn 1468, perhaps to enjoy one of the boating picnics Luigi Pulci mentions, among the absorbing sights he presumably saw in its carefully planned garden were the box borders Giovanni had described only four years before, which made 'una festa cum molte arme della chasa, e arme de' chasati, dove à maritate le sue figliuole, e de' chasati delle nuore sue, e maximamente quelle della chasa delli Strozzi, del quale è la mia honorevole compagnia'[7]. Bernardo, on the other hand, quickly became part of the Medici circle.

[1] *Zibaldone*, ff. 68v–69r: 'el quale fu riputato el più bello e il più dengno huficio che ssi desse mai nella nostra città di Firenze, e di grandissima autorità' (f. 68v). Cf. Rubinstein, *Government*, pp. 221–22.

[2] Perosa, p. 91. It was perhaps no coincidence that Donato also ceased to be *sospetto* in 1462: Garin, "Donato Acciaiuoli", pp. 89–90. For the two men's discussions on ethics, see *ibid.*, pp. 61–64.

[3] Wind, "Platonic Tyranny and the Renaissance Fortuna", pp. 491–6. Ficino's letter to Rucellai (Perosa, pp. 114–16) is the only evidence of their even knowing each other; cf. R. Marcel, *Marsile Ficin (1433–1499)*, Paris, 1958, pp. 235, 289–90. Bernardo, however, did become an intimate of Ficino's (*ibid.*, see references in the index).

[4] Perosa, p. 35. However, if Giovanni's use on his buildings of the device of the ring and feathers (see p. 29, n. 4 above) was a direct reference to its Medici connotations, this would certainly be an open statement of his regard.

[5] There is not one letter to Cosimo. With Piero de' Medici Rucellai always uses the more formal "voi", calling him 'Hono [revole] come maggiore fratello' (MAP, XVII, 360, 15 February 1464); Lorenzo, to whom he gives the 'tu', is addressed as 'K[arissi]mo come figluolo' (*ibid.*, CXXXVII, 142, 27 April 1465) or later as 'Karissimo parente' (*ibid.*, XXV, 50, 11 May 1471) and 'Figliuolo karo' (*ibid.*, XXIX, 1205, 23 December 1473). Giovanni's letter of 27 June 1464 to Piero announcing his daughter-in-law Caterina's imminent death conventionally ends: 'Disiderre[i] ora avere il consiglo vostro e di Chosimo quello vi pare si debbi fare circha l'onoranza sua, perchè tanto si seghuiterà quanto ne consiglarete' (*ibid.*, XVI, 157). On Cosimo's own death, it was Bernardo, not his father, who wrote a formal letter of condolence (*ibid.*, CLXIII, f. 39v).

[6] Alessandra Strozzi, *Lettere*, pp. 385–86, mentions this intriguing incident when writing to her son Filippo on 29 March. For the Ardinghelli, see pp. 72, n. 5 and 92–93 below.

[7] Perosa, p. 21. Giovanni's letter to Lorenzo of 15 October 1468 began: 'Io ti scrissi circha a un mese fa e dipoi tel dissi a boccha a Quarachi . . .' (MAP, XXI, 109). For Pulci and the picnics, see below, p. 81.

The one personal touch in his father's first letter to Piero is a sentence asking him to urge Bernardo 'a studiare sollecitamente perchè mi rendo cierto che farà più conto dell'amunizione vostre che delle mie'[1]: nine years later Giovanni was to enlist Lorenzo's help—his younger son, it seems, was deliberately annoying a certain 'Messer Tomaso [Soderini ?]'—so that 'arò tenpo a mettello ad ordine che ci farà onore chom' è usato di fare'[2]. Even before the wedding Bernardo was indispensable to Lorenzo's *brigata* of boon companions, whom Giovanni's daughters also joined on one occasion in April 1465[3].

It is almost as if Giovanni Rucellai preferred to leave the social and personal duties attendant on the Medici *parentado* to his son, who relished them all more than was perhaps absolutely necessary, and devoted himself, in a spirit which owed more to traditional aristocratic mores than to novel courtly impulses, to exploiting the new relationship, both for his own sake and for the other 'belli parentadi'[4] he had made. 'Chome per altra v'ò detto', Giovanni wrote to Piero de' Medici on 15 February 1464, 'per gli amici e parenti miei che io stimo sapete che male posso dineghare il servire'. The claim is often repeated in the *Zibaldone*[5] and confirmed by the stream of letters he and Bernardo sent to the Medici on behalf, among others, of kinsmen, other relations, friends and faithful domestic servants. Giovanni's letters have none of the courtly hyperbole even some aristocratic Miceans were using at this time[6]. Along with much other evidence, they suggest that his concerns remained very much the same after as before the Medici marriage—his economic affairs, his building programme and the welfare of the circle of his kinsmen and relations, now enlarged to include the city's leading family—for all that he was properly sensible of the dramatically improved environment in which he could now pursue them.

There were quite as many old as new friends at the June wedding which, despite its boasting about the Medici connection, was a characteristic attempt by Giovanni not to reject his past but to merge it with his future. The names of three of the four knights who accompanied Nannina to her husband suggest older ties and experiences dear to Giovanni: Messer Carlo Pandolfini, his maternal first cousin; Messer Manno Temperanni, his very near neighbour and a man influential in Lion Rosso and beyond[7]; Messer Giovannozzo Pitti, a cousin of Pandolfo Rucellai's brother-in-law

---

[1] *Ibid.*, XVII, 343, 7 November 1462.

[2] *Ibid.*, XXIX, 1205, 23 December 1473. This cryptic note is rather hard to interpret.

[3] On the Laurentian *brigata*, see Rochon, *Jeunesse*, pp. 88 ff., 251 ff. Bernardo's pre-1466 letters to Lorenzo are full of intimate allusions: MAP, CXXXVII, 134, 15 March 1466; 243, 29 March 1466; 961, no date, but belonging to the same series. The April party is mentioned in I. Del Lungo, *Gli amori del Magnifico Lorenzo*, Bologna, 1923, p. 32. It seemed natural to Carlo Scala, when writing to Lorenzo on 14 December 1465, to recommend himself also to Bernardo (MAP, VII, 427; a reference I owe to Alison Brown).

[4] Perosa, p. 118. Elsewhere Rucellai mentions with pride marriages other than the Medici match; pp. 21, 145, n. 1.

[5] MAP, XVII, 360, a letter recommending 'Michelagnolo Tanagli, gienero di Francesco Vettori [whose son Piero had married one of Rucellai's daughters]'. On one's duties to relations, see Perosa, pp. 4 ff., 10–13, and many aphorisms in the unpublished *Zibaldone*: e.g., 'Non ti fidare in colui che non ama i suoi parenti chè chi non ama le sue cose non amerà l'altrui' (f. 36r).

[6] Some of these letters are referred to below, pp. 73 ff. See too Kent, *Household and Lineage*, pp. 97–98, for still others. Only one phrase, quoted below, p. 79, n. 4, from a letter of 9 May 1471 to Lorenzo, suggests a certain willing compliance on Giovanni's part.

[7] In general, see Perosa, p. 28. Interestingly, though all four knights had very solid Micean traditions, Pitti and Temperanni were by 1466 both dissidents who had signed the anti-Micean *sottoscrizione*: Rubinstein, *Government*, p. 157. On Temperanni, see *ibid.*, pp. 27, n. 4, 28, 130, n. 1, 144, 157, 159, 196, and other references. He lived directly opposite Giovanni, on the corner of Via Vigna Nuova and Via de' Palchetti (see Cambi, *Istorie, ed. cit.*, XX, p. 324), and was often at *gonfalone* meetings, for example as Gonfalonier of Company in December 1444, when he was chairman of the important meeting which decided to pay for a choir for San Pancrazio; see above, p. 47, and Diplomatico, San Pancrazio di Firenze, 21 December 1444. When Rucellai, as *procuratore* of Alessandra Strozzi, sold property to Bernardo Rinieri in October 1460, the *mezzano* was Messer Manno, 'il quale riputo in luogho di padre,' Rinieri wrote (Conv. Sopp., 95, 212, f. clviir).

Buonaccorso whose father Luca was a particularly esteemed *parente*[1]. The fourth knight, Messer Tommaso Soderini, also had Rucellai connections, but of a more tenuous and ambiguous kind[2]. At each dinner 'chomunemente si convitava . . . 50 cictadini tra parenti e amici e vicini de' principali della cictà', those 'kinsmen and relatives and neighbours'[3] who had sustained him in the past. The '25 honorevoli anella' given to the bride came from members of this circle. Apart from the rings donated by Giovanni himself, and by his two sons, grandchildren, wife, mother and married daughters, there were gifts from two of Bernardo's paternal first cousins and, further afield, from a neighbour and paternal kinsman Bingeri di Iacopantonio Rucellai[4]. A Strozzi connection, Caterina Ardinghelli, and Messer Tommaso Soderini and Stoldo Frescobaldi also gave rings[5]. Gifts of food and wine were provided by some, among them Giovanni's client cousin Adovardo di Carlo Rucellai[6], two relations by marriage, Zanobi da Diacceto e Iacopo Venturi (Giovanni's son-in-law) and Rinaldo della Luna, a kinsman of the banker's first business partner. Zanobi, 'a noi stretto parente', and Venturi were later to be among those friends Giovanni and Bernardo recommended to the Medici[7].

Rucellai's celebrated account of the wedding—and his later correspondence with the Medici—provide an unusual glimpse of several (perhaps connected) client groups which clustered round Giovanni and gave him some established, indeed independent, identity in the complex Florentine social structure: the peasants from the rural districts where he was a major landowner and certain other followers whom it is harder to identify. The nature and importance of the allegiance these men gave to Giovanni is difficult to analyse; it is evident, however, that he was the centre of a small social network, a patron-client group—one of dozens in Renaissance Florence about which we need to know more—whose membership, united by bonds such as economic dependence or geographical propinquity, was drawn from several social classes and looked to one or more magnates for leadership and for access to still higher powers[8]. In this sense, his other social connections aside, Giovanni was an important man in his own right, the head of his own small pyramid when in June 1466 he attached himself very near to the apex of the Florentine-wide patronage group which the Medici had been busily building up for a generation[9]. Like Florence's leading family, he too had had and

---

[1] See above, p. 29.

[2] This Soderini was a close relative, but also rival, of Francesco di Tommaso Soderini, who had married one of Palla Strozzi's daughters in 1415 (P. Litta, *Celebri famiglie italiane*, Milan, Disp. 141[1861], vol. IX [1868], tav. iii–iv). Giovanni Rucellai stood surety to the politically suspect Francesco in 1437: Otto di Guardia e Balìa, 224, f. 73r and see too Perosa, p. 51. Piero di Messer Tommaso Soderini was to be Rucellai's banking partner in 1478 (Arte del Cambio, 15, f. 65v), the year after he witnessed the notarial act by which Giovanni's grandson married into the Malaspina family (see p. 92, n. 2 below).

[3] Perosa, p. 28; cf. p. 9.

[4] He was also a *parente* through his marriage to a Pandolfini (*Zibaldone*, f. 223v).

[5] Perosa, pp. 29–30. Caterina Ardinghelli was Messer Palla Strozzi's niece, the daughter of his brother Niccolò. For Giovanni's part in the complicated affairs of these Ardinghelli and Strozzi, see below, pp. 92–93.

[6] Perosa, p. 30, and below p. 76.

[7] *Ibid.*, pp. 30–31. Rucellai so describes Zanobi, a kinsman of his brother Filippo Rucellai's wife Francesca da Diacceto, in a letter of 22 August 1472 (MAP, XXVIII, 448). Iacopo Venturi was recommended to Lorenzo by Bernardo Rucellai on 14 April 1483 (*ibid.*, XLVIII, 187), and 12 June 1485 (*ibid.*, LI, 316); he had been the arbiter in a 1465 dispute involving Rucellai (NA, B 1184 [Ser Girolamo Beltramini, 1457–78], inserto 8 [56]).

[8] Recent important contributions to this subject have been made for Florence by Brucker, in "The Structure of Patrician Society in Renaissance Florence", *Colloquium*, I (1964), pp. 2–11; *Renaissance Florence*, pp. 89 ff.; *Civic World*, chap. I, and by D. V. Kent, *Rise of the Medici*, esp. chaps. 1–2. See too the interesting remarks of C.-M. de la Roncière, "Pauvres et pauvreté à Florence au XIVe siècle", in *Études sur l'histoire de la pauvreté*, ed. M. Mollat, Paris, 1974, ii, pp. 742–43. For clientage in Europe in general, see Heers, *Le Clan familial*; cf. my remarks in "A la recherche du clan perdu: Jacques Heers and 'Family Clans' in the Middle Ages", *Journal of Family History*, II (1977), pp. 77–86. D. V. Kent and I are currently preparing a study of patronage and client groups in Medicean Florence.

[9] D. V. Kent, *Rise of the Medici, passim*.

was still to have his servants, even perhaps his creatures whose contribution to his career may have been far greater than the sources permit one to say.

It was to this group of 'più servidori e amici della chasa' that Rucellai gave, on the occasion of the wedding, seventy pairs of cloth stockings with his device (*alla divisa*), presumably the Rucellai arms if not some more personal insignia[1]. These 'friends' were not apparently Giovanni's domestic servants or *famigli* who were separately consigned '12 paia di chalze a divisa'[2], but their willingness to wear his livery probably means that they were of humbler origin than he, men such as his rural factors and leading tenants perhaps, or the unknown 'Guasparre di Tomaxo amico nostro di casa' mentioned by Bernardo in a letter[3]. One of Giovanni's close associates, who would have been among the *famigli* wearing the stockings, was his servant Marco di Bartolo da Vicchio. Of Marco, often mentioned in documents and his proxy in the land purchase of 1461 which helped finance the façade of Santa Maria Novella, Giovanni wrote to Piero de' Medici that 'portogli amore e disidero assai fagli questo bene'[4]. Domenico di Piero da Signa, another manservant, was 'mio amicissimo' according to Bernardo Rucellai, whom he had nursed through a serious illness in 1472. For Domenico's sake Giovanni later risked offending Messer Bartolomeo Scala, the republic's chancellor, when recommending the *famiglio* for a position with the Signoria[5]. In this as in some other respects, Giovanni Rucellai's actions were surprisingly consistent with his advice in the *Zibaldone*, where in 1457 he had counselled his sons 'essere liberali et cortesi a' servi di casa', whose loyalty should be rewarded with humanity and help. He was a master who talked to his dependents, one who thought it better to be loved than feared, though he honestly admitted that in one's dealing with servants 'noi siano tanto dilicati, che noi arabiamo incontenente che ci manca alcuna pichola cosa della nostra volontà!'[6].

There were other clients and friends of the family who if they did not wear the stockings provided

---

[1] Perosa, p. 29; cf. Heers, *Le Clan familial*, pp. 242–3, and his *Fêtes, jeux et joutes dans les sociétés d'Occident à la fin du Moyen Age*, Montreal-Paris, 1971, pp. 77 ff. In his 1465 will, Giovanni ordered 'xxiiii sui signi, videlicet insignium domus de Oricellariis circa lectulum ipsum' (NA, L 130 [Ser Lionardo da Colle, 1441–95], no. 31). Another contemporary example confirms that the expression refers to a heraldic device (cf. Molinari, *Spettacoli fiorentini*, p. 17).

[2] Perosa, p. 34. His establishment seven years later consisted of 'tre...famigli in chasa e quattro in cinque serve, cioè schiave, e uno maestro per insegnare a' fancugli' (p. 121).

[3] MAP, XXI, 154, to Lorenzo de' Medici, undated but between 1464–9 (see Rochon, *Jeunesse*, p. 57, n. 142). In 1473, Giovanni had 'tre fattori salariati alle mie possessioni' (Perosa, p. 121).

[4] The brief note is worth quoting in full for its businesslike pursuit of the manservant's interests: 'Io disiderrei darvi faticha che voi fussi operatore che Marcho mio famiglo fusse messo in palagio per maziere in luogho d'uno ch'è morto stanotte; egl'è stato mecho anni 15 e portogli amore e disidero assai fagli questo bene. Racomandovelo quanto più stretamente posso, non avendo voi fatto inpresa per altri' (MAP, VII, 378, undated). I have not been able to discover if the petition was successful; in the 1440s, however, Piero di Giorgio, one of Giovanni's *famigli*, had become 'famiglio in palagio' (Conv. Sopp., 88, 23, ff. 2r, 13v, 14r). For Marco's witnessing notarial acts for his master, see NA, B 397 (Ser Baldovino Baldovini, 1465–68), f. 158r; C 407 (Ser Pierozzo Cerbini, 1456–65), f. 120r; V 298 (Ser Nastagio Vespucci, 1450–69), f. 124r; see p. 49, n. 4 above for his important role as proxy purchaser. The 'Nanni di Bartolo da Vicchio, uno fattore in villa', mentioned in Rucellai's 1458 tax report was presumably Marco's brother (Cat., 816, f. 63r).

[5] 'Sendo venuto il tenpo che la nuova Signoria potrà eleggiere lo schanbio di quello tavolacino che rifiutò a mia stanza, ti priegho che tu provegha in quello modo ti pare che in suo luogho sia eletto Domenicho di Piero da Signa mio famiglo, aportatore di questa; e anchora sarebbe di bisogno che tu fussi operatore che Messer Bartolomeo Schala chancielliere non ci noiasse per chagone di cierta autorità che gli fu concieduta di potere elegiere uno tavolacino per servire la persona sua' (MAP, XXV, 443, 29 August 1476). Giovanni softened the letter with a postscript saying that 'Puoi molto larghamente fare fede al chancelliere che quello tavolacino che rifiutò non arebbe rifiutato se non perch'io fussi servito per questo mio famiglo in suo luogho'. Bernardo had also recommended Domenico to Lorenzo on 5 December 1472: 'è stato sempre mio amicissimo ma hora in questa malattia s'è portato in modo verso di me che io giudicho potere per pochi huomini operarmi a chui io sia più obrigato' (*ibid.*, LXXIII, 401). His father reported Bernardo's serious illness as early as August of that year (*ibid.*, XXVIII, 448). Domenico also witnessed a notarial act for the Rucellai (NA, G 620 [Ser Simone Grazzini, 1472–94], ff. 3r, 14r–v).

[6] Perosa, p. 13.

by Giovanni served, and were rewarded by, him and his sons in a not dissimilar spirit. These included relatively obscure men of his own class, such as Simone Mazzinghi, 'amico nostro' and 'molto familiare di Pandolfo e mio dimestico'[1], or the mysterious 'Canpolo' [Giampaolo] of one of Giovanni's letters[2], or coming 'new men', the Bongianni or Borgianni brothers for example, whose father had done business with Giovanni in 1458 and who later became very faithful followers of the Rucellai[3]. Closely associated with these Rucellai for many years were a number of notaries, often local men, on whose efficiency and discretion Giovanni depended. In his early days there had been Palla Strozzi's notary, Ser Tommaso Carondini, and at the time of the wedding in 1466 Ser Baldovino Baldovini, his 'k[arissi]mo amico', also from Lion Rosso[4]. Later still Ser Antonio and Ser Niccolò Ferrini, from another *gonfalone* of the quarter of Santa Maria Novella, worked a good deal for the Rucellai. In 1495 Ser Antonio, this 'amico di casa nostra' as Giovanni's grandson was later to describe him when recommending Zanobi Ferrini to the Medici, together with Ser Lionardo Beltramini da Colle, who with his brother Ser Girolamo and their father Ser Giovanni turn up in other documents[5], helped Paolo di Pandolfo to ransack the private family archive for the missing register made in Giovanni's day[6].

Rucellai's country following can be more certainly identified. For Bernardo and Nannina, as for Pandolfo ten years earlier, there were gifts in kind from a number of rural communes and *contadini* closely linked with the Rucellai. Several men 'da Quarachi', including tenants, each gave 'paia 2 di paperi' while 'più huomini da Charmignano', near the Poggio a Caiano estate and still good olive country, excelled themselves with '1 magnificho ulivo in sun un carro'. This relationship—the reciprocity of which Giovanni acknowledged by providing '4 vitelli per dar mangiare a' chontadini[7]', —drew its strength from Giovanni's long association with these districts, especially Quaracchi and nearby Brozzi, northwest of Florence towards Pistoia and only a few kilometres from Campi, the

---

[1] Bernardo Rucellai to Lorenzo de' Medici, MAP, XXIX, 573, 3 August 1473.

[2] On 23 October 1473, Giovanni wrote to Lorenzo that 'Io disidero usare una chortesia a Canpolo per la buona sua conpagnia di 50 anni fa . . .' (MAP, XXIX, 1205). This is presumably the 'Ciampolum ser Zenobii civem florentinum' Rucellai appointed his *procuratore* on 5 March 1474 (NA, F 239 [Ser Niccolò Ferrini, 1471–77], f. 595ʳ), and who had owed him a small sum in 1458 (Cat., 817, f. 216ᵛ). A Strozzi letter of 1475, addressed to 'Campolo di Ser Zanobi', has a recommendation to Bernardo Rucellai (CS, III, 247, f. 6ʳ⁻ᵛ).

[3] Descended from a *tintore*, Mino di Borgianni di Mino Guarzini (Cat., 72, f. 36ʳ⁻ᵛ, a reference I owe to Florence Edler de Roover), Iacopo and Francesco, who were fifteen and twelve respectively in 1458, came from the quarter of Santa Croce: see their father's *portata*, ibid., 805, ff. 939ʳ ff., with a reference to dealings with Rucellai. In 1474, Iacopo became Giovanni's banking partner, Francesco joining him in 1478: Arte del Cambio, 15, ff. 49ʳ, 54ʳ, 59ʳ, 65ᵛ. After Giovanni's death in 1481, Iacopo appears in Bernardo Rucellai's letters to Lorenzo de' Medici as a trusted confidant (MAP, LI, 164, 169, 179, June–August 1482), and Rucellai vigorously supported Francesco's political career (ibid., XLVIII, 111, 19 October 1482) and, 'per l'interessi sai ho con lui', Iacopo's concerns (ibid., 268, 1 December 1484). For the latter's relationship with Pandolfo in the 'nineties, and on the Bongianni brothers in general, see Ristori, "Un mercante savonaroliano", pp. 45–46; and Spedale di San Matteo, 30, f. 322ʳ, and *passim*.

[4] On both men, see above, pp. 24; 28, n. 4; 64; and on Carondini, Kent, *Household and Lineage*, p. 134, n. 49. Ser Baldovino's manuscript life of Antoninus came to be owned by Pandolfo Rucellai (Morçay, *Saint Antonin*, p. viii).

[5] Ser Lionardo drew up Giovanni's last will and a number of other acts, as did Ser Girolamo. Elaine Rosenthal kindly drew my attention to a number of the latter's protocols. On 5 March 1474, two of four procurators appointed by Rucellai were the Beltramini brothers (NA, F 239, [Ser Niccolò Ferrini, 1471–77], f. 595ʳ). Their father Ser Giovanni witnessed Pandolfo's emancipation in an act of Ser Girolamo's (ibid., B 1184 [Ser Girolamo Beltramini, 1457–78], inserto 3, f. 21). Rucellai, as *procuratore* of Alessandra Strozzi, sold some of her property to this man in 1459 (CS, III, 116, f. 55ʳ).

[6] Spedale di San Matteo, 30, f. 357ʳ⁻ᵛ, a letter of Paolo Rucellai to his father Pandolfo dated 23 October 1495. For the reference to Ser Antonio, see the letter of 17 February 1514, from Giovanni di Bernardo Rucellai to Lorenzo de' Medici, pub. by Kent, "Due Lettere", pp. 568–9; see too pp. 566–7.

[7] Perosa, pp. 30–32. For Pandolfo's wedding in 1456, there had been gifts from the *popoli* of Quaracchi, Petriuolo, Peretola and San Donnino (BNC, II, IV, 374, f. 131).

original home of the Rucellai family where most of them still concentrated their estates and villas: 'Rispecto alle possessioni abbiamo su questa strada, tegnano molte amicitie nel contado di Pistoia perchè è necessario spesso affatichiano e' parenti e gl'amici', Bernardo told Giuliano de' Medici in May 1474[1].

At the Quaracchi *possessione,* which had been in his line since at least his grandfather's day, Giovanni let to the same peasant tenants and their families for several generations. Here at his country home commercial leases did not rule out the existence of enduring relationships between peasant and lord. In every *catasto* report of the fifteenth century—from 1427 to 1480—'Pippo del Re' or his son Antonio were leasing from Giovanni. Even earlier, in 1406, the name of Antonio di Dino da Quaracchi was associated with the estate, as were his sons and grandsons until at least 1458. Nanni del Ciochero da Quaracchi and his son or grandson, and a number of men all possessing the name 'Tante', were similarly prominent there for some forty years[2]. It was in conversation with men such as these, the *antichi* of this parish set in 'il più bello sito di quello piano', that Giovanni discussed the weather and harvests at Quaracchi, noting down many interesting details in the *Zibaldone* where he also copied a *ricordo*, mentioning his grandfather, from an old book brought him by an ancient peasant who clearly understood his landlord's preoccupations[3]. Giovanni's pleasure garden at the villa included a wood which was semi-public, intended not only for 'noi di chasa e del paese' but for travellers who could rest there and enjoy the other 'chose molte gentile'[4]. This, and his bequest of dowries for poor girls born and brought up in the district, were among the 'molti benefici' Giovanni had given his rural dependants[5]. Further research might well show that a close relationship between urban lords and their rural clients lasted longer into the Renaissance period, and was in several senses more important and at times less antagonistic than has been assumed[6]. Giovanni presumably did not regard the peasants of this mild farming country so close to Florence as a source of armed retainers—as the *contadini* of the wilder Mugello were for the Medici[7]—but one would like to know more about this small rural society of which he was a leader and whence he drew some of his wealth and standing.

The Medici connection confirmed Giovanni's leading position in yet another respect, among his

---

[1] MAP, V, 807, 6 May; see too a much later letter of 17 December 1490, from Cosimo Rucellai, recommending to Ser Andrea da Foiano certain 'amici mia da Pistoia' (*ibid.,* LXXVI, 236). For the Campi district and the Rucellai, see Kent, *Household and Lineage*, pp. 130, 234–7, 257, n. 106.

[2] Precise references would make a very long list; this statement is compiled from the following *catasti*: Cat., 43, ff. 867r–70v; 367, ff. 597r–600v; 620, parte ii, ff. 574r–v, 579r; 460, ff. 493r–97r; 672, ff. 535r–v, 570r–71r; 707, ff. 402r–404r; 816, ff. 60r–63v; 919, ff. 376r–80v; 1011, ff. 341r–44v. The 1406 reference to Dini comes from Pupilli, 17, f. liiiv. Bartolo di Giovanni di Nanni del Ciochero witnessed a land purchase at Quaracchi for Giovanni in 1462 (NA, V 298 [Ser Nastagio Vespucci, 1450–69] f. 124r). Salvestro di Nanni del Ciochero rented the lands devoted to Santa Maria Novella in 1461 (Conv. Sopp., 102, 308, f. 95v). At Quaracchi Giovanni held a little land *a sua mano*, but most of it was leased by fixed rent or *a mezzo*. Here see P. J. Jones, "From Manor to Mezzadria: A Tuscan Case-Study in the Medieval Origins of Modern Agrarian Society", in *Florentine Studies*, ed. N. Rubinstein, London, 1968, pp. 193–241.

[3] *Zibaldone*, f. 225r: the *ricordo* concerns a famine in 1370, and Messer Paolo's attempts to find bread, 'per tutto dal ponte a Peretola per insino al ponte a San Donino'. Perosa, p. 23, gives the quotation. See *Zibaldone*, ff. 66v–67r, for Giovanni's jottings and his references to the opinions of 'tutti gl'antichi huomini e donne' and 'alchuno uomo anticho'.

[4] Perosa, p. 21.

[5] *Ibid.*, pp. 23, 122, and p. 93 below. Rucellai does not appear to have been the patron of the church of San Piero a Quaracchi (see E. Repetti, *Dizionario geografico-fisico-storico della Toscana*, Florence, 1841, iv, p. 689), but the rector there for at least thirteen years, Ser Lionardo di Giovanni, witnessed an important act concerning several lines of the Rucellai family in February 1460 (NA, B 385 [Ser Baldovino Baldovini, 1450–59], f. 327r); cf. Orlandi, *S. Antonino*, i, p. 173, for a reference to him in 1447.

[6] But cf. de la Roncière, "Pauvres et pauvreté", p. 743.

[7] D. V. Kent, *Rise of the Medici*, pp. 337–8; cf. pp. 40, 117.

Rucellai kinsmen, one of whom, a distant cousin, claimed to be a *parente* of Lorenzo in 1477 apparently because of the 1466 alliance[1]. Giovanni was always respectful of his Rucellai ancestry, happy to have been born of 'buona stirpe, cioè di nobile sangue' as he wrote in 1464[2]. His repeated advice to his sons to help paternal kinsmen was quickly followed by Bernardo, who recommended to the Medici in the first year of his marriage a very distant Rucellai cousin, poor but a 'buono huomo', because 'così mi costrigne a ffare il debito della casa', and then, some years later, another *consorto* older than himself, Mariotto di Piero[3]. Giovanni's leadership was explicitly acknowledged by his eight Rucellai cousins who in late 1465 and early 1466 made him their agent in settling the affairs of the lineage's *spedale* at Osmannoro. 'Chome prochuratore di tutti e miej chonsorti della nostra famigla' he gave the hospital into the hands of the Austin Friars on 12 March 1470, demanding from them a tribute of fish which, appropriately enough, 'debbino chonsengnare nella logga de' Rucellaj'[4]. Adovardo di Carlo, who was to have 'la prima parte, e lla maggore . . . per memoria che il primo fondatore di detto luogho [the *spedale*] fu Cennj di Nardo Rucellaj suo anticho'[5], was a genuine client of his distant cousin Giovanni, and a close friend of Pandolfo[6]. As devoted in his way to corporate Rucellai affairs as the far richer man, Adovardo encounters Giovanni several times in this period and afterwards, for example because of their shared interest in the lineage's chapel of St. Catherine the Martyr. For this in his will of February 1465, Adovardo's father had given Giovanni certain responsibilities[7]. Other distant Rucellai kinsmen worked or acted for Giovanni at this time, Filippo d'Amerigo in Venice[8] and Antonio di Sandro, of a collateral line, as an agent in Florence[9].

Less in the public eye were Rucellai's activities on behalf of his brothers' children (hardly distinguished young men whom he helped as he had their fathers). No doubt remembering his own early life, Giovanni became responsible for the three sons of Donato in mid-1460, and for some years they lived near him in the same parish[10]. In 1473 Agnolo di Donato and his brothers were Giovanni's partners in a 'compagnia d'arte di lana', a practical attempt to share his experience and affluence which miscarried in the economic crises of the following years[11]. Presumably Giovanni's influence also lay behind the choice of career made by Silvestro, Paolo's bastard son, who became a respected Dominican of Santa Maria Novella[12]. Filippo, the rather ugly 'Pippo Lungo', was Giovanni's

---

[1] See Kent, *Household and Lineage*, p. 263, n. 132. The cousin was Giovanni di Cardinale. However, another man of this line, Bernardo di Piero di Cardinale, was still a very influential Rucellai leader at this time.

[2] Perosa, p. 118; see above, pp. 16–17, and Kent, *Household and Lineage*, pp. 274–78, for Giovanni's interest in Rucellai traditions.

[3] Pub. in *ibid.*, pp. 154–5: see too pp. 201–2 for Mariotto's successful nomination to the *Otto*. This Rucellai had been in debt to Giovanni in 1458 (Cat., 816, f. 62ᵛ).

[4] The quotations are in Kent, "Loggia", p. 399: see too pp. 397–401.

[5] *Ibid.*

[6] Kent, *Household and Lineage*, p. 181.

[7] NA, P 339 (Ser Piero da Campi, 1457–1518), no. 28; Kent, *Household and Lineage*, pp. 268–70. I now find that Adovardo witnessed the important notarial act of 1477 concerning Cosimo di Bernardo's betrothal to a daughter of Marquis Gabriello Malaspina (see below, p. 92 n. 2).

[8] See above, p. 35. Lorenzo di Giovanni di Cardinale may also have represented Rucellai in Constantinople in 1470, though I am not sure of this: *ibid.*, p. 68, but cf. above, p. 36, n. 2.

[9] NA, B 1184 (Ser Girolamo Beltramini, 1457–78), inserto 7(38), 14 March 1463; B 397 (Ser Baldovino Baldovini, 1465–68), ff. 221ᵛ–22ʳ, 4 July 1467. In March 1465 Pandolfo Rucellai had advanced 200 florins to Antonio, thus enabling him to gain control over two farms, the 'fondo dotale' of his wife (Cat., 919, f. 71ᵛ [Antonio's *portata*]).

[10] NA, C 407 (Ser Pierozzo Cerbini, 1456–65), ff. 145ʳ–46ᵛ; cf. f. 120ʳ. Their tax report for 1469 is Cat., 919, f. 78ʳ. They also owned 'una mezza bottegha per non divisa chon Giovanni Rucellai nostro zio'.

[11] Cat., 1011, f. 58ʳ. Agnolo di Donato bought a house in Giovanni's street from the abbot of San Pancrazio in June 1477, a transaction which suggests the banker's influence: *ibid.*, and Conv. Sopp., 88, 57, f. 10ʳ. His two brothers rented a house from Tommaso di Neri Ardinghelli, another close connection of Giovanni's (Cat., 1012, ff. 28ʳ–29ʳ).

[12] Orlandi, *Necrologio*, i, pp. 177–8. Father Orlandi (ii, p. 294) suggests Fra Andrea Rucellai's influence. See too Passerini,

favourite brother—there had been talk of naming one of Bernardo's sons after him[1]—and his child Ridolfo apparently also found a special place among Giovanni's family. Ridolfo was recommended as a *veduto* Gonfalonier of Justice, a great honour, by his first cousin Bernardo on 3 June 1485[2]. Later in the Savonarolan period, he followed Pandolfo's far less worldly example by becoming a Dominican friar, persuading his wife to take religious vows, so the story runs, only to find when he came to reverse his hasty decision that she would not change hers[3]. Giovanni Rucellai's brothers and nephews neither had nor acquired his sense of judgement, perhaps because of his very willingness to come to their rescue.

The Strozzi theme in Rucellai's life became at once more complex and less prominent after the early 1460s. He and his sons were still and long remained in touch with various members of the family—Bernardo recommended to the Medici several Strozzi, connected by marriage to Pandolfo, as 'amorevoli e buoni parenti'[4]. With Palla's heirs his continued relations were complicated, and for a while disturbed, by the intricate terms of the various agreements, some of them secret, by which Rucellai had come to own, with the obligation to sell back on request, parts of Strozzi's estate. Two acts of 1470–71 made between Giovanni and the heirs represent an attempt to sort out the legal and financial ambiguities and may reflect Strozzi disquiet at Rucellai intentions. By this time Palla's surviving sons and grandsons in Ferrara apparently neither wanted nor expected to receive back the Florentine lands in question, their main concern being to ensure that they were compensated for the modest prices Giovanni had paid under the original agreements[5].

The details are obscure and in some respects contradictory. The properties became legally Giovanni's in 1470–71—and another tied ex-Strozzi estate had certainly been cleared of obligation around the same time[6]—but one of Palla's grandsons, Bardo, could claim in 1497 that he still had

---

Rucellai, tav. xvi, and Paolo's last tax report written in Giovanni's hand; Cat., 816, f. 1044r. In the *Zibaldone*, f. 2r, Giovanni calls Silvestro 'non legiptimo nato a Napoli'. Two recently consulted acts of 1465 show Pandolfo's role in his cousins' affairs after Paolo's death (NA, B 1184 [Ser Girolamo Beltramini, 1457–78], inserto 8 [70], [79]).

[1] See Poliziano's story, quoted in Kent, *Household and Lineage*, p. 47, and above, p. 20, n. 1. On 3 February 1462, the abbot of San Pancrazio noted that 'fece Giovanni di Paolo Rucellai l'uficio per l'anima di Pippo Lungo suo fra[tello]' (Conv. Sopp., 88, 23, f. 51r). It is possible that Donato's death was not so solicitously attended to (cf. f. 46r).

[2] MAP, LI, 314.

[3] See Passerini, *Rucellai*, pp. 130–2, and G. M. Brocchi, *Vite di santi e beati fiorentini*, Florence and Pisa, 1765, parte 2, ii, pp. 339–47. Cammilla, Ridolfo's wife, became a *beata*. He remembered her still, generously, in his last will of 7 April 1513, in which he named as heirs his sister and Pandolfo Rucellai's grandson Filippo (NA, F 235 [Ser Antonio Ferrini, 1500–31], f. 126r–v). For further evidence of Ridolfo's relations with Giovanni's family, see Kent, *Household and Lineage*, pp. 61–62 (Decima Reppublicana, 23, f. 377r; NA, F 239 [Ser Niccolò Ferrini, 1471–77], ff. 804v–805v, 833r–v).

[4] Quoted in Kent, *Household and Lineage*, p. 98, n. 155. See too Bernardo's recommendation of one Girolamo Strozzi on 17 August 1472 (MAP, XXVIII, 416). Messer Roberto Strozzi in Ferrara ended a letter to Filippo Strozzi by asking to be remembered to 'Giovan Ruccellai et figliuoli et a Strozzo nostro' (CS, III, 131, f. 9r, 17 November 1471; cf. a similar Ferrarese letter of April 1485, *ibid.*, 133, f. 139r).

[5] NA, B 1186 (Ser Girolamo Beltramini, 1468–71), unfoliated, 19 October 1470, is an agreement between Giovanni Rucellai and Niccolò di Messer Palla and Bardo and Messer Lorenzo di Lorenzo di Messer Palla (there is a number of lacunae and cancellations). It is followed by an almost identical act, but without dates and with even more gaps, apparently between Rucellai and the two Strozzi grandsons, Niccolò's name having been cancelled; the document concerning him alone is in fact at 4 November 1471. There is also a copy of the *compositio* with the grandsons, dated 4 August 1471 and without lacunae, in AS Ferr., Notarile antico, Giacomo Vincenzi, matricola 177, pacco 16/5, unfoliated. See above, pp. 46–49. Cf. Diplomatico, Strozzi Uguccione, 5 April 1475, which throws light on these documents, and several letters by Bardo and Lorenzo Strozzi to Filippo Strozzi in mid-1475, asking for his help to pay to Giovanni Rucellai the *sodamenti* for the purchases made from Palla many years before. In fact they had asked Rucellai himself that 'ci sodi per una parte ed è stato contento' (CS, III, 133, f. 17r, 29 May 1475; cf. *ibid.*, 247, ff. 9r, 11r).

[6] See *ibid.*, 180, ff. 127r–28r, a declaration made in Ferrara and dated 24 July 1464, in which Bardo and Messer Lorenzo renounce all such rights over a house their mother had sold to Girolamo Giachinotti in 1460; see also Diplomatico, Strozzi Uguccione, 5 April 1475. For the original terms, similar to those usually asked of Rucellai, see NA, G 616 (Ser Simone Grazzini, 1460–62), ff. 53r–56v, the sale document. Rucellai had been the *procuratore*.

'qualche ragone . . . nel poggio a chaiano' and that Pandolfo Rucellai agreed with him[1]. Earlier, however, throughout the 'seventies and after Poggio had been sold, Bardo and his brother Messer Lorenzo had sought and copiously received Giovanni's help in their attempt to win back their Florentine house from some Ardinghelli relations[2]. The incident does not suggest that either of them then regarded Giovanni as having betrayed the trust their grandfather had placed in him in his last will of 1462, not to say for thirty years before that date. Even after the Medici betrothal, Strozzi had had no hesitation in giving Giovanni wide powers as executor, both in Venice and Florence, and in naming as his associates Pandolfo and Filippo d'Amerigo Rucellai, Giovanni's distant cousin and Venetian agent. 'Confidomi nella virtù sua e nella dilectione che cci porta', Palla had written of Giovanni, whom nonetheless he regarded from a realistic, not wholly uncritical position. One of the most interesting passages in this will is Palla's long account of a dispute he had had with his son-in-law, apparently in the early 'forties, concerning a piece of Strozzi property which the younger man had bought without his permission. This action earned what might seem, given Giovanni's proved devotion, an over-sharp rebuke, which was nevertheless accepted humbly and with protestations of loyalty[3]. Rucellai's sense of commitment to Palla's heirs, especially to the third generation, was probably less intense, but it may not be merely a lapse into biographer's partiality to suggest that he had little cause to be ashamed of his dealings with them, for all that Bardo Strozzi claimed that Pandolfo wanted in 1497 'sharichare la choscienzia [about Poggio] e andare in paradiso'[4]. This statement may tell us as much about Pandolfo, who by then had renounced Giovanni's world and preoccupations to follow Savonarola, as about his father and his activities, which could hardly withstand scrutiny from that severe point of view. 'Sempre nostro padre e noi suoi figliuoli' had considered these Strozzi 'per buoni e cari parenti', Bernardo told the widow of Giovanfrancesco di Palla, his father's former partner, in an intimate letter of 14 October 1482. Perhaps the last word should be left to Pandolfo's more worldly brother[5].

Giovanni's acquisitive spirit burnt if anything harder and brighter in his more comfortable Medicean period, when his need for funds for building came at a time of economic difficulty for

---

[1] This passage is from a letter to Savonarola, pub. by G. Biagi, "Spigolature savonaroliane", *Rivista delle biblioteche e degli archivi*, IX (1898), p. 83. Judging from the available documents, I cannot see how such a claim could be justified for the *possessione* at Poggio (just after 4 August 1471 Rucellai confidently went ahead to settle its future [Perosa, pp. 25–26]). The villa itself is not mentioned in the 1470–71 acts but might have been included in one of the private pacts to which one finds references. The alienation of all or part of the estate, bought by the Medici and in 1497 to be sold by the commune to 'una persona aliena', was the rub. However, the letter's text appears to be corrupt (Gino Corti was unable to trace the original for me, from Biagi's reference), and one cannot be certain about the whole affair.

[2] See below, pp. 92–93. By means of Filippo Strozzi, Bardo was in correspondence with Pandolfo Rucellai in June–July 1482 (CS, III, 247, ff. 173ʳ, 175ʳ) and again in 1494 (*ibid.*, 133, f. 164ʳ; cf. below, p. 92). He recommended himself 'al mio nipote Chosimo Rucellai vostro chonpagno' in a letter to Alfonso Strozzi of 3 March 1496 (*ibid.*, f. 173ʳ).

[3] AS Ferr., Archivio Bentivoglio, lib. 6, 34, ff. 43–45, and *passim*; the quotation is at f. 55.

[4] Biagi, "Spigolature savonaroliane", p. 83. Pandolfo had probably come to dislike many things his father had done and stood for, not just his banking activities (see above, p. 32) but his building programme, which would have been offensive to a Savonarolian. Interestingly, an entry of 6 May 1497 in a *ricordanze* belonging to San Marco notes that in the will Pandolfo had made before becoming a friar, he had retained "cierta quantità di danari et iuri[s]ditione sopra le chose sua di fare e dispensare chome gli paressi per ischaricho della coscientia sua" (Biblioteca Medicea-Laurenziana, S. Marco, 903, fol. 9ʳ). Apparently the will, which has not so far come to light, was concerned with 'restitutione'. A further testament, dated 22 April 1496, has now been brought to my attention by Gino Corti: NA, G 429 (Ser Giovanni da Romena, 1496–97), fols. 357ʳ–58ʳ. Its terms differ from those described in the above *ricordo*, but one clause also concerns a provision "pro exoneratione sue conscientiae et dicti Iohannis eius patris" (fol. 357ᵛ).

[5] Biblioteca Communale, Forlì. Autografi Piancastelli, 1902, 14 October 1482 (from a photocopy kindly sent me by Professor W. Vichi). The context is, admittedly, a refusal to help Luisa Strozzi with her financial problems, but Bernardo's account of his own misfortunes was quite true (see below, p. 90), and he concluded by saying that 'tucto quello possiamo o vaglamo qui [Milan] e a Firenze ne potete così disporre come de' più cari parenti che abbiate'.

many Florentine businessmen. His genuine concern for his network of friends and relations did not imply neglect of his own interests. The very first surviving letter to the Medici, of 7 November 1462, was to seek Piero's help in extracting 425 florins 'ch'io debbo avere da figliuoli di Bartolomeo da Chastagniuolo' of Milan. Milanese citizens 'non possono essere presi in persona sanza licienza del ducha', and so Giovanni asked Piero for a letter to the Duke 'tanto chalda quanto essere possa che li piacia dare detta licienza e anchora d'essere operatore che mi sia fatto il dovere ecc.', and suggested he write others to 'Messer Agnolo [Acciaiuoli] o ad altri' whose intercession might be useful[1]. The ready availability of such high level personal and diplomatic help would have delighted Rucellai all the more since the Signoria's formal letter of 15 June 1461 to the Duke on this very issue had not persuaded the Milanese to take action[2]. Medici backing on this, or similar occasions, must often have been effective: Giovanni confidently expected 'buono frutto' from Lorenzo's attempts, with Pigello Portinari, 'rischuotere cierti danari ch'io resto avere da Piero del corte milanese' in April 1465[3]. A little later he was grateful to learn 'che avevi dato principio a parlare con Pigiello del favore ti richiesi di parlare chol Magnifico Conte Ghuasparre per chagione de' danari. . .'[4]. In the preceding year Cosimo himself had sent word to Rucellai, a restless creditor, to be patient[5].

Tighter economic circumstances after December 1464, when the Strozzi letters are full of disastrous bankruptcies, may have intensified the sharp way with creditors any 'sollecito e diligente' medieval businessman had to adopt[6]. In the short or even medium run, however, Giovanni emerged from the 1460s in remarkably good condition: his 'ricordo del 1464', with its happy acknowledgement 'della buona fortuna che [messer Domenedio] m'à conceduta nel mio traffichare' could as well have been written in very late as in early 1464[7]. Unlike his ex-partner Giovanfrancesco Strozzi, Rucellai was not among the bankrupts of whom Piero di Dietisalvi wrote on 26 December 'noi siano stati parechi dì molto attoniti per la ruina de' falliti da Firenze'[8]. There were however

[1] MAP, XVII, 343. Giovanni's tax report of 1458 lists dealings with these men (Cat., 817, ff. 209ᵛ, 211ʳ).

[2] Signori—Carteggio, Missive, Registri, 43, ff. 141ᵛ–42ʳ.

[3] Pub. by Kent, "Letters", p. 349, with 'corte milanese' incorrectly given as 'arte milanese'.

[4] MAP, XX, 154, 18 May 1465. However Giovanni did not always quickly or automatically get his way with the Medici. A letter of 15 October 1468 to Lorenzo asks for his intercession with Betto Rustichi over some disputed woods (ibid., XXI, 109), but three years later, though the matter had gone to arbitration, it was in effect still unsettled, Lorenzo's 'speaking' to Betto not having produced the desired result: 'e Betto si tira adrieto e dicie che la madre non se ne contenta e fra pochi dì si parte di qui e va podestà; e anchora ci è peggio chè 'gl'à fatto taglare uno boscho a questi dì che per santenzia [sic] m'era stato giudichato, sichè io sono in pigiore grado che inanzi che tu gli parlassi. Io non so indovinare ma ongni picholo acienno ch'io avessi che questa fusse la tua volontà resterrei più che paziente e mai più ne farei parola. Piaciati dimostrarmi la tua intenzione e volontà' (ibid., XXV, 50, 9 May 1471). Giovanni was probably right in thinking that Lorenzo, for reasons of his own, did not wish to press Rustichi who, having arrived at Peccioli as podestà, wrote to him on 22 May that 'vi fo questa per richordarvi che essendo io in questo luogho se gli schadessi più una chosa che un'altra, fate dua versi e farassi il bisogno' (ibid., XXVII, 293). These boschi were ex-Strozzi lands, which the Mercanzia had awarded to the abbot of San Pancrazio in 1466, according to Rustichi himself (Cat., 917, f. 186ʳ), from whom they did eventually go to Giovanni (ibid., and f. 378ʳ; 1011, f. 342ᵛ, and above, p. 48, n. 3).

[5] MAP, XI, 531, Cosimo to Piero de' Medici, 23 January 1464: 'Attendo come avisi Niccholò serà pochi dì et chome ci sia si prenderà partito del podere di Piero da Ghagliano et quanto più tosto viene tanto sia meglio, perch'e' creditori della 'redità ànno chominciato a richiamarsi, cioè Giovanni Rucie[ll]ai, al quale mandai a dire non seghuitasse più avanti che innanzi uscisse secondo mese sarebbe paghato'. In June 1455 Giovanni had told Michele Brancacci that he was now pressing 'l'amicho tuo da Todi' only because 'i miei conpagni se ne cominciano accruciare' (Acquisti e Doni, 140, inserto 8 [3]).

[6] See Alessandra Strozzi, Lettere, pp. 333 ff., the first reference being to 13 December; according to Agnolo Acciaiuoli, the 1464 failures were worse than any since 1339 (p. 350). See too CS, III, 249, ff. 161ʳ⁻ᵛ, 281ʳ.

[7] Perosa, p. 117.

[8] CS, III, 247, f. 123ʳ, to Filippo Strozzi. Giovanfrancesco's failure, first reported on 22 December (Alessandra Strozzi, Lettere, p. 350), was then much mentioned, not least because Alessandra feared that he would disgrace his kinsmen (pp. 336,

unrecoverable debts and ten years later, in a petition to the Signoria, Giovanni had become fully aware of the problems associated with the earlier wave of bankruptcies[1]. Indeed his cousin and partner Stoldo Frescobaldi left the bank in early 1465; 'e di poi sono stato sanza aviamento', as he reported to the tax officials in 1469, 'e questo fu per la perdita grande cho' faliti'[2]. Rucellai at once began a new firm with his two sons on 25 May 1465[3], and his current account with Filippo Strozzi reveals vigorous trading in large sums two years later[4]. By the early 'seventies, Stoldo Frescobaldi was again in business as a banker and merchant, though not in partnership with his cousin, whom he perhaps regarded as insufficiently cautious[5]. From about 1467 to 1474, Rucellai's major partner was Iacopo di Francesco Venturi, who had married his daughter Margherita in 1455. Another *compagno* after 1469 was Bertoldo di Bartolomeo Corsini, who had earlier been employed by Rucellai[6]. As little as we know about it, 'el bancho di Giovanni Rucellai e de' compagni' was, according to Dei, the second biggest within Florence in 1470[7]. Though in 1469 other men of affairs had had even more justification than usual to complain of business difficulties, Giovanni's report to the *catasto* officials did not attempt to hide the flourishing state of his own operations, more limited as they had become with his withdrawal from Venice:

> Truovomi più traffichi, cioè la mia chonpagnia di Firenze, dove fo la risidenza nel bancho di Merchato Nuovo, il quale tengho a ppigione da' Chapitani della Parte [Guelfa]. E chosì una ragione in Pisa e chosì arte di lana in Firenze, ne' quali tutti traffichi ò più e diversi chonpagni. . .[8].

This *portata* also reveals that in 1469 Giovanni possessed more rural land than ever before or after: a villa and its big estate (*possessione*) at Quaracchi, at least six farms, a mill, two vineyards, extensive woods and dozens of other *pezzi* of land, some of it arable. He controlled another prize, but the details of part of the large estate at Poggio a Caiano, whose villa Giovanni also bought after the

---

342, 354); cf. CS, III, 249, ff. 161ᵛ, 281ʳ. When precisely Giovanni's association with Strozzi ended is not clear (it was still in existence in July 1462 [see p. 36, n. 3 above]), but obviously it was over by 1464, though Giovanni went on trying to collect its outstanding debts: see e.g. a document of 1473 in NA, F 239 (Ser Niccolò Ferrini, 1471–77), f. 595ʳ.

[1] See below, pp. 87–88.

[2] Cat., 906, f. 734ᵛ. His last partnership with Giovanni listed in the guild records is in 1463 (Arte del Cambio, 15, f. 10ᵛ). On 20 March 1465, however, the consuls formally approved the dissolution of a newly created company (*ibid.*, 19, unfoliated).

[3] Arte del Cambio, 15, ff. 15ʳ, 17ʳ (1465–66). His sons are not again mentioned by name as their father's *compagni* until Bernardo appears in 1478 (f. 65ᵛ). It is always assumed that Pandolfo at least was long active in the bank (see R. de Roover, "Il Trattato di Fra Santi Rucellai", pp. 3–5, 13), and certainly he appears in many documents as his father's right-hand man; see for two examples above, p. 50, and NA, C 407 (Ser Pierozzo Cerbini, 1456–65), f. 145ʳ. He is mentioned a number of times, once as a consul, in the deliberations of the Bankers' Guild in the late 1460s (Arte del Cambio, 19, unfoliated).

[4] See "Libro segnato A di Filippo di Matteo Strozzi, 1466–71", in CS, V, 17, ff. cv, cxxxviii, cxxxxiiii, clxi, clxx, clxxviii, clxxxxvii. I owe this reference to F. Melis, *Documenti per la storia economica dei secoli XIII–XVI*, Florence, 1972, pp. 86, n. 1, 87, who cites an unpublished thesis on this Strozzi register by F. Bigazzi. The business relationship had survived the crisis revealed in NA, B 1184 (Ser Girolamo Beltramini, 1457–78), inserto 7 (8), 13 July 1462.

[5] Archivio Frescobaldi, 44, unfoliated. Stoldo continued to do business with Rucellai until the mid-seventies, however (*ibid.*, 12, *passim*). He and his brother Lamberto were taxed 21 florins in 1469 (Cat., 906, f. 735ᵛ), more than in 1458 (*ibid.*, 788, parte i, f. 436ᵛ).

[6] Arte del Cambio, 15, ff. 20ʳ, 23ʳ, 26ʳ, 32ᵛ, 36ᵛ, 41ʳ. Bertoldo and at least one other Corsini appear as employees of Giovanni in Filippo Strozzi's register (see n. 4 above for the reference).

[7] "Memorie storiche", in Bayerische Staatsbibliothek, Munich, cod. ital. 160, f. 133ᵛ. Melis, *Documenti*, p. 87, describes Rucellai's bank as 'assolutamente sconosciuta'.

[8] Cat., 919, f. 379ʳ. See above, p. 79, n. 8, on the Venetian firm; however, Giovanni probably maintained some interests there, Filippo Rucellai continuing to represent him, as a document of 1471 shows (Diplomatico, Strozzi Uguccione, 12 September 1471). Rucellai was the richest man in the quarter of Santa Maria Novella in 1470, according to Dei: G. C. Romby, *Descrizioni e rappresentazioni della città di Firenze nel XVᵒ secolo*, Florence, 1976, p. 60.

report was drawn up, do not appear because its income was not taxable[1]. A little of this property came in payment for bad business debts[2]. Almost all, however, had been bought over the years, directly from Messer Palla or from men in possession of ex-Strozzi lands, most concentratedly at Poggio, where by 1470 with the purchase from Neri Venturi of the villa 'Ambra' and then (from himself in effect) of several tracts whose income had been used for the façade, Giovanni had reassembled the great *possessione* reported by his father-in-law in 1427 and shortly after dispersed. In 1474 this estate alone produced an annual income of 444 florins[3].

Both villas, especially Quaracchi, were also places of rural retreat and recreation usually, judging by Giovanni's letters, in spring and autumn. Giovanni liked to study and comment on the unfolding of the seasons at Quaracchi[4]. In late March 1466 Bernardo told Lorenzo de' Medici that he expected to have 'parechi giorni di buon tempo' at Quaracchi and Peretola (indeed his natural son was named Tommaso Masini da Peretola)[5]. Even Lorenzo's sister grew to like the villa so much after her marriage that she was nicknamed 'la Quaracchina' by Luigi Pulci[6]. The poet refers to 'festi giorni' spent on the river there with the Medici *brigata* and, in the private language of the circle, remembered them in his satire on women's cosmetics, 'Le galee per Quaracchi'[7]. The 'bello e grand'orto, chopioso di buoni fructi' was full of delights. There was box clipped into a riotously incongruous collection of figures, including dragons, centaurs, philosophers, cardinals and Cicero, so reminiscent of Pliny the Younger's descriptions of 'the box-shrubs, clipped into innumerable shapes' at his Tuscan villa. There were the boat for fishing and the charming four-wheeled carriage, drawn by two or four horses, 'dipinta e gentile, nel modo che s'usano in Lonbardia'[8]. Giovanni's loving description of his garden is perhaps the most attractive in the *Zibaldone*, in which he also wrote

---

[1] Cat., 919, ff. 376r–80v. In 1427, his brothers and he had owned the then smaller Quaracchi estate, two farms and a storehouse in Campi (*ibid.*, 43, ff. 867r–70v). On Poggio, see n. 3 below. Most of this acquired property was in the same fairly small area, north and north-west of Florence towards Pistoia, where Giovanni's ancestral estates lay. By 1467 he held a little land *a livello* further afield, in the Pisan *contado* (*ibid.*, 919, ff. 378r, 379r, and NA, B 397 [Ser Baldovino Baldovini, 1465–68], ff. 221v–22r).

[2] See the references in Cat., 919, f. 377v.

[3] On Giovanni's gradual reassembling of the estate and villa at Poggio, see above, pp. 48–49 and my "Poggio a Caiano", pp. 250–57. 'Ambra' itself was bought on 20 September 1469. In an undated document apparently drawn up at the time of the sale to the Medici (1474), the income from rents and produce was estimated at about 2,000 lire or 444 florins (Spedale di San Matteo, 30, ff. 299r–v; see too below, p. 88). Having paid for the two properties attached to Poggio in 1460–61—and having consigned them to the Company of St. Peter the Martyr—(see p. 49 above), Giovanni then apparently bought them back in May 1468, the proceeds going towards the façade as originally agreed. Conv. Sopp., 102, 308, f. 95v, lists only the repurchase of one of these tracts, but presumably the other was treated in the same way since both appear in the 1469 *catasto* as belonging to Giovanni (Cat., 919, f. 378r). Conv. Sopp., 102, 309, f. 33r, under the year 1477, nicely summarizes the original deal: 'et fornito quella [the façade] si debbino vendere dette possessione a detto Giovanni o a sua heredi, volendole per pari pregio et il prezo di dette possessioni etiamdio spendere in detta facciata o in adornamento d'essa'.

[4] See above, p. 75.

[5] MAP, CXXXVII, 243, 961. Passerini, *Rucellai*, tav. xvi, pp. 143–4, notes that Bernardo had a child by a woman from Peretola named Masini; Mazzini, *Opere di Giovanni Rucellai*, p. xiv, mentions Messer Giovanni di Bernardo Rucellai's close friendship with this man without realizing that the two were half-brothers.

[6] See his letter to Lorenzo of December 1470 in *Morgante e Lettere*, ed. D. De Robertis, Florence, 1962, p. 962; cf. p. 969. See too Nannina's letter written in Pulci's hand from Quaracchi, on 19 April 1473, in De Robertis, "Supplementi all'epistolario del Pulci", p. 568. Pulci witnessed a document for Giovanni in Florence on 5 March 1474: NA, F 239 (Ser Niccolò Ferrini, 1471–77), f. 595r.

[7] These 'festive days' were recalled in his *Stanze per la giostra*: cf. Rochon, *Jeunesse*, pp. 29–30, 93, 126–7, nn. 315, 322. *Le galee* has been published by G. Volpi in his edition of *Le frottole*, Florence, 1912, pp. 23 ff.; see Pulci's reference to it in a letter of 1472 to Lorenzo (*Morgante, ed. cit.*, p. 978; cf. p. 1062). In general see Nigro, *Pulci e la cultura medicea*, pp. 8–10, 62–3; Nigro points out that Pulci's early patron Messer Francesco Castellani, a son-in-law of Palla Strozzi, probably gave him an entrée to the Rucellai (pp. 5–7).

[8] Perosa, pp. 20–23. Rucellai's description is well analysed by G. Masson, *Italian Gardens*, London, 1966, pp. 62–63. See Pliny, *Letters*, V.6.36, trans. B. Radice (Loeb Classical Library), London, 1969, I, pp. 348–9; cf. pp. 342–3. Patricia Simons kindly pointed these passages out to me.

—a dictum interestingly enough repeated later by his son Bernardo—that 'l'agricultura . . . è vita beata e felicità non conosciuta'[1].

There is no reason to attribute Rucellai's pleasure in country life, or his investment in land (a long pursued policy which even in the 'sixties coincided with very vigorous commercial activity) to anything other than his combining absorption in his own and Messer Palla's affairs with putting into practice the advice to maintain a mixed portfolio—'mi piace non tutti denari nè tutte possessioni, ma parte in questo, parte in questo altro'. This he copied into the *Zibaldone* from the pseudo-Pandolfini in 1457 when he had a far smaller proportion of his total wealth in land than did the Medici[2]. Here there are few traces of Giovanni's having or developing a *rentier* mentality (he was never a notable urban landlord) and none of a 'retreat' to the land by a businessman grown over-cautious in the conviction that, as one of Francesco Datini's associates had much earlier put it, 'almeno quelli [posisioni] non corerano rischio di mare, nè di fattori, nè di conpangni, nè di faliti'[3]. His final acquisition of the whole Poggio estate was prompted by several motives, among them perhaps an irrepressible desire to build a new villa on this attractive site which had once been his father-in-law's[4]. Ownership was the signal for expensive improvements, including the creation of a whole new farm from *boschi* and of several plantations of trees to be cut for timber. Whatever Giovanni's building plans, Poggio a Caiano was also to be a working estate, and an unusually profitable one. The three or four thousand mulberry trees he planted there were a nicely judged investment at a time when, as he himself had noted a little earlier, the Florentine silk industry was making huge profits[5]. At this point and most others, it is hard and perhaps fruitless to distinguish between Giovanni the landed gentleman and 'improver' and Rucellai the astute man of business.

Behind Giovanni's continued drive to make money was the need to pay for the building programme, substantially complete after great expenditure by about 1470, though some work on the façade of Santa Maria Novella continued after that date[6]. The extraordinary demands on Rucellai's purse during this decade of furious activity, when several projects were under way simultaneously, forced him to begin to raise money by selling off his *Monte* shares. This he had begun to do after about 1458 and even more purposefully, as a result of the worsening economic conditions, from 1464 onwards. As he explained in a petition for tax relief presented to the Signoria in August 1474, 'in exhibendis

---

[1] *Zibaldone*, f. 34ʳ. Bernardo finished a long diplomatic letter to Lorenzo on 20 January 1483 (MAP, XLVIII, 155): 'Ho inteso el piacere che pigli più ogni dì della agricultura, che è felicità non conosciuta et nihil homine libero dignius'.

[2] Perosa, p. 9. In 1458 Giovanni's taxable urban and rural property was valued at approximately 5,200 florins, his total wealth amounting to 22,537 florins; of course his real estate's proportional value would have gone up sharply were his new palace, and his Quaracchi villa, to have been added (Cat., 816, ff. 60ʳ–63ᵛ). Not much under half of the Medici's large fortune was then in real estate: de Roover, *Rise and Decline*, p. 26.

[3] Quoted in F. Melis, *Aspetti della vita economica medievale: (Studi nell'Archivio Datini di Prato)*, Siena, 1962, p. 61. It was advice that Francesco followed (pp. 61 ff.). Ponte has shrewdly pointed out that Rucellai does not quote passages from the pseudo-Pandolfini in praise of life *in villa*: see "Etica ed economia nel terzo libro 'Della Famiglia' ", p. 299, and his review of Perosa in *Rassegna della letteratura italiana*, LXIV (1960), pp. 470–73. See n. 1 above, however. On the 'retreat' to the land, and for evidence of continuing mercantile initiative, see R. A. Goldthwaite, *Private Wealth*, Princeton, 1968, pp. 246–7, and *passim*. Even in 1469 Rucellai's urban property consisted only of his palace, a small dwelling beside it, two and a half shops and a house in Pisa: Cat., 919, f. 376ʳ⁻ᵛ.

[4] See my "Poggio a Caiano", pp. 250–57.

[5] These details of the improvements are from Spedale di San Matteo, 30, f. 299ʳ⁻ᵛ; see above, p. 81.

[6] This emerges from the *ricordi* in Perosa, pp. 25–26, and the documents pub. by Dezzi Bardeschi, *Facciata*, pp. 21–22. The façade of course bears the date 1470, and Dezzi Bardeschi is probably right in suggesting that Giovanni's remarks in 1473 (Perosa, p. 121) also imply that it was substantially finished (*Facciata*, p. 18). In 1479, however, 60 florins a year were still to go, for as long as a decade, 'nel fornire la faccia et porta di legname' (*ibid.*, p. 22); cf. Cat., 1011, f. 343ᵛ, where in 1480 the scribe also noted that Rucellai had allocated property for 'le faccia e porta' which in ten years would go to the Guild whether the façade was 'finita o non finita'.

hedificiis publice et privatim ipse credebat facere sumptibus ex lucro et fructibus, at ipse expendebat de capitali'[1]. Unfortunately one cannot work out what his 'grandissima spesa' was. On the one project for which there are any figures at all—the marble façade—it is possible that Giovanni had to provide money from sources other than the allocated income of the several parts of the Poggio estate, which can have yielded no more than about 3,500 florins, at most, between 1448 and 1479[2]. Much of Giovanni's time in the 'sixties must have been devoted to the practical problems, made worse by the economic climate, created by these schemes. The death of Benedetto Toschi in mid-1464, for example, removed a willing ally at San Pancrazio where the Holy Sepulchre chapel was not yet completed. Giovanni was concerned to ask Lorenzo de' Medici, on a visit to Rome, to recommend him to the Cardinal of Pavia—whom he may have met as Pope Pius II's secretary—'e cche tu lo preghassi che in quello che poteva piaciermi de' fatti del munistero di San Branchazio . . .', recalling to the prelate 'el parentado che noi abbiamo insieme ecc.'. In particular Lorenzo should ask 'che alla sua S[ignoria] piaciesse eleggiere per ghovernatore del detto munistero Don Giovanni Borromeo monacho in detto luogho, e cchosì ti piacca di fare chè llo riputerò in grandissimo piacere'[3]. Borromeo had been prominent in the financial affairs of his monastery during Rucellai's activities there[4].

The excitement of seeing his plans completed and his dreams fulfilled, whatever the financial or nervous cost, made up for the practical problems of the 1460s and the accumulated vicissitudes

---

[1] Provvisioni, Registri, 165, f. 124^v, 26 August 1474. This petition also gives the information that Rucellai's *Monte* shares in 1469 had a face value of 17,373 florins and a real value, calculating at 24%, of 4,169 florins. His 1469 *catasto* yields a higher, but comparable, figure of about 4,429 florins (Cat., 919, ff. 376^r–80^v). Eleven years earlier, when one converted at only 20%, he had had shares with a market value of some 8,835 florins (*ibid.*, 816, ff. 60^r–63^v). However, the real run on his *Monte* holdings came in 1474 (below, p. 88).

[2] This is in any case a very approximate figure, calculated as follows. From 1448 onwards—strictly speaking 1452—Giovanni had 60 florins per annum from part of the Poggio estate; with interest this would have been a tidy sum by the time the façade was begun (ruling out the charge that the funds were diverted elsewhere!). Further, these lands provided this income right through to 1479, Quaracchi then taking up the burden. The adjacent Poggio properties consigned in 1461 produced 90 florins a year until they were 'sold' back to Giovanni in 1468, when the sale price (340 florins certainly and probably 750 more) also went to the façade, a welcome injection of cash at what was probably a crucial time: for references, see p. 49, n. 4, and p. 81, n. 3 above. I am grateful to Richard Goldthwaite for his opinion that 3,500 florins might have paid for the façade of Santa Maria Novella, if the marble was bought from the cathedral workshop and if a partial revetment only was necessary. When the friars of Santa Croce contemplated a façade for that church in 1476, however, they had in mind a cost of 10,000 florins, consigning 'agli operai di decta chiesa certi debitori di decto convento per lasci facti al convento e tanti che fanno la somma di fiorini diecimila incirca, et sono tali debitori che se non interamente tutta la somma, se fussi chi gli volessi riscuotere se ne ritrarrebbe al meno gran parte' (Provvisioni, Registri, 167, f. 147^r, 28 September 1476). Only new information on both projects can help here.

[3] MAP, XXIII, 289, undated but of March–April 1466 (see Kent, "Letters", p. 342, n. 6). The cardinal had been given the church *in commendam* on Toschi's death (D. F. Tarani, *La Badia di San Pancrazio in Firenze*, Pescia, 1923, p. 25). Apart from being Pius II's secretary, Ammannati had been educated in Florence and was a friend of Rucellai's cousin Donato Acciaiuoli (see G. Calamari, *Il confidente di Pio II: Cardinale Iacopo Ammannati-Piccolomini [1422–1479]*, Rome–Milan, 1932, i, pp. 29 ff., and *passim*). He seems to have lived with one of Giovanni's Rucellai kinsmen at this time (A. Della Torre, *Storia dell'Accademia Platonica*, p. 330, n. 6).

[4] Borromeo became a monk there in 1450 (Conv. Sopp., 88, 23, f. 100^r), and is often subsequently mentioned in this and other records of the convent (e.g. ff. 31^v, 39^r); Giovanni may also have favoured him on account of his own early connections with the Borromeo (see above, p. 20). If 'ghovernatore' means 'abbot' rather than 'administrator', Don Giovanni did not win the position, which went to Vincenzo Conci on 10 November 1466 (Tarani, *La Badia di San Pancrazio*, p. 25). A year later, Borromeo was the *priore* of another Vallombrosan community (Conv. Sopp., 88, 63, f. 43^r). Rucellai seems to have co-operated quite well with Toschi's successor: see e.g. *ibid.*, f. 44^r (when in September 1468 the church borrows from him 'uno boticino da bianco'), and 41, f. 2^r, where Rucellai is credited with 112 florins in November 1466 'e'quali ci prestò per lo spacio delle nostre bulle di Santo Pancratio pagò per noi a Rinaldo della Luna e compagnia'. In the 1470s he was procurator of the convent in litigation concerning its and Lion Rosso's rights over certain ex-Strozzi woods: Mercanzia, 7247, unfoliated, 14 June 1477. I owe the reference to Alison Brown.

of Rucellai's earlier life. His attitude to his buildings and other expenditure in the *ricordo* of 1464 still retains traces of nervousness, as well it might since some of his projects were barely begun and the road to bankruptcy in Florence was littered with unfinished buildings. Wise spending 'non è minor virtù che il guadangnare', he wrote, 'et credo che m'abbi facto più honore l'averli bene spesi ch'averli guadagnati e più chontentamento nel mio animo'[1]. By 1473 spending had become not just a virtue but, as Filarete suggested and Alberti more austerely agreed, an almost voluptuous pleasure. In the intervening years Giovanni had put his own and others' doubts to the test and from experience could say that 'achordomi che anchora sia maggore dolcezza lo spendere che il ghuadangnare'. All reserve about his activities as a patron had disappeared: 'm'ànno dato e danno grandissimo chontentamento e grandissima dolcezza, perchè raghuardano in parte all'onore di Dio e all'onore della città e a memoria di me'[2]. Even so, at the age of seventy he may have longed to start yet another project — at Poggio a Caiano. No building was begun there. Rather the existing *casa da signore* was repaired, a prudent course of action after 1469. There are, however, grounds for believing that he and Bernardo had thought quite specifically about the question[3].

There is scattered evidence to suggest that Giovanni, ever sensitive to public opinion, was right in his assessment of his buildings' impact, long and carefully calculated, on the city. Filarete's early reference to the palace was followed by its appearance, admittedly unnamed and without distinguishing architectural features, in the 'chain map' of 1472 and then as a landmark in Cambi's chronicle[4]. When one of the Sforza visited Florence in March 1471 there was a stir of preparation at several notable households including, the Sienese ambassador reported, 'in casa . . . di Giovanne Rucellario'[5]. Much earlier Giovanni had quoted Cicero as saying that 'nella casa d'un uomo richo sono da essere ricevuti molti forestieri e debbono essere honorati con largità imperoché altrimenti faccendo l'ampla casa sarebbe a disonore del Signore', and we may guess that the palace in the Via della Vigna Nuova, which had become that 'più bella casa di questo quartiere' Alessandra Strozzi had dreamed of creating for her sons in 1448, had been designed (and proved) to be just such a show place[6]. Pius II very quickly and practically expressed his admiration for it and perhaps for the Loggia project; there is little evidence of the reception given the façade of Santa Maria Novella but Vasari's statement that 'fu finita . . . con molta sodisfazione dell'universale', especially the portals, rings true[7].

Benedetto Dei has left the only strictly contemporary comment on the banker's building activities as a whole. Unintentionally—it was his normal practice—the chronicler as it were rebuked Giovanni for omitting in the *ricordo* of 1473 any reference to his having built for his family's sake (and for his

---

[1] Perosa, p. 118.

[2] *Ibid.*, p. 121. According to Alberti, ordinary people built from necessity but the rich for 'pleasure and delight' (*Ten Books on Architecture*, trans. J. Leoni and ed. J. Rykwert, London, 1965, p. 100). Filarete wrote that 'Non è altro lo edificare se none un piacere voluntario, come quando l'uomo è innamorato': *Trattato di Architettura*, ed. A. M. Finoli and L. Grassi, Milan, 1972, i, p. 41.

[3] Kent, "Poggio a Caiano", pp. 250–57.

[4] For Filarete, see p. 41 above. G. Boffito and A. Mori, *Piante e vedute di Firenze*, Florence, 1926, reproduce the map opposite p. 144. Cambi placed Manno Temperanni's house by saying that 'stava nella Vingnia insul chanto di verso el ponte della Chasa di Giovanni Ruciellai, che si chiama la via de' Palchetti' (*Istorie, ed. cit.*, XX, p. 324).

[5] Pub. by M. Mansfield, *A Family of Decent Folk, 1200–1741: A Study in the Centuries Growth of the Lanfredini . . .*, Florence, 1922, p. 285.

[6] Alessandra had more modestly and traditionally hoped to achieve her end by adding an existing house to her own (*Lettere*, p. 39). Giovanni's 1457 reference to Cicero, in *Zibaldone*, f. 23ᵛ, comes from the passage of the *De officiis* which he uses again in 1464 (see p. 52, n. 2 above): *De officiis, ed. cit.*, pp. 142–3.

[7] *Opere, ed. cit.*, ii, p. 541. For an early reference by a Dominican friar, see Orlandi, *Necrologio*, ii, p. 507.

remaining silent about the identity of the architect) by not once mentioning the patron by name. Dei rather ascribed Giovanni's achievements to the Rucellai family. Old Ugolino Rucellai would have appreciated Dei's reference to the Loggia 'della ricca e potente casa de' Rucellai'[1]. Even Giovanni's tomb Dei mentioned as 'lle sepolture de' Medici e Ruciellai', a phrase which could easily have included family sepulchres other than his own, though the sentence ended consolingly 'e mill'altre degnie ch'è un'altra Roma novella'[2]. Benedetto was not trying to belittle what he called 'la famosa muraglia che ànno fatto la gran chasa de' Ruciellai', and Giovanni would have understood the impulse to incorporate his own activities, and those of several of his kinsmen 'in più luoghi'[3], into one Rucellai achievement. It was a feeling he in part shared and had acted on—all his buildings had a Rucellai context, not least to ensure that his very memory, about which he cared so much, was preserved.

Giovanni had much to be grateful for in 1473. More than most men are ever able he had, despite an often hostile environment, finally reconciled conflicting claims in his private and public life, and had found thereby acceptance, contentment, a sense of security, and above all a means of self-expression which thoroughly absorbed him. Almost every preoccupation of his life appears, satisfactorily or triumphantly brought to an end and neatly catalogued, in his *ricordo* of that, his seventieth, year: he was able to take 'grandissimo contentamento' in his legacy to poor country girls as well as in his grander acts of munificence[4]. There had been inevitable blows, for example the deaths of his wife and mother in 1468 and 1471 respectively. This 'savio huomo e buono'—as a contemporary describes him—could find consolation in noting their long and virtuous lives and in the contemplation of his children and grandchildren, especially his 'due figluoli huomini, Pandolfo e Bernardo, della qualità che sono', all of whom lived with him in the grandpaternal household he himself had never known as a child[5]. He had become, he wrote matter-of-factly, 'al pari o inanzi di qualunche altro cittadino del quartiere nostro di Sancta Maria Novella, e forse che pochi in tutta la città ne sono che mi debino passare inanzi'[6].

Rucellai's statement that he took more pride in his achievements because 'si può dire ch'io abbi fatte in tempo d'aversità . . . che m'è chonvenuto navichare molto a punto e ssanza errore, e tanto più è da maraviglarsi ch'io mi sia chondotto in questi termini'[7] is as much a sober summary of how he had coped with his tortuous affairs, in particular perhaps a reference to the careful course he had had to steer between the Strozzi Scylla and the Medici Charybdis, as a complacent piece of self-congratulation by a born trimmer. This passage also reminds us that, though Giovanni believed with many of his contemporaries that fortune could usually be controlled by 'il buono ghoverno e il senno e la prudenza'[8]—and was no doubt flattered by Marsilio Ficino's reference to his 'opere' as evidence that a prudent man can resist 'colpi fortuiti'—it is nevertheless not clear to what degree, or

---

[1] "Memorie storiche", Bayerische Staatsbibliothek, Munich, cod. ital. 160, f. 127ᵛ.

[2] "Cronica", Manoscritti, 119, f. 35ʳ.

[3] *Ibid.*, f. 36ᵛ. The Munich manuscript (see n. 1 above) contains the reference to the 'Muraglia della degna casa de' Rucellai in più luoghi' (f. 134ᵛ).

[4] Perosa, p. 122.

[5] The first quotation is from a letter of 1472, published by Foster, *Villa at Poggio a Caiano* (p. 57, n. 2 above), ii, n. 162, pp. 349–50; for the second, see Perosa, pp. 118, 119, 121. In 1469, Giovanni's household comprised ten persons and three generations: himself, Pandolfo (a widower, with five children) and Bernardo and Nannina with their son Cosimo (Cat., 919, f. 379ᵛ). On grand-paternal families, see my *Household and Lineage*, pp. 29–30, 33–35, and *passim.*

[6] Perosa, p. 120.

[7] *Ibid.*, p. 122.

[8] *Ibid.*, p. 103.

for how long after 1462, Rucellai accepted the more subtle Ficinian view that the very best course of action was to make 'a peace or league' with Fortuna, 'conformando la voluntà nostra colla sua e andare volentieri dov'ella acenna'[1]. To be sure, Giovanni's adoption of the device in which the goddess Fortuna navigated a ship in full sail may show his interest in the Ficinian idea[2].

In the last resort, however, even at this time of superlative serenity, Giovanni did not overestimate the importance of his own skilled navigation, rather believing, without any apparent sense of contradiction, that his great happiness did not stem 'da mie virtù nè da mie opere, ma per grazia di Dio'[3]. And when in the very next year he found himself suddenly a much poorer man he declared, perhaps with a revived, rather more old-fashioned awareness of the goddess's arbitrary nature, that he had been 'perchosso dala fortuna'[4].

---

[1] *Ibid.*, pp. 114, 116. See Wind, "Platonic Tyranny and the Renaissance Fortuna", pp. 491–6, for an ingenious but perhaps rather forced analysis. Rucellai's application to Antonio Ivani for advice on the same question in 1476 (see below, p. 87) suggests that he did not long stay persuaded, if he ever was, by Ficino's case. Cf. Perosa, below, pp. 140 ff., and Preyer, below, p. 201. See now F. Kiefer, "The Conflation of Fortuna and Occasio in Renaissance Thought and Iconography", *Journal of Medieval and Renaissance Studies*, IX (1979), esp. pp. 2–7.

[2] On Rucellai and this emblem, see A. Warburg, "Le ultime volontà di Francesco Sassetti', pp. 231 ff.; Gilbert, "Bernardo Rucellai", pp. 103–4; Preyer, below, pp. 200–01. Rucellai may well have used the sail device for reasons less precise and knowing than Wind suggests (p. 492). It was not uniquely his—in Florence the Pazzi had employed it, as had the Estensi of Ferrara even earlier (see Preyer, *loc. cit.*; and p. 44, n. 4 above). It is also possible that he used it before the Ficino letter was written, 'probably' between 1460–62 (Perosa, p. 176, n. 114). So far as I know, discussion of these questions has also not taken into account a Quattrocento version of the *stemma* in the Rucellai courtyard which is in the Bargello. Of uncertain provenance—now placed within an early sixteenth-century della Robbia garland—it is reproduced in A. H. Marquand, *Andrea della Robbia and his Atelier*, Princeton, 1922; 1972 reprint, ii, p. 255, fig. 298; cf. I. B. Supino, *Catalogo del R. Museo Nazionale di Firenze* (*Palazzo del Podestà*), Rome, 1898, p. 440.

[3] Perosa, p. 120; cf. p. 118, where in 1464 he thanked God for having guarded and defended him 'da molti mali e noie e aversità, come dà il mondo, ch'io arei potuto avere, che noll'ò avute'.

[4] The phrase occurs in his tax report for 1480: 'Solevo fare bancho in Merchato Nuovo ... e per essere stato perchosso dala fortuna è chonsumato quello vi missi per il chorpo' (here I have used the copy in Archivio di Monte, Catasto-Duplicati, 66, f. 406ʳ).

VI. 'PERCHOSSO DALA FORTUNA', 1474–81

Understandably Giovanni's interest in Fortuna, his uncertainty about 'che cosa sia veramente la fortuna', revived in the later 1470s. Through his son-in-law Domenico Bartoli he asked the Volterran humanist Antonio Ivani in 1476 precisely that question and another which had also concerned him in the preceding decade, 'la cagione che la natura humana comunemente è più inclinata al male che al bene'. Ivani responded eagerly in words which, though they show the provincial intellectual's elation at being asked learned advice by a Florentine 'citadino non meno potente che diligente', may also reveal something of the state of mind of Rucellai, who in that city 'copiosa de nobilissimi ingiegni, non habi ogiumai trovato sufficiente expositore'[1]. Bernardo Rucellai put the family's position in terms identical with his father's in a letter to Luisa Strozzi written just one year after Giovanni's death. We would willingly have helped you, Bernardo told her, 'se la fortuna come sapete non ci avessi percosso'[2].

Even for a man accustomed to them Fortune's blows had struck extremely hard and suddenly. As Giovanni explained in a succinct note added in his own hand to the *ricordo* he had dictated to a secretary in 1473:

> [Di poi l'anno 1474 ebbi una grande perdita nella mia conpangnia di Pisa, ghovernata per Ridolfo Paghanelli, che m'inghannò e rubò per vie torte e feciomi danno f. ventimila, per modo che insieme con altra aversità di richo sono diventato povero. Che Dio di tutto sia lodato][3].

Despite Rucellai's sense of well-being only a year before (one shared by Benedetto Dei)[4], there had been suggestions of trouble ahead. According to the banker himself the Pisan company had been losing money for three years[5], and in a letter of April 1473 Nannina Rucellai mentions the poor pickings available for pilgrims at Quaracchi that year[6]. January 1474, however, saw Giovanni first acting to forestall a crisis which had become really threatening by mid-year. In that month he sold some property to raise money. Perhaps he had been made more aware of his situation by a rebuff that by then can hardly have been made on political grounds, the refusal of some unnamed citizen to marry one of Pandolfo's daughters[7].

On 26 August 1474 Giovanni made a successful petition for tax relief to the Signoria, using the unexceptionable argument that he now owned well under half as much as he had when the assessment was made in 1469. His tax was reduced from forty-six to eighteen large florins. Though he acknowledges the long-term causes of his financial difficulties, including capital expenditure on

---

[1] Ivani's reply to Bartoli's request, made when the Florentine was captain of Sarzana, is pub. by P. Landucci Ruffo, "L'epistolario di Antonio Ivani (1430–1482)", *Rinascimento*, 2ª s., VI (1966), pp. 188–92. I owe this important reference to Alison Brown. Bartoli had long been a close associate of his father-in-law, whom he accompanied to Rome in 1450 (Perosa, p. 67). In the 1470s Donato Acciaiuoli was in correspondence with Ivani (Garin, "Donato Acciaiuoli", p. 92).

[2] Biblioteca Comunale, Forlì, Autografi Piancastelli, 1902, 14 October 1482.

[3] Perosa, p. 122.

[4] Romby, *Descrizioni . . . di Firenze*, p. 45.

[5] See p. 88 below.

[6] Nannina sent a deserving pilgrim on to Lucrezia de' Medici 'per limosina, perché in verità questo anno, come dovete havere compreso meglio di me, hanno trovati pochi danari': pub. in De Robertis, "Supplementi all'epistolario del Pulci", p. 568.

[7] For the sale in January, see the reference to the 1474 petition in the following note. In a letter of the same month to Lorenzo de' Medici, Bernardo Rucellai refers to the breakdown in the marriage negotiations, adding that his family was now turning 'a quelli che volentieri sono voluti essere nostri parenti', namely Carlo di Lionardo del Benino (MAP, XXI, 348).

building and 'perditiones factas cum fallentibus ab anno 1464 citra', Rucellai emphasizes the recent loss at Pisa of 'supra vii milia florenorum intra spatium trium annorum vel minus'. (His private figure of 20,000 suggests both successful tax evasion and a more serious blow than he could publicly acknowledge). He suddenly had so many debts, Giovanni went on, 'quod ut satisfacere creditoribus et restitueret deposita pro quibus fuit ei necesse solvere intra xx dies aut pauciores, postquam ablatum fuit sibi creditum, ut notum est omnibus, ingentes quantitates pecuniarum per plura et plura milia florenorum'[1]. Late May and June was the period of maximum pressure, and Giovanni's first major response to it reveals how desperate was his predicament. On 29 May the banker agreed to sell his newly consolidated estate at Poggio a Caiano to Lorenzo and Giuliano de' Medici, who formally clinched the deal two weeks later, buying the *possessione* in two instalments, one immediately for the price of 2,000 florins *di suggello* and the second three years later for 4,333 large florins[2]. The petition mentions another as well as an earlier sale of land, and by 1480 there were to be still more[3]. Another quick source of ready cash was the sale of *Monte* shares. Since 1469 he had alienated shares with a face value of 12,528 florins, Giovanni told the Signoria, sales which yielded 3,006 florins. The records of the *Monte* officials generally confirm Rucellai's account; on 30 June 1474 he sold credits of 4,000 florins to Domenico Bartolini alone and made other substantial alienations[4].

Still vigorous and courageous in his seventies, Rucellai did not at once go out of business. Presumably the Pisan enterprise collapsed but the wool shop owned by Giovanni and his nephews and managed by Tommaso Frescobaldi lasted until 1476 when the partnership was dissolved, leaving Agnolo di Donato Rucellai with 'panni e llane sode e debitori di mimifattori'[5]. The Florentine bank survived until January 1478, when it was replaced for one more year by a company bearing Rucellai's name but having as *compagni* his son Bernardo, Piero di Tommaso Soderini and the faithful Bongianni brothers[6]. In his last tax report Rucellai officially reported the death of this, his last banking company, struck down by fortune:

> è chonsumato quello vi missi per il chorpo, sono rimasto chon debito et è mmi chonvenuto finire la chonpagnia … e [ò] mandato la grida e rinunziato alla pigione del bancho alla Parte Ghuelfa e il magazzino a' Chapitani d'Orto San Michele[7].

Despite his fighting back, these had been bitter years. In September 1479, for example, the *operai* of the church of Santo Spirito, to whom he had failed to pay 320 florins on time, voted 'che contro

---

[1] Provvisioni, Registri, 165, ff. 124ᵛ–26ʳ, 26 August 1474. Concerning his Pisan losses, it is possible that Giovanni's figure in the *Zibaldone* includes all the losses following, but not directly caused by, Paganelli's dishonest activities. The petition mentions that in all 15,000 florins had 'melted away' (f. 124ᵛ), a figure more comparable to the 20,000 mentioned in Perosa, p. 122.

[2] For details see my "Poggio a Caiano", pp. 250–57.

[3] See below, p. 89.

[4] Fol. 125ʳ of the petition (see n. 1 above) gives the overall figures; in fact he had sold shares with a face value of 14,331 florins, and bought 1,802 florins' worth. Archivio del Monte, 903, f. 62ʳ, gives Giovanni's holdings as 13,832 florins in 1474, then lists the dramatic sales. A year earlier (see *ibid.*, 902, f. 65ʳ) the income from these shares had gone straight to the taxation officials to defray his taxes. I am grateful to Anthony Molho for helping me to find and interpret these references.

[5] Cat., 1011, f. 58ʳ.

[6] Arte del Cambio, 15, ff. 41ʳ, 45ʳ, 49ʳ, 54ʳ, 59ʳ, 65ᵛ. Henceforth until 1487, when this register of partnerships ends, there are no companies run by Giovanni nor, after his death, by his sons. Michele Strozzi addressed a letter to Filippo Strozzi 'care of' Rucellai's bank in November 1477: CS, III, 132, f. 70ᵛ. De Roover, and then others, have suggested erroneously that Giovanni had cannily withdrawn from banking by 1470 (*Rise and Decline*, pp. 374–5; cf. Preyer, *Giovanni Rucellai*, pp. 7, 237, n. 23).

[7] Cat., 1011, f. 344ʳ. Among Pandolfo Rucellai's surviving papers, however, there are scraps of evidence, including business letters to Giovanni Rucellai from France—two of them, of 1480, registered with his own hand—which show Giovanni's commercial activities continuing until that year. There was even some trade after his death. See Spedale di San Matteo, 30, ff. 51 ff. This interesting *carteggio* was discovered by Renzo Ristori, who plans to publish parts of it.

Giovanni Rucellai et compagnia si procedesse all'arciveschovado in fargli schomunichare et in fare dare loro bando di cessante'. This humiliating threat Rucellai only averted by belatedly offering payment in grain[1], and it is hardly surprising that a letter of Nannina's written two months earlier suggests a family atmosphere full of tension[2]. Iacopo Venturi, Rucellai's son-in-law, had left the bank some time in 1475 and reported his losses there to the *catasto* officials five years later[3]. More embarrassingly, and in the same semi-public place, the brothers of another ex-partner Bertoldo Corsini, whose association with the bank had ended in 1473–74, sneeringly called Giovanni a 'buono merchatante' and accused him of bad faith and malpractice:

> E più ci troviamo Berttoldo nostro fratello oblighato nella chompagnia fè chon Giovanni Rucellai a fiorini 1,200 larghi chè anchora detta ragione ha debito; e' quali fiorini 1,200 larghi il detto Giovanni per più sententie è chondannato a ppaghargli ch'egl'à in mano e à gli tenuti già 7 anni che finì detta ragione. Lui chome buono merchatante ha fatto chonto gli paghi Bertoldo nostro, perchè si sta in chasa del chontinovo e ha transferiti e' beni suoi ne' nipoti e dice esser fallito; in modo che chi ha avere da detta ragione si fa a Berttoldo e dubitiamo non habbia a esser la nostra disfactione. . .[4].

Corsini's specific charges cannot now be investigated, but certainly Rucellai had acted illegally in 1477 when he sold to the Medici that part of the Poggio estate which was still pledged to the Bankers' Guild. He cannot have hoped completely and permanently to conceal such a sale—his postponing it for three years after the original purchase may indeed suggest that he tried to avoid infringing the agreement—and presumably intended to present a *fait accompli* which had bought him time and made available much needed cash before the Guild retaliated. This it did in June 1479 in an arbitrated judgment which compelled Rucellai similarly to cede the income of a large part of his Quaracchi estate[5]. There is no firm evidence of Giovanni's transferring important assets to his 'nipoti' (whether nephews or grandsons)[6]. If he was not quite 'fallito' his economic position in 1480 was indubitably grave, especially by comparison with earlier days. No longer even the richest Rucellai—one of his kinsmen could still sign a begging letter of 1475 to Lorenzo de' Medici 'G[i]ovanni Rucellai el più povero' but he had made his point[7]—our Giovanni now owned and controlled much less land. His estate had been diminished not only by ordinary sales but also by alienations in lieu of payment for debts, to Pandolfo's *parente* Buonaccorso Pitti for example, who explained that a transaction with Giovanni had been made 'per chagioni d[e'] suoi sinistri'[8]. All Rucellai's *Monte* shares had gone. According to him even 'una masseria di bestiame grosso e minuto' was no longer his because in spring 1479 the beasts 'mi furono predate dal chavaliere Orsino nella pastura di

---

[1] Conv. Sopp., 122, 128, f. 34^r; see too ff. 27^v, 34^v. I am grateful to Ann Fuller for this reference, and to Julius Kirshner for the information that such a threat of excommunication was nothing out of the ordinary.

[2] See p. 66, n. 2 above.

[3] Cat., 1014, parte i, f. 14^r; Arte del Cambio, 15, ff. 45^r, 49^r, 54^r.

[4] *Ibid.*, ff. 41^r, 45^r. The quotation is from Cat., 996, f. 200^v. On Bertoldo di Bartolommeo Corsini, see L. Passerini, *Genealogia e storia della famiglia Corsini*, Florence, 1858, p. 129.

[5] Dezzi Bardeschi, *Facciata*, p. 22. Interestingly, Giovanni's own account of the matter is less than frank (Perosa, p. 27). The 1477 sale document is in NA, B 735 (Ser Antonio Bartolommei, 1476–82), ff. 63^{r-v}.

[6] It is, however, true that his nephews Agnolo di Donato and brothers were his business partners (see p. 76 above), and that the January 1474 property sale was to them (p. 87 above).

[7] For this letter, see Kent, *Household and Lineage*, p. 297, and n. 5.

[8] Pitti's comment, in Cat., 996, f. 303^v, was explained by Rucellai himself: 'per danari avea avere da me Lorenzo suo figliuolo, overo dal bancho mio, che per non potere paghario gli chonsegniai in vendita il detto podere' (*ibid.*, 1011, f. 343^r). Fols. 341^r–44^v give Rucellai's total situation in 1480.

Ghuardistallo presso a Chanpiglia'[1]. Bernardo's letters to his Medici brother-in-law in the years just after Giovanni's death suggest a continuing and urgent financial crisis. Again and again he wrote for help in obtaining a tax reduction, adding to one diplomatic letter from Milan on 12 July 1482 a reference to 'sgravo nostro':

> Io ti priego se mai debbo impetrare gratia da te che vogla questa volta ridurci in termine da potere vivere come tuoi parenti, che come intenderai da Iacopo [Bongianni] lo puoi fare con giustificazione di Iddio e degl'uomini[2].

Some years later Giovanni's heirs still possessed outstanding debts and unprocured assets. A letter to Savonarola of 1496 sought the friar's aid in excommunicating these Rucellai for an alleged debt now thirty years old[3].

It was only in this last difficult part of his life that Giovanni became more conservative in his business advice to his sons. His counsel was that they should withdraw from trading unless they gave it their meticulous personal supervision. It was better to be known as 'mercatanti, ma in facto che voi siate botteghai, cioè che'l fondamento del ghoverno sia chome costumano fare e' lanaiuoli, e' setaiuoli et di simili, d'avere le sustantie del traffico più tosto in Firenze che di fuori in mercatantie, danari et debitori'; and to deal in ready cash or short term loans and exchange, avoiding 'di torre danari in diposito per trafficarli se già non fussi a certe stagioni di carestie'. This late passage, with its insistence on the necessity of finding sound associates ('egl'è da ffar maggior conto de l'uomo che governa che del danaio o del credito') and its near-obsession with keeping affairs in one's own hands to avoid destruction 'in uno punto', must reflect Giovanni's unfortunate experiences with his Pisan manager Ridolfo Paganelli. It does not, however, constitute an unqualified rejection of the bustling values of Giovanni's long life. He had in mind the period 'dopo la morte mia'—as his own extreme reluctance to withdraw from business also suggests—aware no doubt that Bernardo had little interest in or capacity for mercantile pursuits and that Pandolfo may already have lost his zest for them, and perhaps for all things secular, since his younger brother was to be infuriated by his lack of enthusiasm for preserving their mutual patrimony in the early 1480s. 'Bastivi il conservare' was sensible—and not necessarily universally relevant advice—at a time of sudden economic crisis when Giovanni himself was a very old man and his sons' capacity and inclination to manage anything other than a manufacturing enterprise were in doubt[4]. Rucellai had not withdrawn from trade and

---

[1] *Ibid.*, f. 344ʳ. This report mentions no *Monte* shares, though Archivio del Monte, 908, f. 76ʳ, gives Rucellai credits of 103 florins. Bernardo and Nannina had somewhat larger holdings (ff. 26ᵛ, 108ᵛ).

[2] MAP, LI, 169; nos. 140, 151, 156, 164, 171 and 179 all belong to this series. See too *ibid.*, XLVIII, 170, 194, and a letter on the same subject to Ser Niccolò Michelozzi (172). In 1484 Filippo Strozzi offered to lend Bernardo money when Rucellai was a *Monte* official (CS, III, 247, f. 250ʳ, 1 October), the sum being the very large one of 5,600 florins. Bernardo accepted the offer several years later (Goldthwaite, *Private Wealth*, p. 66).

[3] Spedale di San Matteo, 30, f. 345ʳ⁻ᵛ, 23 May, by Pandolfo Benvenuti. Pandolfo Rucellai had sent Benvenuti to his brother Bernardo, who 'mi mandò a Pagolo di Pandolfo e va di qua e va di là sanza concluxione niuna'; this letter is now published in full by Fumagalli, "I Trattati di Fra Santi Rucellai", p. 299. In October 1494 Carlo del Benino, Pandolfo Rucellai's son-in-law, declared himself a debtor of Giovanni's bank (Spedale di San Matteo, 30, f. 548ʳ⁻ᵛ). An undated copy in Bernardo's hand of a document in BNC (Fondo Ginori Conti, 29, 102), shows Giovanni's heirs seeking support from the royal family of Naples 'per la executione de una sententia che ànno . . . contro a Colantonio di Marino dall'Aquila'.

[4] The passage is in Perosa, p. 19; its dating presents difficulties (Perosa, p. xv). For two interpretations of Giovanni's advice and its significance, see Martines, *Social World*, pp. 35, n. 64, 291–2, and R. de Roover, "The Story of the Alberti Company of Florence, 1302–1348, as revealed in its Account Books", *Business History Review*, XXXII (1958), pp. 43, 45, n. 20. One of Bernardo's outbursts against his brother is in MAP, LI, 164, 28 June 1482. A Bernardo Rucellai was active as a merchant in Pisa at this time, but I suspect he was Bernardo di Piero di Cardinale (1417–93) (M. E. Mallett, "Anglo-Florentine commercial Relations, 1465–1491", *Economic History Review*, XV [1962], p. 259; *id.*, "Pisa and Florence in the Fifteenth Century . . .", in *Florentine Studies*, pp. 437, 439). Giovanni's Bernardo appears to have lived from landed income, and he acquired further lands *a*

banking—let alone become a *rentier*—and had struggled almost to the end to save something of his life's work as a great man of affairs.

Ridolfo Paganelli was among the few of Rucellai's close business associates who had not been or become his relation. Though the merchant did not himself make the point, after 1474 he must bitterly have regretted ignoring his own and the pseudo-Pandolfini's advice to ensure fidelity by employing men from among one's paternal kinsmen or *parentado*[1]. It was probably no coincidence that during this last decade of his life Rucellai found the time in February 1476 to write, on four tightly packed folios of the *Zibaldone*, a detailed account of 'tutto il parentado nostro', a complement to his much earlier 'notizia della discendenzia della nostra famiglia de' Rucellai'. This description, though it excludes the marriage alliances of most of his Rucellai kinswomen because 'sono grandissimo numero per modo si tirano drieto tutta la città', still manages to include, in an austere listing of the connections of his grandfather's line alone, some hundreds of names and scores of maternal first and second cousins. If the majority of those named have not appeared in the present account of Giovanni's life, yet almost every important figure we have mentioned, his paternal kinsmen aside, can be found there among these numerous *parenti* or their friends[2].

That his Medici relations had come to his rescue would have reconfirmed Giovanni's life-long belief in the efficacy of bonds of relationship by marriage and maternal and paternal blood. In April 1474 Lorenzo and Giuliano had bought land from him at Calenzano[3], and in the next month made the agreement about Poggio a Caiano. The details were left to the Medici, 'chè con cognati e parenti abbiamo a ffare, non con istrani', Bernardo Rucellai wrote on 29 May. Very probably Lorenzo took the initiative—and his motives were by no means disinterested—but the Medici ability to buy quickly such an estate, and to help in the legal complications that inevitably were to follow, would have made his offer irresistible, if not particularly welcome[4]. A letter written by Lorenzo to the abbot of San Paolo in Rome on 23 July 1474, 'promettendo quando lui servissi e' Rucellai di ducati 1,000, pagharli quando e' Rucellai non pagassino', also suggests financial support in Giovanni's greatest crisis[5]. Medici influence cannot have been irrelevant to the success of Rucellai's request in August for tax relief, which was passed with an unimpressive two-thirds majority of black beans, and to his attaining consolingly important political posts in 1475 and 1480[6].

The betrothal in 1477 of the nine-year-old Cosimo di Bernardo to the even younger daughter of Gabriello Malaspina, Marquis of Fosdinovo, brought the Rucellai a superb dowry of 4,000 large florins as well as helping to bolster their self-esteem. This very distinguished match with an ancient

---

livello; see Decima Repubblicana, 22, ff. 195ʳ–98ʳ; 63, ff. 226ʳ–27ᵛ; MAP, XLVIII, 127, letter of 22 November 1482 by Bernardo to Lorenzo de' Medici asking his advice and help concerning 'possessioni . . . per investirvi dentro qualche somma di danari rispecto a coteste nostre gravezze'.

[1] Perosa, pp. 3 ff. Rucellai presumably chose Paganelli, who had represented him in Pisa as early as 1461 (NA, B 1184 [Ser Girolamo Beltramini, 1457–78], inserto 6 [22]), because he was a Pisan specialist who owned property there and before 1469 had been the manager of the Quaratesi company which had long rented the house Giovanni owned in Pisa (Cat., 905, f. 674ᵛ; and Mallett, "Pisa", in *Florentine Studies*, p. 438). Paganelli himself makes no reference to Rucellai in his tax returns for 1469 and 1480 (Cat., 905, ff. 674ʳ–75ʳ; 993, ff. 241ʳ–42ʳ). He was not well off, but the latter report reveals that he had recently acquired some land.

[2] *Zibaldone*, ff. 223ʳ–24ᵛ.

[3] For the sale see NA, G 620 (Ser Simone Grazzini, 1472–94), ff. 3ʳ, 14ʳ–ᵛ, a reference I owe to Alison Brown. Lorenzo mentions the sale in 1480 (Cat., 1016, parte ii, f. 464ʳ) but Giovanni does not.

[4] For this letter and the other details, see my "Poggio a Caiano", pp. 251–2.

[5] *Protocolli del carteggio di Lorenzo il Magnifico per gli anni 1473–74, 1477–92*, ed. M. del Piazzo, Florence, 1956, p. 520; see pp. 90, 135 for later letters on Giovanni's behalf.

[6] Sixty-six votes against were recorded from a total of 236: Provvisioni, Registri, 165, f. 126ʳ. See above, p. 67.

feudal family—the Marquis had been a *condottiere* in Florence's service—was personally arranged by Lorenzo, as Bernardo made clear in an unusually effusive letter to his mother-in-law Lucrezia Tornabuoni on 6 June:

> per fare mio debito v'aviso Lorenzo vostro avere dato per donna a Cosimo mio, o vogliano dire più tosto suo, una figluola del M[agnifi]co Marchese Gabriello Malespina, parentado come intendete degnissimo in tucte le parti e molto più che alla qualità nostra non s'aspectava'.

'Non potremo essere più lieti nè più contenti', he continued, not only 'per le buone conditioni e qualità del Marchese' but because here was further evidence of 'l'affectione che ogni dì maggiore riconosciano in Lorenzo', who as always 'à mostro le cose nostre essergli all'animo come di cari parenti suoi, e figluoli miei stimare suoi proprii'[1]. Bernardo did indeed speak for his father, who added to an earlier passage on his family's marriage alliances a *ricordo* in his own hand which expressed, intensely but less sophisticatedly, his pleasure at a *parentado* which 'seghuita gl'altri narrati dirinpetto di degnità e avanzagli mediante il grado della signoria e il sanghue nobile'[2].

Always mindful of the obligations as well as the advantages of the ties of *parentado*, Giovanni in his consistent way still continued to pursue the interests of his Strozzi *parenti*, despite his increasing age, his many preoccupations and his grandson's new connections with an ancient family whose blood the Rucellai conceded to be gentler than Strozzi's 'nobile sangue'[3] and their own. Among the Strozzi correspondence in 1492–93 there are copies, in Bardo di Lorenzo di Messer Palla's curious hand, of some eight letters or extracts sent by Giovanni to Messer Lorenzo the copyist's brother in the 1470s, all concerning Rucellai's vigorous activities as a middleman in an attempt by Palla's grandsons in Ferrara to win back their ancestral Florentine house from their Ardinghelli relatives. The negotiations were long and tedious—these letters alone cover the years 1473 to 1480[4] —and even at the age of seventy-six Rucellai mentions that 'ho dato la vostra lettera a Nic[col]ò Ardinghelli e larghamente parlato insieme del fatto della chasa'[5].

These are Giovanni's most personal letters, and make one regret more than ever the loss of his correspondence with those relations and friends with whom he felt most at ease; when he made a mistake about some financial detail he admitted to the Strozzi that the seemingly very recalcitrant Niccolò Ardinghelli 'si fece beffe di me'[6]. Their contents confirm what their existence suggests, that Rucellai's social and personal concerns and his shrewd instincts had changed remarkably little since his youth. On 10 May 1480, having advised Messer Lorenzo that both he and his sons thought

---

[1] MAP, LXXX, 48. Maguire, *Women of the Medici*, pp. 104, 211, publishes and translates the letter, and Lucrezia's pleased note to Lorenzo two days later.

[2] *Zibaldone*, f. 6ʳ, which also gives the dowry. According to Giovanni the arrangement was made on 5 May, which explains Bernardo's apology to Lucrezia a month later (see preceding note) for the secrecy surrounding the negotiations. For the Marquis and his family, see Litta, *Famiglie*, VIII (1855), "Malaspina", tav. xiv. For the relevant notarial act, see NA, B 1184 (Ser Girolamo Beltramini, 1457–78), inserto 11 (8), 7 June 1477.

[3] Perosa, pp. 54, 61, 63, 118.

[4] The letters were recovered as part of Bardo's attempts to document his claims,—but I see no reason to doubt their authenticity, especially as the copies were sent privately to Bardo's kinsman Michele; on these men see my " 'Più superba' ", pp. 311–323. They are in CS, III, 139, ff. 23ʳ–24ᵛ and are dated 6, 27 February 1473; 7, 22 May 1473; 20 March 1479; 10 May 1480; 12 August 1480; one is undated and another copy, of a letter written by Pandolfo Rucellai on 8 November 1483, is on the same theme. From f. 17ʳ onwards there are other letters explaining the context of the Rucellai letters. An important judgement in the case is in Diplomatico, Strozzi Uguccione, 3 January 1470. As Caterina Ardinghelli explained in 1469: 'Non abbiamo chasa in Firenze nè altrove per abitare; torniamo in chasa fu di Messer Palla di Nofri Strozzi per certe ragioni leghate da Nofri detto a detta m[onn]a Caterina': Cat., 917, f. 253ʳ. On Giovanni, and the Ardinghelli and Strozzi, see above, pp. 70; 72, n. 5.

[5] CS, III, 139, f. 24ʳ, 20 March 1479.

[6] *Ibid.*, f. 23ʳ, 22 May 1473.

that Niccolò was prolonging the issue because he knew his position was weak, Giovanni went on earnestly to counsel these Strozzi, not themselves remarkably easy men with whom to deal, that the best way to break the deadlock was 'di rimanere d'achordo per mezzo d'amici e di parenti'. Indeed, he summed up:

> si facci quello si può di non venire a rottura cho' llui e che più tosto questa chosa s'abbi achon[i]are d'achordo che per via di piato, che sarà più honore dell'una parte e dell' altra e più chonservazione del parentado[1].

These were matters that had always been close to Giovanni's heart and much of the best of him can be found in these later letters. When, however, Niccolò remained obdurate, Rucellai was not above bluffing him in the service of his Strozzi friends. While 'cho' llui per altre facende', Giovanni reported to Messer Lorenzo on 12 August 1480, he had told Niccolò that various documents in the case had been submitted 'a' famosi dottori'. Niccolò, taken in by these wily tactics, showed signs of indecision whereupon Rucellai, sensing victory, advised a sharper line with this man who had refused honourably to submit the matter to arbitration, suggesting to Lorenzo that: 'quando voi diliberate scrivergli sopra a cciò abbiate a stare fermo di volere la chasa libera e che lla si chonoscha di ragone da uno chollegio di dottori, ho altri dottori'. Giovanni ended this, his last surviving letter, with the declaration that 'io per voi sono apparechiato a ffare hogni chosa sopra a cciò'[2].

Happily we know a little more of Giovanni Rucellai's last few months than that he was working for, and writing letters to, Palla Strozzi's grandson. Before his death in late October 1481 there were to be consolations for his business losses and 'altra aversità'. He was, for example, able to spend part of the autumn of 1480 at Quaracchi. There, on 10 September, he witnessed a notarial act drawn up al fresco in his garden[3]. A month later his autumnal pleasure in his creation was enhanced when a meeting of the parishioners of San Piero a Quaracchi, 'parendo loro che le bellezze e gentilezze del gardino mio da Quaracchi desse loro fama', obliged the parish 'a mantenere e chonservare le bellezze e gentilezze del detto gardino alle spese del detto popolo'. The men of Quaracchi did this 'of their own free will', Giovanni stated, to acknowledge 'avere riceuti molti benefici da me'. There is no reason to suppose that he had bullied his tenants into this action when he found himself in considerable financial difficulty[4]. Indeed he appears to have been moved by what was, almost certainly, his dependents' grateful thoughtfulness, since his reference to it—probably the last entry made in the Zibaldone—comes on the same folio as the note on the judgement of 1479 which had compelled him to pledge part of this beloved estate (and even a portion of the garden, the fine 'via d'albori grandi, con vite di raverusti su detti albori' that ran down to the Arno) to the Bankers' Guild in compensation for Poggio a Caiano[5].

Upon his return to Florence from Quaracchi Giovanni seems to have stayed much at home. 'Si sta in chasa del chontinovo' wrote Bertoldo Corsini, who implies that he was skulking there to avoid his creditors[6]. That might indeed have been true, however much the experience may have been

---

[1] Ibid., f. 24r.

[2] Ibid., f. 24r–v.

[3] NA, S 94 (Ser Salvi di Cenni di Ser Salvi, 1469–89), ff. 70v–71v.

[4] Perosa, p. 23. The notary was Ser Salvi di Cenni, but unfortunately I cannot find the act in his protocols (see preceding note).

[5] Perosa, pp. 23, 27. Compare Giovanni's description of the treed walk in ibid., p. 21, with the terms of the 1479 judgement in Dezzi Bardeschi, Facciata, p. 22. The arbiters clearly realized that Quaracchi was dear to Rucellai since he was given ten years to nominate another estate which could produce a similar revenue. One of them, Recco Capponi, had married his daughter to Stoldo Frescobaldi's son in 1475: Conv. Sopp., S. Pietro a Monticelli, 153, f. xxviir.

[6] See above, p. 89.

softened by the possession of such an elegant house, the expression of his own identity, into which to retreat. Rucellai was also now a very old man whose thoughts were more than ever concentrated upon his death and his hopes of the after-life, for which he had also provided. In late February 1481 the abbot of San Pancrazio, 'a volontà e beneplacito di Giovanni di Pagholo di Messer Pagholo Rucellai' gave special permission 'che ogni venerdì, quando altro impedimento non fussi di festa o di morti, che detto Giovanni volessi si conti [sic] la messe allo suo altare del sepolcro'[1].

The convent's sacristan noted in his register some months later that on 28 October 'se sopellì Giovanni Rucellai padre di Pandolfo e di Bernardo: si misse in una chas[s]a per serbanza', presumably the 'capsa marmorea' which, according to his will of 1465, was to be situated as his sons decided in his burial place 'in cappella quam ibidem fecit edificare'. In that testament Rucellai, who had spent so freely on this chapel and his other enterprises, had forbidden the ostentatious display of wealth or worldly position at his funeral, regarding with abhorrence 'sumptuosas impensas maxime in cereis candelis aut fanalibus aut in vexillis seu banderiis tam domesticis quam publicis et tam domesticis quam publicis signis decoratis', especially the so-called *drappelloni*. These austere last wishes were probably more or less respected. The amount of wax consumed at the funeral was no larger than that used for other distinguished parishioners buried at that time. Though there were present forty religious 'tra preti e monaci e preti secolari', most of these would have been accounted for by the Vallombrosan monks of San Pancrazio and Santa Trinita, and the Dominican friars of Santa Maria Novella, whom Giovanni, neatly summing up so much of his life's concerns, had given permission to attend. Perhaps another last request was honoured, that around his funeral bed there should be placed not personal devices (of which there were arguably enough in the Holy Sepulchre chapel), but only 'xxiiii sui signi, videlicet insignium domus de Oricellariis'[2].

As these conditions made in his hey-day imply, there may always have been a strain of personal austerity in Rucellai. It was to emerge in Pandolfo, Fra Santi Rucellai, as other sides of Giovanni's character were writ large in Bernardo. Possibly the experiences of his last seven years also gave Giovanni Rucellai second thoughts about how he had spent his life and his wealth, to the extent that he may have half anticipated his own elder son's subsequent Savonarolan revulsion against the exhibitionistic piety, and confident Quattrocento belief in mankind's ability to handle Fortuna, which he himself had personified. There is, for example, his late sense of not having solved the problem of fortune's nature[3]. Yet it is hard to resist the conclusion that, despite such twinges of fear and uncertainty as he may have felt, Giovanni Rucellai died a basically contented man, consoled and surrounded by the buildings which inevitably enough have inserted themselves into this account of his last year, confident that he had ensured that his memory would live on. Indeed it has. The *Zibaldone* would lose much of its interest, and the present volume would not exist, had Giovanni Rucellai not been the patron of some of the finest early Renaissance buildings. If man was indeed born to procreate and to build[4], his had been an exceptionally full and well-spent life, as his own sons noted in the *Zibaldone* upon their father's death. Giovanni would have been the first to appreciate

---

[1] Conv. Sopp., 88, 63, f. 77[r]. Giovanni was still active on San Pancrazio's behalf, he and Pandolfo being arbiters in a dispute concerning the convent in late 1477 (*ibid.*, 41, f. 167[r]).

[2] The references to his burial are *ibid.*, 67, ff. 49[v], 116[r]; cf. for other funerals ff. 49[v], 50[r]. For the will see NA, L 130 (Ser Lionardo da Colle, 1441–95), no. 31.

[3] See above, p. 87.

[4] See above, p. 13.

the judgement, made 'da più uomini antichi della famigla nostra de' Rucellai', which Pandolfo and Bernardo recorded there:

> la chasa nostra non n'ebbe mai niuno che meritasse tante dengne lode e chommendazioni, e che magg[i]ore onore abbi fatto alla famiglia nostra poi che ll'ebbe principio che'l detto Govanni nostro padre, chonsiderato massimamente e' dengni parentadi, la richezza, l'essere stato ghrande merchatante e di ghran fede e chredito, e mediante le muragle fatte per lui tenporali e spirituali, e paramenti di brochato d'oro e altre dengne chose: per modo che ci è paruto meritamente farne memoria in questo libro che Dio gli choncieda della sua santa ghrazia[1].

---

[1] *Zibaldone*, f. 66ʳ, beginning: 'Memoria chome noi Pandolfo e Bernardo Rucellai figluoli di Govanni autore di questo libro faciano fede d'aver inteso da più uomini antichi. . .'. There is a modernized and not always accurate partial transcription in Marcotti, *Mercante fiorentino*, p. 42. The rich *paramenti* in San Pancrazio are described in an inventory of 1466 (NA, G 680 [Ser Griso Griselli, 1439–80], inserto 26).

Postscript (see p. 45, above)

The Vanni or Giovanni Rucellai who wrote the official version of Masaccio's tax declaration reporting his death—see L. B. Watkins, "The Brancacci Chapel Frescoes: Meaning and Use", unpub. Ph.D. dissertation, University of Michigan, 1976, pp. 212–13, and J. Beck (with the collaboration of G. Corti), *Masaccio: The Documents*, Locust Valley, New York, 1978, p. 26 —was not our Giovanni but his cousin Vanni di Paolo, a secretary to the catasto officials: D. Herlihy and C. Klapisch-Zuber, *Les Toscans et leurs familles*, Paris, 1978, pp. 83–84.

ALESSANDRO PEROSA

LO ZIBALDONE DI GIOVANNI RUCELLAI

LO ZIBALDONE DI GIOVANNI RUCELLAI

I

Di Giovanni Rucellai esiste, nel Palazzo gentilizio di via della Vigna Nuova a Firenze, un ritratto a olio su tela, non firmato, della seconda metà del '500, probabilmente di scuola vasariana (Frontespizio). Il Rucellai—rappresentato di tre quarti seduto davanti al suo tavolo di lavoro—campeggia sullo sfondo di un irreale paesaggio urbano, che vede allineati, come in un sapiente 'collage', al di là di un'ampia finestra su cui si solleva una pesante tenda di colore oscuro, i monumenti ch'egli aveva fatto edificare: da un lato gli edifici privati (il Palazzo e la Loggia), dall'altro quelli sacri (S. Maria Novella e il Sepolcro di S. Pancrazio)[1].

L'ignoto autore del quadro ha voluto, evidentemente, rappresentare, emblematicamente, Giovanni Rucellai nel ruolo di Mecenate legato al prestigioso nome di Leon Battista Alberti, cui il Vasari nelle *Vite* aveva attribuito in blocco la paternità delle opere che il Rucellai aveva fatto costruire[2]; ma ha anche cercato, se non erro, di adombrare un altro lato, meno ovvio, della personalità del Rucellai, quello cioè dell'uomo impegnato culturalmente. Giovanni Rucellai vien qui infatti rappresentato nelle sembianze idealizzate—che non sapremmo dire quanto rispondano alla realtà[3]—di un antico filosofo o patriarca. Egli indossa ricche vesti ad ampie pieghe e il suo volto sereno e pensieroso è incorniciato da una folta capigliatura e da una barba fluente che gli scende a mezzo il petto. Colla mano sinistra sembra indicare un libro spalancato sul tavolino, di cui si riesce a decifrare una parte del titolo (*Delle Antichità*), stampato nel margine superiore dell'unica pagina visibile. Accanto al libro si scorgono alcune lettere dissigillate, che recano l'anacronistico indirizzo (in stile e grafia del '500): 'All'ill.mo sig. Giovanni Rucellai Firenze', che, evidentemente, funge da biglietto di presentazione del personaggio ritratto. La collocazione in primo piano del volume, che presumibilmente trattava delle antichità di Roma, non sembra casuale. A prescindere dal fatto che si sia voluto, in questo modo, alludere alla descrizione che il Rucellai stesso ha fatto, in alcune pagine del suo Zibaldone, delle 'anticaglie' e delle cose mirabili della città di Roma[4], si ha l'impressione che l'ignoto ritrattista, attribuendo un valore emblematico al libro di argomento antiquario squadernato sul tavolo, abbia voluto proporci l'imagine di un Rucellai coinvolto intellettualmente in quel processo culturale di riscoperta dell'antico, che l'Alberti stava attuando in campo architettonico. Comunque stiano le cose, par certo, che a un secolo di distanza dalla sua morte, Giovanni Rucellai appariva agli occhi dei suoi concittadini e dei suoi discendenti, non solo come un

---

[1] *Mostra dei Tesori segreti delle Case fiorentine*, Firenze, 1960, pp. 25 s., tav. 39. Questo ritratto è stato descritto da G. Marcotti, *Mercante fiorentino*, pp. 40 s., e da G. Biagi, "La vita privata dei Fiorentini", in *La vita italiana nel Rinascimento*, Milano, 1899, pp. 86 s. Per quanto concerne l'attribuzione, una mia scolara, Gloria Cecchi, ha proposto dubitativamente (ma con buoni argomenti di carattere stilistico) il nome di Giacomo Coppi, che tra il 1570 e il 1572 collaborò col Vasari nella decorazione dello Studiolo del granduca Francesco. Cfr. Kent, sopra, p. 10, n. 2. Sul Coppi v. F. Noack, in Thieme-Becker, *Allgemeines Lexikon der bildenden Künstler*, VII, Lipsia, 1912, p. 378; L. Berti, *Il Principe dello Studiolo*, Firenze, 1967, pp. 84, ss., fig. 76.

[2] Vasari, *Vite*, a cura di G. Milanesi, II, Firenze, 1878, pp. 540 ss. Da notare che il Vasari ritiene, erroneamente, che il committente del Palazzo e della Loggia non sia Giovanni ma Cosimo Rucellai.

[3] Non possediamo, che io sappia, un ritratto contemporaneo del Rucellai, ma è probabile che qualcuno tra gli artisti ch'egli protessse o che hanno lavorato per lui (cfr. Perosa, p. 24) ne abbia immortalato l'immagine in opere che non ci sono pervenute.

[4] Perosa, pp. 67–78.

grande Mecenate, ma anche come un uomo di cultura, che—soprattutto per i suoi noti legami coll'Alberti—non si poteva ritenere fosse rimasto estraneo o indifferente al rinnovamento spirituale del suo tempo.

II

A definire nei suoi giusti limiti la personalità e la cultura del Rucellai, e a soddisfare la curiosità di chi ancor oggi vorrebbe sapere qualcosa di più sul celebre patrono dell'Alberti, provvede il voluminoso Zibaldone, che si conserva manoscritto a Firenze in casa dei conti Rucellai, ed ha più volte attirato l'attenzione degli studiosi[1]. Di questo codice—di cui ho dato una descrizione dettagliata nella prefazione al volume *Il Zibaldone Quaresimale* nel 1960[2]—mi limiterò ora a fornire soltanto alcuni dati essenziali, ricordando che si tratta di un ms. cartaceo di 258 ff., scritto in varie riprese da una decina di amanuensi, e riveduto e integrato qua e là dallo stesso Rucellai, che di sua mano ha effettuato frequenti aggiunte nei margini o in parti di foglio rimaste bianche. Il ms. è composto di 27 fascicoli; i fascicoli XXIV–XXVI—che contengono testi non pertinenti alla primitiva compagine dello Zibaldone—furono scritti verso la metà del '500; il fascicolo XXVII è rimasto bianco. Il foglio di guardia del codice è in membrana e nel verso contiene su due colonne l'indice sommario del contenuto dello Zibaldone, scritto in rosso da uno degli amanuensi, con aggiunte, d'inchiostro diverso, di mano del Rucellai e di altri copisti.

Nei vari fascicoli del codice il Rucellai ha fatto copiare un abbondante materiale di natura e provenienza disparate. Ai ricordi personali e di famiglia si intrecciano consigli ed ammaestramenti ai figli, memorie di avvenimenti storici, narrazioni di viaggi e descrizioni di fenomeni naturali, raccolte di estratti, note e sentenze di vari autori antichi, medioevali e contemporanei, copie di atti e documenti di famiglia, di lettere di parenti, amici ed umanisti, di cronache fiorentine, di volgarizzamenti di autori classici, ecc. Come si può constatare anche da questo breve sommario, lo Zibaldone del Rucellai rientra in un genere di opere—'ricordanze', 'cronache familiari', 'commentari domestici', ecc.—che ebbero una larga diffusione nel tardo Medioevo e durante il Rinascimento, e recano preziose testimonianze sulla vita privata, la situazione economica e finanziaria, gli interessi pubblici e le aspirazioni culturali degli uomini d'affari toscani dal XIV al XVI secolo. Questi libri di ricordanze ci sono pervenuti in buon numero, ma giacciono in gran parte inediti in biblioteche ed archivi pubblici e privati, anche se dagli inizi del secolo questa produzione memorialistica abbia suscitato un crescente interesse sia da parte di storici e di cultori della lingua e letteratura nazionale, sia da parte di studiosi dell'economia e della società tardomedioevale e rinascimentale, e alcuni di questi testi—i più interessanti—siano stati pubblicati integralmente per la prima volta o ristampati in edizioni più corrette che nel passato, oppure fatti conoscere parzialmente in saggi monografici o in opere di carattere generale[3].

---

[1] Ricorderò L. Passerini, *Rucellai*; G. Temple Leader, *Autografo tolto dallo Zibaldone di Giovanni Rucellai fiorentino*, Firenze,1872, che per un certo tempo fu il proprietario del codice; e G. Marcotti, che publicò vari estratti dello *Zibaldone* nel suo *Mercante fiorentino* e in due articoli usciti nello stesso anno: "Il giubileo dell'anno 1450 secondo una relazione di Giovanni Rucellai", in *Archivio della Società romana di Storia patria*, IV, 4 (1881), pp. 563–80; "Descrizione di una tromba terrestre avvenuta nel 1456", *Atti della R. Accademia dei Lincei*, s. III, Transunti, V (1881), pp. 252–5. In epoca più recente se ne sono occupati A. Warburg ("Francesco Sassetti's letztwillige Verfügung", 1907, in *Gesammelte Schriften*, Lipsia, 1932, I, pp. 127–58, 350–65 = *La Rinascita del paganesimo antico*, Firenze, 1966, pp. 211–46); P. O. Kristeller (*Supplementum Ficinianum*, I, Firenze, 1937, p. XXIX; II, pp. 169–73, 330); R. Valentini e G. Zucchetti (*Codice Topografico della Città di Roma*, IV, Roma, 1953, pp. 399–419).

[2] Perosa, pp. xi–xviii.

[3] Per notizie più dettagliate sui libri di ricordanze si vedano, tra l'altro: D. Velluti, *La Cronica domestica scritta fra il 1367 ed*

Libri di questo genere—pur derivando da una comune matrice, cioè dai libri contabili, che col tempo erano diventati sempre più numerosi e specializzati—presentano contenuti, strutture e sviluppi assai vari, che rispecchiano in genere le diverse personalità ed esigenze degli uomini di affari che li compilavano per uso proprio e per ricordo e ammaestramento della famiglia. Nei libri di ricordanze più comuni si alternano cronologicamente, in forma di diario, notazioni di carattere finanziario—che riguardano l'attività commerciale, agricola o artigianale, i contratti, le compere e le vendite, ecc.—con memorie che concernono la famiglia, il casato (genealogie, nascite, matrimoni, morti, ecc.), e, in certi casi, gli avvenimenti cittadini di maggiore rilievo[1]; in altri—come ad es. nelle *Mescolanze* di Michele Siminetti, che si trovano in un codice di Dresda[2]—sono riuniti alla rinfusa ricordi personali, memorie di avvenimenti storici e un'infinità di testi di vario genere e provenienza (documenti, lettere, testi di carattere religioso, astrologico e letterario, volgarizzamenti, ecc.); nei libri, infine, di più ampio respiro e di maggiore pretesa letteraria—come ad es. i *Ricordi* di Giovanni di Paolo Morelli o di Buonaccorso Pitti[3]—la narrazione estesa di fatti personali e di avvenimenti storici arricchita da ampi *excursus* di carattere morale o didattico (da servire da esempio ed ammaestramento ai figli e ai discendenti), dalla descrizione di viaggi e paesaggi, da annotazioni di carattere psicologico, ecc.

Lo Zibaldone del Rucellai ha vari punti di contatto con tali opere (soprattutto in quei settori che concernono le tradizioni della casata e i ricordi di famiglia), ma se ne discosta per una diversa impostazione generale e per strutture e contenuti delle singole parti che spesso divergono dai tipi più tradizionali.

Per poter valutare però adeguatamente gli elementi che hanno concorso a dare allo Zibaldone l'attuale sua fisionomia, è necessario, prima di ogni altra cosa, sottoporre il manoscritto ad un attento esame codicologico. Lo Zibaldone non è un'opera organica ed omogenea, ma ha subito nel tempo—con ritmo non costante—progressivi accrescimenti, che ne hanno via via modificato la fisionomia originaria. Parti nuove si sono aggiunte alle antiche, pagine rimaste bianche sono state invase da più recenti scritturazioni, nuovi amanuensi hanno preso il posto degli antichi. Il Rucellai stesso è intervenuto più volte e di suo pugno ha segnato nel testo o nei margini notizie più recenti riguardanti eventi di famiglia, maturatisi dopo la prima stesura del testo. La ricostruzione del processo che ha portato lo Zibaldone alla sua attuale consistenza è affidato pertanto a un'opera paziente di analisi delle singole parti del codice e di ripulitura dalle incrostazioni che via via si sono venute a depositare sullo sfondo originario del contesto. Nella prefazione del già citato volume antologico di testi tratti dallo Zibaldone[4], ho indicato in dettaglio la via percorsa, dimostrando che, in base a testimonianze interne (riferimenti cronologici) ed esterne (raggruppamento dei fascicoli, mani di copisti, indice, ecc.) era possibile distinguere vari strati nella composizione del libro; in un *Indice generale* poi, aggiunto alla prefazione, ho elencato—perchè il lettore potesse più agevolmente

---

il 1370, a cura di I. Del Lungo e G. Volpi, Firenze, 1914, pp. XII–XXIV; A. Sapori, *Le Marchand italien au Moyen Age*, Parigi, 1952, pp. 5–10; C. Guzzoni degli Ancarani, *La Cronica domestica toscana dei secoli XIV e XV*, Lucca, 1920; P. J. Jones, "Florentine Families and Florentine Diaries in the Fourteenth Century", in *Papers of the British School at Rome*, XXIV (1956), pp. 183–205; C. Bec, *Les Marchands écrivains à Florence 1375–1434*, Parigi, 1967; Kent, *Household and Lineage*, pp. 75–6, 113–5, 272–8; F. Pezzarossa, "La memorialistica fiorentina tra Medioevo e Rinascimento", *Lettere italiane*, XXXI (1979), pp. 96–138.

[1] Fra i tanti ricorderò, per la sua singolarità, il memoriale-diario di un artista: Neri di Bicci, *Le Ricordanze (10 marzo 1453–24 aprile 1475)*, a cura di B. Santi, Pisa, 1976. Neri lavorò per il Rucellai nel 1455 (cfr. pp. 28 s.).

[2] G. Buchholz, "Die 'Mescolanze' des Michele Siminetti auf der königlichen öffentlichen Bibliothek zu Dresden", *Zeitschrift für vergleichende Litteraturgeschichte und Renaissance-Litteratur*, II (1889), pp. 340–59.

[3] G. Morelli, *Ricordi*, a cura di V. Branca, Firenze, 1956; B. Pitti, *Cronica*, rist. da A. Bacchi Della Lega, Bologna, 1905.

[4] Perosa, pp. xii ss.

rendersi conto della struttura dello Zibaldone—i brani contenuti nel codice, con l'indicazione dei fascicoli e dei fogli in cui si trovavano, e delle mani che li avevano trascritti[1].

Sono riuscito così ad isolare un nucleo centrale più antico (che per brevità ho chiamato Zibaldone *vetus*) dalle successive sovrapposizioni ed aggiunte, e ad appurare che questo primo Zibaldone constava di nove fascicoli, o per dir meglio di due gruppi, rispettivamente di sette e due fascicoli, scritti da due amanuensi diversi. I primi sette fascicoli (ff. 1–70, di cui i ff. 3r, 49r–50v, 61v–70v bianchi) comprendevano—come si può constatare dall'*Indice*—, oltre al preambolo, un blocco di notizie di carattere genealogico; una serie di ammaestramenti ai figli sul governo della famiglia, l'educazione dei figli, l'utilità della masserizia (con relativa appendice di *auctoritates* su liberalità, prodigalità e avarizia), la fortuna, la partecipazione alla vita pubblica, ecc.; un florilegio di precetti morali e di definizioni di vizi e virtù desunti da raccolte trecentesche; una sorta di catechismo; la descrizione di due visite del Rucellai, a Roma per il giubileo del 1450 e nel contado fiorentino in seguito ad una tempesta nel 1456. I fascicoli ottavo e nono (ff. 71–88, di cui i ff. 85r–88v bianchi) comprendevano una *Cronaca* di Firenze del Rucellai, e poi, in coda, un blocco disordinato di notazioni disparate, dicerie, ricordi ricavati da fonti spesso non facilmente identificabili.

Questo primo nucleo dello Zibaldone fu costituito nell'estate del 1457. 'Questo libro—dice il Rucellai nel preambolo—fu ordinato et scripto per me, Giovanni di Pagholo di messere Pagolo Rucellai, mercatante et cittadino fiorentino, questo anno 1457, nel castello di Sancto Giminiano, dove mi truovo colla mia famiglia, fuggito la pestilentia che in detto tempo era nella nostra città di Firenze; il quale ò principiato per dare notitia et amaestramento a Pandolfo et a Bernardo miei figliuoli di più chose ch'io credo abbia a essere loro utile; et fia una insalata di più erbe, come s'intenderà pe' lettori; il quale libro si chiama il Zibaldone quaresimale'[2]. E altrove, ricordando le morìe che avevano colpito la città di Firenze dopo il 1348, il Rucellai annoterà: 'Nell'anno 1457 avemo un'altra morìa, che cominciò di luglio . . . la quale io fuggi' con tutta la mia famiglia nel castello di San Gimignano, e quivi ordinai la presente opera'[3].

Dal preambolo risulta evidente quale fosse lo scopo principale, che il Rucellai, sin dall'inizio, s'era proposto di raggiungere con questo Zibaldone. Come altri autori di Ricordanze[4], egli intendeva—in un momento importante della sua esistenza—'dare notitia et amaestramento' ai figli di 'più chose' che egli riteneva potessero essere loro utili; e per attuare questo programma progettava un'opera, che pur conservando alcune strutture tipiche medioevali, obbedisse ad una certa impostazione unitaria, e in qualche modo adombrasse quei trattati umanistici che il Rucellai leggeva ed ammirava e dai quali avrebbe tratto, come vedremo[5], cospicui materiali. Lo Zibaldone sarebbe stato, è vero, un'insalata di più erbe, ma—almeno nelle intenzioni del suo autore—avrebbe dovuto distinguersi da tante opere consimili per una diversa organizzazione della materia.

Abolito il sistema della notazione cronologica che in genere compariva nei libri di Ricordanze, nei diari e nelle cronache familiari, il Rucellai ha tentato di raggruppare i suoi materiali secondo argomenti o temi di carattere generale, cercando di dare (almeno agli inizi) al suo Zibaldone una

---

[1] Perosa, pp. xxi ss.

[2] Perosa, p. 2.

[3] *Zibaldone*, f. 26br. Cfr. p. 123 e n. 4.

[4] L'intenzione pedagogica è, si può dire, essenziale in quasi tutti i libri di Ricordanze. Scopo di questi libri è infatti di offrire, rievocando i tempi trascorsi e l'esempio dei maggiori, utili documenti e modelli di comportamento ai figli e ai discendenti. L'intento moralistico-pedagogico è meno esplicito nei libri domestici di carattere più tecnico; esplode invece in quei libri di maggiore pretesa letteraria, come ad es. nei già citati *Ricordi* del Morelli (ed. Branca, pp. 205–85).

[5] Cfr. pp. 111 ss.

parvenza di organicità. Indizi non trascurabili di carattere formale confermano quest'ipotesi. Il Rucellai si è valso, ad es., nella stesura dello Zibaldone *vetus*, dell'opera di due amanuensi, che pur non essendo—come si può arguire dai numerosi errori di trascrizione—particolarmente colti rivelano dalla grafia un certo grado di professionalità. La presenza poi di vari elementi decorativi (titoli scritti in rosso, iniziali dipinte in rosso e azzurro, l'iniziale del primo foglio dorata e contornata da un fregio floreale colorato in verde, azzurro e rosa, ecc.) sottolinea l'intenzione del Rucellai di dare al suo libro, anche esteriormente, la fisionomia di un'opera concepita organicamente e con un certo impegno. Si aggiunga che il Rucellai ha fatto copiare di getto il materiale che doveva entrare a far parte dello Zibaldone *vetus*, e ha—presumibilmente—fornito egli stesso ai due amanuensi le minute dei testi 'ordinati' (come egli dice nel preambolo) secondo un suo disegno personale, avvalendosi di appunti, minute, documenti, libri, ecc. di vario genere in suo possesso. Nello Zibaldone infatti—oltre a singoli documenti (lettere, testamenti, atti vari appartenenti a diversi periodi), che il Rucellai ha fatto riprodurre integralmente o in forma riassuntiva—s'incontrano talvolta note o ricordi, che ci riportano, per quanto concerne la data di stesura, ad anni precedenti al 1457[1], e non mancano riferimenti ad altri libri dell'archivio di famiglia[2], e in modo particolare ad un 'libro memoriale', cui il Rucellai rimanda i figli qualora desiderino avere maggiori notizie su alcuni argomenti marginali[3]. Ma la testimonianza più importante a questo proposito è costituita da un libro del 1456 (scritto, dunque, un anno prima dello Zibaldone), di cui ci sono pervenuti degli estratti in alcuni codici del sec. XVII, che ci danno la possibilità di valutare adeguatamente, attraverso utili raffronti, le modifiche nella disposizione della materia e nel testo apportate dal Rucellai nella redazione definitiva del 1457[4]. Singolare infine il preambolo, che si discosta dalla tradizionale *invocatio*, con cui si aprono, in genere, i libri di Ricordanze[5]. Il Rucellai ha voluto, sin dall'inizio, prendere le distanze dalla tradizione e presentare un libro di ricordi un po' diverso dal consueto. Questa sua intenzione appare evidente anche dalla scelta del titolo. Egli ha infatti voluto che il suo libro si chiamasse *Zibaldone quaresimale*, precisando che si sarebbe trattato di 'una insalata di più erbe'.

Poco si sa sulla storia della parola 'zibaldone' e sul suo etimo. I dizionari più comuni della lingua italiana—che sotto 'zibaldone' indicano 1) una vivanda composta di molti e svariati ingredienti, 2) una mescolanza confusa di cose diverse, 3) un quaderno o scartafaccio di appunti segnati senz'ordine[6]

---

[1] *Zibaldone*, ff. 81a^v ('la chiesa di Santa Maria del Fiore . . . insino a questo tempo, che siamo nel 1449'), 83b^r ('la leggie della grazia . . . del nostro Signore Giesù Christo in sino al presente dì è durata anni 1451'), ecc.

[2] Perosa, p. 25.

[3] *Zibaldone*, ff. 29b^r–30a^r ('E volendo sapere, figliuoli miei, qual sia . . . andrete al libro memoriale a. . . .'). Ci sono una trentina di rimandi a questo libro—sempre introdotti dalla stessa formula—per inchieste su argomenti anche assai stravaganti. Il Rucellai ha lasciato in bianco il numero della pagina, in cui doveva trovarsi il passo cui rimandava.

[4] Gli estratti del libro del 1456 (andato perduto insieme alla quasi totalità dei documenti e libri appartenuti al Rucellai) si trovano nei mss. Vat. Barb. lat. 5004, pp. 376–88 (segnalato da Dezzi Bardeschi, "Complesso monumentale", pp. 16, 41), Naz. II. IV. 374, pp. 126–31 della Biblioteca Nazionale Centrale di Firenze, e CS, ser. iii, 79, pp. 57–9 dell'Archivio di Stato di Firenze (segnalati da Kent, "Letters", p. 343). Da notare che negli estratti contenuti nel codice dell'Archivio di Stato (che riguarda personaggi della famiglia Strozzi) figurano frequenti rimandi del Rucellai ad altri suoi libri scomparsi (ad es. ad un 'libro delle Ricordanze, coreggie bianche', ad un 'libro rosso', ecc.).

[5] I preamboli dei libri di Ricordanze seguono, in genere, uno schema convenzionale, che—come ha rilevato di recente A. Petrucci, *Il libro di Ricordanze dei Corsini (1362–1457)*, Roma, 1965, pp. lxiv ss.—si ispira, in gran parte, alla tecnica del documento notarile. I punti obbligati sono: 1) invocazione (Dio, la Vergine, questo o quel Santo, la corte celeste, ecc.); 2) nome dell'autore e possessore del libro; 3) contenuto; 4) titolo. Valga un esempio tra i tanti: 'Al nome sia dell'onnipotente Idio e della sua groriosa Madre . . . questo libro è di . . . el quale libro si chiama Richordanze ed è segnato . . . in sul quale farò richordo d'ogni lavoro, ecc.' (Neri di Bicci, *Ricordanze*, ed. Santi, p. 1).

[6] N. Tommaseo–B. Bellini, *Dizionario della lingua italiana*, IV, 2, Torino, 1861; e tra i più recenti C. Battisti–G. Alessio, *Dizionario etimologico italiano*, V, Firenze, 1966 e G. Devoto–G. C. Oli, *Vocabolario illustrato della lingua italiana*, Firenze, 1967. Utili osservazioni in P. G. Goidanich, "Denominazioni del pane e di dolci casereci in Italia", *Memorie della R. Accademia delle Scienze*

—non registrano il passo del Rucellai. L'esempio più antico riportato dai lessici è tratto dal *Pataffio* (poemetto in terza rima probabilmente della prima metà del sec. XV), ove 'zibaldone' viene interpretato come 'miscuglio di parole'[1]. Due giovani colleghi, R. Bessi e G. Tanturli, hanno però richiamato la mia attenzione su due testimonianze più antiche: la Bessi su un verso (v. 368) di una frottola di Franco Sacchetti (seconda metà del sec. XIV), in cui il poeta chiama 'zibaldone' l'oscuro e confuso guazzabuglio di parole, che egli ha composto e trascritto, immagazzinando 'molti strani vocaboli de' fiorentini'[2]; il Tanturli su un passo del volgarizzamento della *Invettiva* di Cino Rinuccini (che dovrebbe risalire agli inizi del sec. XV), in cui viene riferita l'opinione di taluni, che facendosi beffe del 'coronato poeta messer Francesco Petrarca', dicono che il suo *De viris illustribus* è 'un zibaldone di quaresima'[3]. Anche per il Rucellai 'zibaldone' ha il significato di minestrone o insalata quaresimale di più erbe; ed è assai probabile che, in mancanza di altre testimonianze, egli sia stato il primo a dare questo titolo a un libro di Ricordanze; soltanto più tardi, verso la fine del secolo, furono chiamati zibaldoni—nel significato traslato più comune del termine—non tanto i libri di Ricordi, quanto le raccolte miscellanee di varie opere o di vari autori, i quaderni o registri di appunti, ecc.[4].

Cessato il pericolo della pestilenza, il Rucellai—dopo aver fatto eseguire ai suoi fidati amanuensi, contemporaneamente alla stesura dello Zibaldone *vetus*, la trascrizione su una quarantina di fogli a parte di un'ampia silloge di epistole di Seneca volgarizzate (che non è chiaro se nel suo primitivo disegno avrebbero dovuto entrare a far parte integrante dello Zibaldone)[5]—fece ritorno in città,

---

dell'Istituto di Bologna, *Classe di scienze morali*, s. I, VIII (1913–14), pp. 64–6. W. Th. Elwert ("Ital. Zibaldone", *Paideia*, X [1955], pp. 303–7, rist. in *Studi di letteratura veneziana*, Venezia, 1958, pp. 63–70) ritiene—a torto, come spero, in altra occasione, di poter dimostrare—che la parola 'zibaldone' derivi dal nome di un ipotetico 'physico magistro Cibaldone', al quale in alcune stampe viene attribuito il volgarizzamento in terza rima della versione latina del terzo libro del *Liber medicinalis Almansoris* di Rhazes, in cui si tratta dei vari alimenti e dei loro effetti sull'uomo.

[1] B. Latini, *Pataffio e Tesoretto*, Napoli, 1788, p. 92. Il *Pataffio*, ritenuto un tempo opera di Brunetto Latini, è stato attribuito di recente da F. Ageno ("Per l'identificazione dell'autore del *Pataffio*", in "Tre studi Quattrocenteschi", *Studi di Filologia italiana*, XX [1962], pp. 75–84) al fiorentino Raimondo Mannelli (1388–1464). Non ha invece alcun valore documentario la testimonianza di 'zibaldone', che talvolta viene addotta per designare 1) l'opera di Antonio Pucci, composta intorno al 1362 e giunta autografa nel codice Tempi 2 della Biblioteca Laurenziana, e 2) la miscellanea di testi volgari copiata da una mano della metà del sec. XV nel codice Laur. Conv. Sopp. 148 bis, che nei vari dizionari ottocenteschi viene Zibaldone Andreini dal nome di uno dei suoi possessori. In ambedue i casi si tratta di denominazioni posteriori, che non appartengono alle opere originarie.

[2] F. Sacchetti, *Il libro delle Rime*, a cura di A. Chiari, Bari, 1936, p. 161.

[3] *Invettiva contro a cierti caluniatori di Dante e di messer Francesco Petrarca e di messer Giovanni Boccacci . . . composta pello . . . uomo Cino di messer Francesco Rinuccini . . . ridotta di grammatica in vulgare*, in Giovanni da Prato, *Il Paradiso degli Alberti*, ed. A. Wesselofsky, I, II, Bologna, 1867, p. 309. Di 'zibaldone', nel significato di minestrone che si serve soprattutto in quaresima, o di piatto composto di vari intingoli, si hanno anche testimonianze più recenti. Si vedano, ad es., V. Magazzini, *Coltivazione toscana*, Firenze, 1634, p. 12 ('La sera di Quaresima, per colazione, mandorle tagliate, pinocchi, uve passere et anici confetti in zibaldone, olive, una mela o pera e poco pane, ecc.'); G. B. Fagioli, *Rime piacevoli*, I, Lucca, 1729, p. 137 ('Pare il mio piatto un zibaldone o pozza di variati intingoli composto'), ecc. Il Goidanich, "Denominazione del pane", p. 66, osserva che 'zibaldone ancor oggi in Toscana (Pisano) significa una minestra intrugliata di più cose e mal riuscita'. Cfr. G. Malagoli, *Vocabolario pisano*, Firenze, 1939.

[4] Da una nota di possesso, di mano della seconda metà del sec. XV—che figurava nel foglio di guardia del codice BNC, Pal. 359 (che comprende vari testi volgari del sec. XIV) ed è stata poi erasa—si ricava: 'Questo libro è di Lorenzo . . . chiamato un zibaldone perchè tracta di più chose diferenziate'; al f. 90ᵛ del codice BNC, II.IX.42 (che contiene, di mano dell'autore, ricordi di viaggi, notizie storiche, sentenze morali, ecc.) si legge: 'A dì 15 di Gienaio 1484 (= 1485). Questo libro è di Giannozo di Bernardo. . . . Salviati, citadino fiorentino. Chiamasi zibaldone, ischritto in più volte et in vari tempi chome si vede'; ad un suo zibaldone (che doveva contenere la prima stesura delle sue poesie) rimanda Filippo Scarlatti in due passi (ff. 58ʳ e 372ʳ) di una raccolta di versi, allestita tra il 1468 e il 1481, che ci è pervenuta nel codice Venturi Lisci 3 (cfr. M. Ferrara, "Il codice Venturi Ginori di rime antiche", in *La Bibliofilia*, LII [1950], pp. 45, 78, 92 e E. Pasquini, "Il codice di Filippo Scarlatti", in *Studi di filologia italiana*, XXII [1964], pp. 436, 464); analogamente, ad un giovanile zibaldone di sonetti e commenti di Lorenzo de' Medici fa allusione Piero da Bibbiena in una lettera al Magnifico del 1486 (cfr. M. Martelli, *Studi laurenziani*, Firenze, 1965, pp. 128 s.).

[5] Perosa, p. xiv.

interrompendo il lavoro, che così alacremente aveva iniziato nel forzato ritiro di S. Gemignano. A Firenze il Rucellai fu riafferrato dai suoi negozi, e per qualche tempo non ebbe più la possibilità e l'occasione di attendere allo Zibaldone. Quando, alcuni anni dopo, lo riprese in mano, ne fece un uso alquanto diverso, e abbandonando il primitivo disegno, vi accolse testi e documenti di disparato valore e provenienza. Nella citata prefazione al volume edito nel 1960, io ho cercato, anche per questa parte dello Zibaldone (che, si badi, è la più voluminosa) di individuare—in base ai dati cronologici che i documenti riprodotti offrivano, e ad un attento esame delle scritture dei vari amanuensi impiegati e della composizione e struttura dei singoli fascicoli—le varie tappe percorse dal Rucellai nell'opera di continuazione dello Zibaldone dopo il suo rientro a Firenze fino agli ultimi anni della sua lunga esistenza[1]. Il Rucellai ha agglutinato ai nove fascicoli, che come s'è visto, costituivano lo Zibaldone *vetus*, nuovi fascicoli o gruppi di fascicoli, fatti trascrivere da uno stuolo di amanuensi, professionalmente meno abili dei loro predecessori di S. Gemignano, ed ha via via riempito di proprio pugno o per mano altrui, in tempi diversi, gli spazi e i fogli che, per vari motivi, sia nei fascicoli che componevano lo Zibaldone *vetus*, sia nei fascicoli aggiunti posteriormente, erano rimasti bianchi.

Per quanto concerne il contenuto dei fascicoli, venuti man mano ad ingrossare la primitiva compagine dello Zibaldone, colpisce, anzitutto, il fatto che—come si può rilevare in dettaglio dal già citato *Indice generale*—un gran numero di essi sia stato riservato alla trascrizione di parti di testi storici o letterari. Prescindendo dai fascicoli XV–XIX, copiati a S. Gemignano—che comprendono, come s'è visto, il volgarizzamento delle Epistole di Seneca—nello Zibaldone è confluito un numero non indifferente di fascicoli (XI–XIV, XIX–XXIII)—per un totale di circa un'ottantina di fogli— che contengono trascrizioni più o meno ampie di alcune opere storiche, come ad es., un'adespota Cronachetta fiorentina dal 450 al 1336 (ff. 98^r–100^r), la *Istoria* di Goro Dati (ff. 179^r–203^v) e parte della *Storia fiorentina* di Domenico Buoninsegni (ff. 101^r–122^v, 124^r–138^v, 204^r–220^r).

Rispetto allo Zibaldone primitivo, le parti aggiunte non sembrano obbedire ad un programma o piano organico di sviluppo dell'opera, ma costituiscono un insieme alquanto prolisso e discontinuo, che lascia uno spazio più ridotto ad interventi e contributi personali del Rucellai. Se si eccettuano due interessanti 'ricordi', rispettivamente del 1464 e del 1473 (ff. 61a^v–62a^v, 227^r–227^v), la descrizione del matrimonio di Bernardo nel 1466 (ff. 49^r–50^v) e quella della villa di Quaracchi (ff. 62b^v–63a^v) e alcune serie di appunti, ricordi, consigli, ecc., riuniti disordinatamente ai ff. 65a^v ss. e 94a^r ss., la gran parte dello Zibaldone *recentior* si distingue, più che altro, per il suo valore documentario: dalle copie di documenti di famiglia e di importanti lettere—come quelle del Ficino (ff. 64a^v–65b^r), di Giovanni da Viterbo e di Donato Acciaiuoli (ff. 85a^r–87b^v, 88a^r–93a^r)—ecc. alle trascrizioni già ricordate di testi storici e letterari.

Chiarita, da un punto di vista strutturale, la compagine dello Zibaldone, si dovrà ora procedere allo studio dei contenuti, all'identificazione cioè e alla caratterizzazione dei materiali che vi sono entrati a far parte, distinguendo, caso per caso, i contributi personali del Rucellai da ciò che invece deriva da fonti medioevali e umanistiche che egli ha utilizzato liberamente. Da uno studio analitico di questi testi, risulta—come si vedrà—che soltanto una piccola parte dei materiali riuniti nello Zibaldone è originale. A prescindere dai documenti di famiglia, dalle lettere, e dalle opere storico-letterarie trasferite di peso nello Zibaldone, si rileva che perfino parti (come ad es. i consigli ai figli), che si doveva presumere fossero, per la loro particolare natura, contributi originali del Rucellai non

---

[1] Perosa, pp. xiii–xv.

sono altro che abili composizioni musive, cui prestano le loro tessere alcune opere di contemporanei e diffuse raccolte medioevali.

La figura del Rucellai va pertanto ricostruita di scorcio e in gran parte per via indiretta, attraverso le scelte che egli ha effettuato, le inchieste che ha promosso, e il modo con cui ha reagito di fronte a certe situazioni culturali e politiche del suo tempo. Si tratta, evidentemente, di un'operazione assai delicata, dalla quale tuttavia emergono, con sufficiente chiarezza, i tratti più salienti della personalità del Rucellai e della sua cultura e gli interessi ch'egli ha nutrito per il mondo della natura, della storia e dell'arte; e attraverso la sua figura acquista particolare rilievo un tipico aspetto della società mercantile del '400, in cui l'impatto tra cultura tradizionale e cultura umanistica avviene con un certo ritardo e in forme talvolta laboriose e impacciate.

Lo Zibaldone del Rucellai è dunque un libro voluminoso, discontinuo e farraginoso. Quando anni or sono mi si offrì l'occasione di curarne la pubblicazione, fui costretto, ovviamente, a procedere a delle scelte. Scartato un criterio di discriminazione che si fondasse esclusivamente—o quasi esclusivamente—sulla distinzione esteriore di edito e di inedito, la mia attenzione si è rivolta soprattutto a quelle pagine dello Zibaldone che si prestavano a delineare, con particolare efficacia e vivezza, gli aspetti più notevoli della figura del Rucellai, e a sottolineare i rapporti che egli aveva intrattenuto cogli uomini del suo tempo. Ho pertanto escluso deliberatamente, sia quelle parti che riproducevano opere già note (Seneca, Cronache fiorentine, ecc.), sia quelle pagine (notizie episodiche di avvenimenti di interesse limitato, memorie frammentarie e disordinate, ecc.), che ritenevo fossero meno indicative per i fini, essenzialmente culturali, che mi ero proposto. Ho raggruppato quindi il materiale prescelto—indipendentemente da considerazioni cronologiche—secondo affinità di contenuto, distribuendolo in tre parti, a loro volta suddivise, a seconda della materia, in vari capitoli secondari. In ciascuna di queste parti ho raccolto materiali che si riferivano a uno dei tre temi generali—1) la storia della casata, il governo della famiglia e il mecenatismo; 2) la storia di Firenze e la vita civile; 3) la condotta morale, la fortuna e la grazia divina—che a mio avviso ricorrevano con maggiore insistenza sia nelle pagine più antiche che in quelle più recenti dello Zibaldone, ed erano essenziali per la ricostruzione della figura del Rucellai.

Alla tripartizione della materia, adottata nel volume antologico del 1960, mi sono attenuto anche nella stesura di questo saggio, che si appoggia prevalentemente sui testi già pubblicati, ma si vale, quando l'occasione lo richieda, anche di quelle parti dello Zibaldone rimaste finora inedite.

III

Il tema della famiglia è tra i tre quello che ha maggior spicco nello Zibaldone del Rucellai. Ed è naturale sia così, se si pensa che lo Zibaldone—pur colle note riserve—è sostanzialmente un libro di ricordanze, ed è quindi imparentato con quei libri, che per la loro stessa natura ed origine, erano destinati, in gran parte, alle annotazioni e descrizioni di avvenimenti, che riguardavano la vita, in tutti i suoi aspetti, della famiglia e della casata. Sulla famiglia, come nucleo a sé e come elemento costitutivo di agglomerati di più vaste proporzioni (la casata, la consorteria, ecc.) che vantano comune ascendenza e identità di tradizioni, si è concentrata, in questi ultimi anni, con particolare interesse, l'attenzione degli studiosi della società mercantile fiorentina tra la metà del '300 e la metà del '500[1]. Pur giungendo talvolta a conclusioni divergenti, essi hanno concorso a chiarire vari aspetti inediti dell'organizzazione familiare di quest'età, e a sfatare preconcetti che da tempo pesavano sulla storiografia in questo settore. Attraverso lo studio documentato di alcune famiglie campione si è cercato di individuare le strutture e le caratteristiche più salienti della famiglia alto borghese fiorentina di questo importante periodo di transizione, ponendo in rilievo—più che la sua funzione politica—l'importanza che essa ebbe nell'organizzazione della società civile e della economia; e, soprattutto, si è tentato di chiarire—nell'innegabile evoluzione e trasformazione che i gruppi familiari subirono nel passaggio dalla civiltà medioevale a quella rinascimentale—di qual natura fossero i rapporti tra i singoli membri nell'ambito più vasto della casata e della consorteria.

I materiali, che concernono la famiglia e la casata del Rucellai, sono concentrati, in buona parte, nelle prime pagine dello Zibaldone *vetus*, e si possono suddividere in due sezioni distinte, la prima di carattere documentario, la seconda di carattere normativo. Il Rucellai stesso—obbedendo ad un preciso disegno—ha voluto sottolineare questa partizione, ponendo in rilievo la priorità e gli scopi diversi delle due sezioni. 'E prima—dice all'inizio, subito dopo il preambolo[2]—mi pare di dovervi dare notitia della discendenzia della nostra famiglia de' Rucellai et d'altre cose appartenenti all'onore della casa degna di memoria'; 'Secondariamente, Pandolfo et Bernardo, miei figliuoli—dice all'inizio della seconda sezione[3]—mi pare di dovervi confortare a seguitare, ecc.'.

Nella prima sezione—che comprende i ff. 1a^r–6b^r dello Zibaldone *vetus*—il Rucellai ci dà, anzitutto, una completa genealogia della sua famiglia 'et maximamente di quelli che al dì d'oggi n'è discendentia perchè degli autri—egli dice—non ò vera notitia che sono spenti, benchè di loro sono stati discendenti assai'[4]. Pur limitandosi a un asciutto catalogo di nomi—che in qualche modo anticipa l'opera di quegli estensori di alberi genealogici di famiglie patrizie, che tanta fortuna ebbero nei secoli del principato[5]—il Rucellai elenca con scrupolo i nomi di tutti i Rucellai maschi appartenenti al ramo principale della famiglia, che risale a Nardo di Giunta (vissuto all'inizio del sec. XIV), accennando appena di sfuggita ai rami laterali, in gran parte estinti.[6]

All'albero genealogico il Rucellai fa seguire delle notizie biografiche su alcuni dei suoi antenati—ad es. su Ferro venuto a Campi dalla Bretagna, che fu il capostipite di tutta la casata; su Nardo di Giunta, 'che fu il primo che diè principio d'onore alla nostra famiglia'; su suo figlio Bencivenni, detto Cenni, che murò intorno al 1355–6 la cappella dedicata a Santa Caterina in Santa Maria Novella; sul figlio di costui Naddo, che, insieme agli altri consorti di casa Rucellai, fu tra 'i primi a levarsi in arme per la cacciata del duca d'Atene'; sul proprio avo, sul padre e sul suocero Palla Strozzi, su cui il Rucellai indugia, come vedremo in seguito, con particolare insistenza, ecc.—, e dà ampi ragguagli ai ff. 4b^r–5a^r e 5b^v di due documenti che riguardano da vicino la consorteria dei Rucellai, e si riferiscono, il primo al patronato della famiglia sulla cappella di S. Caterina, che, in seguito a contestazioni sorte tra gli eredi di Cenni di Nardo, alcuni ponevano in dubbio,[7] il secondo alla

---

[1] Ricorderò, tra le opere più recenti che direttamente o indirettamente trattano della famiglia nel Rinascimento: L. Martines, *Social World*, pp. 50 ss., 199 ss.; R. A. Goldthwaite, *Private Wealth*; G. A. Brucker, *Renaissance Florence*, New York, 1969, pp. 90 ss.; E. Sestan, "La famiglia nella società del Quattrocento", *Convegno internazionale indetto nel V° Centenario di Leon Battista Alberti*, Accademia Nazionale dei Lincei, Roma, 1974, pp. 235–58; Kent, *Household and Lineage*. Sempre utile il libro di N. Tamassia, *La famiglia italiana nei secoli XV e XVI*, Palermo, s.d. (1911). Le famiglie campione scelte dal Goldthwaite e dal Kent sono, rispettivamente, gli Strozzi, i Guicciardini, i Gondi e i Capponi nel primo caso, i Capponi, i Ginori e i Rucellai nel secondo.

[2] *Zibaldone*, f. 1a^r.

[3] Perosa, p. 3.

[4] *Zibaldone*, f. 1a^r.

[5] Martines, *Social World*, p. 57; Goldthwaite, *Private Wealth*, pp. 266 s., 270 ss.

[6] Passerini, *Rucellai*, pp. 19 ss.; Kent, *Household and Lineage*, pp. 274–5.

[7] Kent, *Household and Lineage*, pp. 257, 267 s.

donazione fatta dall'ottuagenario Ugolino Rucellai a Giovanni 'ricevente per tutta la famiglia de' Rucellai' di una bottega 'sotto la casa sua', perchè si costruisse una loggia 'per honore della famiglia, per aoperarla per le letitie et le tristitie, ecc.'[1]. Non sarà inopportuno rilevare che parte di queste notizie biografiche e documentarie figurano anche nei mss. BNC II.IV.374 e ASF, CS, ser. III, 79, che—come ho già detto[2]—ci hanno trasmesso degli estratti di un libro perduto del Rucellai che recava la data del 1456. Non si può sapere, ovviamente, in quale misura questi estratti del '600 riproducano l'originale, ma da una collazione effettuata delle parti che questi codici hanno in comune collo Zibaldone, ho potuto appurare che il testo della prima redazione del 1456 era molto più conciso, e divergeva da quello definitivo inserito nello Zibaldone *vetus*. Il Rucellai, evidentemente, ha riscritto e ampliato i testi riguardanti la sua famiglia che dovevano entrare a far parte dello Zibaldone.[3]

La sezione documentaria si conclude con un lungo elenco di 'tutti quelli che sono stati dello ufficio de' Signori Priori et Gonfalonieri di giustitia della nostra famiglia de' Rucellai ... cominciando nel 1302 insino a questo anno 1457'[4]. L'importanza di una famiglia nell'età che precede il principato era commisurata, a Firenze, com'è noto, al numero dei suoi membri che fin dai tempi più antichi avevano tenuto le magistrature più importanti della città (priorato e gonfalonierato di giustizia). Molte famiglie di alto livello sociale tenevano pertanto un priorista, un libro cioè che registrava queste cariche e, in certi casi, forniva anche interessanti notizie storiche al riguardo. Libri di questo genere—che coll'inizio del sec. XVI diventano sempre più frequenti—ci sono pervenuti, e spesso hanno un aspetto lussuoso e sono decorati cogli stemmi di famiglia. L'elenco che troviamo nello Zibaldone fa le veci di uno di questi libri, e rivela, indirettamente, l'intenzione del Rucellai di sottolineare, in questo modo, la preminenza della sua famiglia tra quelle più in vista in città[5].

Memorie e documenti relativi ad avvenimenti che riguardavano la sua famiglia e la sua casata il Rucellai ha inserito nello Zibaldone anche dopo la compilazione dello Zibaldone *vetus*. Dal 1457 fino alla morte egli ha trascritto o fatto trascrivere nello Zibaldone—in genere in fogli o parti di foglio rimasti in bianco—testimonianze sulla sua famiglia, che ne arricchivano la storia e ne aumentavano il prestigio.

Come prima cosa il Rucellai ha aggiornato la genealogia della sua famiglia, segnando le variazioni intervenute dopo il 1457[6], e ha aggiunto alla lista dei priori e dei gonfalonieri di giustizia i nomi dei

---

[1] Perosa, p. 20. L'atto notarile originale, redatto da ser Antonio Salamone (ASF, NA, S 16, 1434–37, f. 178), è stato segnalato da Kent, "Loggia", p. 398, n. 5.

[2] Cfr. p. 103 e n. 4.

[3] Il libro del 1456 si trovava nel sec. XVII in casa di Piero e di Giovanfilippo, figli di Benedetto Rucellai, quando fu utilizzato dal sen. Carlo Strozzi. Sia nel codice della Nazionale che in quello dell'Archivio di Stato (che riproduce soltanto le notizie attinenti a Palla Strozzi e alla sua famiglia) gli estratti sono preceduti da un titolo quasi identico. Un confronto minuto tra queste due serie di estratti e lo Zibaldone del 1457 non è qui possibile; mi basterà far presente che nella redazione definitiva sono state riprese (con variazioni dell'ordine di esposizione e del testo) tutte le notizie che figurano negli estratti del libro del 1456, salvo una—il ricordo delle nozze del figlio Pandolfo (cfr. p. 103, n. 2)—che il Rucellai, evidentemente, ha voluto obliterare.

[4] *Zibaldone*, f. 6a[r].

[5] Goldthwaite, *Private Wealth*, p. 273; Sestan, "La famiglia nella società del Quattrocento", p. 237; Kent, *Household and Lineage*, pp. 198 ss.

[6] Delle aggiunte, fatte dal Rucellai dopo il 1457, alla genealogia della sua famiglia, si potrebbero arrecare vari esempi; mi limiterò a ricordare, tra i nomi aggiunti, al f. 1a[v] quelli di Filippo, Giovanni e Andrea, figli di Ubertino, nati rispettivamente nel 1463, 1467 e 1469 (Passerini, *Rucellai*, tav. VII); sempre nello stesso foglio, quelli di Piero, Stefano e Cosimo, figli di Giovanni, nati rispettivamente nel 1460, 1462 e 1464 (Passerini, *Rucellai*, tav. VIII); al f. 2a[r] quelli dei nipoti Paolo, figlio di Pandolfo, nato nel 1464, e Cosimo, Piero, Palla e Giovanni, figli di Bernardo, nati rispettivamente nel 1468, 1473, 1474 e 1475 (Passerini, *Rucellai*, tav. XVII e XVI); e così via.

consorti che avevano ottenuto queste cariche dopo tale data[1]. Il Rucellai ha poi fatto ricordo, in uno spazio rimasto bianco al f. 5b[v], dei fidanzamenti di Pandolfo e di Bernardo, avvenuti, rispettivamente, nel 1453 e nel 1461. Da notare che nello Zibaldone *vetus* mancava ogni accenno sia al fidanzamento (1453) che al matrimonio (1456) di Pandolfo[2]; qui invece il Rucellai non solo ha ricordato i due avvenimenti, ma ha aggiunto un'interessante postilla sull'utilità che parentadi con famiglie di alto livello sociale ed economico avevano arrecato alla sua famiglia negli ultimi anni[3]. Egli sapeva troppo bene che in una società rotante intorno al nucleo familiare, il matrimonio—per i vincoli che stabiliva tra famiglia e famiglia—era un istituto assai importante, sia dal punto di vista del prestigio sociale e politico, sia dal punto di vista economico-finanziario[4]. Non ci meraviglieremo, quindi, che più tardi il Rucellai abbia fatto trascrivere, alla fine del V fascicolo (ff. 49a[r]–50b[v]), la narrazione dettagliata delle nozze di Bernardo, celebrate nel 1466, in cui egli insiste nella descrizione degli apparati suntuosi apprestati per questa festa, che si svolse dinnanzi alla Loggia di via della Vigna; elenca gli inumerevoli doni presentati alla sposa da parenti, amici, comunità rurali, popolani, ecc.; descrive il suo ricco corredo nuziale; ed infine fa memoria delle ingenti spese—un totale di 6,638 lire—che egli aveva dovuto sostenere per questo matrimonio[5].

Altri amanuensi hanno poi copiato al f. 69b[v] un ricordo della nascita, avvenuta nel 1468, del nipotino Cosimo, figlio di Bernardo[6]; al f. 70a[r] un estratto dell'atto notarile col quale il Rucellai nel 1470 'come prochuratore di tutti . . . i chonsorti della . . . famiglia' cedeva ai frati di S. Agostino l'ospedale di S. Bernardo in Osmannoro, e al f. 70b[v], di seguito a questo documento, un riassunto (poi ripetuto con varianti ai ff. 94b[r] e 95a[r]) del testamento, che Ugolino di Nardo aveva fatto nel 1357, dal quale risultava che l'ospedale di S. Bernardo apparteneva a tutti i figliuoli di Nardo di Giunta Rucellai, 'sicchè in effetto'—sottolinea il Rucellai—apparteneva 'a tutti e' discendenti di Nardo'[7].

Ma quel che più conta, il Rucellai ha fatto trascrivere nel febbraio del 1476 nelle ultime pagine

---

[1] Dal 1458 al 1480 sono stati priori e gonfalonieri di giustizia nove membri della famiglia Rucellai. Giovanni stesso vi figura due volte: priore nel 1463, gonfaloniere nel 1475; suo figlio Pandolfo priore nel 1469.

[2] Nel libro del 1456 veniva dato, invece, un certo rilievo al matrimonio di Pandolfo. A p. 131 del codice BNC II.IV.374 si trova infatti una descrizione sommaria (e frammentaria) di questo matrimonio: 'Ricordanza che a dì 30 di maggio 1456 Pandolfo, mio figluolo, menò la Caterina di Buonaccorso Pitti a cavallo con pifferi et trombetti, accompagnata da Gio., et fessi le nozze a Quaracchi, e il dì della ritornata si mangiò nella via; era la strada . . . [sic]. E appresso sarà nota dell'anella li furon donate et da cui, et così delle cose ci furon presentate:

L'anella furon 26, cioè etc.
Dal popolo di Quaracchi 2 vitelle
Dal popolo di Petriuolo
Dal popolo di Peretola
Dal popolo di S. Donnino
Dal Bastio dalla Sala
Dall'abate di S. Brancatio una stanghata di paperi, etc.'.

[3] Il Rucellai, infatti, osserva: 'E come si può intendere per quello ch'è scritto in questa carta, e' pare che la chasa nostra da ciento anni in qua abbi per 'redità avuto d'aver fatti e' principali parentadi della città: prima messer Paolo, mio avolo, con messer Donato Acciaiuoli; Paolo, mio padre, con messer Vieri de' Medici; io con messer Palla de li Strozzi; Bernardo, mio figluolo, con Piero di Chosimo de' Medici, che in quelli tenpi tutti sono stati e' primi de la città; Pandolfo, mio figluolo, con Bonaccorso di messer Lucha Pitti, com'è detto di sopra'. Cfr. Perosa, p. 145.

[4] Martines, *Social World*, pp. 57 ss.; Brucker, *Renaissance Florence*, pp. 92 ss.; Kent, *Household and Lineage*, pp. 91 ss. Martines cita a tale proposito alcuni interessanti passi dei *Ricordi* del Morelli (ed. Branca, pp. 208 ss., 253, ecc.).

[5] Perosa, pp. 28–34, 145 s. Notizie su cerimonie nuziali, corredi di sposa, ecc. sono frequenti nei libri di Ricordi. Cfr. G. Niccolini, *The Chronicles of a Florentine Family*, Londra, 1933; G. Biagi, *Due corredi nuziali fiorentini. Da un libro di Ricordanze dei Minerbetti*, Firenze, 1899; ecc.

[6] Perosa, pp. 35, 146.

[7] L'atto notarile, redatto da ser Matteo di Cenni d'Aiuto, non ci è pervenuto. Cfr. Kent, "Loggia", p. 399; id., *Household and Lineage*, pp. 234–6, 243 s.

dello Zibaldone (ff. 223ʳ–225ʳ), a mo' di conclusione, un 'ricordo' del proprio parentado che fa da 'pendant' e completa, su diversa scala, le notizie sulla casata dei Rucellai, fornite, come s'è visto[1], all'inizio dello Zibaldone *vetus*. In queste pagine il Rucellai, diversamente che nella genealogia del 1457, ha preso come punti di riferimento alcune donne di casa sua (l'avola Caterina Acciaiuoli, la madre Caterina Pandolfini, la moglie Iacopa Strozzi e la di lei madre Marietta, ecc.), delle quali ha elencato, coll'abituale precisione, fratelli e sorelle, figli e figlie coi relativi consorti e discendenti. Il Rucellai (pur limitandosi ai familiari più stretti, e trascurando—come egli dice—'i parentadi della consorteria de' Rucellai delle fanciulle uscite e delle entrate, che son grandissimo numero, per modo si tirano drieto meza la città')[2] ha tessuto un ampio arazzo familiare, in cui compaiono, in virtù dei matrimoni contratti, le figure più prestigiose della Firenze del suo tempo. Se poi si tien conto, che il Rucellai, uscito da poco da un grave infortunio finanziario[3], stava tentando, ormai in tarda età, di risalire con fatica la china, si comprenderà come egli abbia cercato, proprio nelle ultime pagine del suo Zibaldone, di lasciare un segno tangibile del suo prestigio sociale, ponendo in risalto, coll'implicito richiamo a così illustri parenti ed affini, gli stretti vincoli che lo legavano ad un ambiente privilegiato su cui poteva contare.

Ai documenti di famiglia illustrati finora, si affianca nello Zilbaldone *vetus*, come s'è detto[4], una sezione di carattere normativo, in cui il Rucellai impartisce ai figli una serie di consigli sul governo della famiglia. Queste pagine—insieme a quelle che seguono nello Zibaldone, sulla liberalità, la vita civile, ecc.—sono indubbiamente tra le più significative dello Zibaldone. I materiali, di cui il Rucellai si serve, non sono originali, ma sono tratti, spesso alla lettera, da fonti facilmente individuabili. L'impasto che ne deriva è tuttavia molto efficace, perchè, nello stesso tempo, mette a fuoco il punto di vista del Rucellai su problemi considerati essenziali dalla società mercantile cui egli apparteneva, e sottolinea la sua capacità di operare scelte efficaci, combinando in un contesto unitario elementi di disparate provenienze.

All'organizzazione ed al governo della famiglia, intesa in senso lato (come nucleo basilare della vita sociale ed economica) si sono interessati, fra Tre e Quattrocento, mercanti, educatori, religiosi, umanisti, ecc. che ne hanno trattato, più o meno ampiamente, nelle loro opere[5]. Consigli (ai figli, alle spose, ad amici, ecc.), ammonimenti, riflessioni, ricorrono spesso nei memoriali domestici (ad es. nei *Ricordi* del Morelli)[6], in certe raccolte di lettere (ad es. in quelle del Mazzei e della Macinghi Strozzi)[7], in alcuni opuscoli di tendenza ascetica (ad es. nella *Regola del governo di cura familiare* del Dominici, e nelle prediche di S. Bernardino)[8], ecc. Una fortuna immensa, tra il secolo XIII e il XV, ha poi avuto l'epistola *De gubernatione rei familiaris* (o *Lettera a Raimondo*), attribuita falsamente a S. Bernardo. Di questa lettera, sia nell'originale latino che nelle versioni che ne furono fatte nelle principali lingue europee, ci sono pervenuti numerosissimi codici e stampe[9].

---

[1] Cfr. p. 107.   [2] *Zibaldone*, f. 225ʳ.

[3] Perosa, p. 122.   [4] Cfr. p. 107.

[5] V. Lugli, *I trattatisti della famiglia nel Quattrocento*, Bologna, 1909.

[6] Morelli, *Ricordi*, ed. Branca, pp. 205–85. Cfr. p. 102, n. 4.

[7] L. Mazzei, *Lettere di un notaro a un mercante del secolo XIV*, con altre lettere e documenti, a cura di C. Guasti, Firenze, 1880; Alessandra Macinghi negli Strozzi, *Lettere di una gentildonna fiorentina del sec. XV ai figliuoli esuli*, a cura di C. Guasti, Firenze, 1877.

[8] G. Dominici, *Regola del Governo di cura familiare*, a cura di D. Salvi, Firenze, 1860; id., *Trattato delle dieci questioni e lettere a Madonna Bartolomea*, a cura di A. Levasti, Firenze, 1957; San Bernardino, *Le prediche volgari dette nella Piazza del Campo l'anno 1427*, a cura di L. Bianchi, Siena, 1880–7. Passi di queste prediche che riguardano il governo della famiglia, sono indicati da Lugli, *I trattatisti*, pp. 63 ss., e da Sestan, "La famiglia nella società del Quattrocento", pp. 240 ss.

[9] Limitandosi ai soli incunabuli, si registrano ventidue edizioni del testo latino (= *GW* 3960–3981), cinque di una versione

Orbene, il Rucellai, nella compilazione dei suoi ammaestramenti ai figli, non si è servito di nessuno di questi testi sulla famiglia, che pur avevano una larga diffusione negli ambienti mercantili della prima metà del '400. Ha però fatto trascrivere più tardi in alcuni fogli rimasti bianchi nel fascicolo X dello Zibaldone[1] una lettera inviatagli da Donato Acciaiuoli, che altro non era se non un nuovo volgarizzamento della pseudobernardiana epistola *De gubernatione*. Da un rapido confronto effettuato tra questa redazione e qualcuna delle altre pervenuteci, ho potuto constatare che la redazione Acciaiuoli era incompleta e che, per quanto concerneva il testo—pur accogliendo e-spressioni e frasi che già comparivano in precedenti redazioni—non concordava, in senso stretto, con nessuna di esse. E' verisimile che l'Acciaiuoli abbia ritradotto la lettera dello Pseudo-Bernardo, servendosi come falsariga di un precedente volgarizzamento; abbia soppresso alcune parti che riteneva meno pertinenti alla condizione del Rucellai; e abbia infine spedito la lettera al Rucellai intestandola come se si trattasse di cosa propria ('Donato Acciaiuoli disidera salute all'umanissimo ciptadino Giovanni Ruciellai') e non di una versione di un'epistola che già circolava da due secoli. Comunque stiano le cose, è significativo il fatto che del contenuto di questa lettera si sia fatto portavoce un uomo come Donato Acciaiuoli (che, come vedremo, era uno degli esponenti più qualificati della nuova cultura umanistica)[2], e che il Rucellai stesso abbia apprezzato il contenuto e il significato di questo opuscolo, e, garantito dal nome di chi glielo aveva inviato, abbia voluto che figurasse nel suo Zibaldone insieme agli altri ammaestramenti ai figli. In questa lettera—com'è stato autorevolmente osservato—poco entrava la morale e nulla il cristianesimo, tanto è vero che Geremia da Montagnone la considerava come 'economica'[3]. Nonostante la sua presunta origine, la lettera era destinata a rimanere cosa laica e a diffondersi, in prevalenza, tra i laici. Ed è questa, forse la ragione principale, per cui è piaciuta all'Acciaiuoli, che, al corrente degli interessi del Rucellai, deve aver pensato che, inviandogliela, avrebbe contribuito a far conoscere al suo secondo cugino un testo sulla famiglia che godeva meritata fama. E' infatti probabile che il Rucellai non avesse letto, prima di allora, questa epistola, dato che non se ne trovano tracce negli ammaestramenti impartiti ai figli nello Zibaldone *vetus*. Gli ammaestramenti a Pandolfo e a Bernardo derivano, come ora vedremo, da un'altra fonte, una fonte coeva di maggior rilievo e importanza.

Quando nel 1457 il Rucellai era impegnato a 'ordinare' e a far copiare lo Zibaldone *vetus*, erano usciti da poco i quattro libri della *Famiglia* di Leon Battista Alberti, che a buon diritto è considerata l'opera più significativa della trattatistica sulla famiglia di quegli anni[4]. A dire il vero, l'opera dell'Alberti—per varie ragioni che non è qui il caso di esporre—non ha avuto nel '400 la fortuna che noi oggi ci aspetteremmo, e non è un caso che, per averne un'edizione integrale a stampa, si

___

tedesca (= *GW* 3982–3986), cinque di una versione francese (= *GW* 3987–3991), due di una versione fiamminga (= *GW* 3993–3994), un'edizione in italiano (= *GW* 3992), e una in spagnuolo (= *GW* 3995). Della versione italiana—che ci è stata tramandata da un numero stragrande di mss. (la sola Biblioteca Riccardiana di Firenze ne possiede diciassette)—abbiamo diversi rifacimenti e redazioni, di cui non è sempre facile identificare gli autori. Uno di questi volgarizzamenti è stato stampato nel '400 (in un incunabulo privo dell'indicazione del luogo e dell'anno di stampa), altri, considerati come preziosi testi di lingua, sono stati pubblicati, in gran numero, durante il secolo scorso (cfr. F. Zambrini, *Le opere volgari a stampa*, Bologna, 1884, I, col. 63, 65–7); un'edizione recente ha poi curato G. De Luca, *Prosatori minori del Trecento*, I, *Scrittori di religione*, Milano–Napoli, 1954, pp. 817–24.

[1] *Zibaldone*, ff. 93ʳ–93ᵛ.

[2] Cfr. p. 144.

[3] De Luca, *Prosatori minori del Trecento*, p. 817.

[4] Le varie vicende della composizione dei quattro libri della *Famiglia* dell'Alberti (che si protrasse per circa dieci anni, dal 1433/4 al 1443) sono esposte sinteticamente da C. Grayson, in L. B. Alberti, *Opere volgari*, a cura di C. Grayson, I, Bari, 1960, pp. 379–80.

siano dovuti attendere quattro secoli[1]. Un particolare favore ha invece incontrato il terzo libro, detto *Oeconomicus*, che più degli altri tre trattava temi che potevano interessare il pubblico cui indirettamente si rivolgeva. Il libro ha avuto vita autonoma, e, preceduto da una lettera di dedica a Francesco d'Altobianco Alberti, è giunto a noi in più copie manoscritte[2]. Ma quel che più conta è che questo terzo libro della *Famiglia* è stato ampiamente rimaneggiato, e il rifacimento—definito un 'infelice travestimento' da F. C. Pellegrini, che lo studiò e confrontò coll'originale[3]—soppiantò, si può dire, l'originale albertiano, e godette nei secoli un favore sproporzionato ai suoi meriti. Eseguito, molto probabilmente, su un testimone della tradizione autonoma del terzo libro della *Famiglia*[4], il rifacimento—giunto a noi in due redazioni contenute, rispettivamente, in tre e sette manoscritti del sec. XV, e stampate, la prima da A. Bonucci nel 1849, la seconda da D. M. Manni nel 1734[5]—è adespoto e anepigrafo, ma già nel sec. XV—come risulta da una nota di possesso del Pal. 789, f. 1v ('Questo libro è di Raffaello di Francesco Minerbecti e chiamasi Dialogho d'Agniolo Pandolfini', ecc.)—veniva attribuito ad Angelo Pandolfini. L'attribuzione al Pandolfini era motivata dal fatto che nel rifacimento i personaggi di casa Alberti (Giannozzo, Lionardo, Adovardo), che sono gli interlocutori del terzo libro della *Famiglia*, erano stati sostituiti da personaggi di casa Pandolfini (Agnolo, Carlo, Filippo, ecc.). E' quindi probabile che il rifacimento sia stato allestito in ambienti vicini al Pandolfini, certamente dopo il 1443, in cui avvenne l'ultima revisione della *Famiglia*[6], e molto probabilmente dopo la morte di Angelo Pandolfini (1446), che è il personaggio più in vista del dialogo. Se infatti si pone a confronto, dal punto di vista dei contenuti e dello stile, il libro dell'Alberti colle due redazioni del rifacimento—come acutamente è stato fatto di recente da Judith Ravenscroft[7]—si nota che chi ha rifatto il testo, non solo ha proceduto per tappe sulla via di una sempre più accentuata semplificazione del tessuto originario e ad una progressiva normalizzazione del lessico—in modo che il libro dell'Alberti trovasse così più agevole circolazione tra coloro che avrebbero potuto usufruirne—ma ha, soprattutto, concentrato la sua attenzione su uno degli interlocutori, Agnolo Pandolfini, lasciando in ombra gli altri. Agli Alberti—ormai distanziati nel tempo—si è voluto sostituire un personaggio di attualità, di cui erano universalmente riconosciuti prestigio e saggezza, e che poteva—per analogia di ceto, ideali e cultura—porsi come tramite tra il mondo rappresentato nella *Famiglia* e la società mercantile fiorentina del suo tempo. Del resto l'Alberti stesso—definendolo 'uomo grave, maturo, integro, quale e per età e per prudenza sempre fu richiesto e reputato fra' primi nostri cittadini'—ne aveva fatto uno degli interlocutori del suo dialogo *Profugiorum ab aerumna libri*, composto, a quanto sembra, intorno al 1441–42[8], e prima di lui Matteo Palmieri nel dialogo *Della Vita civile*, completato intorno al 1439–40, aveva assegnato al Pandolfini il compito di dimostrare ai suoi interlocutori—'seguendo in questo la natura de' vecchi, che sono larghi predicatori di quello che per tutta la vita hanno di detti e di fatti raccolto'—'quello

---

[1] La *Famiglia* completa fu stampata per la prima volta nel 1844 (L. B. Alberti, *Opere volgari*, a cura di A. Bonucci, II, Firenze, 1844). Dei tredici mss., elencati dal Grayson (Alberti, *Opere volgari*, I, pp. 367–76), soltanto tre contengono l'opera intera, due hanno i primi tre libri e due i primi due. Per la diffusione autonoma del terzo libro cfr. la n. seg.

[2] Questo libro, diffuso autonomamente intorno al 1440, ci è pervenuto in cinque mss. del secolo XV, ed è stato stampato per la prima volta nel 1843 (L. B. Alberti, *Il Padre di Famiglia*, a cura di F. Palermo, Napoli, 1843).

[3] F. C. Pellegrini, "Agnolo Pandolfini e il 'Governo della Famiglia' ", *GSLI*, VIII (1886), pp. 1–52.

[4] Non esistendo ancora un'edizione critica di quest'opera, non è possibile—come ha giustamente osservato il Grayson (Alberti, *Opere volgari*, I, pp. 409 s.)—stabilire rapporti precisi tra i mss. che ce ne hanno tramandato il testo e la tradizione manoscritta del terzo libro della *Famiglia*.

[5] Alberti, *Opere volgari*, ed. Bonucci, V, pp. 9–227; A. Pandolfini, *Trattato del Governo della Famiglia*, Firenze, 1734.

[6] Alberti, *Opere volgari*, ed. Grayson, I, p. 380.

[7] J. Ravenscroft, "The Third Book of Alberti's *Della Famiglia* and its two *Rifacimenti*", *Italian Studies*, XXIX (1974), pp. 45–53.

[8] Alberti, *Opere volgari*, ed. Grayson, II, pp. 107 e 442.

che . . . si richiede all'onesto vivere di ciascuno cittadino virtuoso, secondo gli approvati amaestramenti degli antichi sapientissimi padri nostri'[1]. Non c' è quindi da meravigliarsi se il rifacitore del terzo libro della *Famiglia*, adeguandosi al cliché che proprio in quegli anni si stava formando intorno alla figura del Pandolfini, gli abbia assegnato la parte del saggio padre di famiglia, che 'secondo la natura de' vecchi' è buon 'predicatore', e, polarizzando su di lui la sua attenzione, abbia quasi inavvertitamente alterato la struttura della fonte albertiana, trasformandone il tessuto dialogico in una sorta di monologo, cui gli altri interlocutori—più comparse che personaggi—si limitano, nei loro interventi, ad assentire in coro.

Il rifacimento Pandolfini (che d'ora in poi indicheremo col titolo di *Trattato del Governo* e citeremo dall'edizione fiorentina del 1734 indicata a p. 112, n. 5), affiancandosi e sostituendosi all'originale albertiano, circolò e si diffuse tra i mercanti fiorentini della metà del '400, e fu da essi sentito come patrimonio comune cui attingere con la massima libertà. Prova ne è un ms. della prima redazione, il codice 354 del fondo Vittorio Emanuele della Biblioteca Nazionale di Roma, appartenuto, come si rileva dalle note di possesso, a Guglielmo e ad Antonio Pazzi, in cui i nomi dei Pandolfini, che vi erano stati scritti originariamente, sono stati abilmente cancellati e sostituiti da nomi della famiglia Pazzi (Antonio, Francesco, Guglielmo, Giovanni)[2].

Ma la testimonianza più singolare e significativa della diffusione del *Trattato del Governo* è offerta proprio dallo Zibaldone del Rucellai. Che al Rucellai fosse rimasta sconosciuta l'opera dell'Alberti, lo si arguisce da vari indizi, ma soprattutto dal fatto che i consigli sull'educazione dei figli, che egli dà nello Zibaldone (e mancano nel *Trattato del Governo*) non derivano dal primo libro della *Famiglia*, ove l'Alberti espone i suoi principi pedagogici, ma dal primo libro della *Vita civile* di Matteo Palmieri, che per questa parte pedagogica integra la fonte principale di questa sezione normativa dello Zibaldone, che è per l'appunto il *Trattato del Governo* attribuito al Pandolfini. E' da queste due opere che il Rucellai ha tratto, quasi esclusivamente, i materiali entrati a far parte dello Zibaldone in cui ha condensato i consigli ai figli sul governo della famiglia e sull'educazione.

Pandolfini e Palmieri appartenevano, colle dovute riserve e distinzioni, allo stesso milieu cittadino cui appartenevano i Rucellai[3]. Per di più Giovanni Rucellai era imparentato coi Pandolfini, essendo figlio di Caterina di Filippo Pandolfini e quindi nipote di Angelo, il protagonista del *Trattato del Governo*. Di rapporti diretti tra il Rucellai e il Palmieri non si hanno, che io sappia, testimonianze, se si eccettua il fatto, in sé trascurabile, che il Rucellai ha inserito, come vedremo, nello Zibaldone, poche righe, in versione volgare, dell' inizio del *De Temporibus* del Palmieri[4]. Il Rucellai ricorda invece in varie occasioni nello Zibaldone il parentado Pandolfini, un'avola, i cugini, le loro mogli, i loro figli, ma soprattutto, e con grande affetto, sua madre, che era rimasta vedova quando egli aveva appena tre anni (nel 1406) e non s'era più risposata per poter badare ai suoi quattro figli[5]. Il Rucellai rammenta anche di essere stato ospite di Agnolo Pandolfini nella sua villa di Ponte a Signa nel 1423–4 per sfuggire al contagio della peste che imperversava a Firenze[6].

---

[1] M. Palmieri, *Della Vita civile*, a cura di F. Battaglia, Bologna, 1944, p. 11. Per la data di composizione del dialogo v. G. Belloni, "Intorno alla datazione della *Vita civile* di M. Palmieri", *Studi e problemi di critica testuale*, 16 (1978), pp. 49–62.

[2] C. Grayson, "La redazione Pazzi del *Governo della Famiglia*", GSLI, CXXX (1953), pp. 514–9.

[3] Non è qui il caso di insistere su particolari biografici e notizie bibliografiche riguardanti il Pandolfini e il Palmieri. Per un primo orientamento si veda Vespasiano da Bisticci, *Le Vite*, ed. A. Greco, Firenze, I, 1970, pp. 563–7; II, 1976, pp. 261–84. Tra le opere più recenti sarà utile consultare Martines, *Social World*, pp. 138–42, 191–8, 313 ss.

[4] Cfr. p. 121.

[5] *Zibaldone*, ff. 4b[r], 5a[r], 223[r–v]; Perosa, pp. 26, 28, 29, 44, 51, 53, 118. Sui rapporti Rucellai–Pandolfini cfr. Kent, pp. 14–20 sopra.

[6] *Zibaldone*, f. 26a[r]. Cfr. p. 123, n. 4.

E' probabile—e documenti d'archivio potrebbero confermarlo—che, in seguito alle difficili condizioni in cui era venuta a trovarsi la famiglia della sorella, Angelo Pandolfini abbia contribuito concretamente ad allevare, educare e poi avviare ai traffici Giovanni ed i suoi fratelli. Se così fu, il Rucellai potè sperimentare di persona l'efficacia dell'esempio e dell'insegnamento del Pandolfini, e ravvisare nella persona dello zio la figura ideale del saggio padre di famiglia, che anche i trattatisti del tempo concorrevano ad esaltare, tramandandola ai posteri. Comunque stiano le cose, non reca meraviglia, che a distanza di anni, il Rucellai stesso—assumendosi il ruolo di capo famiglia cui spettava il compito di ammaestrare i figli sul governo della famiglia—si sia posto come modello da emulare la figura dello zio, scomparso ormai da più di dieci anni, e si sia appropriato di alcune parti del discorso che gli veniva attribuito nel *Trattato del Governo*[1].

Il Rucellai s'è, dunque, giovato per questa sezione dello Zibaldone della *Vita civile* del Palmieri e dell'anonimo *Trattato del Governo* di netta derivazione albertiana. Egli è ricorso cioè (ed è questo uno dei risvolti più imprevedibili e importanti dello Zibaldone), per trattare i temi della famiglia e dell'educazione, a fonti diverse da quelle cui tradizionalmente attingevano i libri di Ricordanze. Le fonti utilizzate sono il prodotto di una nuova cultura, e rivelano un significativo impatto del Rucellai colla trattatistica umanistica. In questo genere letterario gli umanisti, com'è noto, hanno dato le prove migliori della loro capacità di inquadrare esperienze di vita vissuta in un tessuto letterario, in cui, sia dal punto di vista dello stile e dei contenuti, erano presenti e operanti le ideologie e i paradigmi del passato. Indipendentemente dalle loro polemiche sull'uso del volgare, gli umanisti legati alla borghesia mercantile si sono valsi dello strumento linguistico più idoneo per agire in profondità su un ceto, che, per certi aspetti, era ancora legato—come nel caso del Rucellai— a idee e prodotti della cultura tradizionale, ma che, spinto da una nuova situazione ambientale, si stava lentamente accostando a un nuovo tipo di spiritualità e di cultura. Nel caso specifico il Rucellai ha attinto, tramite il Palmieri e lo Pseudo-Pandolfini (in realtà l'Alberti), a Quintiliano, a Cicerone, ad Aulo Gellio, all'*Oeconomicus* di Senofonte, ai primi trattati di pedagogia del '400, ecc.[2]

Chi, d'altronde, voglia rendersi conto in dettaglio del sistema adottato dal Rucellai nell'utilizzazione sia del Palmieri che del *Trattato del Governo* o di eventuali fonti minori, non ha che da scorrere le note della mia edizione dello Zibaldone, in cui sono indicati, caso per caso, i singoli passi delle fonti cui si riferisce il testo del Rucellai[3]. Potrà allora rendersi conto che il Rucellai ha concentrato la sua attenzione di preferenza su alcuni temi, che egli riteneva di maggior interesse, scegliendo qua e là, dalle opere che aveva a disposizione, quei materiali che rispondevano ai suoi intenti e rientravano nel suo programma. Egli ha così costruito degli ampi mosaici, formati da un numero notevole di tessere collegate tra di loro da un esile tessuto connettivo. In qualche caso però non è stato possibile individuare la fonte di cui si faceva portavoce il Rucellai, e quindi—tenendo anche conto dei contenuti—s'è dovuto ragionevolmente supporre che si trattasse di osservazioni scaturite da una diretta esperienza personale.

---

[1] Sul rapporto padre-figlio nella struttura della famiglia mercantile v. Kent, *Household and Lineage*, pp. 45, 54–9.

[2] Non si conoscono, che io sappia, studi dettagliati sulle fonti dei libri della *Famiglia* dell'Alberti. Ancora utile l'ampio commento scolastico di F. C. Pellegrini (Firenze, 1911), riveduto da R. Spongano (Firenze, 1946). Per quanto concerne il primo libro del Palmieri—oltre a G. B. Gerini, *Scrittori pedagogici italiani del secolo decimoquinto*, Torino, 1896, pp. 205–27—si veda D. Bassi, "Il primo libro della *Vita civile* di Matteo Palmieri e l'*Institutio oratoria* di Quintiliano", *GSLI*, XXIII (1894), pp. 182–207; L. Rainaldi, "Di una fonte comune della *Vita civile* di Matteo Palmieri e del *De educatione liberorum* di Maffeo Vegio", *GSLI*, CXXX (1953), pp. 495–507.

[3] Perosa, pp. 139–43.

Per quanto concerne l'educazione dei figli, il Rucellai si è valso esclusivamente di quella parte del primo libro del dialogo della *Vita civile* che tratta appunto quest'argomento. Il Rucellai—seguendone il filo—ha cercato di dare un conciso estratto del discorso del Palmieri, cavando dal contesto e riversando nello Zibaldone, con lievi modifiche formali, i passi ritenuti più efficaci e pertinenti. Gli estratti si susseguono nello stesso ordine in cui compaiono nel contesto del Palmieri, ma sono significative certe omissioni o variazioni. Il Rucellai ha, ad. es., trascurato i riferimenti storici, le parti a carattere filosofico, soffermandosi e dando risalto a particolari che si riferivano all'ambiente mercantile[1].

Con criteri analoghi il Rucellai ha attinto al *Trattato del Governo*, trascrivendo passi che riguardavano i fattori, l'impiego dei propri capitali, la masserizia, la spesa, la liberalità verso amici, congiunti e servi, la vita civile, ecc. Il Rucellai ha concentrato la sua attenzione su quelle parti del *Trattato del Governo* che avevano maggiore attinenza colla sua professione di mercante e colla vita civile. Ha perciò trascurato—per fare qualche esempio—i passi in lode della villa e l'ampia sezione in cui il padre di famiglia dà consigli alla moglie sul modo di contenersi nel governo di sé stessa e della casa; ha poi sorvolato su gran parte del lungo ragionamento tenuto dal vecchio padre di famiglia circa il fare masserizia del proprio animo, che l'autore del *Trattato del Governo* imagina sia stato udito un tempo dal Pandolfini, e che ricalca, con modifiche, tagli e incongruenze, l'analogo discorso del vecchio sacerdote, riferito da Giannozzo nel terzo libro dell'Alberti[2].

Nell'esposizione il Rucellai ha variato liberamente la successione che le singole parti hanno nel contesto del *Trattato del Governo*, e ha raccolto e trascritto spesso *ad verbum* nello Zibaldone i materiali di cui serviva (passi, frasi, sentenze, ecc.) dai luoghi più disparati del *Trattato*, aggregando al tema centrale anche brani che derivavano da sezioni diverse[3]. Si ha perciò l'impressione che il Rucellai, durante la lettura del *Trattato*, abbia registrato a parte i passi più significativi in cui si imbatteva, compilando una specie di elenco di *flores* cui attingere al momento opportuno.

Tuttavia non tutti i passi dello Zibaldone, che riguardano il governo della famiglia, trovano riscontro nel *Trattato*. Ce ne sono alcuni che sembra rispecchino opinioni personali del Rucellai. Il Rucellai ha per es. introdotto, a proposito dei fattori, un interessante *excursus*, in cui raccoman-

---

[1] Il Rucellai—tanto per citare qualche esempio—sottolinea che tra gli insegnamenti da impartire ai giovanetti ci deve essere la musica e 'l'aresmetrica, cioè l'abacho ... perchè fa l'animo atto e pronto a esaminare le cose sottili' (Perosa, p. 14). Il Palmieri non parla affatto dell'aritmetica, bensì della geometria, alla quale meglio si addice il giudizio che egli ne dà—e che il Rucellai mutua trasferendolo all'aritmetica—circa l'efficacia che essa ha sull'affinamento delle qualità intellettuali dei giovani (Palmieri, *Vita civile*, p. 23). In questa sostituzione si riflettono gli interessi pratici del Rucellai, che riteneva fondamentale, per la preparazione del mercante, lo studio dell'abaco. Al Palmieri invece il piano delle materie d'insegnamento veniva suggerito da Quint. *Inst.* I. 10, 26 e 34–5. Significativa è anche la chiusa di questo brano sull'educazione. Il Rucellai trae lo spunto dal passo della *Vita civile*, in cui il Palmieri esorta chi è ormai alle soglie dell'adolescenza a 'considerare le forze del suo ingegno, quelle insieme col corpo esaminare, et eleggere quella vita a che si sente più atto e nella quale spera vivere migliore e più degno ...' (Palmieri, *Vita civile*, p. 40), ma traduce il concetto del Palmieri in termini più appropriati alla sua mentalità e condizione, dandogli un valore alquanto limitativo. 'Di poi—egli dice—si vogliono mettere e' figliuoli a quell' arte o vero mestiero a che si sentono più atti, et in qualunche exercitio abbiate l'occhio, dare loro buono, experto et praticho maestro' (Perosa, p. 15).

[2] Cfr. Alberti, *Opere volgari*, ed. Grayson, I, pp. 173 ss. Il ragionamento del 'vecchissimo padre di famiglia', le lodi della vita in villa e i consigli alla moglie, in *Trattato del Governo*, pp. 13 ss., 37 ss., 55 ss.

[3] Scorrendo l'apparato di note della mia edizione dello Zibaldone (Perosa, pp. 140 ss.) in cui sono indicati i passi del *Trattato del Governo* recepiti dal Rucellai, ci si può fare un'idea precisa dei criteri che egli ha seguito nell'impiego di questi materiali. Egli, ad es., ha spezzettato in una quindicina di parti l'ampio discorso sui fattori, che Agnolo fa nel *Trattato del Governo*, pp. 42–44, e ha convogliato nel gruppo compatto degli ammaestramenti ai figli sui fattori due 'ricordi' (Perosa, p. 7, nn. 36 e 37), tratti dal *Trattato del Governo*, pp. 16 e 84 ss., che non derivano, come gli altri, dalla sezione del *Trattato*, che tratta dei fattori, ma da altre sezioni (ad es. da quella in cui si discute sull' utilità o meno di fare prestiti ai Signori), che non hanno gran che a vedere con tale tema.

dando ai figli di controllare in proprio l'attività dei loro collaboratori, li esorta a farsi 'domandatori', ad andare cioè in mercato per interrogare mercanti e sensali sulla situazione del mercato italiano e straniero e sulle effettive condizioni finanziarie dei vari operatori economici ('Quando de' giovani mercatanti tornano di fuori, chi da Vinegia, chi da Roma, chi da Ginevra, chi da Bruggia, fatevi loro incontro con fare loro motto, rallegrandovi della tornata loro, et domandategli di novelle, et infine tirategli da parte. . .')[1]. Sempre in questo capitolo, il Rucellai, dopo aver esortato i figli, sulla falsariga del *Trattato*, a utilizzare come fattori i propri familiari, confessa che egli, personalmente, non ha potuto seguire sempre questa linea di condotta 'perchè in casa della nostra famiglia, nel tempo mio, ci sono stati pochi giovani atti al mio exercitio et da essere factori soficienti. . .'[2]. Il Rucellai, quasi presentisse il guaio che doveva capitargli quindici anni dopo, aveva le sue buone ragioni per essere, se non diffidente, certo prudente nell'impiego di estranei come fattori. Egli subirà infatti nel 1474 'una grande perdita' nella sua compagnia di Pisa 'ghovernata per Ridolfo Paghanelli, che—com'egli dirà—m'inghannò e rubò per vie torte e feciomi danno f. ventimila. . .'[3]. Un riflesso di questa situazione si può forse cogliere (ma la datazione è incerta) in un brano aggiunto più tardi nello Zibaldone, in cui il Rucellai consiglia ai figli di non seguitare più il traffico dopo la sua morte, ma di finirlo qualora non siano in grado di attendervi personalmente; e, nel caso abbiano deciso di seguitarlo, s'ingegnino di trovare buoni compagni o fattori, di cui possano fidarsi. Il Rucellai in ogni caso—sempre secondo la testimonianza di questa aggiunta seriore—avrebbe desiderato che i figli ridimensionassero su basi più modeste l'attività mercantile, e pur avendo nome di 'mercatanti', si accontentassero in fatto di essere dei 'botteghai', per non trovarsi esposti con grosse partite di merci e forti somme di denaro[4]. Nello Zibaldone *vetus*—in uno dei già citati capitoli derivati dal *Trattato del Governo*—il Rucellai aveva invece consigliato ai figli una prudente diversificazione del 'portafoglio', cioè un'equa ripartizione del capitale in 'denari contanti', in 'denari del Monte' e in 'possessioni'[5]. Tuttavia anche in questo caso, seguendo la sua fonte, egli aveva dimostrato una certa diffidenza nei riguardi della 'moneta' ('niuna cosa si truova meno stabile, meno durabile che la moneta . . . piena di sospetti et d'infiniti pericholi')[6]; e nella chiusa—sviluppando il discorso della fonte in base ai dati che gli offriva l'esperienza personale—aveva espresso il suo punto di vista sull'instabilità delle ricchezze a Firenze, sui sistemi di tassazione, e sulla necessità dell'aiuto dei 'buoni amici' e dei 'buoni parenti' per ottenere sgravi fiscali e prestiti[7].

E' ovvio quindi che—anche in vista dei vantaggi che gli potevano derivare—il Rucellai stimasse opportuno mostrarsi, verso amici, congiunti e consorti, il più possibile liberale e cortese, e tale comportamento consigliasse a Pandolfo e a Bernardo[8], aggiungendo un interessante *excursus*—che non figura nel *Trattato del Governo*—in cui viene esposta una singolare teoria sulla cortesia che, in particolare, i ricchi dovrebbero usare verso i poveri, per sfuggire all'invidia che costoro nutrono nei loro riguardi, in quanto sanno di essere vittime di un sopruso, che risale a quando 'la terra et le possessioni et l'avere' erano 'comuni tra tutte le genti, secondo le ragioni naturali' e non esisteva il concetto di proprietà[9].

[1] Perosa, p. 6.
[2] Perosa, p. 5.
[3] Perosa, p. 122.
[4] Perosa, p. 19; Martines, *Social World*, pp. 35 n. 64, 291 s. Per la datazione v. Perosa, p. xv.
[5] Perosa, p. 8; Goldthwaite, *Private Wealth*, p. 248.
[6] Perosa, pp. 8 s.; Kent, *Household and Lineage*, p. 155.
[7] Perosa, p. 9.
[8] Perosa, pp. 10–13.
[9] Perosa, p. 12; cfr. infra, p. 118. Non mi è stato ancora possibile identificare la fonte diretta di questo brano del Rucellai.

Il Rucellai indugia con particolare insistenza nello Zibaldone *vetus* sui temi della liberalità, della masserizia, della spesa, ecc. Agli ammaestramenti ai figli su tali argomenti, desunti dal *Trattato del Governo*, egli fa seguire un'interessante appendice, in cui compaiono due serie di *auctoritates*—tratte da vari autori e da varie raccolte—circa la virtù della liberalità[1]. Nel primo elenco il Rucellai fa 'nota di più auctori che anno detto dello spendere moderatamente e del servire gli amici e i parenti'[2]; nel secondo fa 'nota di detti di più autori che anno scripto dello spendere con larghezza e del servire gli amici con grande liberalità forse più che non richieda la ragione'[3]. Le *auctoritates*, che il Rucellai registra senza un particolare ordine nei due elenchi, sono tratte (ma il Rucellai, come al solito, non lo indica) 1) dal *Trattato del Governo*; 2) dal *Fiore di Virtù*; 3) da altre fonti che non sempre è stato possibile identificare.

1) Il Rucellai riproduce in questi elenchi, con lievi varianti di testo, un buon numero di passi del *Trattato del Governo* già utilizzati nel contesto degli ammaestramenti ai figli, e passi dello stesso *Trattato* che non compaiono tra gli ammaestramenti. Questa procedura rafforza l'ipotesi—già da noi formulata—che il Rucellai, nella composizione degli ammaestramenti, si sia servito di precedenti spogli effettuati durante la lettura del *Trattato*.[4]

2) Il *Fiore di Virtù*, composto agli inizi del sec. XIV (e attribuito, sembra a torto, al frate bolognese Tommaso Gozzadini) riunisce in una quarantina di capitoli sentenze di autori classici, cristiani, ecc. su virtù e vizi, filtrate attraverso i più noti florilegi medioevali (ad es. il *Liber philosophorum*, i trattati di Albertano da Brescia, lo *Speculum doctrinale* di Vincenzo di Beauvais, la *Summa* di Peraldo, ecc.)[5]. L'opera ebbe una grande diffusione anche durante il '400 e gli inizi del '500—come risulta dal gran numero di mss. e di edizioni a stampa che ce l' hanno tramandata[6]—soprattutto tra i ceti e gli ambienti più popolari—i bottegai, i mercanti, i religiosi, le donne, gli artigiani, gli artisti (figura ad es. tra i libri di Leonardo, che se ne servì per la compilazione del suo Bestiario[7]), ecc.—in quei settori cioè che, culturalmente, erano ancora legati alla tradizione. Non fa quindi meraviglia che anche il Rucellai si sia servito del *Fiore di Virtù* e ne abbia trascritto nello Zibaldone alcuni passi del cap. I ('Che cosa è amore e benevolenza') e quasi integralmente, ma disordinatamente, il cap. XI, che tratta appunto 'Della virtù della liberalità appropriata all'aquila'[8].

3) Di alcuni passi trascritti nei due elenchi dello Zibaldone è indicata la fonte classica (Seneca, Ovidio, Tullio *De officiis*, Aristotele, Giovenale, ecc.), ma non mi è stato finora possibile reperire il florilegio da cui probabilmente sono stati tratti. Talvolta la fonte è indicata genericamente con espressioni come 'Un savio disse . . .', 'Un nostro cittadino disse . . .', 'Un savio nostro anticho',

---

I concetti qui espressi sulla proprietà discendono da S. Tommaso (*Summa theol.*, II–II, q. 66, a. 2), e sono stati ripresi e trattati da S. Antonino (*Summa theol.*, I, tit. 13, c. 2, par. 11; II, tit. 1, c. 14, par. 1; III, tit. 3, c. 2, par. 2; ecc.). Cfr. R. Morçay, *Saint Antonin*, Tours–Paris, 1914, pp. 377 ss.; A. Pfister, *Die Wirtschaftsethik Antonins von Florenz*, Friburgo, 1946, pp. 26 ss., 124.

[1] *Zibaldone*, ff. 20b[v]–25b[r]. Questi elenchi non figurano tra le parti dello Zibaldone pubblicate in Perosa.

[2] *Zibaldone*, f. 20b[v].

[3] *Zibaldone*, f. 22b[v].

[4] Cfr. p. 115. I passi del *Trattato del Governo*, che gli elenchi hanno in comune cogli ammaestramenti ai figli, sono indicati in Perosa, pp. 141–3 alle nn. 64, 82–3, 117–8, 120, 123, 126, 128–30, 135, 138–40.

[5] C. Frati, "Ricerche sul *Fiore di Virtù*", *Studi di Filologia romanza*, VI (1891), pp. 247–447; M. Corti, "Le fonti del *Fiore di Virtù* e la teoria della 'nobiltà' nel Duecento", *GSLI*, CXXXVI (1959), pp. 1–82.

[6] Anche limitandosi alle sole stampe del sec. XV, nell' *Indice generale degli incunaboli* sono registrate più di quaranta edizioni del *Fiore di Virtù*, a partire dalla *princeps* del 1471 fino alla fine del secolo (*IGI* 3927–3970).

[7] E' menzionato nell'elenco dei libri adoperati (e probabilmente posseduti) da Leonardo, che figura al f. 210a[r] del Codice Atlantico. Cfr. Leonardo da Vinci, *Scritti letterari*, a cura di A. Marinoni, Milano, 1952, p. 240.

[8] *Fiore di Virtù*, Roma, 1740, pp. 9 e 49–57.

'Uno nostro cittadino savissimo huomo disse . . .', ecc.[1]. Da notare che in questi elenchi sono stati inseriti anche alcuni brani adespoti (come ad es. quello sulla cortesia che i ricchi devono usare verso i poveri) che figuravano già tra gli ammaestramenti ai figli[2].

Il Rucellai, sia negli ammaestramenti ai figli sui temi della liberalità e della spesa, sia negli elenchi contrapposti di *auctoritates*—che fanno loro da supporto—si muove con una certa cautela, e, condizionato in parte dalle fonti che utilizza (prima fra tutte il *Trattato del Governo*), non sembra assumere una posizione decisa in merito. Tuttavia, l'interesse e l'insistenza, colle quali egli affronta la casistica inerente a tali temi nel momento in cui sta allestendo e 'ordinando' lo Zibaldone *vetus*, non sono affatto casuali, ma rispondono agli interrogativi che gli vengono posti da una situazione di fatto, in cui si è decisamente impegnato. Il Rucellai infatti—travalicando i confini degli interessi strettamente familiari—sta ora dando, coll'esempio e coll'azione, una risposta più precisa e su più vasta scala al dilemma circa l'opportunità o meno di mostrarsi liberali e d'impegnarsi in forti spese. Egli sta progettando e, in parte, dando corso a un vasto piano di costruzioni edilizie a lunga scadenza, in cui avranno modo di rivelarsi concretamente la sua liberalità e il suo mecenatismo. Nello Zibaldone *vetus*—a dire il vero—compare un solo documento che riguardi tali attività, l'estratto cioè di un atto del 1456 dal quale risulta la donazione da parte di Ugolino Rucellai a Giovanni e ai suoi consorti di una bottega perchè vi costruisse una loggia 'per honore della famiglia'[3]. Ma da recenti studi, che arricchiscono di nuovi dati le notizie che già si possedevano al riguardo, si è potuto appurare che già nel 1448 il Rucellai, avendo acquistato parte delle proprietà di Poggio a Caiano, appartenute a suo tempo a Palla Strozzi, ne aveva vincolato le rendite (e il ricavato di un'eventuale vendita) per la costruzione di una cappella nella Chiesa di S. Pancrazio o per il completamento della facciata di S. Maria Novella; e che nel 1455 egli aveva dato inizio ai lavori per la ristrutturazione del Palazzo di via della Vigna, secondo il primitivo disegno a cinque archi[4]. I lavori per la cappella di S. Pancrazio e la facciata di S. Maria Novella avevano avuto effettivamente inizio nel 1458, un anno dopo la compilazione dello Zibaldone *vetus*, quelli per la costruzione della Loggia qualche anno dopo.

Il Rucellai, negli anni in cui progettava e intraprendeva tale programma edilizio, si trovava all'apogeo della sua fortuna finanziaria. Dal Catasto del 1458 risulta che egli era al terzo posto nella graduatoria dei fiorentini più tassati, e che su un imponibile di 21,464 fiorini (19,406 colle deduzioni) doveva pagare una tassa di 102, 17, 2 ff.[5]. Il suo programma edilizio non rispondeva però soltanto a necessità, pur comprensibili e legittime, di carattere finanziario (l'impiego di capitali in investimenti immobiliari), ma soprattuto all'esigenza, vivamente sentita, di rafforzare il proprio prestigio e quello della famiglia nell'ambito delle élites cittadine. Il Rucellai e i suoi contemporanei sapevano troppo bene, che il patronato delle arti e la pratica della virtù della magnificenza, connotavano positivamente il mecenate e la sua famiglia sia negli ambienti religiosi che in quelli civili, e davano loro lustro tra i contemporanei e gloria tra i posteri[6]. Le opere fatte costruire—dirà più tardi

---

[1] *Zibaldone*, ff. 21b[v], 22a[v], 23a[v], 24b[v].

[2] Perosa, pp. 12–3, 141–2 e nn. 87, 89, 91. Cfr. p. 116.

[3] Perosa, p. 20. Cfr. p. 108.

[4] Ricorderò tra gli studi più recenti che affrontano la cronologia dei monumenti fatti erigere dal Rucellai: Dezzi Bardeschi, "Complesso monumentale"; *id.*, *Facciata*; Kent, "Loggia"; B. Preyer, "The Rucellai Loggia", *MKHIF*, XXI (1977), pp. 183–98; cfr. *id.*, pp. 179–207 infra.

[5] ASF, Cat. 817 (S. Maria Novella, Lion Rosso, 1457/8), f. 74[r]; R. de Roover, *Rise and Decline*, p. 31.

[6] 'Boni viri—dice l'Alberti in un passo famoso del prologo del *De re aedificatoria*—, quod parietem aut porticum duxeris lautissimam, quod ornamenta postium columnarum tectique imposueris, et tuam et suam vicem comprobant et congratulantur vel ea re maxime, quod intelligunt quidem te fructu hoc divitiarum tibi familiae posteris urbique plurimum decoris ac dignitatis adauxisse' (L. B. Alberti, *L'Architettura*, a cura di G. Orlandi, I, Milano, 1966, p. 13). Un concetto analogo viene espresso

il Rucellai—'raghuardano in parte all'onore di Dio e all'onore della città e in memoria di me'[1]. I Rucellai esercitavano da tempo una specie di patronato sulle chiese di S. Pancrazio e di S. Maria Novella; colla costruzione del palazzo di via della Vigna e della Loggia (destinati a diventare il simbolo dell'elevato stato sociale ed economico raggiunto dalla famiglia), Giovanni Rucellai conseguiva lo scopo ambizioso di allinearsi colle maggiori e più potenti casate fiorentine[2]. Non bisognerà poi dimenticarsi, che in questo momento il Rucellai stava tentando—come vedremo in seguito[3]—di accostarsi ai Medici, e quindi riteneva giustamente che, elevando con tali iniziative edilizie il rango della sua casata, avrebbe acquisito quelle possibilità di approccio, che la mancata partecipazione alla vita politica e amministrativa non gli garantiva.

Di questo programma e delle varie motivazioni che l'hanno promosso c'è ben poco, come s'è visto, nello Zibaldone *vetus*, anche se ai problemi connessi ai concetti di liberalità e spesa nell'ambito dell'organizzazione familiare, il Rucellai abbia dedicato particolare attenzione sia negli ammaestramenti ai figli che nell'appendice di *auctoritates*. Nelle parti più recenti dello Zibaldone si coglie invece l'eco della nuova situazione, che veniva allora delineandosi e maturando. Sull'opportunità di spendere per opere di prestigio il Rucellai non sembra aver più dubbi e riserve, e in più luoghi traspare la sua soddisfazione e il suo orgoglio per le opere fatte eseguire con largo dispendio di sostanze. Due memorie—rispettivamente degli anni 1464 e 1473—in cui il Rucellai fa ricordo delle 'molte e infinite grazie' che gli ha 'facto messer Domenedio'—sono molto interessanti al riguardo[4]. In ambedue il Rucellai, più o meno colle stesse parole, ringrazia Iddio non tanto perchè gli ha concesso grazia nel guadagnare, 'ma anchora nello spenderli bene, che non è minor virtù che il guadangnare'[5]. 'Il ghuadangnare e lo spendere—dice il Rucellai—sono del numero de' grandi piaceri che gl'uomini piglino in questo mondo, e ffassi difichultà quale sia il maggiore di questi due'. 'Io—continua il Rucellai—non avendo mai fatto altro da cinquanta anni in qua se non ghuadangnare e spendere . . . achordomi sia maggiore dolcezza lo spendere che il ghuadangnare'[6]. Perciò 'credo—aggiunge il Rucellai nella prima delle due memorie—che m'abbi facto più honore l'averli bene spesi ch'averli guadangnati e più chontentamento nel mio animo. E maximamente delle muraglie che io ò facte della chasa mia di Firenze, del luogo mio da Quarachi, della facciata della chiesa di Sancta Maria Novella e della logia principiata nella Vigna dirinpetto alla chasa mia; e anchora della chappella chol sancto Sipolcro . . . facta fare in Sancto Branchazio. . .'[7].

Queste opere sono elencate, con lievi varianti, anche in un'aggiunta marginale al f. 3b^r, e poi nella 'memoria' del 1473 (ove, tra l'altro, il Rucellai si vanta, a proposito del Palazzo, di aver fatto d'otto case una, 'chè tre—egli dice—ne rispondevano nella via della Vigna e cinque di drieto')[8];

---

dall'Alberti anche nel terzo libro della *Famiglia*, ove Leonardo, secondo cugino di Leon Battista, osserva che 'accade tale ora a fare qualche spesa la quale appartenga allo onore e fama di casa, come . . . in edificare nel tempio . . . e in molti luoghi dentro e fuori della terra, a Sancto Miniato . . . e simili nostri publici e privati edifici' (*Opere volgari*, ed. Grayson, I, p. 210). Cfr. A. D. Fraser Jenkins, "Cosimo de' Medici's Patronage of Architecture and the Theory of Magnificence", *JWCI*, XXXIII (1970), pp. 162–70; Kent, *Household and Lineage*, pp. 284 ss.

[1] Perosa, p. 121.

[2] Si veda, per l'importanza che veniva attribuita, da un punto di vista sociale, alla costruzione di un palazzo gentilizio, Martines, *Social World*, p. 281; Goldthwaite, *Private Wealth*, pp. 68, 271; Brucker, *Renaissance Florence*, p. 121; Fraser Jenkins, "Cosimo de' Medici's Patronage of Architecture", p. 162; Kent, ' "Più superba" ', pp. 311–23.

[3] Cfr. pp. 133 s.

[4] Perosa, pp. 117–20, 120–2.

[5] Perosa, p. 118.

[6] Perosa, p. 121.

[7] Perosa, p. 118.

[8] Perosa, p. 121.

ma, con nostro grande disappunto, nè in questi passi nè in altra parte dello Zibaldone, il Rucellai—
in ciò uniformandosi ad una consuetudine dei suoi tempi—fa il nome dell'autore (Leon Battista
Alberti?) o degli autori, che queste opere avevano ideato, progettato e costruito[1]. Egli ha tuttavia
inserito, o fatto inserire, tra le pagine più recenti dello Zibaldone, varie copie o estratti di documenti
che si riferivano, in qualche modo, a questi monumenti[2]; un'ampia descrizione della sua villa di
Quaracchi, che è una delle pagine più personali e vivaci dello Zibaldone[3]; e al f. 69a[r], di suo pugno,
un elenco prezioso delle opere di scultura, pittura e tarsia, che egli allora possedeva (ma non sono
più reperibili), e recavano le firme di illustri maestri, quali Domenico Veneziano, fra Filippo Lippi,
Giuliano da Maiano, Antonio Pollaiolo, Maso Finiguerra, Andrea Verrocchio, Andrea del Castagno,
Paolo Uccello, Desiderio da Settignano e Giovanni Bertini[4].

IV

La città di Firenze, la sua storia e la vita civile sono al centro degli interessi del Rucellai. Numerose
le tracce nello Zibaldone dell'attaccamento che il Rucellai ebbe per la sua città, i suoi monumenti,
la sua storia più recente. Egli dichiara, ad es., in un 'ricordo' del 1464, di essere grato a Dio per aver
avuto i natali 'nella parte d'Italia la quale è la più degna e più nobile parte di tutto il Cristianismo, ed
ènne la provincia di Toschana', e appresso per essere nato nella 'ciptà di fFirenze, la quale è riputata
la più degna e la più bella patria che abbi non tanto il Cristianesimo ma tutto l'universo mondo[5].'

Documenti, memorie ed estratti di cronache fiorentine occupano una parte rilevante dello
Zibaldone, come si può constatare dall'*Indice generale* del codice, premesso, come s'è già detto,
all'edizione antologica del 1960[6]. Nello Zibaldone *vetus*—accanto a documenti di carattere familiare
e a una descrizione delle morìe che hanno funestato Firenze dal 1348—figura una *Cronaca* di Firenze
dal 1400 al 1457 composta dal Rucellai, che è uno dei pezzi più interessanti dello Zibaldone[7]. Nelle
parti più recenti dello Zibaldone la documentazione storica si fa più fitta. Oltre ad alcune interessanti
memorie del Rucellai sulle condizioni climatiche e la produzione agricola degli anni dal 1458 al
1474[8], fa spicco in questi fascicoli la presenza massiccia di testi storici d'argomento cittadino, che fa
supporre che il Rucellai abbia accarezzato l'idea di raccogliere nello Zibaldone una silloge di
Cronache o di parti di Cronache fiorentine a documentazione degli avvenimenti più importanti del
recente passato.

---

[1] Fraser Jenkins, "Cosimo de' Medici's Patronage of Architecture", p. 169.

[2] Ricorderò, tra l'altro: una copia della bolla, con cui papa Paolo II concedeva, in data 22 giugno 1471, un'indulgenza ai
visitatori della cappella di S. Pancrazio (Perosa, pp. 24 s.); due 'memorie', rispettivamente del 1471 e del 1479, riguardanti le
possessioni di Poggio a Caiano (Perosa, pp. 25–7); un estratto del testamento del Rucellai redatto in data 13 dicembre 1465 dal
notaio ser Lionardo da Colle (ASF, NA, L 130, 1441–95, n° 31), che contempla la futura destinazione del Palazzo di via della
Vigna Nuova (*Zibaldone*, ff. 3a[r]–3b[r]; Marcotti, *Mercante fiorentino*, pp. 69–71); ecc.

[3] B. Patzak, *Palast und Villa in Toscana*, Lipsia, I, 1912, pp. 105 s. (n. 443 s., tav. LXII); II, 1913, pp. 97–103 (nn. 162–9). Il
Patzak riteneva che il piano del giardino della villa di Quaracchi fosse dovuto all'Alberti, e a tale proposito citava alcuni passi
del *De re aedificatoria*. Concetti, in parte analoghi, sono sviluppati da L. Bek, "Ut ars natura—ita natura ars. Le ville di Plinio e
il concetto del giardino nel Rinascimento", *Analecta Romana Instituti Danici*, VII (1971), pp. 136 ss.

[4] Perosa, pp. 23 s.

[5] Perosa, p. 117.

[6] Perosa, pp. xxi–xxiv.

[7] Perosa, pp. 44–62.

[8] *Zibaldone*, ff. 66b[r]–67a[r]. In queste brevi memorie—che varrebbe la pena di pubblicare—il Rucellai non solo ci fornisce
interessanti notizie e vivaci descrizioni sulla situazione climatica stagionale di quegli anni, ma ci dà anche utili ragguagli su rac-
colti, prezzi di prodotti agricoli (vino, olio, grano), ecc., con riferimenti alle proprietà di Quaracchi e di Brozzi.

Rimandando a più tardi l'analisi della *Cronaca* del Rucellai che figura nello Zibaldone *vetus*, mi soffermerò per ora sui testi inseriti nella seconda parte dello Zibaldone. Ricorderò anzitutto due brevi testi adespoti, e cioè: 1) un computo sommario—con un significativo accenno alla fondazione di Firenze ('Dal principio di Roma in sino al cominciamento di Firenze sono anni 667')—degli anni trascorsi dal principio del mondo al 1470, che non è altro che un volgarizzamento con varianti dell'inizio del *Liber de Temporibus* composto da Matteo Palmieri tra il 1446 e il 1448[1]; 2) una cronaca per sommi capi di Firenze e di Toscana dall'anno 450 (in cui 'fu disfatta la ciptà di Firenze per Totile, ecc.') fino al 1336 (in cui i Fiorentini fecero lega coi Veneziani contro 'quelli della Scala'), che ritroviamo—senza però che si possa inferire un rapporto di reciproca dipendenza—adespota e anepigrafa, con varianti, ai ff. 1ʳ–3ᵛ del codice Panciatichiano 92 della Biblioteca Nazionale di Firenze[2].

Questo manoscritto—appartenuto ad Antonio Bonsignori—contiene, oltre alla 'Cronachetta', i libri quarto, quinto e sesto della *Istoria fiorentina* di Domenico Buoninsegni (ff. 4ʳ–104ʳ) e l'intera *Istoria di Firenze* di Goro Dati (ff. 104ᵛ–155ᵛ). Ed è proprio su questi due storici coevi che il Rucellai —vedi caso—ha concentrato la sua attenzione. Ad essi infatti egli ha consacrato un'ottantina di fogli dello Zibaldone (i fascicoli XI–XIV e XIX–XXIII), aggiunti in varie riprese allo Zibaldone *vetus*[3]. Il Rucellai ha fatto copiare in questi fascicoli da più mani, quasi integralmente, l'*Istoria* del Dati, e ampi estratti dell'*Istoria fiorentina* del Buoninsegni, guardandosi bene dall'indicare, in ciascuno dei due casi, i nomi degli autori. L'*Istoria* del Dati, composta nel 1409–10, abbraccia gli anni dal 1380 al 1406, e fu stampata dal Manni nel 1735 e poi dal Pratesi nel 1904[4]; quella del Buoninsegni, composta tra il 1450 e il 1466, va dalla creazione del mondo al 1460, e fu stampata in due riprese, dal Marescotti nel 1580–1 i primi sei libri (attribuiti erroneamente al figlio di Domenico, Piero), dal Landini nel 1637 gli ultimi due[5]. L'*Istoria* del Dati e gli estratti del Buoninsegni, inseriti nello Zibaldone, presentano numerose varianti e anomalie testuali rispetto alle edizioni a stampa, ma—in mancanza di un'edizione critica (chè tale non è quella del Pratesi!) di queste due opere, e nell'impossibilità, per ora, di procedere ad una collazione sistematica dei numerosi mss. che ce l'hanno trasmesse—non sono in grado di stabilire a quale codice o gruppo di codici facciano capo i manoscritti utilizzati dal Rucellai. Dalla *Istoria fiorentina* del Buoninsegni—che è suddivisa in otto libri nel codice più autorevole, il ms. BNC II.IV.41—il Rucellai ha fatto copiare (sembra intorno al 1465), ai ff. 101ʳ–122ᵛ dello Zibaldone, parte del secondo libro e l'intero libro quinto, che si riferiscono, rispettivamente, agli anni 1342–3 e 1378–85; poi, da un'altra mano, ai ff. 124ʳ–211ʳ, il quarto libro, che abbraccia gli anni dal 1368 al 1376[6].

La scelta dei due autori da parte del Rucellai e le preferenze accordate (nel caso del Buoninsegni)

[1] *Zibaldone*, f. 70ᵛ. M. Palmieri, *Liber de temporibus* (1–1448), a cura di G. Scaramella, RR.II.SS., XXVI, 1, Città di Castello, 1906, p. 7. Un volgarizzamento anonimo del *Liber de temporibus* si trova nel codice Laur. Ashb. 668. Da un confronto effettuato tra i due testi, sembrerebbe si tratti dello stesso volgarizzamento, che lo Zibaldone tramanda in una versione ridotta, non immune da sviste, omissioni ed errori.

[2] *Zibaldone*, ff. 98ʳ–100ʳ.

[3] Per la composizione di questa sezione dello Zibaldone e i relativi problemi cronologici rimando a Perosa, pp. xv ss.

[4] G. Dati, *Istoria di Firenze*, ed. G. Manni, Firenze, 1735; *L'Istoria di Firenze di G.D. dal 1380 al 1405 . . .*, a cura di L. Pratesi, Norcia, 1904.

[5] *Historia fiorentina di M. Piero Buoninsegni nuovamente edita in luce*, Firenze, 1581; *Storie della città di Firenze dall'anno 1410 al 1460 scritte . . . da Domenico Boninsegni*, Firenze, 1637.

[6] Buoninsegni, *Historia fiorentina*, pp. 336–62, 604–71, 531–604. Da segnalare che l'inizio del quinto libro (pp. 604–32) è stato riscritto nello Zibaldone ai ff. 211ʳ–220ʳ dall'amanuense che ha copiato il quarto libro e non s'è accorto che il quinto libro già figurava nello Zibaldone ai ff. 109ʳ ss.

a certi brani dell'*Istoria* piuttosto che ad altri, sono molto significative. Sul Dati e sul Buoninsegni, che pur ebbero al loro tempo—come risulta dalla tradizione ms.—una larga diffusione, si è concentrata, in questi ultimi anni, l'attenzione degli studiosi, che ne hanno rivalutata l'importanza, ponendo in risalto (soprattutto nel caso del Dati) gli elementi innovatori, che rispetto alla storiografia del '300 le loro opere offrivano[1]. Le due storie, sia per la loro collocazione cronologica e per gli argomenti che trattano, sia per la loro impostazione metodologica, si collocano tra la storiografia degli umanisti e quella medioevale in lingua volgare, e costituiscono un valido anello di congiunzione tra la tradizione cronachistica e le esigenze storiografiche di una società in via di formazione. Se poi si tiene conto che sia il Dati che il Buoninsegni erano originariamente dei mercanti e coprivano uffici nell'ambito delle arti e delle più importanti magistrature della città[2]—appartenevano cioè ad una classe che, direttamente o indirettamente, era rimasta coinvolta, da un punto di vista politico, economico e ideologico, agli avvenimenti più salienti che essi narravano—si capirà come ad essi si rivolgesse di preferenza l'attenzione di molti contemporanei (il Dati morì nel 1435, il Buoninsegni nel 1466), che, come il Rucellai, appartenevano al loro stesso milieu. Essi hanno esercitato la stessa funzione culturale, che in altro settore, come abbiamo visto, hanno esercitato il *Trattato del Governo* e la *Vita civile*, quella cioè di porre in contatto la borghesia mercantile colla cultura umanistica, cui altrimenti sarebbe rimasta preclusa. Del resto già Vespasiano da Bisticci—che ha tracciato un rapido profilo del Buoninsegni—osservava che Domenico compose 'una cronica volgare, acciò fusse comune a tutti quegli volessino legere ... avendola messer Lionardo fatola latina, gli parve bastassi a' litterati, e per questo la fe' volgare. Songli molto obrigati quegli sono al presente e quegli veranno pe' tempi. . .'[3]. Il Buoninsegni ha infatti utilizzato come fonti, soprattutto per i fatti più recenti, le due opere storiche del Bruni, composte intorno al 1439–40, ma non bisogna dimenticare che egli si è anche largamente servito delle cronache di Giovanni Villani e dei suoi successori, e quindi ha condensato e filtrato, attraverso un più aggiornato strumento narrativo, materiali che provenivano dalle più disparate fonti umanistiche e cronachistiche.

Per quanto concerne i contenuti, il Rucellai, con sicuro intuito storico, ha centrato la sua attenzione e operato le sue scelte su alcuni avvenimenti chiave della storia fiorentina degli ultimi cento anni. Dal Buoninsegni, ad es., egli ha scelto—anche per ragioni di famiglia—le pagine che trattano del governo dispotico del duca d'Atene e della sua cacciata[4], e quelle in cui è ampiamente descritto

[1] Per il Dati si veda H. Baron, *The Crisis of the Early Italian Renaissance*, Princeton, 1955, I, pp. 62 s., 140–60; II, pp. 471 s., 506–13 (tr. it. di R. Pecchioli, Firenze, 1970, pp. 83–5, 185–206); *id.*, "A crucial Date in the History of Florentine Historiography", in *From Petrarch to Leonardo Bruni*, Chicago, 1968, pp. 138–50; C. Varese, "Una 'Laudatio Florentinae Urbis': la *Istoria di Firenze* di Goro Dati", in *Storia e politica nella prosa del Quattrocento*, Torino, 1961, pp. 65–91; Bec, *Marchands écrivains*, pp. 151–73. Per il Buoninsegni cfr. Martines, *Social World*, pp. 321 s.; A. Molho, "Domenico di Leonardo Buoninsegni's *Istoria fiorentina*", *Renaissance Quarterly*, XXIII (1970), pp. 256–66; *id.*, "Buoninsegni Domenico", *DBI*, XV, Roma, 1972, pp. 251 s.; G. M. Anselmi, "Machiavelli e l'*Istoria fiorentina* di Domenico di Leonardo Buoninsegni", *Studi e problemi di critica testuale*, IX (1974), pp. 119–32.

[2] Per l'attività mercantile svolta dal Dati e dal Buoninsegni e le cariche pubbliche che essi ebbero si veda F. Flamini, "Leonardo di Piero Dati poeta latino del sec. XV", *GSLI*, XVI (1890), pp. 2 s.; Baron, *Crisis*, II, p. 506 (tr. it., p. 186); Martines, *Social World*, pp. 32, 321 s., 372 (catasto del 1427); Bec, *Marchands écrivains*, pp. 151 s.; Molho, *DBI*, p. 251; ecc. Si ricordi che il Dati è anche autore di un importante libro di ricordanze (*Il libro segreto* [*1384–1434*], a cura di C. Gargiolli, Bologna, 1869).

[3] Vespasiano, *Vite*, ed. Greco, II, pp. 407 s.

[4] Buoninsegni, *Historia fiorentina*, pp. 339, 345, 351, 355. Il Buoninsegni dice che Naddo, figlio di Cenni Rucellai, fu preso dal duca d'Atene e confinato a Perugia; ritornato poco dopo, con garanzie di sicurtà, fu impiccato 'con una catena in collo'; il padre, per disperazione, si fece frate di S. Maria Novella. La storia di Naddo è raccontata dal Rucellai sia nel già cit. libro del 1456 (BNC II.IV.374, p. 128), sia—con qualche variante—all'inizio dello Zibaldone *vetus* (ff. 3b^v–4a^r). Naddo—dice il Rucellai—era stato accusato dal duca d'aver 'rubato il Comune; per la qual cosa n'è seguito che essendone molto isdegnati il resto degl'uomini della nostra famiglia de' Rucellai e parendo loro esserne molto vituperati, furono i primi a levarsi in arme per la cacciata del detto duca d'Atene. . .'. Ricorderò poi che al f. 82a^v dello Zibaldone è trascritta una 'pistola del re Ruberto mandata al ducha

il tumulto dei Ciompi con le implicazioni politiche che ne seguirono; dall'*Istoria* del Dati (accolta integralmente nello Zibaldone) il Rucellai ha potuto, invece, farsi un'idea precisa su due fatti tra loro intimamente collegati (le guerre col Visconti e l'acquisto di Pisa), che rappresentavano un momento cruciale nella storia della sua città.

Gli avvenimenti, cui il Rucellai si interessava, avevano avuto un'importanza decisiva sul destino di Firenze, sia in fatto di politica interna che di politica estera, e avevano inciso profondamente nello sviluppo sociale, politico ed economico dell'oligarchia che deteneva il potere. Non a caso un uomo, come Gino Capponi, esponente di primo piano della classe dominante, figura—forse a torto, come i più oggi ritengono—come autore di una storia in volgare, sia del tumulto dei Ciompi che dell' 'acquisto' di Pisa[1]; e a quest'ultima opera (l'abbia scritta Gino o, più probabilmente, Neri su appunti del padre) si richiamano—confermando implicitamente, che l'interesse, condiviso da Giovanni Rucellai, per la vicenda pisana era rimasto vivo per tutto il secolo—gli umanisti Matteo Palmieri—che intorno al 1450 (poco prima della stesura dello Zibaldone) la utilizza come fonte per la composizione in latino del suo *De captivitate Pisarum liber*, dedicato appunto a Neri Capponi—e Bernardo Rucellai, figlio di Giovanni, che, verso la fine del secolo, traduce in latino l'opuscolo, attribuendolo espressamente a Neri Capponi[2].

Mancano, invece, tra i brani tratti dal Buoninsegni, testimonianze sulla peste. Questo flagello periodico ha un posto di particolare rilievo in cronache, storie, epistolari, opere letterarie, ecc. a partire dalla famosa morìa del 1348, che sconvolse la città, ne turbò la composizione sociale, produsse gravi danni economici, alimentò conflittualità di classe e rivalità nel campo stesso operaio, che portarono alle successive lotte dei Ciompi[3]. Anche il Rucellai—che come si ricorderà iniziò la composizione del suo Zibaldone proprio in un periodo di forzato esilio a causa della peste—ritenne che fosse cosa di cui far memoria, ma invece di attingere a una cronaca, come per gli altri avvenimenti importanti della città, si servì questa volta di un documento di famiglia. Egli, infatti, ha fatto copiare nello Zibaldone *vetus* 'una scriptura antica' di suo nonno Paolo di Bingeri 'che fa ricordo della morìa dell'anno 1348', e poi, di seguito, ha elencato, a partire dal 1400 fino al 1457, le morìe che si succedettero a Firenze, indicando, volta per volta, il numero delle vittime, e i luoghi dov'egli s'era rifugiato insieme alla famiglia[4].

---

d'Atene quando gli venne a notizia che aveva presa la singnoria della cipptà di Firenze nel 1340 vel circha'. La lettera porta la data del 19 settembre 1342. Il testo di questa lettera si trova anche, con alcune varianti e con la firma di re Roberto, nella *Cronica di Giovanni Villani*, XII, 4 (ed. Firenze, 1845, IV, pp. 11–12).

[1] G. Capponi, *Caso o tumulto de' Ciompi dell'anno 1378* e *Commentari dell'acquisto ovvero presa di Pisa seguita l'anno 1406*, in *RR.II.SS.*, XVIII, Milano, 1731, coll. 1103–26, 1127–48. La storia del tumulto dei Ciompi fu ripubblicata, in edizione critica, col titolo di *Cronaca (1378)* da G. Scaramella nella nuova edizione dei *RR.II.SS.*, XVIII, 3, Bologna, 1917–34, pp. 13–34. Lo Scaramella attribuisce l'opuscolo ad Alamanno Acciaiuoli, che fu priore nel 1378 ed ebbe modo di seguire da vicino le varie fasi della rivolta. Quest'ipotesi, e quella più plausibile, che assegna a Neri di Gino la stesura dei commentari sulla conquista di Pisa—accolte dal *Repertorium fontium historiae Medii Aevi*, II, Roma, 1967, pp. 104 s.; III, Roma, 1970, pp. 124 s.—non sembrano condivise da G. Folena ("Ricordi politici e familiari di Gino di Neri Capponi", in *Miscellanea di studi offerta a Armando Balduino e Bianca Bianchi per le loro nozze*, Padova, 1962, p. 30) e dal Bec, *Marchands écrivains*, p. 228. Cfr. M. Mallett, "Capponi Gino" e "Capponi Neri", *DBI*, XIX, Roma, 1976, pp. 26 s., 70.

[2] M. Palmieri, *De captivitate Pisarum liber*, a cura di G. Scaramella, *RR.II.SS.*, IX, 2, Città di Castello, 1904, p. XVIII. La versione latina di Bernardo Rucellai fu pubblicata per la prima volta, col titolo di *De bello Pisano*, a Londra nel 1724, di seguito al *De bello Italico Caroli VIII commentarius*. Si noti che l'opuscolo sulla guerra di Pisa è dedicata a Pier Capponi, nipote di Neri.

[3] Bec, *Marchands écrivains*, pp. 32, 325, 344 n. 215; Brucker, *Renaissance Florence*, pp. 55 s.

[4] *Zibaldone*, ff. 25ar–26br. Il Rucellai ricorda le morìe del 1400 ('che fu l'anno de' bianchi'), 1411 ('la quale io fugi' a Pisa'), 1417 ('la quale io fugi' a Modona e a Furlì'), 1423–4 ('la quale io fugi' a 'Rezo e poi al Ponte a Signa, al luogo d'Agnolo di Filippo Pandolfini, mio zio'), 1430 ('la quale io fugi' prima a 'Rezo e poi all'Ancisa'), 1437–8 ('la quale io fugi' a Monte Varchi e poi a Pisa la famiglia mia, ma io stetti il forte di detto tempo a Genova in exercitio mercantile'), 1449–50 ('la quale io fugi' a Gobbio e poi a Perugia e poi alla Petraia, al luogo di messer Palla di Nofri degli Strozzi, mio suocero') e 1457 ('la quale io

Il Rucellai non si è limitato a raccogliere (come s'è visto finora) documenti storici e testi altrui, ma ha voluto egli stesso cimentarsi nella compilazione di una breve *Cronaca* di Firenze. Poichè 'nell'età nostra, dall'anno 1400 in qua—dice nel preambolo—sono state nella terra nostra, cioè nella cipttà di Firenze, molte cose nuove e grandi e dengnie di farne memoria, io . . . farò qui a presso memoria di quelle ch'io ò vedute e intese, ecc.'[1]. Il Rucellai, in queste poche pagine, narra, anno per anno—con rapidità, precisione e una certa vivacità di stile—gli avvenimenti di mezzo secolo, dalla morìa del 1400 alla 'maravigliosa e mirabile fortuna' dell'agosto del 1456; facendo seguire, a mo' d'appendice, a questa notizia, che praticamente conclude la *Cronaca*, la copia di tre lettere da Napoli (due indirizzategli dal fratello Paolo, rispettivamente in data 8 e 14 dicembre 1456, una inviata da Giannozzo Manetti alla Signoria in data 8 dicembre), in cui si descrive con dovizia di particolari, il violento terremoto, che nella notte fra il 4 e il 5 dicembre sconvolse gran parte dell'Italia meridionale[2].

Il Rucellai si affida, quasi interamente, alla propria esperienza personale, alla memoria e alle testimonianze dei contemporanei, e non indica mai nè cita fonti particolari, orali o scritte. La *Cronaca* non reca grandi novità—come si può constatare, effettuando, caso per caso, gli opportuni riscontri colle testimonianze tratte da cronache e storie contemporanee (dal Buoninsegni al Rinuccini, dal Bruni al Poggio, dal Cavalcanti al Palmieri, ecc.)[3]—ma è tuttavia degna di particolare attenzione, perchè contribuisce ad una più approfondita conoscenza del Rucellai attraverso le scelte che egli ha effettuato e la valutazione che egli ha dato di certi avvenimenti del più recente passato. Il Rucellai, infatti, pur dando il dovuto rilievo alle vicende politiche, concentra di preferenza la sua attenzione sui fatti di carattere economico—come ad es. sui commerci di Firenze per mare coll'Oriente e la conseguente coniazione del fiorino largo di galea; sull'andamento delle 'graveze'; sull'istituzione del catasto 'che—a quanto dice il Rucellai—contentò molto il popolo e molte riccheze grosse se ne disfeciono, perchè in verità il modo del detto chatasto offendeva più le riccheze grandi che lle mezane o lle picchole'); sulle rendite del Monte e sulla dote delle fanciulle 'in sul Monte', ecc.[4]; e anche quando parla di guerre, di paci e di alleanze, valuta sempre quanto siano costate al popolo fiorentino e quali vantaggi o perdite ne abbia ricevuto. 'Dal 1413 al 1423, che

fuggi' con tutta mia famiglia nel castello di San Gimignano, e quivi ordinai la presente opera'). Sempre nello Zibaldone *vetus*, al f. 81b[r] c'è in latino un 'Rimedio spirituale contro al male della pestilenzia'. Cfr. A. Corradi, *Annali delle epidemie occorse in Italia dalle prime memorie fino al 1850*, I, Bologna, 1865, pp. 188–299 (che abbracciano gli anni dal 1348 al 1457). In quest'opera, assai utile, sono elencate, per ciascuna epidemia, le fonti consultate e la bibliografia relativa.

[1] Perosa, p. 44.

[2] Perosa, pp. 55–60, 157–8. Di questo violento terremoto ci sono giunte numerose testimonianze in lettere e cronache contemporanee (cfr. Perosa, p. 157 n. 37). Di gran parte della prima delle due lettere inviate al Rucellai dal fratello Paolo, in data 8 dicembre, esistono altre tre copie. La prima si trova nel BNC II.IV.128, ff. 105[r]–106[r], trascritto da Giovanni di Iacopo Pigli; la seconda in una miscellanea di scritti e ricordi in volgare del codice Ricc. 1030, ff. 7[v]–8[r], ov'è attribuita erroneamente a Giannozzo Manetti; la terza fu inserita nella "Cronaca Varignana" (cod. 432 della Bibl. Universitaria di Bologna), che fa parte del *Corpus Chronicorum Bononiensium*, edito dal Sorbelli in *RR.II.SS.*, XVIII, 1, 20–1, Bologna, 1927, pp. 246–8. Il testo della lettera, in tutti e tre i casi, presenta numerose varianti e alterazioni, dovute in gran parte ai trascrittori; d'altra parte è probabile, che anche il Rucellai abbia modificato qua e là il testo della lettera prima di farla copiare nello Zibaldone.

[3] Ho indicato nelle note che accompagnano la mia antologia di passi dello Zibaldone (Perosa, pp. 147 ss.) i riscontri che, caso per caso, m'era stato possibile istituire tra il testo del Rucellai e le più importanti cronache e storie contemporanee.

[4] Perosa, pp. 46 s., 150 n. 12, 152 n. 16, 153 n. 18, 155 n. 26. Sarà opportuno ricordare che Pandolfo Rucellai, figlio di Giovanni, scrisse—dopo aver preso nel giugno 1495 l'abito domenicano e aver cambiato il proprio nome in quello di fra Santi—due opuscoli in volgare, in cui trattava di materia finanziaria, e precisamente, uno sui cambi (dedicato al Savonarola) e l'altro sul Monte comune e sul Monte delle doti. Le due opere furono pubblicate da R. de Roover, "Il Trattato di Fra Santi Rucellai sul cambio, il Monte comune e il Monte delle doti", *ASI*, CXI (1953), pp. 24 ss., e recentemente, sulla base di tutta la tradizione ms., da E. Fumagalli, "I Trattati di Fra Santi Rucellai", *Aevum*, LI (1977), pp. 289–332. Cfr. R. Ristori, "Un mercante savonaroliano: Pandolfo Rucellai", in *Magia, astrologia e religione nel Rinascimento*, Varsavia, 1974, pp. 30–47.

ssono anni 10, avemo una pacie molto tranquilla e sanza sospetto—dice il Rucellai—et il comune aveva pocha spesa di giente d'arme, et non si ponevano graveze o poche, per modo che lla terra ne venne molto pechuniosa e riccha'[1]. La situazione però s'era modificata radicalmente sia a causa della guerra con Filippo Maria Visconti, durata dal 1423 al 1428, nella quale—dice il Rucellai—'portamo grande spesa', sia a causa della guerra di Lucca, durata dal 1429 al 1433, durante la quale—nota il Rucellai—'il comune di Firenze' aveva corso 'grandissimi pericoli, perchè il danaio era molto manchato per la lunga guerra, e se la rotta fosse venuta per lo contradio eravamo spacciati'[2]. Interessante il giudizio che il Rucellai dà sulla guerra tra lo Sforza, il comune di Milano e i Veneziani nel 1449, e poi, tra lo stesso Sforza, i Veneziani e il re di Napoli tra il 1451 e il 1454. Il Rucellai fa notare, che l'aver ricusato i Fiorentini, per ben due volte, di entrare nella lega bandita da Venezia, 'fu tenuta non picchola scioccheza', di cui erano responsabili i 'principali ciptadini, che avevano il governo nelle mani' e nutrivano una 'grande affezione e amicizia' nei riguardi del conte Francesco. 'Si conoscieva—dice il Rucellai—che, essendo queste tre comunità (cioè Firenze, Venezia e Milano) d'acchordo e colleghate insieme, egli era uno spengniere e' signori e lle gienti d'arme d'Italia, et ragionevolmente ne doveva seguitare una lunga, buona e tranquilla pacie in tutta Italia, perchè non sarebbe stato nè singniore nè prencipe inn Italia nè fuori d'Italia che avesse avuto ardire di voler fare contro a tre comunità tanto potenti'[3]. Ma, a prescindere da tali valutazioni politiche (in cui è evidente un atteggiamento polemico contro la politica filosforzesca di Cosimo de' Medici), la guerra—aggiunge il Rucellai—aveva assorbito notevoli capitali, perchè s'era dovuto 'sopprire non tanto per noi quanto in parte pel ducha di Milano'), e i 'danari del Monte' non erano mai scesi, come per questa guerra, 'in tale bassezza di pregio'[4]. C'era poi anche una ragione personale alla radice dell'opposizione del Rucellai a questa guerra contro i Veneziani. La rottura con Venezia—città che godeva delle simpatie del Rucellai, che ne aveva tessuto un caldo elogio in altra parte dello Zibaldone *vetus*[5]—aveva avuto infatti gravi ripercussioni sul commercio fiorentino, perchè i Veneziani, per ritorsione, avevano 'accomiatato' dalla loro città i mercanti fiorentini, concedendo loro soltanto quindici giorni di tempo per 'sgombrare le persone el le sustanze a ppena della testa'. Il Rucellai stesso aveva subito le conseguenze di questa situazione, e nella *Cronaca* lo dichiara con una certa enfasi: 'E io Giovanni Rucciellai ne so ragionare—egli dice—perchè v'avevo la conpangnia insieme con Giovanfranciesco di messer Palla degli Strozi, mio congniato, e lasciamovi del chuoio e del pelo'[6].

---

[1] Perosa, pp. 46, 151 n. 14. Il giudizio, troppo ottimistico, che di questi anni, ormai lontani, dava il Rucellai, è stato recentemente ridimensionato da A. Molho, *Florentine Public Finances*, pp. 1–2; G. A. Brucker, *Civic World*, pp. 400–1.

[2] Perosa, p. 47; Molho, *Florentine Public Finances*, pp. 156–7.

[3] Perosa, pp. 52, 155 n. 27.

[4] Perosa, pp. 53, 156 n. 30.

[5] *Zibaldone*, ff. 84b^r–84a^v: 'E si dicie quello che è il vero, che la ciptà di Vinegia è meglio posta ciptà per fare merchatantia che alcuna altra ciptà del mondo, non perchè di terre marine non ci sieno delle meglio poste quanto al mare (chè ci sono molte terre poste in più comodo sito al navichare per mare e a llevante e a ponente che none Vinegia), ma la chagione perchè si dicie che Vinegia è posta in più comodo sito per fare merchatantia che niuna altra, si è perch' ell'à più commodità allo spaccio delle merchatantie per terra ferma che niuna altra ciptà, et massimamente per essere vicina alla Magnia e per avere comodità di condurvi le merchatantie parte per aqua e parte per charrette con pocha spesa ... e ancora per essere vicini alla provincia della Lonbardia, che per essere grande provincia e bene popolata vi si spaccia merchatantia assai, et perchè il forte d'essa è posta in piano e la pianura v'è grande, vi sono grossi fiumi, per gli quali fiumi si può condurre la merchatantia da Vinegia là con molta comodità e con picchiolissima spesa, et niuna altra nazione che navichi, o Gienovesi o Fiorentini o altri, non può stare al pari di loro, per averle a conduciere co' muli e altre bestie con molto maggiore spesa di loro. Et però sono di questa oppenione che non possa mai manchare a quella ciptà fare grandi facciende di merchatantie, et credo che quando fusse disfatta, o per guerre o per altro, fino a' fondamenti, che sarebbe nicistà di nuovo riedificharla per essere in detto buono sito, o veramente riporne un'altra lì vicina per sopprire a quello medesimo'. Cfr. Kent, sopra, p. 36.

[6] Perosa, p. 53.

Il Rucellai si esprime in prima persona soltanto qui e in un passo in cui accenna alla visita fatta nell'agosto del 1456 ai luoghi del contado fiorentino colpiti da una furiosa tempesta[1]. Nei libri di ricordanze la narrazione di fatti storici s'intreccia in genere a quella di vicende personali o di famiglia. Nello Zibaldone invece la *Cronaca* ha una sua collocazione autonoma e il Rucellai cerca di mantenere nell'esposizione un certo distacco dai fatti che narra, tanto è vero che di alcuni avvenimenti (ad es. la cacciata dei Medici, il loro ritorno, il confino degli Strozzi, ecc.), che avrebbero avuto un'influenza decisiva sulla storia della città e sulle sorti della sua famiglia, egli si limita a dare un resoconto sommario, senza alcun particolare intervento personale[2].

Di una più diretta partecipazione del Rucellai ad avvenimenti registrati succintamente nella *Cronaca*, recano invece testimonianza due 'memorie', che nello Zibaldone *vetus* precedono la *Cronaca*, e furono evidentemente composte prima della sua stesura. Nella prima 'memoria' il Rucellai dà notizia della visita fatta alle chiese e alle 'anticaglie' di Roma, in occasione del giubileo del 1450[3]; nella seconda egli fa un vivace resoconto del sopralluogo effettuato alle zone colpite dalla violenza— come egli dice—'d'una mirabil fortuna, che fu nel contado di Firenze uno lunedì mattina innanzi dì, a dì 22 d'agosto 1456'[4]. Il violento fortunale—che è ricordato da molte fonti contemporanee[5]— si abbattè sulla campagna circostante a Firenze all'alba del 23 (e non del 22, come dice il Rucellai) agosto, che cadeva appunto di lunedì. Il Rucellai 'pochi dì appresso', montato a cavallo, e 'in compagnia di Bartolomeo Ridolfi et altri' percorse per tutto il giorno le zone colpite, registrando puntualmente i danni sofferti da uomini e animali, alberi e coltivazioni, case, chiese, castelli, ecc. Di questa sua descrizione il Rucellai—prima di curarne l'inserzione nello Zibaldone—fece eseguire delle copie, che ci sono giunte per altre vie in redazioni diverse[6].

Ma di gran lunga più significativa è la prima delle due 'memorie' del Rucellai, che descrive il viaggio fatto a Roma per il giubileo. 'Trovandomi nella città di Perugia l'anno 1449 colla mia famiglia—dice il Rucellai—per rispecto della pestilentia ch'era nella nostra città di Firenze, et essendo principiato il giubileo, terminai andare a Roma . . . et col nome di Dio parti' da Perugia a dì 10 di febraio 1449 (= 1450) in compagnia della buona memoria di Lorenzo di messer Palla delli Strozi, mio cognato, et di Domenicho di Giovanni Bartholi, mio genero. Et ritornamo in Perugia a dì 8 di marzo . . . e nel tempo che noi stemo a Roma, osservamo questa regola, che la mattina montavamo a chavallo andando a vicitare le 4 chiese notate di sopra [San Pietro, San Paolo, San Giovanni

---

[1] Perosa, p. 55: 'Nel 1456 a dì 22 d'agosto fu una maravigliosa e mirabile fortuna. . . . E io Giovanni Ruciellai andai personalmente in detti luoghi a vedere, udire e sentire, ecc.'.

[2] Perosa, pp. 48–9, 154.

[3] Perosa, pp. 67–78, 159–63. La descrizione del Rucellai, oltre che dal Marcotti e da Valentini e Zucchetti (già citati a p. 100, n. 1), è stata pubblicata da H. P. Horne, "An Account of Rome in 1450", *Revue archéologique*, s. IV, X (1907), pp. 82–97.

[4] Perosa, pp. 78–82, 163. Anche questa descrizione è stata pubblicata (come s'è visto a p. 100, n. 1) dal Marcotti.

[5] Ricorderò, tra le tante testimonianze che potrei addurre, una lettera di Poggio al cardinale Domenico Capranica (*Poggii Epistolae*, ed. Th. de Tonellis, III, Firenze, 1861, pp. 229–39: *Ep.* XIII 30); Buoninsegni, *Storie*, p. 116; F. Rinuccini, *Ricordi storici*, a cura di G. Aiazzi, Firenze, 1840, p. LXXXVI; M. Palmieri, *Annales*, a cura di G. Scaramella, *RR.II.SS.*, XVI, 1, 2, Città di Castello, 1903, pp. 176 ss.; N. Machiavelli, *Istorie fiorentine*, VI, 34 (*Tutte le Opere*, a cura di M. Martelli, Firenze, 1971, p. 789).

[6] Una copia di questa descrizione, inviata sotto forma di lettera in data 28 agosto a Napoli, ci è giunta nella trascrizione imperfetta in dialetto napoletano, che ne ha fatto il cronista Angelo de Tummulillis (*Notabilia temporum*, a cura di C. Corvisieri, Roma, 1890, pp. 63–8); un'altra copia è stata inserita da Giovanni de' Pigli—che dice di averla avuta da uno degli accompagnatori del Rucellai—in una raccolta autografa di scritti di vari autori volgari (BNC II.IV.128, ff. 96r–99r); una terza copia, infine— eseguita da certo Matteo Rinaldi—ha trovato posto nel *Priorista* di Paolo de' Petriboni (ASF, Conv. Sopp., C 4, 895, ff. 172r ss.) da dove è passata in G. Cambi, *Istorie*, ed. Fr. Ildefonso di San Luigi, I (*Delizie degli eruditi Toscani*, *XX*), Firenze, 1785, pp. 338–45. Dal Petriboni (ripreso poi dal Cambi) si ricava che anche l'arcivescovo di Firenze, S. Antonino, lontano parente del Rucellai, s'era recato sui luoghi del disastro.

Laterano, Santa Maria Maggiore], et dipoi drieto a mangiare rimontavamo a chavallo et andavamo cerchando et veggiendo tutte quelle muraglie antiche et cose degne di Roma, et la sera, ritornati a casa, ne facevo ricordo...'[1]. Dopo questo preambolo, incomincia la descrizione dei monumenti visti dal Rucellai, il quale segue nell'esposizione un ordine ben preciso. Il primo posto spetta alle quattro chiese maggiori (alle quali il Rucellai dedica quasi la metà dell'intera 'memoria'), seguono poi i monumenti dislocati in Trastevere, le chiese minori (circa una ventina), gli archi di trionfo, le colonne, le terme, i teatri, i palazzi, singoli monumenti come il Carcere Tulliano, il Campidoglio, il tempio della Pace (basilica di Costantino), le Capoccie, e in fine le Torri, le Mura, le Porte, ecc. Di ogni chiesa, di ogni monumento, di ogni opera d'arte antica e moderna, il Rucellai offre, con vivacità di stile, una descrizione circostanziata. Egli ne indica la grandezza (che talvolta confronta con quella di analoghi monumenti fiorentini)[2] e ne illustra le strutture, indugiando nella descrizione delle parti decorative ed ornamentali e dei materiali impiegati. Il Rucellai sottolinea con frequenti apprezzamenti o giudizi ammirativi (che pur nella loro semplicità adombrano quel certo gusto per l'arte e le antichità, che non poteva mancare in un mecenate e collaboratore dell'Alberti) la bellezza o la eccezionalità di un monumento o di un'opera d'arte[3]; e accompagna le sue descrizioni con notazioni di carattere storico, mitico o leggendario, elencando, ad es., le numerose reliquie, che la pietà popolare venerava nelle chiese romane, o indulgendo, secondo la tradizione medioevale, a dicerie, favole e superstizioni, che circolavano da secoli (ma che il Rucellai prudentemente introduce, quasi sempre, col dubitativo 'si dice'). Il Rucellai ha, evidentemente, visitato, se non tutti, gran parte delle chiese e dei monumenti che descrive; tuttavia, è lecito supporre, che nella stesura di questo 'ricordo', egli abbia seguito, servendosene come di una falsariga, qualcuno di quei *Libri indulgentiarum et reliquiarum*, compilati ad uso dei pellegrini che visitavano la città eterna. Questi libri—di cui ci è giunto, in mss. dei secoli XIV e XV e in stampe della fine del '400, un numero cospicuo di edizioni in latino, tedesco, italiano, francese ed inglese[4]—consistono di due parti, la prima delle quali è un epitome assai breve degli antichissimi *Mirabilia*, mentre la seconda, molto più estesa, contiene una lista delle reliquie e delle indulgenze delle chiese di Roma, che i romei dovevano visitare. La conoscenza da parte del Rucellai di uno di questi libri è molto probabile, se si tien conto, sia delle numerose coincidenze che si possono rilevare nelle descrizioni degli stessi monumenti—che ho messo, in parte, in evidenza nelle note che accompagnano la stampa di questo testo[5]—sia del fatto, che non sembra conciliabile col sistema di notazione giornaliera delle cose viste, la catalogazione che il Rucellai ne fa

---

[1] Perosa, pp. 67–8.

[2] Perosa, pp. 68 ('Sancto Pietro, di grandeza quanto la chiesa di Sancta Croce di Firenze vel circha'), 69 ('Sancta Maria Maggiore, della grandeza di Sancta Maria Novella di Firenze'), 70 ('Sancto Giovanni Laterano, lunga et largha quanto la chiesa di Sancta Croce di Firenze vel circha'), 75 ('Le terme di Diocritiano ... di grandezza quanto mezo il prato Ognisancti di Firenze'), 77 ('Testaccio, che è uno monte pocho meno che 'l monte di Sancto Miniato di Firenze').

[3] Aggettivi come 'bello', 'bellissimo', 'maraviglioso', 'mirabile', 'notabile', 'gentile', 'gratioso', 'piacevole', ecc.—riferiti a chiese, chiostri, tabernacoli, mosaici, colonne, pavimenti, portici, e (come dice il Rucellai) ad altre 'gentileze'—ricorrono con grande frequenza in questa descrizione. Un dipinto in S. Paolo, attribuito a Giotto, è 'di perfecte et buone figure', e 'cosa molto buona' è detta la 'nave degli Appostoli', mosaico in S. Pietro, 'che si dice essere di mano di Giotto'.

[4] Cfr. L. Schudt, *Le guide di Roma*, Vienna, 1930. Un particolare rilievo meritano, a tale proposito, la guida in inglese del teologo agostiniano John Capgrave (*Ye solace of Pilgrimes*, ed. C. A. Mills, Londra, 1911) e la descrizione di Roma in lingua tedesca del borgomastro di Norimberga Nicola Muffel (*Beschreibung der Stadt Rom*, ed. W. Vogt, Tubinga, 1876), ristampate, recentemente, da Valentini e Zucchetti, *Codice Topografico*, IV, pp. 325–49, 351–73.

[5] Perosa, pp. 159–63. Utile strumento di consultazione—per identificazioni, riferimenti, ecc.—la raccolta di descrizioni antiche, medievali e rinascimentali della città di Roma, che R. Valentini e G. Zucchetti hanno pubblicato, col titolo di *Codice Topografico della Città di Roma*, in quattro volumi delle *Fonti per la storia d'Italia dell'Istituto storico italiano per il Medio Evo* (voll. LXXXI, LXXXVIII, XC, XCI, Roma, 1940–53. Cfr. Kent, sopra, p. 51 n).

per gruppi di monumenti affini (chiese, archi, colonne, ecc.) secondo lo stile dei *Mirabilia* e dei *Libri indulgentiarum*.

Al testo della *Cronaca* e all'appendice di lettere, che riguardano il terremoto di Napoli del 1456, il Rucellai ha fatto seguire alcune pagine, in cui ha cercato di esprimere, in rapida sintesi, un suo giudizio complessivo su quel mezzo secolo di storia fiorentina, di cui egli aveva narrato le vicende[1]. 'Egli è oppenione—dice all'inizio—che l'età nostra dal 1400 in qua abbi da contentarsi più che niuna altra età che ssia stata poi che Firenze fu hedifichata'[2]. Il Rucellai ha colto, in queste pagine, con una certa lucidità, l'importanza del grande momento storico-culturale in cui era vissuto e viveva, e si è reso conto che, con l'inizio del secolo, s'era dischiusa una nuova età, contraddistinta, oltre che dal rafforzato prestigio politico della città e dal maggior benessere economico della collettività, da un autentico rinnovamento della cultura e delle arti. Sulla scia di quegli umanisti—dal Salutati al Bruni, dal Dati al Rinuccini—che all'inizio del secolo avevano vissuto in pieno la complessa crisi politico-culturale di Firenze e rendendosi conto della posizione chiave che la città era venuta assumendo nel quadro della politica nazionale, ne avevano esaltato la capacità di resistenza e i grandi meriti procuratisi in ogni settore della vita pubblica e privata, il Rucellai riprende il tema—a loro tanto caro—della *laudatio Florentinae urbis*, della glorificazione cioè della città, dei suoi ordinamenti, della sua cultura e della sua prosperità economica[3].

In questa acuta e ampia rassegna delle realizzazioni conseguite, in ogni campo, dai Fiorentini dall'inizio del secolo, il Rucellai pone in evidenza, tra l'altro, il prestigio politico e militare raggiunto da Firenze in questo periodo ('però che dal 1400 in qua s'è fatto aquisto di Pisa, di Cortona e del Borgo a San Sipolcro e di Poppi, ecc. . . . e si diè principio al navichare per mare con ghalee grosse da merchato'[4]); ricorda l'incremento edilizio che città e contado hanno realizzato colla costruzione di 'chiese, spedali, chase e palazi, dentro e fuori con bellissimi adornamenti di conci alla romanesca, cioè al modo facievano gli antichi Romani'[5]; accenna all'uso sempre più diffuso, tra uomini e donne, di 'vestimenti ricchi, ben fatti e puliti', splendidamente ornati di 'richami, gioie, perle', ecc., di masserizie 'con chopia di panni d'arazo, spalliere e panchali', ecc.[6]; sottolinea il progresso verificatosi nella lavorazione della seta ('il mestieri della seta—dice—non lavorò mai tanti drappi quanto in questo tenpo, e mai si feciono i più ricchi drappi d'oro e di seta di maggior pregio che al presente'[7])

---

[1] Perosa, pp. 60-2.

[2] In un 'ricordo' del 1464 il Rucellai, riprendendo questo concetto, ringrazierà Dio per avergli concesso di vivere 'nell'età presente, la quale si tiene per li intendenti ch'ella sia stata e sia la più gioconda età che mai avessi la nostra ciptà poi che Firenze fu edificata, per le chagioni e ragioni che sono narrate in questo libro . . .' (Perosa, p. 118).

[3] Si veda, a tale proposito, Baron, *Crisis*, I, pp. 163 ss.; II, pp. 514 ss. (tr. it., pp. 209 ss.); Varese, *Storia e politica*, pp. 65 ss.; Bec, *Marchands écrivains*, pp. 173, 374 ss., 379 ss.; Brucker, *Renaissance Florence*, pp. 126, 162, 170.

[4] Perosa, pp. 60-1.

[5] Perosa, p. 60. Tornerà qui a proposito ricordare che il Rucellai, più di dieci anni dopo, inserì nello Zibaldone un elogio delle chiese fiorentine, pronunciato dal servita fra Mariano Salvini, che fu vescovo di Cortona dal 1455 alla morte, avvenuta agli inizi del 1477 (cfr. Eubel, *Hierarchia catholica Medii Aevi*, II, Münster, 1901, p. 154)—in un incontro che egli aveva avuto col Rucellai il 30 luglio 1469 nella chiesa dei Servi. L'elogio dalle chiese si estende ai conventi, ai monasteri, agli ospedali, ai 'palazi e chasamenti di cittadini', in genere a tutta Firenze, che dal vescovo viene definita come 'la più bella, più nobile, più gentile che città del mondo, per modo che i Fiorentini ànno la più dengna patria che abbi tutto il Christianesimo' (Perosa, pp. 65 s., 159). Sul Salvini cfr. C. Piana, *La Facoltà teologica dell'Università di Firenze nel Quattro e Cinquecento*, Grottaferrata, 1977, pp. 160-8.

[6] Perosa, p. 61.

[7] Perosa, p. 61. In una successiva 'memoria' (*Zibaldone*, f. 94b^v) il Rucellai fornisce alcuni dati interessanti sulla lavorazione della seta a Firenze negli anni 1459 e 1460. 'Si fece—dice—in Firenze grandissimo lavorare di drappi di seta, per modo che in un anno di tenpo si consumorno l[ibbre] 100 m[igliaia] di seta e montorno e' drappi che si feceno in detto tenpo circa f[iorini] 600 m[igliaia], e lavoravasi chom 1500 in 1600 telaia [di seta e montorno e' drappi] in su tale botegha, cioè una bottegha sola che in uno anno di tenpo lavorò l[ibbre] 8 m[igliaia] di seta e montorno e' drappi f[iorini] 40 m[igliaia] tutti in detto anno solo in detta botegha'. Cfr. Brucker, *Renaissance Florence*, p. 85; Molho, *Florentine Public Finances*, p. 4.

e nella lavorazione dell'oro filato, ecc. Il Rucellai dedica poi particolare attenzione alla situazione finanziaria, che giudica positivamente ('la ciptà riccha di danari contanti e di merchatantie e di possessioni, crediti di Monte più ch'a niuno altro tenpo'), facendo notare che il colmo della ricchezza s'era verificato 'da l'anno 1418 a l'anno 1423'—quando, secondo il Rucellai, i mercanti fiorentini possedevano sui due milioni di fiorini in 'chontanti e merchatantia' (senza contare gli investimenti immobiliari e in titoli del Monte)—cui era succeduto un progressivo impoverimento, dovuto alle guerre e alle forti tassazioni, che avevano consumato 'assai richeze'[1].

Ma la parte più interessante di questa rassegna finale è quella in cui il Rucellai esprime il suo punto di vista sulla rinascita delle lettere e delle arti e sui personaggi che in questo periodo ebbero un ruolo dominante nella vita politica e culturale di Firenze. Il Rucellai ricorda infatti che in quegli anni le lettere—per opera di 'più singulari huomini inn iscienzia', che hanno 'rivochato a lucie antica leggiadria dello stile perduto e spento'—s'erano 'ringientilite con latino pulito e ornato più che a niuno altro tenpo da Tulio in qua'; e che le arti, a loro volta, avevano sfornato un gran numero 'd'architettori, maestri di scoltura, d'intaglio e di scharpello', per modo che se n'era 'condito tutta Italia', tanto è vero che 'dal tenpo de' Gientili in qua' non c'erano stati 'simili maestri di lengname, di tarsie e commessi, di tanta arte di prospettiva che con pennello non si farebbe meglio, dipintori, disengniatori singulari e con grande arte, misura e ordine e per modo che Giotto o Cimabue non sarebbono stati sofficienti disciepoli, ecc.'[2].

Il Rucellai incastona quindi nel corpo di questa rassegna i medaglioni di 'quattro notabili cittadini dengni di memoria'. Sono Palla Strozzi e Cosimo de' Medici, ancora in vita quando il Rucellai componeva lo Zibaldone, e Leonardo Bruni e Filippo di ser Brunellesco, morti ormai da più di dieci anni. Di Palla il Rucellai dice, elencandole, che possedeva 'tutte e sette le parti della felicità'; di Cosimo che era 'ciptadino ricchissimo . . . huomo di grandissimo naturale, potentissimo . . . e di gran seguito . . . per forma che . . . disponeva del governo della ciptà come se propio ne fussi stato singniore'; di Leonardo Bruni, che era stato 'dottissimo e singularissimo in grecho, ebraicho e latino, famoso quanto alchuno che ssia stato da Tulio in qua, dal quale la eloquentia latina è stata risucitata'; di Filippo Brunelleschi, che era stato 'maestro d'architettura e di scoltura, perfetto gieometrico, di grande ingiengnio naturale e fantasia nelle dette arti quanto niuno altro che fussi mai dal tenpo de' Romani in qua, risucitatore delle muraglie antiche alla romanescha'[3].

Dei quattro Grandi il Rucellai non discorre soltanto qui, ma anche in un *excursus* inserito nel contesto della *Cronaca*[4]. I due testi presentano notevoli somiglianze. Il Rucellai ha riprodotto, quasi letteralmente, nella rassegna finale, i giudizi su Cosimo, sul Bruni e sul Brunelleschi espressi precedentemente nella *Cronaca*, ma ha invece notevolmente ridotto il brano che riguardava Palla. A Palla, infatti, egli aveva concesso nell'*excursus* un più largo spazio, dilungandosi soprattutto su quel motivo delle 'sette parti della felicità', che era diventato, a quanto sembra, un tema d'obbligo per chi si interessasse dello Strozzi.

Questo motivo, infatti, ricompare, con varianti, in un breve profilo di Palla, che figura in altra parte dello Zibaldone *vetus*[5], e, in redazione più antica, in quel libro del 1456, di cui ci sono pervenuti, come s'è visto in precedenza, degli estratti nei codici ASF, CS, s. III, 79, pp. 57 ss. e BNC

---

[1] Perosa, p. 62. Cfr. Brucker, *Renaissance Florence*, pp. 82, 160 ss.; Molho, *Florentine Public Finances*, pp. 156–7.
[2] Perosa, pp. 60–1.
[3] Perosa, p. 61.
[4] Perosa, pp. 54–5, 157.
[5] Perosa, pp. 63–4, 158–9.

II.IV.374, pp. 126 ss.[1]. Di Palla, sia nello Zibaldone che nel libro del 1456, il Rucellai discorre a proposito dei vincoli di parentela che lo legavano a lui, avendone sposato la figlia Iacopa. 'Nel tempo che io la tolsi—dice il Rucellai nello Zibaldone—decto messere Palla era il più potente et maggiore cittadino della terra nostra et il più riccho, et era opinione che tutto il Cristianesmo non avessi cittadino più richo di lui.' Le sue ricchezze—di cui il Rucellai specifica l'entità—consistevano in 'denari sul Monte, possessioni, denari contanti, casamenti, masseritie drento alla città et di fuori nel contado, arienti, libri et gioie'. Queste ricchezze si erano però consumate—aggiunge il Rucellai—per due ragioni: per le gravezze pagate, a causa delle guerre, dal 1423 al 1433, e 'per cagione di suoi confini, però che per ghare et divisioni cittadinesche fu confinato a Padova. . .'[2]. Il Rucellai ricorda poi che il giorno del suo matrimonio (nel 1428) Leonardo Bruni, venendogli incontro, s'era rallegrato con lui, perchè aveva 'fatto parentado col più felice huomo' di questo mondo, che possedeva tutte sette le parti della felicità, di cui il Bruni stesso gli aveva recitato l'elenco. Il nome del Bruni non figura nè nella *Cronaca* nè nel libro del 1456, in cui si fa riferimento alle 'sette parti della felicità'; appare invece nella *Vita* di Palla Strozzi di Vespasiano da Bisticci ('Diceva messer Lionardo d'Arezo in loda di messer Palla, che il più felice uomo che avessi la sua età era messer Palla di tutte le parti che si richiegono all'umana felicità ecc.'[3]), e poichè è poco probabile che lo Zibaldone sia stato la fonte diretta di Vespasiano, bisognerà ritenere che l'attribuzione a Leonardo Bruni di questa diceria su Palla fosse diffusa e universalmente riconosciuta.

Una delle parti della felicità di Palla consisteva—secondo queste testimonianze—nell' 'essere virtuoso di scienza; et lui era dottissimo di tutte le scienze e intendeva il latino, il greco e ll'ebraicho'[4]. A parte l'evidente esagerazione per quanto concerne la conoscenza dell'ebraico (che il Rucellai stesso, stranamente, attribuiva anche a Leonardo Bruni[5]), le benemerenze dello Strozzi nel campo degli studi classici (soprattutto del greco) sono troppo note, perchè io vi ritorni sopra. Legato ad uomini come il Crisolora, il Filelfo, l'Argiropulo, Andronico Callisto[6], ecc., lo Strozzi apprese il greco sin da giovane, e coi larghi mezzi di cui disponeva mise insieme una delle più ragguardevoli biblioteche umanistiche dei suoi tempi, che in parte si può ricostruire alla luce di un inventario del 1431 e di due testamenti, rispettivamente del 1447 e del 1462[7].

Il Rucellai rende omaggio, più volte, alla cultura del suocero, e in una breve nota dello Zibaldone, scritta, a quanto sembra, intorno al 1470 (quando cioè Palla era già morto) dà un elenco 'dell'opere o vero libri, che messer Palla di Nofri Strozzi traslatò di grecho in latino'[8]. Sono registrati diciannove

---

[1] Cfr. p. 103 e n. 4.

[2] Perosa, p. 63. Il Rucellai precisa che Palla 'aveva solamente in sul Monte del comune di Firenze fiorini dugento migliaia scripti, che a quel tenpo valevano 51 per cento', aveva 'possessioni di valuta di fiorini ottanta migliaia', e la sua rendita 'solo delle cose stabili passava fiorini quindici migliaia'. Quanto alle tasse, il Rucellai sostiene che Palla, dal 1423 al 1433, 'pagò in comune di gravezze ordinarie . . . fiorini ciento sesanta migliaia'. Risulta che Palla pagò di prestanze nel 1403 fiorini 121, ma nel Catasto del 1427 ebbe d'imponibile netto fiorini 101,402. Cfr. Martines, *Social World*, pp. 316 ss., 359 e 372.

[3] Vespasiano, *Vite*, ed. Greco, II, p. 142. Cfr. Bec, *Marchands écrivains*, p. 368.

[4] Perosa, p. 54.

[5] Perosa, p. 61.

[6] Per i rapporti tra Palla Strozzi e Andronico Callisto si veda A. Perosa, "Inediti di Andronico Callisto", *Rinascimento*, IV (1953), pp. 3–15.

[7] Inventari e testamenti di Palla Strozzi sono stati pubblicati e studiati da L. A. Ferrai, "La biblioteca di S. Giustina di Padova", in G. Mazzatinti, *Inventario dei mss. italiani nelle biblioteche di Francia*, II, Roma, 1887, pp. 549–661; V. Fanelli, "I libri di messer Palla di Nofri Strozzi", *Convivium*, I (1949), pp. 57–73; G. Fiocco, "La casa di Palla Strozzi", *Memorie dell'Accademia dei Lincei, Classe di scienze morali*, s. VII, V (1954), pp. 361–82; A. Diller, "The Greek Codices of Palla Strozzi and Guarino Veronese", *JWCI*, XXIV (1961), pp. 313–21; G. Fiocco, "La Biblioteca di Palla Strozzi", in *Studi di bibliografia e di storia in onore di T. De Marinis*, II, Verona, 1964, pp. 289–310.

[8] Perosa, p. 64.

pezzi (che dovrebbero corrispondere ad altrettanti codici), ma le indicazioni che per ognuno di essi dà il Rucellai sono molto sommarie, nonostante che egli si prenda cura, di volta in volta, di precisare se si tratta di opere 'emendate', 'assai emendate', 'assai corrette', 'non emendate', 'non corrette', ecc. Gli autori sono sette (Simplicio, *Commento alla Fisica d'Aristotele*, 5 mss.; Giovanni Crisostomo, *Omelie*, 2 mss.; Gregorio Nazianzeno, *Sermoni*, 4 mss.; Plutarco, *Morali*, 1 ms.; Ermogene, *Retorica*, 1 ms.; Demostene, *Sermoni*, 2 mss.; Platone, *Sermoni*, 4 mss.), ma soltanto in tre casi (per le *Omelie* del Crisostomo, per i *Morali* di Plutarco e per il *Commento* di Simplicio al primo libro della *Fisica d'Aristotele*) è detto espressamente che si tratta di traduzioni dal greco. Che Palla attendesse a Padova 'a tradurre opere di sancto Giovanni Grisostimo di greco in latino', si sapeva da una testimonianza di Vespasiano da Bisticci[1]; non risultava invece che egli avesse realizzato un programma così vasto di versioni dal greco, come sembrerebbe dal titolo che l'elenco ha nello Zibaldone. Se si tien conto che gran parte delle opere ivi elencate risultano 'non corrette' o 'non emendate', si potrebbe supporre che si tratti di traduzioni intraprese da Palla coll'aiuto dell'Argiropulo e di Andronico Callisto rimaste allo stato di abbozzo e in tale forma pervenute al Rucellai dopo la morte del suocero; ma si potrebbe anche ritenere che le opere greche che Palla ha realmente tradotto siano soltanto quelle espressamente indicate nell'elenco, e che negli altri casi si tratti puramente di libri scritti di sua mano o più semplicemente di libri appartenuti alla sua biblioteca. Sappiamo infatti, dall'antico inventario del 1431, che Palla possedeva codici greci di Demostene, Platone e del Crisostomo[2]; che tra i codici lasciati da Palla a S. Giustina ce n'erano tre che contenevano l'esposizione di Simplicio alla *Fisica* di Aristotele ed erano stati scritti tra il 1441 e il 1443 da Palla stesso e dall'Argiropulo[3]; che allo Strozzi infine era appartenuto il codice Vat. Ottob. gr. 22 della *Retorica* di Ermogene, copiato nel 1458 dal cretese Giovanni Roso[4].

L'attenzione (commista a sentimenti di affetto e di ammirazione) che il Rucellai dedica a Palla Strozzi, non è dovuta soltanto a ragioni di parentela, ma anche, e soprattutto, a comunanza di ideali politici e di interessi economici. Se non è vero (come è stato dimostrato recentemente)[5] che il Rucellai abbia iniziato la sua attività mercantile sotto la guida o a fianco dello Strozzi, è tuttavia certo che, dalla cacciata in esilio del suocero fino alla sua morte (1434–1462), egli fu uno dei più validi collaboratori finanziari di Palla, che—come risulta da vari documenti[6]—lo fece suo agente e procuratore nel disbrigo di vari negozi, e intrattenne con lui continui rapporti di affari. Il Rucellai fu anche amico e socio in affari dei figli di Palla, suoi cognati, tanto è vero che con uno di loro, Giovanfrancesco, egli costituì una compagnia a Venezia, che, come s'è visto, subì notevoli perdite durante la guerra col duca di Milano[7]. Il Rucellai d'altronde, da questi suoi rapporti con Palla e gli Strozzi trasse cospicui vantaggi, perchè potè accapparrarsi—evidentemente a prezzi di favore—varie proprietà

---

[1] Vespasiano, *Vite*, ed. Greco, II, p. 160.

[2] Fiocco, "Biblioteca di Palla Strozzi", p. 310, n[i] 250, 268 e 270; Diller, "Greek Codices", pp. 315–6.

[3] Fiocco, "Biblioteca di Palla Strozzi", pp. 295–6; Diller, "Greek Codices", p. 314.

[4] Diller, "Greek Codices", p. 317.

[5] Kent, *Household and Lineage*, p. 95, n. 140; sopra, p. 19.

[6] Kent, *Household and Lineage*, pp. 98 s.; Fiocco, "Casa di Palla Strozzi", pp. 379 (n[i] 9, 12), 381 (n[i] 29, 34), 382 (n[i] 37, 41). A rapporti di affari tra il Rucellai e gli Strozzi si accenna più volte negli estratti strozziani del libro del 1456 (ASF, CS, 79, pp. 57 ss.). Il Rucellai fa riferimento, ad. es., a copie di 'scritte', 'partite', 'lettere' (tra cui una del 1452 scrittagli da Palla per 'chiarezza di sua faccende fatte per lui'), inserite in un 'libro delle Ricordanze coreggie bianche', che cita più volte. Interessante il 'ricordo' a p. 57 che qui trascrivo: 'Ricordo che mess. Palla mi fe' fine di cose ministrate di suo, et simile Lorenzo suo figliuolo come suo procuratore, come appare al libro Rosso a c. 165; e ancora del mese di gennaio 1452 mi scrisse una lettera ch'egli era ben contento di più cose fatte per lui di commissione di Gio. Francesco suo figliuolo, la qual lettera è chopiata alle Ricordanze a c. 43 coreggie bianche...'.

[7] Cfr. p. 125.

del suocero (ad es. quelle di Poggio a Caiano) e utilizzarne le rendite per sovvenzionare le sue imprese edilizie[1].

Questa parentela collo Strozzi, ma soprattutto la identità di interessi e di ideali che lo legava a lui, non giovò politicamente al Rucellai; come, ovviamente, non gli giovò l'aver fatto parte della balìa del settembre 1433, che aveva deliberato l'invio al confino di Cosimo de' Medici[2]. In un 'ricordo' del 1473 il Rucellai ammette di essere stato 'non accetto ma sospetto allo Stato anni 27, cioè dal 1434 al 1461'[3]. Dall'esame dei documenti d'archivio di cui possiamo disporre, risulta che il Rucellai —finchè non si imparentò coi Medici—fu quasi completamente tagliato fuori dalla vita pubblica della città.

Prima della cacciata e del successivo ritorno di Cosimo, il Rucellai aveva coperto—agli inizi del suo *cursus honorum*—alcuni uffici amministrativi: ufficiale della Grascia nel 1429, ufficiale della Condotta nel 1430, cassiere della Camera del Comune nel 1432, ufficiale dell'Onestà nel 1433, degli Otto di custodia nel 1434[4], oltre a membro, come s'è visto, della balìa del settembre 1433. Dopo il ritorno di Cosimo, il Rucellai non fece più parte di alcuna balìa tra il 1434 e il 1458[5], nè risultò tra i vincitori negli squittini dei Tre Maggiori Uffici (Signori, XVI Gonfalonieri e XII Buoni Uomini) del 1444, del 1448 e del 1458[6]. Vinse invece nello squittino del 1453, ma il suo nome fu cassato per evidenti ragioni politiche[7]. Gli Accoppiatori avevano infatti ricevuto dalla Balìa del 1452 (che si richiamava a quella del 1434) l'autorità di estrarre (cioè eliminare) fino a 20 nomi dalle borse dei Tre Maggiori Uffici[8]. Essi si valsero di questa prerogativa il 21 giugno 1455, e una delle vittime di questo provvedimento—come risulta dal registro delle loro Deliberazioni[9]—fu appunto il Rucellai, il cui nome fu pertanto cancellato nel registro dell'imborsazione della Signoria del 1455[10]. Il Rucellai riuscì tuttavia negli scrutini di quartiere del 1439 e del 1445 per la nomina ad uffici amministrativi 'intrinseci' di non primaria importanza[11]. Prima del 1461 il Rucellai fu infatti ufficiale del Banco nel 1440, regolatore delle entrate e delle spese nel 1441, ufficiale di Pratica e Banco nel 1444, camarlingo delle Gabelle di Pisa nel 1445, ufficiale dei Difetti nel 1447, ufficiale dell'Abbondanza nel 1452[12].

Si spiega così la presenza nello Zibaldone *vetus*—di seguito ai precetti sul governo della famiglia— di una serie di ammaestramenti a Bernardo e a Pandolfo, in cui il Rucellai consiglia ai figli di astenersi —pur con qualche riserva e cautela—da ogni forma di partecipazione alla vita pubblica[13]. Anche questi passi, come quelli analoghi sulla famiglia, provengono, quasi integralmente, dal *Trattato del Governo*, attribuito al Pandolfini, cioè, in definitiva, dal terzo libro della *Famiglia* dell'Alberti[14]. 'Non

---

[1] Perosa, pp. 25-7, 121.
[2] ASF, Balìe, 24, ff. 10v–11r, 22r–23v.
[3] Perosa, p. 122.
[4] ASF, Tratte, 80, ff. 72v (=64v), 49r (=51r), 341r (=218r), 176r (=112r), 14r (=21r); cfr. Kent, sopra, p. 22, n. 5.
[5] Rubinstein, *Government*, pp. 244-91.
[6] ASF, Tratte, 49, ff. 23-38. E' il 'campione' di quelli che furono imborsati pel quartiere di S. Maria Novella per i Tre Maggiori nel maggio 1449, in base allo squittino del 1448. In questa imborsazione furono mescolate le polizze rimanenti degli squittini del 1434, 1439 e 1444 con quelle del 1448, ma il nome di Giovanni Rucellai non si trova nel registro di questa imborsazione.
[7] ASF, Tratte, 1151, f. 415r.
[8] ASF, Balìe, 27, f. 191v (=199v); Rubinstein, *Government*, p. 43.
[9] ASF, Tratte 16, f. 16r; Rubinstein, *Government*, p. 45.
[10] ASF, Tratte, 61, f. 60r.
[11] ASF, Tratte, 49, f. 48r (in mg.: 'obtinuit in 39').
[12] ASF, Tratte, 80, ff. 447r (=314r), 25r (=32r), 472r (=339r), 339r (=216r), 63v (=61v), 465r (=332r).
[13] Perosa, pp. 39-43, 146. Cfr. Bec, *Marchands écrivains*, pp. 282 ss., 344; Brucker, *Renaissance Florence*, p. 126.
[14] I passi del *Trattato del Governo* (ed. Tartini del 1734), mutuati dal Rucellai, sono indicati in Perosa, p. 146.

vi consiglio—dice il Rucellai, rivolgendosi ai figli—che voi cerchiate o disideriate ufici e stato. Niuna cosa meno stimo, niuna cosa mi pare in fatto di minore onore che ritrovarsi in questi stati publici: e sapete perchè? Non sono da pregiagli nè da desederagli pe' pericoli, per le disonestà, per le ingiustitie che ànno i' lloro, e perchè non sono stabili nè durabili', ecc.[1]. Il brano è una requisitoria contro la vita infelice dello 'statuale', che è servo e vittima del potere, e va incontro ad un'infinità di disagi, non ultimo quello di dover trascurare i suoi interessi privati. 'Per le cose publiche— ammonisce il Rucellai—non lasciate le vostre private, però che a cui mancherà in casa meno tro- verrà fuori casa; le cose publiche . . . non sovengono alle necistà familiare, gli onori di fuori non pascono la famiglia in casa'[2]. Eppure il Rucellai avrebbe gradito che i suoi figli fossero 'nelle borse' e venissero 'onorati come gli altri cittadini, se non fusse per altro che per mostrare non essere a sospetto al reggimento, ma essere accetti e in gratia de' cittadini'[3], e sarebbe anche stato—come lo pseudo Pandolfini e l'Alberti— favorevole ad una partecipazione alla vita civile, se si fossero verificate condizioni diverse, se cioè 'ne' priori magistrati per guidare le cose publiche' ci fossero stati cittadini, che amano, 'la pacie, la equalità, l'onestà, l'umiltà, l'umanità, la tranquillità di tutta la città, ecc.'. Ma ciò non realizzandosi, e non potendo 'uno solo' provvedervi, quando 'e' molti non s'acordano a farlo', è necessario—conclude il Rucellai—'lasciare lo stato a chi piace'[4].

Alberti, Pandolfini e Rucellai, consigliando ai loro figli e discendenti di astenersi dalla vita pub- blica, rispecchiano uno stato d'animo diffuso negli ambienti dell'alta borghesia mercantile, da tempo in crisi in seguito al progressivo mutamento e deterioramento di una situazione politica che portava, per successivi gradi, al principato. Il libro dell'Alberti si riferiva ad altri tempi e ad altre situazioni; ma non per questo perdeva agli occhi dei contemporanei di Cosimo il valore paradigmatico e normativo, che anche per la parte politica era propensa ad attribuirgli la restia oligarchia mercantile fiorentina.

Il Rucellai ha circoscritto, come s'è visto, agli anni tra il 1434 e il 1461 il periodo in cui è stato 'sospetto allo stato', anche se in realtà la marcia di accostamento ai Medici e alle famiglie dominanti— pur tra alti e bassi—fosse iniziata già prima del fatidico 1461. Comunque il 1461 è stato—almeno formalmente—l'anno della svolta, l'anno in cui il figlio Bernardo ha ottenuto in sposa la Nannina di Piero di Cosimo de' Medici. Da allora il Rucellai entra nel giro della politica medicea, ottenendo, come risulta dai documenti di archivio, varie cariche pubbliche di un certo rilievo. Il 19 aprile 1463— in base all'autorità concessa agli Accoppiatori il 28 dicembre 1458 'de reducendis . . . de illis qui non obtinuissent in novo scrutineo tunc celebrato' (lo squittino del 1458)—fu restituito nelle borse dei Tre Maggiori, e in seguito a questa 'reductio' eletto 'a mano' dagli Accoppiatori priore nella Signoria dei mesi di maggio e giugno del 1463[5]. Veduto (cioè tratto), ma non seduto (cioè fatto) per il Gon- falonierato di giustizia della Signoria dei mesi di luglio e agosto 1465, fu membro della Balìa del settembre 1466[6]. Dal 1° luglio di quest'anno, e poi successivamente per il secondo semestre degli anni 1467, 1468, 1472 e 1473, fu eletto nel Consiglio dei Cento[7], e nel luglio 1471 fu nominato Accoppiatore per l'anno 1471–72, della qual nomina e della soddisfazione ch'egli ne provò, è

---

[1] Perosa, p. 39.
[2] Perosa, p. 43.
[3] Perosa, p. 39.
[4] Perosa, p. 42.
[5] ASF, Balìe, 29, f. 20ᵛ (=26ᵛ); Tratte, 17, ff. 34ᵛ–36ᵛ, 45ᵛ; 94, f. 26ʳ; Rubinstein, *Government*, pp. 108, 123–4.
[6] ASF, Balìe, 30, f. 10ʳ (=14ʳ); Rubinstein, *Government*, p. 298.
[7] ASF, Tratte 336, ff. 29ᵛ, 40ʳ, 44ʳ, 63ᵛ, 70ᵛ. Da notare che il Rucellai fu eletto nel Consiglio dei Cento anche il 1° luglio 1469, ma perdette l'ufficio perchè inserito nello 'Specchio' (*ibid.*, f. 48ᵛ).

rimasta un'interessante testimonianza nello Zibaldone[1]. Gonfaloniere di giustizia nella Signoria dei mesi di luglio-agosto 1475, fece parte dei Settanta dall'aprile 1480 in poi[2]. Accanto a queste, il Rucellai tenne, durante questo periodo, anche cariche minori: fu maestro della Zecca nel 1462, ufficiale del Monte negli anni 1464–5 e 1468–9, ufficiale del Banco per l'anno 1467–8, approvatore degli Statuti delle Arti per l'anno 1474[3].

Il Rucellai ha la coscienza di aver saputo condurre, per ventisette anni, un'abile azione politica, dimostrando spiccate capacità di adattamento e di inserimento in un contesto politico inizialmente ostile. 'M'è chonvenuto navichare molto a punto e ssanza errore—dice il Rucellai nel già citato 'ricordo' del 1473—ma ll'essere stato in aversità mi dà più dolcezza che ss'io fussi stato sempre in prosperità. Che Iddio sia lodato e ringraziato d'ongni chosa, amen'[4].

V

L'indagine, a questo punto, si sposta sulla personalità etico-religiosa del Rucellai e sulla sua concezione della vita e del mondo. Il Rucellai, come s'è visto, fu soprattutto un uomo d'azione, impegnato nella pratica mercantile e nelle attività economico-finanziarie. E' stato finora abbastanza agevole farsi un'opinione sul comportamento che egli tenne nei riguardi della vita pratica (il governo della famiglia, l'educazione dei figli, la liberalità, il mecenatismo, la partecipazione alla vita pubblica, ecc.), ma è assai meno facile trarre ora dalle pieghe dello Zibaldone e coordinare in una visione unitaria e organica gli elementi che concorrono a delineare e a definire la sua più profonda spiritualità. La sua condotta, in questo campo, non è stata, infatti, lineare, nè poteva esserlo, perchè il Rucellai non ha seguito una precisa corrente di pensiero, ma ha continuamente oscillato tra valori tradizionali e aspirazioni ad una spiritualità più moderna e vivace.

Il Rucellai è sostanzialmente legato—nè si può negarlo—ai valori religiosi della tradizione cattolica. Egli legge e s'interessa di testi di devozione e di pietà, e per l'educazione ricevuta—che si presume non fosse dissimile da quella di un Datini, di un Mazzei, di un Morelli—segue con diligenza le pratiche del culto. Il Rucellai—gioverà ricordarlo—è per tradizione di famiglia, patrono e benefattore di Santa Maria Novella e di San Pancrazio; egli gode quindi nell'ambito del quartiere e della parrochia una posizione di prestigio, che lo rende bene accetto agli ambienti ecclesiastici, ma che anche gli procura concreti benefici mondani. D'altra parte, vivendo a contatto con una cultura che si sta rinnovando, e che presenta soluzioni più aperte e articolate ai problemi etico-religiosi tradizionali, il Rucellai avverte gli stimoli delle nuove proposte e, pur mantenendosi nell'alveo della tradizione, cerca di instaurare un dialogo proficuo coi più qualificati rappresentanti della cultura umanistica, per ottenere da essi risposte adeguate agli interrogativi che gli stanno più a cuore.

Questi due momenti coesistono, con diversa intensità di accento e con diverse sfumature, in tutte le parti dello Zibaldone. Se però si tien conto, che col passar degli anni, il Rucellai ha sviluppato comportamenti diversificati sia nei riguardi della tradizione che della nuova cultura, non sarà

---

[1] ASF, Balìe, 31, f. 1r (=9r); Tratte, 1148, f. 27v (=II fasc., f. 3v); *Zibaldone*, ff. 68av–69ar: 'Memoria chome del mese di luglio 1471, chome io Govanni Rucellai fui eletto dalla Singnoria del numero degl'acchopiatori ... el quale fu riputato el più bello, el più dengno hufficio che si desse mai nella nostra città di Firenze e di grande stima, autorità . . .'; Rubinstein, *Government*, pp. 222, 240, 302.

[2] ASF, Balìe 31, f. 92v (=100v); Tratte, 94, f. 27v; 336, f. 112v; Rubinstein, *Government*, p. 317.

[3] ASF, Tratte, 81, ff. 56r (=47r), 65r–65v (=58r–58v), 151r (=158r), 68v (=62v).

[4] Perosa, p. 122.

inopportuno, penso, tenere d'occhio, più in questo che nei capitoli precedenti, la distinzione tra le parti che appartengono allo Zibaldone *vetus* e quelle aggiunte successivamente.

Appartengono alla tradizione i testi di carattere morale e religioso, che il Rucellai ha raccolto in due sezioni distinte nella seconda metà dello Zibaldone *vetus*[1]. Una di queste sezioni consiste in una sorta di catechismo della dottrina cristiana, che raggruppa vari testi di carattere religioso o liturgico, e precisamente: 1) un'illustrazione della Messa e dei suoi simboli (ff. 41a^r–43b^v)[2]; 2) un'esposizione del 'simbolo della fede cattolica composto da Attanasio vescovo grecho' (ff. 43b^v–44a^v)[3]; 3) un elenco dei 'dieci comandamenti di Dio', dei 'dodici articoli della fede', dei 'sette doni dello Spirito sancto', dei 'sette peccati mortali', delle 'sette opere della misericordia spirituale', delle 'sette beatitudini', delle 'quattro virtù cardinali', delle 'quattro tempora', dei 'digiuni comandati dalla Chiesa', delle 'feste comandate', ecc. (ff. 44a^v–45b^r)[4]; 4) alcuni frammenti di inni mariani (ff. 46a^r–46a^v)[5]. Seguono alcune curiose notizie sul modo di dir messa (ff. 47a^r–47b^v)[6], e vari consigli d'ordine morale e religioso (soprattutto sul tema dell'elemosina) da parte di due frati francescani, 'maestro Antonio d'Arezo' e 'frate Girolamo da Firenze', che andranno identificati, rispettivamente, col teologo Antonio Neri ('de Nigris') di Arezzo, e col frate Girolamo della Stufa di Firenze (ff. 48a^r–48a^v)[7].

Nell'altra sezione—che nello Zibaldone precede il gruppo di testi religiosi di cui s'è fatto testè parola—il Rucellai ha fatto trascrivere, rispettivamente ai ff. 30b^r–32b^r e 36b^r–40b^v, due serie di *excerpta* tratti da due fonti ben precise, che egli, come al solito, non nomina, ma che in realtà sono gli

---

[1] *Zibaldone*, ff. 30b^r–32b^r, 36b^r–40b^v (fasc. III–IV) e 41a^r–48a^v (fasc. V).

[2] Testi in volgare anonimi dei secoli XIV e XV sulla simbologia della Messa—non dissimili da quello contenuto nello Zibaldone—furono pubblicati in varie occasioni durante lo scorso secolo. Ricorderò, ad es., le edizioni curate da G. Manuzzi (*Meditazione sopra l'arbore della Croce . . . coll'aggiunta degli Ordinamenti della Messa . . .*, Firenze, 1836, pp. 81 ss., e *Trattato della Messa e della maniera di assistervi e del paramento del prete*, Forlì, 1850) e da A. Ceruti ("Sposizione della Messa e transito della Vergine Maria", *Propugnatore*, VI, 4–5 [1873], pp. 403–18). Cfr. Zambrini, *Opere volgari a stampa*, I, col. 446, 657, 953, 1014, App. col. 148.

[3] Versioni analoghe, ma con varianti, di questo testo furono pubblicate da A. Ceruti (*Il libro della Regola Pastorale di S. Gregorio Magno*, Milano, 1869, pp. 251–4) e da G. Bartoli (*Il simbolo Atanasiano, volgarizzamento del sec. XIV*, Pistoia, 1883). Cfr. Zambrini, *Opere volgari a stampa*, I, col. 491–2, App. col. 148.

[4] Raccolte del genere, da utilizzare soprattutto nell'istruzione religiosa dei giovani, dovevano circolare in gran numero a Firenze nel sec. XV. Un tipico modello è offerto dal 'Libreto de la doctrina christiana, la quale è utile e molto necessaria che i puti pizoli et zovenzelli l'impara . . .' di S. Antonino, che, a decorrere dall'edizione veneziana del 1473 (=GW 2159), figura di seguito all'edizione volgare del *Confessionale*, Omnis mortalium cura (=*Specchio di coscienza*). Cfr. Zambrini, *Opere volgari a stampa*, I, col. 377 ss.

[5] Il Rucellai ha fatto trascrivere, tra l'altro, le prime tre strofe in volgare dei 'Septem gaudia beatae Mariae virginis', il cui testo latino completo (accompagnato da un volgarizzamento veneto, che coincide su per giù con quello impiegato dal Rucellai) si legge in *Hymni Latini Medii Aevi*, ed. F. J. Mone, II, Friburgo Brisg., 1854, pp. 165 ss.

[6] Il Rucellai dà notizia, ad es., dell'uso—invalso, in certe occasioni, presso alcune corti (dell' 'imperadore dei Cristiani' e del re di Francia), città (a 'Colognia nella Magna') o conventi (Sant' Antimo)—di celebrare o partecipare alla Messa armati. In modo particolare egli si sofferma sulla Badia di Sant' Antimo nel Senese, fondata, secondo la tradizione, dall'imperatore Carlo Magno, che ai 'monaci neri' ivi istallati e al loro abate Guglielmo aveva concesso vari privilegi ('scripti—come dice il Rucellai—in giunchi, cioè in carta di giunchi, come sono le nostre Pandette, che noi abbiamo a Firenze'), tra i quali quello di far assistere, di fianco all'altare, alla celebrazione delle Messe solenni, un 'huomo . . . armato . . . colla spada ingniuda in mano in defensione della fede di Christo a chi volesse contradirla'. Altre notizie sulla Messa il Rucellai dà al f. 97a^v, dove spiega 'a che fine la notte di Natale si chantino tre Messe'; al f. 30a^r, invece, egli rimanda al suo 'libro memoriale' (cfr. p. 103) chi volesse conoscere la ragione per cui i fedeli si alzano in piedi al Vangelo e si siedono all'Epistola, e perchè 'il prete in ciaschuna Messa si volge cinque volte al popolo'. Da notare che il Rucellai non indica mai le fonti dalle quali ha tratto queste notizie.

[7] Debbo al cortese interessamento del padre C. Piana l'identificazione di questi due frati francescani. Antonio di Cipriano Neri, morto interno al 1450 all'età di 70 anni, fu decano della Facoltà di Teologia di Firenze nel 1424, predicò per vari anni in S. Maria del Fiore, ed ebbe nel 1432 l'incarico di leggere Dante nello Studio. Su di lui cfr. Piana, *Facoltà teologia*, pp. 35, 133–4, 249, 287. Il fiorentino fra' Girolamo della Stufa, è ricordato fra i predicatori francescani che più da vicino riuscirono ad emulare l'oratoria di San Bernardino da Siena, conquistandosi per la sua facondia una grandissima fama in tutta Italia. Cfr. C. Piana, "I processi di canonizzazione su la Vita di S. Bernardino da Siena", *Archivum Franciscanum Historicum*, XLIV (1951), p. 410; D. Cresi, "Elenchi di illustri Frati Minori in un'opera inedita di Mariano da Firenze", *Archivum Franciscanum Historicum*, LVII (1964), p. 198.

Ammaestramenti degli antichi di Bartolomeo da San Concordio e il *Fiore di Virtù* attribuito al frate Tommaso Gozzadini. Al *Fiore* e alla popolarità che l'opera ottenne nei secoli XIV e XV s'è già accennato a proposito dell'utilizzazione che il Rucellai ne fece per i suoi ammaestramenti ai figli sulla liberalità[1]; analoga diffusione e popolarità—come si ricava dal numero notevole di mss. che ce li hanno tramandati—ebbero i *Documenta antiquorum*, che il domenicano Bartolomeo da San Concordio compose in quegli stessi anni (agli inizi del '300) e volgarizzò col titolo di *Ammaestramenti degli antichi*[2]. Gli *Ammaestramenti* sono un'opera enciclopedica di filosofia morale, suddivisa in vari trattati, distinzioni, capitoli, ecc., che raggruppa una silloge di *auctoritates* in servizio del *dictamen* così religioso che civile. Il metodo di Bartolomeo consiste nell'avanzare un'affermazione parenetica, e quindi sostenerla con una filza di citazioni tratte da autori antichi e dai Padri della Chiesa. Gli *Ammaestramenti*, concepiti organicamente, rivelano nelle strutture e nei contenuti dottrinari, la presenza costante di S. Tommaso d'Aquino, che il frate s'è posto come modello.

Il Rucellai ha tratto degli *excerpta* da tre rubriche della distinzione terza e da una rubrica della distinzione nona degli *Ammaestramenti*. Le tre rubriche della distinzione terza—che allineano citazioni da S. Girolamo, Cicerone, i Vangeli, 'Agellio' e da una quantità di luoghi di Seneca—trattano, rispettivamente, dell' 'abitare seco', di 'come la mattina e la sera l'uomo dee spezialmente se medesimo curare', e del fatto che 'l'uomo non dee intendere a molte cose'[3]. Sono temi, come ognun vede, che dovevano attirare, in modo particolare, l'attenzione del Rucellai, il quale, pur apprezzando il loro significato spirituale e religioso, fondato sul principio dell'introspezione, vi coglieva, probabilmente, anche un risvolto pratico, cioè la conferma di un tipo di condotta nella vita di ogni giorno, che egli da saggio mercante, aveva adottato e consigliato ai figli sulle orme del *Trattato del Governo*[4].

Che poi il Rucellai abbia voluto includere nello Zibaldone anche la rubrica della distinzione nona che tratta delle 'otto cose . . . che sono utili a ben ricordare'[5], non deve sorprendere, se si pensa all'importanza che all'arte della memoria (alla *memoria artificialis*) veniva attribuita nei più svariati campi dell'educazione, dell'oratoria religiosa e civile, delle lettere e delle arti nei secoli del Medioevo e del Rinascimento[6]. Bartolomeo da San Concordio ha raccolto, anche in questo campo, tra i primi, l'eredità di San Tommaso, che muovendo dal *De memoria et reminiscentia* di Aristotele e dalla pseudociceroniana *Rhetorica ad Herennium*, aveva rifondato su nuove basi la trattazione della memoria. Bartolomeo da San Concordio nel brano che il Rucellai ha fatto trascrivere, cita infatti largamente Aristotele, 'Tullio' e 'Tommaso', ma insieme a loro, anche altri autori, come ad es. S.

---

[1] Cfr. p. 117.

[2] Sul frate domenicano Bartolomeo da San Concordio (Pisa) (1262–1347) e i suoi *Ammaestramenti* cfr. A. De Rubertis, "Fra' Bartolomeo da S. Concordio . . .", *Memorie domenicane*, LXIV (1947), pp. 158–69; C. Segre, s.v. "Bartolomeo da San Concordio", *DBI*, VI (1964), pp. 768–70. Nelle citazioni degli *Ammaestramenti* mi servo dell'edizione di Brescia del 1817.

[3] Bartolomeo da San Concordio, *Ammaestramenti*, III, 1–2, 4, pp. 17–21, 23–5.

[4] Significativi, a tale proposito, i passi in cui il Rucellai consiglia ai figli di far 'masserizia' del tempo. Egli dice, ad es.,: 'Et perchè l'una opera non mi confonda l'altra e truovimi averne cominciate alcune et fornitene niuna . . . piglio questa reghola, che la mattina, quando mi lievo, penso fra me stesso: "Oggi che ò io a ffare di fuori? Tali e tali cose". Annoverole e a cciascuna pongho il tenpo suo: queste istamani, queste oggi, quest'altre stasera' (Perosa, p. 18). E ripete: 'Fate masseritia del tenpo . . . fate come ò fatto io. La mattina v'ordinate a tutto il dì et seguite quello vi si richiede; po' la sera, innanzi vi posiate, ricogliete in voi quello avete facto il dì . . .' (Perosa, p. 8).

[5] Bartolomeo da San Concordio, *Ammaestramenti*, IX, 8, pp. 75–9. Questo capitolo è stato ripubblicato di recente da G. De Luca, *Prosatori minori del Trecento*, Milano–Napoli, 1954, pp. 60–3.

[6] F. A. Yates, *L'arte della memoria* (tr. it. di A. Biondi), Torino, 1972, pp. 79–84. A Bartolomeo da San Concordio fu attribuita anche la paternità di un 'Trattato della memoria artificiale', che altro non è che il volgarizzamento della sezione sulla memoria della *Rhetorica ad Herennium*.

Girolamo, Gregorio, Platone, Vegezio, Seneca, ecc., e perfino Gaufredo da Vinsauf, di cui Bartolomeo aveva scritto un commento di tipo grammaticale[1].

Il secondo gruppo di *excerpta* di questa sezione dello Zibaldone è tratto, come s'è detto, dal *Fiore di Virtù*. L'ampia scelta del Rucellai non abbraccia tutta l'opera, ma si arresta al cap. XX[2]. Il Rucellai da ognuno di questi venti capitoli (che contemplano le seguenti virtù e vizi: 'amore e benevolenza', 'invidia', 'allegrezza', 'tristizia', 'pace', 'ira', 'misericordia', 'crudeltà', 'liberalità', 'avarizia', 'correzione', 'lusinga', 'prudenza', 'pazzia', 'giustizia', 'ingiustizia', 'lealtà' e 'falsità') ha scelto, senza seguire l'ordine di successione che esse hanno nell'originale, un manipolo di sentenze di disparata provenienza, di cui talvolta (soprattutto nei primi capitoli) ha soppresso i nomi degli autori che pur figuravano nel *Fiore di Virtù*.

Il Rucellai ha tratto dunque buon frutto dalla consultazione dei due florilegi del primo '300, che anche in pieno secolo XV circolavano diffusamente in ambienti di origine popolana, tra artigiani ed artisti, e tra quei borghesi del ceto mercantile, che si erano formati alle scuole dell'abaco ed erano rimasti sostanzialmente estranei all'educazione umanistica, anche se in molti casi—come farà il Rucellai—reagivano con vivacità agli stimoli e alle sollecitazioni che il contatto con ambienti culturali di élite esercitava su di loro.

Non bisognerà poi dimenticare che testi come il *Fiore di Virtù* e gli *Ammaestramenti degli antichi* non venivano apprezzati soltanto per il loro contenuto morale e per il loro impianto tomistico, ma esercitavano un notevole fascino anche perchè, tramite le continue citazioni di *auctoritates* del mondo antico, avvicinavano alla sapienza e alla morale dei classici chi, ancora ignaro di latino, non era in grado di accostarvisi direttamente. Nel Rucellai stesso, che pur accettava gli insegnamenti morali basilari fornitigli da testi legati alla tradizione medioevale, la lettura di questi florilegi deve avere contribuito ad acuire l'interesse per la cultura e la civiltà degli antichi. Non farà quindi specie che ben cinque fascicoli dello Zibaldone *vetus* (fasc. XV–XIX, ff. 138–63)[3] siano riservati ad un gruppo di ventidue lettere di Seneca—le *Epistole* 8, 13–16, 30, 36, 39, 40, 41, 47, 56, 59, 61, 69, 70, 74, 84, 90, 91, 105 e 123—nella versione del notaio fiorentino Andrea Lancia, vissuto nella prima metà del sec. XIV[4]. Il Rucellai non conosceva il latino, ma Seneca morale—che gli era, tra l'altro, familiare per le frequenti citazioni che ne facevano i florilegi medioevali—egli desiderava leggerlo, approfittando del volgarizzamento del Lancia, e voleva altresì che una scelta delle sue lettere entrasse a far parte dello Zibaldone, perchè figli e discendenti ne potessero trarre giovamento[5]. Troppo spesso si dimentica che i volgarizzamenti di autori antichi—e perfino le citazioni di classici greci e latini, che s'incontrano in florilegi come gli *Ammaestramenti* e il *Fiore*—hanno suscitato in territori,

---

[1] G. Manacorda, "Fra' Bartolomeo da San Concordio grammatico e la fortuna di Gaufredo da Vinsauf in Italia", *Raccolta di studi ... dedicati a F. Flamini*, Pisa, 1918, pp. 139–52; A. Wilmart, "L'art poétique de Geoffroi de Vinsauf et les commentaires de Barthélemy de Pise", *Revue bénédictine*, XLI (1929), pp. 271–5. Da notare che Bartolomeo cita l'opera (la 'poetria novella') e non l'autore, per cui non ci si deve meravigliare se il Rucellai (che evidentemente non sapeva chi avesse scritto la 'poetria novella') ha sostituito il nome dell'opera della fonte con l'indicazione generica 'un altro filosofo'.

[2] *Fiore di Virtù*, pp. 4–97.

[3] Cfr. Perosa, pp. xiv, xxiv.

[4] Perosa, p. 172. Andrea Lancia, notaio fiorentino (c. 1280–c. 1360), fu fecondo volgarizzatore di testi classici (*Eneide*, Valerio Massimo, *Ars amandi* e *Remedia amoris* di Ovidio, ecc.), anche se non di tutti i suoi volgarizzamenti gli si possa attribuire la paternità con ragioni altrettanto valide. Del volgarizzamento delle *Epistole a Lucilio* esistono numerosi mss., ma il testo ha subito varie interpolazioni e rimaneggiamenti. Il testo delle lettere trascritte nello Zibaldone è molto vicino a quello dato dalla stampa fiorentina del Tartini, curata da T. Bonaventuri e da G. Bottari (*Volgarizzamento delle Pistole di Seneca e del Trattato della Provvidenza di Dio*, Firenze, 1717). Cfr. *Volgarizzamenti del Due e Trecento*, a cura di C. Segre, Torino, 1953, p. 569.

[5] Passi delle lettere di Seneca sono citati frequentemente nello Zibaldone, come si può constatare dall' *Indice dei nomi* in Perosa, p. 241.

come quello fiorentino e in parte quello bolognese, culturalmente avanzati e ricettivi, un interesse sempre più vivo per la cultura classica contribuendo a dissodare il terreno per l'impianto e la crescita della pianta vigorosa dell'umanesimo. Di Bartolomeo da San Concordio, ad es., che compilò anche un robusto volgarizzamento di Sallustio, più volte utilizzato dal Rucellai[1], è stato detto, giustamente, che 'ebbe parte nell'opera di diffusione della cultura che doveva sfociare nell' Umanesimo'[2].

Sallustio, ma soprattutto il Seneca delle Epistole a Lucilio, nei volgarizzamenti, rispettivamente, di Bartolomeo da San Concordio e di Andrea Lancia, sono anche gli autori latini, che ricorrono più di frequente in una delle parti più significative dello Zibaldone *vetus*, nella sezione cioè in cui il Rucellai affronta il problema della fortuna e del caso[3]. 'Io m'achordo, Pandolfo et Bernardo—dice rivolgendosi ai figli—che sia utilissima materia di darvi a intendere che chose è fortuna et che cose è caso; e appresso, inteso che è fortuna et che è il caso, che voi intendiate se e il senno e la prudenza e il buono ghoverno dell'uomo può risistere a' casi della fortuna o non in tutto o in parte. E perchè gli oppenioni sono variati, vi farò qui di sotto nota di detti di più filosofi et altri autori, seperati l'uno dall'altro quelli che ànno tenuto una oppenione et quelli n'ànno tenuto un'altra'[4].

Il Rucellai, come si vede, in questo preambolo—che ha la forma consueta del consiglio ai figli—delinea con grande chiarezza la partizione del suo trattatello sulla fortuna. Egli si chiede anzitutto che cosa sia fortuna e caso, e risponde allegando varie definizioni, tratte dalla *Consolatio* di Boezio (nel volgarizzamento di Alberto della Piagentina), dalla *Fisica* e dai *Magna Moralia* di Aristotele (probabilmente da un florilegio di sentenze aristoteliche, qual è ad es. il *De bona fortuna*), da un'epistola familiare del Petrarca, e dall'*Altercatio Hadriani et Epicteti philosophi*, che si fa risalire al II o III sec. dopo Cristo, e si diffuse, con successo, in svariate redazioni interpolate, nel Medioevo e alle soglie dell'età moderna. Il Rucellai fa poi seguire due elenchi di sentenze di autori che hanno sostenuto pareri contrastanti circa la possibilità di resistere ai colpi di fortuna. Nella prima lista— di autori che hanno manifestato 'oppenioni che contro a' casi della fortuna non si possa resistere'— sono riprodotti un famoso brano del VII canto dell'*Inferno* di Dante Alighieri e un sonetto adespoto sulla fortuna (che è stato attribuito, tra l'altro, ad Antonio Pucci), e passi della *Catilinaria* di Sallustio (nel volgarizzamento di Bartolomeo da San Concordio), del *Dittamondo* di Fazio degli Uberti, di varie epistole di Seneca (nella versione del Lancia). Nella seconda lista, assai più ricca—di autori che hanno sostenuto 'oppenione in contrario, cioè che la prudentia, il senno e il buono ghoverno possi risistere a' casi della fortuna, e se none in tutto, nella maggior parte'—figurano un lungo brano dell'*Acerba* di Cecco d'Ascoli, un'ottava del poemetto *La Sfera* di Gregorio Dati, la parafrasi di alcuni versi di Lucano (di cui non è facile individuare la fonte), e citazioni, più o meno ampie, dal volgarizzamento della pseudobernardiana *Epistola de gubernatione rei familiaris*, dalla *Giugurtina* di Sallustio (nel volgarizzamento di Bartolomeo da San Concordio), dai *Magna Moralia* di Aristotele (cioè dal *De bona fortuna* già citato) e, come sempre, da un gran numero di epistole di Seneca (nella solita versione del Lancia).

---

[1] Perosa, pp. 171–2, 175. Le opere sallustiane, volgarizzate da Bartolomeo da San Concordio, ci sono giunte in numerosi codici, e furono pubblicate, per la prima volta, da G. Cioni (*Di C. Crispo Sallustio, Della Congiura Catilinaria e della Guerra Giugurtina libri due, volgarizzati da Frate Bartolommeo da S. Concordio* . . ., Firenze, 1790). Un'edizione critica parziale della *Catilinaria* ci ha dato recentemente C. Segre, in *Volgarizzamenti del Due e Trecento*, pp. 405–45. Cfr. F. Maggini, "Appunti sul 'Sallustio volgarizzato' di Bartolomeo da S. Concordio", in *I primi volgarizzamenti dai classici latini*, Firenze, 1952, pp. 41 ss.

[2] C. Segre, *DBI*, p. 769.

[3] Perosa, pp. 103–12.

[4] Perosa, p. 103.

Quest'antologia presuppone larghi spogli di autori, enciclopedie, volgarizzamenti. Nelle note—che ho aggiunto a questi testi—ho cercato di identificare, via via, i passi citati nello Zibaldone, e di indicare le fonti di cui il Rucellai s'era servito nella scelta del materiale[1]. Non sempre, però, sono riuscito nel mio intento, perchè le citazioni del Rucellai sono spesso di seconda mano e da testi che hanno subìto varie interpolazioni. Mancano poi, in alcuni casi, le indicazioni degli autori e delle opere da cui i singoli passi sono stati desunti; talvolta le attribuzioni che figurano nello Zibaldone sono errate o confuse[2].

C'è poi, strettamente connesso a quanto s'è detto finora, il problema di fondo, se cioè il Rucellai si sia servito, come in tanti altri casi, di una silloge sulla Fortuna preesistente, o abbia personalmente raccolto i vari brani e le sentenze che compongono il florilegio. Non è facile dare una risposta sicura a questo dilemma, ma da alcuni indizi, da non sottovalutare, sembrerebbe che la seconda ipotesi sia la più probabile. Sembrerebbe confermarlo il fatto che tra le parti aggiunte allo Zibaldone *vetus*, figura, inseritavi qualche anno dopo, una lettera al Rucellai (indicata, a dire il vero, col titolo di 'opera') di un 'ser Giovanni di messer Nello da San Gimignano', che contiene la versione volgare e un'interpretazione molto minuta di un passo dell'*Altercatio Hadriani et Epicteti*, di cui il Rucellai aveva chiesto la spiegazione all'amico[3]. Il 'ser Giovanni' di questa lettera è Giovanni Martini di S. Gemignano, figliuolo di messer Nello, celebre giureconsulto, ed egli stesso notaio, professore di grammatica e poeta[4]. È probabile che il Rucellai si legasse d'amicizia al Martini durante il forzato esilio del 1457 a S. Gemignano. Imbattutosi, mentre stava raccogliendo materiale per il capitolo sulla fortuna, in un passo dell'*Altercatio*, di cui non riusciva a venire a capo perchè scritto in latino, il Rucellai si è rivolto al Martini perchè glielo traducesse e spiegasse. Il Martini ha risposto con questa 'opera', dando tre interpretazioni—tutte e tre errate—del passo dell'*Altercatio*. Il Rucellai ha scelto la prima delle tre e l'ha fatta inserire, tra le definizioni di fortuna e caso, nell'antologia che stava curando[5].

Orbene, da quest'episodio mi sembra si possa arguire: 1) che il Rucellai non conosceva il latino[6]; 2) che egli non riproduceva meccanicamente una raccolta volgare preesistente, ma metteva insieme —probabilmente coll'aiuto di qualche amico o collaboratore più aggiornato e più colto di lui che fosse in grado non solo di attingere direttamente alle fonti, ma eventualmente di spigolare da recenti opere sulla fortuna[7]—le singole 'autorità' che facevano al caso, servendosi, quando si trattava di testi scritti in latino, dei volgarizzamenti esistenti, oppure ricorrendo—quando tali volgarizzamenti non ci fossero—alla collaborazione di persona più dotta di lui.

In ogni caso, comunque siano andate le cose per ciò che concerne la genesi dell'antologia, una

[1] Perosa, pp. 170–5.

[2] Si possono vedere, a tale proposito, le nn. 4 e 5 a p. 170, la n. 7 a p. 171, le nn. 21, 23 e 25 a p. 173, le nn. 29 e 30 a p. 174, e le nn. 38 e 40 a p. 175.

[3] Perosa, pp. 112–4. Cfr. *Altercatio Hadriani et Epicteti philosophi*, ed. L. W. Daly–W. Suchier, Urbana, 1939, p. 105. Il passo dell'*Altercatio* è riprodotto da Perosa, p. 171, n. 9.

[4] Perosa, p. 175 s.; F. Flamini, *La lirica toscana del Rinascimento anteriore ai tempi del Magnifico*, Pisa, 1891, pp. 291–2, 602–3; Martines, *Social World*, pp. 267, 269–71, 303, 340.

[5] Perosa, pp. 104, 171 n. 9.

[6] Passi in latino nello Zibaldone si contano sulle punta delle dita. Segnalerò ai ff. 80b^v–81a^r 'un detto di Senecha', ripetuto pari pari al f. 83b^v; un passo dal titolo 'De liberis et postumis heredibus instituendis' del *Digesto* (=Dig. 28, 2, 13), e un 'rimedio spirituale contro al male della pestilenzia'; al f. 97a^v alcune citazioni dalla Scrittura a proposito delle tre messe che si cantano nella notte di Natale. In tutti questi casi (fatta eccezione per il rimedio contro la peste) il testo latino è accompagnato dalla relativa versione volgare.

[7] Non è possibile dimostrare una diretta dipendenza dell'antologia del Rucellai da qualcuno dei tanti trattati o scritti sulla fortuna, che circolavano ormai da quasi un secolo, anche se, ovviamente, si possono sempre scoprire delle coincidenze nell'uso di certe fonti canoniche.

cosa è certa, che 'fortuna' e 'caso' era materia, alla quale il Rucellai era profondamente interessato, e la posizione stessa di rilievo, che la silloge ha nello Zibaldone *vetus*—inserita com'è tra gli ammaestramenti sul governo della famiglia e quelli sulla partecipazione alla vita civile—sembra indicarlo chiaramente[1]. Il Rucellai, contrapponendo—come aveva già fatto a proposito della virtù della 'liberalità'[2]—due liste di *auctoritates* a sostegno di due soluzioni opposte, si era uniformato—è vero—alla tecnica espositiva di certi florilegi medioevali, ma—contrariamente a quanto si sarebbe indotti a credere—aveva anche voluto sottolineare l'interessamento che egli nutriva per la complessa casistica connessa ai problemi di 'fortuna' e 'caso', di cui riteneva opportuno offrire un'ampia e rigorosa documentazione. Egli si era reso conto che problemi di carattere etico-filosofico che incidono così profondamente sull'azione umana, proponevano spesso soluzioni e scelte alternative, che lasciavano margini al dubbio e richiedevano continue verifiche dalla realtà. Il Rucellai aveva voluto, pertanto, che i figli avessero presenti le risposte di segno opposto che la tradizione letteraria e filosofica dava al quesito se si possa resistere ai casi di fortuna, anche se egli, da parte sua—accordandosi alla propria esperienza e all'opinione dei più—già s'era formato un'idea in proposito. Le conclusioni, che egli aveva tratto dalla valutazione delle testimonianze raccolte nella silloge, sono espresse sinteticamente nel preambolo, ove, rivolgendosi ai figli, il Rucellai dice: 'Come vedrete, e' più s'acordano che fortuna niente sia se none un nome, e comprenderete che il buono ghoverno e il senno e la prudenza giova molto a ogni caso averso et tengono stretti et legati i casi fortuiti per modo che pocho o niente possono nuocere e il più delle volte il savio si difende da loro'[3]. Il Rucellai, quando scriveva queste parole (dalle quali traspare uno spiraglio di fiducia nelle proprie possibilità) si considerava, come abbiamo visto, ancora in disgrazia, anche se in realtà la sua politica di avvicinamento ai Medici (affiancata dal prestigioso programma edilizio varato proprio in quegli anni) stava già dando i suoi frutti, e autorizzava un certo ottimismo, che facesse da contrappeso al diffuso e radicato pessimismo nei riguardi della partecipazione alla vita pubblica, che traspare da tante pagine dello Zibaldone *vetus*. Il Rucellai, di fronte alla propria esperienza e agli esempi delle alterne vicende cui soggiacevano ricchezze e cariche pubbliche, s'era dovuto, ovviamente, chiedere quanto contasse —nel raggiungimento del benessere e della felicità—l'azione degli uomini, e quale incidenza avessero su di lei le forze imprevedibili del caso e della fortuna.

Prescindendo, tuttavia, dalle motivazioni di carattere personale, che ebbero, ovviamente, un peso determinante sui suoi orientamenti, non bisognerà dimenticare che il Rucellai si inseriva e si muoveva in un contesto culturale—basti pensare all'Alberti—in cui il tema della fortuna aveva una posizione di particolare rilievo. Senza voler entrare in particolari—che storici del pensiero, delle lettere e delle arti hanno, d'altronde, abbondantemente illustrato[4]—basterà considerare l'importanza che hanno avuto, nell'età del Rinascimento, le discussioni su fato, fortuna e caso, e come dal Mussato al Machiavelli temi del genere—inseriti nel processo di sviluppo della civiltà umanistica—

---

[1] Si consulti a tale proposito—per farsi un'idea più precisa della sistemazione delle singole parti dello Zibaldone—l' *Indice generale del ms.* in Perosa, pp. xxi ss.

[2] Cfr. p. 117.

[3] Perosa, p. 103.

[4] Sul concetto di fortuna nel Rinascimento, e sulle opere filosofiche, letterarie e artistiche, che ne fanno oggetto di discussione o di raffigurazione, esiste una bibliografia vastissima; qui mi basterà ricordare—oltre ai contributi fondamentali di Warburg, *Gesammelte Schriften*, 'ad indicem'—i lavori di A. Doren, "Fortuna im Mittelalter und in der Renaissance", *Vorträge der Bibliothek (Warburg*, I, 1922–23), Lipsia, 1924, pp. 71 ss.; H. R. Patch, "The Tradition of the Goddess Fortuna in Roman Literature and in the Transitional Period", *Smith College Studies in Modern Languages*, III (1922), 3, pp. 131 ss., 4, pp. 179 ss.; *id., The Goddess Fortuna in Medieval Literature*, New York, 1967; F. Kiefer, "The Conflation of Fortuna and Occasio in Renaissance Thought and Iconography", *Journal of Medieval and Renaissance Studies*, IX, 1 (1979), pp. 1–27. Cfr. Kent, sopra, pp. 35, n. 5; 70, n. 3; 86, n. 1.

abbiano trovato larga accoglienza in opere di varia provenienza e fattura (come ad es. in trattati, dialoghi, orazioni, versi, cronache, ecc., per non parlare dei libri di ricordanze dei mercanti, molto sensibili a tali problemi). Quest'interessamento e l'insistenza con cui sin dagli albori del primo umanesimo è stata affrontata la tematica sulla fortuna non è casuale, ma risponde a stati d'animo e a incertezze spirituali e ideali, che—in un periodo di crisi, più o meno manifesta, dei valori tradizionali—implicano più sottili e sofferti rapporti tra l'uomo, la trascendenza e quelle forze soverchianti della realtà circostante, contro le quali il comportamento dell'uomo va a cozzare.

Alcuni anni dopo, condotta ormai a un felice approdo la propria navigazione, il Rucellai si è riproposto, con maggiore consapevolezza ed intensità questi stessi problemi, che ha cercato di approfondire e di chiarire a sé stesso e ai propri figli, sia ricorrendo al parere di alcuni qualificati interlocutori, ai quali ha posto due quesiti—se cioè sia più facile bene o male operare, e se l'uomo abbia la possibilità di difendersi dai colpi di fortuna—; sia interrogando sé stesso in due significativi 'ricordi', in cui, tentando di fare un bilancio della propria vita e dei propri successi, egli si è posto, implicitamente, il problema del rapporto tra azione umana e grazia divina.

I due 'ricordi' sono, rispettivamente, del 1464 e del 1473, e—sia nel contenuto che nella forma— non presentano sostanziali differenze[1]. C'è solo da notare che il primo dei due si conclude con un ampio brano—un caldo e vibrante ringraziamento al Signore per i benefici e le infinite grazie ricevute—tratto da un anonimo volgarizzamento di un raffazzonamento medioevale dei *Soliloquia* di S. Agostino[2]. In tutti e due i 'ricordi' la vena religiosa è molto profonda e le conclusioni che il Rucellai trae da questo processo di introspezione sono espresse all'inizio del secondo 'ricordo'. 'Io chonoscho'—dice il Rucellai—che questo benessere non procede 'da mie virtù nè da mie opere, ma per grazia di Dio, preghandolo che mi chonceda grazia ch'io ne sia chonoscente e non ingrato, perchè in verità m'à fatto più grazie ch'io non gl'ò chieste nè disiderate'[3].

Le inchieste sulla fortuna e sul tema se sia più facile bene o male operare furono promosse dal Rucellai, una prima volta negli anni che vanno dal 1461–2 al 1464, quando cioè, in seguito al fidanzamento del figlio Bernardo colla Nannina de' Medici, egli aveva da poco raggiunto un più sicuro stato sociale e politico; una seconda volta—stando a testimonianze che non figurano nello Zibaldone —nell'anno 1477, quando cioè, in seguito a gravi perdite finanziarie subite tre anni prima, il Rucellai poneva ogni sforzo nel risalire la china per mantenere almeno in parte l'antico splendore[4].

Nel primo caso i due quesiti erano stati posti dal Rucellai, rispettivamente, al filosofo Marsilio Ficino, per quanto concerne il tema della fortuna, e al frate domenicano Giovanni da Viterbo e al filosofo Donato Acciaiuoli, per quanto concerne il secondo tema; nel secondo caso, invece, i due quesiti erano stati posti—tramite il genero del Rucellai, Domenico Bartoli, che allora copriva la carica di capitano di Sarzana—al filosofo e politico sarzanese Antonio Ivani. Le risposte del Ficino, di Giovanni da Viterbo e dell'Acciaiuoli ci sono pervenute sia nello Zibaldone che in altre fonti

---

[1] Perosa, pp. 117–22.

[2] Perosa, pp. 119–20, 117–8. Il raffazzonamento medioevale dei *Soliloquia* di S. Agostino ebbe una grande diffusione in età umanistica, sia nel testo latino che nel volgarizzamento anonimo, giunto a noi, variamente interpolato, in un'infinità di codici e in sei incunabuli (= *GW* 3015–3020). Di quest'opera esiste anche un'edizione degli inizi del secolo scorso: *Volgarizzamento dei Soliloquij di S. Agostino*, Verona, 1830, pp. 22–5.

[3] Perosa, p. 120.

[4] Perosa, p. 122. Dei danni subiti nel 1474 il Rucellai stesso ha lasciato memoria in calce al 'ricordo' del 1473. 'Di poi—egli dice—l'anno 1474 ebbi una grande perdita nella mia conpagnia di Pisa, ghovernata per Ridolfo Paghanelli, che m'inghannò e rubò per vie torte e feciomi danno f. ventimila, per modo che insieme con altra aversità di richo sono diventato povero. Che Dio di tutto sia lodato'.

manoscritte[1]; la lettera dell'Ivani, indirizzata al Bartoli, non figura nello Zibaldone, ma ci è giunta tra le lettere dell'epistolario dell'Ivani[2].

In questa lettera l'Ivani risponde soltanto al quesito se sia più facile bene o male operare, rimandando, per ciò che concerne la fortuna, ad una lettera-opuscolo *De fortuna*, che egli aveva composto alcuni anni prima[3]. A parte il contenuto dottrinale della lettera al Bartoli—cui farò cenno in seguito—mi preme per ora porre in risalto il passo, in cui l'Ivani, pur protestando la propria inadeguatezza a formulare risposte così impegnative, pone in risalto, riferendosi al Rucellai, il suo continuo, vivace interessamento per questi problemi, che le risposte fornitegli precedentemente (da Giovanni da Viterbo, dall'Acciaiuoli, eventualmente da altri) non erano riuscite, a quanto sembra, ad appagare completamente. 'E l'una e l'altra di queste propositioni—dice l'Ivani—bisognerebbe di più perspicace ingiegno ne lo investigare e di magior facilità ne lo explicare che in me non sonno, maximamente essendovi mosso per satisfare—come proponesti—a un certo desiderio dil nobile huomo Giovanni Rucellai, vostro honorato cittadino et amorevole suocero, che meritamente in luogho di padre havete, el quale sicundo voi havendo investigato assai per esser chiaro—quanto per humana ragione si può discernere—qual sia la verità di questi duo difficili motivi, ho preso admiratione che essendo egli citadino non meno potente che diligente, nato e nutrito in sì ampla città copiosa de nobillissimi ingiegni, non habi ogiumai trovato sufficiente expositore. Il perchè mi diffido di me medesimo, el quale habito puoi dire in contado et ho poca doctrina e mancho pratica'[4].

Nei 'ricordi' e nelle inchieste promosse dal Rucellai vengono riproposti, in forma diversa e con impegno più deciso, temi e motivi già presenti nello Zibaldone *vetus*. Il quesito stesso, se sia più facile fare il bene o il male—che anche Bartolomeo da San Concordio si era posto in una rubrica dei suoi *Ammaestramenti*[5]—era già affiorato timidamente in alcune pagine dello Zibaldone *vetus*. 'Vorrei sapere—s'era chiesto il Rucellai—dove noi siamo più inchinati o a ffare il male o il bene'. Senza prendere posizione in merito, egli s'era limitato—anche in quell'occasione—a far seguire a quest'interrogativo sia la sentenza di chi riteneva che 'avendo fatto abito di fare bene, sarebbe più malagievole a ffare il male e così per averso', sia quella opposta, espressa in due passi, rispettivamente, dell'*Etica* di Aristotele ('Dicie Aristotile nell'eticha sua nel secondo libro al nono chapitolo che il bene si può fare solamente inn uno modo e che il male si fa in molti modi, et che perciò è grave chosa e fatichosa essere buono, et lieve et agievole a essere reo...') e del Vangelo di S. Matteo ('Disse Christo nel Vangelo di San Matteo che lla via d'andare a ddanazione dello inferno era larghissima e spaziosissima'), che si ritrovano—vedi caso—anche tra le testimonianze arrecate, a tale proposito, da Bartolomeo da San Concordio[6].

---

[1] Perosa, pp. 85–102, 114–6, 125–35. Alle pp. 164 e 176 gli elenchi dei mss. che, al di fuori dello Zibaldone, ci hanno tramandato i testi di Giovanni da Viterbo, Donato Acciaiuoli e Marsilio Ficino.

[2] P. Landucci Ruffo, "L'epistolario di Antonio Ivani (1430–82)", *Rinascimento*, VI (1966), pp. 188–92. L'Ivani fu in rapporti cordiali con molti uomini politici ed umanisti del suo tempo, primo fra tutti Marsilio Ficino (per cui cfr. Kristeller, *Supplementum Ficinianum*, II, pp. 243–50). Sull'Ivani si veda ora R. Fubini, "Antonio Ivani da Sarzana: un teorizzatore del declino delle autonomie comunali", in *Egemonia fiorentina ed autonomie locali nella Toscana nord-occidentale del primo Rinascimento: vita, arte, cultura*, Pistoia, 1978, pp. 113–64.

[3] L'epistola *De fortuna*, indirizzata il 1° dicembre 1474 a Giovanfrancesco di Sarzana, è stata pubblicata da A. Altamura, "Quattro epistole inedite di Antonio Ivani", *Studi e ricerche di letteratura umanistica*, Napoli, 1956, pp. 32–4.

[4] Landucci Ruffo, "Epistolario di Antonio Ivani", p. 188.

[5] Bartolomeo da San Concordio, *Ammaestramenti*, IV, 5, pp. 41–3.

[6] *Zibaldone*, f. 81a[v]. Il Rucellai—come risulta da un rimando che si legge al f. 29b[r] dello *Zibaldone* ('E volendo sapere quale sia più agevole o a fare il male o a fare il bene, andrete al detto libro memoriale a c...')—doveva aver raccolto materiali che riguardavano questa 'dubitazione' anche in quel 'libro memoriale', andato perduto, cui egli accenna in alcune pagine dello Zibaldone (cfr. p. 103).

Nello Zibaldone *vetus*—s'è visto—gli interessi spirituali del Rucellai erano orientati, praticamente, in due direzioni: verso la religiosità e la cultura tradizionali e verso una problematica più aperta, connessa ai concetti di fortuna, caso, ecc. Questa distinzione persiste, *grosso modo*, anche nelle pagine dello Zibaldone degli anni successivi, e si esprime, da un lato nei 'ricordi' sulla grazia, pregni di religiosità, e dall'altro nelle inchieste sul valore dell'azione umana e sulla fortuna. Il Rucellai, che filosofo non era, e che a temi di tal genere si accostava da profano, affidandosi più alla sua sensibilità di uomo pratico che non all'impianto sistematico della ragione, si era reso conto che problemi così complessi si prestavano a soluzioni alternative, che non escludevano la coesistenza di comportamenti apparentemente diversi. Esperienze spirituali, inchieste filosofiche, ecc. traevano, comunque, origine da una matrice comune, dai dubbi cioè e dagli interrogativi che affioravano dall'azione di ogni giorno; e non è un caso che tali dubbi se li sia posti, con tanta sofferta vivezza, un uomo che, come il Rucellai, aveva concentrato tutti i suoi interessi sulla vita pratica.

Tra lo Zibaldone *vetus* e le aggiunte successive c'è però un salto di qualità, che è dovuto in parte anche alle mutate condizioni in cui era venuto a trovarsi il Rucellai dopo il 1461. Nello Zibaldone *vetus* il Rucellai si era limitato a far parlare le voci del passato. Egli aveva scelto e raccolto per sè e per i suoi figli testi religiosi e liturgici che rappresentavano la pietà popolare e la tradizione, sentenze tratte dal *Fiore di Virtù* e dagli *Ammaestramenti degli antichi*, e aveva appoggiato le sue conclusioni sulla fortuna su liste di *auctoritates* desunte da autori classici o da autori volgari di un più recente passato. Si trattava di preferenze significative, ma la presentazione dei materiali era alquanto schematica e la personalità del Rucellai rimaneva sostanzialmente nell'ombra. Il suo atteggiamento cambia nelle pagine più recenti dello Zibaldone. Il Rucellai si sente più sicuro di sé, e ostenta un certo compiacimento per i suoi successi, che trapela sia nei due 'ricordi', sia, indirettamente, nel tono stesso delle risposte che i suoi interlocutori danno alle inchieste da lui promosse. Egli non interroga più i testi del passato, ma—come nei 'ricordi'—sé stesso, oppure, come nelle inchieste, i suoi contemporanei più rappresentativi, che immedesimandosi nelle sue preoccupazioni spirituali, sono in grado di fornirgli risposte più immediate e adeguate; e nelle scelte che in questi casi egli fa, si dirige, con fine intuito, ai rappresentanti dei tre filoni più significativi della filosofia del primo Rinascimento, e cioè al tomismo nell'ambito della tradizione, al neoaristotelismo e al neoplatonismo nell'ambito della cultura umanistica.

Per sapere se sia più facile bene o male operare, il Rucellai si è rivolto ad un frate domenicano, Giovanni da Viterbo, e ad un umanista, Donato Acciaiuoli. Le risposte, in forma di lettera-trattato, dei due filosofi interpellati, sono state trascritte nello Zibaldone, ma esistono a parte: nel codice Magl. VI. 162, ff. 87^r–101^v della Biblioteca Nazionale di Firenze, le minute autografe, con correzioni e varianti, del testo volgare e di una redazione latina—destinata, ovviamente, ad ambienti umanistici —della lettera dell'Acciaiuoli, e nel codice II.IV.192, ff. 195^r–209 della stessa Biblioteca gli autografi della lettera di Giovanni da Viterbo e della redazione definitiva in volgare della lettera dell'Acciaiuoli, oltre al frammento di una seconda lettera autografa di Giovanni da Viterbo al Rucellai, mutila dell'inizio, che non figura nello Zibaldone.

Le vicende di questa polemica sono facilmente ricostruibili. Nella sua lettera, che reca la data del 15 agosto 1464, l'Acciaiuoli ricorda che la discussione era sorta un anno prima, quando, essendo insieme al Rucellai 'de' priori della libertà' e 'avendo insieme più volte ragionamenti di chose morali', il Rucellai gli aveva chiesto 'quale era più difficile o bene o male operare'. 'Risposi—dice l'Acciaiuoli—che mi pareva che fussi più difficultà a bene operare, assegnando alchune ragioni che allora mi occhorsono.' Più tardi però—soggiunge l'Acciaiuoli—egli aveva ricevuto dal Rucellai 'uno libello' di 'autore incerto' (la lettera di Giovanni da Viterbo), che sosteneva una tesi contraria alla sua, per cui ora si vedeva costretto a mettere per iscritto le sue ragioni, per sottoporle all'autorevole giudizio del suo parente[1]. Il Rucellai, evidentemente, insoddisfatto della discussione avuta coll'Acciaiuoli, s'era rivolto per un parere a Giovanni da Viterbo, e il domenicano gli aveva risposto colla lettera autografa pervenutaci nel ms. della Nazionale, che il Rucellai aveva fatto copiare nello Zibaldone. Successivamente il Rucellai aveva inviato la lettera del frate all'Acciaiuoli, che presane visione aveva risposto appunto con quella del 15 agosto. Trascritta anche questa nello Zibaldone, il Rucellai ne aveva mandato al frate l'originale, perchè ne prendesse conoscenza ed eventualmente controbattesse. Il domenicano, effettivamente, aveva risposto, compiegando alla propria la lettera dell'Acciaiuoli. Il Rucellai, a questo punto, aveva trasmesso tutto il materiale all'Acciaiuoli, senza preoccuparsi di far trascrivere nello Zibaldone la seconda lettera del frate nè di trattenere presso di sé il testo originale della prima lettera dell'Acciaiuoli. Il Rucellai, evidentemente, confidava che l'Acciaiuoli gli avrebbe restituito, con comodo, le lettere che gli appartenevano. Questa restituzione, invece, non ebbe mai luogo, e i singoli pezzi rimasero fra le carte Acciaiuoli, che sono conservate nel codice II.IV.192 della Biblioteca Nazionale di Firenze[2].

Dei due personaggi, ai quali si rivolge il Rucellai, l'Acciaiuoli è figura ben nota agli studiosi del Rinascimento. Scolaro dell'Argiropulo, commentatore dell'*Etica Nicomachea* di Aristotele, umanista e diplomatico, ha trovato di recente in Eugenio Garin il biografo che ne ha messo in evidenza gli interessi per la speculazione etico-politica, che aveva le sue radici nel primo umanesimo fiorentino, dominato dalla figura di Leonardo Bruni[3]. Mi basterà soltanto rammentare che l'Acciaiuoli era anche parente (secondo cugino) del Rucellai, e che in questo stesso Zibaldone gli veniva attribuito un volgarizzamento della pseudobernardiana epistola *De gubernatione rei familiaris*[4]. Il frate domenicano dovrà invece identificarsi con quel Giovanni Nanni da Viterbo, che latinizzò il suo nome in Annio, e fu una strana figura di teologo, profeta, astrologo e antiquario[5]. Il Nanni—che morì a Roma nel 1502—fu uno dei più abili e fortunati falsari della Rinascenza, ed una sua raccolta, con commento, di diversi autori 'de antiquitatibus loquentium' (indicata, comunemente, col titolo di *Antiquitates*), stampata a Roma nel 1498, e poi più volte riedita e in parte volgarizzata durante il secolo successivo, ebbe una notevole diffusione e rinomanza. Il Nanni fu anche predicatore efficace. Nel 1480 stampò a Genova un trattato *De futuris Christianorum triumphis in Saracenos*—frutto di una lettura tenuta nel 1471 in una chiesa di quella città—in cui prediceva, fondandosi sull'interpretazione di passi dell'Apocalisse e su considerazioni e calcoli astronomici, l'imminente declino della potenza turca in Oriente. Nel 1464 il Nanni si trovava a Firenze, dove iniziava verso la fine di

---

[1] Perosa, p. 91. Il Rucellai era stato priore insieme all' Acciaiuoli nei mesi di maggio e giugno del 1463. Cfr. ASF, Priorista di Palazzo, f. 202[v].

[2] Per un'esposizione più dettagliata di questa vicenda cfr. Perosa, pp. 164–5.

[3] Sull'Acciaiuoli cfr. A. Della Torre, *Storia dell'Accademia Platonica di Firenze*, Firenze, 1902, pp. 322 ss.; E. Garin, "Donato Acciaiuoli cittadino fiorentino", in *Medioevo e Rinascimento*, Bari, 1954, pp. 211–87; A. D'Addario, "Acciaiuoli Donato", *DBI*, I (1960), pp. 79–80; Martines, *Social World*, pp. 348–9.

[4] Cfr. p. 111.

[5] Sulla figura e attività del Nanni—oltre ai lavori indicati in Perosa, p. 165, n. 2—si veda A. Zeno, *Dissertazioni vossiane*, II, Venezia, 1753 ss., pp. 186–92; R. Weiss, "An unknown epigraphic Tract by Annius of Viterbo", *Italian Studies presented to E. R. Vincent*, Cambridge, 1962, pp. 101–20; *id.*, "Traccia per una biografia di Annio da Viterbo", *IMU*, V (1962), pp. 425–41. L'identificazione del frate interlocutore del Rucellai col Nanni è corroborata da un confronto di scritture, dato che nell'Archivio segreto Vaticano (AA. Arm. I–XVIII, 5029, f. 188) esiste una lettera autografa del Nanni a papa Alessandro VI, che rivela una grafia molto simile a quella delle lettere al Rucellai contenute nel già cit. codice II.IV.192 della Nazionale di Firenze (cfr. A. Mercati, "Comunicazioni antiquarie dell'Archivio segreto Vaticano [2. Una supplica di Annio da Viterbo ad Alessandro VI]", *Rend. della Pont. Accad. Romana d'Archeologia*, XIX [1942–3], pp. 415 ss.).

novembre un corso sulle sentenze di Pietro Lombardo. Ospite del Convento di S. Maria Novella, non gli sarà stato difficile entrare in contatto col Rucellai, la cui famiglia, da antica data, esercitava una sorta di patronato su quella Chiesa[1].

Il frate, premesso che il bene e il male, di cui si fa questione, sono il bene e il male morali, ricorre a S. Tommaso, ove trova che 'mos' significa due cose, cioè 'la naturale inchinazione delle cose' oppure la 'consuetudine alla qual l'uomo s'avezza'. Pertanto 'i beni morali o vizii' si chiameranno 'quegli che l'uomo à o per naturale inchinatione o per consuetudine e exercitio acquistati', e quindi 'l'agevolezza dell' adoprare alcuna volta verrà per natura, alcuna volta per consuetudine alla qual l'uomo s'avezza'. Ma l'uomo—dice Giovanni da Viterbo—è composto di . . . due parti contrarie, l'una spirituale e l'altra corporale, di cui la prima è 'inchinata per natura alle virtù', la seconda 'è inchinata a ogni cosa corporale', ed è proprio quest'inclinazione corporale che l'uomo segue durante la giovinezza assuefandovisi. Stando così le cose, le risposte che si possono dare circa l'agevolezza a fare il bene o il male variano a seconda che si consideri l'agevolezza che l'uomo ha 'per natural inchinazione di ragione' ovvero quella che ha per 'natural complessione di corpo', o ancora quella che ha 'per consuetudine'. Soltanto nel primo caso l'agevolezza si volge, in senso univoco, verso il bene, essendo 'le vertù . . . natural dono degli uomini, per natura intendi propria dell'uomo che si chiama esser ragionevole', ma è soltanto questo caso che va preso in considerazione 'perchè il principal bene de l'uomo è lla ragione, la quale è ppiù possente che non è la complessione del corpo, e anque che non è la consuetudine', e d'altra parte, poichè 'secondo la ragione siano agevoli a vertù e al bene', consegue che 'absolutamente l'uomo più agevolmente fa 'l bene che 'l male'. Come la pietra 'più agevolmente . . . va in giù che in alto, perchè andare in giù gl'è propria natura e non andare in su', così l'uomo 'esser ragionevole', per natura è inclinato a 'viver secondo il bene della ragione' e trova meno impedimenti e meno fatica a compiere opere virtuose che non opere viziose. La maggiore facilità nel fare il male piuttosto che il bene è soltanto apparente, e si fonda—dice il frate—sulla 'consuetudine' al male, alla quale s'avezza il fanciullo, quando, innanzi abbia l'uso di ragione, è ancora soggetto agli stimoli della carne; ragione per cui 'i padri fanno bene da fanciullezza inchinare i figlioli a vertù e guardallo dalle cattive compagnie acciò che, quando fia giovene gli si' difficile il male e agevole il bene'. Il duplice significato di 'mos' è anche corroborato—nota il domenicano—da un fatto linguistico, che cioè 'in lingua grecha v'è differenzia nello scrivere: chè quando "ethos" significa la consuetudine alla quale l'uomo s'avezza, scrivano per "e" longo, che gle chiamano "ita" . . . ma quando significa naturale inchinatione scrivano per "ipsilon", che è chome "fio" nostro'[2].

La definizione, che Giovanni da Viterbo dà di 'mos' e gli argomenti che egli adduce, derivano da due luoghi, rispettivamente, del *Commento all'Etica* di Aristotele e della *Summa Theologica* di S. Tommaso. Aristotele nel famoso inizio del II libro dell'*Etica Nicomachea* aveva precisato 1) che la virtù morale nasceva dall'abitudine, da cui aveva tratto—con una lieve modifica—anche il nome; 2) che nessuna virtù etica era insita nell'uomo per natura; 3) che l'uomo aveva per natura soltanto disposizione a ricevere la virtù, e tale disposizione attuava mediante l'abitudine[3]. S. Tommaso,

---

[1] L. G. Cerracchini, *Fasti teologali ovvero notizie istoriche del Collegio de' Teologi della sacra Università fiorentina*, Firenze, 1738, p. 165: 'Giovanni Nanni . . . li 27 novembre (1464) comincia a leggere ed interpretare il primo libro delle *Sentenze* (di Pietro Lombardo), essendo già per tale lettura stato incorporato come Baccelliere'.

[2] Perosa, pp. 85–91. La confusione tra ε e υ rivela che Giovanni da Viterbo era ancora completamente digiuno di greco. 'Fio' era il nome dell'ultima lettera dell'alfabeto nei libri di scuola del Medioevo e corrispondeva a 'y' greca. Cfr. R. Sabbadini, *Il metodo degli umanisti*, Firenze, 1922, p. 4.

[3] Arist. *Eth. Nic.* II. I. 1103a, 1: ἡ δ' ἠθικὴ ἐξ ἔθους περιγίνεται, ὅθεν καὶ τοὔνομα ἔσχηκε μικρὸν παρεκκλῖνον ἀπὸ τοῦ ἔθους.

premesso che la virtù morale era 'in parte appetitiva', per cui comportava una qualche inclinazione in qualcosa di appetibile, e che tale inclinazione era 'vel a natura, quae inclinat in id quod est sibi conveniens, vel ex consuetudine, quae vertitur in naturam', aveva attribuito, nel commento a questo passo aristotelico, una duplice accezione a 'mos', trovando conferma di ciò nel fatto che 'in graeco ethos per "e" breve scriptum significat morem sive moralem virtutem; ithos autem scriptum per H graecum quod est longum significat consuetudinem'[1]. E nella *Summa*, riproponendo il problema, aveva specificato che 'mos ... duo significat; quandoque enim significat consuetudinem ..., quandoque vero significat inclinationem quandam naturalem, vel quasi naturalem, ad aliquid agendum', aggiungendo che questi due significati, mentre in latino erano indicati da una stessa voce, in greco si distinguevano, perchè ' "ethos", quod apud nos morem significat, quandoque habet primam longam et scribitur per H, graecam litteram; quandoque habet primam correptam et scribitur per ε'[2].

Il testo aristotelico ha subìto, come si vede, nell'interpretazione dell'Aquinate una strana deformazione, dovuta in gran parte alla sua scarsa conoscenza del greco, in parte ai condizionamenti che il suo stesso impianto filosofico (che si proponeva scopi tanto diversi) doveva esercitare nell'interpretazione di Aristotele. S. Tommaso leggeva Aristotele nella versione di Roberto Grossatesta, emendato da Gugliemo di Moerbeke, e si giovava per indicazioni di carattere linguistico del corpo di glosse che il vescovo di Lincoln aveva inserito nella sua traduzione dal greco, e spesso si prestavano—come in questo caso specifico—ad incomprensioni ed equivoci[3]. In Aristotele infatti la definizione di virtù etica è univoca ed implica la deduzione di ogni atto morale dalla 'consuetudo', colla esplicita esclusione di ogni condizionamento naturalistico. La virtù etica non è un dato naturale, ma un abito, che si acquisisce con l'esercizio degli atti virtuosi. In S. Tommaso l'accento è posto con particolare insistenza sul concetto di inclinazione naturale, che è caratteristico dell'etica tomistica, ma non trova un esatto equivalente nella formulazione aristotelica. S. Tommaso sembra trasferire su un piano diverso l'aristotelica disposizione naturale a ricevere la virtù (la 'naturalis aptitudo'), attribuendole una funzione preminente, strettamente connessa coll'atto morale. E' soprattutto in rapporto a questa esigenza che trova una giustificazione plausibile la formulazione di una duplice definizione di 'mos', che a S. Tommaso è suggerita dall'accostamento effettuato da Aristotele, con diverso intendimento, delle due parole greche ἦθος ed ἔθος.

Giovanni da Viterbo richeggia molto da vicino, nella lettera al Rucellai, le argomentazioni di S. Tommaso, di cui era, ovviamente, un fedele seguace[4]. Completamente diverso è invece l'atteggiamento di Donato Acciaiuoli, che come s'è visto sostiene la tesi opposta a quella del frate. Confutata la distinzione tomistica, che il suo antagonista aveva accettato in pieno, e corretta l'interpretazione errata, che S. Tommaso aveva dato dei due termini greci—e che Giovanni da Viterbo aveva ulteriormente peggiorato confondendo 'epsilon' con 'upsilon'—l'Acciaiuoli punta direttamente su Aristotele, di cui riproduce il passo sulla definizione di 'virtus moralis' nel testo originale greco, facendolo seguire da una versione latina, che è una contaminazione di quella del Bruni con quella dell'Argiropulo. L'Acciaiuoli dimostra che l'identità di 'mos' e di 'inclinatio' non ha senso e

---

[1] Thom. Aq. *In Arist. Eth. Nic.* 247.

[2] Thom. Aq. *Summa theol.* 1/2, q. 58, a. 1.

[3] La notula del Grossatesta—edita da E. Franceschini, "Roberto Grossatesta, vescovo di Lincoln, e le sue traduzioni latine", *Atti del R. Istituto Veneto di Sc., Lettere ed Arti*, XCIII (1933), pp. 85 s.—è riprodotta in Perosa, p. 168, n. 24.

[4] Il Weiss ("Traccia per una biografia", p. 427, n. 2) segnala un codice—il Vat. lat. 729—della prima parte della *Summa theologica* di S. Tommaso con postille marginali e correzioni interlineari di mano di Giovanni da Viterbo.

non quadra colla speculazione aristotelica, ove la 'naturalis aptitudo' a ricevere la virtù è cosa assai diversa della 'inclinatio' tomistica. La virtù etica non è un dato naturale, ma un abito acquisito con l'esercizio degli atti virtuosi. Aristotele dice 'apertissimamente . . . le virtù morali acquistarsi per consuetudine' e nega 'essere in noi da natura'. Il bene perciò—conclude l'Acciaiuoli—si conquista con fatica nell'azione quotidiana, superando le difficoltà che l'umano operare fatalmente incontra[1].

L'Acciaiuoli, quando nel 1464 prese parte alla disputa con Giovanni da Viterbo, era appena uscito da un robusto tirocinio di studi aristotelici sotto la guida dell'Argiropulo, che dal 1457 stava svolgendo nello Studio una serie di corsi sulle opere di Aristotele[2]. All'*Etica Nicomachea* l'Argiropulo aveva dedicato due anni scolastici, il 1457 e il 1458. Delle sue lezioni l'Acciaiuoli ci ha tramandato la stesura originaria nel ms. autografo II.I. 104 della Nazionale di Firenze. Più tardi, rimaneggiato questo materiale, egli ha dato forma a quel commento alla *Nicomachea*, che si trova nel ms. II.I.80 della Nazionale, e poi fu più volte dato alle stampe, a cominciare dall'edizione fiorentina del 1478. In questo commento il passo di Aristotele, che costituiva il punto di attrito tra le due opposte interpretazioni di Giovanni da Viterbo e dell'Acciaiuoli, viene illustrato con grande copia di argomentazioni. L'Acciaiuoli—in polemica col neoplatonismo ('Notandum quod philosophus videtur etiam hoc afferre propter Socratem et Platonem, qui dixere virtutes inesse nobis a natura')— insiste sull'origine sperimentale e non naturale dell'esercizio della virtù ('a consuetudine oritur . . . non a natura'), e chiarisce il significato che bisogna attribuire al concetto di 'aptitudo naturalis'[3]. In realtà, a Firenze, negli anni dello Zibaldone, era in atto, soprattutto in virtù dell'insegnamento dell'Argiropulo, una riscoperta e rivalutazione in chiave 'umanistica' (e filologica) dell'etica e della politica aristoteliche, che affondavano le loro radici nell'attività di traduttore e di interprete di Leonardo Bruni. Il Bruni, come si ricorderà, figurava tra i quattro Grandi, che il Rucellai aveva indicato come gli uomini più rappresentativi della prima metà del '400; e non a caso, il Rucellai stesso aveva fatto trascrivere nello Zibaldone la *Canzone della felicità* del Bruni, che esaltava l'etica aristotelica del giusto mezzo[4].

Il nuovo Aristotele è una delle colonne su cui poggia la speculazione etico-politica degli umanisti, e oscura l'Aristotele degli scolastici, letto nelle versioni latine medioevali e interpretato, generalmente, attraverso il filtro delle *Summe* e dei *Commenti* di S. Tommaso[5]. La sostanziale divergenza tra i due contendenti viene sottolineata, non soltanto dalla diversa lettura di Aristotele, ma anche dalla diversa natura delle *auctoritates* che ognuno di essi schiera a sostegno della sua tesi. Giovanni da Viterbo—oltre a S. Tommaso e ad Aristotele—cita infatti il *De fide orthodoxa* di Giovanni Damasceno nella versione del pisano Burgundione, la *Vita di S. Antonio abbate* di S. Atanasio nella traduzione di Evagrio, le postille a S. Paolo di Pietro di Tarantasia (che fu poi papa Innocenzo

---

[1] Perosa, pp. 91–102.

[2] Interesserà, a tale proposito, la testimonianza di Vespasiano da Bisticci (*Vite*, ed. Greco, II, pp. 25–6): 'In primo udì da llui (dall'Argiropulo) a casa tutta la Loica d'Aristotile . . . Uscito de la Loica, cominciò andare allo Studio a udire l'Etica d'Aristotele, et ricoglieva in iscritti tutto quello che diceva messer Giovanni in voce. Aveva la mano velocissima et era bellissimo iscrittore di lettera corsiva. . .'. Sull'Argiropulo si veda G. Cammelli, *Giovanni Argiropulo*, Firenze, 1941 e E. Bigi, "Argiropulo Giovanni", *DBI*, IV (1962), pp. 129–31.

[3] D. Acciaiuoli, *Expositio Ethicorum Aristotelis*, Firenze, 1478, f. giiʳ (= *GW* 140).

[4] *Zibaldone*, ff. 34aᵛ–35bᵛ. Cfr. Leonardo Bruni Aretino, *Humanistisch-philosophische Schriften*, a cura di H. Baron, Lipsia, 1928, pp. 149–54, 169. Il Bruni è ricordato tra i Grandi della città di Firenze in Perosa, pp. 48, 54–5, 61, 63. Cfr. p. 129.

[5] Per un orientamento più preciso sulla diffusione dell' etica aristotelica nel sec. XV, si veda: E. Garin, "Le traduzioni umanistiche di Aristotele nel secolo XV", *Atti e Memorie dell'Accademia fiorentina di Scienze morali 'La Colombaria'*, n.s., II (1947–50), pp. 55–104; id., "La fortuna dell'etica aristotelica nel Quattrocento", in *La cultura filosofica del Rinascimento italiano. Ricerche e documenti*, Firenze, 1961, pp. 60–71.

V), le *Institutiones* di Lattanzio, e molti passi della Bibbia, di cui il frate era un profondo conoscitore. L'Acciaiuoli allega invece passi dell'*Expositio super libros de anima Aristotelis* di Egidio Romano, delle lettere di S. Paolo, del *contra Iulianum* di S. Agostino, delle *Sentenze* di Isidoro di Siviglia e del *De legendis libris gentilium* di S. Basilio, che Donato leggeva nella versione latina di Leonardo Bruni, soffermandosi soprattutto sul mito di Ercole al bivio, tanto caro alla simbologia letteraria ed artistica del Rinascimento. L'Acciaiuoli dimostra di conoscere assai bene, non solo—com'è ovvio—Aristotele, ma anche S. Tommaso, e di questi due autori—visti in un'ottica diversa da quella tradizionale— egli offre una gamma assai varia di testimonianze a sostegno della sua tesi[1].

Non sappiamo per quale dei due interlocutori si sia dichiarato il Rucellai, ma è legittimo sospettare che egli abbia sentito più vicina alla sua mentalità e alla sua esperienza la soluzione prospettata dall'Acciaiuoli. Una riconferma, comunque, sul piano dottrinale, egli la ebbe, come s'è visto, alcuni anni dopo, quando il sarzanese Antonio Ivani, da lui interpellato sulla medesima 'dubitazione' tramite il genero Domenico Bartoli, gli rispose—uniformandosi evidentemente a quella che egli doveva ritenere fosse la soluzione che meglio si attagliava alla personalità del Rucellai—che 'l'humana natura . . . è più inclinata a' vicii che facile a le virtù', e quindi 'el peccare più facile ch'el bene operare', confermando con argomenti diversi (tra i quali anche l'influsso esercitato dai pianeti) la risposta data dall'Acciaiuoli[2]. Il Rucellai, sia allora—dopo cioè il tracollo finanziario subito nel 1474—sia precedentemente—nel lungo periodo in cui era stato 'sospetto allo stato'—aveva potuto valutare personalmente quanto fosse difficile 'navichare' con prudenza e virtù; anche perchè, durante la difficile navigazione, egli era stato costretto più volte a venire a patti con forze—come la fortuna e il caso—che agivano imprevedibilmente sul corso della vita umana.

E' appunto sul tema della fortuna che si indirizza, come s'è visto, la seconda inchiesta promossa dal Rucellai. Il Rucellai s'è rivolto a Marsilio Ficino, per sapere 'se l'uomo possa rimuovere o in altro modo remediare alle cose future et maxime a quelle che si chiamano fortuite'. Il Ficino risponde con una lettera in volgare, che ha avuto una larga diffusione autonoma, come si può arguire dai numerosi codici, che oltre allo Zibaldone, ce l'hanno tramandata[3].

La lettera del Ficino si può dividere in tre parti. Nella prima parte il Ficino afferma che non il volgo ma soltanto l'uomo prudente è capace di resistere alle vicende della fortuna. 'Imperò che— dice il Ficino—quando considero la confusa vita del misero volgo, truovo che a' futuri casi non pensano gli stolti, e se pensano non provegono a' ripari . . . sì che in questa considerazione l'animo pare che mi dica la fortuna essere sanza riparo; ma quando dall'altra parte mi rivolgo nella mente l'opere di Giovanni Rucellai e d'alcuni altri, a' quali la prudentia è regola ne' loro effetti, veggo le

---

[1] I passi di Aristotele, di S. Tommaso e degli altri autori citati da Giovanni da Viterbo e da Donato Acciaiuoli sono stati identificati e registrati da Perosa, pp. 165–71, nn. 3–53. Quanto al mito di Ercole al bivio e la sua diffusione nel Rinascimento, si veda E. Panofsky, *Hercules am Scheidewege*, Lipsia, 1930, pp. 53 ss., 155 ss.

[2] Landucci Ruffo, "Epistolario di Antonio Ivani", p. 189.

[3] Perosa, pp. 114–6, 176. La lettera è stata pubblicata per la prima volta, incompleta, dal Warburg ("Francesco Sassetti's letztwillige Verfügung", pp. 149–50); è stata poi riedita integralmente da G. Bing nella ristampa degli scritti del Warburg (*Gesammelte Schriften*, I, pp. 147–8) e da P. O. Kristeller (*Supplementum Ficinianum*, II, pp. 169 ss.). L'edizione che io ho curato— e che il Kiefer ("Conflation of Fortuna", p. 6, n. 16) non sembra conoscere—si fonda, oltre che sullo *Zibaldone*, su altri sette codici, che ho indicato e sommariamente descritto in Perosa, p. 176. La lettera del Ficino non è datata. E' stata trascritta nello *Zibaldone* verso la fine del 1464 (Perosa, p. xiii), ma—tenuto conto che nei mss. compare in genere in un gruppo di cinque lettere ficiniane in volgare, disposte in ordine cronologico—è probabile che sia stata composta precedentemente, forse tra il 1460 e il 1462. All'esegesi del contenuto filosofico della lettera hanno contribuito, tra gli altri, il Doren ("Fortuna im Mittelalter", pp. 118, 121)—che stranamente confonde il Rucellai col Sassetti—e il Kristeller (*Il pensiero filosofico di Marsilio Ficino*, Firenze, 1953, pp. 320–1).

chose venture essere antevedute e alle vedute posto riparo, et in questa cogitatione lo 'ntelletto mi giudica el contrario di quello che nella prima considerazione mi diceva'[1]. La prudenza è dunque per il Ficino la virtù basilare di cui necessitano gli uomini che vogliono premunirsi dai colpi della fortuna; ma essa—spiega il Ficino nella seconda parte della lettera—non si acquista soltanto cogli sforzi umani, ma è un dono della natura, quindi di Dio. 'L'uomo prudente—dice il Ficino—à potestà contro alla fortuna, ma con quella chiosa che gli dette quello sapiente: "Non haberes hanc potestatem nisi data esset desuper" '[2].

Analogamente, la fortuna stessa, pur manifestandosi 'fuori dell'ordine che comunemente da noi si conosce e desidera', segue una sua legge e un suo ordine, che sono voluti da 'chi sopra a nostra natura cognosce et vuole (cioè Dio); sì che quello che per rispecto a noi si chiama fortuna e caso, si può chiamare fato rispecto della natura universale et providentia rispecto del principio intellectuale'[3].

La conclusione qual'è? Ce lo dice il Ficino stesso nell'ultima parte della sua lettera: 'Tenendo queste cose di sopra tractate, ci acosteremo alla segreta et divina mente di Platone . . . et finiremo la pistola in questa morale sentenzia: che buono è combattere colla fortuna coll'arme della prudentia, pazientia e magnanimità; meglio è ritrarsi et fugire di tal guera. . .; optimo è fare co llei o pace o triegua, conformando la voluntà nostra colla sua e andare volentieri dov'ella acenna, acciò ch'ella per forza non tiri'[4].

L'accenno a Platone suscita dei problemi. Secondo Edgar Wind, il Ficino avrebbe avuto in mente un passo del quarto libro delle *Leggi* (709b–c), in cui Platone sottolinea il contributo, che nel governo delle cose del mondo—che alcuni attribuiscono quasi esclusivamente alla fortuna (τύχη), altri al binomio Dio-fortuna—reca (secondo una terza e più moderata opinione) l'abilità dell' uomo (la τέχνη); è infatti di somma utilità poter disporre, in occasione di una tempesta (καιρῷ χειμῶνος), di un buon pilota che conosca l'arte della navigazione[5]. Il Ficino nell'*argumentum* che precede la sua versione latina di questo libro delle *Leggi* si è soffermato con particolare attenzione su questo passo, dandone un'interpretazione abbastanza singolare. Al governo dell'umana società—egli dice—'tria conducere arbitratur, Deum videlicet fortunamque et artem, quae tria humana omnia gubernare dicuntur'. Ma poichè è da Dio che procedono sia le cose governate dalla fortuna che le cose governate dall'arte, accade che 'neque fortuna neque ars . . . Deo valeat adversari, quippe cum semper ab ipso utraque moveantur'. Fortuna ed arte poi, tra loro, o 'consentiunt invicem aut forte dissentiunt'. 'Si dissident, aut fortuna superat artem aut ars fortunam'. Valga un esempio: 'dum movet deus spheras, interdum per fortunam in mari commovet tempestatem, tempestas quatit navem'. Ma nello stesso tempo anche Dio muove la stessa nave 'per animum . . . gubernatoris, id est per artem ipsam a Deo continue dependentem'. Orbene, se l'abile nocchiero dirige la nave allo stesso porto cui la indirizza la tempesta, si potrà dire che 'ars simul cum fortuna consentit', se ciò invece non avviene, 'ars et fortuna dissentiunt' e di conseguenza 'vel ars cedit fortunae, vel arti fortuna'. Tutto questo però accade per volere della divina provvidenza, che predispone e dirige armonicamente ogni cosa 'ad finem sibi soli notum'. Se questa divina predisposizione è tale 'ut artem necessario superatura sit', si chiama fato; se invece è tale 'ut exuperare inertem possit, et superari ab arte', si chiama

---

[1] Perosa, p. 114.

[2] Perosa, p. 115. La citazione è tratta dal Vangelo di S. Giovanni (*Ioh.* 19, 11).

[3] Perosa, p. 115.

[4] Perosa, p. 116.

[5] E. Wind, "Platonic Tyranny and the Renaissance Fortuna: on Ficino's Reading of *Laws* IV, 709A–712A", in *Essays in Honor of Erwin Panofsky*, New York, 1961, pp. 491–6 (tr. it. di P. Bertolucci: E. Wind, *Tirannia Platonica e fortuna rinascimentale*, Milano, 1971); Kiefer, "Conflation of Fortuna", p. 6.

fortuna. Perciò—conclude il Ficino—'neque diffidas artem quandoque vincere posse fortunam'[1].

L'interpretazione che il Ficino dà del passo delle *Leggi* fa violenza, come ognuno vede, al testo di Platone. Il Ficino, in questo, come in tanti altri casi, cerca di adeguare alla propria concezione teologica l'esegesi platonica. Analogie tra le argomentazioni della lettera al Rucellai e il commento alle *Leggi* ci sono, ma non è detto che col generico accenno 'alla segreta et divina mente di Platone' il Ficino abbia inteso riferirsi—come vorrebbe il Wind—ad un passo preciso di Platone, e non abbia piuttosto voluto dire che il contenuto filosofico della sua lettera rientrava nell'ambito della sua concezione neoplatonica. Comunque stiano le cose, è poco probabile che il Rucellai conoscesse le *Leggi* di Platone e gli *argumenta* della versione ficiniana, al punto di saper cogliere e apprezzare l'allusione, che il Ficino avrebbe fatto, in forma così generica, al testo delle *Leggi*; ed è altrettanto poco probabile che da questo passo (in cui è introdotto il paragone della nave e del nocchiero), il Rucellai—sia di propria iniziativa o per esplicito suggerimento del Ficino—abbia tratto lo spunto per l'emblema della 'Fortuna nautica', che nel cimiero dello stemma della sua casata, posto nel cortile del Palazzo di via della Vigna, è rappresentata, com'è noto, da una donna nuda, ritta su una navicella, mentre, fungendo da albero maestro, regge un'ampia vela, gonfiata dal soffio di un vento favorevole.

Anche a prescindere dal fatto che non si può escludere a priori che l'assunzione da parte del Rucellai dell'emblema preceda cronologicamente la lettera del Ficino, studi recenti hanno dimostrato che l'impresa della vela, adottata dal Rucellai, era già diffusa in Italia da qualche decennio. Volker Herzner, ad es., ha posto in rilievo che anche gli Estensi—come risulta da due medaglie (una del 1444 e l'altra degli anni 1441–43), fatte eseguire al Pisanello dal marchese Lionello—e i Pazzi—per concessione avuta nel 1442 da René d'Anjou—si fregiavano di quest'impresa[2]. D'altronde, la grande diffusione che l'emblema ebbe negli anni successivi—a cominciare da una serie di incisioni di origine fiorentina, attribuite un tempo a Baccio Baldini, a finire alla 'Fortuna' di Rubens del Museo del Prado[3]—faceva di per sé stessa supporre—indipendentemente da ogni altra considerazione—che la 'Fortuna nautica' del Rucellai non fosse l'esclusiva progenitrice di questa numerosa famiglia che si è diffusa e propagata in zone e aree tanto diverse e lontane. Ciò non toglie, tuttavia, che—sia per i dettagli dell'invenzione che per i pregi formali dell'esecuzione—l'emblema del Rucellai debba considerarsi opera di originale squisitezza, che ancor oggi esercita un fascino particolare.

Chi per primo ideò e disegnò quest'emblema, creò qualcosa di sostanzialmente nuovo, staccandosi decisamente dalla tradizione figurativa medioevale, e soltanto in parte accogliendo spunti che provenivano dalla tradizione classica. Nel Medioevo la fortuna è stata costantemente raffigurata

---

[1] Platone, *Opera*, tr. M. Ficino, Lione, 1548, p. 530 (M. Ficino, *Opera omnia*, II, Basilea, 1561, pp. 1496–7).

[2] V. Herzner, "Die Segel-Imprese der Familie Pazzi", *MKHIF*, XX (1976), pp. 13–32. Le due medaglie del Pisanello in G. F. Hill, *A Corpus of Italian Medals of the Renaissance before Cellini*, Londra, 1930, I, pp. 9 s., II, tav. 5, n° 26 e tav. 6, n° 32; e in G. Paccagnini, *Pisanello alla corte dei Gonzaga*, Venezia, 1972, pp. 112, n° 68, 113, n° 72. Quanto ai Pazzi, l'impresa della vela—oltre che nel collare, che il giovane Renato Pazzi indossa nell'affresco della Madonna del Trebbio di Andrea del Castagno—è riprodotta, a scopi ornamentali, sia nella cappella di famiglia in Santa Croce, sia nella facciata e nel cortile del palazzo di via del Proconsolo.

[3] Testimonianze sul significato e la diffusione dell'emblema della 'Fortuna con vela' nell'iconografia rinascimentale sono raccolte nei lavori del Warburg (*Gesammelte Schriften*, I, pp. 75, 146 ss., 360, 364 s., tav. XX, figg. 36, 38), del Doren ("Fortuna im Mittelalter", pp. 121, 130 n. 125, 132, 143, tav. VI, figg. 14, 16, 17, 20), di A. M. Hind (*Early Italian Engraving*, Londra, 1938, pp. 27 (A.I.6), 34 (A.I.19), 95 (A.IV.37), 96 (A.IV.38), tav. 6, 19; 57), di E. Wind (*Giorgione's Tempesta*, Oxford, 1969, pp. 3, 20 s., figg. 21, 22, 57), del Kiefer ("Conflation of Fortuna", pp. 1 ss. e figg. 1 ss.), ecc. Di grande utilità i repertori di imprese, immagini, emblemi dell'Alciato, del Cartari, del Conti, del Ruscelli, del Ripa, ecc., e quel *Liber Fortunae ... centum emblemata et symbola centum continens* di Jean Cousin, che, pronto per la stampa già nel 1568, vide la luce soltanto alla fine del secolo scorso (J. Cousin, *The Book of Fortune*, a cura di L. Lalanne, Parigi, 1883). V. anche Preyer, *infra*, p. 200; e Kent, *supra*, p. 86.

simbolicamente da una ruota in perpetuo movimento, che solleva gli uomini e abbassa i potenti; dai Romani è stata, invece, rappresentata con una figura femminile, che regge una cornucopia nella mano sinistra e un timone nella destra, cui si aggiungono, in alcuni casi, quali attributi, la prora di una nave, un globo ecc. In questa simbologia sono evidenti i richiami al mare, e la Fortuna romana— sia sotto specie di 'Fortuna redux' o di 'Fortuna Antia' ('domina aequoris' in Hor. *Carm*. I. 35, 6), sia confusa coll'orientaleggiante 'Isis Pharia'—è stata onorata anche come dea della navigazione[1].

Se poi ora dal versante figurativo ci si sposti a quello letterario, si trova che—accanto all'immagine della ruota, che ricorre sporadicamente nei classici, ma diventa d'uso comune nei testi letterari del Medioevo e del primo Rinascimento[2]—è costante la presenza—sia in opere letterarie antiche che recenti—di espressioni, immagini, metafore, ecc., che, in connessione col tema della fortuna, alludono alla violenza dei flutti, al variabile soffio dei venti, alle difficoltà della navigazione. Gli esempi non mancano, ma si fanno sempre più numerosi ed insistenti nel Quattrocento (soprattutto nella prosa dei memorialisti, degli storici, ecc.)[3], anche perchè—per un processo facilmente intuibile—nelle lingue romanze (ed anche nelle lingue di alcuni popoli dell'area balcanico-mediterranea) il termine 'fortuna' ha assunto il significato (che nel latino classico non aveva) di 'fortunale', cioè di tempesta[4].

In base a tali considerazioni, sembra verosimile che chi tra i primi ha foggiato l'immagine della 'Fortuna colla vela' si sia ispirato, più che alle immagini e parole di Platone e del Ficino, a questa tradizione letteraria, che forniva gli elementi essenziali per dare alla fortuna una nuova e più incisiva rappresentazione figurata. Il Rucellai ha, ovviamente, fatta sua questa soluzione, che trovava consona alla sua condizione e ai suoi ideali, e ha utilizzato l'emblema non solo per decorare il cimiero del suo stemma, ma altresì—come già del resto avevano fatto i Pazzi—per ornare in forma schematica (colla raffigurazione di una vela o di una successione di vele) la superficie del Santo Sepolcro in S. Pancrazio o i fregi della facciata del Palazzo di via della Vigna o della chiesa di S. Maria Novella.

Ritornando ora—dopo questo breve *excursus*—alla lettera del Ficino, credo si possa affermare con grande probabilità, che le teorie sulla fortuna ivi esposte abbiano trovato buona accoglienza nel Rucellai, anche se egli, presumibilmente, non sarà stato in grado di seguire fino in fondo i tortuosi giri del pensiero ficiniano. Una cosa, comunque, pare certa, che Marsilio Ficino ha saputo immedesimarsi col suo interlocutore, individuarne le aspirazioni e i dubbi, e trovare una risposta filosoficamente adeguata agli interrogativi che egli si poneva. Sostenendo che la capacità di previsione umana

---

[1] Si consultino, per la rappresentazione della Fortuna nell'antichità, gli articoli Fortuna, Isis (Euploia, Pelagia, Pharis), Kairos, Tyche, ecc. in Roscher, *Ausführliches Lexikon der griechischen und römischen Mythologie*, e in Pauly-Wissowa, *Real-Encyclopädie*. Si veda anche Warburg, *Gesammelte Schriften*, I, p. 149, n. 2; Doren, "Fortuna im Mittelalter", pp. 73 s., 135, n. 130.

[2] Il Doren ("Fortuna im Mittelalter", pp. 79 ss.) reca un gran numero di testimonianze dell'impiego della imagine della ruota in testi letterari antichi, medioevali e rinascimentali, sia in latino che nelle varie lingue nazionali.

[3] Numerose testimonianze letterarie di tal genere ricorrono sia in testi classici (cfr. ad es. la voce 'Fortuna' nel *Thesaurus linguae latinae*, VI, Lipsia, 1912–26, coll. 1175–95) che in opere medioevali e rinascimentali. Citerò, fra le testimonianze più recenti, due esempi che mi sembrano particolarmente significativi. Il riminese Marco Battagli (*Marcha*, a cura di A. F. Massera, in *RR.II.SS.*, XVI, 3, Città di Castello, 1912–3, p. 47), a metà del secolo XIV, parlando di Francesco Ordelaffi, dice che fu il 'primus eorum magnatum qui vela fortune ventis libere relaxavit', esponendosi più volte, nei pericoli, 'fortune fluctibus tanquam navis'. Egli poi trae da ciò una conclusione che forse il Rucellai avrebbe sottoscritto, che cioè 'audaces fortuna iuvat, quoniam audaces motum fortune proprium consecuntur'. Francesco Filelfo, in una delle sue satire (*Satyrae*, Milano, 1476, f. 45r = VI, 4, 7–8), rivolgendosi nel 1433 a Cosimo de' Medici (e non al Rucellai, come erroneamente intende Mancini, *Alberti*, p. 419, n. 1) gli fa notare come, al momento della disgrazia, sia stato abbandonato da amici e parenti: 'Te cognati carique propinqui—gli dice—deseruere tui, fortune vela sequentes'. Cfr. Doren, "Fortuna im Mittelalter", pp. 132 ss.; Patch, *Goddess Fortuna*, pp. 101 ss.

[4] Cfr. Du Cange, *Glossarium mediae et infimae latinitatis*, III, Niort, 1884, pp. 574 ss.; A. Ernout-A. Meillet, *Dictionnaire étymologique de la langue latine*, I, Parigi 1951 (III ed.), p. 443; Battisti-Alessio, *Dizionario etimologico*, III, p. 1695; Warburg, *Gesammelte Schriften*, I, p. 148, n. 1 = *La Rinascita del paganesimo antico*, p. 235, n. 1; Patch, *Goddess Fortuna*, p. 107; Bec, *Marchands écrivains*, pp. 301–4; Wind, *Giorgione's Tempesta*, pp. 3, 20 n. 7, fig. 57.

poteva cospirare colla fortuna, perchè sia questa che quella traevano la loro origine da Dio che provvedeva al loro accordo finale, il Ficino è riuscito non solo a riconoscere nel Rucellai—che egli, con una certa compiacenza ed adulazione, discrimina dal 'misero volgo'—un uomo privilegiato, capace di cogliere, per la sua prudenza e saggezza, nelle vicende umane, l'accenno divino, e di conformare, pertanto, il proprio comportamento ai disegni voluti da Dio e attuati dalla fortuna, ma anche a dare, in qualche modo, una formulazione filosofica al primitivo sentimento religioso del Rucellai, il quale—com'è evidente dai due 'ricordi' del 1464 e del 1473—attribuiva, con antica fede popolare, alla grazia divina la concessione dei molteplici beni di cui aveva finora goduto.

L'immagine del Rucellai, che si ricava frammentariamente e per via indiretta da questa lettera, passa, ovviamente, attraverso il filtro dell'ottica ottimistica del Ficino, e andrà quindi accettata con qualche riserva. Il Ficino, rendendo merito al Rucellai di aver saputo, con saggezza e prudenza, dar prova di abile adattamento, ha sottolineato, involontariamente, uno degli aspetti—il conformismo—che più ci lasciano perplessi nella valutazione etico-politica di questa e di tante altre figure di rilievo della storia del Rinascimento. C'è infatti il fondato sospetto che parole come 'prudenza', 'saggezza', 'virtù' coprano, ottimisticamente, qualità non altrettanto nobili; e che la divina fortuna, con cui si deve fare 'o pace o triegua' 'conformando la propria volontà colla sua ... acciò ch'ella per forza non tiri' rischi, in definitiva, di identificarsi colla volontà del principe o del signore, col quale è giocoforza venire a patti, per trarne il maggiore profitto personale, come il Rucellai stesso, da un certo momento in poi, s'era sforzato di fare, rivelandosi, anche sotto questo aspetto, uomo del suo tempo.

BRENDA PREYER

THE RUCELLAI PALACE

THE RUCELLAI PALACE

I. INTRODUCTION

Giovanni Rucellai was one of many Florentines who, in the middle of the fifteenth century, constructed a new palace. He followed the normal pattern by building in the neighbourhood where his family was concentrated. Beginning with his father's residence, he gradually acquired property to incorporate into his new building, rather than buying a new site all at once. The restricted possibilities of this site had important consequences for the building as a whole. The palace was constructed not as one coherent project but rather in distinct phases as Giovanni first focused on the interior and then added a façade. Later, after acquiring one more house, he extended both façade and interior. This is why a detailed exploration of the interior of the Rucellai Palace is necessary for a balanced assessment of the building. The façade, though certain constraints were imposed on its design because it had to harmonize with the interior, is both superb in quality and a remarkable stylistic statement.

The palace stands on the corner of the via della Vigna Nuova and the via dei Palchetti (Pls. 4, 12, 24). Its façade covers the three houses that Giovanni owned on the via della Vigna, but breaks off abruptly at the right edge of his property. The façade was executed by leaving the street wall standing, and giving it a revetment of *pietra forte* masonry. The stones are set in courses of several different heights, with the blocks of the drafted masonry emphasized by vertical and horizontal channels. Played against the design of the masonry field is another system. A bench and accompanying back-rest (*spalliera*) form its base. The three main storeys, separated by entablatures with friezes, are divided into seven bays and part of an eighth by pilasters of three different orders. The whole façade is capped by a projecting stone cornice; above, and set back slightly, is a low row of colonnettes that opens the third-storey *altana*, visible only from a distance. The bays are equal in width, except that those with the doors are slightly wider. Centred within each bay are the windows. The ground floor has two sets—one small and inconspicuous, the other square and defined by projecting frames. On the upper storeys biforate windows with frames of drafted masonry fill the bays (Pl. 27). Each window is divided by a colonnette which, together with two pilasters on the inner façades of the frames, carries an architrave; above open two semi-circular lights and an oculus. In the spandrels are carved emblems of three interlinked diamond rings. On the frieze above the ground floor are alternating emblems—diamond rings with two feathers linked by looping ribbons to wreaths with three feathers. The diamond ring with two feathers and the three interlinked diamond rings, often considered Medicean, have frequently been used for dating the façade. Another emblem, a wind-filled sail, is repeated across the length of the second frieze. The emblems, which also appear in three places inside the palace, are discussed on pp. 198–201 below.

This study will concentrate on the construction and architectural character of the whole building, interior and exterior. It will follow a roughly chronological order by considering first the acquisition of the site, next the interior, then the façade. Finally, there will be an assessment of Giovanni as a builder[1].

[1] Most of the material presented here derives from my dissertation "Giovanni Rucellai and the Rucellai Palace" (Harvard University, 1976). The co-operation and hospitality of Count Bernardo Rucellai were indispensable for my investigations, and I acknowledge them with the greatest appreciation. Others whom I would like to thank for advice, suggestions and assistance are: James Ackerman, Beverly Brown, Howard Burns, Suzanne Butters, Harriet Caplow, John Coolidge, Gino Corti, Caroline Elam, Richard Goldthwaite, Margaret Haines, Rab Hatfield, F. W. Kent, Ulrich Middeldorf, Niccolò Rucellai, Howard Saalman, Piero Sanpaolesi, Beatrix Smith, Janet Smith, Peter M. Smith, Franklin Toker, Diane Zervas. The staffs of the Archivio di Stato and the Kunsthistorisches Institut in Florence were especially helpful. To the Art Department, University of Texas at Austin, I am grateful for assistance in preparing the manuscript.

II. THE ACQUISITION OF THE SITE

An understanding of how the pieces of land for the site were bought is vital for all aspects of the building. It is crucial for dating the façade, undoubtedly the most important architectural feature of the palace. The interior has its own intrinsic interest, representing the practical approach towards the design of living quarters found in all but the most extravagant Florentine palaces. When the original constituent houses are related to the interior, the plan is found to depend in major elements upon the walls that outlined them; this in turn has important implications for dating the façade.

Until recently, little had been done to clarify the acquisition of the site. The first to trace the process by systematic use of tax records was Charles Randall Mack[1]. A more comprehensive picture can be drawn if evidence from other sources is combined with that of the tax documents, and if the palace basement and previously unpublished plans are brought into the study[2]. Mack considered the façade a single project datable after 1461, but the information we now have regarding the site will lead to substantially different conclusions (below, pp. 179–84).

Of the several types of document to be used, the most important are the tax records, dependent on the initial *catasto* declarations of 1427[3], and revised with information about current holdings in 1431, 1433, 1442, 1447, 1451, 1458, 1469 and 1480. The value of this source for the study of housing, and of palace-building in particular, lies in the requirement that citizens list all their real estate, along with recent sales of property. Each piece was defined by its boundaries (*confini*), which could be streets or the property of neighbours. These are usually accurate for 1427, but later are less complete and often simply refer to a previous tax declaration. If a piece of property produced income, it was assigned a taxable valuation, derived by capitalizing its annual rent at seven per cent. The tax officials analysed the reports, and noted in the margins, with comments, transfers of property and valuations, referring to entries from other books. Because owner-occupied property was not taxed, these records unfortunately do not give the value of many important houses in the city.

Since the tax declarations often raise as many questions as they answer, a useful supplement is the notarized contract of sale, often providing more accurate boundaries and a summary of the important rooms and spaces of the building concerned. Another informative type of notarial document is the division, usually written for brothers, recording the break-up of an entire patrimony or the division of a family house into separate living quarters. These sources enable us to reconstruct a vivid picture of the process of acquiring a site.

In the *Zibaldone* Giovanni Rucellai states: 'From eight houses I made one . . . three were on the via della Vigna and five were behind'[4]. Of these eight houses, one was Giovanni's ancestral house. The other seven were bought in four stages: two early, before 1442, three in 1445–6, the remaining one on the via della Vigna in 1458, and the last house at the back, which was never incorporated into

---

[1] C. R. Mack, "The Rucellai Palace. Some new Proposals", *AB*, LVI (1974), pp. 517–29.

[2] I am most grateful to Count Bernardo Rucellai for making the plans available and to the Kunsthistorisches Institut in Florence for photographing them. The plans of the ground floor, mezzanines, first, second and third floors are a set and are dated ca. 1846 by a recent pencil note. The plan of the basement is dated 1968. The plans are inaccurate in certain particulars. In Pl. 6, the vaults between walls C and G are wrongly drawn. In Pl. 7 the wall on the via dei Palchetti should start perpendicular to the via della Vigna, and then turn east at a slight angle north of wall D; and the north-south wall north of the court is shown too thick. In Pl. 9, wall J is shown too thick south of the court, too thin south of the western gallery.

[3] For the *catasto* see D. Herlihy and C. Klapisch-Zuber, *Les Toscans et leurs familles. Une étude du catasto florentin de 1427*, Paris, 1978 (especially Part I, Chap. 2).

[4] ' .. d'otto chase n'ò fatto una, chè tre ne rispondevano nella via della Vingna e cinque di drieto' (Perosa, p. 121).

the palace by Giovanni, in 1467. The clearest way to discuss them will be in the order of their acquisition. (Here constant reference will be made to house numbers, as on Pl. 5.)

The house where Giovanni's father, Paolo di Messer Paolo Rucellai, had lived, and in which Giovanni and his brothers grew up (House 1) was on the corner of the via della Vigna Nuova and the via dei Palchetti (sometimes called the via degli Stamaiuoli in the documents). When Paolo died in 1406, leaving his nineteen-year-old wife Caterina with four small sons, an inventory of the estate was made, including a list by room of all the contents of the house[1]. The house itself had a *volta* (cellar), seven rooms, and some sort of loggia. The original building was not very large, and by the late 1420s the family had already begun their acquisition of neighbouring residences, although their first purchase was not initially used to increase their living space. In 1428 Giovanni and his brothers bought the house behind on the via dei Palchetti (House 2) for 220 florins from the heirs of Benedetto di Ser Francesco dell'Arte della Lana, who had to raise money to pay back their mother's dowry when she remarried[2]. This house had been described in 1427 as 'domus cum volta, lodia, cameris et salis', and valued at 157 florins[3]; so a good price was paid for it. Tax records through the year 1447 show that it continued to be valued at 157 florins, and that it was not occupied by the family, but rented out during this period[4].

By 1429 the family was renting the next house east on the via della Vigna (House 3), thus almost doubling their living space[5]. Giovanni's prospective marriage to Iacopa di Messer Palla Strozzi may have been a reason for the expansion into House 3. The distant cousins who owned this house moved two houses up the street to larger quarters (House 9)[6]. After the division of 1442 between the four Rucellai brothers, Giovanni and Filippo owned the family's main house (House 1) and the three younger brothers had equal shares in House 2 behind[7]; but by 1447 Giovanni had full possession of both houses, his brothers having moved away (Doc. IV). For House 3 the brothers had paid rent through 1433, but it was mentioned in 1442 among the goods that were understood by all the brothers to belong to their mother, Mona Caterina. In her tax report of 1442 she recorded that she had bought it from the heirs of the men who had previously owned it[8]. The opportunity to buy perhaps arose when one or more of the widows remarried, forcing the children to gather cash to repay the dowry[9]. Caterina listed the house in her 1451 tax report, but Giovanni and the neighbour on the east gave each other as *confini*, showing they understood the house to belong to Giovanni's property (Docs. V, VI)[10]. Houses 1 and 3 had been used jointly as early as 1429, and probably even after the 1442 division Giovanni and his mother continued to live in them together, regardless of

---

[1] ASF, Pupilli, 17, ff. 51r–53r.

[2] ASF, Pupilli, 46, f. 13r refers to the sale; I have not found the sale document itself.

[3] ASF, NA, C 189 (Ser Tommaso Carondini, 1425–27), f. 119v; Cat., 76, f. 290v.

[4] ASF, Cat., 367, f. 597r; 462, f. 514r; 620, f. 574r; 672, f. 535r.

[5] ASF, Cat., 367, f. 597r.

[6] A document of 1429 regarding the boundary between San Pancrazio and the remodelled house of Piero di Giovanni Rucellai and his brothers certainly refers to this house. See Dezzi Bardeschi, "Complesso monumentale", p. 41, n. 52.

[7] ASF, NA, B 1994 (Ser Matteo Boccianti), ff. 84r–92v; Cat., 620, f. 574r.

[8] ASF, Cat., 620, f. 302r.

[9] *Ibid.*, f. 541r. The documentary evidence is neither full nor clear. Antonio, Piero, and Paolo filed a tax return together in 1433, but all were dead by 1442 when the tax records were next revised (ASF, Cat., 462, ff. 30r–32v; 620, f. 541r–v). In that year Antonio's son Giovanni mentioned that real estate had been assigned to him by the courts in compensation for his mother's dowry; presumably she too was dead. He said nothing about when the litigation took place, nor did he refer to House 3; we do not know if he sold it to Caterina, or if the courts sold it in order to raise money for the other widows' dowries.

[10] See also ASF, Cat., 707, f. 424r.

legal ownership. The point is important, for House 3 is part of the new interior I believe Giovanni Rucellai to have constructed by 1452.

The remaining property on the via dei Palchetti to be used in the palace was bought in 1445 and 1446. First Giovanni acquired two small houses (4 and 5) separated from House 2 by one piece of land (Docs. I, II). The seller, Lionardo di Benedetto di Como, charged 80 florins for each house, forty florins more than he had paid for them. Lionardo had received one in 1433 as part of the dowry of his Rucellai wife (from a branch of the family only distantly related to Giovanni), had bought the other one from S. Maria Nuova, and had lived in both concurrently; but he sold them to Giovanni when he needed money to buy a large house on the via degli Orafi from another Rucellai[1]. With House 6, at least, Giovanni got a bargain. For in 1446 he made the unusual purchase (Doc. III) of the 'land only' between House 5 and House 2. The notarial record specifies that the vendor deliver the cleared site whenever Giovanni should ask for it. In 1431 the property had carried a value of 105 florins[2], admittedly a high figure for what must have been a very small house, but Giovanni managed to acquire the land with the house already razed for only thirty florins.

The documentation and circumstances concerning House 7, which Giovanni bought in 1458, are more complicated. The boundaries of this house, which I shall call 'Iacopo Antonio's house' are placed in all documents between Houses 3 and 9. In 1436 Iacopo Antonio di Bingeri Rucellai paid 425 florins for the house, on which he had had an option[3]. The house remained in Iacopo Antonio's name until his death in 1456, and was still in the possession of his young children in 1458, although rented out for 20½ florins a year, so that the tax valuation was only 292 florins[4]. When Giovanni Rucellai bought this house in 1458 he paid 1,000 florins, more than for all his other houses put together. Evidently this price was not consistent with its true value, though it was large and situated on the via della Vigna. The Pupilli officials, guardians of Iacopo Antonio's children, had a duty to get the best price possible. The estate had been depleted by the repayment of the widow Piccina's dowry, and the heirs were still looking for the money to cover a 600-florin business debt of their father to Giovanni's brother Filippo[5]. The document of sale explains that the house, rather than pieces of farmland, was being sold because the officials expected a better return on the rental of the land than of the house. They 'judged that [the house] would be bought by someone who would gain great convenience from it and for that convenience the buyer would not mind if he had to give 25 soldi per lira for it' (there being, of course, 20 soldi in a lira)[6]. The officials sold the house by a form of auction, advertised by the town criers. Somebody else offered 700 florins, but Giovanni's bid of 1,000 florins was clearly intended to top any other.

The eighth and last house at the back was acquired from the neighbouring monastery of S. Pancrazio in 1467, although Giovanni had already arranged to buy it in 1457[7]. The conditions of the

---

[1] ASF, Cat., 671, f. 389[r–v]; 707, f. 90[v].

[2] ASF, Cat., 367, f. 85[r].

[3] ASF, Cat., 620, f. 293[r].

[4] ASF, Cat., 816, f. 269[r].

[5] ASF, Pupilli, 76, f. 8[v].

[6] 'Arbitrorono [sic] gli ufficiali detti che ella si comperasse per chi ne potesse pigliare grande commodità, et a chagione di quella così facta commodità non churerebbe il compratore darne soldi venticinque per lira' (ASF, Diplomatico, Strozzi-Uguccione, 22 September–10 November 1458). A portion of this document, which gives all the background of the sale, is transcribed as Document XIII.

[7] 1467 is not a simple date of sale, for this house has a rather complex history. In 1425 San Pancrazio had sold it to Antonio *cimatore* for 150 florins *ad vitam*, with the understanding that it revert to the monastery upon the death of his last son (ASF, NA, C 189 [Ser Tommaso Carondini, 1425–27], ff. 34[r]–35[v]). In 1457 San Pancrazio made an agreement with Giovanni Rucellai to

sale were carefully designed to protect the monks' privacy: Giovanni was not to raise the walls or build anything above the existing chimneys, and he was not to make any new windows in the wall towards S. Pancrazio (Doc. IX). Giovanni did not in the end make use of this house for his palace[1], but terms of the 1457 contract imply that he was ready to do so. It may well be that he had decided to assure himself of the possibility of expanding in this direction should the negotiations for Iacopo Antonio's house fall through.

Before the relationship of all these houses to the present palace is explored, some general remarks may be made about the process of acquisition. Already in 1428 the family were thinking of expanding their own residence; with the purchase of House 3 they had a sizeable block of contiguous real estate. Soon after the division in 1442, Giovanni evidently persuaded his mother and brothers to give him control of this property, and he quickly seized the opportunity to buy the remaining houses on the via dei Palchetti. Though wealthy, Giovanni could not simply buy up at once an area on which to build his palace, and the process of assembling the site was a complicated one. There is, however, little evidence to confirm his statement in the *Zibaldone* that he had great difficulty in persuading the owners to sell[2]. Five of the six houses acquired were sold because their owners needed cash: three of those came from orphans, and two from a man who in any case was moving away. We can be certain that Giovanni exerted pressure only in the case of House 6, because of the location, and even then we do not know that the owner was unwilling to sell. I incline to the interpretation that Giovanni had to wait quietly for changes in his neighbours' circumstances before he could begin to discuss buying their houses. Equally, while the purchases were mostly from members of the Rucellai family or their relations by marriage, they do not reflect a co-operative effort on the part of the whole clan to facilitate Giovanni's acquisition of land. In each case there was a good reason for the sale, whether to repay a dowry, or to finance the purchase of a new house, or to cover a business debt, and Giovanni was obliged to pay a good, or even, as in the case of House 7, an exorbitant price.

Giovanni had to keep himself informed of neighbourhood gossip, in order to be ready at the right moment to 'help' others with the appropriate amount of cash. Presumably he also had to be on good terms with his neighbours and not antagonise them by seeming too anxious to move them out. In addition, there were several elements of luck involved in his successful assembling of the site. Most important was the fact that, as the eldest brother, he received the prime property on the corner. From here he could expand up the via della Vigna Nuova and the via dei Palchetti. There was probably little competition for the small houses on the via dei Palchetti, as there was no other ambitious landowner in Giovanni's part of the block. On the via della Vigna side the houses were larger and the owners more prominent. Not until Iacopo Antonio's death in 1456 could Giovanni contemplate the possibility of buying House 7, and as we shall see, this changed his plans for both interior and façade. With House 9 Giovanni abandoned the cautious and patient policy which had worked so well hitherto, and applied direct but unsuccessful pressure on its owner, Giovanni d'Antonio Rucellai (see below, p. 183). It is worthy of note that Giovanni di Paolo's designs on House 9 began by 1458 and continued throughout the 1460s, when he had not only vast economic power but the best

exchange the house for a furrier's shop owned by Giovanni in a different part of town (Doc. IX). The *baratto* could go into effect only after Cristofano d'Antonio's death in 1467, when Giovanni gained control of the house (ASF, Cat., 919, ff. 376^r, 307^v).

[1] It was long considered a unit separate from the palace, as in ASF, Cat., 919, f. 376^r; Decima repubblicana, 23, f. 335^r.

[2] '. . . e anchora [ò] soperito a chonperare e' siti da potere murare che mi sono chosti danari assai, perché m'è chonvenuto dare s. 30 per lira, oltre alla faticha del disporre i venditori a vendere (e quasi è stata chosa inpossibile) . . .' (Perosa, p. 121). Giovanni's unsuccessful attempt to buy House 9 perhaps coloured his recollections about all the other houses. See below, pp. 183–84.

political connections as well. That both were insufficient to sway Giovanni d'Antonio is proof that money and influence were not necessarily the only requirements for building a palace in Renaissance Florence.

To resolve the important question of how far the palace was built new from the foundations or created by remodelling the original houses, it is essential to identify as precisely as possible the boundaries of those houses. Here the plan of the present palace basement (Pl. 6) is of great use. The basements of Florentine houses large and small consisted of vaulted spaces with earth floors. They served both for storage, and to insulate the ground-floor from dampness and cold. In the Rucellai Palace there is a basement under the front rooms only, except for two narrow arms running north from the eastern portion. The variety of configurations and materials in the walls and vaults indicate that they were not built in a single project, but are survivals of the component houses brought together to form the present palace.

It can be shown that walls dividing the original houses were retained in the basement and used wherever feasible as bearing walls in the new palace. This helps to reconstruct the areas of the houses on the via della Vigna with a fair degree of probability. The three houses on the front referred to by Giovanni in the *Zibaldone* appear clearly on the basement plan, divided by walls C and B. Houses 1 and 3 originally had basements similar in plan, with an intermediate wall dividing each house from front to back. This wall survives entire in House 3, but in House 1 was partially demolished, while two square piers were inserted to the east of it to support a new wall (G). Plate 6 shows that these piers break through the groin vaults and are placed too close to the intermediate wall of House 1 to have been an integral part of the original construction. The boundary between Houses 1 and 2 may well coincide with wall D (Pl. 5), but the original configuration of House 2 and the northern termination of House 3 are difficult to determine. The evidence of the basement is no help for these or the other houses on the via dei Palchetti.

It seems likely that the original walls and the basement vaults of House 7 are preserved on the present plan (Pl. 6). The cellar here has a strange configuration, with two irregular arms on either side of a solid area, which probably corresponds to the court (*curia*) mentioned in the sale document. It was common practice to leave intact the ground beneath an open court, or even to fill it in during remodelling, so as to avoid the risk of seepage by rain water. The western boundary of House 7 is probably wall B, which corresponds above ground to the wall separating the fifth and sixth bays on the façade (Pls. 4, 5). After a jog to the west this wall continues north as wall F, which lies almost directly above the western side of the shorter basement arm. At the back, House 7 can be shown from *catasto* evidence to extend to the area of the present triangular court (once part of House 8: Pl. 5)[1].

The reconstruction of the area of House 7 will be of prime importance to the building history, for the interior of the entire palace can be understood as consisting of two sections divided by wall B–F (Pl. 5). This wall in fact must have formed the basis for partition of the palace between Giovanni's two sons in 1492 (Doc. XXI). Pandolfo, the older son, was assigned 'the large house, that is, court with loggia, stables, and cellar and whatsoever is built over it along its breadth and height'[2]. Bernardo got 'the small house, which was bought by the said late Giovanni their father from [the heirs

---

[1] The court is probably the one that was being built by Giulio Rucellai in 1743 (ASF, Notarile Moderno, 23966 [Ser Antonio Pratesi], ff. 71v–73r).

[2] 'Domum magnam videlicet curiam cum lodia et stabulis et volta et quicquid super inde hedificatum est per suam latitudinem et altitudinem' (Doc. XXI).

of?] Iacopo Antonio Rucellai'[1]. Bernardo received 750 florins from Pandolfo in compensation for his smaller share. In 1492 Iacopo Antonio's house could still be thought of as a separate structure, and as the document states, could be made entirely independent merely by closing up doors. Wall B–F is the one wall that could divide a large and small portion of the whole palace. All later inventories and descriptions support this interpretation of the size, location and integral survival of Iacopo Antonio's house. I believe that Giovanni Rucellai first built a palace interior bounded on the east by wall B–F, that a few years later he added a façade of five bays, and that he extended both the interior and the façade after the acquisition of House 7 in 1458.

There is no doubt that the interior of the fifteenth-century palace stopped on the east at wall A (Pl. 5), which is also the place where the façade's revetment breaks off. The house immediately east of the palace (House 9) was acquired as late as 1654 by Giovanni di Paolo di Giovanni Rucellai from a member of the della Rena family[2]. The implications of Giovanni's unsuccessful attempts to acquire House 9 are discussed below (pp. 183–84, 205–06).

Although the houses on the via della Vigna have the greatest importance because of their relationship to the façade, it is worth trying to reconstruct the houses on the via dei Palchetti side. Here the bearing walls do not all survive, and the documents must be interpreted without the aid of the basement plan. The one fixable point is House 8, bought from S. Pancrazio. Its northern wall must be wall I, as is made clear from the anxiety of the monks that they might be overlooked from the house (Pl. 12 shows the relationship of Giovanni's property to the monastery). Since Giovanni did not incorporate this house into his palace, the wall between it and House 4, which I take to be wall H, marks the northern boundary of the fifteenth-century palace, which has no obvious exterior termination on the via dei Palchetti. On the ground-floor plan (Pl. 5) a heavy and continuous wall (wall E) goes from the via dei Palchetti to beyond the north-east corner of the courtyard. This is probably the re-used dividing wall between Houses 4 and 5. The two small houses (5 and 6) can be taken to fall within the area of the present courtyard, their party wall therefore demolished. House 2 probably began as we have seen at wall D, though the original wall may not have been straight, and House 3 may have extended a little further into the area allocated to House 2 on Plate 5. We have no way of knowing if the northern boundary of House 2 coincides with wall J.

The evidence about the acquisition and location of the original houses gives several pointers to the date and planning of the palace. Most important is that the property over which Giovanni had gained control by 1446 was bounded on the north and east by wall H and wall B–F. Not until 1458 was he able to add Iacopo Antonio's house, going to wall A. Certain walls that belonged to the original houses were retained and used in the new palace interior (B–F, C, E, H). Wall G is the one major wall that was definitely built new; it forms the left side of the *androne* on the ground floor and of the *sala* on each of the upper storeys. Wall J is also likely to be new, while wall D remains a question. When Giovanni Rucellai built his palace by amalgamating and remodelling existing structures, he was following normal practice. Many Florentine palaces of the mid-fifteenth century incorporate old walls in their plans. This is especially evident in the *androni* of the Spinelli, Neroni-Gerini, Boni-Antinori, and Pazzi Palaces, while only the Medici and Pitti Palaces were built new from the foundations.

---

[1] 'Domum parvam, que empta fuit per dictum olim Johannem eorum patrem ab heredibus [?] Jacobi Antonii de Oricellariis' (Doc. XXI).

[2] ASF, Notarile Moderno, 23966 (Ser Antonio Pratesi), f. 63r (a reference only to the contract). In 1655 this Rucellai wrote, 'Ricordo come questo presente anno si fece la scala a chiocciola nella casa della Rena' (AR, XXXI, 4, f. 22v). On the first-floor landing of the spiral staircase is a corbel with the initials GR and the date 1655. The lateral passageway in the basement near the north of wall A was opened to House 7 after acquisition of House 9. It is a remnant of the original cellar of House 9 which was cut off from the front cellar area when the court above was constructed with the typical solid core.

III. THE INTERIOR

The interior arrangement of the fifteenth-century palace survives largely unchanged. This section explores the existing interior and reconstructs, where possible, the areas that have been remodelled. A rough date for the interior can be determined. It is important for dating the façade, because the relationship between the two projects shows that the interior was built before the façade. Also to be investigated are planning and the use of rooms.

The western part of the interior comprised Giovanni Rucellai's property before the purchase of Iacopo Antonio's house in 1458. It can be studied more fully than the addition, because more documents relate to it and because it contains most of the original architectural details. The history of ownership for both portions, summarized in the Appendix at the end of this chapter, is important for understanding the circumstances occasioning the documents, some of which are late. While the palace has always remained in the Rucellai family, divisions of the whole building, starting in 1492, have followed wall B–F (see above, pp. 160–61). The most important documents to be used in connexion with the interior are a division from 1531 of the larger portion, an inventory of this same part from 1548, and several notes referring to both parts of the palace in the late seventeenth and early eighteenth centuries.

a. DESCRIPTION AND RECONSTRUCTION OF THE LARGER PORTION

Giovanni's will of 1465 describes the palace only in general terms: 'Una domus magna cum lodia curia puteo ortulis voltis subtus et super terram stabulis coquinis salis cameris palcis veronibus et aliis pluribus edifitiis' (Doc. XVII). The first really helpful information about the interior is contained in the record of arbitration made for the division in 1531 of the larger portion between two pairs of Pandolfo di Giovanni's grandsons (Doc. XXII). The *confini* list Palla di Bernardo on the east (in the smaller portion) and on the north the house on the via dei Palchetti (8 on Pl. 5), owned by Pandolfo's line but not considered to belong to the palace itself. This confirms that the area being divided lay between walls H and B–F. In the absence of evidence to the contrary, the description contained in this document can be understood to reflect the fifteenth-century arrangement of the interior.

The first pair of brothers, Pandolfo and Giovanni, were given the ground-floor room between the *androne* and the street corner, a mezzanine room above it 'at the head of the first stair', and the entire first floor of the house (lines 37–44). They received in addition the western side of the third-floor terrace, and another room near it (lines 44–52), the western half of a ground-floor room 'which is used partly as a stable and partly to hold wood' (lines 52–59), and half the basement (lines 59–61). To the other pair of brothers, Filippo and Leonardo, was assigned all the rest of this portion; specifically mentioned are the large ground-floor room at the right of the *androne*, half the basement, half the stable, all the rooms above the *primo piano*, and the rest of the terrace (lines 65–76). The courtyard, *loggia*, well, entrances, and stairs were to be held in common.

Most of the rooms referred to are easily located on the plans (Pls. 7, 9–11). In 1531, as now, there were two main ground-floor rooms on the front of the palace, one on either side of the *androne*. The style of the corbels in the eastern room shows that its vaulting system belongs to the fifteenth century. The ground-floor room at the south-west corner retains major walls on the west, south, and east, but has undergone alterations in connexion with the staircase at the north. The room now has a high rounded ceiling, but there must once have been another level between it and the first floor.

The courtyard and its southern arm, the *loggia*, were not to be divided, but for the remaining area of the ground-floor mentioned in the document—a room used as a stable and for wood storage— two possible locations appear on the plan: along the eastern side of the court or north of the court between wall E and the via dei Palchetti house at wall H. The area not recorded in the document must have been open to the court in 1531. That originally the eastern arm of the court was not a separate space can be proved in conjunction with analysis of the courtyard and reconstruction of its original appearance.

The *loggia* is a large hall with vaults supported on three sides by corbels and on the north by a row of six columns. It stands as it did in the fifteenth century except that the last bay on the north-east has been closed by a wall. Originally, column 2 (Pls. 7, 13) was free-standing and carried an arch to the engaged column at wall F, leaving five arched openings. Some scholars have believed that wall K, running north from column 2, conceals a colonnade resembling that of the western arm[1]. But Count Bernardo Rucellai reports that probes made after World War I revealed no vestiges of columns; and Professor Sanpaolesi found a piece of evidence that refutes the notion that the court-yard turned here with a third arcaded arm: a portion of the lower string-course on the wall above the arches of the *loggia* continues behind wall K and re-emerges indoors on the southern wall of the mezzanine[2]. This surviving fragment from the original courtyard shows that the eastern vaults on both the ground-floor and the mezzanine are later additions, and that the open space of the court continued eastward at least to the end of the moulding, half way into the present vaulted area. The long vaulted spaces on the second floor and the mezzanine above it are not referred to in the 1531 document, and were built with wall K only around 1700 when this whole area was remodelled[3]. The fifteenth-century courtyard was open to wall F on the ground floor and probably had a canti-levered passage overhead, at the level of the first storey only. The western wall of this passage, sup-ported beneath by half-vaults rising from wall F, would have joined the *loggia* at the point where

---

[1] C. R. Mack, "The Rucellai Palace. Some new Proposals", *AB*, LVI (1974), pp. 524–5; in correspondence, Rudolf Wittkower hinted at the same idea.

[2] P. Sanpaolesi, "Precisazioni sul Palazzo Rucellai", *Palladio*, n.s. XIII (1963), p. 61. Professor Sanpaolesi did not indicate how much further east the courtyard originally extended.

[3] Document XXIV reflects a heated dispute about this wall, built by the owner of the larger part of the palace, against whose actions the owner of the smaller portion protested. Documents XXIV and XXV were written by a man who was responsible for the material constituting the bulk of the Rucellai Archives, but his identity is not precisely clear. He was either Abate Filippo (1661–1737) or his brother Francesco Maria di Giovanni di Paolo di Giovanni di Pandolfo (1666–1752; see Passerini, *Rucellai*, tav. XVII.) Possibly both brothers produced many documents. In any event, the Archivist, as we shall call him (or them), combed the public records for documents involving the Rucellai, making accurate notes. After years of research he knew so much about the history of his family that he was able to fabricate documents; among them is a series of letters purporting to be by Giovanni Rucellai, including the famous one to his mother about the dispatch to Jerusalem of a mission (with an engineer!) to measure the Holy Sepulchre. (Kent, "Letters", reaches conclusions similar to mine.) Other fanciful reconstructions of family history include a life of Bernardo "l'Istorico", and an inflated description of his famous marriage festivities (AR, XIX, 16). The Archivist's style usually makes his work easy to spot, but sometimes tantalizing statements require careful analysis to deter-mine whether their source is his imagination or his research. It should be noted that by the time he started his studies, the family archives were no richer in fifteenth-century material than they are today. In the volumes of the Archivist's work that I have seen there is no information that could not have been found in the public records or in other sources still now available to scholars. It is clear, furthermore, that the Archivist could not find many of the same documents which are known today only from references. But on the subject of the palace interior, the Archivist is a trustworthy, if sometimes confusing, source, as his description shows (Docs. XXVa and b).

the moulding now stops in the mezzanine. Arrangements similar to this are found in numerous Renaissance palaces in Florence.

Giovanni Rucellai's will indicated that the palace had *veroni* (covered spaces overlooking a court and open to it); the 1531 division mentions only one *verone*, without saying if it was east or west of the court. The eighteenth-century description confirms that there was a *verone* at the east of the court. The owner of the smaller part of the palace stated that a room on his first floor was 'opposite the kitchen of the palace, there being nothing [in between] but the wall [wall F] and the aforementioned *verone* of the first [larger] portion' (Doc. XXVb). In the Bartolini Palace the *verone* is very like the one here proposed for the Rucellai courtyard (Pl. 14).

The western arcade was built with the *loggia*, for the southern and western walls of the court are joined by binding masonry; also, the string-course just above the arcades is identical on both walls (Pl. 15), and the corbels of the western arm (except for one obvious replacement) are of the same style as those in the *loggia* (Pl. 17a–c)[1]. Above the western arcade there is one storey only. No document makes clear reference to this area, and it has been completely remodelled, leaving no evidence upon which to base a reconstruction of its original appearance.

On the north, wall E belongs to the original plan, and does not replace a colonnade, for the corbel set into the northwest corner of the courtyard (Pl. 17c) has not simply been cut in half by a new wall; rather, it is specially adapted to be centred on the corner, so that half of both lower leaves and almost the entire upper leaf are exposed. On none of the complete corbels in the courtyard or the *androne* are the leaves at the edges so complete. In the rooms behind there are no old vaults or architectural details to affect the conclusion that wall E always bounded the court. In this area north of the court, then, were the stable and wood store of the 1531 document.

The garden mentioned in the 1465 will was probably in the northern part of the courtyard, exposed to the southern sun, for the marginal notes for House 5 in the 1469 tax report say that this house was 'where the garden is' (Doc. XX). The stable behind could have been entered from the court's western arm, or directly from the via dei Palchetti. After Giovanni Rucellai's death, the garden must have been removed, as it is not mentioned in the 1531 division or in any of the later documents.

To summarize, the fifteenth-century courtyard was built in one project. On the ground-floor it followed the existing arrangement except on the east, where it was open to wall F. Here on the first floor, a narrow *verone* projected into the court. The superstructure on the west, north, and east terminated with the first floor, while only on the south above the *loggia* was it higher. The courtyard thus appeared considerably more open than it does today, and it would have received more light and air. Its rather irregular arrangement was not unusual for buildings of the period. In only the most extravagant palaces in Florence was a premium put on the creation of a courtyard with four arcades.

---

[1] One other factor, the column capitals, should not be used for argument. The capitals of the courtyard as a whole can be divided by style into three groups. Capitals 1, 3, 4, and 6, all on the *loggia* arcade (Pls. 15, 16a), are close in design and execution to the corbels and therefore are probably original. The *loggia*'s remaining columns (2 and 5) have capitals identical to the one on the northernmost column of the west arcade (9) (Pl. 16b, c). These capitals resemble the first group in some details, but they differ in overall design. The volutes in the second group push up from under a plate-like, protruding calathos instead of emerging from above and bending around a banded calathos. The peculiar prominence of the calathos is unusual for fifteenth-century capitals; all three capitals of the second group may be later replacements. Definitely later are capitals 7 and 8 (Pl. 13). Since the corbels within both arms exhibit a narrow range of style, one would expect the same consistency of the original capitals. Those of the first group are close in style to the corbels, and all capitals may once have resembled them. Bernhard Patzak noted the difference between the capitals of the *loggia* and the western arcade, stated that the latter capitals date from the sixteenth century, and concluded that the *loggia* originally stood alone (see his *Die Renaissance- und Barockvilla in Italien. Palast und Villa in Toscana*, Leipzig, 1912–13, II, pp. 36–37). He did not deal with the fact that capital 9 is identical with two capitals of the *loggia*, nor did he note that the corbels all the way round the southern and western arms of the courtyard belie the idea of a two-stage project.

Bernardo Rossellino's name has been mentioned in connexion with the courtyard, on the basis of Antonio Billi's attribution to him of the *modello* for the Rucellai Palace[1]. But the style of the architectural details has no parallel in Bernardo's work. Only four of the *loggia* capitals appear to be original (Pls. 15 and 16a; see p. 164, n. 1). The closest analogies to them are in the Cardini Chapel in S. Francesco at Pescia, dated 1451 and attributed to Andrea di Lazzaro Cavalcanti[2], where the capitals of the outer engaged columns are similar to those at the Rucellai *loggia* (Pl. 16d), both in proportions and in general design. There are certain differences: at Pescia the upper leaves do not grow from the base of the capitals, the button-flowers are larger, the volutes have no leaves and are divided at the corners of the capitals, and the calathos includes egg-and-dart mouldings (also present on most of the corbels in the Rucellai courtyard). At Pescia the carving of the leaves, especially of the serrated leaf edges, is crisper. Stegmann and Geymüller noted a similarity between the Pescia capitals and some at the Florentine Baptistery. The capitals of the Rucellai courtyard were executed by a group of stone-cutters who worked from a design close to Cavalcanti's; the designs at both projects were perhaps inspired by the capitals at the Baptistery. On the southern and western arms of the courtyard, the corbels are similar in style to the four original capitals, and though they are less uniform in design and execution, the two groups are clearly related (Pls. 16a, 17a–c). A characteristic of capitals and corbels is a fussiness of detail that is all the more apparent because of the crude carving. The quality of some of the corbels is not good, especially where the veins of the leaves degenerate into mere vertical channels.

Documentary evidence accords with general stylistic characteristics to give a date early in the 1450s for the courtyard. The houses on the via dei Palchetti were still intact in 1447, but by 1451 work had begun, as is indicated by the marginal notes to Giovanni Rucellai's tax report. The officials made an incomplete list of the houses that had been taken off the tax rolls and incorporated into Giovanni's new house, and they added above: "We have sworn testimony from Nofrio di Biagio, building master, who says he tore them down" (Doc. VI). The list includes House 2, approximately where the new *loggia* was built (Pl. 5). It was finished by 1452, when the painters Apollonio di Giovanni and Marco del Buono painted 'a tondo in the ceiling of the loggia' (Doc. VII). The reference could only be to the *loggia* of the palace, since the Rucellai Loggia across the street was built in the 1460s[3]. There is in fact a terracotta *tondo* about five feet in diameter in the centre of the vault of the *loggia* (Pls. 15, 17d). It shows within an enclosing garland an emblematic display; one of the emblems, three interlinked diamond rings, is usually associated with the Medici. As a consequence one might think that this *tondo* is a replacement made only after the 1461 betrothal, but there are reasons for identifying the *tondo* with the one mentioned in the document[4]. Too little comparative material exists to date it by style, but the price of nine florins provides a clue, as it is very high, either for the detailed painting of this object or for an entirely different fresco *tondo*. The price can be compared to the 4½ florins (20 lire) paid by Giovanni Rucellai to Neri di Bicci for a job that would appear from the

---

[1] C. von Stegmann and H. von Geymüller, *Die Architektur der Renaissance in Toscana*, Munich, 1885–1907, III, "L. B. Alberti", p. 9.

[2] Stegmann and Geymüller, *Architektur*, III, "Andrea di Lazzaro Cavalcanti", p. 2. See for the chapel and its patrons: *La chiesa di S. Francesco*, Pescia, 1930, pp. 27–30; the date of the chapel comes from an inscription, but the fresco on the back wall was painted by Neri di Bicci only in 1458: G. C. Lensi Cardini, *Storia della famiglia. Appendice*, Florence, 1973, p. 148.

[3] See my article in *MKHIF*, XXI (1977), pp. 187–8.

[4] The other candidate, the stone *tondo* with heraldic display of Rucellai arms and Fortuna, is not on the ceiling of the *loggia*, but on its wall facing the court. Ellen Callmann did not know the terracotta *tondo*, and speculated that Apollonio's work might be identifiable with the *altana* frescoes, which were not accessible to her (*Apollonio di Giovanni*, Oxford, 1974, p. 35). See the Appendix at the end of chap. IV (pp. 198–201 below) for arguments against a Medicean significance for the emblems.

verbal description to have been larger[1]. The document regarding the *tondo* is Carlo Strozzi's version from the lost Bottega Book, and Strozzi probably made only a summary of the original entry. Therefore, though the document mentions only painting in connexion with Giovanni Rucellai's *tondo*, there is the strong possibility that the payment covered other work as well. Nine florins would be a reasonable price for manufacture and installation, in addition to the colouring, of the existing *tondo*. The document thus gives a date of 1452 at the latest not only for the terracotta *tondo*, but for the *loggia* with its columns, corbels, and vaults, as well as for the rest of the courtyard.

The *androne* [16], the long narrow entrance-way linking the façade portal with the *loggia*, was built at the same time or shortly after, as can be shown by the style of its corbels and by consideration of its placement. Its ceiling reaches almost as high as the *loggia*, but a door divides it into two separately vaulted spaces, and its awkward proportions are masked (Pls. 7, 18a and d). Its corbels (Pl. 18b and c) are an entirely different group from those of the court. No two are identical, for palmettes, decorative volutes, wings, shells, and wreaths are sprinkled over them and combined with mouldings, leaves, and bases of various types. The style is derived from the ornate capitals of the Rossellino and Michelozzo workshops, as on the S. Egidio tabernacle and the portal of S. Agostino at Montepulciano, both of about 1450. Although the *androne* corbels are different in design from the capitals and corbels of the court, the execution of the two groups is not dissimilar. The leaves of the *androne* corbels are even more fleshy and inarticulate, perhaps because of their slightly smaller scale; the abacus in both groups is the same, as is the handling of the egg- and-dart moulding (when it appears). Finally, the volutes have similar springiness. Certainly a number of stone-carvers must have been working on the court and *androne*; but for both areas the same designer set up the patterns. There is one set of corbels in Florence close in style to those with fluted fields in the Rucellai *androne* (Pl. 18a and d). They are in the Spinelli Cloister at S. Croce, datable about 1452[2]. Possibly all these details were produced by the same workshop; in any case, the Spinelli examples substantiate a date in the early 1450s for the Rucellai *androne*[3].

Analysis of the palace basement showed that the foundation piers of wall G intrude into the original configuration of House 1; wall G was therefore built to form the west wall of the new *androne*. Its precise placement must have been dictated by the desire to centre the *androne* with the *loggia*. Because the plan of the *loggia* is slightly irregular, the columns are displaced to the east in relationship to the corbels; the *androne*, like the *tondo* in the ceiling, is centred with neither the corbels nor the columns, but opens at an intermediate point. Despite the limitations presented by the existing wall C, the two spaces were evidently carefully coordinated.

The ground-floor room between the *androne* and the *loggia* on the south-west corner of the palace has been rebuilt since the fifteenth century. The 1531 document clearly indicates that above this room there was a mezzanine level, no trace of which survives. Further stipulations in the document will help in reconstructing the staircase and the rooms related to it built by Giovanni Rucellai.

---

[1] In 1455 Neri di Bicci painted in Giovanni's house 'five arches of imitation stone, and a coat-of-arms in relief with a helmet, and two half-figures [of] a woman and a boy in fresco' (Doc. VIII). This notice is sometimes used to show that the palace interior in general was ready for decoration by 1455, but it is better interpreted to refer only to the courtyard. The 'coat-of-arms in relief with a helmet' is very probably the stone *tondo* on the northern wall of the *loggia* (Pl. 15). The five painted arches may have decorated the half-vaults supporting the destroyed *verone*; the half-figures are lost. See also below, p. 201, n. 4.

[2] H. Saalman, "Tommaso Spinelli, Michelozzo, Manetti, and Rossellino", *JSAH*, XXV (1966), p. 152.

[3] According to Mack, '[since] Bernardo [Rossellino's] role in designing the interior of the Rucellai Palace is uncontested, the design of these corbels supports his authorship of the cloister' ("Rucellai Palace", p. 524). I think that the evidence is too weak for a firm attribution of either project to Rossellino.

The present staircase is the second remodelling, perhaps of the late eighteenth century. Occupying the whole area between walls D and G, it turns in three wide, gentle ramps and reflects a fashion in stairs which developed in the sixteenth century[1]. In contrast, fifteenth-century planners thought in purely functional terms, and their staircases were unobtrusive and as compact as possible—narrow and steep. Most surviving staircases from Florentine palaces of this period have for each storey two equal ramps, one doubled back on the other[2].

The staircase in the palace encloses remains of an earlier one, which for convenience can be called the 'hidden' staircase. Its surviving portion, located between the long ramps of the present staircase, consists of most of the first ramp up from the first floor; a modified second ramp continues to the second floor (Pl. 19a)[3]. Stylistic and documentary evidence rules out the possibility that the hidden staircase is the original one. It disrupts the south-west corner of the palace with an inefficiency uncharacteristic of the fifteenth century. Nor does it fit the description in the 1531 division: the first pair of brothers was assigned a *scriptoio* 'at the head of the first stairs and above the ground-floor room' listed separately from the *sala principale* and the other rooms on the first floor (lines 39–41). The *scriptoio* must have been located between the ground and first floors, but the hidden staircase leaves too little space for a room at a mezzanine level; further, stipulations made in the document regarding access to the staircase cannot be correlated with the hidden staircase. The passage is made less confusing by the addition of numbers for the three doors in question:

> . . . we wish that at the top of the stairs, that is, to the left of the door [1] going into the *sala* assigned to Pandolfo and Giovanni, be made a doorway [2] which will be used by Filippo and Lionardo to go upstairs; and that the door [3] which was used previously to go upstairs, which is next to the *sala*, be bolted on both sides; now in order that the wooden wings of the door [1] of Pandolfo and Giovanni's *sala* not block the new doorway [2] we wish that the first door be partially closed off.

On the second floor similar changes were to be made (lines 102–120; see Pl. 19b).

The passage implies that there was no landing on either storey between the top of the stairs and the door leading into the *sala*. In order to separate the two households effectively, a change was needed to allow the second pair of brothers to go from the ground floor to their own quarters on the second floor without passing through the first floor *sala*. Now the hidden staircase is not the one referred to in the document, since it was placed within a hallway that made it a closed unit of circulation (Pl. 19a); one would not need to enter the *sala* on the first floor in order to reach the second floor. Furthermore, nowhere 'to the left' (i.e. north) of any conceivable door along wall G could a second door have been located to facilitate access to the upper floor. Finally, the hidden stair would have allowed little space for the room on the mezzanine level mentioned in the document.

---

[1] See, for interesting comments about staircases, P. Frankl, *Principles of Architectural History* (tr. and ed. J. F. O'Gorman), Cambridge, Mass., 1968, pp. 80–83.

[2] There are fifteenth-century staircases of this type in Florence at the da Uzzano-Capponi, Antinori, Ricasoli, Strozzi, Corsi-Horne, and Gondi Palaces; most early sixteenth-century examples have a similar configuration (Serristori, Ridolfi); the seventeenth-century plans of the Medici Palace show that it too originally had a small two-ramp staircase. (See W. A. Bulst, "Die ursprüngliche innere Aufteilung des Palazzo Medici in Florenz", *MKHIF*, XIV [1970], pp. 372–3, Figs. 3–4.) Howard Saalman's reconstruction of the Pazzi Palace staircase follows the type ("The Authorship of the Pazzi Palace", *AB*, XLVI [1964], p. 393, n. 32). The Spinelli Palace has an exceptional fifteenth-century stair system. The normal parallel ramps with a common wall rise to the first floor, and open on a broad landing overlooking the court. The stairs up to the second floor start at the back of this landing and have first a short ramp and then a long one set at a right angle to it. This irregular arrangement allows the *sala* on the first floor to be large, by keeping the stairs from cutting into it.

[3] On the first floor the landing of the hidden staircase is still partially visible.

The inventory of 1548 indicates that this room, and those above it, were not mere closets but well-furnished living spaces.

Plate 19b is a reconstruction of the first Rucellai staircase, in a plan that conforms with both fifteenth-century practice and the 1531 description. The two equal ramps are set parallel to the bearing wall D and run east-west. The height (19 cm.) and depth (29 cm.) of the individual steps were dictated by the space available; they are not out of line with early staircases from other palaces[1]. This arrangement of the staircase is the only one that can incorporate the several exits mentioned in the 1531 division. The second ramp opens directly into the *sala* [1], a narrow doorway [2] could have been cut into the wall separating the ramps, and the far wing of the first door could be kept closed so it would not block the new doorway. The third door must have been just to the north and still in the *sala*. The staircase in the sixteenth-century Ridolfi Palace at via Maggio 7 has undergone the same kind of alteration, notably the cutting of a second door through the wall between the two ramps, and the closing of a third door.

The staircase as reconstructed would have had one ramp down to the basement and two ramps per storey from the ground-floor up to the third floor. The plan leaves space at the front of the palace, between the via dei Palchetti and wall G, for a room at the top of the first ramp to be entered from the landing, and another above it, entered from the *sala*. Each room would have had a ceiling about three metres high, low by fifteenth-century standards but not disproportionate with the size of the rooms. These rooms, and two more above them, appear in the 1548 inventory. The inventory does not list a third mezzanine room between the second storey and the terrace. Part of this area is still visible, and the original ceiling beams with their consoles are large in scale, confirming that they were built for a high room. All these rooms took advantage of the desirable space on the front corner, an area that a fifteenth-century planner would not have sacrificed to circulation. The same sort of mezzanine room above the ground-floor is found in the Spinelli and Antinori Palaces as well as in recent reconstructions of the Medici and Pazzi Palaces. The Rucellai staircase was unusual for the period only in the fact that it did not lead into a hall outside the *sale* on the main floors. This must have been the feature which led a later owner of the palace to rebuild the whole area.

Evidence from the basement shows that the staircase was planned with wall G, for the new pier on the north is connected by binding masonry to an arch that runs to an engaged pier in wall D. This arch re-inforced the foundations of wall G to support the staircase. The staircase, at least up to the first floor, was thus part of the same phase of construction as the *androne* and *loggia*; probably it was built all the way up to the third floor at this time[2].

Though the interior of the original palace was for the most part, I believe, built in a single campaign before the façade, Giovanni Rucellai may later have remodelled some areas. The two important

---

[1] Spinelli H. 17.5, D. 27.5; Antinori H. 17, D. 33.5; Strozzi H. 18, D. 38. (Measurements of depth are given without the overhanging lip.)

[2] The reconstruction of the staircase is neat, but perhaps too neat. A large problem is raised by the fact that the floor of the second mezzanine would have hit the façade at a point beneath the architraves of two first-floor windows (see Pl. 20). The façade was built later than most of the interior, and one explanation for the discrepancy might be that the mezzanine room too already existed, and that the façade design could not be adjusted to it. But the evidence is too tenuous to be used for argument. It is worth speculating if there might be connexions between three disconcerting aspects of the reconstruction: the relatively low ceiling of the corner room on the first floor, the disjunction of façade and interior in the room above, and the absence of a third mezzanine above the second floor. Neither the hidden staircase nor any alternative reconstruction that I can devise accords with the information in the documents while allowing for (a) a higher ceiling for the first floor room, (b) a mezzanine above that consequently had a higher floor coinciding with the window architraves, (c) a room beneath the *altana* with a floor a good bit higher than that of the other rooms on the second storey, but accessible from them.

remaining sets of architectural details appear to be later than those already investigated, though the rooms they decorate are bounded by walls preserved from the original houses and by walls whose positions were established by the *loggia* and *androne*.

All or most of the original House 3 is replaced by the *camera terrena grande* [10]. Its side walls (B and C) follow the lines of the walls between Houses 1, 3, and 7. On the north wall D may be an old wall, but if not, it was built with the *loggia*. The vaulting system (with corbels) ends on the south 1.35 metres short of the façade wall, and the central corbel meets a broad spur, a remnant of a dividing wall for which foundations survive between walls B and C (Pls. 6, 21a). The arrangement is clumsy, but it certainly dates from the fifteenth century. The area between corbels and façade forms two low storage rooms [11] lit by the lowest façade windows; above, the square windows light the main room[1]. The walls of the room must have been built by 1452, but there is some question whether it was vaulted then, for its corbels are very different from those in the *androne* and the courtyard, as well as from any details on the façade (Pl. 21b). All nearly identical, they are not made of *pietra serena* but of a dark brown, finely grained stone. In design they are no more evolved than those of the *androne* (Pl. 18c), but their refined execution places them far from the workshop that carved the details of the *androne* and courtyard. In contrast to the flaccid treatment of all the other corbels, these are so crisply and precisely carved that they can almost be called dry. They resemble in design and proportions corbels in the Spinelli Palace, datable soon after 1458[2], although certainly the two sets were executed by different hands (Pl. 21c). The Spinelli corbels are more lively, both in the elaboration of the central stalk and in the quality of the carving. The Rucellai corbels seem rather frozen in comparison, with their flatter forms and careful separation of leaves from volute-stalks, and they look like a refined later version of the Spinelli type; consequently the vaulting of this room could date from about 1460. A possible explanation for the late corbels and the peculiar plan is that the room may have been redone only after the façade had been built.

On the first floor, the *sala principale* [19] covers the combined areas of the *androne* and the *camera terrena grande*, and is the largest room on the floor, with three windows on the façade. Its ceiling has five large beams placed parallel to the façade and resting on elaborately carved wooden consoles. The rest of the structural system, reflected in the second floor *sala* (Pl. 22a), was plastered over to accommodate the present painted decoration (probably late eighteenth-century). The consoles are of the highest quality (Pls. 22b, c; 23a, b). Their function as supporting elements is expressed by the elegant curve of the volute, pressing against the wall but yielding slightly under the weight of the beam. The large acanthus leaf sweeps up under the volute to soften and elaborate its surface. The consoles are identical in handling, although among the ten there are three different designs[3].

Nothing from mid-fifteenth-century Florence in carved wood approaches the quality of these consoles, except perhaps the doors of the Pazzi Chapel, surely by Giuliano da Maiano. Although Giovanni Rucellai's *Zibaldone* mentions that there were works by Giuliano in the palace[4], I hesitate to attribute to him the Rucellai consoles, because nowhere in his oeuvre is there found the same virtuoso naturalism in the handling of sculptural form. In the Antinori Palace (usually

---

[1] An arrangement similar to this, but without the lowest windows, is found at the Strozzi Palace, in the ground-floor rooms on either side of the north entrance.

[2] Saalman, "Tommaso Spinelli", pp. 160–4.

[3] Professor Otello Caprara suggests that originally the consoles would have been left unpainted, and that the natural wood would have been selectively highlighted with gold (*lumeggiato*).

[4] Perosa, p. 24.

attributed to Giuliano) there are consoles which seem directly related to those at the Rucellai Palace[1]. Some have almost identical structures and analogies in details (Pls. 22b, 23c); others use the same method for articulating the veins (Pl. 23b and d). However, all the Antinori consoles are much cruder than those at the Rucellai Palace, where the artist reveals great sophistication and sureness of hand. The differences between the two sets are entirely a question of quality. In the consoles of the Rucellai *sala*, unlike the corbels of the room just below, the forms are refined, but also very alive. There is no indication that they represent a drier version of something that had been done before. For this reason, the Rucellai consoles are likely to be the models for those at the Antinori Palace, rather than the reverse. The building history of the Antinori Palace is still unclear, but its consoles probably date from 1465–1470. The building history of the Rucellai Palace would suggest that its consoles are earlier. They also have stylistic characteristics in common with the first-storey capitals of the façade; particularly noticeable in examples from both groups is the treatment of the veins of the leaves as broad rounded troughs. The consoles are finer than the capitals, but they may have been designed at the same time (about 1455). The consoles perhaps in fact do not belong to the original structure of the ceiling. The north and south beams are narrower than the rest because they are partly embedded in the walls. The corner consoles were not specially adapted to these beams, but were just shaved off, or left unfinished, on the side towards the wall (Pls. 20, 23a)[2]. This suggests that the beams and consoles were not produced together, and that the consoles were inserted some time after the ceiling structure was up. If so, the room could have been built with the rest of the house and more elaborately decorated later.

The areas dealt with so far involve the greatest number of problems and yield the richest material for understanding the interior. Most of the remaining rooms in the larger part of the palace still follow the original plan, but have been extensively remodelled. For example, doors and windows, which might have given some indication of articulation and of circulation patterns, have been moved or stripped of their old frames. North of the *sala* the area above the *loggia* is divided in half by a thin wall to form two rooms overlooking the court [4–7]. The ceilings in both, as in several rooms in the smaller part of the palace, were given false vaults of cane mesh and were frescoed in the eighteenth century, so that the original beams are not visible[3]; the slightly different heights of the two ceilings, echoed in the floor-levels of the rooms above, indicate that the dividing wall is original. The western gallery and the remodelled *verone* [5?, 20], neither in its original form, flank the courtyard and connect the front rooms with the service area in the back.

The plan of the second floor, in the major bearing walls, follows that of the first (Pl. 10). The northern wing and the western gallery, and originally the *verone* on the east as well, were not carried up, but otherwise the differences consist only in a greater number of minor walls. The old beamed ceilings are still visible in the *sala* [25] (Pl. 22a), the Archive [27], and the rooms directly south of the court [26, 28]. Spanning the narrower dimension of each room, they probably reflect the original systems of the corresponding first-floor rooms, since in the *sale* of both storeys the beams follow one pattern. As was standard practice for the floor above the *piano nobile*, the consoles are simple.

The nineteenth-century plan shows the essential structure of the third floor, though it has been

---

[1] For general treatments of the palace see M. Trionfi Honorati, "Il palazzo degli Antinori", *Antichità viva*, VII (1968), pp. 65–80; and L. Ginori Lisci, *I palazzi di Firenze*, Florence, 1972, I, pp. 241–8.

[2] This is common in fifteenth-century buildings.

[3] Documents for the frescoes were found by Ginori Lisci (*Palazzi*, I, pp. 215–16 and n. 13); see also G. Ewald, "Some unpublished Works by Giovan Domenico Ferretti", *Apollo*, LXXXVIII (1968), p. 281.

remodelled twice subsequently (Pl. 11). Wall B, wall D, and parts of wall G go up through this storey. The frescoes discussed by Professor Salvini (below, pp. 241–52) were painted in the front room, the *altana*, on the thin wall running east-west between the façade wall and wall D. Toward the street the space is opened by colonnettes with crude Ionic capitals that are in no way related to the fine work on the façade. The *altana* columns are evenly spaced and on a building of five equal bays would have lined up perfectly with the rest of the façade, two to a bay; but because of the wider central bay on the façade revetment, they move gradually out of phase (in relationship to the façade) to either side of centre. From the *altana* some steps lead up to a narrow terrace resting on the exterior cornice. The third floor is thus sunk behind the cornice, which was used to hide the *altana* and keep it from interfering visually with the façade. Giovanni Rucellai's *altana* with colonnettes is one of the earliest surviving in Florentine palaces; it was a form that became very popular, particularly on buildings with *intonaco* façades (Gianfigliazzi, Canacci and Buondelmonti Palaces), where, however, the columns are larger and placed only one to a bay. I think it possible that the façade Giovanni originally envisioned for his palace was of this more modest type, perhaps decorated with *sgraffiti*.

b. THE INVENTORY OF 1548

Few physical alterations seem to have been made in the palace for at least a century after it was built. We have no direct information about living patterns during Giovanni Rucellai's lifetime; but it is unlikely that they altered radically in old buildings where, as with the Rucellai, the occupants were not leaders of the changing Florentine society. A rather late document about the larger part of the palace provides useful information, much of which can be projected back to the fifteenth century.

The sons of Paolo di Pandolfo di Giovanni and his wife Lorenza, in pairs, had divided this portion in 1531, but in 1542 one of them, Pandolfo, had reunited it by purchasing the other share. He died later that year, and in 1548 an inventory was made by the Pupilli officials who took charge of the estate for the heirs after the death of Lorenza, their grandmother and guardian. The inventory[1] does not give the boundaries of the 'casa grande de' Rucellai', but since Iacopo Antonio's house was still owned by Bernardo's line, the area covered extended only to wall B–F. The northern boundary was wall H[2]. The officials began on the first floor [rooms 1–7 on the plans], then went to the basement [8], to the *loggia* and through the entire ground-floor [9–16]; next they proceeded to the mezzanine [17–18], completed the first floor [19–23], continued to the second mezzanine [24] and the second floor [25–28], and ended with the third floor and its terrace [29–33]. The following discussion will change this route slightly, so as to start from the basement and to consider the entire first floor as a unit[3]. Except where the furniture was built-in, the items listed in the inventory are probably not the same as were in the palace in the fifteenth century; but new pieces are likely to have followed in type the early furnishings in each room.

---

[1] ASF, Pupilli del Principato, 2649, no. 63. It does not seem useful to publish this document, which is 45 sides long; the spaces mentioned have been added to the plans and keyed to them with numbers. Another inventory was made when Pandolfo died in 1542, but its listing of rooms is too incomplete to be helpful (ASF, NA, C 393 [Ser Domenico Cennini, 1541–49], ff. 53ᵛ–54ᵛ).

[2] House 8 on the via dei Palchetti had belonged to Lorenza, but she had willed it to a daughter (*ibid.*, f. 204ᵛ).

[3] Two studies were particularly helpful for this inventory: Bulst, "Palazzo Medici", and A. Schiaparelli, *La casa fiorentina e i suoi arredi nei secoli XIV e XV*, Florence, 1908.

The basement (*volta*) [8] was treated as a unit and the contents listed show that it was used primarily for storage of wine casks. On the ground-floor, the officials went first into the *loggia*, where benches were attached to the wall and there were two tables. The *camera terrena grande* had two pairs of chests and a round table, but little other furniture. Access in 1531 was from the *loggia*, so the room is likely to have been a supplementary living space, used primarily during the hot summer months. Attached to it was a *scriptoio* [11] which must be the space between the façade and the southern wall of the main room; the furniture listed in the inventory—three chairs, a bench and a small bed—must simply have been stored here, because the area is very small. Through the thick spur wall is cut an opening not shown on the plans; it may have been there in 1548, since the inventory mentions only one minor space.

The officials next went to the courtyard, with its well [12], and then to the stable and adjoining chicken coop [13–14], a conversion of the wood-storage area of the 1531 document. The *camera terrena in su la via overo granaio* [15] is the remaining room, in the south-west corner. Neither granary nor chicken coop was mentioned in Giovanni Rucellai's will, and during his lifetime it is unlikely that the spaces were so used. Finally, the *andito* is the *androne* [16]. The 1548 inventory thus correlates well enough with what can be seen from the plans and conjectured from other documents. As in 1531, the eastern area adjoining the court was not yet a separate space.

After finishing the ground-floor the officials went upstairs, stopping on the mezzanine level at the *camera a meza schala overo scriptoio* [17]. In it were a bed and flanking tables and a number of smaller items. Listed as attached to this room is a smaller one [18] in which the officials found no furniture.

On the first floor the inventory lists four major rooms: *sala principale* [19], *camera in su la sala grande di verso la via* [1], *camera principale in su la sala* [4], *anticamera allato alla sudetta camera* [6]. These rooms must be between façade and court: the *sala principale* is the largest, the room 'towards the street' is the destroyed one on the corner, and the remaining two are those directly south of the court. As a block they formed the family's main living quarters. Auxiliary spaces [2–3, 7] clearly associated verbally with three of these rooms cannot be found on the plans. They were probably small closet-like areas added after the palace was built and later removed. They may have resembled the minor spaces, all part of the original structure, next to the *camera terrena grande*, and in two rooms in the smaller portion of the palace (see below, pp. 176–77).

The *camera in su la sala grande di verso la via* [1] was filled with furniture, much of it elegant[1], arranged in a logical manner round the bed and near the door, and there were many works of art. All contents of the chests were listed, so that the inventory of the *camera* with its *cameretta* and *scriptoio* fills a full twelve sides of the total forty-five. The room must have been an important living space and a pleasant one, as it was on the sunny front corner of the palace.

The *camera principale in su la sala* [4] is one of the two rooms south of the court, the other being the *anticamera allato alla sudetta camera* [6]. The *camera principale* contained fewer pieces of furniture than the corner room, but they were probably the prize items in the house[2]. In this room were the personal belongings of Lorenza; its designation as *camera principale* suggests that it was the quarters

---

[1] 'Uno quadro di noce intarsiato con otto cassette, uno forziere alla viniziana acanto al'uscio di decta camera, uno altro forziere simile acanto al decto, uno lettuccio di noce con panchetta et spalliera et quattro pivioli et con suo cassino, uno cassone a sepoltura di noce intarsiato, uno altro cassone simile, uno letto semplice, dua paia di casse di noce intarsiate a quattro serrami intorno al decto letto, una guardaroba di noce con tre cassette et suo armarino'. No valuations are given in the inventory.

[2] 'Uno letto et lettuccio grande con la spalliera apichati insieme con panchette atorno, tutte di noce alla antica intarsiate; uno paio di cassoni alla antica grandi dipinti et dorati, con spalliera di tela dipinta a verzura et cornice et base dipinte et messe a oro, col'arme de' Rucellai et Ginori'. The late Lorenza was a Ginori.

of the head-of-household. In the *anticamera* were a *lettuccio*, a bed, and two pairs of chests[1], as well as a fireplace. The fireplace still in wall D in the eastern room identifies this as the *anticamera* and the room next to it as the *camera principale*. In both rooms were many paintings and a few pieces of sculpture.

Eight sides of the inventory were devoted to the *camera principale* with its *cameretta*, four sides to the *anticamera* and *soffitta acanto*, but only one to the *sala principale* [19]. Unlike the other three rooms it had no bed or chests filled with personal items, and it was evidently a rather formal room. It had a fireplace, benches attached to the wall, thirteen chairs, and a table six *braccia* long. The *sala* was fitted out with a basin set into the wall (*aquaio*), and, in 1548 at least, had birds in three cages. The inference from the 1531 document that the stairs opened directly into the *sala* is confirmed by the reference within the *sala* to an *armario acanto al' uscio si va su*; the door to a stairway leading only upward implies that there was a second door opening on a stairway going down.

From the *sala principale* the officials went to the *andito si va in cucina* [20], which must be the *verone* east of the court, attested in documents both earlier and later than 1548[2]. Although the western gallery is not clearly referred to, the inventory is so complete that this must be the *cameretta* [5] of the *camera principale*.

The remainder of the first floor is listed as the kitchen area: the *cucina* itself, and the *soffitta* and *cameretta di decta soffitta o camera* [21–23] connected with it. This block of rooms occupied the area between wall E and wall H. The whole section north of the courtyard was a service wing with shelter on the ground-floor for animals and wood, and kitchen with servants' quarters on the first floor, all situated well away from the family's living area.

As the officials went up to the second floor, they stopped in the second mezzanine room [24: *camera a meza schala di sopra*]; like the first one [17] above the granary, its furnishings show that it was lived in[3]. This upper room differed from the other in that no *cameretta* was incorporated within its space. On the second floor the four main rooms followed the same plan as below, but there were no rooms north of the courtyard, nor were there galleries to its sides. The kitchen [26] mentioned in the inventory (and already existing on this floor in 1531) may have been above the *anticamera*, since there is still a fireplace in wall D on the second floor as well as on the first. The *camera grande* [28] would then correspond to the *camera principale* below, while the *camera in su di sala di su la via* [27] would be the room on the street corner.

The second floor was more sparsely furnished than the *piano nobile*. Only its *sala grande* [25] was fitted out with large pieces, though again there was no bed[4]. In the *camera grande* were a cupboard, a chest, two chairs and a small bed. The 'kitchen' [26] had no cooking utensils, only a bed and a pair of chests; the corner room [27] had similar furniture. The inventory of the second floor required less than four pages. This is understandable, because only Lorenza and her three small grandchildren had

---

[1] 'Uno lettuccio inpiallaciato di noce, con una panchetta et sua spalliera, con trespioli; uno letto di legniame di albero; dua paia di casse intorno a decto letto, inpiallaciate di noce con tarsie; uno altro paio di casse all' antica appichate'.

[2] The *andito* had 'una tavola d'albero con trespoli di braccia 4 incirca'. Unless the table was stored in pieces, it seems large for the reconstructed *verone*.

[3] 'Uno armario di guardarobe con sue cassette, una tavola d'alboro di braccia 4 incirca, uno letto in su dua panchette con regoli, uno forziere dipinto col'arme, uno cassonetto di braccia 3 incirca, uno armario alto braccia 3½ a 4 palchetti'.

[4] 'Quattro siede pichole con corame, uno cassone di noce antico, una cassa grande a dua serrami di braccia sei incirca, uno paio di casse grandi a dua serrami, 2 panche da letto di braccia 5½ l'una, una tavola corniciata di noce di braccia 6 con li sua trespoli, una pancha di braccia 10 incirca buona, 4 pezi di panche tra grande e pichole intorno alla sala, uno paio di casse a dua serrami di braccia 6 incirca'.

lived in the palace since 1542 and the second storey probably had little use. None of the small auxiliary rooms listed for the first floor appear in the inventory of the second floor. The first floor was
always more heavily used, and perhaps the small rooms were added to it some time after the interior
was completed, to suit new requirements of later inhabitants, while on the second floor the need
never arose for such closet-like spaces. The second floor (and the second mezzanine) may have retained longer than did the main floor the original arrangement of the interior, with the four unen-
cumbered spaces following the plan of the bearing walls and of the one intermediate wall running
south from the court. Surviving wood consoles on the second floor are all simple, and the ceilings
of rooms 26 and 28 are lower than that of the *sala* [25]. The storey above the *piano nobile* was thus not
designed for show; but it was important as a living space, for in the mid-fifteenth century, ten to
twenty people lived in Giovanni Rucellai's palace (including Iacopo Antonio's house)[1].

A *camera o soffitta a tetto* [29] in which kitchen utensils are listed, did not form a second level to
room 26 or 28 on the second floor, where the ceilings are directly under the roof. It was thus on the
third floor with the *colombaia* [30] and the *pollaio di sopra* [31], in the area where the chickens were
kept in 1531 (Doc. XXII, lines 47–49). On the terrace [32], which in the document includes the
altana, were potted plants[2]. The frescoes, plants, and pleasant spaciousness of the area lead one to
expect that it was in frequent use, especially during the summer, but in 1548, the only item of
furniture found in it was a six-*braccia panchaccia*. The room behind [33] had no usable furniture at all.

Inventories are normally used by art historians to identify works of art. Giovanni inscribed in the
Zibaldone an extraordinary list of artists whose works he had in the house[3]. Unfortunately not one of
the art objects listed in 1548 is so described as to permit the inference that it dates from the fifteenth
century. While some works owned by Giovanni may be hidden in the inventory, most appear to be
from the sixteenth century; even those would be difficult to identify, for there is no indication of
size or of artists' names, though subject matter and support are usually stated. Just a few items of
furniture can be dated—the benches in the *loggia* and *sala principale* probably installed by Giovanni,
a pair of chests with Ginori and Rucellai arms executed in the late fifteenth century when Lorenza
and Paolo were married—but none can be identified with surviving pieces. The fine set of wooden
doors on the main portal, not mentioned in the inventory, can be dated by style to about 1460
(Pl. 29)[4].

An inventory can be valuable for understanding the interior of a house and the life of its inhabitants.
The Rucellai inventory has been useful, but it does not provide all desirable information, in part
because of its late date. Even though most rooms had not changed radically in size or use since the
death of Giovanni Rucellai, the document evokes only indirectly the fifteenth-century palace.
Presumably the *camera principale* and its *anticamera* functioned as a suite for the head of the household;
the bed kept in the latter room was probably used by a servant. The main service area was clearly
north of the court. The *sala principale* seems to have been sparsely furnished, but the impression given

---

[1] In 1458 Giovanni listed nine *bocche* in his tax report; his mother also lived with him, although she filed a separate report
(ASF, Cat., 816, ff. 63ᵛ, 64ʳ). In 1475 living in the house were Giovanni, his son Pandolfo with six children, and Bernardo and
Nannina with at least four children (Passerini, *Rucellai*, tavv. XVI and XVII). In 1473 Giovanni listed in his household seven or
eight servants and slaves, as well as a teacher (Perosa, p. 121); many of these people must have lived in the palace.

[2] The potted plants (shown in Jacopo Zucchi's view in the Palazzo Ruspoli in Rome) were called *horticini* in the 1531 document (lines 83–85); they should not be confused with the *ortuli* of Giovanni Rucellai's will, which were listed in a sequence of
spaces that allowed the inference that they were on the ground floor.

[3] Perosa, pp. 23–24.

[4] They are similar in design and execution to the doors of San Felice, and they seem related in handling to the *sala principale*
consoles.

by the inventory may be deceptive[1], for its size and location certainly made it the most important room in the palace. Unlike most other rooms, it had no bed; the benches all around, the large table, and many chairs indicate that it was used for family eating and for entertaining[2]. Florentine palace builders devoted an extraordinary amount of space to their *sale*. That in the Pazzi Palace took up more than half the front of the house—five of the nine windows; in the Medici Palace the *sala* occupied a similar proportion of the *piano nobile*[3]. In these two buildings, the *sale*, with splendid ceilings, were truly grand. Like the Rucellai *sala*, they were probably formally furnished. The Rucellai *sala* was not just another room in the house, but the one which suggested to visitors the character of the whole interior and the pretensions of the owner.

The western portion of the interior had a centralized *androne* and courtyard, a large *sala* with related suite of rooms, service areas at the rear, and a staircase going from basement to top floor. All these were deftly arranged within the confines of the site, and the palace plan is entirely self-sufficient. The two key planning decisions involved the *sala* and the courtyard. The *sala* had to be large and on the front. Though the court could have been built further south, Giovanni preferred to devote a large space to the *loggia* and the rooms above; perhaps he also wanted the service wing to be a unit separated from the main part of the house. The construction of the interior may have been phased so that Giovanni and his family could live in one area while the other was being built, for I have found no evidence that they rented other quarters during these years.

Giovanni's remodelling of several small houses for his new interior accords with normal procedure in all but the most lavish contemporary palaces. Although the birth of Renaissance palace planning occurred at the Medici Palace, within the city only the Tornabuoni, Pitti, and Strozzi rivalled it in scale, because few men could hope to acquire more than a few houses if they wanted to build in their crowded ancestral neighbourhoods. The restricted sites and the re-use of standing walls meant that plans could not be abstractly conceived. The chief developments in Renaissance interiors after the Medici breakthrough took place in villas and in the residences of popes and princes throughout Italy. In Florence, the power of even very wealthy individuals was not sufficient to enable them to buy up large sites; they had a frugal preference for adapting old elements instead of razing to rebuild; and in devising their plans they were guided as much by utilitarian as by aesthetic considerations.

The interior of the Rucellai Palace is rather modest, but the façade has an entirely different character, and it was evidently conceived only after completion of the interior. The decision to use only three main levels in the new stone revetment meant that the *altana* had to be concealed. In the *androne*, which had been carefully centred with the *loggia*, one can see even more clearly that the design of the façade reflects a subsequent change in planning. While the third pilaster is placed almost directly in front of wall G, the fourth pilaster is considerably east of wall C, and on this side the door-frame barely clears the wall. The arched intermediate doorway in the *androne* and the doorway to the *loggia*

---

[1] According to John Shearman, 'restricted furnishing of *sale* is consistent throughout all properties [of the Medici]' ("The Collections of the Younger Branch of the Medici", *BM*, CXVII [1975], p. 17). Shearman reasoned that *sale* were frescoed and therefore wall decorations did not appear in the inventories; the absence of personal effects is another indication of the special use of these rooms.

[2] Bulst thinks that *sale* generally were dining rooms, although the *sala grande* of the Medici Palace was probably not so used every day. See for these and other important remarks about room utilization his "Palazzo Medici", especially pp. 387–91.

[3] I am grateful to Drs. Margaret Haines and Arnoldo Moscato for making possible a visit to the Pazzi Palace and for sharing with me their expertise; for the original Medici Palace layout, see Bulst, "Palazzo Medici", p. 374, fig. 4. See also p. 167, n. 2 above for the measures taken to ensure that the *sala* of the Spinelli Palace be large.

have frames of carved stone, but there is none on the inside of the façade doorway, which further-more is rectangular (Pl. 18d). The central corbel above this doorway is off-centre, and the square window of the façade has to be blind, since the *androne* vaults block it (Pl. 4). If the façade and *androne* had been planned together, the door would have opened to the centre of the *androne*, the vaults would have arched above the door so as to allow for an open square window, and a central corbel would not have been used on this wall. Probably before the new façade was built, the main portal was tall and rounded, and was logically related to the vaulting system, like the doors inside the *androne*.

The measurements of the façade bays are precisely equal, except for the central bay, and they could not be perfectly co-ordinated with the existing interior. That is why the windows in the *sale* are only roughly centred with the walls. On the other hand, the discrepancy between friezes on the façade and floor-levels of the interior (Pl. 20) has little significance: façades of this period always have the windows resting on the horizontal membering dividing the storeys; but the floors inside are four to six feet lower, and the front windows are reached by steps[1].

C. THE ADDITION

The division between Giovanni's sons in 1492 states that the whole palace 'was made and con-structed in two stages, namely the large house and the small house, which at present are . . . one house, [and] are being used as one house'[2]. In the context of a division of living quarters, the refer-ence is certainly to the interior. The 'small house' must be understood as an addition to the original palace. After 1458 Giovanni remodelled Iacopo Antonio's house entirely, removing its courtyard and most interior walls, and extending walls D and J into the new house. The floor-levels were rebuilt to make them correspond with those in the original palace. All this work could have been done at the same time the façade was being added to the house, but probably Giovanni co-ordinated the new property with his old interior earlier. The result was two large rooms on each of the three main storeys; behind wall J the rooms were not so carefully planned, and they were for the most part carried up only through the first storey. As in the original palace, the third storey was built only between wall D and the façade; the columns of the *altana* were continued east of wall B. No decora-tive detail, except some wood consoles of the standard type, survives in this new part of the palace. The large rooms on both the ground-floor and the *piano nobile* all have false vaults now; the structural ceilings of course must still exist above. Probably there was nothing about them worth keeping visible, in contrast to the *camera terrena grande* and the *sala* of the original palace. In the first ground-floor room the false vault extends only to the thin wall at the front, but in the little mezzanine room (Pl. 8) there is no evidence of the main ceiling system. Therefore this little room and the one below it belong to the fifteenth-century arrangement. Although the plan resembles the *camera terrena grande*, the short north-south wall could not have supported similar stone vaults. Above the false vault there is probably a wood ceiling carried by beams parallel to the façade and starting about five feet in. Access to the mezzanine would have been by a ladder until the house next door was bought and rebuilt. Upstairs, adjacent to the second big room (Pl. 9), the two little closets have two

---

[1] The only exception is the Pitti Palace, where the windows go down to the floor.

[2] '. . . fuit facta et constructa in duabus vicebus, videlicet domum magnam et domum parvam, que ad presens sunt . . . una domus utuntur pro una domo . . .' (Doc. XXI).

levels and can likewise be shown to be old. In the original palace, only in the *camera terrena grande* were the minor spaces that we know about through the 1548 inventory similarly built into the structure of the rooms. The integration of storage areas with the architecture of the interior in Iacopo Antonio's house may indicate that in a period of about ten years one aspect of planning had already changed.

Giovanni did not add a stone staircase to this portion—in the eighteenth century there were still simple wood stairs that by then reached only the first storey (Docs. XXVa and XXVb). But in the years when the palace was divided along wall B–F, some access to the upper floors must have existed. On the second storey, in the middle of the front room, is a wood staircase, and the room has two levels. This strange arrangement dates from the eighteenth century, for it is similar to that described in Document XXVa as a recent improvement for the first storey, where it has since been removed.

The interior of the addition duplicated no essential areas of the original palace. Even though Giovanni Rucellai wanted to buy House 9 next door, there is no evidence to suggest that he aspired to build a double palace for his sons. Iacopo Antonio's house was used simply to provide more living space for Giovanni's expanding family. The real excitement of the purchase for Giovanni lay in the possibility of showing his control over a larger area by extending the showy façade of his original palace.

d. APPENDIX: THE HISTORY OF THE OWNERSHIP

(See also Table III)

Larger Portion

1492	In division between Giovanni Rucellai's sons, this portion goes to Pandolfo di Giovanni[1].
1494 (s.c.)	Pandolfo gives it to his son Paolo[2].
1531	Division between two pairs of Paolo's sons[3].
1542	Filippo, the surviving brother from one of the above pairs, sells out to Pandolfo, who owns the other half of larger portion[4].
1542–1620	On death of Pandolfo di Paolo, ownership passes to son Giovanni, who lives until 1620.
1576–1578	Giovanni reunites larger and smaller portions with purchase of the latter[5].
1622	In division between Giovanni's sons, this portion goes to Benedetto[6].
1743	Giulio, one of Benedetto's great-grandsons, buys smaller portion, reuniting palace[7].

---

[1] ASF, NA, F 237 (Ser Antonio Ferrini, 1470–99), Busta 1492–5, ff. 50r–50v (see Doc. XXI).
[2] ASF, NA, F 237 (Ser Antonio Ferrini, 1470–99), Busta 1493–5, 30 January 1493 (s.f.).
[3] ASF, NA, B 2699 (Ser Zanobi Buonaventura), ff. 19v–22r (see Doc. XXII).
[4] ASF, NA, C 393 (Ser Domenico Cennini, 1541–9), ff. 33r–35v.
[5] ASF, Notarile Moderno, 305 (Ser Angiolo Favilla), ff. 20v–22r; 309, ff. 120v–125r.
[6] AR, XII, 5, 4.
[7] ASF, Notarile Moderno, 23966 (Ser Antonio Pratesi), ff. 62v–65r.

Smaller Portion

1492	In division between Giovanni's sons, this portion goes to Bernardo di Giovanni[1].
1576–1578	Giovanni di Pandolfo buys from heirs of Bernardo di Palla di Bernardo and reunites with larger portion[2].
1622	In division between Giovanni's sons, this portion goes to Paolo[3].
1696	Division between Paolo's grandsons assigns this portion to Abate Filippo[4].
1722	Given by Abate Filippo to his brother Francesco Maria[5].
1743	Bought from Francesco Maria by owner of larger portion: the palace is again united[6].

---

[1] See above, p. 177, n. 1.
[2] See above, p. 177, n. 5.
[3] See above, p. 177, n. 6.
[4] AR, XII, 5, 2.
[5] Reference in ASF, Notarile Moderno, 23966 [Ser Antonio Pratesi], f. 63r.
[6] See above, p. 177, n. 7.

IV. THE FAÇADE

a. CONSTRUCTION AND DATING

The first section of this chapter will investigate how and when the façade was built. No construction books or other direct records have ever been found, but physical and stylistic evidence, used in conjunction with the available documents, provides clues for dating. Only after the phases and dates of construction have been established will the design be analysed and the attribution to Alberti explored.

The façade was dated 1446–1451 by Del Badia, who found that in the tax report of 1446 (1447 s.c.) Giovanni Rucellai listed his property as several houses, whereas in 1451 he listed only one (Docs. IV, VI)[1]. Del Badia's date was accepted for years by most scholars, and many still follow it, but the evidence from the tax records is not as clear as he thought. In 1451 Giovanni's mother still reported House 3 (which would have constituted the fourth and fifth bays) as her own, even though Giovanni included it within his *confini* (Doc. V). While there must have been free movement on the interior between the houses of mother and son, Caterina would not have listed her house separately if the properties had been united on the exterior by the façade. The fact that in 1458 she mentioned no house[2] does not necessarily mean that the façade was up by then, because the 'official' unification of her house with her son's can be interpreted strictly only in terms of the interior. The question of whether documents refer to the interior or the new façade must always be weighed carefully.

The assumption that some of the emblems on the façade were borrowed from the Medici has led to another line of reasoning for establishing the date. Maryla Tyszkiewicz observed that the decoration of the friezes could have appeared only after 1466, the year Bernardo di Giovanni Rucellai married Nannina di Piero de' Medici. She wrote that the three diamond rings in the windows 'speak of the noble connection,' but did not explain how any of these emblems could have been inserted after construction of the façade which she still dated 1446–1451[3]. Wolfgang Stechow, with more logic, suggested that 1466 (or possibly 1461, when the couple was betrothed) should serve as a *terminus post quem* for all the Rucellai buildings embellished with 'Medicean' emblems[4]. Howard Saalman considered the palace one of a group of buildings inspired by Alberti and executed by the Rossellino workshop after Bernardo Rossellino's return to Florence from Rome about 1455. Although Professor Saalman initially proposed that the façade was built in the late 1450s, he has recently revised the date to after 1461 to account for the appearance of the emblems[5]. Charles

---

[1] I. Del Badia, "Palazzo e Loggia dei Rucellai. Illustrazione storica", in Riccardo and Enrico Mazzanti and Torquato Del Lungo, *Raccolta delle migliori fabbriche antiche e moderne di Firenze*, Florence, 1876.

[2] ASF, Cat., 816, f. 64ʳ. The tax officials in their marginal notes did not comment on the disappearance of House 3 from the rolls, perhaps because it had not been rented for income for so many years. I have found no indication that a legal document was ever made for its transfer to Giovanni.

[3] M. Tyszkiewicz, *Bernardo Rossellino*, Florence, 1928, pp. 22–24 (pp. 12–13 in typescript translation at the Kunsthistorisches Institut in Florence [tr. R. Rosmaryn, ed. A. Markham]).

[4] W. Stechow, "Marco del Buono and Apollonio di Giovanni", *Bulletin of the Allen Memorial Art Museum* (Oberlin College), I (June 1944), p. 12, n. 19.

[5] H. Saalman, "Tommaso Spinelli, Michelozzo, Manetti, and Rossellino", *JSAH*, XXV (1966), p. 162–3; Antonio di Tuccio Manetti, *Life of Brunelleschi* (tr. C. Enggass, ed. H. Saalman), University Park and London, 1970, p. 31. In conversation Professor Saalman maintained that the emblems could not have been used by the Rucellai before their alliance with the Medici, which he

Randall Mack too thought that the emblems indicated that the façade was begun after 1461[1]. This is an argument that should be rejected. More substantial new evidence, both visual and documentary, favours an earlier date. Furthermore, material assembled in the Appendix on Emblems at the end of this chapter weakens the thesis that the Rucellai diamond rings must be connected with the Medici, and proposes a different source for them.

The most significant observations about the façade came in Piero Sanpaolesi's article analysing the masonry[2]. During the last restoration in the early 1960s, Professor Sanpaolesi found that the façade is made up of fewer, and larger, blocks than is indicated by the surface design. Nearly all horizontal channels follow the actual lines of the blocks, but often a long block has intermediate vertical channels so that it looks like more than one piece of stone. Some blocks used for the pilasters spread into the adjacent masonry field. The most important implication of this construction method is that the bays were not built as separate units. In general, the revetment would have been applied from west to east, course by course along the entire width of the façade. In principle, Professor Sanpaolesi's discoveries about the façade are valid, but the drawing he published to show the actual stonework is unfortunately not entirely accurate (Pl. 25)[3]. He worked from the drawing to develop a new theory about construction of the façade. He observed that most pilasters are connected in at least one course with the drafted masonry to the east. But on the ground-floor the blocks stop neatly at the eastern edge of the sixth pilaster, except for the capital. On the second floor six blocks straddle the fifth and sixth bays. Professor Sanpaolesi noted the thick wall on the interior behind bays V and VI, and he surmised that the façade may have been planned originally for five bays only, giving a palace with a centralized doorway. He concluded that the façade was actually begun with five bays; that by the time the workers reached the level of the first capitals, Giovanni Rucellai had acquired the house next door; that the revetment was then continued over the ground-floor of the new house; and that on the upper storeys it was built without a break over the entire width of the present façade.

Professor Sanpaolesi's conclusions are suggestive. Before his article, the façade had always been treated as a whole, and was assumed simply to be unfinished; speculation about the original plan gave it eight, or even eleven bays, to form a regular palace with two or three doors. When Professor Sanpaolesi's arguments regarding the phases of construction are refined and supplemented with analysis of the friezes, capitals, and cornice, an even more startling possibility emerges. There is strong visual evidence that the revetment of the last two bays was executed separately from that of the first five bays not on the ground-floor only, but on the entire façade. The most significant and

---

had assumed was long in planning and only made official in 1461. But he agreed that Cosimo's letter of November 1461 informing Pierfrancesco of the family's recent thoughts on the selection of a husband for Nannina implies, on the contrary, that the matter had been entirely in flux (Doc. XIV). Professor Saalman adjusted his dating of the façade accordingly.

[1] C. R. Mack, "The Rucellai Palace. Some new Proposals", *AB*, LVI (1974), pp. 521, 523.

[2] P. Sanpaolesi, "Precisazioni sul Palazzo Rucellai", *Palladio*, n.s. XIII (1963), pp. 61–66. Early restoration on the façade, for the most part confined to projecting portions, is easily visible on the photograph in C. von Stegmann and H. von Geymüller, *Die Architektur der Renaissance in Toscana*, Munich, 1885–1907, III, "L. B. Alberti", Bl. 2. It includes the following replacements of stone: the bench and its base; parts of the lower half of the *spalliera* from the fourth bay eastward; nearly all the cornice above the *spalliera*, along with the bases of the first pilasters and the rippling moulding between them; bottoms of all four door-jambs; perhaps the consoles of the doors; cornices of both doors; first course of stone above the second door; pieces near the top of the *cornicione*; finally, the upper part of the sixth window on the second floor may also have been replaced in the nineteenth century— in the Brogi photograph it looks very new (Pl. 4). During the Sanpaolesi restoration stone was replaced on the bench, parts of the cornices above the friezes and doors, the windows' colonnettes and bases, and the *cornicione*. A few blocks in the masonry field are obviously new, as are some capitals in the *altana*. I am convinced that neither the friezes nor the pilaster capitals have been replaced or reworked, with the possible exception of the abaci of the ground-floor capitals.

[3] I have added the code to Professor Sanpaolesi's drawing as a key to bays and details of the façade.

noticeable differences between the two parts occur in the capitals and the sail frieze of the first storey. Capitals B1, 3, 4, 5, and 6 resemble one another in overall treatment (Pls. 26b, c and 27); capital B2 has a different design, but it is executed with the same vigour as the other five. Capitals B7 and B8, of the same type as B2, differ from it in handling. The leaves are larger, they are less articulate in veining and lobes, and the volutes are scrawny. The overall effect is of a frozen elegance that has lost all the liveliness of the model. The second frieze has the same kind of distinction in style; on the last two bays, the sails are flatter and catch less light (Pl. 4). Plate 27 shows that the ropes all repeat the pattern of the sail above capital B6. In the first five bays, these ropes had tossed about in a variety of configurations. In capitals C7 and C8 of the second storey, the lower leaves are taller than in the other six (Pl. 28a, b). The change continues above these capitals: between the consoles of the cornice, identical rosettes are repeated above the sixth and seventh bays, whereas previously a number of types of flower were used (Pl. 28a). Also on the ground floor, the capitals of the last two bays are distinguished from the rest by more bulbous egg-and-dart cushions (Pls. 26a, 27). To all this may be added the differences in the leaf-garlands above the doors and in the ribbons fluttering from the coats-of-arms.

Almost everywhere in the last two bays the changes in handling from the first five bays reveal a pattern of rather insensitive repetition which indicates that the two eastern bays are later and were executed by a different set of workers from the rest. But in the first frieze there are no discernible differences. It is odd that most other details show such an incapacity to copy, while this lively and intricate passage seems to be entirely continuous in style across the façade. One peculiarity, however, suggests that the second part of this frieze was designed separately, despite its high quality: its composition does not follow the logical arrangement present in the first five bays, where one emblem (the wreath) is centred over the doorway. At the same point above the second door there is only a loop of the ribbon (Pls. 4, 27).

The stylistic evidence does not corroborate Professor Sanpaolesi's hypothesis that the revetment of the ground-floor was carried out in two parts only up to the first capitals, and that then the rest of the seven-bay façade was executed as a unit. His argument depends on the assumption that the uppermost block on the ground-floor crosses bays V and VI, and that there were six such blocks on the first floor. Without new scaffolding one cannot check all these details, but a clear break between capital A6 and the masonry to the east is evident even from the street (Pl. 27). It is much more difficult to be certain about the six blocks on the second floor. There appears to be a join all the way up the eastern edge of pilaster B6, perhaps stopping beneath the last two courses. One course of pilaster C6 may also extend into the sixth bay; and so do both friezes. The blocks that go beyond the sixth pilasters are few in number compared with every other bay[1]. Therefore, even though the building line between the two parts of the façade is not straight, it is noticeable. Its significance will be explored shortly. The stylistic differences in the two parts of the façade, and the seam in the masonry, definite though ragged, just at the point where those differences begin, indicate that the façade was built in two parts, and that the first part was completed before the second was begun. The two sections of the façade, like the two parts of the interior, are divided by wall B.

For the dates of the façade, stylistic criteria are not very helpful. There was no precedent for the use of classical orders on a private palace in Florence[2]; nor do later buildings in the city make

---

[1] I have checked this point carefully with binoculars.

[2] I disagree with Kurt Forster ("The Palazzo Rucellai and Questions of Typology in the Development of Renaissance Buildings", *AB*, LVIII [1976], pp. 109–113). There are problems with the two salient examples used by Forster to suggest

important reference to the Rucellai Palace. The character of the details suggests no more precise date than the 1450s. The elaborate capitals on the first floor are derived from a type used by Michelozzo in the late 1440s at the S. Miniato tabernacle, and are closer in handling to an example at the Spinelli Cloister, datable about 1452 (Pls. 26c, 28c). One other consideration, the relationship with the Piccolomini Palace in Pienza of 1459–1462, should not be used for determining the date of the Rucellai façade, for without a secure chronological sequence, interpretations of the nature of this relationship can only be subjective. The best procedure is to work with the evidence from the stonework, the interior, and the documents.

The first five bays are placed between the via dei Palchetti and wall B, and the central bay between walls C and G, all standing when the façade was designed. These walls are screened by the pilasters and adjacent masonry. Because the bays, except for the central one, are equal in width, the openings to the interior could not be precisely centred between the walls. But continuation of the façade across Iacopo Antonio's house required that the additional windows be shifted much further west inside the front rooms; and the unfinished eighth windows hit wall A. Evidently the façade was not only built first in five bays, but that was the limit of the original design. The revetment of Iacopo Antonio's house is an addition to a façade that in its original conception had been sensitively adapted to existing conditions.

If the façade design had been made after 1458, it would have been made for all three houses on the via della Vigna Nuova. It must pre-date the acquisition of Iacopo Antonio's house, unless we are to believe that a man who had recently paid the high price of 1,000 florins for the house next door would then have had a façade designed that did not include the new purchase. The 1458 sale document seems in fact to refer to this first part of the façade: 'From his old house Giovanni . . . is building . . . a large and agreeable edifice which is understood not yet to be completed, at least in breadth, and which he will be able to complete together with the above-mentioned house which is being bought'[1]. The wording of the text perhaps reflects the perplexity of the officials. They 'understood' that the house (façade)[2] was not completed, but they added the qualification 'at least in breadth'. The implication is that in some other respect the five-bay façade was finished. Since it was not built bay-by-bay, it must have stood all the way up to the *cornicione*. The site of Iacopo Antonio's house was not wide enough for the necessary three additional bays to make an eight-bay façade, but how did Giovanni Rucellai persuade the officials to include in the sale document the phrases about needing the house to complete the palace?

The five-bay façade was begun some time after 1452, for it clearly belongs to a project separate from the datable *androne* (see p. 176). The façade took several years to build, and as it was substantially completed by 1458, the design could have been made about 1455. The revetment may have reached the first frieze by early 1456, with a building-line at the edge of the sixth pilaster, from the

---

that the Rucellai pilasters were not innovative. The building in one of Fra Angelico's Vatican frescoes is probably the artist's own invention, and does not necessarily reflect contemporary buildings, any more than do the churches represented in the same series. The *sgraffiti* of the Palazzo Gerini were dated about 1450 by the Thiems (G. and C. Thiem, *Toskanische Fassaden-Dekoration in Sgraffito und Fresko, 14. bis 17. Jahrhundert* [Kunsthistorisches Institut in Florenz, Italienische Forschungen, 3. Folge, 3. Bd.], Munich, 1964, p. 60); but Heikamp's doubts and his dating of the decoration in the 1460s seem justified (D. Heikamp, review of Thiem, *Kunstchronik*, XIX [1966], p. 76).

[1] '. . . Iohannes, prole nobilis, magnum atque placabile de sua antiqua domo construit et construi fecit hedifitium, quoddam edifitium nondum perfectum esse comprenditur saltem in latitudine, et quod perfici poterit una simul cum suprascripta emenda domo' (Doc. XIII).

[2] For two reasons I do not think that this refers to the interior. During these years remodelling of the interior was minor in scale; and the adjective *spetiosi* used in the next sentence of the document more appropriately evokes the façade.

ground up to the first frieze. Soon after Iacopo Antonio died in January 1456, Giovanni may have decided to try to buy House 7, for he was certainly familiar with the estate's financial situation, the eventual catalyst for the sale. Giovanni had a design only for the five-bay palace, but with the possibility of buying the neighbouring property, his ambitions regarding the façade may have changed significantly, as he realized that it might be extended by several more bays[1]. If this theory is correct, he continued the revetment of his old property while waiting for the opportunity to buy House 7, but to influence the Pupilli officials and the other guardians of Iacopo Antonio's heirs[2], he ordered that the remaining two storeys be built as if the façade was meant to continue eastward. This would explain why the friezes and a few blocks of the masonry field extend slightly beyond the sixth pilasters[3]. Nowhere, however, do they cross the middle of wall B, since the sixth pilasters are placed slightly to its west. While Giovanni's high bid secured for him Iacopo Antonio's house, the officials included in the record of sale the peculiar allusion to completing the façade as additional justification for allowing the orphans' house to be sold. The officials had been sure that they could get a good price, because there was 'someone who would gain great convenience' from the house. Giovanni evidently had made clear to them, both in conversation and by his jagged façade, that he was determined to buy. The extremely high price paid is proof of his resolution, and reinforces the notion that he was prepared to use other extraordinary means to secure the house[4].

The original termination of the five-bay façade has an analogy in the present façade. Its ragged edge is the result of Giovanni's unsuccessful attempt to buy House 9. Early in 1458 its owner, Giovanni d'Antonio Rucellai, wrote in his tax report that he had rented out his house for three years because he was going away. He added that after his return he wanted to live in the house again (Doc. XII). While the most obvious motivation for this statement was an attempt to limit taxation on the rent to three years, the defensive tone may also reflect uneasiness about the intentions of Giovanni di Paolo, who was making no secret of his hopes for House 7 and who had probably already approached Giovanni d'Antonio about buying House 9. After the success with Iacopo Antonio's house, Giovanni di Paolo must have tried to pressure his relative by again using the same strategy as for the earlier section and covering House 7 with revetment while leaving the eastern edge unfinished as we still see it today. Giovanni d'Antonio continued to refuse to sell and it comes as no surprise that he included in his will of 1470 a long *fidecommesso* prohibiting sale or rental of his

---

[1] An additional factor in Giovanni's decision to expand may have been connected with the Loggia project across the street. See below, pp. 205–06.

[2] Their mother, a daughter of Carlo d'Agnolo Pandolfini, cared for them until August 1457; the Pupilli officials took over in February 1458 (ASF, Pupilli, 75, f. 131r).

[3] I am uncertain just how the five-bay palace would have been finished on the east. The pilasters certainly provided clean terminations; and the cornice, probably considerably higher than the roof of House 7, might have been continued around the corner as on the via dei Palchetti. But the friezes would have presented a real problem, still apparent at Giuliano da Sangallo's Palazzo della Rovere in Savona. Raphael found an imaginative solution at the Palazzo Pandolfini; he pulled the frieze out from the plane of the wall, at the palace's southern edge, so that it has a corner to turn before it runs into the building-line.

[4] The reference to the palace in Filarete's treatise (Doc. XVI) is eloquent, but cannot be used for dating the façade because of its own uncertain date. Confirmation that the façade was in place by January 1462 comes from a notarial document in which the location of the transaction was given as '... in domo seu palatio habitationis infrascripti Johannis ...' (Doc. XV). There is an analogy in documents written by this notary's father for Cosimo de' Medici. In 1440 and 1451 the location was given as 'in domo habitationis infrascripti Cosime de Medicis' and 'in domo habitationis dictorum Cosime et Pierfrancisci'; in April 1456 the phrase ran 'in palatio sive domo habitationis dicti Cosime' (ASF, NA, B 1182 [Ser Giovanni Beltramini], ff. 68r, 111r, 115v). The change in wording indicates the transfer of Cosimo's household to his new palace. In the fifteenth century the word *palatium* was used for buildings of great size, importance, or impact; it would not apply to the Rucellai Palace if the façade were barely begun (as would be the case if the 'Medicean' emblems were used to give a *terminus post quem* of November 1461).

house[1]. The revetment of House 7 should be dated before 1470, because after Giovanni d'Antonio's will and death a week later, the unfinished edge would no longer have carried the meaning that Giovanni di Paolo had intended for it—a dramatic 'temporary solution' to the completion of his palace.

A *terminus post quem* for the second stage of the façade can be derived from Giovanni di Paolo's will of 1465. It lists as a boundary of the house he was placing under *fidecommesso* '[property] formerly of the heirs of Jacopo Antonio di Bingeri Rucellai' (Doc. XVII). Giovanni had bought that property seven years previously, had not rented it out, and must have used it since 1458, remodelling its interior along the present lines. His reason for not including Iacopo Antonio's house in the *fidecommesso* must therefore have been that he had not yet extended the façade over it[2]. The late date of the second stage of revetment (1465–1470) helps explain why Iacopo Antonio's house could still be remembered in 1492 as a separate entity from the 'large house' (Doc. XXI).

Giovanni Rucellai's actions regarding the houses of both Iacopo Antonio and Giovanni d'Antonio reflect a change in attitude from the patience with which he acquired the other houses. After having put together a comfortable interior, he built a façade small in dimensions but prepossessing in style and extravagant in cost. As the impressive results of his efforts became visible to the city, his ideas became more grandiose. As if in recognition of this possibility, he included in his *Zibaldone* a warning from St. Bernard: '. . . one must build more for necessity than just because one wants to do it, because in the course of building one's desire to continue does not diminish, but grows'[3]. Giovanni's ambition to extend his palace façade led him to gamble twice; the second time he lost[4].

b. STYLE AND ATTRIBUTION

The novelty of the Rucellai pilasters has claimed such great attention that critics have under-emphasized other aspects of the design[5]. Furthermore, the building has usually been dealt with on the assumption that it was originally meant to have at least eight bays. Analysis of the style will substantiate the conclusion that the original façade consisted of only five bays; more important, it will suggest the architectural thinking underlying the design.

Of the greatest importance for the effect of the façade is the precision of execution, most consistent in the first five bays. Probably a thick cushion of mortar covered any irregularities in the old wall, permitting the smooth laying of the new stones. From a distance the pilasters look like solid vertical blocks and the cornices seem continuous strips. The joins in the channels of the masonry field are invisible. The frequent use of the same block for part of a pilaster and an adjacent unit in the masonry

---

[1] ASF, NA, C 666 (Ser Bartolommeo Corsi, 1467–73), ff. 162r–v. Earlier wills of 1450 and 1456 make no such stipulation

[2] In 1540 the palace's second part (Iacopo Antonio's house) was judged to be free of the *fidecommesso*; the reason given was that it had been built after Giovanni had made his will (Doc. XXVI). Whether or not this was strictly true for the interior, the important point is that the court read the *confini* in the will carefully, and used them as the basis for the decision.

[3] The whole passage reads: 'Due cose principali sono quelle che gli uomini fanno in questo mondo: la prima lo'ngienerare; la seconda l'edifichare. Ma San Bernardo dicie che si debbe hedifichare più per neciessità che per voluntà, perché hedifichando, la voluntà non mancha ma crescie' (*Zibaldone*, f. 83v). Cf. Kent, above, p. 52, n. 6.

[4] For the whole of the preceding section, I owe much to stimulating conversation with Howard Saalman, though our views did not always correspond.

[5] Only Hans Kauffmann has published an extensive analysis of the façade, but I cannot agree with his conclusion that the architecture is pictorial and anti-structural in character. See his "Über 'rinascere', 'Rinascita' und einige Stilmerkmale der Quattrocentobaukunst", *Concordia Decennalis. Festschrift der Universität Köln zum zehnjährigen Bestehen des Deutsch-Italienischen Kulturinstituts Petrarcahaus*, Cologne, 1941, pp. 123–46 (especially pp. 128–9).

field must have required particularly careful measurement because the two parts of the block lie in different planes. The joins within the masonry field occur at one edge, rather than in the centre, of the channels[1], so the relationship of each block to its neighbour had to be carefully planned.

Within the first part of the façade there is only one obvious 'mistake'; in the fifth bay of the second floor, the lower part of the window frame slips out of the established courses. This carelessness may indicate that supervision of construction had become lax. Probably it does not mean that the area in question was executed only with the later portion, where yet another pattern is used for the frames, because the sixth capital and the related cornice details are consistent in style with the rest of the first portion. The quality of execution falls elsewhere in the second portion: channels are broader and they are not uniform, joins are more apparent, and in the seventh bay two masonry courses above the square window have settled crookedly.

Because the last two bays are an addition to the original plan, the five-bay façade should first be considered alone. Its design is composed of three elements: the masonry field, the pilaster-entablature system, and the apertures. The relationships between them all are rich and varied. The masonry field is articulated into a pattern of blocks, on the lowest floor irregular in height. On the upper storeys, above the arches framing the windows, the courses settle into a height equal to that of the narrowest courses below[2]. In all three levels the irregular vertical channels contribute to the appearance of a random pattern within the strict confines of the bays. The smooth pilasters, unbroken lines of the cornices, and flowing friezes are strongly distinguished from the masonry field. These elements form a closed system that may be thought of as a grid that organizes the masonry field. The entablatures divide the façade into three areas of slightly diminishing height, and the pilasters, which also narrow slightly, subdivide each storey into bays. Apertures, the third element of the design, are centred in all bays, and within each storey they are of the same dimensions, except in the wider central bay with its door and larger windows. The frames of the biforate windows, resting on the entablatures and enclosed by the pilasters, are anchored to the grid system. On the ground floor, the central square window is related to the lintel of the door, and gives a rationale for the placement of the windows lined up with it. The lowest windows are simply voids within a single course of masonry.

The relationship between the pilaster system and the masonry field is complex, even ambiguous, and may be interpreted in either of two ways. If the pilasters and entablatures are understood as a grid laid over a continuous masonry field, their slight projection enables one to imagine them as separable from the wall, with the channelled horizontals only periodically covered by the pilasters. The square windows and the irregular height of the masonry courses on the ground floor make the horizontal association across the bays especially strong at this level. The random arrangement of the blocks on all three storeys reinforces the sensation that the masonry field is a continuous wall surface, even behind the pilasters. Because in no two bays is the drawing of the field the same, the bays are not perceived as a series of identical units.

Alternatively the pilasters and entablatures can be understood as the emerging structure of the

---

[1] This practice is absent in earlier examples of drafted masonry (Davanzati, Minerbetti, della Stufa, Medici Palaces) where the joins occur in the centre of the channels so that each block is cut with half a channel at each of its four edges. The Rucellai technique is followed in many later buildings, such as the Piccolomini Palaces in Pienza and in Siena, and the Spannocchi Palace, also in Siena.

[2] On the top storey one course is slightly lower still and expresses the lower overall height of this level in comparison to the second.

wall—not an overlay but a framework within which the masonry field acts as a filler. A detail en-couraging a reading of the masonry field in separate bays (rather than as a continuous wall) is the vertical channel along the sides of each pilaster. This groove, though no deeper than those marking the individual blocks of the wall surface, sets the pilasters off from the masonry field and suggests that they emerge from a deeper plane. The mass of the pilasters is clearly stated at the south-west corner where the revetment turns on to the via dei Palchetti (Pl. 24c). The pilasters here appear as solid piers, in contrast to Brunelleschi's Palazzo di Parte Guelfa, where at the corner the pilasters on adjacent faces are separate decorative strips that do not touch.

Interpretation of the pilaster system from one point of view as a thin overlay and from another as a projecting structural framework may appear to be contradictory, but these are alternate ways of binding together a complex wall surface. Nowhere is the interrelationship of continuous wall and grid more ingeniously developed than in the *spalliera*, the backrest of the bench, which serves the additional visual function of podium for the entire structure. Its plane surface lies midway between the masonry field and the pilasters; its fabric is related to both. The *spalliera* has long sections in *opus reticulatum* pattern, interrupted by smooth panels that represent socles for the pilasters, with vestigial cornices and bases at the very top and bottom. The socles establish continuity between the pilasters and the bench, so that the grid framework is subtly related to the ground. In addition, the socles divide the *spalliera* into bays and are especially important in preparing at this level for the break made by the door. Much of the intricate thinking present in the whole façade is summed up in the *spalliera*; in it are merged the pilaster system and a channelled surface similar to that of the masonry field. The meeting results in accommodations by both: the diagonals of the *opus reticulatum* have a visual elasticity that is rhythmically broken by the pilaster socles; these do not so much stop the continuity of the diagonal pattern as stretch its fabric. Conversely, the skin of the *spalliera* flattens the socles into the same plane as the *opus reticulatum*. Just above the cornice of the *spalliera* the pilasters and wall surface occupy distinctly different planes, but the profile of the pilaster bases is continued across the width of the bays, becoming a rippling moulding for the masonry field. Only above this point are clear textural and planar distinctions made between masonry field and grid.

The treatment of the *spalliera* shows the careful use of detail to bind two elements of the façade. The same principle governs the interplay of the first- and second-floor windows with the masonry field. The sides of their drafted frames, divided into horizontal courses of two different heights, recall the courses on the ground floor and thus double as masonry field, or wall, since there is no other substance between the pilasters. But the frames keep their primary function of enclosing in-dividual units, for they are differentiated from the masonry field of the ground floor by having no vertical channels. There is a continuity of pattern among all three storeys, but also a subtle transition upwards from the expansive design of the ground floor to the lower frames, and then to the vous-soirs which introduce the change to the low and regular courses above the arches. The masonry field is no longer an element of visual excitement, but becomes a subdued background for the windows.

The designer of the Rucellai Palace façade was particularly concerned with organizing and articu-lating the wall. He rejected the surface treatment traditional for Florentine palaces, where masonry, plaster, or *sgraffiti* spread across large areas and are used as a neutral background for windows and doors. Only a vestige of this remains in the upper floors of the Rucellai Palace. The pilaster system is used to give a new kind of structure to a more complex façade than had ever been seen previously on a private building. Every unit is defined, from the terminations in bench, cornice, and corner pilasters to the individual blocks of the masonry field. The biforate windows are locked into the grid, the square windows and door are related to one another and are framed as separate units, while the smallest windows replace single stones. The façade is a brilliant counterpoint between clarity of definition and the underlying relationships binding the parts.

The planning of the design is evident even within the seemingly random pattern of the masonry field, for certain constant features appear that help organize each separate bay and relate the bays to one another. Comparison with the sixth and seventh bays will reveal differences analogous to those already noted in the drawing and execution of decorative details.

On the ground floor the top, or fourteenth, course of masonry is drafted into three or four blocks in each of the first five bays; in both the sixth and seventh bays it is divided into six blocks. The thirteenth course is a single strip in bays I, II, IV, and V while in III a small block added in the centre expresses the greater width of this bay; in this same course in the last two bays no account is taken of the consistency present in the first five bays. A similar break from an established pattern comes three courses lower where in bays I–V only one block is seen on either side of the windows, while in bays VI and VII the corresponding areas are twice shown as two blocks. On the first floor the blocks above the window frames of bays I–V are about equal in length, while in bays VI and VII many blocks are either very long or very short, forming a different pattern.

Although the three cases mentioned above are the only repetitions in the pattern of the masonry field, the harmonious drawing of the original palace as a whole is evident when compared with the treatment of the last two bays. The differences noted underscore the integrity of the first five bays, and they support the conclusion derived from analysis of the stonework, ornamental detail, and documents—that the last two bays were executed later and by a different team of stone-carvers than the first five bays. This conclusion can now be refined.

It is clear that the masonry field of the five-bay palace was carefully planned, and that its designer took no part in the extension. A detailed eight- or nine-bay design by the first architect was not available to the builders of the last two bays, and there is no evidence that such a plan ever existed. When, after the ground-floor had been completed, Giovanni Rucellai ordered that the revetment above it be extended slightly past the sixth pilaster, he was already overstepping the original design. About ten years later the sixth and seventh bays were added to the original façade, but their treatment reveals that already the subtleties of the design were misunderstood. One more area of evidence will show that the design for the original palace could not have been developed at the site from the architect's rough sketches, but had to be worked out even before the stones could be cut.

Crudely scratched on many of the stones are lines, some forming letters, others abstract signs. The marks appear frequently on the drafted masonry and pilasters, only very occasionally on the architraves and *spalliera*. There are marks on all three levels and across all seven bays. Although many more marks can be seen on the ground-floor than on the upper storeys, one would probably find more even distribution if one could check from scaffolding. On a building where great care was taken to produce the stippled surface of the blocks (see Pl. 26a), these marks must have been incised afterwards for a specific purpose. The entire façade has a total of about fifty different marks, most of which occur at least twice, many several times. They follow no particular order, nor is any mark a code for the function or size of stones. Some, such as stars and crosses, have no expected orientation, but the marks in the form of letters are often upside-down or on their sides. Therefore they did not serve as signs for the directional placement of blocks; rather, they are masons' marks that identified the individual stone-workers who finished the blocks[1].

The conclusion that the palace was built in two parts and by two sets of stone-workers is supported by the masons' marks, for they too change east of the sixth pilaster. Marks that occur frequently on the first part, such as F, O, and B are absent on the second; conversely, the f, F, S, St in the two bays to the right are not found in the first five bays[2]. Only five marks occur on both parts: C, D, J, K, +.

On the first five bays there are about thirty-seven different masons' marks. With so many workers the façade may have been built quickly[3]. The intricacy and quality of the workmanship suggest that the workers were carefully supervised and controlled. The question of how this control was exercised becomes significant when one realizes that the workers did not merely cut blocks to arbitrary dimensions and fit them into whatever spaces were available on the façade. The diverse orientations of the marks indicate that they were incised before the stones were put in place on the wall and therefore that the surfaces were finished on the ground[4]. The stone-workers must have been provided with precise measurements for each block, with its channels on two sides and probably also the intermediate channels where a block is divided into two 'visual' blocks. Specifications for the blocks that stretched from a pilaster into the masonry field would have been more complex. Because no two bays are identical, and because they are bound in construction, a detailed drawing must have been made of each storey to provide the necessary information for the stone-workers. Probably the drawing of the entire façade was done at once[5]. The actual instructions to the stone-workers may have taken the form of sketches for individual blocks[6].

---

[1] I have found similar marks on the following fifteenth-century Florentine buildings: Medici, Neroni-Gerini, Pazzi, Strozzino, Pitti, and Ridolfi-Guidi Palaces, and the Badia Fiesolana. There is no published material about such signs in Renaissance Florence, but I have profited from discussions with Ulrich Middeldorf and Richard Goldthwaite. The marks are found outside Florence, for instance on the staircase of the Ducal Palace in Urbino, at the two Piccolomini Palaces in Siena, at S. Francesco in Rimini, and in Naples at the Cuomo and Sanseverino Palaces. Roberto Pane has concluded that the marks at the latter building (now the Gesù Nuovo) identified the workers ("Architettura e urbanistica del Rinascimento", in *Storia di Napoli*, IV*, Naples, 1974, pp. 380–1). If the Rucellai signs are indeed masons' marks, they fit into a long medieval tradition. Where a building has marks of only two or three configurations, as on the ground floor of the Medici Palace, Suzanne Butters suggests that they refer to the different quarries from which the blocks were taken.

[2] On the two parts of the palace the F and F, the M and M, the K and K, the G and G are consistently different in form.

[3] Account books show that as many as 89 stone-cutters were employed during the first two and one-half years of construction at the Strozzi Palace, a much larger project; see R. A. Goldthwaite, "The Building of the Strozzi Palace: The Construction Industry in Renaissance Florence", *Studies in Medieval and Renaissance History*, X (1973), pp. 173–4. Building practice at the Rucellai Palace seems to have differed from that at the Strozzi, where the stone-cutters were paid by the day (pp. 172–3). There were no masons' marks at the Strozzi Palace, even before the recent cleaning.

[4] In conversation Professor Middeldorf raised an intriguing question about the façade: how is it possible, if the blocks were finished on the ground, for their joins to be so close, their surfaces always to lie in the same plane, and the channels to coincide perfectly? He was particularly concerned about the problem of achieving the smooth surfaces and edges of the pilaster shafts, since so many of their blocks are attached to pieces of the masonry field. He suggested that much of the finishing of the pilasters and channels might have been done after the blocks were in place, following the practice for the fluting of Greek columns. Only one of these questions can be answered definitely. The many masons' marks on the pilasters show that their blocks were finished on the ground; it is still possible that the vertical channels dividing them from the masonry field were evened up after the blocks had been put in place.

[5] It could have been a scale elevation drawing, but Professor John Coolidge suggests an ingenious alternative: to the standing wall a layer of plaster may have been applied to smooth over the irregularities. On to this 'priming' layer something like a *sinopia* drawing may have been made; the masons' marks on the stones would then have been matched to similar indications on the wall. A procedure analogous to this seems to underlie the way in which the surviving model for the Strozzi Palace was made. Before the tiny blocks of wood representing *bugni* were affixed, the entire masonry pattern was incised on the flat 'walls'. With this incised drawing the master architect firmed up his design and communicated to his shop the specific size of the *bugni* to be cut for the model.

[6] The block sketches would have been more precise than those made by Michelangelo for the San Lorenzo façade and for

Two independent kinds of evidence—analysis of the design and of the masons' marks—have suggested that a drawing was used for the Rucellai façade. It is instructive to compare the Rucellai design with that of the drafted masonry on the Medici Palace. In contrast to the division into bays with the periodic interruption of the masonry field by pilasters, the Medici first storey is organized by evenly-spaced windows, above which the field is continuous. An identical design is used for the areas between all windows, and one drawing could have been made and then repeated across both façades. Above the springing of the arches the masonry spreads across the bays in a random pattern for which no drawing would have been necessary. The Medici drafted masonry differs from that of the Rucellai in two important technical respects: each visual block is an actual block, and each block is channelled round its full perimeter so that joins are at the centre of the channels. The pattern above the windows may have been dictated by nothing more precise than a well-trained foreman's judicious choice of stones for the appropriate courses as the carvers finished with them[1]. At the Rucellai Palace, because of the grid system, this practice would have been not only inefficient but probably impossible. It is difficult to imagine that the foreman can have composed each course of masonry within the confines of the bays by choosing from blocks that had not been specially measured. Certainly for the identical details above and to the sides of the square windows, stones were cut for specific locations. Even though the rest of the masonry field does not follow a logical pattern, practical considerations must have dictated the careful planning of each detail before the blocks were cut.

As in few other buildings, the design and execution of the Rucellai façade are interrelated. No detailed elevation drawings, precise in scale, survive from the fifteenth century but one must have been used here[2]. Even such a drawing, however, would not be sufficient to ensure the resolution of the numerous questions arising in even the best-planned project. Either the architect himself or a foreman who perfectly understood his ideas must have been present to supervise construction. Before proposing Alberti as the architect, we must consider the other contender for the honour, Bernardo Rossellino. Comparison with the palace he designed and built for Pius II in Pienza from 1459 to 1462 (Pl. 30)[3] will show that Rossellino was neither architect nor foreman at the Rucellai Palace.

When on the basis of Del Badia's reading of Giovanni Rucellai's tax reports the Rucellai façade was dated 1446–1451, its relationship to the Pienza palace seemed clear enough, and all scholars agreed on the precedence of its design. They of course assumed that the whole Rucellai façade, with the eighth bay completed, formed the basis for the east (piazza) and west sides of Pius' palace. Only Dr. Mack has made the specific proposal that the chronological relationship should be reversed. His dating of the Rucellai façade on the basis of the 'Medicean' emblems has already been weakened by analysis of the physical evidence and of the documents. This discussion will therefore follow the usual understanding of the direction of influence, but with one difference: only the first five bays,

---

the Medici Chapel, which specified the form of the stones as they came from the quarry and not their finished form. See C. de Tolnay, *Michelangelo, IV: The Tomb of Julius II*, Princeton, 1954, pp. 155–6 and figs. 124–85; J. S. Ackerman, *The Architecture of Michelangelo*, New York, 1961, *Catalogue*, pp. 14–17.

[1] I can see no masons' marks on the first floor of the Medici Palace.

[2] Diane Zervas helped me measure the lower courses of the Rucellai masonry. We had expected the lengths of the blocks to be rationally related to the *braccio* unit used for the ground-floor pilasters. Many of the fractions used are small, however. This evidence works against my hypothesis that a scale drawing was used for the design.

[3] For Bernardo Rossellino's authorship, see Stegmann and Geymüller, *Architektur*, III, "Bernardo Rossellino", p. 9. General studies of Pienza are L. H. Heydenreich, "Pius II. als Bauherr von Pienza", *Zeitschrift für Kunstgeschichte*, VI (1937), pp. 105–46 and E. Carli, *Pienza. La città di Pio II*, Rome, 1966. For documents of payment, see E. Müntz, *Les arts à la cour des papes*, Paris, 1878, I, pp. 300 ff. and A. Rossi, "Spogli vaticani", *Giornale di erudizione artistica*, VI (1877), pp. 130 ff.

constructed by 1458, constitute the Rucellai precedent. Close observation of the 'copy' at Pienza strengthens the case for dating the Rucellai façade earlier; it also reveals important aspects of Rossellino's attitude toward the Rucellai design.

The Rucellai theme of drafted masonry and grid is used on three sides of the palace in Pienza (there is a garden loggia on the fourth). Also similar are the rectangular ground-floor windows and doors, and the biforate windows on the upper floors. But Pius's palace is much bigger, with an interior based on the plan of the Medici Palace, which Pius would have seen on his visit to Florence in April 1459 (Pl. 31)[1]. The salient borrowing is the large centralized courtyard with one broad arm that provides a transition to the garden (at Pienza on the south, at Florence on the west). In both buildings the main portal is on the side opposite the garden. The plans are also similar in the general arrangement of large rooms and hallways round the courtyard.

The Rucellai five-bay façade was thus adapted to a palace of grand plan. While Pius's description of Pienza did not acknowledge the debt to either Florentine precedent, one comment implies the struggle encountered in lengthening the Rucellai example to make it conform to a different plan:

> They placed a very tall and splendid door in the middle of the north side; this was to be the principal entrance. On the east side, which faces the town square, since a door could not occupy the centre, two doorways were added for the sake of symmetry, one of them closed by the wall but so built as to present the appearance of a closed door; the other remained open for ordinary use. They did the same thing on the west side[2].

Pius stressed the issue of centralized doorways because he was recalling the five-bay Rucellai façade. Especially on the north side he wanted the door to be in the centre, since this was the main façade and he wished the entrance to be co-ordinated with the plan. To cover the wider interior, the Rucellai's odd number of bays was retained but one more was added at each edge for a total of seven. True to the Rucellai example, the bay with the door is wider than the others. On the east 'the door could not occupy the centre'. Pius gave no reasons, but they again presumably involved the plan: the garden loggia, added to the square Medicean plan, lengthened the east façade from seven to eight bays. Even if the side of the loggia had not been included in the façade, and there had been only seven bays, a doorway in the centre would have resulted in unfortunate relationships both to the church and to the courtyard. Pius preferred to use all eight available bays, and 'for the sake of symmetry' to accent the new design with two doorways. The door on the right, 'open for ordinary use', leads into the north arm of the court; the other doorway could not be co-ordinated with the plan, and is blind. But Pius' architect had the five-bay Rucellai façade in mind, and retained the concept of the wider central bay. With the eight bays and two doors on the east (and west) at Pienza, there were two central bays, but they were now between the doors; both were made wider than the rest[3].

The two-door façade for Pius's palace coincidentally anticipates the present Rucellai façade. When Pius visited Florence in 1459, he had occasion to see the original Rucellai Palace, and he may also

---

[1] For Pius' visit, see R. Hatfield, "Some unknown Descriptions of the Medici Palace in 1459", *AB*, LII (1970), pp. 232–49; W. A. Bulst ("Die ursprüngliche innere Aufteilung des Palazzo Medici in Florenz", *MKHIF*, XIV [1970], p. 386) also notes the dependence of the Pienza plan upon that of the Medici Palace.

[2] 'In latere quod aquilonem spectat, portam in medio altissimam et magnificam collocarunt, quae praecipua esset. In orientali latere, quod oppidi plateam respicit, cum medium porta tenere non posset, ad servandam semetriae gratiam duae ianuae additae sunt, quarum altera muro obducta clausae vestigium prae se ferret, altera ad quotidianum usum mansit aperta. In occidentali latere idem fecere' (*Pii Secundi Ponteficis Maximi Commentarii*, Rome, 1584, p. 426; translation by P. M. Smith).

[3] The central bays on all three façades are considerably wider than the flanking bays, though the latter are not uniform in width.

have heard of the plans for extending the revetment over Iacopo Antonio's house. Nevertheless, the centralizing principle of the five-bay palace was imitated. But the wider central bay was doubled and used out of its proper context of emphasizing the door. This small point of difference is symptomatic of Rossellino's misunderstanding of the Rucellai façade.

Elsewhere, subtleties of the Rucellai design are exaggerated at Pienza, as in the heights of the storeys and widths of the pilasters; the workmanship as a whole is much rougher, notably in the handling of drafted masonry and of pilaster capitals. The effect of the execution is due in part to the use of tufa, which is coarser than the *pietra forte* of Florence; and provincial masons were less skilled in carrying out details. Some changes are attributable to preferences of the patron. Pius rejected the emblematic decoration of friezes and window-sprandrels, although the high quality of carving in the piazza fountain shows that he could have found someone to execute a complicated frieze if he had wished. His loving (though inaccurate) description of the large windows suggests that it was he who dictated their greater height within the bays. But other divergences from the Rucellai precedent are due to Rossellino, and they reveal a general misinterpretation, mixed with an instinct for a more traditional Florentine conception of a palace façade. If one thought that he indeed designed the Rucellai Palace and that it post-dates the palace in Pienza, further differences between the two might be seen as the result of his greater experience after the Pienza venture. The purpose now is not to prolong the argument against that sequence, but to explore the changes Rossellino made when he re-used the Rucellai design at Pienza, and thereby to test the attribution of the Florentine building to him.

The drawing of the masonry field of the Pienza palace nowhere gives the impression of having been designed, as is so apparent at the Rucellai Palace. Instead, blocks are generally short and the pattern is merely choppy. With few exceptions one feels that the stones were taken from a heap on the ground and simply fit on the wall into a course of the correct height. The ground floor, where the drafting pattern is continued across the pilasters, gives an impression of unrelieved stoniness, with none of the elegant rhythms of the Rucellai Palace. These pilasters seem to be embedded in the wall, and in pushing out its surface they convey a sense of underlying structure in a much more specific way than at the Rucellai. But above, the pilasters are smooth and are twice considerably diminished in width. Such changes in texture and in mass make the grid difficult to see as a consistent structural system; in the upper floors it seems, to a far greater extent than at the Rucellai, a decorative overlay. The tight relationship between the biforate windows and pilasters is abandoned. Within the bays the windows are narrower and, in the absence of framing at their sides, the wall is allowed to spread. Rossellino returned to the traditional Florentine mode of accenting the upper windows with an arch only[1], and he gave up the individualizing frames of the lower windows[2]. His windows rhythmically interrupt the wall, but they do not affect it. He used the pattern established on the ground floor for all three storeys, and he did not attempt to imitate the subtle transitions of the Rucellai stonework.

Although Pius may have been responsible for major decisions at his palace, he would not have been involved in details. Rossellino's design is coherent enough to represent a critique, retrospective in character, of the Rucellai façade[3], but his treatment also shows that in many respects he did not

---

[1] See, for example, the Palazzo Vecchio and the Davanzati, Medici, Strozzino, Pitti, Antinori and Strozzi Palaces.

[2] The frames of the Rucellai ground-floor windows are novel for Florence, and are found on none of the palaces cited in the preceding note, except for the Strozzi. Such frames were also included in the Spinelli Palace design of about 1458.

[3] Frommel sees in the Pienza Palace a rejection by Rossellino of many of Alberti's innovations, in favour of a return to the style of the Medici Palace (C. L. Frommel, *Der römische Palastbau der Hochrenaissance*, Tübingen, 1973, I, p. 28).

understand the Florentine building. On the side façades, the peculiar widening of the central bays is a flagrant misinterpretation of a subtle point of emphasis. The relationship between grid-system and wall has lost the delicate balance, as well as the firmness, present in the Rucellai Palace. As builder and designer at Pienza, Rossellino proved equally oblivious of the beauty of execution in the Rucellai model. Since he did not comprehend the subtleties of the Rucellai design, it is not surprising that he made no effort to duplicate the careful masonry composition by having each block cut for a specific location.

Despite all the extenuating variables of material, workmanship and patron at Pienza, clearly Rossellino's was not the mind that created the Rucellai Palace. His activity at Pienza works not for but rather against the notion that he was architect or foreman for Giovanni Rucellai. This conclusion contradicts the earliest source for the attribution, the early sixteenth-century *Libro di Antonio Billi*, which credited Rossellino with the model[1]. Vasari, too, rejected Billi, and stated that Alberti designed all the Rucellai buildings—the palace, the Loggia, the façade of Santa Maria Novella, the chapel in San Pancrazio[2]. His basis for these attributions still entirely eludes historians, for no earlier valid sources are preserved that connect any of these projects with Alberti[3]. The attribution of the Rucellai Palace to Alberti can be substantiated only by analysis of its relationship to his treatise and to his documented work—San Francesco in Rimini, San Sebastiano and Sant' Andrea in Mantua—and to the Santa Maria Novella façade, the authorship of which has never been questioned (Pls. 32, 33)[4].

Each of Alberti's buildings presents a new solution to the problem of the façade. Not only did he work with a different kind of design in each case, but he drew on diverse ancient sources. Thus he did not evolve a consistent language of architecture, and in this respect his production contrasts with Brunelleschi's. As a group his churches are strikingly varied. San Sebastiano and San Francesco, for instance, differ as much as would seem possible within the oeuvre of one architect. In contrast to the rich sculptural qualities of San Francesco, San Sebastiano is conceived in terms of the stark contrast between the flat wall surface and voids with simple articulation; the framing pilasters and

---

[1] Billi's text reads: 'Fu Bernardo architettore suo [Antonio Rossellino's] fratello che fecie il modello della casa de Rucellai, oggi di mess. Lorenzo di mess. Piero Ridolfi [the words 'oggi ... Ridolfi' are cancelled], et della loggia de Ruciellai fecie il modello Antonio di Migliorino Guidotti' ([Antonio Billi], *Il Libro di Antonio Billi*, ed. C. von Fabriczy, Westmead, 1969 [reprinted from *ASI*, VII, series 5, 1891], p. 322). Rossellino died in 1464 and therefore was not involved in the revetment even of Iacopo Antonio's house. If the denial to Rossellino of the Rucellai Palace were not clear from the Pienza comparison, Billi would have to be given more weight, for he may be correct in the attribution of the Rucellai Loggia to Antonio di Migliorino Guidotti. See my article in *MKHIF*, XXI (1977), p. 194.

[2] Vasari, *Vite*, ed. G. Milanesi, Florence, 1906, II, pp. 541–3.

[3] In the *Zibaldone* Giovanni Rucellai included material about his buildings and about Brunelleschi, but he never mentioned Alberti. Bernardo di Giovanni Rucellai in his *De Urbe Roma* showed admiration for Alberti, but did not indicate that his family had a special relationship with the great man (see P. Pozzetti, *Leo Baptista Alberti*, Florence, 1789, pp. 34, 36; Mancini, *Alberti*, pp. 103, 486.) Pozzetti claimed to have found a late fifteenth-century reference to Alberti as architect of the Santa Maria Novella façade in Fra Giovanni Caroli, *Vitae nonnullorum fratrum beatae Mariae Novellae*. According to Pozzetti a manuscript of this work contains the following passage: 'Si Templi illius frontem, ac reliquum faciei decus inspicias, egregium profecto, ac magnificum sese intuentium oculis offert, et opera Leonis Baptistae Alberti celeberrimi Architecti marmoreo tabulato, et monumentorum insigni vallo contenta' (Pozzetti, *Alberti*, p. 39). Even Mancini could not trace the manuscript Pozzetti used (Mancini, *Alberti*, p. 461), and I too have looked for it without success. I question its authenticity because the passage quoted above appears without the section 'opera Leonis Baptistae Alberti celeberrimi Architecti' in an autograph manuscript of the book (Laurenziana, Plut. 89, inf. 21, f. 3ᵛ [new page numbering]).

[4] Much in the following discussion is derived from R. Wittkower, *Architectural Principles in the Age of Humanism*, 3rd ed. London, 1965, pp. 33–56. Other important sources are: C. Ricci, *Il Tempio Malatestiano*, Rome and Milan, 1924; C. Grayson, *Alberti and the Tempio Malatestiano*, New York, 1957; E. Marani and C. Perina, *Mantova. Le Arti*, II, Mantua, 1961; E. Marani, ed., *Il Sant' Andrea di Mantova e Leon Battista Alberti*, Mantua, 1974; E. J. Johnson, *S. Andrea in Mantua*, University Park and London, 1975.

architrave barely project from the wall, all decorative elements are eliminated, and even the pediment is austere. But there is one common denominator in all Alberti's churches. The façades are organized with a profound understanding of systems of classical orders. While the use of classicizing elements is of course common in Quattrocento architecture, Alberti's façades are the only ones designed by 1470 in which such elements are the true basis of the design.

This quality of Alberti's churches can best be understood through comparison with Bernardo Rossellino's Pienza Cathedral façade, the most interesting of contemporary examples (Pl. 34)[1]. It is still based on the medieval type of the cathedral of Assisi, where the broad rectangular façade is divided by two string-courses and topped by a gable, and where buttresses on the façade reflect the interior divisions for nave and aisles. At Pienza, Rossellino added classicizing details to this format, but he integrated them only superficially. He applied to the three bays a double order of columns carrying arches, and provided the lower columns with imposing pedestals encasing the buttresses. But the second order of columns has only a string-course to rest on. The gable is nearly classical in proportion, and has a modest cornice of egg-and-dart and dentile mouldings; but again the scale and unity of the form are disrupted with the decorated strips carried up from the buttresses.

For Alberti the great resource of ancient architecture was not just the beauty of its detail but the structural implications—the possibility of binding together all forms within systems that give clear expression to the interrelationships of the parts. Only he was able to use with true understanding the ancient orders which he could then embellish at will. With the interlocking design of the Rucellai Palace, the whole wall is composed to be woven with the grid. In this sense it is closest to Sant' Andrea in spirit; the decorative emphasis of the surface is akin to that of S. Francesco. Certain forms resemble features of all three documented churches—the doorway seems related to that of San Sebastiano, the rounded windows occur at Sant'Andrea, the podium and embellished frieze at San Francesco. But similarities of detail are too rare to be used for an attribution to Alberti, because he was an architect of such inventiveness and wealth of imagination that his buildings have almost too many variables from which to distil a 'style' in traditional art-historical terms.

One idea none the less underlies all Alberti's architecture, the documented buildings as well as the Rucellai Palace. It involves the significance he attached to the supporting elements. When Rudolf Wittkower analysed Alberti's church façades, he observed a shift from the use of engaged columns at the first two to pilasters at San Sebastiano and Sant' Andrea. Wittkower felt that this represented an important change in Alberti's thinking. He proposed that the passage from *De re aedificatoria*, 'the principal ornament in all architecture certainly lies in the column'[2], applied to the earlier buildings, and that after the composition of the treatise Alberti modified his theory to favour the pilaster as more suitable decoration for the wall. Wittkower's interpretation failed to account for the consistency of Alberti's attitude towards the column and pilaster (or pier), both in theory and practice throughout his career. Several passages in the treatise show that Alberti considered them less diverse in nature than Wittkower tried to demonstrate[3].

---

[1] Although the interior was built at Pius' stipulation as a hall church, the façade is Bernardo's and, incidentally, it is the one major building in which his own ideas seem to predominate.

[2] 'In tota re aedificatoria primarium certe ornamentum in columnis est' (Leon Battista Alberti, *L'architettura* [*De re aedificatoria*] [tr. G. Orlandi, notes by P. Portoghesi], Milan, 1966, Bk. VI, Chap. xiii [p. 521]). I shall henceforth cite this edition.

[3] 'Paries si erit plus satis gracilis, tunc aut novissimum alterum parietem applicabimus veteri, ut fiat unus, aut impensae vitandae gratia ossa tantum interstruemus, hoc est pilas columnasve trabeales' (X, xvi [p. 991]). 'In prominentibus erunt columnae aut rotundae aut quadrangulae' (VI, xii [p. 519]). 'Columnas natura nimirum primo praebuit ligneas et rotundas; post id usus effecit, ut aliquibus locis haberentur quadrangulae' (I, x [p. 73]). See also the first passage quoted below, p. 194, n. 2.

Wittkower acknowledged a contradiction in the references to the column as ornament and as residue of the wall[1]. But in stating that the first interpretation was the primary one, he did not link the use of columns (and pilasters) to a concept of architecture which is fundamental both to Alberti's treatise and to all his buildings. For Alberti the system of orders should give to the wall a structure analogous to that of animal skeletons (*ossa*):

> Among the chief elements of walls, and perhaps even the most important, are their corners and the pillars or columns, or anything else of that kind, set and incorporated in the walls. This is because they take the place there of [actual] columns supporting the beams and arches of the roof; all these things are called the 'bones' [of the building]. And the vertical elements on each side of the openings are edges or jambs, which at the same time have something of the character of corners and columns. Moreover, the top of the openings, too, i.e. the lintel, will itself be reckoned among the 'bones'—whether it be laid as a straight beam or drawn into the form of an arch. For may I not say that an arch is nothing else than a curved beam? And what should I call a beam but a column laid horizontally? Those elements, on the other hand, which lie and extend between these chief or leading parts will properly be termed 'fillings'[2].

While there is no evidence that Alberti actually followed his own recommendation that the stones of the *ossa* be large and be set deep into the wall, so as to strengthen it[3], his columns and pilasters always have a dual function as ornament and structure.

At San Francesco the ornamental nature of the columns, fluted and embellished with elaborate capitals, is clear; but the columns with the podium and entablature also suggest a structural framework for the wall. Alberti took some pains to articulate this concept of emerging structure, or residue of the wall, according to Wittkower. The entablature breaks out above the four columns, and the frieze and cornice wrap round the projections, uniting the wall with the columns and implying that both belong to the same fabric. The podium upon which both wall and columns rest is carried around the flanks of the church, and there it supports piers, which are of course also to be seen as the remainder of the wall (after the arches between them have been cut away). Now the piers are set precisely the same distance in from the edge of the podium as are the bases of the façade columns. In effect, columns and piers are equated in relationship to the podium, and both are to be understood as vestiges of the wall.

For his later churches Alberti used no columns, only pilasters. Wittkower, thinking that this signified an important change for Alberti, overstressed the factor of ornament in Alberti's attitude

---

[1] Wittkower used the following passage for the second meaning: 'ut de columnis et de his, quae ad columnas pertinentt dicendum sit, quando ipsi ordines columnarum haud aliud sunt quam pluribus in locis perfixus adapertusque paries. Quin e, columnam ipsam diffinisse cum iuvet, fortassis non inepte eam dicam firmam quandam et perpetuam muri partem excitatam ad perpendiculum ab solo imo usque ad summum tecti ferendi gratia' (I, x [p. 71]).

[2] 'Sunt et inter primarias parietum partes, vel in primis praecipuae, anguli et insertae conceptaeque seu pilae seu columnae seu quidvis istiusmodi, quod quidem substinendis trabeationibus arcubusque tectorum illic columnarum sunt loco: quae omnia ossium appellatione veniunt. Sunt et apertionum stantia hinc atque hinc labra, quae angulorum columnarumque insimul naturam sapiunt. Praeterea et apertionum tectum, hoc est superliminare, sive recto sit positum trabe sive arcu ductum, ipsa inter ossa computabitur: nam esse arcum quidem non aliud dicam quam deflexam trabem; et trabem quid aliud quam in transversum positam columnam? Quae autem inter has primarias partes intercurrunt atque extenduntur, recte complementa nuncupabuntur' (III, vi [pp. 195–197]; tr. M. Baxandall). Alberti elsewhere equated the supporting members with the *ossa*: 'Ossa enim aedificii, naturam secuti, hoc est columnas et angulos et eiusmodi, numero nusquam posuere impari' (IX, v [p. 819]). See also the first quotation in n. 3, p. 193 above. David Friedman first suggested to me that the Rucellai design should be linked to Alberti's concept of *ossa*.

[3] 'Similia esse angulis ossa in pariete et apertionum latera condecet, et eo firmiora, quo maioribus ponderibus fortassis fuerint substituenda' (III, vii [p. 203]). 'Atqui hac una in re a complementis ossa ipsa differunt: quod in his media inter crustas infarciuntur fractitio et commutilato quocunque datur lapide, opere prope congestitio et tumultuario; in his alteris nulli aut perquam modici immiscentur lapides incerti, sed tota totum id intimum ordinario extexunt opere' (III, viii [p. 207]).

towards the column. While the form of the support at San Sebastiano is changed, its more important meaning is still consistent with the concept of *ossa*. The key to the strange arrangement of the pilasters is found again in their primary function as expressions of structure. In order to suggest a reinforcement of the wall, Alberti placed the outer pair at the very corners. The inner pair flanks three levels of openings that almost cut away the wall. The impression that the central bay represents a gap in the wall is strengthened by the broken entablature and the arch above which spans the void. In the two-dimensional design the pilasters are important as framing elements, but they work also as visual reinforcements of the wall.

The design for Sant' Andrea was developed from that of San Sebastiano: the central arch became a major motif while the three tiers of openings were moved to the sides (Pl. 32). The wall's mass is more openly expressed by the vault and its projecting framing; the subsidiary order of pilasters encasing the portal could therefore be more decorative than usual for Alberti. The colossal order, no longer placed at the edge of the openings, seems simply to be applied to the wall, and where it overlaps the lower architrave its contact with the wall is made remote. In addition, the moulding round the shafts indicates the ornamental nature of these pilasters. Yet the pilasters at Sant' Andrea are more closely bound to the wall than in any other building: inside the mouldings the shafts are literally embedded in the wall.

Alberti's expression of supporting elements as *ossa* changed in his three documented churches. From the columns of San Francesco, which convey openly a sense of being the supporting structure of the wall, the pilasters of San Sebastiano and Sant' Andrea are more subtle manifestations of the same relationship. At the very core of his architectural style is the articulation by the supporting members both of structure and of ornament. As in the churches, at the Rucellai Palace the two aspects were welded in a way that would not have been possible for any other Quattrocento architect.

The palace façade was designed after San Francesco, but before Santa Maria Novella (Pl. 33). The diverse problems that the two Florentine buildings posed are central for an assessment of their styles. Wittkower's analysis of Santa Maria Novella showed its close relationship to San Francesco. Alberti was working under difficult conditions at the second church, where existing revetment on the lower half and a round window above had to be fitted into the façade. These constraints certainly affected his attitude towards the design, and perhaps encouraged him to adapt for it the solution adopted at San Francesco. Wittkower's theory that in Alberti's façades the replacement of columns with pilasters reflected a basic change in thinking about the relationship of support to wall worked well because his discussion was limited to the churches. James Ackerman, however, suggested that the Rucellai façade might complicate such a tidy explanation[1]. The relative chronology of the palace to Santa Maria Novella is now clear: the palace façade was begun about 1455 but that of the church not until two years later[2]. If Alberti was already using pilasters in 1455, he evidently did not hold the column and pilaster to be so different as Wittkower supposed.

Specific connexions with the Medici Palace will be investigated in the next section, but the strong

[1] J. S. Ackerman, review of Wittkower, *Architectural Principles*, *AB*, XXXIII (1951), p. 197.

[2] The date of 1458 for Santa Maria Novella proposed by Wittkower (p. 45) is based, I think, on documents in the Rucellai Archives that are late copies of those published by Dezzi Bardeschi, *Facciata*, pp. 21–22; Dezzi Bardeschi's documents give 1440 as the initial date of purchase of land later used to finance the Santa Maria Novella façade, but 1440 is a scribe's error and should be corrected to read 1448 (see ASF, Arte del Cambio, 105, f. 16ᵛ and Cat., 703, f. 74ʳ). Dezzi Bardeschi's documents show that 1458 is only a *terminus ante quem* for commencement of the façade; other data I have found suggest that construction began in 1457.

Florentine palace tradition may have suggested to Alberti both the three-storey elevation and the rounded windows of the upper floors. Contrary to that tradition, the ground-floor of the Rucellai Palace is only minimally differentiated from the others; the architect was interested in giving the façade an unprecedented cohesiveness. This is surely why he used drafted masonry on all three floors. The façade had to screen an interior that determined the general location of the horizontal divisions on the exterior. Although the *altana* also existed, Alberti excluded it from the design. The door was already in the centre, which he subtly emphasized by widening that bay slightly. The resulting five-bay arrangement is in accord with his known preference for an odd number of bays. His important innovation was that he chose to define and at the same time to link the storeys by orders of pilasters. There is no strong evidence supporting Forster's proposal that a gradual development in palace architecture can be reconstructed to provide enough antecedents so that the Rucellai classical orders need not be thought remarkable[1]. The three tiers of orders were inspired directly by the Colosseum. The palace design with arches inserted between the pilasters makes it look like a flattened version of the Roman building; it can also be seen as a synthesis of the Colosseum's arcaded tiers and top-storey pilasters. While the ancient source is obvious, equally clear is Alberti's rethinking of every element. He made an important decision when he transformed the engaged columns of the Colosseum to pilasters, playing the stable grid against the intricate pattern of the drafted masonry. No clear ancient precedent was available to him for the combination of pilasters with this type of masonry. Elsewhere at the palace he adapted ancient architecture inventively. He incorporated the distinctive *opus reticulatum*, using it for an ornamental podium to dignify the building, and making the pilasters merge with it. As a result of the height gained with the base, the remaining wall beneath the *cornicione* is very nearly square. This permitted Alberti to contrive pleasing proportions for the pilasters and bays[2]. The *cornicione* provided a logical termination for the pilaster system, and it permitted screening of the troublesome *altana*. At the Colosseum a minor cornice separated the second and third storeys, and Alberti's use of the *cornicione* is derived more directly from that at the Medici Palace, while the form itself has numerous sources in Roman architecture. The rectangular door, used for the first time on a Florentine palace, refers again to ancient architecture, although Brunelleschi had already re-introduced this type of door at the Ospedale degli Innocenti. For the existing Rucellai interior, an arched doorway would have been more appropriate, but the choice of a form that works so well with the grid of the façade is an important illustration of the care with which Alberti treated every detail.

Alberti's activity as architect of the Rucellai façade may have extended beyond the design. The question of his role in his projects has been the subject of much scholarly discussion. L. H. Heydenreich expressed a common view: 'He remained to the end the advisor who laid down the general lines and occasionally gave instructions for details'[3]. Most scholars have used the comparison with the Pienza palace to reject the claim that Rossellino designed the Rucellai façade, but many still cling to the notion of his involvement by assigning to him the execution. They are thus able to give

---

[1] See p. 181, n. 2 above.

[2] The proportions are investigated in P. von Naredi-Rainer, *Musikalische Proportionen, Zahlenästhetik und Zahlensymbolik im architektonischen Werk L. B. Albertis*, Dissertation, Graz, 1975, pp. 51–62. With an entirely different methodology from mine, Naredi-Rainer's interesting (and for the most part convincing) work comes to similar conclusions. He supports Alberti's authorship of the Rucellai Palace and finds the proportions of the five-bay design to be characteristic of Alberti, while those of the eight-bay façade are not. He thus specifically rejects the notion that an eight-bay palace was designed by Alberti. Furthermore, he favours the interpretation that the Rucellai façade was the misunderstood model for Pienza.

[3] L. H. Heydenreich and W. Lotz, *Architecture in Italy 1400 to 1600*, Harmondsworth, 1974, p. 27.

Billi's statement some weight[1], and they have a respectable name to attach to the execution of an Albertian building. But *De re aedificatoria* is filled with the preoccupations of a man concerned with the technical aspects of building, even though Alberti did not include specific comments about directions to stone-workers. Because he was not on the site for the whole construction of his churches, he seems to have made, or to have made, detailed models from which the buildings were executed by trusted foremen. Letters written in connexion with the two documented projects carried out during his lifetime, S. Francesco and S. Sebastiano, prove that he paid close attention to the progress of the work and insisted on being consulted about proposed changes[2]. Documents found recently suggest that his interest and participation in actual building operations have been greatly underestimated[3]. The assumption that he held himself aloof from such activity should be revised, and we should recognize that he was often kept away from the construction sites because of commitments related to his employment by the Church.

Mancini did not know what Alberti did during the pontificate of Callistus III, and few documents have been found to trace his movements in the years 1455 to 1458[4]. His presence in Florence during this period can be proposed on the basis of the Rucellai façade. It was a project where the execution was crucial for the success of the design. Everything about the façade suggests that someone extremely knowledgeable directed the work. Alberti certainly made a detailed drawing[5]. If he was in any case in Florence, he may well have wished to supervise the construction, leaving, however, many duties to a foreman who still cannot be identified[6].

---

[1] Del Badia seems to have been the first to propose this compromise between Vasari and Billi (see p. 179, n. 1 above). Sometimes a further piece of evidence is used to bolster the case for Rossellino as foreman: his 1458 tax report records a credit in Giovanni Rucellai's bank for 169½ large florins. It has been suggested that the money was owed Rossellino for work on the palace, but it is too much for an architect's or supervisor's fee: at the Strozzi Palace the supervising architect received 36 florins per year (Goldthwaite, "Building of the Strozzi Palace", p. 124); and Baccio d'Agnolo was paid two florins per month to supervise construction of the Bartolini Palace (L. Ginori Lisci, *I palazzi di Firenze*, Florence, 1972, I, p. 174). Another possibility, that the money represents a payment to Rossellino as a contractor, is also unlikely. Account books survive for three major Florentine palaces—Medici, Strozzi, Bartolini—and all show that the patron paid artisans directly for most labour and materials. The money owed Rossellino by Giovanni should be understood as a normal deposit, left in the bank until Rossellino could find a good investment for it, for instance in land. (The *catasto* of 1458 shows that he had been buying land since the later 1440s; see for a transcription: F. Hartt, G. Corti, and C. Kennedy, *The Chapel of the Cardinal of Portugal, 1434–1459*, Philadelphia, 1964, pp. 177–84.)

[2] For S. Francesco, see Ricci, *Tempio Malatestiano*, pp. 587–90; for S. Sebastiano see the discussion in Marani and Perina, *Mantova. Le arti*, II, pp. 119–27.

[3] A forceful case for Alberti's involvement at San Sebastiano, with a new document showing that he was even concerned with the scaffolding, is made in G. Guidetti, "Leon Battista Alberti direttore della fabbrica di San Sebastiano", in Marani, ed., *Il Sant' Andrea di Mantova*, pp. 237–41. Johnson found another such document about a different building (*S. Andrea in Mantua*, p. 113 [note 52]).

[4] *Alberti*, p. 369. 1455–58, the proposed dates for construction of the Rucellai façade, coincide with the years of Callistus III's reign; some time in 1455 Alberti was in Mantua (S. Lang, "The Programme of the SS. Annunziata in Florence", *JWCI*, XVII [1954], p. 299).

[5] The drawing here proposed would have been very different in character from the one recently published by Howard Burns ("A Drawing by L. B. Alberti", *Architectural Digest*, XLIX [1979], pp. 45–56).

[6] Very little is known about Nofrio di Biagio, who by 1451 had torn down Giovanni Rucellai's houses on the via dei Palchetti (Doc. VI); but he could have worked on the façade only for a short time, since he died in October 1456. (His will and his widow's repudiation of the inheritance are in ASF, NA, B 2008 [Ser Matteo Boccianti], ff. 87r–88v, 104r–v. Dr. Kent has found the suggestive information that in September 1456 Nofrio, with a number of *scarpellatori*, witnessed the will of Messer Manno Temperani in the house across the via dei Palchetti from the Rucellai Palace [ASF, NA, S 16 (Ser Antonio Salamoni, 1434–57), ff. 201r–204r]). Luca Fancelli, who according to Vasari (*Vite*, II, pp. 545–6) executed Alberti's buildings in Florence, was in the city during the period when the Rucellai façade was constructed, but only for two, or possibly three, short visits, in summer 1456 and September 1458 (see W. Braghirolli, "Luca Fancelli, scultore, architetto e idraulico del secolo XV", *Archivio storico lombardo*, III [1876], p. 613; Braghirolli wrote that Fancelli was in Florence from May to October 1456, but James Lawson has demonstrated to me from the evidence of letters that the visit was much briefer. For a recent discussion of Fancelli see P. Carpeggiani, "Luca Fancelli architetto civile nel contado mantovano: ipotesi e proposte", *Civiltà mantovana*, IV [1969], pp. 87–114).

C. APPENDIX: THE EMBLEMS

If the first five bays of the façade were built about 1455–1458, what of the three interlinked diamond rings displayed on the spandrels of the biforate windows, and the diamond ring with two feathers on the first frieze[1]? These are usually taken to be Medicean emblems, and some scholars have assumed that Giovanni Rucellai would not have displayed them before the betrothal in 1461 of his son Bernardo to Nannina, the daughter of Piero di Cosimo de' Medici[2].

Unfortunately, there is no reliable contemporary literary or documentary information to explain the origin of the use of the diamond ring as an emblem by either the Medici or the Rucellai. In the *Zibaldone* Giovanni Rucellai noted only how his family had acquired the lion on its coat-of-arms. From the Medici side, we have to wait until 1556, when Paolo Giovio tried to interpret the various Medici *imprese*. As have many writers after him, Giovio attempted to link specific *imprese* to particular members of the Medici family, reporting that Clement VII thought the diamond ring with three feathers to be a variation invented by Lorenzo the Magnificent[3]. That is hardly possible, since the same emblem occurs on the San Miniato tabernacle built by his father Piero in 1448–1449.

The Medici used diamond rings elsewhere also as an emblem before the betrothal in 1461. For example, inside their palace, the corbels on the ground floor, already in place by the late 1440s, are decorated with diamond ring and two feathers. The three interlinked diamond rings cannot be found so early, but they occur on the title-page of a book owned by Piero di Cosimo, probably dating from the mid-1450s[4]. Neither of the emblems appears in works patronized by the Rucellai before Giovanni's buildings. Nor are they to be found, in the period in question, on objects or buildings associated with other Florentine families. If investigation of the emblems is limited to their use by the Medici and the Rucellai, the conclusion is not illogical that Giovanni may have adopted the emblems as a result of the kinship established by the engagement, for he was proud of the alliance, and derived considerable benefits from it.

There are difficulties with this attractive argument. In fifteenth-century Florence a man did not commonly take over the emblems of the family into which his son married. I know, indeed, of no such case. A different sort of doubt is raised by the display on the existing *tondo* in the courtyard *loggia* (Pl. 17d). If the *tondo* is the one referred to in the document of 1452 (see pp. 165–66 above), it would then represent a significantly early use by Giovanni Rucellai of the three diamond rings. Even in 1452, the emblematic display could have been inspired by the Medici, and it might even

---

[1] The latter emblem alternates on the frieze with a doughnut-shaped wreath of knobbly surface with three feathers projecting from its centre. This too is strongly suggestive of a Medici emblem, but I have found it only on Rucellai projects.

[2] The betrothal took place in late November or early December 1461 (Document XIV). If Giovanni Rucellai's diamond rings were derived from the Medici, there would be a parallel in another Medici marriage, early in the sixteenth century. After Maria Salviati (herself a grand-daughter of Lorenzo the Magnificent) married Giovanni delle Bande Nere, the Salviati incorporated diamond rings into the *sgraffito* decoration of their villa (G. and C. Thiem, *Toskanische Fassaden-Dekoration*, pp. 89–91). However, a nearly contemporary use of the diamond ring by Giovanni Bartolini on corbels and on a ceiling in the Bartolini Palace is not based on ties of marriage with the Medici; perhaps it resulted from the friendship between the builder's brother and Leo X? (See, for this line of the Bartolini family, Fr. Ildefonso di San Luigi, "Istoria genealogica delle famiglie de' Salimbeni di Siena e de' Marchesi Bartolini Salimbeni di Firenze", *Delizie degli eruditi toscani*, XXV, Florence, 1786, pp. 354–401).

[3] *Ragionamento sopra i motti, disegni d'arme, e d'amore, che communemente chiamano imprese*, Venice, 1556, p. 31. For extensive discussion of the use of emblems by the Medici, see now F. Ames-Lewis, "Early Medicean Devices", *JWCI*, XLII (1979), pp. 122–43.

[4] The MS. is listed in Piero di Cosimo's inventory of 1456 (F. Ames-Lewis, *The Library and MSS. of Piero di Cosimo de' Medici*, Ph.D. thesis, University of London, 1977, p. 380). For a similar device see Ames-Lewis, "Early Medicean Devices", p. 126 and pl. 37 f.

have been conceived in homage to them. But both possibilities are doubtful, especially in view of evidence that permits a different approach towards the questions of the source of the Rucellai diamond rings and the mode of transfer of such emblems.

Outside Florence the use of diamond rings as emblems was much more extensive than has generally been recognized. They occur in a variety of permutations throughout Italy. In Milan, Francesco Sforza used them in combination with other emblems[1]. An intarsia door in the Ducal Palace at Urbino also shows diamond rings; Federigo da Montefeltro may have displayed them to honour his Sforza wife; she was of the Pesaro line of the family, and at the Ducal Palace in Pesaro the main portal is decorated with a chain of diamond rings. In Ferrara, the diamond ring appears about 1455 as one of the many emblems in the illuminated Bible of Borso d'Este[2]. I have seen no earlier examples, but I take seriously the assertion in a seventeenth-century account by Marco Cremosano that it was one of the emblems conferred by Niccolò III d'Este upon Francesco Sforza's father in 1409[3]. Its association with the Este house would already have been well established. Later members of the family used the diamond extensively. It appears on medals of Ercole and his bastard brother Rinaldo, from about 1471 and 1469[4]; it was so strongly connected with Ercole that in 1471 his supporters took it as a rallying cry during the struggle for power against his nephew Niccolò[5]; and later Ercole's brother Sigismondo based the masonry of the Palazzo dei Diamanti on the motif. Thus we have the use of a common emblem, in similar but not identical forms, by the Medici, Giovanni Rucellai, Francesco Sforza, Federigo da Montefeltro, the Pesaro Sforza, and a number of the Este. The diamond can hardly have been adopted independently by each man. Indeed, a significant link can be shown to have existed between Giovanni Rucellai and the Este, at a date long before the Medici-Rucellai alliance: in 1446 the Este already counted Giovanni Rucellai among their faithful friends. A letter of 10 September 1446 from Lionello d'Este to Palla Strozzi remarks: '. . . and similarly it was unnecessary to relate how faithfully in the past Giovanni Rucellai your son-in-law acted for and served our house. . .'[6]. At present, only one instance of Giovanni's service to the Este can

---

[1] See illustrations in *Storia di Milano*, VII, *L'età sforzesca dal 1450 al 1500*, Milan, 1956, pp. 7, 41, 92, 180, 293, 540. Francesco Sforza used three diamond rings as early as 1455 (E. Pellegrin, *La bibliothèque des Visconti et des Sforza ducs de Milan au XVe siècle*, Paris, 1955, p. 412). While Giovanni Rucellai had dealings with Milan, he was not close to Francesco Sforza.

[2] Kindly pointed out by Charles M. Rosenberg.

[3] Reported in P. Mezzanotte and G. Bascapè, *Milano nell' arte e nella storia*, Milan, 1948, pp. 144, 151. See also Ames-Lewis, "Early Medicean Devices", p. 130.

[4] G. F. Hill, *A Corpus of Italian Medals of the Renaissance before Cellini*, London, 1930, nos. 103–4.

[5] L. Chiappini, *Gli Estensi*, Varese, 1967, p. 146.

[6] Letter found by F. W. Kent in AS Ferr., Archivio Bentivoglio, mazzo 2, 8–2, Lettere, 1446–1566 (under date):

Spectabilis et clare vir amice nostre honorande. El non bisognava che ad volere impetrare da nui quello che per vostra littera ce havetti chiesto, ce ricordassi quanto vui siati stato bon amico dela felice memoria del Signore nostro padre, né anche quanto siati nostro; e simile è stato superfluo ramentare quanto fidelmente Johanne Rucellai vostro genero per lo passato habia operato ssé e servito casa nostra, perché tuto già bon pezzo sapiamo e di continuo havemo inteso e cognosciuto quanto e voi e lui habiati amato l'honore e bene de questa nostra casa. Aliegramente e di prompto cuore e bona voglia senza fare altra publica o solenne scriptura de salvoconducto per ogni bon rispecto assecuremo, affidemo, e per questa nostra faciamo pieno e' salvoconducto a Giovanni predeto vostro genero [added in margin: e Giovanni Francesco vostro figliolo] e soi compagni e compagnia per ogni e singule robbe siano de che conditione se vogliano che se ritrovi[no] essere o per l'advenire passasseno in e per le terre nostre de epsi Giovanni [added in margin: e Giovani Francesco predeto] [e] soi compagni e compagnia, e che a lhoro spectino e sia de sua ragione che quanto sia per noi; e per alcuno credito habiamo contra la Magnifica Comunità de Firenze per dinari debiamo havere dela camera del monte non serano in alcuna dele nostre terre e luoghi ritenute né arrestate e serano lassate spazare e andare al suo camino senza alcuno nostro impedimento. Siché statene vui Messer Palla e anche Giovani e soi compagni de bon animo e senza alcuna tema che le robbe de la compagnia serano questo [*sic*] e per nui e per decta cagioni salve da ripresaglia securamente. Se altro possemo per voi e per Giovanni, scrivetelo che nui il faremo voluntiera. Ex Ferrara die x Septembris 1446.

Lionellus Marchio Estensis

be documented: in 1434 he was agent for Niccolò III, procuring in Florence a list of items that included carved coats-of-arms[1]. By 1453 ties between the Este, Strozzi, and Rucellai had probably become even stronger, since another letter shows that business of the Rucellai-Strozzi firm was conducted from Ferrara[2], and Giovanfrancesco Strozzi eventually settled there.

Lionello's letter suggests the possibility that the Este conferred on Giovanni the privilege of displaying the diamond ring[3]. While there are no certain cases of transfer of emblems from one Florentine family to another during the fifteenth century, there are many instances of the nobility of other states giving heraldic privileges to Florentines. The most significant example for the present discussion again involves the Este: in 1475 Ercole granted to Iacopo and Giovanni Lanfredini permission to use Este arms and devices. This was done in a most official manner, through letters patent[4]. Other letters patent, with similar purpose and effect, survive. In 1465 the King of France gave Piero de' Medici and his heirs the privilege of using three fleurs-de-lis on their coat-of-arms; and in 1453 René d'Anjou issued letters patent allowing Otto Niccolini and his heirs to use two fleurs-de-lis[5]. These three cases suggest that the honorary use of emblems was normally thus conferred. Procedure evidently already followed a standard form and demonstrated strong ties of friendship. It is possible, then, that Giovanni Rucellai's diamond rings come from the Este. If they derive from the Medici, this would be a case unique for the fifteenth century, because it would involve the conferring of an emblem within Florence by a bourgeois family.

Furthermore, if the Rucellai emblems are dependent upon the Medici alliance, what of the fourth emblem found on the façade of the Rucellai Palace as well as on Giovanni's other buildings? The wind-filled sail (*vela gonfa*) on the second frieze has never been associated with the Medici, but investigation of the reasons why Giovanni used it reinforces the conclusion presented above about the origin of his diamond rings[6]. Passerini explained it as an allusion to commercial prosperity, adding that other members of the family besides Giovanni used it[7]. He did not name them, however, and I have not found Rucellai sails from the fifteenth century except on Giovanni's buildings[8]. Richa thought the sail might have come from some ancestor of Giovanni who was a ship's captain 'since one sees it used by other Florentine families for that distinction'[9]. All we know about the Rucellai

---

[1] Communication by James Beck.

[2] ASF, MAP, 138, 304 is a letter from the firm 'di Venezia in Ferrara'.

[3] Dr. Ames-Lewis believes that the use of the diamond ring by the Medici derives from their relations with the Este ("Early Medicean Devices", pp. 140–1). The Sforza might seem a more likely source, but I have found no evidence that, during the fifteenth century, recipients of heraldic privileges had the right to confer them upon others.

[4] For the document see M. Mansfield, *A Family of Decent Folk, 1200–1741: A Study in the Centuries Growth of the Lanfredini . . .*, Florence, 1922, pp. 265–6; the key phrase is: '. . . atque Donamus praefati Fratribus eorumque Filiis et descendentibus ut supra, INSIGNIA ac DIVISIAS Nostras et ipsius Domus nostrae Estensis, quae et quos pro eorum libito pingi facere atque deferre possent in Vexillis, Scutis, Armis, Sigillis ac Vestimentis suis, atque suorum, prout eis magis et melius placuerit atque videbitur'.

[5] The Medici letter is translated in J. Ross, *Lives of the Early Medici as told in their Correspondence*, London, 1911, pp. 86–87. Reference is made to the letter from René in G. Niccolini di Camugliano, *The Chronicles of a Florentine Family, 1200–1470*, London, 1933, p. 226.

[6] The origin of some emblems is easily explained. Where the family name itself can be made to refer to a specific object, that object or an allusion to it can be used. For instance, Warburg pointed out that Francesco Sassetti (*sasso*) used a sling in a bookplate and in his chapel at Santa Trinita (*Gesammelte Schriften*, Leipzig, 1932, I, p. 152 = *La Rinascita del paganesimo antico*, Florence, 1966, p. 239). The name Rucellai (Oricellarius) has no such associations.

[7] Passerini, *Rucellai*, "Dell' arme".

[8] Sails, *palle*, and other emblems, including diamond rings, are found on a pair of *cassoni* in the Musée des Arts Décoratifs in Paris; see P. Schubring, *Cassoni*, Leipzig, 1923, nos. 110–111. Werner Weisbach (*Trionfi*, Berlin, 1919, pp. 27–30) may be correct in concluding that these chests were done for the 1466 Rucellai-Medici marriage.

[9] G. Richa, *Notizie istoriche delle chiese fiorentine*, Florence, 1754–62, III, p. 24.

as sailors is that Paolo di Vanni Lapo (1384–1435) was a commander of Florentine galleys[1]. He had no close connection with Giovanni. Warburg's explanation connected the sail to the image of Fortuna, who is shown on a heraldic display of Rucellai arms in the stone *tondo* of the palace courtyard (Pl. 15). Fortuna's dependence upon the winds here echoes a preoccupation of Giovanni's[2]. The sail alone would signify 'wind, wealth, and fate'[3]. Since it is not found in association with the Rucellai before the construction of Giovanni's buildings, we might conclude with Warburg that Giovanni adopted it as a personal *impresa*.

But Giovanni did not have a monopoly on this emblem, even in Florence. It was also used by the Pazzi: it decorates the windows of their palace (probably built in the 1470s); it is inlaid on the back of the wood doors of the Pazzi Chapel (carved in the 1470s); and it hangs from the neck of one of the Pazzi children in the fresco of about 1450 attributed to Castagno from their villa at Trebbio. There was no connection by marriage between the Rucellai and the Pazzi, nor was Giovanni Rucellai close personally or in business to any members of the Pazzi family, so that the common use of the emblem must have developed either independently or from a common source. The Pazzi must have derived the emblem from René d'Anjou, with whom they had strong ties[4]. The identical form of the sail (sometimes attached to a beaded necklace) used by both makes the connexion virtually certain, despite the absence of documentary confirmation. This link does not help to explain why Giovanni Rucellai used the sail, since he had no close relations with René. But Lionello d'Este used a sail, though of different form, on a medal as early as 1444[5]. After his death, in the same struggle for power in which his brother's faction was shouting 'Diamante, diamante', the opposing forces of Niccolò (Lionello's son) countered with 'Vella, vella'[6]. Volker Herzner dismissed the notion of an Este source for the Rucellai emblem, because the two sails look so different, but he did not know of the friendly relations between Giovanni and the Este. If, as suggested above, Giovanni Rucellai's use of the diamond ring depends on his connexions with the Este, then his sail would logically come from them too.

Giovanni's emblems, like those of many other Florentines, were imported, not invented to express personal conceits. They were used to allude to special relationships with noble houses. The differences in form between Giovanni's emblems and those of the Este remain puzzling. The actual appearance of many emblems in fifteenth-century Florence seems not to have been a matter of great importance—the Medici used the diamond ring alone, with two or three feathers, and in other forms, yet no one has been able to discover any significance in the variations[7]. The case of the numbers of *palle* on their coats-of-arms is even better known and reinforces the notion that Florentines treated heraldry rather casually. Only in the early sixteenth century did local families adopt a more punctilious approach; during the same period they developed the practice of conferring emblems upon each other.

---

[1] Paolo was a captain in 1430 and 1431 (M. Mallett, *The Florentine Galleys*, Oxford, 1967, pp. 105, 156).

[2] Warburg, *Gesammelte Schriften*, I, pp. 146–51=*La Rinascita del paganesimo antico*, pp. 232–8.

[3] E. H. Gombrich, *Aby Warburg. An Intellectual Biography*, London, 1970, p. 173.

[4] V. Herzner, "Die Segel-Imprese der Familie Pazzi", MKHIF, XX (1976), pp. 13–32. Herzner's reasoning that Giovanni Rucellai did not use the sail until 1461 is based on an unusual interpretation of Neri di Bicci's *ricordo* (Doc. VIII); he assumes that Neri painted the woman and boy on the carved arms referred to in the preceding phrase (see above, p. 166, n. 1; and his p. 16); he concludes that the present carved *tondo*, with arms and Fortuna, is a later replacement. His citation (n. 13) of a *stemma* at Poppi to support his theory that in 1452 Giovanni was not yet using the sail is also unfounded; the *stemma* was made for Vanni di Paolo Rucellai, not Giovanni di Paolo di Messer Paolo (ASF, Tratte, 67, f. 32r lists the former as *castellano* at Poppi in 1452.) Cf. Perosa, p. 150 above; and Kent, p. 86, n. 2 above.

[5] Hill, *Corpus*, no. 32.

[6] Chiappini, *Gli Estensi*, p. 152.

[7] This general conclusion is supported by Dr. Ames–Lewis's investigations (personal communication).

V. THE PATRON, HIS PALACE AND HIS LOGGIA

After 1445, when the Medici Palace was begun[1], the building of palaces both by members of the ruling clique and by men who were neither allied with the Medici nor very prominent politically was so widespread as to indicate a climate favourable to such enterprises[2]. As a showy private residence, the Medici Palace was a generic example for many later buildings, because of its huge scale and because of the authority of the patron. Its impact on style, however, is not always obvious.

My dating of about 1455–1458 for the original Rucellai façade puts the project at a time when Giovanni was both immensely wealthy, and able to function in most ways as an ordinary citizen, even though he was not permitted to sit on the highest government councils and felt himself mistrusted by the Medici regime. His palace was evidence of his taste and magnificence, in a medium that he knew Cosimo understood. It is important to realize how strongly his façade was influenced by Cosimo's (Pl. 35).

On the Medici Palace, for the first time on a private building in Florence, the street façades were faced entirely with dressed stone. The revetment of the Rucellai Palace may be the first reflection of this important Medici innovation[3]. The Medici Palace also introduced the stone *cornicione* to Florentine domestic architecture. Earlier palaces had been protected by projecting wooden roofs, and that less ostentatious (and less expensive) practice was followed at all other palaces, except the Rucellai, until the Strozzi Palace at the end of the century. Only these palaces, and the Strozzino and Pazzi, have biforate windows. The windows were unusual enough in Florence about 1455 to justify the assumption that Giovanni Rucellai and his architect had in mind the formal precedent of the Medici Palace. The borrowing of both *bifore* and cornice should be understood as Giovanni intended: he was acknowledging his esteem for Cosimo's palace.

Drafted masonry similar to that covering the Rucellai Palace had been used on the ground floors of late Trecento palaces (Davanzati, Minerbetti, della Stufa), and the Rucellai version may have been developed from that tradition. But on the assumption that there is a special relationship between the Medici and Rucellai Palaces, one may reasonably suppose that this type of revetment was adapted from its recent revival on the first floor of the Medici Palace. All elements derived from the Medici Palace are adjusted at the Rucellai to harmonize with the pilaster-entablature system. The cornice is the logical termination for such a design. In comparison with the Medici cornice it is moderate in

---

[1] D. V. and F. W. Kent, "Two Comments of March 1445 on the Medici Palace", *BM*, CXXI (1979), pp. 795–6.

[2] I differ from Howard Saalman, for whom the building of a pretentious palace like Rucellai's was 'a direct affront to the notoriously sensitive Medici', and would have been undertaken 'only after successful family alliances with the dominant house'. See his "The Authorship of the Pazzi Palace", *AB*, XLVI (1964), p. 391. The argument applies no better to the Tornabuoni than to the Rucellai. Lucrezia Tornabuoni married Piero de' Medici in 1443, but the Tornabuoni Palace was probably not begun before 1465 (I thank Caroline Elam for documentation of this). The time gap is too long for the construction to have been dependent on the marriage. At least ten palaces that survive substantially intact were begun between 1445 and 1465. They are: Neroni-Gerini, Ridolfi-Guidi, Strozzino, Rucellai, Lenzi-Quaratesi, Spinelli, Pitti, Gianfigliazzi, Neroni, Boni-Antinori. I hope to publish an extensive study of this group of palaces and their patrons. For an examination of the building boom over the longer period from the later Trecento to the early Cinquecento, see R. A. Goldthwaite, "The Florentine Palace as Domestic Architecture", *American Historical Review*, LXXVII (1972), pp. 977–1012.

[3] This statement depends on the date of the Strozzino Palace, which could have been started about 1451, or as late as 1458. See the assessment by Harriet McNeal Caplow (*Michelozzo*, New York and London, 1977, II, pp. 558–60). Her conclusion that the palace was completed by 1457 may be subject to modification; the last house, bought late in 1457, was on the piazza, and it was probably incorporated into the façade.

projection and mass, so as not to bear down on the subtle relief of the wall below. The *bifore* are given architraves to integrate them with the grid.

Finally, a precedent for Giovanni's emblematic display is to be found in Medici buildings, although my dating of the Rucellai façade and the material assembled on pp. 198–201 above suggest that the emblems did not symbolize the union of the two families. On Cosimo's palace the roundels within the biforate windows are decorated with *palle*, diamond rings with two feathers, or roses. This is the first Florentine palace façade with emblematic allusions to the owner; previously only the family coat-of-arms had been used. At the Rucellai Palace the corresponding roundels were left open, and the emblems were moved to the spandrels. Giovanni also took the opportunity offered by friezes for emblematic embellishment. There are numerous examples of such friezes in works patronized by the Medici, for instance on the San Marco campanile, on the piers of the church at Bosco ai Frati, on the inlaid frieze of the tabernacle at San Miniato al Monte. Such use of emblems in the 1440s in Florence is unique to the Medici, and Giovanni Rucellai's similar display must be understood to have been borrowed from the Medici.

Giovanni was probably responsible for the incorporation of emblems, the cornice, the *bifore*, and the masonry in the Rucellai Palace design. One detail indicates that Alberti had something of a struggle fusing Giovanni's requirements with his own ideas about forms. The design of the upper windows looks as if it derives from a compromise between a Florentine *bifora* and the squared cross-barred window to which Alberti may first have inclined.

Giovanni Rucellai, like all palace builders, sought the admiration of his fellow citizens. The *Zibaldone*'s indirect expression of this hope in the form of a paraphrase from Cicero's *De officiis* is quoted above (p. 55, n. 2). 'We have heard', says Giovanni,

> that Gnaeus Octavius, the first of his family to be elected a consul of Rome, attained very great honour because he built a beautiful palace on the Palatine Hill; the palace was full of renown and impressiveness because it showed good order and measure; it is thought that the palace brought him much good-will and esteem from the people.

It is significant that Giovanni's attention was focused on the possible effects of an impressive house for the furtherance of a political career. His addition to Cicero's text of the awkward phrase "because it [i.e. the palace] showed good order and measure" confirms that Giovanni was likening his house and his experience to those of Gnaeus Octavius.

This passage was entered in the *Zibaldone* about 1464, well after the five-bay façade was built and after Giovanni Rucellai had held high political office. It can nevertheless be argued that one of his motives in building the palace was his hope that he might emulate the ancient Roman. In the event, it was not Giovanni's palace but the marriage alliance with the Medici which reversed his political fortunes. Writing after the fact, however, Giovanni must have felt that his beautiful palace played no small part in his success. He was rich, he had been loyal to Palla Strozzi but irreproachable in his behaviour towards the régime. He was making himself a force to be reckoned with, not least through his magnificent building campaigns.

Giovanni Rucellai thought of the palace almost as an extension of himself. His will of 1465, with its long stipulations for ensuring ownership and occupation by his descendants, conveys the message: Giovanni was mortal but his house would endure[1]. Though he had owned and lived in Iacopo

---

[1] *Fidecommessi* for houses frequently appear in wills of the Quattrocento; Giovanni's desire to tie his palace to the Rucellai family was unusual, if not unique, in the extreme length with which he covered every possible contingency.

Antonio's house for seven years, it was not included in his *fidecommesso*. This fact and the difference in treatment of this portion has already led us to the conclusion that it had not yet received its revetment. Thus, to Giovanni Rucellai, the cherished house was the one with the façade, which was of primary importance as the eloquent expression of his consequence.

In the design, Alberti may have had some idea of re-creating the palace style of ancient Rome[1]. Giovanni's use of Cicero tends to support this interpretation; he probably welcomed the notion that he lived in the most 'Roman' house in Florence. On the other hand, a case cannot be made for a contribution by Giovanni to the selection of the façade's most novel feature, the pilaster-entablature system. Paradoxically, the palace was built for a man who was not an active student of humanist thought in Florence. Furthermore, no evidence exists to suggest that Giovanni was considered by his contemporaries to be knowledgeable about architecture. Disputes involving buildings were frequently arbitrated by other patricians but never, it seems, by Giovanni Rucellai; there are indications that Cosimo de' Medici may have contributed significantly to the style of his buildings[2]. Giovanni's *Zibaldone* occasionally mentions architecture, notably in the account of his visit to Rome. His comments seem to be personal observations, showing that he was sensitive to the impact of architecture, but revealing no particular understanding of design. He was not even fascinated with ancient monuments—his praise goes to medieval Rome, to the magnificent rows of columns and especially to the rich marble decorations. If our object were to characterize his participation in the projects for Santa Maria Novella and San Pancrazio, we would have to consider more closely the attraction for him of medieval marbles. For the classicizing façade of his house Giovanni merely found the architect, indicated a number of elements he hoped could be included in the design, and left the rest to Alberti. When Giovanni involved himself in architectural planning, he was not totally successful.

An understanding of Giovanni's motives may clarify the conditions under which the palace was conceived, but the style of its façade is due solely to the architect. Alberti may have been encouraged by his patron to incorporate features from the Medici Palace, and to spare no expense for materials and labour, but Giovanni had no part in developing the stunning system of organization. And while Giovanni was proud of the new façade, he had little understanding of its ingenuity; the only comment we have by him is the reference to its 'buono ordine e chosa misurata'. Proof that he did not appreciate the genius of his façade is imprinted on its extension, where Alberti was no longer involved. If Giovanni had perceived the subtleties of Alberti's design, he could have insisted that the master in charge of the second portion follow the first five bays more carefully. When not even the patron, to whom Alberti surely explained his ideas, comprehended the design, it is small wonder that the rest of Florence failed to appreciate it.

The foregoing has occasionally shown that Giovanni Rucellai's role as patron was important. With the development of the palace project and the Rucellai Loggia, the nature of his involvement changed.

It is startling to recall that in the late 1420s and 1430s Giovanni, his mother, and brothers had begun to buy property next to the corner house. Leading up to the division of property in 1442, or perhaps shortly afterwards, must have come his decision to build a large new house. By 1452 he had reconstituted six houses into respectable living quarters. A grand façade was, however, not built

---

[1] Howard Burns suggested this.

[2] U. Procacci, "Cosimo de' Medici e la costruzione della Badia fiesolana", *Commentari*, XIX (1968), pp. 80–97. I am convinced that the Medici Palace is as much Cosimo's creation as Michelozzo's.

or even planned in conjunction with this interior, which therefore must have been important in itself for Giovanni Rucellai. Around 1455 the five-bay façade was begun, with a design by Alberti that was wonderfully adapted to the proportions and peculiarities of the standing wall, and to the site as well. The centralized arrangement sets up an axial relationship between the doorway and the via del Purgatorio that extends the visual impact of the palace right down the street (Pls. 12, 24a). This approach to the palace was more important in the fifteenth century than today, for a covered alley, the Volta dei Minerbetti, ran from the largest arch of the Palazzo Minerbetti (on the via Tornabuoni) through to the via del Purgatorio[1].

In the initial façade project, revetment progressed over the ground floor but, on the death of Iacopo Antonio in January 1456, Giovanni continued construction, allowing a few blocks on the first and second storeys to extend past the fifth bay. The façade was completed in this manner, but it must have looked "unfinished". In 1458, when the five-bay revetment had been substantially completed, Giovanni managed to acquire Iacopo Antonio's house. In order to finish the extension, however, he realized that he would need more street frontage and would have to buy the next house (Giovanni d'Antonio's) too. This he never succeeded in doing although he must already have begun the attempt by 1458. So for at least seven years he left the five-bay façade as it was.

Meanwhile, he remodelled Iacopo Antonio's house, co-ordinating it with the original palace interior by extending walls and opening large rooms. The extension of the façade, executed sometime between 1465 and 1470, certainly carried with it Giovanni's fond hope that the façade would eventually be finished neatly; but that was dependent on acquisition of Giovanni d'Antonio's house. The extension was done without Alberti's participation in design or execution. It is interesting to explore further this assertiveness by Giovanni Rucellai, and to connect it with developments across the street at the site that was to become the Rucellai Loggia.

The new loggia and piazza altered the effect of the five-bay palace. When the original façade was designed and built, the character of the site was very different from now, for at the junction of the via della Vigna and the via del Purgatorio there was some opening, but not as large as today's piazza. In April 1456 a distant relative gave Giovanni some land on the projecting eastern corner for the stated purpose that a loggia be built there[2]. However, when the Rucellai Loggia was finally begun seven years later, it was located further east than originally proposed; the new site allowed the opening between the two streets to be enlarged to create the piazza (Pl. 12). Giovanni had to wait until 1462 or 1463 for the larger site, but he must have had designs on it soon after the 1456 donation; otherwise, one assumes, he would have begun the loggia earlier. The location proposed in 1456 would have fitted well with the five-bay palace, but in that year Giovanni was already aspiring to a wider façade. The original loggia would have been tucked under a house, and more important, it would have cut into the space in front of the proposed larger palace. So he worked to obtain a site that would permit him to clear land for the piazza and would also allow room for a grander loggia. After the Rucellai Loggia had been built, the original palace must have looked a little odd, off to one side of the piazza, and the second phase of the façade revetment took place quickly. Evidently the

[1] L. Ginori Lisci (*I palazzi di Firenze*, Florence, 1972, I, pp. 180–2, Fig. 163) presented sixteenth-century evidence showing that the *volta* was open. That it was also considered a thoroughfare is proved by a document of 1459, in which one *confino* for a shop beneath Andrea Minerbetti is given as 'via cum volta supra' (ASF, NA, F 499 [Ser Francesco di Dino], f. 334r). In 1577, in a vain effort to block plans for closing the *volta*, members of the neighbourhood recited the advantages of leaving it as it was. Included is a reference to the 'sfondato, che va riscontro al palazzo de' Rucellai' (ASF, Capitani di Parte, numeri neri, filza ordinaria 1195 [1576–77], ff. 694r–695r. Document found and kindly shared by Caroline Elam).

[2] The complex development of the Loggia project is reconstructed in my article in *MKHIF*, XXI (1977), pp. 183–98.

decision to build a larger loggia together with the piazza was made in 1456 or 1457 and in conjunction with Giovanni Rucellai's determination to extend the palace.

There is still some question as to the ultimate size that Giovanni had in mind for his façade. The
usual assumption is that he would simply have finished off the eighth bay. In support of this would
be not only the regularity of such a two-door palace, but the analogy with the solution put together
at Pienza. But two problems are raised. The eighth bay would cover less than half Giovanni
d'Antonio's house; and the outer edge of the eighth bay would not relate in a logical manner to the
Loggia. When Giovanni succeeded in getting the larger site for the Loggia, he chose to set it perpendicular to the palace, with the columns lining up precisely with the point on the front of Giovanni
d'Antonio's house where a ninth bay would have ended (Pls. 12, 24d). This may be a coincidence,
but the fact is that Giovanni had considerable leeway for the placement of the Loggia. His broadening
of the piazza shows that he was concerned with manipulating the effects of his buildings. It thus
seems strange to think that the siting of the present Loggia was not intended to relate that building
in a meaningful way to the projected palace—especially when with a ninth bay almost the whole
breadth of Giovanni d'Antonio's house would have been used. There is no way of proving the nine-
bay hypothesis, and a major argument against it—the consequent asymmetry of the façade—is not
insignificant. But the idea that Giovanni was thinking ahead to a nine-bay façade gives a rationale
for the placement of the Loggia. And it leads to a vision of a startlingly tight and closely co-ordinated
handling of architecture and space in a fifteenth-century urban complex[1].

All this reveals an interesting attitude on the part of the patron, whether one believes that Giovanni
planned an eight-bay or nine-bay façade. From a purely aethestic point of view, Alberti's design for
the five-bay façade amply compensated for the moderate dimensions of the palace in its original
spatial context, but when the possibility of expansion arose, consideration of size became dominant.
The extension of the palace does not follow a design by Alberti; nor does it accord with his principles, for he surely would have baulked at the two-door idea, not to speak of an asymmetrical
design. Elsewhere I have argued also against his participation in the Loggia. It seems sensible to conclude that he had nothing to do with the conception of the extension, piazza, or present Loggia. All
evidence points rather to Giovanni Rucellai as the main thinker in these new projects, in a single-
minded determination to increase the impact of his buildings[2]. In comparison with his earlier activity
in acquiring the site, his methods became more forceful and direct. One may recall his use of ragged
edges twice on his palace as he tried to buy first Iacopo Antonio's house, then Giovanni d'Antonio's.
Then again there is the case of the Loggia: he waited seven years for a widow to die, and cajoled her
heirs to give him her house for the new site of the Loggia; when one heir refused, Giovanni went
ahead, razing the house and building the Loggia. Giovanni d'Antonio resented such high-handed
tactics, and during his lifetime he resisted pressure from his relative, finally placing on his own
house a prohibition of sale that would be legally binding after his death.

---

[1] The remarks in this paragraph supplement my article on the Rucellai Loggia, and provide what may well be a solution to one
of the major issues left open there. The suggestion that Giovanni Rucellai envisioned a nine-bay palace was made by Beverly
Brown, to whom I am grateful not only for the idea, but for the two supporting arguments regarding the placement of the Loggia
and the probability that Giovanni would have wanted to extend his façade over a reasonably large portion of Giovanni d'Antonio's
house.

[2] I believe that the revetment on the via dei Palchetti side of the palace—half a bay long, without windows—belongs to the
campaign of the 1460s. The stonework beyond the pilasters is sloppy and frequently does not follow the courses on the façade.
But its visual impact is effective; from the west down the via della Vigna, the ragged edge of this masonry is covered by the
house on the opposite corner, and the palace revetment appears to extend down the via dei Palchetti (Pl. 24c).

Giovanni di Paolo's actions also had an enormous effect on the scale of building operations. He was interested in greater size for all three elements—palace, piazza, and loggia. His further ambition was to create an open space in front of the palace that made its whole width visible, thus providing it with an enhancing setting. Just as important, the building and the piazza appeared to be inextricably bound together. On the second side of the piazza, the Loggia reinforces the effect of Rucellai domination in this impressive island. Such then was Giovanni's intention. To some extent he was successful, but his efforts reveal a preoccupation with scale that contrasts sharply with the concern for fine design that governed Alberti.

VI. DOCUMENTS*

I

SALE TO GIOVANNI DI PAOLO RUCELLAI BY LEONARDO DI BENEDETTO DI COMO OF HOUSE 4, ON VIA DEGLI STAMAIUOLI (VIA DEI PALCHETTI)

12 April 1445

ASF, NA, S 17 (Ser Antonio Salamoni, 1436–47)

Venditio pro florenis 80

Item postea, dictis anno indictione et die duodecimo mensis aprilis. Actum in populo Sancti Pranchatii de Florentia presentibus Goro Cini Jacopi Cini rimendatore populi Sancti Michaelis Bisdomini de Florentia et Girolamo Francisci dello Scarfa lanaiuolo populi Sancti Pauli de Florentia et Johanne Andree Petrini setaiuolo populi Sancti Jachopi ultra Arnum de Florentia, omnibus testibus etc.

Leonardus olim Benedicti Chomi de Federigis lanaiuolus populi S. Pranchatii de Florentia, pro se et suos heredes, iure proprio et in perpetuum, dedit vendidit tradidit et concessit Iohanni olim Pauli domini Pauli de Oricellariis dicti populi S. Prancatii, presenti recipienti et ementi pro se et suis heredibus et pro illo vel illis quem vel quos nominaverit in emptorem dictorum infrascriptorum bonorum, unam domum cum terreno et cella, puteo et curia et salis et cameris, contigua cum quadam alia domu dicti Leonardi. Que domus posita est Florentie, in populo S. Pranchatii predicti, in via cui dicitur la via degli Stamaiuoli, cui domui a primo dicta via, a II dicti Leonardi, a III Cristofani Antonii cimatoris, a IIII bona Iachopantonii olim Bingerii de Oricellariis, infra predictos confines etc. Ad habendum etc., una cum omnibus etc. Et cum omni iure etc. Constituens etc. donec etc. Pro pretio et nomine veri et iusti pretii florenorum ottuaginta auri, quod pretium dictus venditor fuit confessus habuisse et recepisse a dicto emptore in pecunia numerata ... [Formulae follow, including the naming of a guarantor of the contract, and the renunciation by Leonardo's wife Brigida to all rights over the house].

II

SALE TO GIOVANNI DI PAOLO RUCELLAI BY LEONARDO DI BENEDETTO DI COMO OF HOUSE 5, ON VIA DEGLI STAMAIUOLI (VIA DEI PALCHETTI)

12 April 1445

ASF, NA, S 17 (Ser Antonio Salamoni, 1436–47)

Venditio pro florenis 80

Item postea, incontinenti, eodem anno indictione et die, loco et coram dictis suprascriptis testibus etc. ad infrascripta omnia vocatis etc.

---

* The transcriptions of Documents 1–3, 9, 13, 17 and 21 are by Dr. Gino Corti. Dr. Corti checked all other documents.

Prefatus Leonardus olim Benedicti Chomi de Federigis, lanaiuolus dicti populi S. Pranchatii, pro se et suos heredes, iure proprio et in perpetuum, dedit vendidit tradidit et concessit Iohanni olim Pauli domini Pauli de Oricellariis dicti populi S. Pranchatii, presenti et ementi pro se et suis heredibus et pro illo vel illis quem vel quos nominaverit in emptorem, infrascripta bona: unam domum cum terreno, curia et puteo et salis et cameris et aliis hedifitiis super se, positam Florentie in populo S. Pranchatii predicti, in via cui dicitur la via degli Stamaiuoli, cui a primo dicta via, a II Niccholai ser Filippi, a III dicti Iohannis, a IIII Jachopantonii Bingerii de Oricellariis, infra predictos confines etc., ad habendum etc. una cum omnibus etc., et cum omni iure etc. Constituens etc. donec etc. Pro pretio et nomine veri et iusti pretii florenorum auri ottuaginta retti ponderis etc., quod pretium dictus venditor fuit confessus et contentus habuisse et recepisse a dicto emptore in pecunia numerata ... [Formulae, as in Document I, follow].

III

SALE TO GIOVANNI DI PAOLO RUCELLAI OF THE LAND (CLEARED) OF HOUSE 6

21 March 1446

ASF, NA, N 127 (Ser Niccolò di Francesco, 1444–1448), f. 143ʳ [the second with that number]

Item postea dictis anno indictione et die xxi mensis martii. Actum Florentie, in populo Sancti Stefani abbatie, presentibus testibus etc. ser Bartolomeo Antonii Johannis Nuti et ser Niccholaio Pieri Bernardi, civibus et notariis florentinis, et ser Antonio Filippi de Prato notario florentino.
Pateat omnibus evidenter quod Niccholaus filius quondam ser Filippi ser Micchaellis Jacobi de Podio Bonizi, civis florentinus, iure proprio etc. dedit vendidit etc. Johanni olim Pauli domini Pauli de Oricellariis de Florentia, et civi et mercatori florentino, presenti et ementi pro se etc., infrascripta bona, videlicet: Terrenum et solum tantum, deducta et excepta superficie unius domus dicti Niccholai, positum Florentie in populo Sancti Pranchatii, in via de' Palchetti, cui a I via predicta, a II et III dicti emptoris, a IIII Jacobiantonii Bingerii de Oricellariis, infra predictos confines etc. Ad habendum etc., que bona etc. precario etc. Et cessit omnia jura etc., ipsumque constituit procuratorem in rem suam etc. Et promixit etc. defensionem generalem etc., et in casu evictionis restitutionem infrascripti pretii et insuper florenorum centum aureorum pro dannis expensis etc. Pro pretio florenorum triginta aureorum etc., quod pretium etc. fuit confessus etc. Et salva etc. eidem venditori tota superficie ipsius domus et soli et iure demoliendi et removendi a dicto solio [sic] et terreno vendito totum [sic] superficiem et edifitium dicte domus existentis super dicto solo vendito, quam superficiem et edifitium promixit deinde demoliri et removeri facere ad omnem ipsius emptoris voluntatem et requisitionem etc. [Formulae follow].

IV

EXCERPT FROM TAX REPORT OF GIOVANNI RUCELLAI

February 1447

ASF, Cat., 672, f. 535ʳ (new pencil foliation)
Acquisition numbers of houses added

Dal catasto di Giovanni Rucellai e fratelli, gonfalone detto a 202 per habitazione.

[1] Una chasa per mio abitare colle maserizie nel popolo di San Branchazio nella via della Vingna, da primo e secondo via da terzo Mona Chaterina mia madre.

Al '51 a conto suo, Lion Rosso 175 per suo uxo.

Dal catasto di Francesco e Betto di Benedetto, Lion Rosso 279.

[2] Una chasa in detto popolo nella via degli Stamaiuoli, da primo via da secondo io medesimo da terzo Jacopo Antonio Ruciellai, apigionata a'Ntonio di Cristofano di Romolo bechaio per pregio di fiorini 11 l'anno.

Al '51 a suo conto in quella di sua abitazione, 175.

Questa che dice una vuole dire 2, ché l'una viene dal catasto di Buonachorso di Lucha, Lion Rosso 38, e l'altra da' catasto d'Antonio di Piero sta al sale, Lion Rosso 117.

[4–5] Un' altra chasa in detto popolo e luogho, che da primo via da secondo e terzo San Branchazio di Firenze da quarto io medesimo, apigionata a Carlo d'Antonio Ruciellai per pregio di fiorini dodici l'anno, la quale conperai fiorini 160 da Lionardo di Benedetto da Como di detto ghonfalone, carta per Ser Antonio di Salamone, sotto dì 28 d'aprile 1445.

Al '51 a chonto suo chome di sopra.

[Canc.: Non si truova] Dal catasto [. . .] è per unire colla casa della sua habitazione, Lion Rosso 223 inn Antonio di Ghuido cimatore.

[6] Conperai adì 21 di marzo 1445 da Nicholaio di Ser Filippo da Poggibonzi cierto terreno d'una chasetta alato a quella di sopra per pregio di fiorini 30, carta per mano di Ser Nicholò di Francesco. Non ò alcuno frutto.

V

EXCERPT FROM TAX REPORT OF GIOVANNI RUCELLAI'S MOTHER, CATERINA, IN HOUSE 3

August 1451

ASF, Cat., 707, f. 406^r

Dal primo catasto di Antonio di Giovanni Ruciellai, Lion Rosso 48; e al '47 a suo conto, Lion Rosso 145 per suo abitare.

Una chaxa per mio abitare nel popolo di Santo Branchazio, da primo via da secondo Jacopo Antonio Ruciellai da terzo e quarto Giovanni Rucellai mio figliuolo; nel primo chatasto la troverete a conto d'Antonio e Piero e Paolo di Giovanni Rucellai, detto ghonfalone.

VI

EXCERPT FROM TAX REPORT OF GIOVANNI RUCELLAI

August 1451

ASF, Cat., 707, f. 402^r

Dal primo catasto suo, Lion Rosso 202; e al '47 a suo conto, 220 per suo

Una chasa nel popolo di San Branchazio di Firenze nella via della Vigna per mio abitare, da primo via della Vigna da secondo via di uxo; al '69, Lion Rosso 376 a Giovanni detto per uso chon altre chase.

Stamaiuoli da terzo Cristofano cimatore da quarto Jachopo Antonio Ruciellai.

Right margin: Avemone fede di mano di Nofrio di Biagio maestro di murare che disse avere disfa[tte?]. Nota che nella casa di sua abitazione v'en drento oltre alla sua, 2 chase dal primo catasto di Bonacchorso di Lucha Ruciellai, Lion Rosso 38 e alla decima [*canc.*: del '47 da Lionardo di Benedetto di Chomo] a suo conto, Lion Rosso 220; e più una chasa [*canc.*: dalle rede] di Benedetto di Ser Francesco dell' arte della lana, Lion Rosso 279, e al '47 a suo conto.

VII

ENTRY FROM BOTTEGA BOOK OF APOLLONIO DI GIOVANNI AND MARCO DEL BUONO

1452

BNC, Magliabechiano 37. 305, p. 110
(*summary by Carlo Strozzi*)[1]

A Giovanni di Pagolo Rucellai dipingono un tondo nel cielo della loggia, 1452, f. 9.

VIII

MEMORANDUM OF NERI DI BICCI

1455

Uffizi Gallery, Library[2]

A dì 6 di giugnio 1455

Lavoro fe' a Giovanni Rucelai

Richordo ch'el sopradetto dì io Neri di Bicci dipintore tolsi a dipigniere da Giovanni Rucelai in chasa sua cinque archi di chonc[i]o chontrafatto e una arme di rilievo chol cimiere e dua meze fighure, 1ª dama e uno gharzone in fresco a tuta sua ispesa e non n'è fatto merchato. A dì 24 di luglio 1455 feci patto chon Giovanni sopradetto del sopradetto lavoro fatto; d'achordo me ne debe dare l. [*canc.*: quindici] venti. l. 20. A libro D a c.10.

---

[1] Ellen Callmann, *Apollonio di Giovanni*, Oxford, 1974, p. 78. This excerpt was earlier published by Schubring with the date given as 1451 and the words "un tondo" omitted (P. Schubring, *Cassoni*, Leipzig, 1923, I, p. 433).
[2] Neri di Bicci, *Le Ricordanze* (ed. Bruno Santi), Pisa, 1976, pp. 28–29.

IX

BARATTO BETWEEN GIOVANNI RUCELLAI AND SAN PANCRAZIO OF HOUSE 8 FOR A SHOP

9 April 1457

ASF, NA, G 678 (Ser Griso Griselli, 1453–1459), ff. 142ʳ⁻ᵛ

[f. 142ʳ] Permutatio facta per capitulum
et conventus Sancti Pancratii de
Florentia, et Iohannem Pauli de Rucellais

In Dei nomine amen. Anno ab eius salutifera incarnatione millesimo quadringentesimo quinquagesimo septimo, indictione quinta et die viiiiᵃ mensis aprilis. Actum in monasterio Sancti Pancratii ordinis Vallis Umbrose, presentibus discretis viris Francisco Bartolomei olim alterius Bartolomei dicti populi Sancti Pancratii, Johanne Laurenzii Foglie populi Sancte Marie Aquaris [Aquaius? Maioris?], testibus vocatis etc.
Convocatis ad capitulum omnibus et singulis monacis etc. monasterii Sancti Pancratii ordinis Vallis Umbrose, de mandato etc. domini Benedicti abbatis etc., ad sonum campanelle etc. ut moris etc. ob quam quidem convocationem etc. convenerunt etc. in loco soliti capituli etc. infrascripti etc.

Dominus Benedictus Angeli, Abbas predictus
Dominus Matheus Antonii de Sancto Godenzio
Dominus Petrus Sandri de Prato
Dominus Benedictus Ughonis de Florentia
Dominus Johannes Ghabrielis de Buonromeis
Dominus Tomasius [. . .] de Florentia
Dominus Johannes Petri de Florenzia

omnes monaci conventus etc. asserentes se esse duas partes et ultra omnium monacorum dicti monasterii etc., et in se residere totam vim dicti capituli etc., ipse abbas una cum eis et ipsi una cum dicto abbate etc. in simul congregati etc., sic que dictis monacis et capitulo etc., idem ex dictis presens dominus Benedictus exposuit etc. quod illis notum esse debet qualiter dictus monasterius Sancti Pancratii habet unam domum cum palchis et aliis edificiis positam in dicto populo et in via que vulgariter appellatur la via degli Stamaiuoli, cui a primo via, a II bona Johanis Pauli de Rucellais, a III bona heredum Jacobi Antonii Bingerii Rucellai, a 4° dicti monasterii Sancti Pancratii. Que domus per antecessorem suum concessa fuit ad vitam Antonii [. . .] cimatoris et domine Laurenzia eius uxoris et Cristofori et Francisce filiorum suorum non nullorum pro pretio florenorum [. . .], ex quibus nunc supervivit Cristoforus Antonii cimatoris, etatis annorum [. . .] vel circa, cuius domus dictum monasterium habebat pro pensione ante dictam concessionem, singulis annis, florenos tredicim. Que domus si ex nunc venderetur ac iure proprius [*sic*] et in perpetuum concederetur post mortem dicti Cristofori, Johanni Pauli Rucellai et suis heredibus. Dictus Johannes offert et vult ex nunc dare et consignare et tradere infrascripto modo dicto monasterio Sancti Pancratii, pro pretio et in cambium dicte domus, unam appotecam ad usum pelliciarii, positam Florentie in populo Sancti Petri Buonconsigl[i]o et in via que vulgariter appellatur la via de' Pellicciai, pro cuius pensione solvitur singulis annis florenos decem et otto et pro dicto pretio eam nunc tenet Nicolaus Iohannis Ugonis pelliciarius. Cui a primo dicta via de' Pellicciai, a 2° platea que dicitur la piaza del lino, a 3° bona Donati Pauli Rucellai, a 4° Cristofori Mathei del Teglia. Cum hoc declarato quod dicta apotheca post mortem supradicti Cristofori solummodo sit et esse debeat et intelligatur dicti monasterii, capituli et conventus Sancti Pancratii et non antea, et cum dicto Johanni et suis heredibus consignabitur et tradetur libera et expedita dicta domus supra posita et confinata. Ante vero mortem dicti Cristofori et consignationem dicte domus, dictus Johannes et eius heredes recipere possint et debeant pensionem dicte apothece, prout et quem ad modum si huiusmodi cambium et permutatio et seu alteratio facta non esset. [f. 142ᵛ] Et etiam cum his pactis et conditionibus. Imprimis, videlicet quod per dictum Iohannem emptorem vel eius heredes et cui concesserint, parietes dicte domus non possint altius erigi nec super illis quicquam altius hedificari quam impresentiarum sit comingnolus tecti dicte domus. Et quod in dictis parietibus qui versus dictum monasterium Sancti Pancratii pergunt, fieri non possit aliqua alia fenestra sine licentia abbatis pro tempore existentis, sed solum illa una remaneat que ibi impresentiarum est, dummodo ita sit alta a palco quod nullus ex ea inferius respicere possit. Et cum pacto quod parietes qui sunt versus monasterium, pro muro comuni habeantur, quod videlicet si dictus abbas vel eius successores prope dictos parietes aliquid hedificarent, ipsis uti possint et valeant tanquam muro comuni. Et cum pacto etiam, considerato quod pro dicta domo, antequam supradictam concessionem ad vitam, solvebatur pro pensione florenos tredecim et impresentiarum fortassis minus solveretur cum potius sit de[te]riorata quam non; et quod pro dicta apotheca nunc solvitur florenos decem et otto, quod secuta morte dicti Cristofori et postquam dictus Johannes vel eius heredes liberam habuerint dictam domum, cum dicta apotheca libera et expedita perveniet ad dictum monasterium Sancti Pancratii supradicti, dictus Iohannes et eius heredes expendere debeant, possint et valeant prout sibi placuerit, ad honorem Dei, in dicta ecclesia Sancti Pancratii supradictam pensionem trium annorum dicte apothece tunc proxime futurorum, videlicet florenos quinquaginta quatuor, pro compensatione dicti melioramenti.

Quapropter viso quod cedit in evidentem utilitatem dicti monasterii Sancti Pancratii quod dicti floreni quinquaginta quatuor in dicta ecclesia expendantur quamvis dictis tribus annis nihil aliud ad dictum monasterium perveniat, et quod postea introitus augentur ut dictum est, sibi abbati supradicti utile ad modum videtur quod fiat dicta ventitio et permutatio dictorum bonorum modis et conditionibus suprascriptis, cum manifeste appareat omnia supra exposita et narrata in evidentem utilitatem dicti monasterii cedere, et quod super hoc ad predicta faciendum et licentiam super predictis omnibus ab eorum superioribus impetrandum constituatur sindacus cum plena potestate hoc faciendi etc . . . [Formulae follow].

X

EXCERPT FROM TAX REPORT OF GIOVANNI RUCELLAI

February 1458

ASF, Cat., 816, f. 60ʳ

| Dal '27 da suo conto, Lion Rosso 202. | Una chasa per mia abitazione posta in detto ghonfalone nella via della Vignia popolo di Santo Branchazio per suo abitare. | Al '69, Lion Rosso 376 a Giovanni per uso. |

XI

EXCERPT FROM TAX REPORT OF LIONARDO DI BENEDETTO DI COMO REGARDING HOUSES 4 AND 5

February 1458

ASF, Cat., 816, f. 536ʳ

Cose conperate e finite da 1427 in qua:
Una chasa posta nela via degli Stamaiuli ghofalone Lio' Rosso conperai da Santa Maria Nuova per pretio di fiorini L, charta per mano di Ser Mate' Soferroni; ne' chatasto era in Bonachorso di Lucha Rucielai in detto ghofalone.
Una chasa posta in detta via e ghofalone, la quale ebi per parte di dota dande Bonachorso detto; ne' chatasto vi stava

Antonio d[. . .] detto Buonasera ch'era [?] in detto ghofalone, e era a sua vita. Le dette ii chase feci a Giovani di Pagholo di Messer Pagholo Rucielai fiorini 160, roghato Ser Antonio di Salamone.
Sono ogi chorte dela sua chasa.

XII

EXCERPT FROM TAX REPORT OF GIOVANNI D'ANTONIO RUCELLAI REGARDING HOUSE 9

February 1458

ASF, Cat., 816, f. 1012^r

Dal '27, gonfalone Vipera 79 da chonto di Ser Piero di Ser Simone Berti e tratta fuori fiorini 131; mettesi per rendita di fiorini xxv chome l'à apigionata; al presente Giovanni e Zanobi Petrini la tengono a pigione chome apare nel gonfalone della Ferza 45.

Una chaxa per suo abitare e per sé e per la sua famiglia, posta nel popolo di San Branchazio di Firenze luogho detto la via della Vingna, da primo via secondo Santa Maria Nuova terzo rede di Jachonp' Antonio Rucellai quarto San Brachazio. E di detta chaxa è stata senpre per nostro abitare e oggi perch'io avevo andare in roccha l'apigonai a Giovanni e Zanobi Petrimi setaiuoli per tre anni; e di poi ala tornata mia e finiti e tre anni la voglio per mio abitare. E da detti ricevetti la pigone inanzi de' detti tre anni per potere andare in detta roccha.

Al '69, Lion Rosso 414 a llui detto per uso.

XIII

EXCERPT FROM RECORD OF SALE OF IACOPO ANTONIO'S HOUSE (7) TO GIOVANNI RUCELLAI

22 September–10 November 1458

ASF, Diplomatico, Strozzi-Uguccione, 22 September 1458

[10 November]
. . . Et inspicientes quod Iohannes quondam Pauli domini Pauli de Rucellariis, civis et mercator florentinus, est contiguus et consors muro communi suprascripte domui sic bannite et sic vendende. Et quod idem Iohannes, prole nobilis, magnum atque placabile de sua antiqua domo construit et construi fecit hedifitium, quoddam edifitium nondum perfectum esse comprenditur saltem in latitudine, et quod perfici poterit una simul cum suprascripta emenda domo. Et ex causa ipsius magni atque spetiosi edificii optulit offitialibus pupillorum antedictis velle dare de et pro pretio prefate domus florenos mille auri, cum alii fuissent qui optulissent florenos settingentos auri eo quod comprendebatur juste pretium esse debere domus ipsius eiusmodi quantitatis florenorum settingentorum auri. Et ex causa ipsius oblationis per eundem Johannem de Rucellariis facte dictis pupillorum offitialibus de quantitate florenorum mille auri omnes excessit et superavit alios in oblatione. Et quod ergo bene merito de iure et secundum statuta et

ordinamenta communis Florentie et dicti eorum offitii prefatus Iohannes quondam Pauli domini Pauli de Rucellariis emptor ipsius domus esse potest et debet ... [Et] dederunt vendiderunt et tradiderunt Iohanni quondam Pauli domini Pauli de Rucellariis, civi et mercatori florentino, presenti et pro se et suis heredibus et sucessoribus ementi et recipienti, unam domum cum terreno, volta, curia, lodia, puteo, palchis, salis, cameris, anticameris, tecto et aliis hedifitiis, positam in populo Sancti Pancratii de Florentia, in via que dicitur la via della Vigna, cui a I dicta via, a II dicti Iohannis Pauli de Rucellariis emptoris, a III Iohannis Antonii del Beccha de Rucellariis predictis, a IIII ecclesie Sancti Pancratii de Florentia, infra predictos confines vel alios si qui forent plures aut magis veriores. Ad[h]abendum tenendum et possidendum utendum fruendum et vendendum ...

XIV

LETTER FROM COSIMO DE' MEDICI REGARDING THE MARRIAGE OF NANNINA DI PIERO DE' MEDICI AND BERNARDO DI GIOVANNI RUCELLAI

November 1461

ASF, MAP, 2, 480[1]

[To] Pierfranciescho di Lorenzo de' Medici a Trebbio.

Io non t'ò avisato prima chredendo che ttu dovessi tornare più presto qui. Et questo è del maritare la Nannina, ché, esaminando quello ci è da ffare, ci è scharsi partiti, chi per uno rispetto et chi per un altro; pure bisogniando fare il meglio che ssi può, ci adriziamo a uno figliuolo di Giovanni Ruciellai; et perché queste chose non si possono tenere per la lungha, rispondici di tuo parere. Et a ffare altro atto della conchrusione ci passerà qualche dì, dicho del giuramento, sicché ci potrai essere a ttempo. Né altro al presente. Che Cristo ti ghuardi. In Firenze a dì xxvi di Novenbre 1461.

Chosimo de' Medici

XV

NOTARY'S REFERENCE TO GIOVANNI'S 'PALATIUM'

January 1462

ASF, NA, B 1184 (Ser Girolamo Beltramini), Busta 6, 22 January 1462 (s.f.)[2]

... in populo sancti pancratii de florentia et in domo seu palatio habitationis infrascripti Johannis ...

---

[1] Letter found and partially transcribed by Rochon, *Jeunesse*, p. 60, n. 170.
[2] In the same *filza*, there are four more references to Giovanni's *palatium* through January 1464.

XVI

EXCERPT FROM FILARETE'S *TRATTATO D'ARCHITETTURA*[1]

1464?

Lodo ben quegli che seguitano la pratica e maniera antica, e benedico l'anima di Filippo di ser Brunellesco, cittadino fiorentino, famoso e degnissimo architetto e sottilissimo imitatore di Dedalo, il quale risuscitò nella città nostra di Firenze questo modo antico dello edificare, per modo che oggi dì in altra maniera non s'usa se none all'antica, tanto in edificii di chiese, quanto ne' publici e privati casamenti. E che vero sia, se vedete che cittadini privati che faccino fare o casa, o chiesa, tutti a quella usanza corrono; intra gli altri una casa fatta in via contrada nuovamente, la qual via si chiama la Vigna, tutta la facciata dinanzi composta di pietre lavorate, e tutta fatta al modo antico.

XVII

EXCERPT FROM GIOVANNI RUCELLAI'S WILL

December 1465

ASF, NA, L 130 (Ser Leonardo di Giovanni da Colle), Testamenti, no. 31, ff. 3ʳ and 4ʳ[2]

Et quod sic predictam domum et eius inhabitationem et possessionem quam scilicet ipse testator ut asseruit totam edificari fecit et a fundamentis ferme erexit propriis sumptibus in dictis eius filiis vel descendentibus aut in aliquibus vel aliquo ex eis ipsius testatoris memoriam conservetur.

... una domus magna cum lodia curia puteo ortulis et voltis subtus et super terram stabulis coquinis salis cameris palcis veronibus et aliis pluribus edifitiis posita Florentie in populo Sancti Pancratii de Florentia in via publica cui dicitur la Vigna videlicet in anghulo dicte vie cui domui a primo dicta via vocata la Vigna a II via publica cui dicitur la via degli Stamaiuoli a III olim heredum Iacobi Antonii Bingerii de Oricellariis a IIII bona dicte ecclesie seu monasterii Sancti Pancratii de Florentia infra dictos confines etc.

XVIII

EXCERPT FROM TAX REPORT OF GIOVANNI RUCELLAI

August 1469

ASF, Cat., 919, f. 376ʳ

Una chasa per mio abitare posta nel popolo di Santo Branchazio nella via della Vigna, da primo e secondo via da terzo Giovanni d'Antonio del Becha Ruciellai	Al '80, Lion Rosso 341 a conto di Giovanni

---

[1] Antonio Averlino detto il Filarete, *Trattato di Architettura* (ed. Anna Maria Finoli and Liliana Grassi), Milan, 1972, I, pp. 227–228. For the unresolved question of the date of the treatise, see the contrasting views of John Spencer ("La datazione del trattato del Filarete desunta dal suo esame interno", *Rivista d'arte*, XXXI [1965], pp. 93–103 [favouring 1461–63]) and Peter Tigler (*Die Architekturtheorie des Filarete*, Berlin, 1963, pp. 7–8 [all probably written in 1464]).

[2] There are two copies of the will. In the other, probably earlier, the third *confino* is given as "heredum Jacobi Antonii Bingerii de Oricellariis"; in an Italian draft at the end of the *filza*, the third *confino* is "delle rede di Jacopo Antonio di Bingieri Rucellai".

da quarto il munistero di Santo Branchazio. Nel 1427 erano più chase che ssi   detto, per abitare. sono disfatte e fattone una.

[Left margin]
Dal '27, Lion Rosso 202 una parte da Giovanni di Pagholo Rucellai per uso; e dal '27, Lion Rosso 279, una parte da Francesco di Betto per rendita di fiorini xi; e dal '27, gonfalone detto 48, una parte d'Antonio di Giovanni per uso; e dal '27, gonfalone detto 38, una parte da Bonachosso Ruciellai per uso; et dal '57, Lion Rosso 24, tutto da Giovanni di Pagholo Ruciellai per uso e chosì si dà.

XIX

EXCERPT FROM TAX REPORT OF BINGERI AND CIPRIANO DI IACOPO ANTONIO RUCELLAI REGARDING HOUSE 7

August 1469

ASF, Cat., 919, f. 116ʳ

	Beni alienati
Intrachiusa nella muraglia di Giovanni Rucellai chome dicie	Una chasa posta nel popolo di San Branchazio chonperò da noi Giovanni Rucellai e àvi murato la sua; e a rinchontro ci dette la chasa che noi vogliamo schontare.

XX

EXCERPT FROM TAX REPORT OF JACOPO D'ANTONIO DI PIERO, REGARDING HOUSE 5

August 1469

ASF, Cat., 920, f. 504ʳ

	Beni alienati
Al '69, Lion Rosso [...] a Giovanni di Pagholo Rucellai, intracchiusa nella sua muraglia dov'è l'orto	Una chasa ... nella via degli Stamaiuoli; era a vita d'Antonio mio padre e rimasta alle rede di Lucha di Messer Giovanni Rucellai insino nel 1433.

XXI

THE DIVISION OF THE RUCELLAI PALACE BETWEEN GIOVANNI'S TWO SONS

8 December 1492

ASF, NA, F 237 (Ser Antonio Ferrini, 1470–1499), Busta 1492–1495, ff. 50ᵣ⁻ᵛ
The notary's handwriting is extremely unclear, and the manuscript is damaged by water

[f. 50ʳ] Laudum divisorium inter fratres

In Dei nomine amen. Nos Pierus olim Francisci de Vectoriis et Iohannes olim Iacobi de Corsis et Bernardus olim Inghilesis Schiatte de Rydofiis, cives florentini, arbitri et arbitratores electi et assumpti a nobilibus viris, videlicet Pandolfo olim Iohannis de Oricellariis ex parte una, et Bernardo fratre carnali dicti Pandolfi et filio dicti olim Iohannis de Oricellariis ex parte alia, prout de compromisso in nos facto, auctoritate, potestate et balia nobis a dictis partibus commissis et attributis constat manu mei notarii sub suo tempore, visis namque dictis compromisso, auctoritate, potestate et balia nobis a dictis partibus concessa et attributa, et maxime supra divisione bonorum omnium [. . .] et viso qualiter vis alienandi non pariter discordiam et non litem accendere possit, volentes dicte partes in quamcunque et quascunque lites et causas cum predictis partibus inter eos existentes [. . .] debito examine [. . .] et eorum bona [. . .] inter dictos fratres laudum divisorium damus, proferimus et laudamus et sententiamus et arbitramur et declaramus, pro tribunali sedentes in loco infrascripto, in hoc modo et forma videlicet.

In primis cum inveniamus et nobis constet inter dictas partes fuisse et esse domus eorum habitationis communis, que domus fuit facta et constructa in duabus vicebus, videlicet domum magnam et domum parvam, que ad presens sunt et [. . .] una domus utuntur pro una domo [. . .] inter dictos fratres volentes dictam domum dividere, prout decet et fieri potest, laudamus sententiamus et declaramus et dividendo damus et imponimus dicto Pandolfo et assignamus domum magnam videlicet curiam cum lodia et stabulis et volta et quicquid super inde hedificatum est per suam latitudinem et altitudinem videlicet cum edificiis de super hedificatis usque ad tectum cum omnibus suis habituris et pertinentiis et cum omni iure et cum omnibus exitibus et introytibus dicte domus magne, ad habendum et ad habitandum [?] etc. Et condemnamus dictum Bernardum fratrem dicti Pandolfi ad disgombrandum dimictendum et relaxandum dictam domum magnam vacuam liberam et expeditam dicto Pandolfo infra sex menses proxime futuros ab hodie et sine aliqua exceptione vel cavillatione.

Item damus et assignamus dividendo in partem et portionem dicto Bernardo domum parvam, que empta fuit per dictum olim Johannem eorum patrem ab heredibus [?] Jacobi Antonii de Oricellariis, cum omnibus suis pertinentiis et edificiis [?], cum eius diricturis usque ad tectum, et cum quodam maghazino quod est iuxta lodiam de Oricellariis, quod vocatur il maghazino dell'avena, cum omnibus adiacentiis et pertinentiis usibus et servitudibus dicte domus parve et maghazini et iuribus [. . .] etc., ad habendum etc. et cedimus iura etc. Et condemnamus [f. 50ᵛ] dictum Pandolfum ad evacuandum, dimictendum, et relaxandum dicto Bernardo dictam domum parvam et maghazinum vacua libera et expedita infra sex menses proxime futuros ab hodie, sine aliqua exceptione vel chavillatione.

Item quia constat nobis quod domus magna assignata dicto Pandolfo est maioris estimationis quam sit domus parva et magazinus predicta, propterea quod in compensationem dictarum partium et pro raguaglio dictorum bonorum condemnamus dictum Pandolfum ad dandum et solvendum dicto Bernardo florenos septingentos quinquaginta auri largos di grossi infra sex menses proxime futuros ab hodie sine aliqua exceptione vel chavillatione.

Item declaramus et laudamus quod omnia hostia existentia inter domum magnam et domum parvam debeant claudi et murari infra dictos sex menses proxime futuros ab hodie, videlicet ultimis diebus dictorum sex mensium sumptibus et expensis amborum dictarum [?] partium.

Item declaramus quod si qua expensa facta fuisset vel declarata fuit per dictum Bernardum in domo magna, quod dictus Bernardus non possit occasione dictarum expensarum aliquid petere vel consequi a dicto Pandolfo, [. . .] quia omnia predicta computamus in suprascripto raguaglio ut suprafacto prout supra imponimus, exceptis duabus colopnis de porfiro alla serpentina hedificatis in dicta domo magna et in cameris dicte domus magne, quas liceat dicto Bernardo extrahere et, ut vulgo dicitur, smurare, et eidem Bernardo libere pertineant et spectent.

Item condemnamus dictas partes ad defensionem dictorum bonorum secundum naturam [?] divisionum etc.
Que omnia etc. Reservamus etc.
Lata data etc. per dictos arbitros et arbitratores pro tribunale sedentes in apoteca mei notarii suprascripti, in populo
Sancti Stephani abbatie florentine, sub anno Domini 1492, indictione XI, die vero viii mensis decembris, presentibus
testibus Francisco Borgianis Mini cive florentino et Aloysio Antonii de Guidottis cive florentino, presente dicto
Pandolfo et dictum laudum et omnia in eo [? . . .] etc. Rogantes etc.

XXII

DIVISION OF LARGER PART OF PALACE BETWEEN TWO PAIRS OF PANDOLFO'S GRANDSONS

13 December 1531

ASF, NA, B 2699 (Ser Zanobi Buonaventura), ff. 19ᵛ–22ʳ

Laudum divisiorium inter fratres

[f. 19ᵛ] In dei nomine amen. Nos Baptista Francisci de Dinis et
Inghileses Bernardi de Lottis arbitri et Johannes Franciscus
Antonii de Nobilibus tertius electi et adsumpti videlicet
dictus Baptista et Inghileses ex compromissaria conventione
5 a Pandolpho olim Pauli Pandolphi de Oricellariis eius nomine
et ut procuratore substituto Johannis eius fratris et modis
et nominibus in compromisso contenctis ex una et Philippo et
Leonardo fratribus et filiis dicti olim Pauli modis et
nominibus in compromisso contenctis ex altera et dictus
10 Johannes Franciscus electus a Dominis otto custodie et balie
civitatis florentie vigore auctoritatis eisdem date a dictis
partibus in dicto compromisso ut de dicto compromisso constare
vidimus publico instrumento manu Ser Philippi Ser Francisci
Lotti notarii florentini sub die 28 ottobris proxime preteriti
15 seu alio veriori tempore et de dicta electione dicti Johannis
Francisci per deliberationem dictorum dominorum otto sub die
16 novembris 1531 seu alio veriori tempore et de prorogatione
compromissi una cum adiunctione dicti tertii demum et sub
die 28 novembris dicti seu alio veriori tempore. Viso igitur
20 dicto compromisso et auctoritate nobis a dictis partibus
data et attributa et auditis differentiis dictarum partium et
omnibus bene consideratis viam arbitrorum et arbitratorum
et amicabilium compositorum eligentes et eam viam quam magis
et melius eligere possumus
25 Dei Nomine repetito Laudamus arbitramur et facimus in modum
infrascriptum videlicet
In prima, trovato come nella heredità di decto Pagolo loro
padre remase una casa la quale in questo modo è confinata,
cioè una casa posta nel popolo di Santo Pancratio di Firenze
30 et in via decta la Vigna, ala quale a primo via 2 via 3 decti

heredi 4 Palla Rucellai infra e predecti o altri più veri
confini, la quale per anchora è commune infra le decte parte;
e intesa la voluntà di decte parte, la quale è che decta casa
tra loro si divida; et per obviare a ogni materia di scandolo
35   el quale spesso si genera per lo stare a commune, però quella
dividiamo nel modo infrascripto.
In prima nella parte di decti Pandolpho et Giovanni vogliamo
che sia la camera prima terrena che è a man [f. 20r] sinistra
al'entrare per l'uscio dinanzi di decta casa. Item una came-
40   retta overo scriptoio che è in testa della prima scala che
è sopra decta camera terrena. Item la sala principale di
decta casa con tucte le camere, anticamera, soffitta, verone, et
cucina cioè tucte le stanze che sono al piano di decta sala
con tucte loro appartenentie come hoggi sono. Item quella
45   parte del terrazo che si contiene tra 'l cammino et muro che è
verso el ponte ala Carraia et habbi l'entrata per l'uscio che
v'è hoggi. Item una stanzetta piccola con un forno nella
quale al presente si tiene polli alato al'uscio entra in decto
terrazo, la quale stanzetta vogliamo che sia di decti Pandol-
50   pho et Giovanni in mentre che viverà Mona Lorenza loro madre,
et dopo la morte di decta Mona Lorenza vogliamo che sia nella
parte infrascripta di decti Philippo et Lionardo. Item la
metà d'una stanza che parte s'adopera per stalla et parte per
tenervi legne, et perché decta stalla et stanza delle legne
55   divide un muro che non è in mezo di decta stanza intera,
vogliamo che decto muro si getti in terra et refaccisene un
altro, el quale sia appunto in mezo di decta stanza intera;
et la parte di decti Pandolpho et Giovanni sia quella che è
verso la via dirieto. Item la metà delle volte di decta
60   casa in verso quella parte che è sotto la parte delle habitatione consegnate loro come di sopra; et perché in decte
volte si va per una prima volta, la quale dà l'entrata a tucte
l'altre, vogliamo che decta prima volta resti a commune fra
decte parte.
65   Et nella parte di decti Philippo et Lionardo salve le cose
infrascripte vogliamo che sia tucto el resto di decta casa,
cioè la camera terrena grande che è a man dextra a entrare
dal'uscio dinanzi di decta casa che ha l'entrata in su la
loggia, et la metà delle volte divise come di sopra, et la
70   metà di decta stanza che s'adopera per stalla et legne come
di sopra, et tucte le stanze che sono dal primo piano in su,
cioè sale, camere, cucine, el resto del terrazo et tucte l'altre
habitatione da decto pia[f. 20v]no in su; et dopo la morte
di decta Mona Lorenza decta stanza de' polli consegnata come
75   di sopra a decti Pandolpho et Giovanni in mentre che viverà
decta Mona Lorenza. Et perché nella parte del terrazo
consegnata a decti Pandolpho et Giovanni come di sopra, v'è
l'uscio donde s'entra in decto terrazo adeo che nella parte
di decti Philippo et Leonardo non è alcuna entrata, vogliamo
80   che l'entrata in decta parte di decti Philippo et Lionardo
sia per la camera che tocca a decti Philippo et Lionardo che

è alato a decto terrazo, e in decta camera si facci uno uscio
che vadi in decto terrazo; et che degli horticini che sono in
su decto terrazo ognuno habbi quella parte che è appiccata
85 con la parte che tocca a ciascuno del terrazo; et che secondo
la divisione soprascripta si facci un muro, o di mattoni o
d'asse secondo che parrà a le decte parte, che divida decto
terrazo e horticini. Et perché in decta casa vi è la loggia
et la corte che non si sono divise, vogliamo che ciascuna di
90 decte parte ne habbi la metà, cioè quella parte che è in verso
le parte consegnate a ciascuna di loro, con questo che e' non
si possa in decta loggia o corte fare muro o obstaculo
alcuno che altrimenti le divida. Item vogliamo che el pozo
che è in decta corte, et l'entrate di fuora dinanzi et di drieto
95 di decta casa, et le vie et scale che vanno in sino al piano
della prima sala data a decti Pandolpho et Giovanni sieno
commune infra le decte parte et che decti Pandolpho et
Giovanni habbino l'uso di potere andare a trovare la parte
del terrazo et pollaio consegnati loro per la parte di decti
100 Philippo et Lionardo, cioè per quella via et scala che vi si
va al presente. Et perché noi desideriamo dare ale decte
parte manco servitù che sia possibile, vogliamo che in capo
della scala, cioè alato al'uscio che entra nella sala consegnata a decti Pandolpho et Giovanni, e a mano sinistra, si facci
105 uno uscio pel quale debbino entrare decti Philippo et Lionardo a trovare la parte loro delle stanze di sopra; et che [f. 21r]
l'uscio che si usava prima per andare di sopra che è
in su la sala si serri con chiavistello dal'una parte et
dal'altra; e a causa che l'uscio del legname di decta sala
110 consegnata a Pandolpho et Giovanni non dia impedimento a
decto uscio nuovo da farsi, vogliamo che decto uscio della
sala s'acconci in modo o dividendolo o in altro modo che e'
non dia impedimento a decto uscio nuovo; et più che nel secondo
piano di decta casa cioè alato al'uscio della sala di sopra,
115 a causa che decti Pandolpho et Giovanni possino ire a trovare
decta parte del terrazo et pollaio consegnata loro, vogliamo
che si facci uno uscio simile a quello che s'è decto del
primo della prima sala; et che di sopra s'acconci come s'è
decto di quel di sotto; et così si serri decto uscio vecchio
120 nel medesimo modo che quel di sopra; et che tucti gli usci,
mura et acconcimi che s'hanno a fare in decta casa secondo
l'ordine soprascripto si debbino fare a spese commune di
decte parte et per tucto el mese di gennaio proxime futuro;
et se alcuna delle parte non volessi concorrere ale spese
125 per fare le cose sopra decte, le possa fare l'altra parte; e di
tucto debba tenere diligente conto et la metà di quello
spendessi gli debba essere facta buona dal'altra; e a così fare
la condenniamo. Item vogliamo che tucte le spese necessarie
che accadessino farsi per mantenimento de' tecti, dale colonne
130 della corte insino ala via, et de' fondamenti di decta casa si
debbino fare a commune fra decte parte, et ciascuna sia tenuta
refare l'altra della metà di quel che spendessi e a così

fare la condenniamo.

Item vogliamo che tucti e legnami che sono nelle stanze di

135 decta casa habbino a restare ciascuno nella stanza dove è al
presente et habbinsi a stimare; et che quella parte che
havessi più che l'altra habbi a refare et ragguagliare l'altra;
e a così fare le condenniamo; et tucte l'altre masseritie di
qualunche sorte s'habbino a dividere et ciascuna delle parte

140 habbi a havere la sua ratha. [Document continues with items unrelated to the house].

XXIII

ASSURANCE BY BENEDETTO THAT ABATE FILIPPO WILL LOSE NO RIGHTS
OVER A COMMON WALL IF BENEDETTO BUILDS ABOVE IT

10 February 1696 (s.f.)

AR, XXI, 6

Essendo che nel palazzo delli illustrissimi Signori Benedetto etc. Rucellai e dell' illustrissimo Signore Abbate Filippo
Rucellai vi sia un muro maestro di grossezza di un braccio che divide la porzione dell' uno da quella dell' altro, qual
muro sia stato e sia comune per indiviso a tutti li detti Signori Rucellai padroni del detto palazzo.
E che li detti Signori Benedetto etc. Rucellai habbino volsuto e vogliono fabbricare nella loro porzione di palazzo
et alzare la loro fabbrica sopra il detto muro comune, e volendo che dalla fabbrica suddetta non se ne possi mai per
alcun tempo dedurre il dominio di tutto il muro a loro favore ad esclusione della comunione di esso con il Signore
Abbate Filippo ma che sempre et in perpetuo consti della comunione di esso con il medesimo Signore Abbate.
Di qui è che in vertù della presente privata scritta da valere e tenere come se fusse un pubblico giurato instrumento
. . . Benedetto etc. . . . . confessano che il muro divisorio che è nel detto loro palazzo che separa le porzioni del medesimo
è sempre stato et è comune per indiviso infra di loro et il detto Signore Abbate Filippo, et che nonostante la fabbrica
che i medesimi alzeranno e che sono per alzare sopra di esso, non deve restar tolta la comunione di detto muro, ma
deve quella non di meno continuare a favore e benefizzio del detto Signore Abbate Filippo al quale convengono che
sia libero il potere fabbricare e valersi di tal muro in qualunque sua occasione et ad ogni sua volontà come cioè padrone
di esso . . .

XXIV

ARCHIVIST'S DIATRIBE AGAINST PAOLO BENEDETTO FOR BLOCKING HIS LIGHT

ca. 1700

AR, XII, 5, 5

Si piglia il presente ricordo per lume a chi verrà doppo di noi, che dal Signor Paolo Benedetto del Signor Francesco di
Benedetto di Giovanni Rucellai essendo egli umor torbido volse, diceva egli, levarsi la soggezione delle 2 finestre
della camera terrena sotto la cucina e della finestra maggiore delle di sotto della nostra porzione di casa e palazzo che

tutte riuscivano nella di lui corte, alimentato il di lui umore da un comune parente mostrando voler murare nella di lui corte dalla nostra parte, che non poté a meno il Senator Giovanni nostro padre di risentirsene restando affatto acciecata la camera terrena, et ancora quasi la cucina, e sì come per opera di più persone l'Auditore Angioli, che fu il Giudice, senza aver riguardo alla struttura del palazzo fatto fabricare da Giovanni di Pagolo di Messer Pagolo Rucellai comune autore, e di più aver ricevuto noi quella porzione nelle divise fatte nel 1622 fra il Senatore e Cavaliere Paolo di Giovanni Rucellai nostro nonno e fra Benedetto di Giovanni Rucellai nonno del medesimo Paolo Benedetto comuni fratelli, che ci dovessi in virtù di dette divise esser mantenute le case nell' istessa forma e valore che furno allora stimate e non peggiorate, e deteriorate, come seguì alla nostra porzione acciecandosi affatto, come ho detto, una camera terrena e quasi la cucina per opera del parente detto di sopra ed altri mossero il detto Giudice a sentenziare che come lume laterale potessi fabbricare. Sì che dalla nostra banda per una distanza di 4 in 5 braccia incirca sopra certi archi bassi tirò un muro e con esso arrivò all' altezza del tetto; e detti archi riuscivano nella corte ove fece al primo piano che rispondeva alla nostra cucina piccoli buchi; e seguitando i consigli del parente e degl' altri fece altri muramenti per la casa e fece attestare per quelli il gran miglioramento che aveva fatto con tali muramenti alla casa che per altro era fidecommessa.

XXVa

ARCHIVIST'S DESCRIPTION OF THE RUCELLAI PALACE

ca. 1722–1734

AR, XIX, 4

Note that he designates the ground-floor as the first
floor, and so on up to the fourth floor (*altana*)

Giovanni di Paolo di Messer Paolo Rucellai della sua casa con altre case ne fabbricò un palazzo con disegno del famosissimo Leon Battista Alberti quale secondo le tradizioni chi dice che dovevono essere XI finestre e tre porte, e chi XIIII finestre e 4 porte. Ne fu solo fatte numero 7 finestre e cominciata l'ottava, e due porte come il tutto si vede uniforme di disegno, d'ordine, e struttura tanto da piedi che fino al cornicione. Questo palazzo per descriverlo si prenderà prima la porzione che presentemente possiede il Signore Paol Benedetto Rucellai quale oltre all'aver una buona loggia et un buon cortile ha una buona scala di pietra che conduce dal pian terreno al piano di mezzo, e di lì con due altre branche simili conduce al terzo piano.

Al secondo piano ha una buona sala che con tre finestre delle 5 del palazzo che ha questa porzione la rende luminosa, ha due buone camere e dopo un camerino. Di sala per un verrone si va alla cucina et a questo piano non vi è altro.

Il Signore Paol Benedetto nelli muramenti che ha fatto ha levato il sopradetto verrone di braccia 5 in 6 in circa et ha raggrandito il sopradetto camerino.

L'altra porzione di detto palazzo fabbricato dal sopradetto Giovanni che consiste in due sole finestre, et una porta in esso vi è la seconda scala del palazzo quale è scoperta, col tetto sopra all' antica e arriva solo al secondo piano di dove per un piccolino ricetto a man ritta si arriva nel salotto del palazzo che a questa porzione fa figura di sala, di lì si passa in un gran bel camerone che con le due finestre che gli tocca risponde su la piazza de' Rucellai; tornando alla scala a mano manca vi è una camera, quale è a tetto che in cambio di stuoia resta di tavole sottili soffittata. Questa stanza dalle conietture che si hanno, pare che potesse servire per mangiarci già che vi è il cammino e vi sono certe aperture d'usci che rincontrano la cucina dell' altra parte. E sì come questa porzione era tanto scarsa di stanze di cucina e di scale, quei due possessori pensorno a farvi quei comodi che più si potessero adattare a cavarne il servizio necessario, onde a mezza la seconda scala del palazzo perché solamente arriva al secondo piano vi fecero un mezzanino, fecero la cucina; la camera poi sopra a detta nuova cucina la divisero in mezzo e ne fecero due stanze. In una delle quali l'Abate Filippo vi ha fatta un alcovina che per anco non è finita. La bella stanza che riesce su la strada e su la piazza Rucellai pure ancora codesta la divisero, e fecero che una camera ricevesse lume dall' altra, e su quella metà divisa che riesce su la strada fecero un mezzanino che riceve lume da certi occhi che sono sopra le finestre; e per andarvi si servirno d'una scaletta di legno larga circa un braccio, e da detto mezzanino per passare nel terzo piano roppero il pavimento superiore, e con altra scala pure di legno vi entrono per mezzo d'una botola come per anco il tutto è in tal forma. I pavimenti tanto del terreno che del secondo piano che del terzo sono tutti ad un piano.

Tutte le stanze del terzo piano sì dell' una che dell' altra parte sono inabitabili e senza intonacare, parte delle quali malissimo impalcate, ma molto più la seconda parte che sì come non vi era comodo di salirvi che per piccola scala di legno rendevasi più difficile l'andarvi, e non pareva mettessi conto con questa impassibilità farvi in esso terzo piano spese.

XXVb

FRAGMENT OF ANOTHER VERSION OF ARCHIVIST'S DESCRIPTION

ca. 1722–1734

AR, XIX, 15

Questa seconda porzione sì come non aveva cucina e mancava d'altre comodità gli mancava ancora quella del pozzo quale fu fatto pare circa l'anno 1520 e ciò da certi contratti e ricordi.

La struttura esteriore dal capo fino ai piedi è tutta medesima e uniforme primo secondo terzo e quarto piano cioè del terrazzo tutti uniscono l'uno con l'altro col cornicione et orticini, vi sono le porte ai i piani una sola presentemente è aperta.

La casa che al presente possiede il Signor Paol Benedetto consisteva dunque nel tempo della fabbrica di sala due stanze et un camerino con un verone et una cucina bislunga. Et il piano di sopra cioè terzo quantunque vi arrivi la prima buona scala del palazzo è inabitabile come è ancora presentemente quantunque il Signor Francesco suo padre in alcuna vi spendesse qualcosa per ridurla un poco meglio.

La parte seconda che possiede Signor Francesco Maria a cui è toccata la seconda scala del palazzo che come si è detto è scoperta all' antica che solo arriva al secondo piano col salotto del palazzo che a questa serve di sala con un gran bel camerone et altro che fu detto potesse servire per desinarvi e cenarvi per essere di rincontro alla cucina del palazzo non vi essendo altro che il muro et il detto verone di mezzo della prima porzione.

Tutto questo palazzo dunque, che presentemente è separato in due porzione, è composto di sala, salotto, 3 stanze buone, un camerino, et altra stanza dove si dice potessero mangiare e cucina.

XXVI

PART OF THE BACKGROUND IN THE SALE OF THE SMALL PART OF
THE PALACE TO THE OWNERS OF THE LARGE PART

1743

ASF, Notarile Moderno, 23966, f. 62ᵛ
(Consult the Genealogy Tracing Ownership of Palace for the names mentioned here: Table III)

. . . fu asserito . . . che . . . Abbate Francesco Maria . . . Rucellai possegga una parte del Palazzo di Casa Rucellai, posto in questa Città di Firenze popolo di S. Pancrazio in via della Vigna . . .; la qual porzione di Palazzo fusse fabbricata da Giovanni di Paolo di Pandolfo [*sic*] Rucellai, dopo che il medesimo haveva fatto il suo testamento sotto dì 3 [*sic*] dicembre 1465 rogato Ser Leonardo di Ser Giovanni di Ser Taddeo da Colle; e però non ostante il fidecommisso strettissimo dal medesimo ordinato sopra la sua casa, fusse per sentenza proferita da i tre Giudici delle Seconde Appellazioni sotto il dì 15 ottobre 1540 in una causa agitata infra Pandolfo di Paolo di Pandolfo Rucellai da una, e Palla di Bernardo Rucellai dall'altra, dichiarato restare detta porzione di palazzo libera, e non soggetta a detto fidecommisso, sopra di che esiste il motivo nel Tribunale del Proconsolo Libro Motivorum 11 a c.344. . .[1].

---

[1] The "Liber Motivorum" in question was damaged by flood in 1966 and is apparently still in storage outside Florence. I have followed the case back through the various appeals in the other *Ruota* books, but they give little information about the basis for the decision. They show that Giovanni's will and the tax records were used in the case; without the missing book we cannot say if other records, perhaps private, were also used.

PIERO SANPAOLESI†

L'ARCHITETTURA DEL PALAZZO RUCELLAI

† Professor Sanpaolesi was unable to see his contribution in proof before his death.

L'ARCHITETTURA DEL PALAZZO RUCELLAI

Devo necessariamente riferirmi allo studio che pubblicai nel 1963[1] e che dava ragione delle fasi costruttive iniziali del Palazzo Rucellai, nel riprendere oggi l'argomento che mi si offre. Non che già allora avessi maturato un esame critico più avanzato, e non ne avessi voluto parlare, ma è vero che quanto espongo ora, nel 1963 non mi era chiaro e devo essere grato alla Dottoressa Brenda Preyer per le sue ricerche d'archivio e le sue precisazioni cronologiche alle quali senz'altro rinvio il lettore[2]. Dirò dunque brevemente il mio argomento perché in parte coincide con quello appunto che ha trattato la Dottoressa Preyer. Vorrei soprattutto portare l'accento su alcuni ulteriori aspetti, forse un po' particolari, ma non meno importanti della vicenda formale di questa facciata e che in quel mio studio mancano. E dico facciata appunto perché è molto chiaro che fra la facciata e la rimanente parte dell'edificio c'è una differenza di concezione e di struttura che indubbiamente ci consiglia di attribuirli a due mani o quantomeno la seconda ad un coordinatore il quale ha utilizzato materiali diversi ma ormai consueti dell'architettura fiorentina. Intanto noto che Giovanni Rucellai ha fatto eseguire una serie di opere di architettura che vanno viste nel loro insieme. Lui stesso nello *Zibaldone*: 'maximamente delle muraglie che io ò facte della chasa mia di fFirenze [la mette subito come prima] del luogo mio da Quarachi, della facciata della chiesa di Sancta Maria Novella e della logia principiata nella Via della Vigna, dirinpetto alla chasa mia; e anchora della chappella chol sancto Sipolcro a similitudine di quello di Gierusalem del nostro Signore Iesu Christo facta fare in Sancto Branchazio e de' paramenti di brochato. . .'[3]. Se osserviamo questo complesso di cose vediamo anche analogamente, per esempio, Cosimo de' Medici aveva dato mano a un gruppo di opere del tutto simili. Il Palazzo, la chiesa di S. Lorenzo, la Cappella, la Sacristia Vecchia e la Villa, che allora era quella di Careggi. E mi limito a Cosimo al quale Giovanni Rucellai fu per lungo tempo sospetto per via della moglie, figlia di uno sbandito, sbandito da Cosimo e riconciliato poi dal matrimonio della figlia proprio di Piero di Cosimo con il figlio maggiore di Giovanni. E mi limito a Cosimo ma, per esempio, si potrebbe dire ugualmente a proposito dei Frescobaldi o di Niccolò da Uzzano o di molti altri i quali intraprendono tutti la stessa carriera di costruttori. Fanno tutti il Palazzo, la Chiesa, la Loggia, la Cappella. E questo non è inutile osservarlo nel quadro della società fiorentina del '400, dove l'emulazione manteneva un equilibrio in certo senso necessario fra i cittadini, ognuno nel suo rango. Poi Giovanni nell'elencare queste cose aggiunge queste costruzioni che:'righuardano in parte all'onore di Dio e all'onore della città e a memoria di me . . .'[4]; questo lo dice da vecchio, e sono tutte in definitiva a memoria di lui, ma in particolare lo è la sua casa. Non tanto per la mole e la destinazione, ma soprattutto perché ne rispecchia, più che qualunque altro edificio la personalità. Il Palazzo Rucellai, o meglio la sua facciata, rigetta le comuni forme della tradizione e propone un modello nuovo, diverso, pieno di umana misura. E' questo che fa dire al Filarete che '. . . Nella città

---

[1] P. Sanpaolesi, "Precisazioni sul Palazzo Rucellai", *Palladio*, n.s. XIII (1963), pp. 61–66.
[2] Preyer, sopra, pp. 155–225.
[3] Perosa, p. 118.
[4] *Ibid.*, p. 121.

nostra . . . oggidì un'altra maniera non s'usa . . ne' publici e privati casamenti. Et che vero sia, se vedete ch'e cittadini privati faccino fare o casa o chiesa tutti a quella usanza corrono, intra gli altri una casa fatta in una contrada nuovamente, la qual Via si chiama la Vignia, tutta la facciata dinanzi composta di pietre lavorate et tutta fatta al modo antico. Sì che conforto ciascheduno ch'investichi et cerchi nello hedificare il modo antico di fare et husare questi modi, che se non fosse più bello et più utile a Firenze non s'userebbe. . .'[1].

L'altro modello, che il proprietario chiama 'chasa' è il disumano, o anche eroico, sogno del Palazzo Pitti, due modi diversi, opposti di fare l'architettura, qui misurata di fronte alla città ed alla sua ampia valle; in Via della Vigna, solo misurata all'uomo.

Firenze allora ci offriva una certa quantità di esempi di trasformazione della vecchia casa, diciamo medievale, cioè trecentesca, di cui potremmo prendere a simbolo il Palazzo de' Mozzi che era uno dei più celebrati, in palazzo privato rappresentativo non più di una consorteria, ma di un cittadino. Questa trasformazione consiste intanto in una diversa distribuzione del complesso dell'edificio, ingressi, stanze, sale, depositi, cucine, stalle, rimesse, ecc., eppoi intanto in una diversa concezione del rapporto fra la facciata, cioè fra la casa che la facciata rappresenta, e la strada pubblica e dunque la città. Ho citato il Palazzo de' Mozzi proprio perché, come del resto si potrebbe citare qualche altro edificio, per esempio il Palazzo Spini, al loro confronto nella casa che si viene definendo come palazzo quattrocentesco, spariscono le botteghe prospicienti la strada mentre l'accesso viene limitato e viene strettamento concepito sotto la forma della porta sola o spesso multipla. Nel Palazzo di Niccolò da Uzzano in Via dei Bardi, ora Capponi, oggi c'è una sola porta; anticamente, e sono ancora bene individuabili, c'erano tre porte. Il Palazzo dello Strozzino, che ha pressappoco la data di costruzione del Palazzo Rucellai, era chiamato il 'Palazzo delle tre porte'. Esso stranamente è costruito nella facciata con lo stesso criterio seguito nel Palazzo Rucellai, quello cioè della scultura fatta su una facciata come su un modello, perché il Palazzo dello Strozzino ha, sì, le tre porte ad arco, ma esse sono ricavate tagliando una parete continua di filari orizzontali[2] e facendo delle finte bozze sugli archi delle tre porte inferiori. E delle finte bozze sulla parete del piano terreno mentre quelle del primo piano sono segnate con una distribuzione che nel Palazzo Rucellai non c'è che al piano terreno, e che è quello della successione di un filare basso e di un filare alto dalle misure ripetute ed alternate. Filare basso e filare alto che sono degli schemi tipicamente ellenistici dei quali possiamo citare il bozzato rustico del basamento del tempio di Apollo a Priene (Tav. 36a), ed il paramento a filari alternati alti e bassi, della scena del teatro di Mileto (Tav. 36b). Perché tutta questa nostra architettura era fondata su di una base indubbiamente culturale. Il problema che si presenta, quindi, nettamente nel Palazzo Rucellai, è che la facciata risulta come in riporto su di un edificio diversamente concepito e cioè, voglio dire, secondo moduli più consueti, e non eccezionali come sono quelli della facciata la quale non obbedisce ad una concezione tridimensionale. Oltretutto è fondamentale, secondo me, rendersi conto che questa facciata doveva essere vista di fronte mentre le simili facciate di Pienza sono viste d'angolo (Tav. 37a). La vista immediata e prima di Pienza è certamente una vista d'angolo tridimensionale. Ne viene in evidenza il fatto che mentre qui noi abbiamo le lesene tutte della stessa larghezza, e non c'è una soluzione d'angolo sulla Via de'Palchetti (Tav. 38), perchè l'ultima lesena è della stessa larghezza delle altre di facciata, ed è l'unica che si trova girato l'angolo della via, a Pienza

---

[1] Antonio Averlino detto Filarete, *Sforzinda*, BNC, cod. Magl. II.I. 140, fol. 59; ed. A. M. Finoli e L. Grassi, Milano, 1972, I, pp. 227-8.

[2] P. Sanpaolesi, "Come disegnava l'architettura L. B. Alberti?", *Scritti di storia dell'arte in onore di U. Procacci*, Firenze, 1977, I, p. 220.

l'ultima lesena è un poco più larga delle altre in facciata rispettando così un antichissimo precetto architettonico. Cioè l'architetto che a Pienza ha costruito il Palazzo Piccolomini, di riflesso a questo nostro fiorentino, ha sentito l'angolo (cioè la terza misura) e lo ha risolto a modo suo, nel modo più ovvio ma efficace. Del resto, direi, a Firenze abbiamo già una premessa a questo problema dell'angolo nei suoi varii aspetti. E' uno dei problemi fondamentali delle strutture rinascimentali. Si pensi al cortile del Palazzo d'Urbino, per esempio, dove il tema è affrontato, dati i tempi, con ben altra maturità. Si pensi alla soluzione che il Brunelleschi ha dato del Palazzo di Parte Guelfa nell'angolo staccando le due lesene per mezzo di una doppia scanalatura del motivo che fa l'angolo (Tav. 37b) e lasciando sul lato corto liberata l'altra lesena opposta senza accenno alla eventuale risvolta perché forse la facciata doveva quasi certamente proseguire lungo la Via delle Terme e non è poi proseguita. Qui, cioè nel Palazzo Rucellai, manca proprio la soluzione d'angolo: quello su Via de' Palchetti. Ma c'era da considerare un'altra questione: il progettista, che qui non possiamo che dire esser l'Alberti, voleva girare l'angolo con lo stesso motivo della facciata o si è trovato nella difficoltà o nell'impossibilità, o nella mancanza di volontà di farlo? E allora perché allo stato dei fatti non ha risolto l'angolo con un sistema architettonico da architetto, visto che tutto fa credere che la facciata in pietra doveva proseguire sulla Via de' Palchetti oltre il limite attuale? E qui dico subito che la mia opinione è che praticamente Giovanni Rucellai avendo in mano il progetto disegnato molto precisamente e perciò, direi, molto coercitivo, abbia poi diretto da sé questi lavori, li abbia portati avanti per fare, in fondo, quello che lui aveva certamente fatto per la distribuzione di pianta che non c'è dubbio è una distribuzione familiare, e dunque sua. Si parte infatti da un'ipotesi iniziale; la corte è là dove soltanto può in pratica essere; la casa è tutta distribuita secondo un criterio personale di Giovanni Rucellai. Non è infatti il tipo del Palazzo Medici dove Michelozzo ha inteso l'edificio come un isolato, (per quanto fosse parzialmente accostato ad un giardino, che poi è stato obliterato dai Riccardi) ed ha concepito l'edificio a pianta centrale e dunque tridimensionale, cioè cortile quadrato, asse verticale del cortile e intorno intorno tutto l'edificio nel suo svolgersi continuo e in certo senso preconcetto. Qui no; qui la forma del terreno era quella che era, e quindi Giovanni che ha intanto seguito certamente come committente, questa distribuzione, ha fatto poi eseguire la facciata, di cui lui aveva in mano il disegno. E essendo lui arbitro non ha sentito quella necessità architettonica che un architetto avrebbe qui previsto e risolto nell'angolo, come ha fatto il Rossellino a Pienza, perché appunto il progetto che il Rucellai ha attuato era costituito dal progetto distributivo secondo la sua volontà di committente e del progetto della facciata, disegnato a sé, dove le coincidenze dimensionali necessarie non caratterizzano una 'struttura'.

Che cosa c'è poi di nuovo in questo complesso di facciata? Sono tante le novità. Intanto spartendolo in tre piani si stava nella tradizione ma adottando i tre ordini sovrapposti l'architetto ha voluto ignorare tutto ciò che in quel momento era consueto a Firenze: cioè il bozzato rustico al piano terreno per sostituirlo con una 'seggetta da via' dove 'l'opus reticulatum' fa da spalliera in ogni campo, e il tutto fa da base all'ordine dorico. E' come un parlar latino di fronte al solito toscano, un segno di approfondita coscienza nel volere e nello scegliere. Ed è il primo che ignora il bozzato per sostituirlo con un ordine architettonico. C'è se vogliamo qualche casa, per esempio, in Via della Vigna Vecchia, nel Palazzo Canigiani accanto al Palazzo di Niccolò da Uzzano in Via dei Bardi, che in un momento prossimo a quello del Palazzo Rucellai, abbandonano anch'essi il bozzato rustico. Però bisognerebbe indagare bene sulle datazioni di questi edifici perché ad esempio; quello di Via della Vigna Vecchia è stato lavorato in sito cioè riutilizzando un vecchio bozzato è stato fatto un nuovo disegno e non so se è possibile datare oggi questa trasformazione. Ma comunque forse potrebbe essere possibile con una ricerca un poco più approfondita seguire questi spostamenti del gusto in un momento in cui tante facciate di pietra forte venivano allineandosi lungo le strade di Firenze rinascimentale. C'è in Piazza S.Trinita il Palazzo Buondelmonti certamente dei primissimi anni del '400 accanto al Palazzo Spini, che non ha al piano terreno un bozzato ma una parete liscia e anche questa era un'antica diversa consuetudine. Nel nostro Palazzo Rucellai i tre ordini si sovrappongono, è stato detto più volte, con lo stesso criterio in certo senso, che aveva ispirato l'uso degli ordini antichi come sul Colosseo; cioè il dorico in basso, un corinzio, che direi un corinzio medievale al primo piano, e un altro tipo di corinzio al secondo piano: tutti su lesene molto schiacciate. L'esecuzione del disegno dei capitelli di queste lesene non ha nessuna parentela con quello che allora si cercava di fare sulla scia del Brunelleschi e con quella che era l'imitazione dell'antico (perché non c'è dubbio che in questo tempo il criterio era proprio l'imitazione dell'antico) come ce lo testimonia insieme alle parole del Filarete il codice di Giuliano da Sangallo che è cominciato nel '65[1] e che ci dice come allora venivano rilevati i capitelli antichi nei luoghi e negli edifici dove potevano essere trovati per usarli poi variamente. I tre ordini si seguono dunque con un disegno schiacciatissimo, le paraste sono appena rilevate di due o tre centimetri sul fondo del bozzato e i solchi del bozzato sono ricavati con un segno molto acuto e netto tale da dare ombra, ma nello stesso tempo di pochissima profondità. E come testimonia quel mio disegno del 1962, l'esecuzione di questa facciata è stata fatta in opera, esclusi i capitelli, ma compresi i fregi; cioè tutto il lavoro di scultura e di incisione, è stato fatto sulle impalcature e questo porta a fare delle considerazioni sulla successione delle facciate per il primo tratto a cinque finestre, che si denota chiaramente soltanto al piano terreno e per pochi filari al di sopra, mentre poi per la parte che segue fino dalla prima cornice al cornicione le bozze, tre o quattro bozze per piano, passano da parte a parte. Allora a meno di pensare che siano state sostituite, ma non lo credo, evidentemente da quella prima bozza passante l'edificio è stato ampliato dai cinque agli otto campi. Osserviamo allora un altro carattere: quello delle due porte ora esistenti. Esso è un carattere anomalo insolito e dunque sospetto e già in una descrizione del Palazzo del 1722–34 si dice '. . . della sua casa con altre case ne fabbricò un Palazzo, con disegno del famosissimo Leon Battista Alberti quale secondo le tradizioni chi dice che dovevano essere XI finestre e tre porte e chi XIIII finestre e 4° porte. . .'[2]. La proposta da me fatta di considerare come originaria la facciata prima cominciata ad una sola porta e cinque assi, aggirava l'ostacolo ma non risolveva il problema di una iniziale proposta. Tornando allora sulla questione delle porte io non sono alieno dal pensare che in fondo la concezione di Giovanni Rucellai fosse invece addirittura per le undici campate, e cioè per le tre porte; e questo lo dice intanto anche un fatto, oggi un po' curioso ed inosservato, e cioè che lo stemma della porta di destra (Tav. 27) è più ricco ed ornato di quello della porta di sinistra come cioè se fosse lo stemma centrale, il più importante di un edificio. Infatti sarebbe stata la porta centrale di un eventuale palazzo a undici campate con tre porte. Tre porte che erano la norma; tre porte il Palazzo Medici, tre porte il Palazzo Pitti, tre porte il Palazzo dello Strozzino, tre porte il Palazzo Capponi. L'unico che non si salva forse in questo elenco è il Palazzo Strozzi; ma è dell' '89. E poi tre porte le ha, sia pure distribuite in modo diverso. Per essere coerente con un mio metodo che spesso m'è stato rimproverato, ma al quale poi tutti s'attengono, ho fatto una ricostruzione grafica di questo palazzo a tre porte [*vedi* nota, p. 237], nella certezza che l'impressione di soddisfazione per aver visto in esso la vera dimensione del Palazzo Rucellai, che io ho provato eseguendolo, a seguito ed a confronto di una considerazione intellettualistica e statistica, sia

---

[1] *Il libro di Giuliano da Sangallo, cod. Vat. Barberiniano latino 4424*, con introduzione e note di Cristiano Huelsen, Lipsia, 1910.
[2] Vedi p. 223 sopra, Doc. XXVa.

provata ed accolta anche da quanti la vedranno. Lo spazio sembra equilibrato, come non c'è dubbio non sia con le otto finestre. I rapporti proporzionali confortano interamente questa proposta dimensione, che con otto finestre era del tutto incongrua. Infatti il gioco delle proporzioni è corretto. Resta solo da dare una ragione distributiva a questa terza porta, che oggi verrebbe a trovarsi fuori della proprietà e non possiamo attribuirle la funzione che è rimasta inespressa. Che cosa avrebbe portato come conseguenza questo allungamento della facciata non sembra oppure esso comprensibile oggi. Si potrebbe immaginare la formazione di un secondo cortile di minori dimensioni, ma tale da dar luce da ambo le parti ad un corpo di ambienti oggi male illuminati, o forse prevedeva la costruzione di una scala più centrale di quella prima costruita, o addirittura dell'ampliamento dello 'scrittoio'. Sono tutte ipotesi possibili. Toccava a Giovanni Rucellai manifestarsi, ma neppure lui ha potuto farlo, forse soltanto perché un vicino 'piccoso', come si dice a Firenze, s'è rifiutato di vendergli quelle due finestre che gli mancavano[1]. Una osservazione che conferma che il progettista era lontano e l'esecutore non poteva trovare nel disegno tutta la carica necessaria per superare certi traguardi, sta nelle lunghe cornici che segnano orizzontalmente la facciata e sono a un tempo base e sostegno dei tre ordini; esse in corrispondenza delle lesene scorrono lisce mentre al piano terreno ci sono basi in risalto. Ma non passerà molto tempo che, come nell'interno della chiesa della Badia Fiesolana, all'incrocio dei bracci, ci sarà anche nella cornice esterna un risalto, che troveremo nella cornice del piano terreno della facciata di S. Maria Novella (c'era solo al piano terreno nell' esterno del S. Giovanni) e diventerà poi un necessario elemento grammaticale, ad esempio, nel Palazzo Bartolini Salimbeni, nel S. Biagio e nel Palazzo Tarugi a Montepulciano; ed a Firenze non c'è né nella facciata degli Innocenti, né nella Cappella de' Pazzi, né nei palazzi dipinti dal Sangallo nelle prospettive di Urbino o di Baltimora, mentre è solo un accenno nelle tribune morte. Queste forme quasi, verrebbe da dire, incompiute, di fronte alla soluzione fondamentale dei tre ordini di lesene sovrapposti, che improuterà di sé tutti gli sviluppi dell'architettura civile e religiosa del '500 italiano, si giustificano solo pensando che l'Alberti non fosse presente a Firenze, a che il suo progetto si limitasse, come disegno particolareggiato, ad un paio o tre campate e che l'esecutore lo abbia eseguito alla lettera e senza discuterlo sapendo che comunque avrebbe fatto invecchiare di colpo tutto quello che a Firenze in fatto d'architettura sapeva di Ghiberti e di Michelozzo. Bisogna risalire al Sangallo, del quale dobbiamo rimpiangere la perdita della facciata del Palazzo di Bartolommeo Scala che era del 65+70 e che a giudicare dal bellissimo cortile, doveva contenere tante 'novità'[2].

Un altro aspetto che sembra abbastanza importante è secondo me il disegno delle finestre; qui le finestre hanno un elemento, che a Firenze, non era mai stato usato. Esso è l'architrave sopra alla colonnina alla base dei due semicerchi. Questo piccolo architrave sopra la colonnina è un ricordo della finestra crociata. Si deve dire che le grandi finestre crociate molte volte non erano altro che un mezzo pratico per potere aprire e chiudere le finestre con maggiore comodità e da ciò era scaturito tanto spesso un nobile motivo architettonico. Noi non ci rendiamo conto di come fosse sempre un problema in questi edifici la manovra delle grandi finestre. E intanto esistevano all'interno anche i grandi sportelloni, ma poi quando si doveva aprire una finestra di grande luce (e qui anche se non è grandissima, è sempre grande) poteva dar luogo a delle difficoltà. Anche questo è un particolare che può aver indotto a disegnare qui il rettangolo, più facile ad aprirsi per la finestra, lasciando poi

---

[1] Vedi a questo proposito i documenti degli acquisti successivi di Giovanni Rucellai in Preyer, sopra, pp. 208–25.

[2] P. Sanpaolesi, "La casa fiorentina di Bartolommeo Scala", *Studien zur toskanischen Kunst: Festschrift für Ludwig H. Heydenreich*, Monaco, 1964, pp. 275–84.

le lunette e l'occhio per una maggior luce come effettivamente avviene. Noi dobbiamo sempre tener presente che le finestre grandi erano necessarie perché, a parte l'impannata, che c'era in moltissime case, piuttosto si usavano i vetri tondi di Venezia i quali assorbono almeno la metà. Quindi era necessario, avviandosi a trasformare l'antica dimora in una casa moderna, risolvere questi problemi i quali sono ancor oggi da tenere assolutamente in considerazione.

L'altro argomento di una certa importanza è proprio quello che ho già appena accennato, del disegno dei vari capitelli sopra le lesene. Questo apparteneva ai doveri dell'architetto. E appartenendogli doveva esser parte importante di quel foglio disegnato, cioè di quel progetto, su carta, e che doveva essere steso in maniera assolutamente tassativa, per poter essere riprodotto da un esecutore nell'edificio costruito. Noi non possiamo immaginare un edificio di questo genere se non disegnato anche nei particolari. Non possiamo pensare cioè che in questo caso fosse lasciata agli scalpellini la libertà di fare capitelli a loro capriccio. Questi capitelli sono e devono essere tutti uguali. Mentre se andiamo, per esempio, a vedere certi aspetti dello stesso S. Spirito o anche del cortile del nostro Palazzo vediamo che fra un capitello e l'altro, data per nota e rispettata la misura generale, essi sono lasciati proprio all'esecuzione dello scalpellino e c'è una notevole differenza fra l'uno e l'altro. Questi invece al piano terreno sono tutti uguali d'ordine cosiddetto dorico e rispondono, come disegno, a quelli del cortile, ora distrutto, del Palazzo dello Strozzino, dove sopra il collare si forma un cilindro a scanalature verticali, una specie di rudentatura, e al di sopra c'è una tavoletta con ovuli e foglie che si ripetono in una forma più plastica, direi, che architettonica e che si ritrova in pochissimi altri casi. Se il dorico fosse stato concepito nella forma antica, sarebbe stati di difficilissima applicazione ad un edificio di questo genere perché implica poi la trabeazione con triglifi, metope e tutte le altre conseguenze che ne hanno reso sempre estremamente difficile l'utilizzazione. A titolo di esempio vedi a Firenze il Palazzo Strozzi del Poeta in Via Tornabuoni. Tanto è vero che, mi pare, in Toscana ce ne siano pochissimi esempi. Anche gli antichi quando scendevano dalle misure del tempio dorico a qualche cosa di più pratico si trovavano in qualche difficoltà, come ad esempio, nel fronte del teatro di Priene in Asia Minore dove il dorico è risolto in una maniera approssimativa appunto perché si è voluto usare nella scena ridotta di un teatro e non di un tempio. E il dorico è un ordine architettonico che oltretutto a Roma non è presente e dove l'Alberti non aveva potuto vederlo. A Roma c'è un solo edificio, ricostruito, che ha colonne doriche di spoglio ed è il S. Pietro in Vincoli; ma non si sa da dove vengono le colonne ivi riadoprate[1]. Altro edificio dorico non c'è. Allora questa scelta fa pensare ad un'interpretazione idealistica di un particolare aspetto dell'architettura ellenistica e quindi colta; delle soluzioni presenti nella nostra facciata si può confermare quella che è la paternità del disegno, cioè la provenienza albertiana dell'invenzione. Ma chi l'ha messo in opera? Un particolare esito di questa scelta sono le porte sulla Via della Vigna per la loro forma rettangolare architravata, quasi senza l'intermedio delle mensole, qui ridottissime, che si trovano sempre collocate fra architrave e pieddritti, ad esempio, nella porta, sempre imitata, dal tempio di Antonino e Faustina, per non citare che questo edificio. Lo spazio per collocare qui una porta arcuata o a timpano c'è e per quest'ultima sappiamo, almeno dall'esempio delle porte che Donatello ha fatto nella Sacristia Vecchia, per non citare il solito Tabernacolo di Orsammichele o le finestre del S.Giovanni che a Firenze era forma ben conosciuta. Si tratta quindi di una scelta precisa divergente essa pure dalla pratica comune. Io ricordo qui che Giovanni Rucellai nel suo viaggio a Roma nel 1449, scrive, a

---

[1] *Ricerche intorno a S. Pietro in Vincoli: L'esplorazione archeologica dell'area*, a cura di A. M. Colini; *Le origini della chiesa*, a cura di G. Matthiae (Atti della Pontificia Accademia Romana di Archeologia, s. III², Memorie, IX), Città del Vaticano, 1966, spec. pp. 70 ss.

proposito della Basilica di S. Paolo fuori le Mura che: '. . . E' due primi filari del mezo sono colonne molto belle di marmo, acanalate, di capitegli et base fatte a uno modo, et simili di grosseza e alteza . . .'[1], cioè di uno stesso 'ordine'. Forse Giovanni Rucellai avrà avuto a Roma, come guida, l'Alberti, può darsi anche se non ne fa cenno. Però ha avuto l'acume di osservare questo fatto, che comunemente a Roma non era osservabile (per esempio S. Maria in Trastevere è tutta fatta di spogli antichi bellissimi, però le colonne sono di granito e i capitelli sono tutti diversi, le basi sono tutte diverse, le altezze sono tutte diverse). Se Giovanni Rucellai dunque ebbe questo particolare ed educato occhio per rilevare un fatto così sottile come quello che le basi sono tutte uguali, le colonne sono tutte uguali, i capitelli sono tutti uguali possiamo pensare ad una certa sua educazione architettonica e ciò fa tornare proponibile per altra via l'ipotesi che l'esecuzione di questa facciata dove le basi, i fusti, i capitelli dovevano essere tutti uguali fra loro sia in gran parte dovuta a lui, mentre la sorveglianza giornaliera sia stata fatta certamente da uno del mestiere magari da Antonio di Migliorino Guidotti, il costruttore della Loggia, sebbene fra la facciata del palazzo e la Loggia corrano delle differenze notevoli. Il Vasari da inizio alla vita dell'Alberti[2] criticandolo (non l'aveva in simpatia) coll'affermare che Leon Battista era un architetto per così dire da tavolino e che quindi aveva commesso un certo errore nella Loggia Rucellai nell'attacco fra le cupolette, le vele d'angolo e il pilastro angolare; e da come lo descrive lui si capisce perfettamente qual'è l'errore. Cioè l'angolo verticale interno del pilastro quadro invece di arrestarsi a una cornice a livello della tavoletta del vicino capitello prosegue e si infila nella volta. Lo stesso errore in senso vasariano lo aveva commesso il Brunelleschi nella Cappella Barbadori, dove il pilastro angolare, che Migliorino Guidotti, chiamiamo così l'esecutore, copia nella Loggia Rucellai, ha nell'interno un risalto verticale che non s'arresta sotto a una cornice ma prosegue e si infila nel pennacchio. C'è da dire che il Vasari all'Alberti attribuiva delle capacità di esecutore molto limitate. Ed è per questa ragione che io ho accennato alla possibilità che quella mancata soluzione dell'angolo sulla Via dei Palchetti dipenda da chi ha dovuto attuare un disegno altrui che è un disegno fatto da un architetto, ma fatto sulla carta e di lontano. Mentre se l'architetto fosse stato sul posto probabilmente avrebbe risolto, come il Rossellino a Pienza, questo fondamentale fatto dell'angolo. E qui viene da dirsi come avveniva questa trasformazione di un disegno immaginato a tavolino e non seguito sul vero. E per l'Alberti noi siamo largamente informati dei suoi edifici. Il S. Andrea di Mantova che certamente l'Alberti non ha seguito, perché quando fu cominciato era già morto, fu disegnato da lui, il quale si comportò, diciamo così, secondo una certa odierna deontologia professionale, in modo scorretto scrivendo al Duca di Mantova che il disegno del Manetti era una brutta architettura e che lui gliene avrebbe fatto uno più bello; e glielo mandò.

Ma in questo caso quali sono le ragioni dell'intervento albertiano? L'Alberti non era stato più a Firenze dal momento che se ne partì la corte pontificia e salvo notizie, che ora non possediamo, non c'è più tornato. Ha avuto sempre rapporti, ha scritto i suoi libri in relazione a Firenze (il *Della famiglia*, *La villa*, ecc.)[3], ma certamente quando il Palazzo Rucellai è stato cominciato intorno al 1452–53 l'Alberti non c'era. E d'altra parte anche dicendo, come io propongo, che qui chi ha sorvegliato l'esecuzione, chi l'ha portata in fondo è stato Giovanni Rucellai, era necessario che accanto a lui ci fosse un tecnico, chiamiamolo così, che dava quanto meno le misure degli elementi, che andava a vedere sul posto, che sceglieva la pietra, che sceglieva la calce ed eseguiva tutti quelli che erano gli

---

[1] Perosa, p. 69.

[2] *Vite*, a cura di G. Milanesi, Firenze, 1909, II, pp. 541-2.

[3] A titolo di *pro memoria* ricordo che il *Della famiglia* è del 1433/4–1443, e la *Villa* è della stessa data.

impegni tecnici e gli aspetti esecutivi dell'edificio. E su questo noi oggi non abbiamo nessuna possibilità di dire chi possa essere stato, quando non mancava chi avrebbe potuto essere a Firenze incaricato di fare una sorveglianza di questo genere, tantopiù che l'edificio non è stato costruito in un numero di anni troppo lungo, anzi per i tempi è stato mandato avanti rapidamente. Non possiamo pensare che la costruzione sia durata più di sei sette anni, se si tien conto che nel 1461 nella piazza e nella Via dei Palchetti e nel Palazzo s'è celebrato il matrimonio della Nannina così minuziosamente descritto da Giovanni di Paolo. Ciò fa ritenere che l'edificio odierno delle otto finestre fosse compiuto da tempo e fosse compiuta anche la Loggia[1]. Ma comunque il nome dell'aiuto del Rucellai è rimasto nell'oscurità e questo porta a fare una serie di considerazioni sulla maniera di condurre una architettura in questo tempo e sulla possibilità di dire che questa certa architettura è di un certo architetto. Prendiamo, sempre nel caso dell'Alberti, il S. Andrea di Mantova[2]. L'Alberti manda il disegno, il mirabile disegno, come dice il Fancelli, ringraziando il Duca di averglielo mandato ed avergli dato l'incarico di eseguirlo, ma il Fancelli che cosa ha fatto e cosa ha fatto in realtà l'Alberti per il S. Andrea di Mantova ? Quale era il programma architettonico a cui il Fancelli doveva attenersi ? C'erano soltanto le misure ? Le misure obbligate? E per di più il S. Andrea di Mantova è in ogni parte regolato da tutta una serie di rapporti proporzionali e rapporti geometrici irrazionali che vincolano l'esecuzione ad una certa dimensione, ma non in maniera assolutamente tassativa perché l'esecuzione sul terreno ha sempre un'importanza e una capacità di suggerire modifiche, di suggerire variazioni; il che è esperienza comune di tutti quelli che hanno fatto una volta un edificio, che hanno messo un mattone sull'altro. Ecco dunque che qui noi vediamo che una grande parte delle strutture degli edifici di questo momento sono, diciamo così, ideati da un architetto da una commissione, e sono poi disegnati ed eseguiti in maniera spesso assolutamente diversa da un'altra serie di esecutori e di architetti e quindi il solo nome tassativo dell'Alberti a questa facciata non si potrebbe dare, come non possiamo dare il solo nome del Brunelleschi alla cupola per ragioni inverse ché l'idea arnolfiana è stata poi modificata in un'infinità di particolari e del Brunelleschi dovremmo dire che si tratta di un altissimo esecutore. Questo è un grande problema della nostra storiografia architettonica che ha bisogno di una penetrazione maggiore nella dinamica della progettazione strutturale e nella dinamica dell'esecuzione, per poter dire con esattezza chi è l'ideatore e chi l'esecutore ed il perché della forma. Se noi possedessimo il disegno della facciata potremmo dunque dire in che cosa differisce questa da quello. Non lo possediamo. Dobbiamo dire che la tradizione attribuisce l'ideazione all'Alberti. Ma l'esecuzione? L'esecuzione rimane sempre una incerta fase dalla quale noi ricaviamo il risultato che è l'edificio stesso. Il bisogno di eliminare questa incertezza è assolutamente inevitabile. E'anche vero che l'edificio non ha solo un padre, ma, come dicevano gli antichi, ha un padre e una madre, il committente e l'esecutore. E in questo caso l'esecutore è ignoto e restiamo nell'impostazione vasariana che è la più antica in materia di attribuzione dicendo che l'Alberti ha fornito il disegno. Del resto dell'Alberti ci è arrivato un disegnino contenuto nella lettera a Matteo dei Pasti per il Tempio Malatestiano dove gli dice '. . . se tu cambi questo disegno tu muti tutta questa musica. . .'[3]. Lui sapeva benissimo, quindi, che l'esecutore avrebbe potuto cambiare qualcosa e lo metteva in guardia; sta attento perché dopo non è più la stessa. E lo stesso io mi permetto di dire della facciata del Palazzo Rucellai dove il cambiamento non è stato volontario ma certamente drastico, per

---

[1] Perosa, pp. 28 ss.

[2] P. Sanpaolesi, "Il tracciamento modulare e armonico del S. Andrea di Mantova", *Mantova nel primo Rinascimento*: *Atti del VI° Convegno internazionale di studi sul Rinascimento, 1961*, Firenze, 1965, pp. 95–101.

[3] C. Grayson, *An autograph Letter from Leon Battista Alberti to Matteo de' Pasti, November 18, 1454*, New York, 1957, p. 17.

il mancato completamento. Sembra infatti di poter dire che Giovanni Rucellai non poté completare l'acquisto di quella porzione che avrebbe consentito di costruire le due ultime finestre, e che in tal modo gli fu impedito di costruire la terza porta. Questa osservazione ci esime dalle facili citazioni dal *De re aedificatoria* o dalla *Famiglia* o da altre sue opere letterarie perché le parole di esaltazione sono qui prive di senso se ripetute a titolo di testimonianza ed inutili se affermazione di una volontà. E' indubbio che il modo attraverso il quale è sorto questo edificio, in relazione alla sua eccezionale importanza formale, indica nel committente una decisa e forte volontà di emergere non tanto sul piano della potenza e della ricchezza, ma su quello della qualità e del gusto. Quasi nello stesso tempo nel quale il Rucellai portava avanti il suo Palazzo, Luca Pitti s'impegnava col suo, dove il tratto distintivo è il gigantesco, sotto ogni aspetto, in assoluto e non in rapporto a quanto si faceva allora a Firenze. Sono due concetti distinti ed in certo modo divergenti, che spiegano le ragioni del successo che ebbe il Palazzo Rucellai, in confronto a quello che non ha avuto il Palazzo Pitti, che non è soltanto un successo di gusto, ma di praticità e di rappresentatività al tempo stesso. Giovanni Rucellai, s'è rivolto dunque ad un architetto disposto a secondare e realizzare una sua volontà, e perciò dobbiamo dar fede all'ipotesi che fra il Rucellai e l'Alberti esistesse un rapporto di amicizia, una stima da lungo tempo, e fondata su precoci contatti diretti, cui possono dar corpo i passaggi da Firenze di Sigismondo Malatesta il primo 'protettore' dell'Alberti architetto e gli stessi viaggi che l'Alberti fece a Firenze e le molteplici ragioni che lo legavano alla città della sua famiglia. Di questa amicizia Firenze ha goduto il frutto più saporito, e cioè quell'edificio, o meglio quella facciata che ha inventato la casa sulla strada, parete o prospetto di fondo di una strada o d'una piazza in dimensione umana, adoprando in modo estremamente penetrante, l'ornamentum e la proporzione su un telaio compositivo di grande semplicità e quindi molto nobile che qui indico nel disegno allegato dove ho segnato la proporzione generale delle tre porte. Si veda come ognuno dei campi delle finestre normali sia tracciato su un rettangolo che determina ogni altra misura. Ma si osservi che i rettangoli comprendono le due paraste e cioè si sovrappongono per tutta la larghezza di una parasta. Il piano terreno è più alto. La maggiore altezza si ottiene aggiungendo il capitello sopra la parasta. Il capitello non è infatti compreso nella misura dei rettangoli e così pure il basamento in opus. Il campo nel quale è la porta è più largo di mezza lesena. Infatti il rettangolo segna esattamente mezza lesena. In tal modo le finestre alte del piano terreno hanno l'angolo sulla diagonale del rettangolo, salvo ovviamente quelle sopra le porte, mentre le altre finestre hanno l'architrave che separa le lunette dalla parte rettangolare e cioè anche l'imposta dell'arco a bozze a livello dell'intersezione della diagonale con l'asse verticale del campo. Le diagonali dei rettangoli così tracciate sono ovviamente tutte parallele fra loro. Ma non è necessario saperlo per godere la straordinaria armonia dell'insieme.

Quando questo contributo, basato sul dattiloscritto mandatoci dall'autore nel 1978, era già in bozze, una stesura ulteriore è venuta alla luce e ci è stata gentilmente comunicata dalla professoressa Carla Pietramellara dell'Istituto di Restauro dei Monumenti della Facoltà di Architettura dell'Università degli Studi di Firenze. Nell'impossibilità di tener conto, salvo in alcuni particolari, dell'ultima versione, ci importa di accennare alla sua disponibilità, su domanda, insieme con la ricostruzione grafica a tre porte (v. p. 232), nel suddetto Istituto.

ROBERTO SALVINI

THE FRESCOES IN THE *ALTANA* OF THE RUCELLAI
PALACE

THE FRESCOES IN THE *ALTANA* OF THE RUCELLAI PALACE

The *altana* of Palazzo Rucellai was originally a covered terrace, with frescoed walls, rising from the roof of the older section of the palace. Soon after 1865, during the severe housing shortage which followed the transfer of the capital of the new-born Kingdom of Italy from Turin to Florence, this terrace was converted into a flat. The *altana* was subdivided and the height of the room lowered by the insertion of a ceiling, which made space for a garret below the old timber roof. In the rearrangement of the lower apartment the plaster there was destroyed, with the single exception of a relatively small part of the northern wall at its western end[1]. A great part of the murals once decorating the back and side walls of the terrace was thus lost. The frescoes of the upper walls, in the garret, are preserved almost complete, with the exception of a few gaps caused by the construction of the transverse dividing walls.

The frescoes were still visible—in their entirety, we may guess—to Crowe and Cavalcaselle, who published a brief commentary on them in the first edition of their famous *New History of Painting in Italy*. Unfortunately these authorities did not describe the paintings in detail and characterized their subjects, laconically and somewhat inexactly, as 'scenes from the lives of St. Benedict and Joseph'[2]. In subsequent years the frescoes suffered the destruction already mentioned and those still extant were whitewashed. It was only in 1950 that murals were rediscovered in the garret (Pl. 41a), transferred to masonite and restored. Larger fragments of the paintings on the walls of the lower storey were revealed in 1967, when the *altana* was modernized. At present most of the detached frescoes hang on the *altana* walls, while three sections are preserved in the *piano nobile* of the palace.

From the point of view of technique, the paintings seem to be monochrome or, more exactly, oligochrome frescoes in *terraverde*, similar to the famous murals by Paolo Uccello and other masters of the fifteenth century in the Chiostro Verde of S. Maria Novella. As their present condition is much poorer than it was over a century ago and the quality of their colour is now much less discernible, I shall quote Crowe and Cavalcaselle's description:

> They are slight bold works of hasty execution and animated movement thrown on a ground of light verde which forms the semitones, shadowed with deeper verde, touched with white in the lights and darkly outlined. They produce an impression similar to that which might be created by a work on coloured paper[3].

The paintings are in an indifferent state of preservation, not only because so much has been destroyed, but also owing to the presence of a network of small lacunae, which have been made good with matching greenish colour. These patchings, though useful in marking out the general outlines

[1] I owe this valuable information to Conte Dr. Bernardo Rucellai and to Dr. Arch. Niccolò dei Conti Rucellai. To both I wish to express my gratitude for the kindness and liberality with which they allowed me to examine the frescoes at leisure and gave permission to have them photographed. There is a colour-plate of my plate 64a in L. Ginori Lisci, *I palazzi di Firenze nella storia e nell'arte*, Florence, 1972, i, pl. 176.

[2] J. A. Crowe and G. B. Cavalcaselle, *A New History of Painting in Italy*, ii, London, 1864, p. 362.

[3] *Ibid.*

of the compositions, blur the details and cause a good deal of confusion to the eye. It is this that makes the identification of the subjects represented unexpectedly difficult.

It is nevertheless easy to recognize that the fresco on the western wall belongs to that group of fourteenth- and fifteenth-century subjects, most popular in Tuscany, known collectively by the time-honoured name "Thebaid" (Pls. 40–45). More detailed identification is less easy, however, not only because of poor surface preservation in general but also, in particular, because of the loss of a great part of the composition. With the single exception of the figure of a fisherman (Pl. 40) the entire lower area is missing. What is still extant is a triangular strip which makes up the uppermost part of the composition (Pl. 41). If we try to read the painting from left to right we first see only a rocky landscape. Then we can just distinguish the figure of an old monk bent forward in the effort of lowering the corpse of another monk into a grave (Pl. 42b). To either side a small lion is scratching the ground to dig the hole. We are doubtless looking at a representation of St. Paul the Hermit's miraculous burial at the hands of St. Anthony Abbot. St. Paul, the story runs, having died soon after he had been visited by St. Anthony, was buried by the Abbot with the help of two lions. From this we realize that the composition should be read, contrary to our habit, from right to left, because nearby to the right are two seated hermits (Pl. 42a). They are Saints Anthony Abbot and Paul fraternally sharing a loaf brought by a raven. What looks in reproduction like a knot on the trunk of the palm tree and two horizontal branches can be seen in the original to be the foreshortened representation of a bird with large open wings. The literary source of the legend is St. Jerome's *Vita Sancti Pauli primi heremitae*, but the episode is also known from other sources, among them the *Volgarizzamento delle vite dei Santi Padri* of Domenico Cavalca (c. 1270–1342)[1]. The oldest representation of the story seems to be a relief on the seventh-century Ruthwell Cross[2]. The immediate model is, however, the Uffizi Thebaid[3] or some similar panel. The iconography goes back at least to the fresco in the narthex of S. Angelo in Formis of the late eleventh century[4].

A little further in the background (Pl. 44) we see the small figures of a donkey and what seems to be a man laboriously walking. If this reading is correct the man could be Abbot Helenos who, sinking under the weight of the food he was bringing to his fellow hermits, was charitably taken up and carried to them by a wild ass. We then see a large cross and further on, sitting before his cell, a monk who seems to be talking to a doe or some other submissive animal (Pl. 43). I cannot identify the episode, but stories of friendly intercourse between the holy fathers and docile animals, or even wild beasts, are not rare in the legend of the Thebaid.

Happily, the scene which follows can be more easily explained. An old bearded monk has halted

---

[1] *Vite*, Bk. i, chap. iii; ed. B. Sorio and A. Racheli, Trieste, 1859, p. 15. This edition is one of many to base its text on that established by D. C. Manni (Florence, 1731–5). The *Vite* were first printed in entirety in Venice, in 1475. See A. Cioni, *Bibliografia de 'Le Vite dei Santi Padri'*, Florence, 1962.

[2] L. Réau, *Iconographie de l'art chrétien*, iii, i, Paris, 1958, p. 112. Owing to a break in the slab only the upper part of the two figures, bending towards one another, is still visible. See F. Saxl, 'The Ruthwell Cross', *JWCI*, VI (1943), esp. pp. 3, 5, 13, 18; repr. in *England and the Mediterranean Tradition*, Oxford, 1945, pp. 1–19; and M. Schapiro, 'The Religious Meaning of the Ruthwell Cross', *AB*, XXVI (1944), pp. 232–45.

[3] This much discussed panel painting, Uffizi, no. 447 (*Gli Uffizi, catalogo generale*, Florence, 1979, no. P 1479), has been variously attributed to Starnina (U. Procacci, 'Gherardo Starnina', *Rivista d'arte*, XV, 1933, pp. 151–90; XVII, 1935, pp. 333–84; XVIII, 1936, pp. 77–94, esp. XVII, pp. 360–79); to Fra Angelico (R. Longhi, 'Fatti di Masolino e di Masaccio', *Critica d'arte*, V, 1940, p. 2ª, pp. 173 ff.; id., *Opere*, VIII, Florence, 1975, pp. 38, 50, 95); to Paolo Uccello (A. Parronchi, *Paolo Uccello*, Bologna, 1974, p. 15); and to the circle of Masolino (M. Boskovits, *Pittura fiorentina alla vigilia del Rinascimento*, Florence, 1975, p. 807).

[4] J. Wettstein, *Sant'Angelo in Formis et la peinture médiévale en Campanie*, Geneva, 1960, p. 28; O. Morisani, *Gli affreschi di S. Angelo in Formis*, Cava dei Tirreni-Naples, 1962, p. 32, pl. 10; G. Kaftal, *Iconography of the Saints in Central and South Italian Schools of Painting*, Florence, 1965, fig. 101.

to contemplate a human skull (Pl. 43). Such an episode occurs in the story of St. Onophrius, whose vision of a skull serves as a warning and a spur to penitence. However, the way in which the pilgrim's stock touches the skull seems to indicate a dialogue between the living person and the dead. Such a dialogue is related of St. Macarius of Egypt, not only in Early Christian sources but also by Cavalca[1]. The dead man describes the flames and tortures of hell, to which devils had brought him. He is rescued by the touch of the saint. The same scene had already been represented, in a very similar way, in the Thebaid fresco of the Camposanto of Pisa—probably under the inspiration of Cavalca, who taught in the Dominican convent of S. Caterina in Pisa until the end of his life. Farther to the right we see a young friar tempted by the devil in the shape of a girl with horns (Pl. 45): a commonplace in the legends of the anchorites, so that it is hardly possible to identify the precise saint intended. An episode of the kind is related of St. Anthony Abbot, but it cannot be he who is shown in this case, since he is always portrayed as a very old man. We also see a dog or wolf holding an animal in its mouth (Pl. 45). Perhaps the reference is to St. Macarius, this time of Alexandria, who, according to Cavalca, once received the gift of a sheepskin from a wolf, having miraculously restored the eyesight of one of its cubs[2]. It is moreover difficult to determine whether the half figure of a monk rising from the rocks behind the wolf has any relation to the story. For the scene in the foreground on the right we may venture a hypothesis: what we see is a young monk pouring out water from a jug before an old hermit, who corresponds very well in type to St. Anthony Abbot. Cavalca records that among St. Anthony's disciples was a young man, called Paul the Simpleton, who made up for his slowness of mind by possessing in extraordinary measure the virtue of obedience[3]. In order to give his obedience full play St. Anthony often asked him to do totally useless things, such as drawing water from a distant well, bringing it back and then pouring it from his jug on to the ground. All this the patient Paul would obediently perform. The monk we see in the background, kneeling on the rocks near the right edge, might be Paul the Simpleton drawing water from the well: unfortunately, slight damage to the frescoes prevents us from seeing whether or not he is holding a jug.

On the eastern wall opposite we can easily recognize the Virgin's Apparition to St. Bernard of Clairvaux (Pl. 47a). Behind a rock spur are three young friars, disciples of the Cistercian saint (Pl. 47b). The right side of the painting is so damaged as to render it impossible to distinguish what was shown there. This scene, later to become popular in Florence (Filippino Lippi, Perugino, Fra Bartolommeo, Puligo), had already made its appearance as the central panel of a polyptych painted about 1360–70 for the Benedictines of the Campora by the Master of the Rinuccini Chapel[4]. In the Rucellai *altana* the setting of the scene and the landscape are somewhat wilder than usual. The artist's intention was probably simply to provide some visual correspondence with the mountainous desert landscape of the Thebaid on the opposite wall.

The frescoes of the main, northern wall are devoted to the story of Joseph the son of Jacob (Genesis xxxvii–xlv). The first scene (Pl. 48a) shows Joseph sleeping on a bed of monumental

---

[1] *Vite*, Bk. i, chap. lviii; *ed. cit.*, p. 74.

[2] *Ibid.*, Bk. i, chap. lviii, p. 85.

[3] *Ibid.*, Bk. i, chap. lxvii, p. 78.

[4] R. Offner, *Studies in Florentine Painting*, New York, 1927, p. 122. L. Marcucci, *Gallerie Nazionali di Firenze. I dipinti toscani del secolo XIV*, Rome, 1965, no. 54 (Accademia no. 8463). L. Bellosi, 'Due note per la pittura fiorentina di secondo Trecento', *MKHIF*, XVII (1973), pp. 179–82, rather convincingly identifies the anonymous painter with Matteo di Pacino, who is recorded in documents from 1359 to 1394. For St. Bernard as patron saint of the Rucellai, see Kent, *Household and Lineage*, pp. 235, 243, 255, 267; cf. *id.*, above, pp. 52, n. 6; 59, n. 6.

proportions and—one would say—of marble, very similar to an altar in shape. This surprising feature is primarily accountable for, I believe, by aesthetic considerations, since the bed is well in keeping with the grandeur of its architectural setting: a lofty hall covered by a barrel vault and drawn in correct perspective instead of a modest bedroom. Secondarily, the assimilation of the bed to an altar may be an allusion to the sacred character of Joseph, whom medieval theology saw as a prefiguration of Christ. The primacy of the aesthetic motive is suggested by the fact that, oddly enough, the representation of the dream of the sheaves is, as it were, concealed in the frieze of the cornice. This implies that the painter's concern with architectural grandeur and harmony is so powerful as to allow him to absorb an essential element of the story into the decorative paraphernalia of a building, without apparent concern for the consequent weakening of the clearness and poignancy of the tale. Further, I can discover no trace of Joseph's other dream of the sun, moon and stars. It is possible that sun, moon and stars were represented in the sky outside the hall to the right, where there is now a gap in the fresco.

The next scene represents the young Joseph relating his dreams to his father and mother in the presence of his brethren (Pl. 48b), gathered together in a room with a panelled ceiling. Round arcades, opening in the background wall, emphasize the perspective construction in a manner slightly reminiscent of Donatello's famous relief of the Banquet of Herod. The animated attitudes and gestures of the figures reflect the feelings of surprise, dismay and outrage aroused by Joseph's words. In the third section Joseph is cast by his brothers into the pit, drawn out of it and sold into slavery (Pl. 53). The first scene from the left translates into action what the biblical narrative presents as a dispute among the brethren (Pl. 54a). In the Bible we are told that when the brethren saw Joseph coming towards them they first decided to kill him but were then persuaded by one of their number, Reuben, to lower him into the well, thus keeping their hands clean from his blood. The painter actualizes the content of the brethren's dispute, showing one of them attempting to beat Joseph with a stick and Reuben intervening in his defence. As for the central episode (Pl. 53), it is difficult to distinguish whether it represents Joseph cast into the pit or taken out of it. The similarity of the two scenes had already perplexed earlier painters, especially when they had no large space at their disposal. In the narthex of St. Mark's in Venice, where Joseph's legend occupies the mosaic decoration of three domes and two lunettes, both moments could have their individual representation: in order to avoid monotony the artist resorted to the device of translating the brief and incidental reference in the text 'sedentes ut comederent panem' ('and they sat down to eat bread') into a banquet scene, which he interposed between the two pit scenes[1]. But in the mosaics of the Florentine Baptistery only one of the pit scenes is represented, namely that of the extraction. In our case the image is perhaps meant to synthesize both moments. The subsequent scene (Pl. 55a) presents no problem of identification: to our left we see Reuben sadly leaning on the edge of the pit (Pl. 56): he has come back intending secretly to draw Joseph out and set him free but, finding the pit empty, fears that the youth may have been killed. This episode appears in St. Mark's, but not in the Baptistery in Florence. We then see, in the right-hand section, two of the brethren cutting the throat of a lamb in order to stain Joseph's tunic with its blood and reporting to their father that the child has been devoured by a wild beast (Pl. 55b). A gap deprives us of the figure of Joseph's despairing mother, familiar from many other representations of the legend.

---

[1] The banquet scene is already present in the Paris Gregory Nazianzenus (BN, MS. gr. 510) and in the Cotton Bible, where it precedes the scene of the extraction of Joseph from the well. See J. J. Tikkanen, *Die Genesismosaiken in Venedig und die Cottonbibel*, Helsingfors, 1889, pp. 66 ff., 107.

At this point we would expect, if not the scene of the Ishmaelites selling Joseph to Potiphar, at least a hint at the episode of Potiphar's wife. It is difficult to understand why this is omitted. The next section (Pl. 57), much damaged, shows a prison in which, through an iron-barred door or window, we distinguish the figure of Joseph. To the left two crowned persons sit conversing, perhaps at a table and certainly beneath a canopy. One of them, holding a sceptre, is doubtless Pharaoh; but who is the second, who seemingly holds something like a ball in one hand and a cup in the other? Does this represent the butler's dream? We read indeed in Genesis xl.10–11: 'videbam . . . calicemque Pharaonis in manu mea. Tuli ergo uvas et expressi in calicem quem tenebam et tradidi poculum Pharaoni' ('Behold . . . Pharaoh's cup was in my hand: and I took the grapes, and pressed them into Pharaoh's cup and I gave the cup into Pharaoh's hand')[1]. The next picture introduces us into Pharaoh's throne-room: in the lobby a solemn halberdier stands guard (Pls. 58, 59), in the hall a man kneels before his lord (Pl. 60). The identification is again uncertain. Perhaps this is the butler telling Pharaoh how he has encountered in prison a young Hebrew who is expert in the interpretation of dreams. His kneeling position might be the visual rendering of the first sentence of his speech to the king: 'Confiteor peccatum meum' ('I do remember my faults this day'). A different hypothesis might, however, be suggested. The figure kneeling before the king, now almost effaced (which prevents us from drawing any inference from its appearance), might represent Joseph himself soon after his final liberation. In a Florentine miracle play of the fifteenth century, *La Rappresentazione di Giuseppe figlio di Giacobbe*[2], Joseph, redeemed from prison, kneels before Pharaoh and begins to explain his dream. Be that as it may, we must bear in mind that important incidents of the story are left unrecounted. There is no direct hint at Pharaoh's dreams and perhaps no scene where one can see Joseph interpreting them. The next picture (Pls. 62, 63, 64b), the first of the lower register, represents Pharaoh crowning Joseph viceroy of Egypt, a solemn scene taking place in a broad hall which opens on a landscape, and is peopled by a number of courtiers whose gestures and attitudes express their surprise and even their anger at this extraordinary event. The next and final extant section shows Joseph selling corn to his brothers (Pl. 64a). A good half of this picture has disappeared and all the subsequent scenes, four in number like the corresponding scenes of the upper register, are lost.

Passing to wider iconological questions, we may first ask ourselves what can be the link between the Thebaid and the legend of Joseph, which would justify the juxtaposition of these subjects. The only apparent analogy between the holy hermits and Joseph lies in the fact that both were considered types of Christ by medieval theology. Like Jesus the hermits retired to the wilderness, and they were all, in particular St. Anthony Abbot, tempted by the devil. As for Joseph, Christian theologians vied with each other in discovering analogies between his life and the life of Christ. At the beginning of the third century Tertullian already declared 'Joseph in Christum figuratur'[3]. Moreover, St. Jerome asserts that Goshen or Gessen where, at the end of the story, Joseph comes to meet his father Jacob who is on his way to Egypt, is perhaps the same as the desert of Thebes: 'nonnulli Judaeorum

---

[1] Two seated crowned men are seen in a miniature of a Byzantine MS. of the sixteenth century, a copy of an early Byzantine codex, published by J. and O. Pächt, 'An unknown Cycle of Illustrations of the Life of Joseph", *Cahiers archéologiques*, VII, (1954), pp. 35 ff. There the scene is included in a cycle of almost a hundred stories from the life of Joseph, based on a text by Ephraim Syrus, and it *follows* the story of Joseph's liberation from prison and of his appointment as viceroy of Egypt. It shows Potiphar in hiding to observe Joseph as he sits in conversation with Pharaoh. In our case this scene *precedes* the crowning of Joseph as viceroy, so that it seems hardly possible that it illustrates the same episode.

[2] A. D'Ancona, *Sacre rappresentazioni dei secoli XIV, XV e XVI*, Florence, 1872, I, pp. 61–96.

[3] *Adversus Marcionem*, lib. iii, chap. xviii (*PL*, ii, col. 346).

asserunt Gesen nunc Thebaidem vocari'[1]. Thus a sort of unity of place would link the story of the anchorites with the legend of Joseph.

The lives of the hermits in the Thebaid can thus be related to the story of Joseph. We have now to enquire what reasons led Giovanni Rucellai to select such subjects for the walls of his *altana*. A recent study of Tuscan Thebaids concludes that:

> the nature of the theme, its sudden and brief appearance in the Tre- and Quattrocento, and its localization in Tuscany, all indicate a close connection with religious movements centered in this region. The religious revivals that swept Europe at this time accorded new importance to the emotional values of faith and to a life imitative of Christ's, qualities which are the essence of the eremitical existence. . . . Not surprisingly many of the monastic reforms that lead to the establishing of new orders were undertaken by monks who had for many years lived as hermits in the mountains and secluded areas of Italy in conscious imitation of the life of penitence and devotion led by their early predecessors[2].

Tuscan representations of the Thebaid were executed chiefly for houses of Augustinian hermits (S. Marta in Siena, the Eremo di Lecceto), of Olivetans (Monte Oliveto Maggiore, S. Miniato al Monte in Florence), or of Vallombrosan friars (the canvas in the Galleria dell'Accademia, Florence, from the Vallombrosan Convent of S. Giorgio dello Spirito in Florence, and probably the famous Thebaid in the Uffizi. This last was once the property of Ignazio Hugford, whose brother Enrico was abbot of Vallombrosa for eighteen years. The related panels in Esztergom, Budapest, England and elsewhere, some of which are older than the Uffizi panel and probably its model, are also likely to have been painted for houses or persons connected with Vallombrosa). The ruined fresco in S. Andrea a Cercina was also painted on the wall of a cloister, though it is not certain that the church was ever monastic in the true sense. Alone among buildings containing a representation of the Thebaid, the Camposanto in Pisa, where the oldest Tuscan example is preserved, was not part of a convent. It belonged to the Cathedral, ruled by Canons Regular[3].

All this serves to increase the surprise with which we encounter paintings of such a subject in a private house. I have been unable to discover any explicit reason for Giovanni Rucellai's choice and must resort to what we may infer of his psychological make-up. Giovanni Rucellai was a merchant and a man of business, a man of action who undoubtedly, like many of his contemporaries, favoured the active life. We may remind ourselves that eulogies of the active life are found in the writings of Leon Battista Alberti[4], with whom Rucellai was on terms of friendship. It seems possible, though not actually demonstrable, that Giovanni, apparently a sincerely religious man, was sometimes assailed by doubts about the moral legitimacy of his calling. Not so long a time, after all, had elapsed since the Church openly condemned trade and business. Sometimes he would ask himself

---

[1] *Hebraicae quaestiones in libro Geneseos*, xlvi. 28 (*Opera*, I, i [Corpus Christianorum, Series Latina, Turnhout, 1959, p. 50]); *Biblia cum Glossis*, Venice, 1495 and *Textus Bibliae cum Glosa Ordinaria*, Lyons, 1520, *ad loc*.

[2] Ellen Callmann, "Thebaid Studies", *Antichità viva*, XIV, no. 3 (1975), pp. 3–4.

[3] For further details see E. Callmann, "Thebaid Studies".

[4] E. Garin, 'Il pensiero di L. B. Alberti nella cultura del Rinascimento', *Convegno Internazionale indetto nel V° Centenario di L. B. Alberti* (1972), Rome, Accademia Nazionale dei Lincei, 1974, pp. 21–41, observes (p. 41) that in the early *Vita S. Potiti* the mode of living based on labour and diligence, which is paradoxically favoured by the devil against the contemplative life preferred by the saint, is the kind of life Alberti had chosen for himself and would steadily favour until he came to write *De Iciarchia*. In *Profugiorum ab Aerumna libri* (*Opere Volgari*, a cura di C. Grayson, Bari, 1966, ii, p. 122) Alberti states that man was not born to lead an inactive life, but 'to win merit through industry and virtue' (see P. Testi Massetani, "Ricerche sugli 'Apologi' di L. B. Alberti", *Rinascimento*, s. 2ª, XII [1972] [*L. B. Alberti: Studi nel V° Centenario della Morte*], p. 106). In the chapter *Erumna* of the *Intercenalia* Alberti cites among the human qualities that are more important than wealth and power 'exercitationis consuetudo, industrie laus' (see *Alcune Intercenali inedite*, a cura di E. Garin, Florence, 1965, p. 51). Praise of active life is frequently met in the *Apologi* (P. Testi Massetani, *loc. cit.*).

whether the best and most Christian way of life would not be one of prayer and devotion. I do not find an explicit discussion on the theme of the active and the contemplative life in his *Zibaldone*. But that he was not unconcerned with moral problems is proved by his seeking the opinions of Fra Giovanni da Viterbo and Donato Acciaiuoli, on whether it is more difficult for man to do good or evil, to exert virtue or to become the prey of vice. He reflects that he owes to God's help and grace not only his birth in such a noble and beautiful city as Florence, and his excellent health, but also his success in business; and he concludes with an almost mystical praise of God[1]. A certain attraction towards the eremitical life is inherent in the favour he showed to the Vallombrosan church and Convent of S. Pancrazio, near his own palace. In short, I believe that Giovanni saw in the two shorter walls at each side of the *altana* a welcome occasion to remind himself of the ideal perfection of monastic life. For this reason he had the left wall painted with scenes from the Thebaid and the right wall with the Apparition of the Virgin to St. Bernard. He was thus able to counterbalance, as it were, the exaltation of the active, mercantile life—a mirror of his own way of living—in the frescoes of the life of Joseph, to which he devoted the main wall. Moreover, in the stories of the hermits and of St. Bernard which he commissioned he found an opportunity to do homage to the memory of his father, Paolo. The earliest promoter of anchoretic life had been, according to the legend, Paolo's namesake, St. Paul the Hermit—whose meeting with St. Anthony and whose miraculous burial are shown in the frescoes. Giovanni similarly invoked good omens for one of his sons, whose name was Bernard. The inclusion in the socle of the coat-of-arms of the Pandolfini, his mother's family, and of the Strozzi, his wife's family, near those of the Rucellai on this occasion reflects once again his solicitude for his own and his relatives' lineage.

As for the story of Joseph, if medieval theology saw in it a prefiguration of Christ's life, what certainly took hold most strongly on men's minds in the early Renaissance were the many vicissitudes, the blows of fate and the final conquest of Fortuna by prudence and industry. Thus Joseph could easily become the exemplar of the active and industrious life, by which a man is hardened to the shafts of adversity. Apropos of this, it is perhaps not too far fetched to cite an apologue by Alberti[2]: a philosopher, comparing the different way in which a loaf of bread and an egg react to the heat of the oven, exclaims: 'En quanti interest inter negotia vitam quam in ocio ducas'. He who has never suffered adversity sweats and is wasted by a moderate warmth (like the egg that lay at the edge of the oven); on the contrary, he who from his youth has been exposed to the blows of destiny acquires éclat and greatness in the most torrid heat (like the bread which was placed in the burning centre of the oven). The story of Joseph, too, offered further scope for reflection on the relationship between fortune and freedom. The problem of fortune and its relationship to man's free will seems to have been one of Rucellai's main intellectual concerns. A substantial chapter of the *Zibaldone* is devoted to a collection of the views on Fortune of many ancient and modern thinkers, writers, and poets from Aristotle to Dante and Petrarch. Finally, Giovanni asks the opinion of the greatest philosopher of his day, Marsilio Ficino[3]. No wonder, therefore, that he found Joseph's vicissitudes and his steady confrontation of adversity especially appealing. On the other hand, Joseph's successful dealings, his service as viceroy of Egypt, and his conservation of corn for future lean years found an echo in Giovanni's own prudent business ethos. In the *Zibaldone* he warns his children to avoid both avarice and prodigality, to put aside money and goods in time of plenty so as to be able to spend

---

[1] Perosa, pp. 85–102, 125–35, 117–22.
[2] No. lviii; P. Testi Massetani, *loc. cit.*, p. 126.
[3] Perosa, pp. 103–16.

them in time of need[1]. Ficino's epistle to Giovanni on remedies against Fortune supplies us with another clue. The philosopher argues that the great majority are so foolish as never to think of the future, or to make provision against adversity. In such conditions, he concludes, nothing can be done. 'But', he goes on:

> when I reflect on the actions of Giovanni Rucellai and of a few other people who have prudence as their rule, I see future events provided for and a way of escape furnished. When I think of this my mind reaches exactly the opposite conclusion to the first. To sum up, I would judge that it is not man or human nature that can withstand the blows of Fortune, but prudent man and human prudence[2].

Here Ficino identifies prudence with foresight. It is true that Ficino's epistle was written some years after the execution of the frescoes, but as the philosopher apparently wished to please the addressee of his letter we may safely infer that he knew very well how proud Rucellai was of his own prudence and how he held foresight to be an important ingredient of a wise action. The reputation of Joseph rested mainly on his gift of foresight, as exemplified in his success both as a dreamer and an interpreter of dreams.

Another reason for our Florentine merchant's predilection for Joseph might perhaps be discovered in the etymology given by St. Jerome, according to which Joseph means 'augmentum', 'increase': a good omen for profit in business[3]. Still more important, the tenor of both St. Jerome's and Nicolaus of Lyra's commentaries on Genesis xliii.23 seems to be a justification of mercantile profit. We remember the suspicions of Joseph's brethren when they find their purchase money restored to them in their sacks, and how they bring it back to assert their innocence and good faith. And we remember how Joseph's steward reassures them: 'Deus vester et Deus patris vestri dedit vobis thesauros in sacculis vestris' ('Your God, and the God of your father, hath given you treasure in your sacks'). St. Jerome explains the passage as meaning that 'all you have has been given you, *scil.* by God'[4]. And Nicolaus of Lyra, a commentator still very popular in the fifteenth century, interprets it: 'that money has been given you by God because of your merits'[5]. Both the biblical text and glosses such as these were well adapted to reassure the merchant about the morality and legitimacy of his profits.

As to the painter, the style and the date of the *altana* frescoes, no help is available from documentary sources. None of the painters listed in the *Zibaldone*[6] among the artists whose work the Rucellai possessed can be held responsible. Indeed, Domenico Veneziano, Filippo Lippi, Pollajuolo, Verrocchio, Andrea del Castagno and Paolo Uccello are all artists of a far superior level. A record of Apollonio di Giovanni and Marco del Buono painting in the loggia does not refer to the *altana*[7].

---

[1] Perosa, p. 16.

[2] Perosa, p. 114: '. . . quando considero la confusa vita del misero volgo, truovo che a' futuri casi non pensano gli stolti, et se pensano non provegono a' ripari, o pure se si sforzono di porre rimedii o nulla o pocho giovano, sì che in questa considerazione l'animo pare che mi dica la fortuna essere sanza riparo; ma quando dall'altra parte mi rivolgo nella mente l'opere di Giovanni Rucellai e d'alcuni altri, a' quali la prudenzia è regola ne' loro effetti, veggo le chose venture essere antevedute e alle vedute posto riparo, et in questa cogitazione lo 'ntelletto mi giudica el contrario di quello che nella prima considerazione mi diceva. Questa tale diversità di poi mi parebbe da ridurre in questa prima conclusione, che a' colpi fortuiti non resiste l'uomo né la natura humana, ma l'uomo prudente et humana prudenzia'.

[3] *Liber interpretationis Hebraicorum nominum*, in *Opera*, I, i, Turnhout, 1959, p. 67.

[4] *Textus Bibliae cum Glosa Ordinaria, Nicolai de Lyra postilla, Moralitatibus eiusdem Pauli Burgensis additionibus Matthiae Thoring replicis*, Lyons, 1520, vol. 1, fol. 109r–v.

[5] *Ibid.*, fol. 110r.

[6] Perosa, pp. 23 f.

[7] E. H. Gombrich, "Apollonio di Giovanni", *JWCI*, XVIII (1955), p. 16; *id.*, *Norm and Form*, London, 1966, p. 11; cf. Ellen Callmann *Apollonio di Giovanni*, Oxford, 1974, pp. 2, 35, 56, 72, 77–81; and Brenda Preyer, above, p. 165.

On the other hand, the sober, austere style of the *altana* frescoes stands in harsh contrast with the charming, flowery and fanciful manner of these well-known *cassone* painters. Nor can the mention of Stefano d'Antonio discovered by Dr. Kent[1], valuable though it is in itself, be taken into account for our purpose because this painter, a pupil of Bicci di Lorenzo, is an epigone of the international late Gothic movement, while the *altana* frescoes unmistakably belong to the new art of the early Renaissance. Not even the information that another painter, Pierfrancesco Fiorentino, is cited in 1461 as witness to an act drafted in the Palazzo can help us. Though sometimes slightly influenced by Castagno, Pierfrancesco derives his style mainly from Benozzo Gozzoli and Baldovinetti[2], is unconnected with Paolo Uccello and, all in all, never attains in his works the quality of our frescoes.

Our situation is one familiar to art historians: we have documents which bear no relation to extant works and we have works which lack the support of any documentary evidence. This being so, we can take as our starting-point the substantially correct evaluation of our frescoes given by Crowe and Cavalcaselle in 1864. 'The subjects', they wrote,

> are composed with some ease and spirit, and the figures are grouped familiarly as if in converse, without a rigid regard for grandeur of distribution. Individually the persons represented are realistically drawn with carefully studied, but coarse muscular limbs and extremities, short waists and long legs. The curly locks and caps of the time, involved zigzag draperies inferior to similar ones in Castagno and Uccelli, may be noticed, together with some types of head reminiscent, as regards character, of those in Fra Filippo's pictures. The painted architecture in some of the scenes is not without perspective; and some panelled ceilings chequered in black and yellow remind one of the manner of Uccelli and reveal the progress of the science in the fifteenth century. Whether by Giuliano [*scil.* Pesello] or not, this is at least interesting as a wall painting of his school[3].

The (later) Italian edition of Crowe and Cavalcaselle adds no new evidence. There, the authors merely state more decidedly that the frescoes 'mostrano un'arte in tutto inferiore a quella di Paolo e di Andrea del Castagno'[4]. Allowing for their slightly academic flavour, characteristic of the aesthetics of the time, these statements give a precise judgement of both the artistic level and the historical position of the work and are still valid.

Crowe and Cavalcaselle's assessment of the good, if not outstanding artistic quality of our frescoes as well as their stylistic connections with Lippi, Castagno and Uccello accord well with what is now known—though not yet accessible in the nineteenth century—of one of the most interesting among the minor painters of the Florentine middle Quattrocento. This is Giovanni di Francesco, alias the Master of the Carrand Triptych, or, according to a recent hypothesis, the Master of Pratovecchio, sometimes called Giovanni da Rovezzano[5]. Giovanni joined the painters' guild in 1442 and worked, about the same time, for or together with Filippo Lippi. Filippo forged Giovanni's signature on a receipt for payment, whence a long lawsuit, lasting until 1455, when Lippi confessed his fault. Giovanni died in September 1459 and was buried in his parish church of S. Ambrogio on the 29th of that month.

---

[1] Above, p. 41.

[2] A. Padoa Rizzo, "Il percorso di Pierfrancesco Fiorentino", *Commentari*, XXIV (1973), pp. 154–75.

[3] *History*, ii, 1864, p. 362.

[4] *Storia della pittura in Italia*, vi, Florence, 1892, p. 13.

[5] Essential bibliography on Giovanni di Francesco: W. Weisbach, "Der Meister des Carrand Triptychons", *Jahrbuch der Preussischen Kunstsammlungen*, XXII (1901), pp. 35 ff.; P. Toesca, 'Il pittore del Trittico Carrand: Giovanni di Francesco', *Rassegna d'arte*, XVII (1917), pp. 1–14; R. Longhi, "Ricerche su Giovanni di Francesco", *Pinacotheca*, I (1928), pp. 34–48; V. Giovannozzi, 'Note su Giovanni di Francesco', *Rivista d'arte*, XVI (1934), pp. 337–65; B. Berenson, *Italian Pictures of the Renaissance*, Oxford, 1932, p. 341; id., *Florentine School*, London, 1963, p. 87; R. Longhi, 'Il Maestro di Pratovecchio', *Paragone*, III, no. 35 (1952), pp. 28 ff.; G. Giustini, 'Un centenario dimenticato: Giovanni di Francesco morto 1459', *L'Arte*, LIX (1960), pp. 5 ff.; Burton B. Fredericksen, *Giovanni di Francesco and the Master of Pratovecchio*, Malibu, 1974.

There is documentary authority for two extant works by Giovanni. The first is the fresco of God the Father giving benediction (Pl. 50), formerly in the lunette of the main doorway of the Loggia degli Innocenti whence it was detached some years ago to hang in the Museo dello Spedale[1]. For this he received payments under the name of Giovanni di Francesco in 1458–59, i.e. shortly before his death. This is also the work that led Toesca to the identification, nowadays generally accepted, of Giovanni di Francesco with the painter of the Carrand Triptych in the Bargello and of other panels once grouped under the name of the Carrand Master. Another triptych now in the J. Paul Getty Museum at Malibu, California, has quite recently been identified with a work painted soon after 1439 for the Convento del Paradiso near the Florentine suburb of Bagno a Ripoli by a certain Giovanni da Rovezzano, whose identity with Giovanni di Francesco seems more than probable. The Getty triptych in turn is clearly the work of the same hand as painted the triptych of Pratovecchio, now divided between its original home of Pratovecchio in the Tuscan Valle Casentino and the National Gallery of London[2]. Once it was realized that the Getty and the Pratovecchio Masters were one and the same, the conflation of the Pratovecchio Master with the Carrand Master was an obvious consequence. From this the identification of this master with Giovanni di Francesco clearly followed. About this painter critics generally agree that he was somewhat of an eclectic, who began his career under the influence of Lippi and still more of Domenico Veneziano and later came under the spell of Castagno and Paolo Uccello. In other words, he has exactly the connections acutely discerned by Crowe and Cavalcaselle in the Rucellai frescoes. The only additional influence is that of Domenico Veneziano, and that is perceptible only in the earlier works, formerly grouped under the name of the Pratovecchio Master. The coincidence of the stylistic sources once found in the *altana* frescoes with those identified by recent criticism in Giovanni di Francesco's later works suggests the attribution of the frescoes to this artist and their dating in the very last years of his life. The date 1457–59 is moreover perfectly compatible with what is now known, thanks to the work of Dr. Preyer on the construction of the palace[3].

Comparison of the frescoes with some of the paintings of Giovanni di Francesco's Carrand phase will prove the point. Focussing attention on the Joseph cycle, where the painter was less bound to conformity with a special genre than in the Thebaid scenes, we find that he tells his story via an exact representation of space and setting. Within this convention he seems to aim at a clear, objective and definite chronicle which avoids synthesis as much as superfluous descriptive detail. The forceful modelling and tension of line in the tradition of Andrea del Castagno gives an impression of energetic action which speaks directly, if not with dramatic intensity. Notwithstanding the unity of space created by skilful perspective, there is no unity of time in his frescoes: each episode, each character demands separate and successive observation. Attitudes and gestures are not summed up or synthesized in a general pattern expressive of the dramatic essence of the situation: they rather follow one another in almost cinematographic sequence. In the scene of Joseph relating his dream to his parents (Pl. 48b), attention is concentrated on the psychological reactions of the characters: the anger and malevolence of the brothers, the instinctive surprise of the mother, the more detached and pensive perturbation of the aged Jacob (Pl. 51). All this is given expression in the rhythmic correspondence of the attitudes and gestures of the figures. It is the same development of the story within a unified spatial setting as may be observed in the episodes of St. Nicholas in the predella of

[1] L. Bellosi—A. Piccini, *Il Museo dello Spedale degli Innocenti a Firenze*, Milan, 1977, p. 11.

[2] M. Davies, *The Earlier Italian Schools* (National Gallery Catalogues), London, 1951, pp. 405 f.; 1961[2], pp. 521 ff.

[3] Above, esp. pp. 179–84.

Casa Buonarroti, which perhaps originally belonged to the Carrand Triptych[1]. In the scene of the resuscitation of the three youths killed by the innkeeper and concealed in barrels (Pl. 66a), for example, the attitudes and movements of all three are co-ordinated in such a way as to give the impression of one person acting in three consecutive instants, rather than of three distinct personages. The effect is somehow of concentrated immediacy. The resuscitation is the central scene. At its left we see the saint throwing three golden bags into the bedroom of the three poor girls and their father. This bedroom is far from the humble chamber required by the story. The painter has been unable to restrain himself from representing it as a handsome hall, adorned with classical pilasters— just as in the bedroom of the Joseph story of the *altana*. The rhythmical distribution of the figures in a clear perspective space is not without a significant relationship with the variety of the attitudes of despondency they exhibit. The scene to the right, where St. Nicholas appears suddenly, after his death, to hold back the sword of an executioner who is putting to death three innocent men (Pl. 66b), does not achieve the same result. This is probably due to the excessive number of bystanders depicted. Only the group of the saint, the executioner and the standing victim is distinctively related by the use of *contrapposto* poses. All the other figures, though crowded together, seem somehow isolated from one another. The painter has no sense of a unity of action and tries without much success to elicit a dramatic atmosphere by the energetic attitudes and harshness of features of the single characters. The scene affords, however, a pleasant variety of costume. It also shows, in the group of the horsemen, a striving for virtuosity in the tradition of Paolo Uccello.

A number of detailed comparisons of the Morellian type may be adduced to corroborate the attribution. The man beating Joseph in the third scene of the *altana* acts with the same tension and, as it were, the same speed as the executioner in the Buonarroti predella, and the shape, position and modelling of his legs are identical (Pl. 54a, b). Joseph's brethren, especially the one in the centre, listening to the narrative of the dream, are very similar in type and in the contours of their curls and beards to the Eternal Father of the Innocenti lunette, the painter's last work (Pls. 49a, 50). A mode of representing inactive hands as hanging limply down, typical of the *altana* frescoes, for example again in the central figure, is also frequently met in other works by Giovanni di Francesco. An instance is the figure of the girl sitting near the bed in the scene of the maidens dowered by St. Nicholas in the Buonarroti predella (Pl. 49a, b). Moreover, the face and the entire figure of Jacob in our fresco may be instructively compared to the Eternal Father in the top cusp of the Carrand Triptych, and the draperies of Jacob's wife and their folds are similar to those of the crowned Virgin (Pls. 51, 52). Physiognomic features similar to those of the youths saved by St. Nicholas are to be seen, for example, in the profile portrait of Pharaoh (Pl. 61a, b) in the fresco. Significant comparisons of detail can also be made between the Thebaid fresco and other works by Giovanni di Francesco: for example the St. Anthony Abbot in the Thebaid is close to the figure of the same saint in the panel at Dijon (Pls. 45, 46). One of the characteristic features of the painter in the *altana* frescoes is the way in which, in representing standing figures, he shows one leg and foot frontally, and the other in profile—a device not unknown to other painters and draughtsmen of the time and ultimately deriving from the antique, but nowhere pursued with such consistency and even stubbornness as here. This characteristic is again encountered not only in works of the Carrand phase but also in the small saints of the National Gallery section of the Pratovecchio triptych (Pls. 64b, 65). This observation, incidentally, will help to dispel such lingering doubts as have recently been

---

[1] U. Procacci, *La Casa Buonarroti a Firenze*, Milan, 1965, p. 192, with literature.

expressed about the identity of the Carrand and Pratovecchio Masters with Giovanni di Francesco[1].

Stylistic connections with the artist's contemporaries suggest that the *altana* frescoes perhaps represent the point of his closest rapport with Paolo Uccello. The figure of the halberdier (Pl. 58) was designed to match Uccello's geometric rigour, and the divergent perspective construction in the final extant scene of the Joseph story (Pl. 62) finds its counterparts in Uccello's almost totally destroyed fresco in S. Miniato al Monte and in his Urbino predella. Moreover, in the *altana* paintings there is a general emphasis, indeed strong stress on perspective construction which is again a feature that Giovanni di Francesco owes to Paolo Uccello. In Uccello, however, the perspective suggests a metaphysical atmosphere in perfect harmony with the abstract and rigorously geometric shaping of his motionless figures. Here, on the contrary, the figures are drawn with a good deal of linear and plastic tension and their lively and rapid gestures are animated by intense movement.

Giovanni di Francesco's painting does not possess the true coherence of *art*, nor does it have the novelty and purity of expression of *poetry*. It is rather, to borrow the useful distinction enunciated more than forty years ago by Benedetto Croce[2], good pictorial *literature*: a fine and interesting document of its epoch. In its choice and treatment of subject, it is also a mirror of some aspects of Giovanni Rucellai's mind and personality.

---

[1] Burton B. Fredericksen, *op. cit.*, p. 26.

[2] Benedetto Croce, *La Poesia*, Bari, 1936, pp. 31–48; G. N. G. Orsini, *Benedetto Croce, Philosopher of Art and Literary Critic*, Carbondale, Ill., 1961, pp. 266–74.

INDEX

TABLES AND PLATES

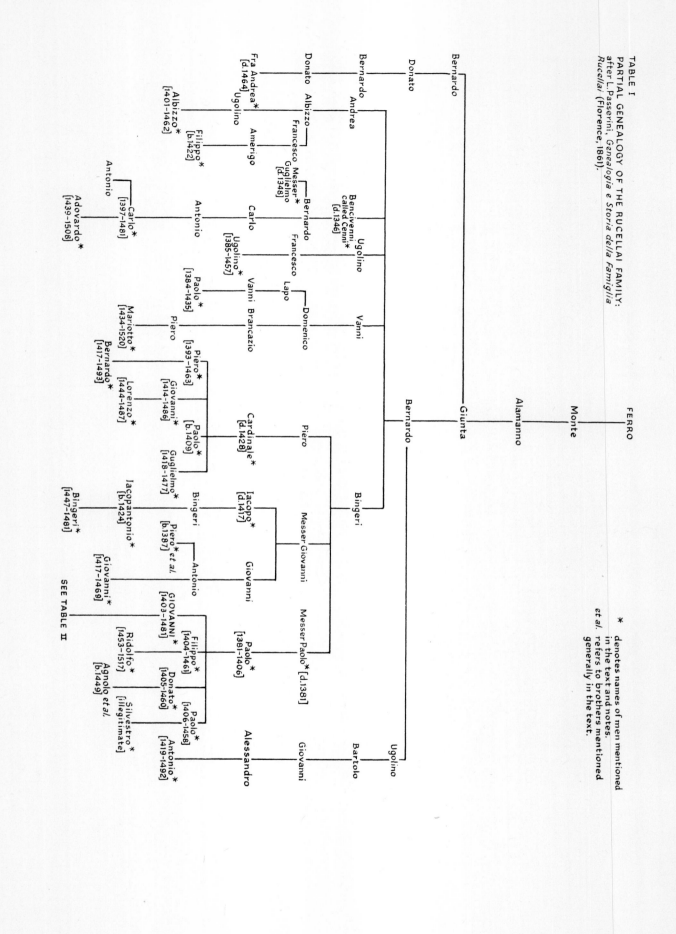

TABLE I
PARTIAL GENEALOGY OF THE RUCELLAI FAMILY:
after L.Passerini, *Genealogia e Storia della Famiglia
Rucellai* (Florence, 1861).

* denotes names of men mentioned
in the text and notes.

et al. refers to brothers mentioned
generally in the text.

TABLE II   (contd. from Table I)

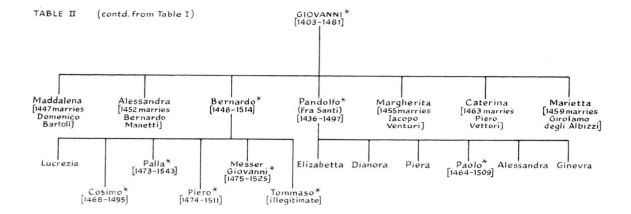

TABLE III

SIMPLIFIED GENEALOGY TRACING OWNERSHIP OF PALACE

LARGER PORTION   SMALLER PORTION

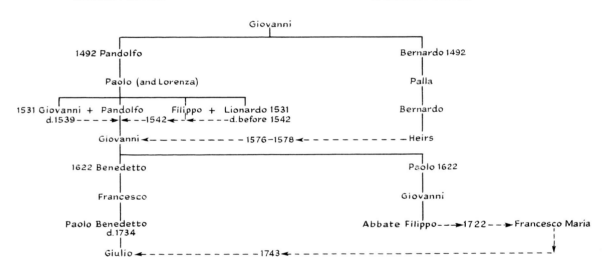

Pl. 1

Andrea Cavalcante, Rucellai Pulpit. Florence, Santa Maria Novella.

Pl. 2

Rucellai Family Chapel (Santa Caterina). Florence, Santa Maria Novella.

Pl. 3

Leon Battista Alberti, Holy Sepulchre. Florence, San Pancrazio.

Pl. 4

Façade.

Pl. 5

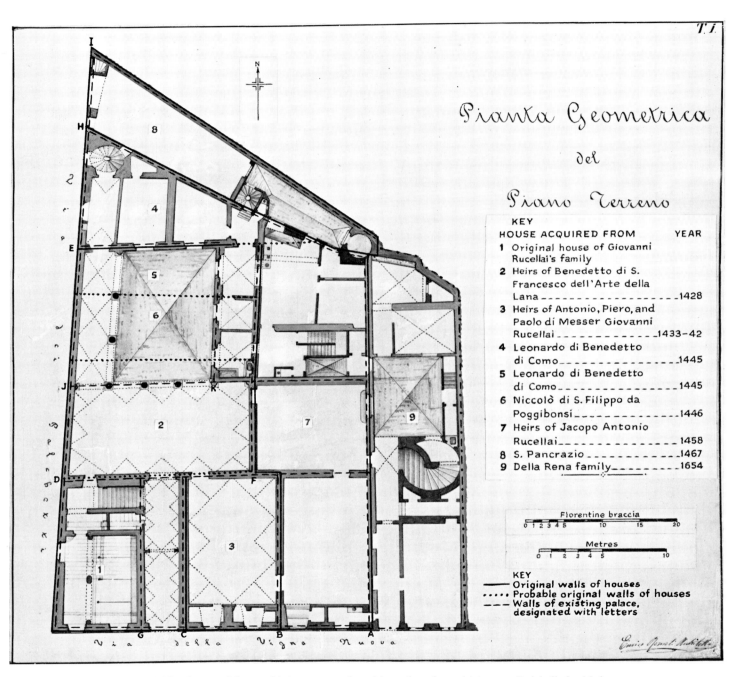

Pianta Geometrica

del

Piano Terreno

KEY

HOUSE ACQUIRED FROM	YEAR
1 Original house of Giovanni Rucellai's family	
2 Heirs of Benedetto di S. Francesco dell'Arte della Lana	1428
3 Heirs of Antonio, Piero, and Paolo di Messer Giovanni Rucellai	1433–42
4 Leonardo di Benedetto di Como	1445
5 Leonardo di Benedetto di Como	1445
6 Niccolò di S. Filippo da Poggibonsi	1446
7 Heirs of Jacopo Antonio Rucellai	1458
8 S. Pancrazio	1467
9 Della Rena family	1654

Florentine braccia
0 1 2 3 4 5   10   15   20

Metres
0 1 2 3 4 5   10

KEY
— Original walls of houses
···· Probable original walls of houses
– – Walls of existing palace, designated with letters

Via della Vigna Nuova

Plan (ca.1846) of ground floor with houses numbered in order of acquisition; walls labelled with letters.

Pl. 6

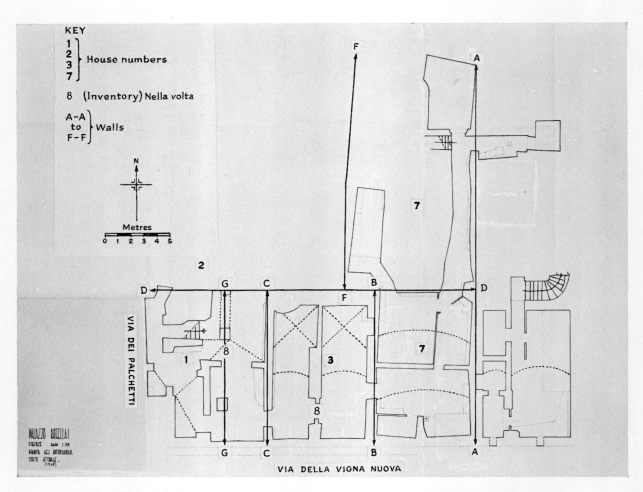

Plan (1968) of basement with spaces mentioned in 1548 inventory; walls labelled with letters.

Pl. 7

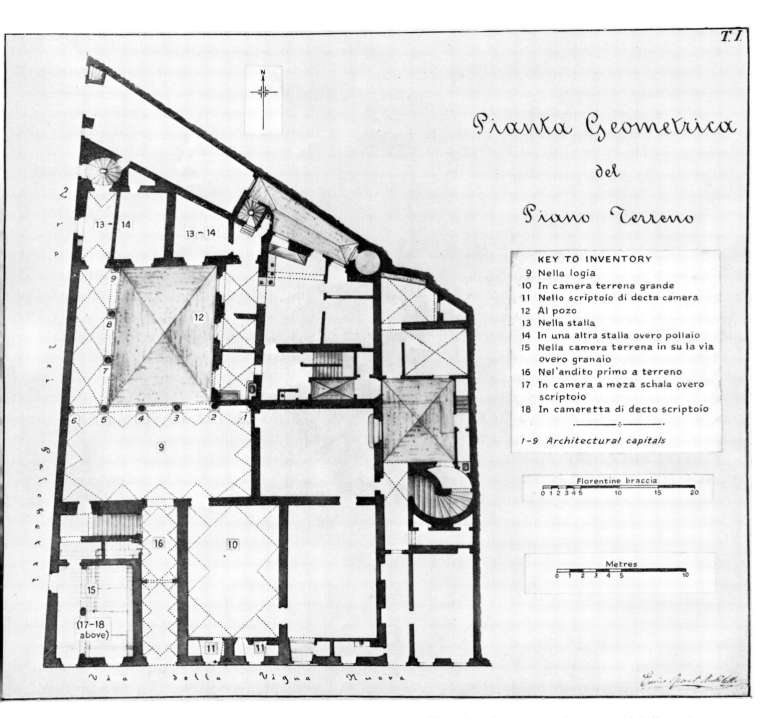

Pianta Geometrica

del

Piano Terreno

KEY TO INVENTORY

9 Nella logia
10 In camera terrena grande
11 Nello scriptoio di decta camera
12 Al pozo
13 Nella stalla
14 In una altra stalla overo pollaio
15 Nella camera terrena in su la via overo granaio
16 Nel'andito primo a terreno
17 In camera a meza schala overo scriptoio
18 In cameretta di decto scriptoio

1-9 Architectural capitals

Florentine braccia
0 1 2 3 4 5   10   15   20

Metres
0 1 2 3 4 5   10

Plan (ca.1846) of ground floor with spaces mentioned in 1548 inventory (bold type); capitals numbered in courtyard (italic type).

Pl. 8

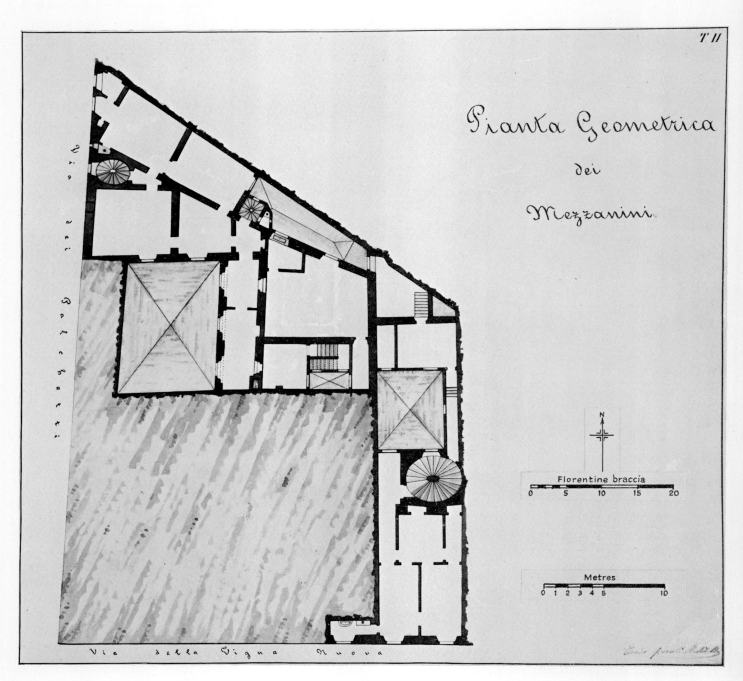

T II

Pianta Geometrica

dei

Mezzanini

Florentine braccia

0 5 10 15 20

Metres

0 1 2 3 4 5 10

Plan (ca.1846) of mezzanines.

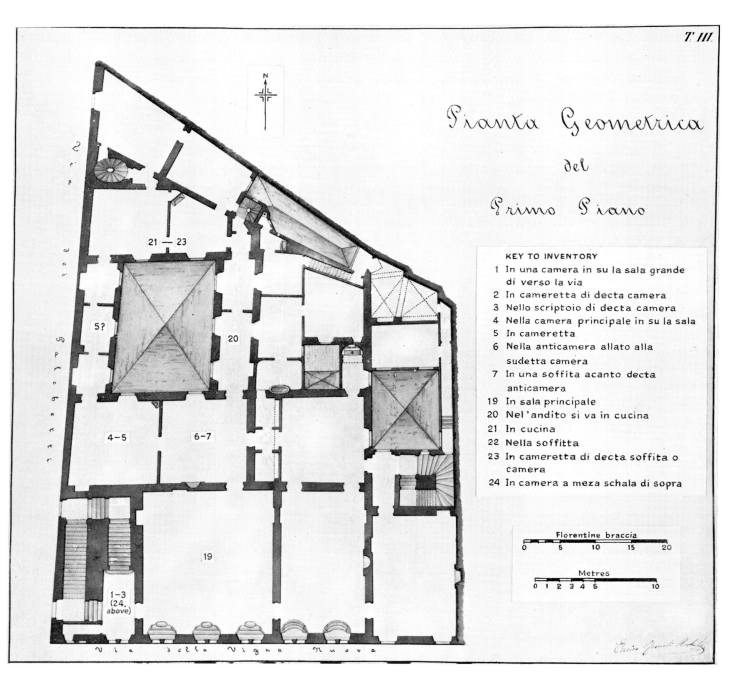

Pl. 9

T. III.

Pianta Geometrica

del

Primo Piano

21 — 23

5?

20

4–5

6–7

19

1–3
(24,
above)

KEY TO INVENTORY

1 In una camera in su la sala grande
   di verso la via
2 In cameretta di decta camera
3 Nello scriptoio di decta camera
4 Nella camera principale in su la sala
5 In cameretta
6 Nella anticamera allato alla
   sudetta camera
7 In una soffita acanto decta
   anticamera
19 In sala principale
20 Nel'andito si va in cucina
21 In cucina
22 Nella soffitta
23 In cameretta di decta soffita o
   camera
24 In camera a meza schala di sopra

Florentine braccia
0   5   10   15   20

Metres
0 1 2 3 4 5   10

Via della Vigna Nuova

Plan (ca.1846) of first floor with spaces mentioned in 1548 inventory.

Pl. 10

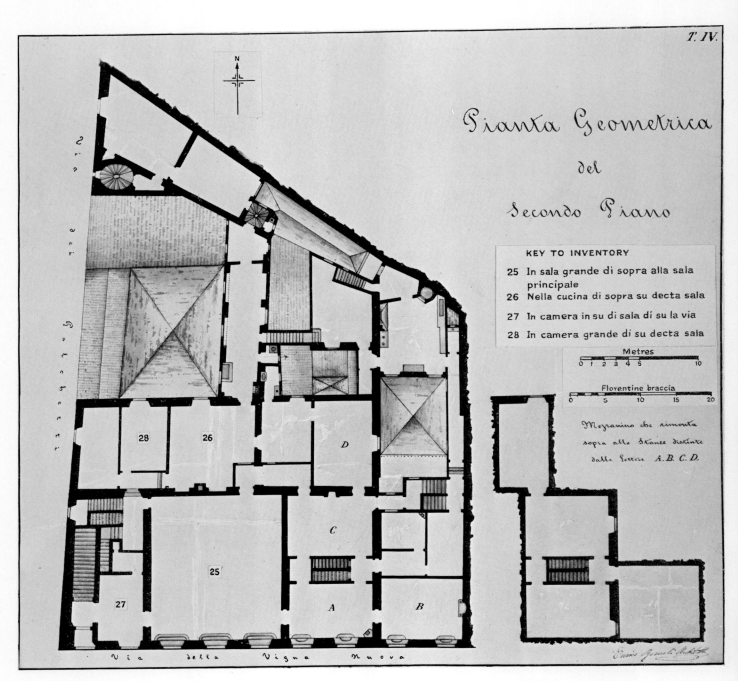

Plan (ca.1846) of second floor with spaces mentioned in 1548 inventory.

Pl. 11

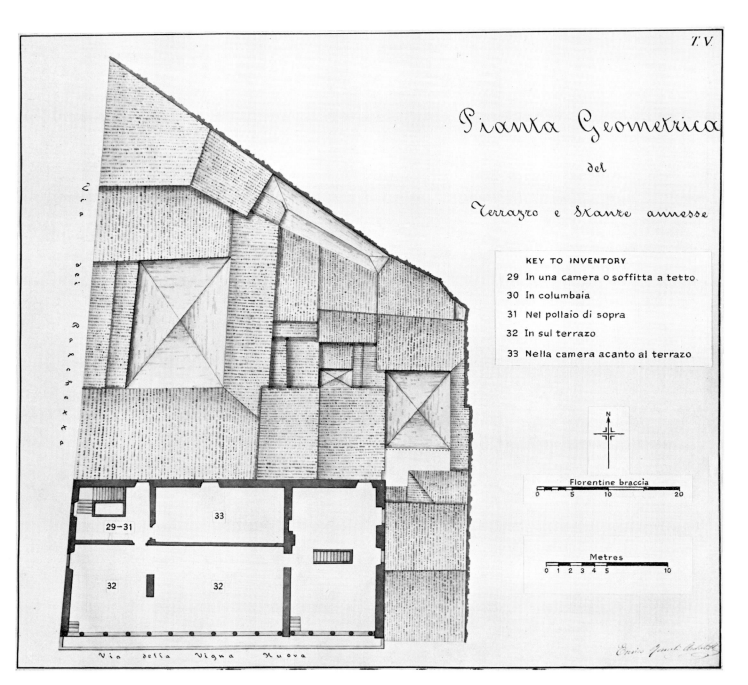

Pianta Geometrica

del

Terrazzo e Stanze annesse

KEY TO INVENTORY

29 In una camera o soffitta a tetto.

30 In columbaia

31 Nel pollaio di sopra

32 In sul terrazo

33 Nella camera acanto al terrazo

Florentine braccia

0   5   10   20

Metres

0 1 2 3 4 5   10

Plan (ca.1846) of third floor (*altana*) with spaces mentioned in 1548 inventory.

Pl. 12

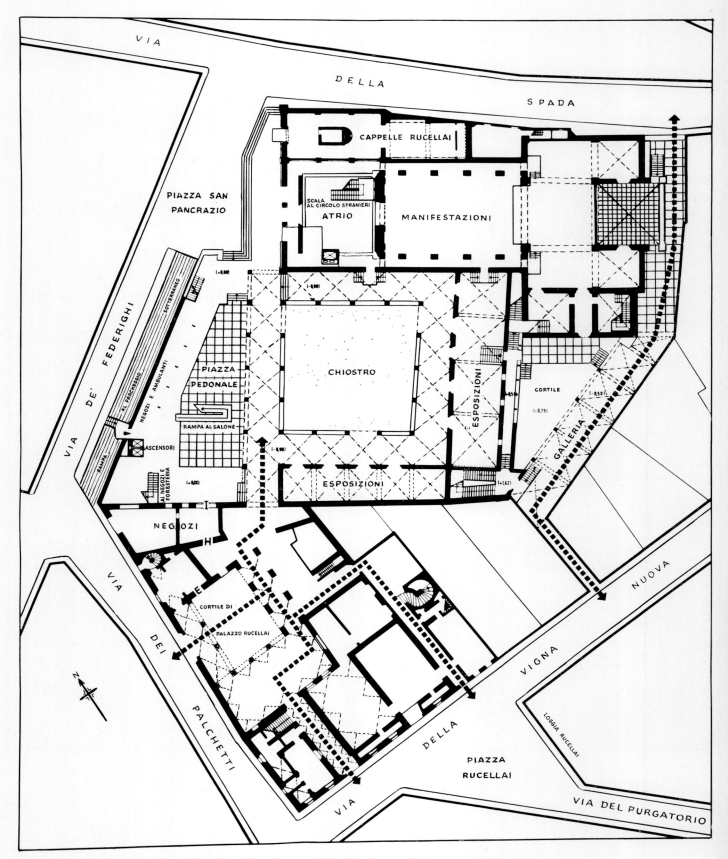

Site plan with palace at south (drawing made for unexecuted project).

Pl. 13

Courtyard from north-west.

Pl. 14

Florence, Bartolini Palace, courtyard.

Pl. 15

Loggia from north.

Pl. 16

a   Courtyard, capital 3.

b   Courtyard, capital 2.

c   Courtyard, capital 9.

d   Pescia, San Francesco, Cardini Chapel, detail.

Pl. 17

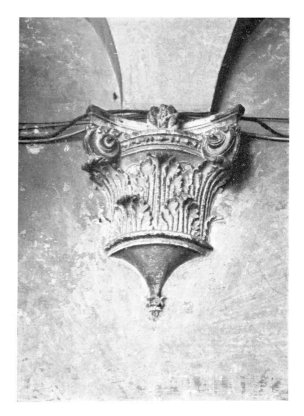

a   Courtyard, corbel.

b   Courtyard, corbel.

c   Courtyard, corbel.

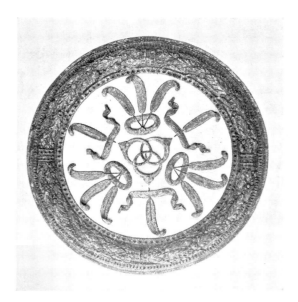

d   *Tondo* in vault of *loggia*.

Pl. 18

a   Southern half from south.

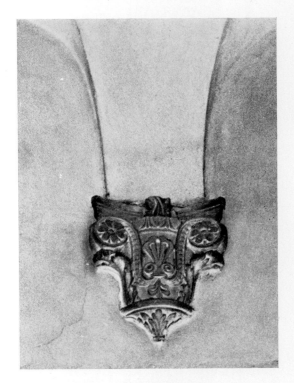

b   Corbel.

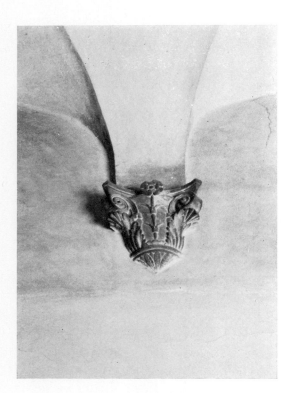

c   Corbel.

d   Southern wall.

Androne

Pl. 19

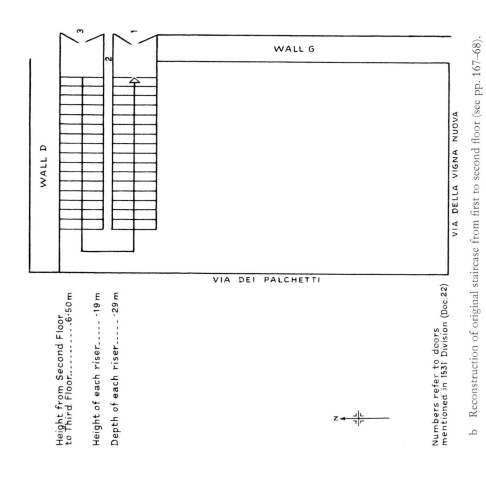

Height from Second Floor
to Third Floor............6·50 m

Height of each riser.......·19 m

Depth of each riser.......·29 m

Numbers refer to doors
mentioned in 1531 Division (Doc. 22)

b   Reconstruction of original staircase from first to second floor (see pp. 167–68).

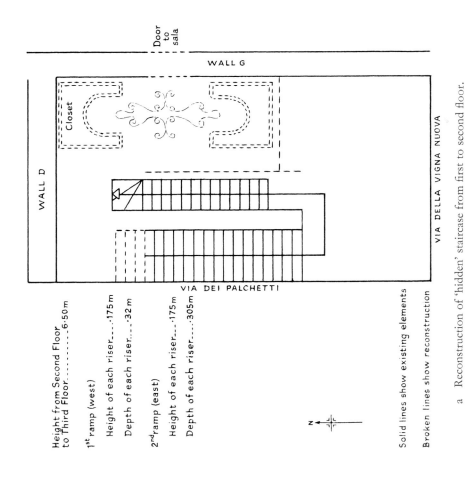

Height from Second Floor
to Third Floor............6·50 m

1ˢᵗ ramp (west)

Height of each riser....·175 m

Depth of each riser.....·32 m

2ⁿᵈ ramp (east)

Height of each riser....·175 m

Depth of each riser.....·305 m

Solid lines show existing elements

Broken lines show reconstruction

a   Reconstruction of 'hidden' staircase from first to second floor.

Pl. 20

Architektur der Renaissance in Toscana

Società San Giorgio

J. Geyer sc.

Elevation and section (From Stegmann-Geymüller, *Die Architektur der Renaissance in Toscana*).

Pl. 21

a *Camera terrena grande,* from north.

b *Camera terrena grande,* corbel.

c Florence, Spinelli Palace, courtyard corbel.

Pl. 22

a   Second-floor *sala*, ceiling.

b   *Sala principale*, console.

c   *Sala principale*, console.

Pl. 23

a   *Sala principale,* console.

b   *Sala principale,* console.

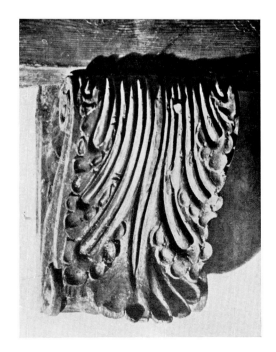

c   Antinori Palace, console.

d   Antinori Palace, console.

Pl. 24

a   Palace from via del Purgatorio.

b   Palace from east.

c   Palace from west.

d   Loggia and eastern termination of palace.

Pl. 25

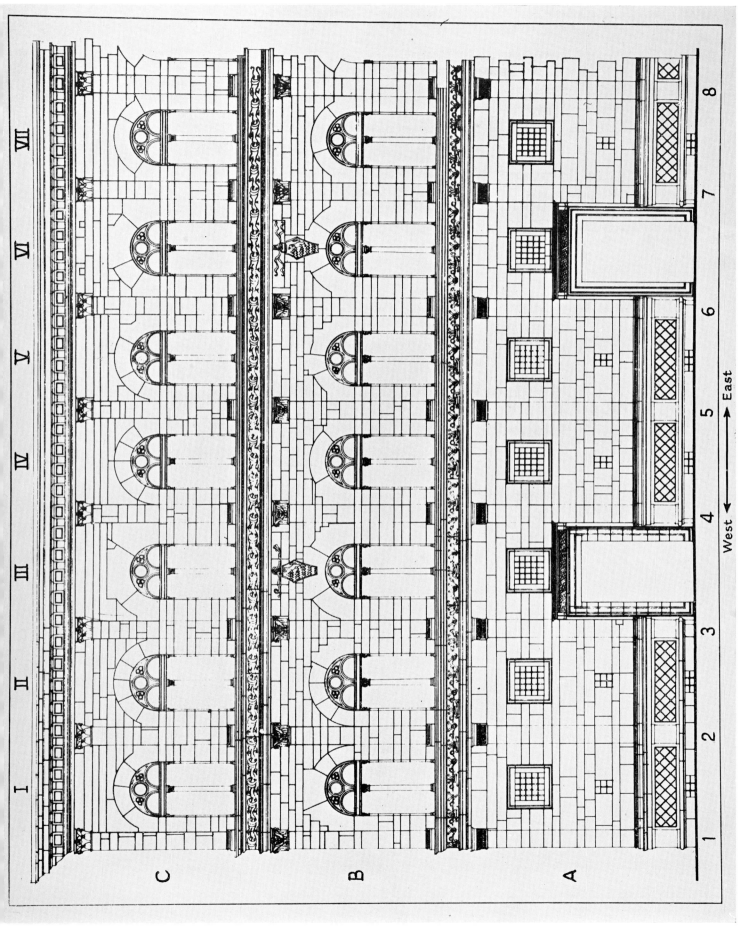

Drawing of 'actual' blocks (From Sanpaolesi, "Precisazioni").

Pl. 26

a   Capital A4.

b   Capitals B1 and B2.

c   Capital B3.

Pl. 27

Bays B V–VII.

Pl. 28

a   Capital C6.

b   Capitals C7 and C8.

c   Florence, Santa Croce, Spinelli Cloister, pilaster capital.

Pl. 29

a   Wooden doors of western portals.

b   Detail of Pl. 29a.

c   Detail of Pl. 29a.

Pl. 30

Pienza, Piccolomini Palace from north-east.

Pl. 31

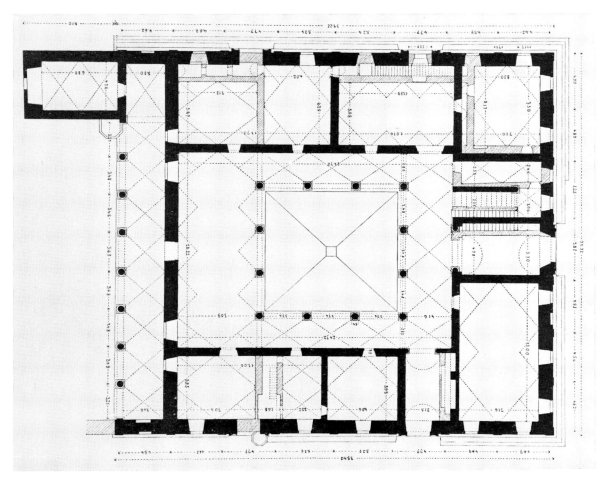

a   Pienza, Piccolomini Palace, ground plan (From Stegmann-Geymüller, *Die Architektur der Renaissance in Toscana*). North to right.

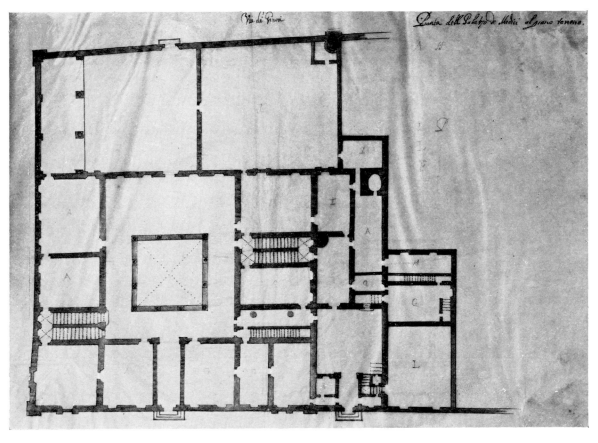

b   Florence, Medici Palace, ground plan. North to right.

Pl. 32

Pl. 32

Mantua, Sant'Andrea, façade.

Pl. 33

Florence, Santa Maria Novella, façade.

Pl. 34

Pienza, Cathedral, façade.

Pl. 35

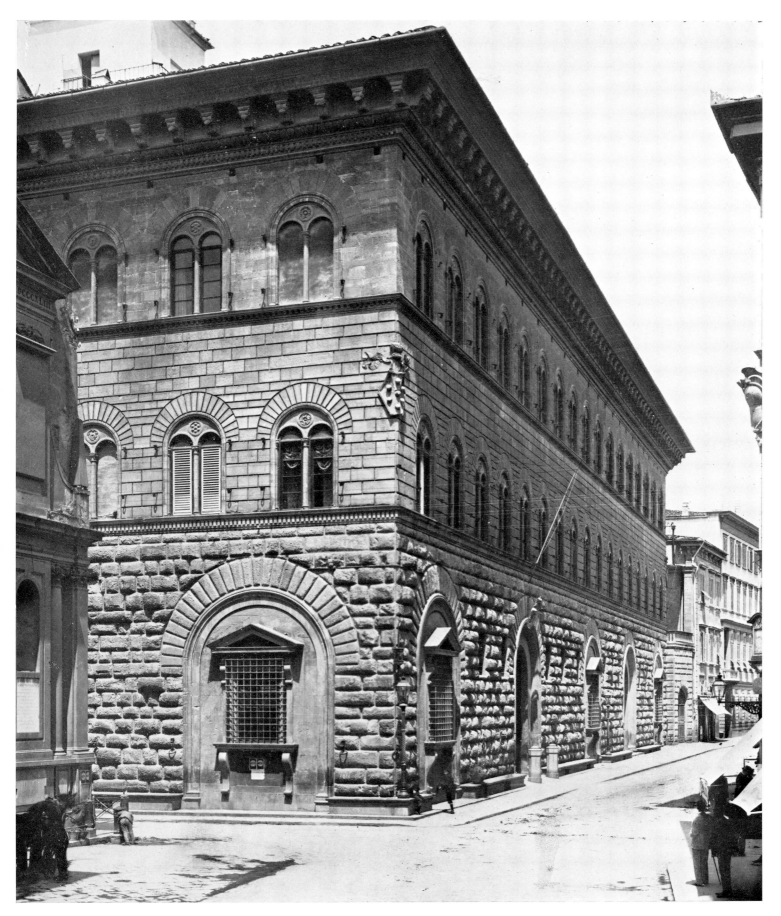

Florence, Medici Palace, façade.

Pl. 36

a   Priene, Tempio di Apollo, basamento.

b   Mileto, Teatro, paramento della scena.

Pl. 37

b   Filippo Brunelleschi, Palazzo di Parte Guelfa, Firenze, angolo.

a   Bernardo Rossellino, Palazzo Piccolomini, Pienza, angolo.

Pl. 38

Angolo del Palazzo Rucellai sulla via dei Palchetti.

Pl. 39

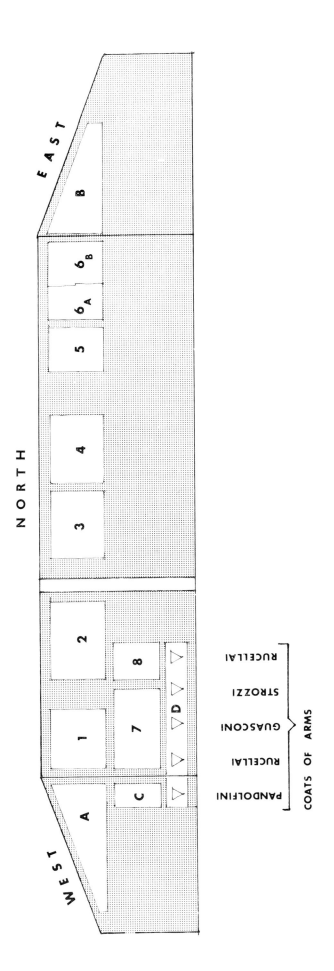

NORTH

EAST

WEST

A   1   2   3   4   5   6_A   6_B   B

7   8

C   D

COATS OF ARMS

PANDOLFINI   RUCELLAI   GUASCONI   STROZZI   RUCELLAI

A   THEBAID SCENES
B   THE VIRGIN'S APPARITION TO SAINT BERNARD
C   A FISHERMAN BELONGING TO DESTROYED THEBAID SCENES
D   COATS OF ARMS
1   JOSEPH'S DREAM OF THE SHEAVES
2   JOSEPH RELATING HIS DREAM
3   JOSEPH CAST INTO A PIT AND SOLD TO THE ISHMAELITES
4   THE BRETHREN STAINING JOSEPH'S TUNIC AND SHOWING THE BLOOD-STAINED CLOTH TO JACOB
5   THE BUTLER'S DREAM (?) - JOSEPH IN PRISON
6   A) A HALBERDIER ON GUARD   B) THE BUTLER OR JOSEPH KNEELING BEFORE PHARAO
7   PHARAO CROWNING JOSEPH VICEROY OF EGYPT
8   JOSEPH SELLING WHEAT TO HIS BROTHERS

Diagram of the *altana*, showing position of the frescoes.

Pl. 40

A fisherman. Detail of the Thebaid, lower portion.

Pl. 41

a Thebaid, left portion.

b The western wall, with the Thebaid fresco, before restoration.

Pl. 42

a   St. Paul the Hermit and St. Anthony Abbot dividing the loaf.

b   St. Anthony Abbot burying St. Paul the Hermit with the help of a lion.

Pl. 43

Thebaid, right portion.

Pl. 44

Onophrius and the ass, a hermit's hut and a cross. Details of the Thebaid.

Pl. 45

Temptation scene, a wolf, St. Anthony Abbot and Paul the Simpleton. Details of the Thebaid.

Pl. 46

Giovanni di Francesco, St. Anthony Abbot presenting a donor to St. James (reversed). Dijon, Musée des Beaux-Arts.

Pl. 47

a   The Apparition of the Virgin to St. Bernard.

b   Three disciples of St. Bernard.

Pl. 48

a   Joseph's dream of the sheaves.

b   Joseph relating his dreams to his parents and brethren.

Pl. 49

a   One of Joseph's brethren. Detail of Pl. 48b.

b   Giovanni di Francesco, one of the maidens given a dowry
by St. Nicholas. Detail of panel. Florence, Casa Buonarroti.

Pl. 50

Giovanni di Francesco God the Father. Florence, Ospedale degli Innocenti.

Pl. 51

Jacob and his wife discussing Joseph's dream.

Pl. 52

Giovanni di Francesco, Coronation of the Virgin. Detail of the Carrand Triptych. Florence, Bargello.

Pl. 53

Joseph beaten, cast into the pit and sold to the Ishmaelites.

Pl. 54

a The man beating Joseph. Detail of Pl. 53.

b Giovanni di Francesco, Executioner. Detail of Pl. 66b.

Pl. 55

a The sadness of Reuben, the staining of Joseph's coat, the coat shown to Jacob.

b Joseph's coat shown to Jacob. Detail.

Pl. 56

The sadness of Reuben. Detail of Pl. 55a.

Pl. 57

Joseph in prison. The dream of the butler (?).

Pl. 58

The halberdier before the throne of Pharaoh.

Pl. 59

The halberdier. Detail of Pl. 58.

Pl. 60

Joseph (or the butler?) kneeling before Pharaoh.

Pl. 61

b One of the youths raised from the dead by St. Nicholas. Detail of Pl. 66a.

a Pharaoh. Detail of Pl. 60.

Pl. 62

Joseph crowned viceroy, Joseph selling corn to his brethren. Socle with coat of arms.

Pl. 63

a   The coronation of Joseph as viceroy. Detail of Pl. 62.

b   The coronation of Joseph. Detail.

Pl. 64

a Joseph selling corn to his brethren. Detail of Pl. 62.

b Courtiers at Joseph's coronation. Detail of Pl. 62.

Pl. 65

Giovanni di Francesco, St. John the Baptist and Saint with arrows. Details of triptych. London, National Gallery.

Pl. 66

a   Giovanni di Francesco, St. Nicholas raises from the dead three youths killed by the inn-keeper. Predella panel. Florence, Casa Buonarroti.

b   St. Nicholas rescues three innocent men from the sword of the executioner. Predella panel. Florence, Casa Buonarroti.